JULIAN OF TOLEDO

Prognosticum futuri saeculi
Foreknowledge of the world to come

Saint Julian of Toledo (AD 642–90). Painting by
Juan de Borgoña (XVIc), Cathedral of Toledo, Chapterhouse.

Ancient Christian Writers

THE WORKS OF THE FATHERS IN TRANSLATION

No. 63

JULIAN OF TOLEDO: PROGNOSTICUM FUTURI SAECULI

FOREKNOWLEDGE OF THE WORLD TO COME

TRANSLATED, EDITED, AND INTRODUCED

BY

TOMMASO STANCATI, OP

Foreword by His Eminence
Cardinal Antonio Cañizares Llovera
Archbishop of Toledo, Primate of Spain

THE NEWMAN PRESS
New York/Mahwah, NJ

Nihil Obstat Ordinis Fratrum Praedicatorum
Fr. Loïc Marie Le Bot OP, Prior.
Apud Conventum SS. Dominici et Xysti,
Romae, Die octava Maii, A.D. MMVIII.

Excerpts from the English translation of the *Catechism of the Catholic Church* for use in the United States of America copyright © 1994, United States Catholic Conference, Inc.

Library of Congress Cataloging-in-Publication Data

Julianus, Saint, Bp. of Toledo, d. 690.
    [Prognosticum futuri saeculi. English]
    Prognosticum futuri saeculi = Foreknowledge of the world to come / Julian of Toledo ; translated, edited, and introduced by Tommaso Stancati ; foreword by Antonio Cañizares Llovera.
        p. cm. — (Ancient Christian writers ; 63)
    Includes bibliographical references (p.   ) and indexes.
    ISBN 978-0-8091-0568-7 (alk. paper)
    1. Eschatology. I. Stancati, Sergio Tommaso. II. Title. III. Title: Foreknowledge of the world to come.
    BT821.3.J8513 2010
    236.09'021—dc22

                                  2010002553

Published by The Newman Press
an imprint of Paulist Press
997 Macarthur Boulevard
Mahwah, New Jersey 07430

www.paulistpress.com

PRINTED AND BOUND IN THE UNITED STATES OF AMERICA

CONTENTS

FOREWORD

St. Julian of Toledo (†690) was the last great Spanish theologian of the seventh century. Following in the wake of great Toledan pastors like St. Eugene (†657) and St. Ildephonse († c. 667), he ruled the Toledan episcopate with zeal and wisdom.

We know the life of St. Julian thanks to the eulogy written for him by the bishop Felix, his disciple and successor. Born in Toledo in 642, Julian was educated at the episcopal school under the direction of St. Eugene. In 679 he was consecrated bishop of the city. He died in 690, before his fiftieth birthday.

The eulogy describes him as an energetic personality and pre-occupied with the idea of a unified Spanish Church. In the liturgical field he accomplished a profound unification of rites and texts. In the field of ecclesiastical discipline he definitively maintained the primacy of the Toledan church. He was a very active participant in the Twelfth, Thirteenth, Fourteenth, and Fifteenth Councils of Toledo and presided over them as metropolitan even though he was not the most senior bishop.

According to the *Mozarabic Chronicle*, St. Julian was of Jewish parentage, which explains why some of his writings were directed toward the conversion of the Jews. His strong character can be seen in his confrontation with the bishop of Rome. The confrontation began when Pope Leo II sent the acts of the Third Council of Constantinople to be signed by the Visigothic bishops. Julian, in the name of the Spanish bishops, sent the pontiff his *First Apologetic*, which approved the received texts and added observations on the opinions of the Spanish Church. Julian's response arrived in the hands of the new Pope Benedict II, who took it as a personal offense. The Spanish bishops then delegated Julian to write a *Second Apologetic*, which was later inserted in the Acts of the Fifteenth Council of Toledo.

Julian wrote numerous works that depended on St. Isidore. In the *First* and *Second Apologetics* he offers a doctrinal justification for the expression *voluntas genuit voluntatem* and refutes the monothelites. His *De comprobatione sextae aetatis* is an anti-Jewish treatise, in which he rebuts the Jewish objections to recognizing Jesus Christ as the Messiah announced by the prophets. The treatise is mostly based on St. Augustine, but Jerome, Tertullian, Gregory the Great, and Hilary of Poitiers are also cited.

St. Julian also wrote a small biblical treatise (*Antikeimenon libri*) in which he comments on and harmonizes all the passages in the Bible that appear to contradict one another. Other works of a historical nature have also come down to us, such as the *Eulogy of St. Ildefonso*, the *Book of the History of Wamba*, the *Insultatio in tyrannidem Galliae*, and the *Judicium*, written against the rebellious Paul of Narbonne and his followers. An *Ars grammatica* is also attributed to Julian, which collects all the grammatical teachings of a Toledan school (probably the episcopal school).

Julian of Toledo's most important work, however, is the *Prognosticum futuri saeculi*. The origin of this work was a dialogue that Julian maintained with Idalius—the bishop of Barcelona, who was in Toledo to attend the Fifteenth Council (688)—on the situation of the soul after death and before resurrection. While it is not an original work in terms of its contents, it became something new thanks to its structure and its manner of ordering eschatological questions around three fundamental themes: death, the situation of the deceased before resurrection, and the final resurrection. In his systematization, Julian of Toledo conceived of the last things in two phases: the final phase, centered on universal resurrection, and the intermediate phase, characterized by the situation of the soul between personal death and the final resurrection. The influence of this work would be notable upon early medieval theology and in the Counter-Reformation, when it became a reference work for Catholic theologians in their disputes with the reformers.

The appearance of a new version of the *Prognosticum* is an event that deserves to be greeted with gladness. The questions treated by St. Julian respond to the inquietudes present in men and women of all epochs. We celebrate, therefore, the authors of this careful translation and hope that this work will help the thought of the Toledan saint, an able witness of the living Tradition of the Church, become better known.

+ *Antonio Cardinal Cañizares*
Archbishop of Toledo, Primate of Spain*

* In December 2008, Cardinal Cañizares Llovera, Archbishop of Toledo and Primate of Spain, was named by the Holy Father Benedict XVI as Prefect of the Congregation for the Divine Worship and Discipline of the Sacraments.

SAN JULIÁN DE TOLEDO
PROGNOSTICUM FUTURI SAECULI

PRESENTACIÓN

San Julián de Toledo († 690) es el último gran teólogo hispano del siglo VII. Siguiendo la estela de grandes pastore toledanos, como San Eugenio († 657) y San Ildefonso († c.667), gobernó la sede toledana con celo y sabiduría.

La vida de San Julián nos es conocida gracias al elogio que sobre él escribió su discípulo y sucesor, el obispo Félix. Nació en Toledo en el 640, fue educado en la escuela episcopal bajo la dirección de Eugenio. En el 679 fue consacrado obispo de la ciudad. Murió en el 690 antes de cumplir los cincuenta años.

El elogio lo describe con carácter enérgico, preocupado por la idea de la unidad de la Iglesia hispana. En el campo litúrgico desarrolló una profunda unificación de ritos y de textos. En el disciplinar sostuvo de manera definitiva el primado de la Iglesia toledana. Partecipó muy activamente en los Concilios XII, XIII, XIV y XV de Toledo, que presidió como metropolita, a pesar de no ser el obispo más anciano.

Según la *Crónica mozárabe*, San Julián sería de origen judío. Su fuerte carácter se percibe en el enfrentamiento que mantuvo con el obispo de Roma. El motivo fue que el Papa León II había enviado a los obispos visigodos las actas del Concilio III de Constantinopla para que las firmasen. Julián, en nombre de los obispos hispanos, escribió al pontífice su *Primer Apologético*, aprobando los textos recibidos y añadiendo observaciones sobre los sentimientos de la Iglesia hispana. La respuesta de Julián llegó a manos del nuevo Papa Benedicto II, quien la interpretó como una ofensa personal. Los obispos españoles delegaron entonces en Julián para que escribiera un *Segundo Apologético*, inserto después en las Actas del XV Concilio toledano.

Julián escribió numerosas obras, dependientes de San Isidoro. En el *Primer Apologético* y en el *Segundo* ofrece la justificación doctrinal de la expresión *voluntas genuit voluntatem* y refuta a los monoteletas. El *De com-*

probatione sextae aetatis es un tratado contra los judíos, donde sale al paso de las objeciones judías para reconocer en Jesucristo al Mesías anunciado por los profetas. El tratado se basa sobre todo en San Augustín, pero también son citados Jerónimo, Tertuliano, Gregorio Magno e Hilario de Poitiers.

San Julián también escribió un pequeño tratado de carácter bíblico (*Antikeimenon libri*) en el que comenta y armoniza todos los pasajes de la Biblia que parecen contradecirse. Nos han llegado también otras obras de carácter histórico, come el *Elogio de san Ildefonso, o el Libro de la historia de Wamba*, con dos adiciones: la *Insultatio in tyrannidem Galliae y el Judicium*, contra el rebelde Pablo de Narbona y sus seguidores. Se attribue además a Julián un *Ars grammatica*, en que se recogen las enseñanzas gramaticales de una escuela de Toledo, probablemente la episcopal.

Sin embargo, la obra más importante de Julián de Toledo es el *Prognosticum Futuri Saeculi*. El origen de este libro está en el diálogo mantenido entre Julián e Idalio – obispo de Barcelona, presente en Toledo para asistir al XV Concilio toledano (688) -, sobre la situación de las almas después de la muerte y antes de la resurrección. Sin ser un obra original en su contenidos, resulta novedosa la estructura y el modo de ordenar las cuestiones últimas en torno a tres temas fundamentales: la muerte, la situación del difunto antes de la resurrección, y la resurrección final. En su sistematización, Julián de Toledo concibe ya las ultimidades según una doble fase: la final, centrada en la resurrección universal, y la intermedia, caracterizada por la situación de alma entre la muerte personal y la resurrección final. El influjo de esta obra será notable en la primera teología medieval y en la contrarreforma, convirtiéndose en obra de referencia para los teólogos católicos en las disputas con los reformadores.

La aparición de una nueva versión del *Prognosticum* es un acontecimiento que merece ser salutado con alegría. La cuestiones tratadas por San Julián responden a inquietudes presentes en los hombres y mujeres de todas las épocas. Felicitamos, por tanto, a los autores de esta cuidada traducción deseando que esta obra ayude a conocer mejor el pensamiento del santo toledano, testigo cualificado de la Tradición viva de la Iglesia.

+ Antonio Cardenal Cañizares
Arzobispo de Toledo, Primado de España*

---

* En el Diciembre 2008, en la solemnidad de Santa Leocadia, Patrona de Toledo, el Sr. Cardenal, don Antonio Cañizares Llovera, fue nombrato como Prefecto de la Congregación para el Culto Divino y la Disciplina de los Sacramentos.

PREFACE

The *Prognosticum futuri saeculi* of Julian of Toledo belongs to that extraordinary series of ancient theological texts, kept for centuries in the libraries of the Old World, that stir the interest of researchers and help them, in a decisive way, to reconstruct the stages of the development of Christian theological thought.

My first contact with Julian of Toledo and his theological works goes back to the end of the 1970s, when, following a course on eschatology at the Faculty of Theology of Southern Italy (St. Thomas Aquinas section) in Naples, the teacher, the Rev. Paolo Pifano, pointed out to us students that Julian, who lived in Spain in the seventh century, was the first theologian to have compiled a systematic work on Christian eschatology. He showed us the *editio critica* of the *Prognosticum*, edited only a few months before by J. N. Hillgarth for the Corpus Christianorum, Series Latina. This news alone, that there existed a "first" treatise on eschatology that was written some five hundred years before the *De novissimis* of the towering figures of the scholastic Middle Ages, was for me a true revelation, testimony to how little I knew about the seventh century of the Christian era and of the great Hispanic-Visigothic theologians of that century.

After further inquiry and extensive consultation, I found my interest sparked still further by the identity of the author, the period in which he lived, and his works. I was struck particularly by the fact that he was only forty-eight years old when he died, almost the same young age as Thomas Aquinas, and that he lived his intense life at the close of the just concluded (in the Western world) patristic epoch, on the one hand, and, on the other hand, at the very dawn of the extraordinary renaissance of theology that occurred in the early Middle Ages. Subsequently, picking up the text of the *Prognosticum*, I was struck by the literary form and the methodology with which the author had compiled the work: *per titula et capitula*, and the fact that he had as the principal sources of his theological reasoning Sacred Scripture and the works of the fathers of the church. To this solid framework he then added his own rational reflections and argumentations. Undoubtedly this was no longer a patristic method but was already developed with a methodological-scientific structure, and all this five hundred years before the Scholastic era!

I had an opportunity to examine the *Prognosticum* more closely when studying the first postconciliar treatise on eschatology, written by C. Pozo, in which he devoted a suitable space to the eschatology of Julian of Toledo. Subsequent treatises on eschatology, even those published up to our own time, have not followed this praiseworthy example and, with some commendable exceptions, have ignored the existence of the *Prognosticum* and its historical and theological importance, an evident sign of a theological view deprived of historical roots and sadly lacking in a broad theological overview.

Subsequently, in my early years of teaching in the Faculty of Theology at the Pontifical University of Saint Thomas—the Angelicum—in Rome, I myself became a teacher of eschatology. I never failed to indicate to the students the particular importance of Julian of Toledo and his *Prognosticum futuri saeculi* to the understanding of the development and the first systematic codification of the Christian Catholic eschatological doctrine. During lessons I often read out a passage from the works of Julian, in a translation intelligible to the class, which always awakened a desire in the students to deepen their knowledge of that interesting text of the early Middle Ages—albeit, owing to a difficulty in understanding the Latin language, in a modern translation.

During some academic years I devoted courses of the second cycle of studies to the *Prognosticum,* and it was really during those lessons that I started to consider the possibility of a translation of the work of Julian of Toledo in the most widely known modern language in the world: English. Finally, in 2006 I resolved to introduce a *prospectus* of translation of the *Prognosticum* to Paulist Press, for the Ancient Christian Writers series. To my delight the publisher approved my project in only a few weeks.

The published volume holds a record: it is the first English translation in the world of the *Prognosticum futuri saeculi* of Julian of Toledo. The book contains a full unabridged translation in the English language, along with notes and a broad historical-theological introduction. The three introductory chapters are devoted to Visigothic Spain, where Julian of Toledo was born and lived his intense life; to the life and works of the primate of Spain; and to a global introduction to the *Prognosticum futuri saeculi.* A fourth and final chapter constitutes a theological commentary on the work.

The introductory chapters have a marked theological-historical character and seek to initiate the reader into the genesis and the contents of the *Prognosticum* and into the eschatological thought of the author in his context. Therefore I offer no comparisons or applications of the eschatological thought of Julian to modern and contemporary eschatology. Instead, his influence on later theology, particularly medieval and Scholastic, and also on some supporters of the Counter-Reformation is very much underlined.

After some centuries of virtual obscurity, therefore, the *Prognosticum futuri saeculi* is about to enjoy a second youth and a new worldwide diffusion, which, I hope, will be even wider than the exceptional diffusion of the manuscript in the Middle Ages. It will confirm the place that is due to this work in the history of Christian theology and will serve as a further demonstration that Julian of Toledo can rightly be called the "father" of Christian systematic eschatology.

It is my hope that the knowledge of this work and its author will contribute to an understanding of the importance that the eschatological dimension, above all in its historical-theological aspect, should have in the life of faith of believers and in the reflection of theologians.

ACKNOWLEDGMENTS

First of all, my grateful thanks go to the successor of St. Julian on the Primatial See of Toledo, His Eminence Card. Antonio Cañizares Llovera, who has graciously accepted the invitation to write the foreword that opens the volume.

I also thank warmly the vicar-general of the Primatial Archdiocese of Toledo, Msgr. Juan Miguel Ferrer Grenesche, who so kindly welcomed me to that ancient royal city on a rainy day in November 2006, when, together with two of my Dominican brethren, I went on pilgrimage to Toledo to implore the intercession of St. Julian for the success of this publishing project. To the vicar-general of the Archdiocese of Toledo, I also owe many thanks for having entrusted to the librarian of the Biblioteca San Ildefonso of Toledo, Mr. Gabriel Salinero Gervaso, an urgent request of mine related to some volumes that were impossible to find in the libraries of the Pontifical Universities and the Spanish library of Rome, as well as in the Italian libraries.

I express all of my gratitude to the Rev. Lawrence Boadt, CSP, editorial director of Paulist Press, for having welcomed my first publishing proposal; to the Rev. Dennis McManus, managing editor of the Paulist Press Ancient Christian Writers series, who has brought to birth the project of translation and has approved, encouraged, and recommended it to the editorial director of Paulist Press. He has followed with discreet attention the progress of the different phases of the English translation of the *Prognosticum* and the editing of the introductory chapters, immediately realizing the theological significance as well as the importance of the project of publishing the first ever English translation of the *Prognosticum*. I thank him for the numerous times that he has kindly visited me at the Angelicum in Rome, always expressing great respect for me and a great enthusiasm for the project of translation, an enthusiasm that, I confess, seemed to me, at times, even superior to my own. I remember my bewilderment when he told me, in April 2007, that at the end of the work of translation, and of the introduction and theological commentary, I would have no choice but to present him with "the best edition in the World of the *Prognosticum futuri saeculi* of St. Julian of Toledo" (!).

A special thanks to my colleague, Prof. Julie Tremblay, professor of dogmatic theology at the Superior Institute of Religious Sciences Mater Ecclesiae, who belongs to the same Faculty of Theology at the Angelicum. The linguistic and stylistic revision of the English text of the volume is due to her patient work. She has always carried out her important assignment with meticulous care, thinking of and proposing optimal linguistic solutions.

A thankful thought I turn to Prof. J. N. Hillgarth. I have not had the pleasure and the honor of personally knowing him; yet I have no difficulty in saying that I have practically lived with him for some years, without meeting him, through the reading and rereading of his several writings devoted to Visigothic Spain, to Julian of Toledo and, particularly, to the *Prognosticum futuri saeculi*. He is, without doubt, the greatest world expert on the works of Julian of Toledo, and it is thanks to him that the figure and the work of the great primate of Spain of the seventh century has been reappraised, furnishing researchers with the text of almost all his works in a critical edition. He has shown the greatness and the vast, unbelievable, worldwide manuscript diffusion in the medieval epoch of the *Prognosticum*. Without his critical edition of the *Prognosticum*, this project of translation of the work into the English language would probably never have been born.

A rapid correspondence with Prof. Hillgarth was developed at the end of 2007 and in the first months of 2008, which led to his agreement to my request to make a final check of the translation of the *Prognosticum*. I warmly thank him for making himself available for this, even though his precious work was soon interrupted by *force majeure*. He has, however, furnished important indications and valuable suggestions for the English translation of the more difficult texts of the *Prognosticum*: the introductory letters, the preface, and the *Oratio ad Deum* of the author.

Many thanks to Padre Maestro Rev. Simon Tugwell, OP, for his good suggestions, and to Prof. Angelo Meriani, from the University of Salerno, for his useful help in the retrieval of some important publications. I heartily thank the Rev. Luca de Santis, OP, fellow traveler from as far back as 1968, for his competent Latinist advice, which was in some cases decisive. He has helped me to resolve some interpretative difficulties of the text of Julian, while momentarily abandoning the peaks of his far more arduous and noble translations of the Greek of the New Testament.

A heartfelt thanks to my Dominican Brothers at the Angelicum, with whom I have cheerfully lived the Christian faith for a long time.

The volume is dedicated to my mother, Dina, and my father, Giorgio, who have transmitted life to me and brought me up in the Christian faith, and to my dear brother, Leonardo, who has recently joined them in the heavenly Church.

Fr. Tommaso Stancati, OP
Potame (Southern Italy)—Rome, the Angelicum,
January 14, 2008
Feast of St. Julian of Toledo (Mozarabic Calendar)

INTRODUCTION

Chapter I

THE HISTORICAL, POLITICAL, AND RELIGIOUS ENVIRONMENT OF VISIGOTHIC SPAIN IN WHICH JULIAN OF TOLEDO WAS BORN AND LIVED

This first chapter seeks to introduce the reader briefly to the historical, political, and religious environment in which Julian of Toledo was born, lived and worked.[1] It does not claim, obviously, to exhaust in these few pages the complex history that led to the birth, development, flourishing, and fall of the Hispanic-Visigothic empire in the Iberian Peninsula. Many matters concerning the history of the empire are, therefore, only touched upon; others are treated in greater detail in the following chapters of the introduction, while many others are not mentioned because they do not directly concern the political, religious, and theological story of Julian of Toledo to which the volume as a whole is devoted.

THE ORIGIN AND THE DEVELOPMENT OF THE VISIGOTHIC DOMINATION OF SPAIN

During the fifth century of the Christian era Spain witnessed great political, social, and religious changes that significantly transformed the status quo of the entire peninsula. This true revolution was provoked by the invasion of the barbarian tribes of the Vandals, Alans, and Swabians, who conquered a large part of the territory. Toward the end of the same century, almost to complete the work, a militarily

3

stronger group of barbarians came to Spain—the Visigoths, who, at the end of a long military campaign, settled in the center of Spain.

In the early years, from 409 to 411, the Visigoths settled in the southwest of Gallia, establishing the kingdom of Toulouse and that of Narbonne. Subsequently their dominion extended to the whole of Spain, and the capital of the empire became the city of Toledo, geographically at the center of Spain and equidistant from the borders of the kingdom. Even though they were a minority people (and remained so throughout their domination of Spain, up to the Arab invasion of 711), the Visigoths were able to carry out a progressive consolidation of their political-military dominion and took control of the greater part of the Iberian Peninsula.[2] In a short time they became dominant over the other barbarian tribes, appropriating the territories conquered by them as well as those of the Hispanic-Roman populations. Gradually they extended their power and dominion, and toward the beginning of the seventh century the whole of Spain and part of southern Gallia made up the Visigothic empire, led by a king who commanded two hundred to four hundred thousand Visigoths, almost all of whom were members of the dominant military class, against around six to nine million Hispanic-Roman citizens. Evidently these numbers are not the fruit of a rigorous statistical analysis but a conjectural estimate, more or less close to the reality.

The Visigothic empire had been born and, after an initial and fierce antibarbarian opposition of the native population, gave life to a new civil and religious society, a new culture and a new art, the Hispanic-Visigothic.

Undoubtedly, however, the invasion of the barbarians started in a negative and difficult way and seriously threatened to destroy centuries of civilization and Hispanic history, lived to a large extent under the dominion of imperial Rome or under the influence of its advanced civilization. Now, with the new despotic masters, things threatened to change for the worse. At the beginning of the conquest, King Ataulf,[3] as the historian Paulus Orosius[4] narrates, with the typical psychology of the conqueror had sought to erase all that was Roman in Spain and to replace that secular culture with Gothic dominion and customs. As a sign of the new epoch, the conquered territory would be called "Gothia" or the Goths' country, and no longer Hispania. Very soon, however, the Gothic king and his successors saw that what still existed of the social structure and of the Roman culture in Iberian territory, rather than being destroyed, ought on the contrary to be assimilated by the invading population, since the latter were almost deprived of a true political and social organization that was not tribal. While the Visigoths were, in fact, militarily very strong, their degree of civilization was completely inferior to that of imperial Rome,[5] a civilization that, by that time, had existed in Spain for centuries.

While this political assimilation changed the thought of the Visigothic leaders relatively easily, things were not so straightforward for the Visigothic population, who not only spoke another language and had very different customs, but had also professed, for about two centuries, a heretical Christian faith,[6] that is to say, Arianism. These elements were in conflict with the Hispanic-Roman culture. But in the end, owing to the indefatigable pastoral work of the Catholic Church of Spain (which mustered all of its strengths and its best pastoral and theological minds to mitigate the barbarian customs), these notable differences were also, if not eliminated, certainly strongly attenuated. This was not least because the Visigothic monarchy had the political and religious intelligence to reject the Arian heresy and embrace the orthodox Catholic faith in addition to adopting the Latin language as the official language of the chancellery of the empire, and adopting the administrative and legal model or system of the Roman Empire, which had been tried and tested for many centuries.

The Catholic Church of Spain, which had battled vehemently against paganism since the beginning of its history, was fully aware that it had been called anew to carry out a similar operation against the barbarians, and this met with complete success. This constant and progressive work of persuasion and influence of the Spanish Church on the dominators was, in the end, broadly successful, and it reached its culmination in King Recared's historical decision in 589 to adhere to the Catholic Church and to its theological doctrine.

The Visigoths' turn toward Catholicism

The Spain of the seventh century into which Julian of Toledo was born and in which he lived and worked had for three centuries, and with varying fortunes, taken the form of the Visigothic empire.[7] However, King Recared and all of the Visigothic people had been Catholic for little more than half a century, ever since the king had rejected Arianism during the solemn celebration of the Third National Council of Toledo.[8] From then on, the progressive integration of the Visigothic minority with the majority native population, which was Hispanic-Roman in terms of its culture and Catholic in terms of the Christian faith, was strongly intensified. Hence, the Arians were introduced to the Catholic liturgy and creed, and the Arian hierarchy, its presbyters and bishops, was welcomed into the Catholic Church.[9]

Some historians (for example, M. C. Díaz y Díaz) maintain that the adherence of the Visigothic people to Catholicism was already a reality before the Third Council of Toledo, and, accordingly, the solemn abjuration of Recared could be considered the consecration of a *fait accompli*. Other researchers, however (for example, E. A. Thompson), believe that the conversion of the king did not automatically lead to the conversion of the Visigothic people, who always remained rather perplexed in the face of the unilateral decisions of the Visigothic kings. Subsequently, in the last years of the sixth century, King Leovigild constantly pursued, for the whole period of his reign, the goal of culturally unifying the populations of the Iberian Peninsula. He started this process with the abrogation of the law that prohibited marriage between Hispanic-Romans and Visigoths.[10] This precaution was very important in furthering the integration of the two peoples, but King Leovigild ultimately did not succeed in furthering his cause.

THE ASSIMILATION OF THE VISIGOTHS INTO THE HISPANIC-ROMAN CULTURE

In a short time the Visigoths discovered the importance and wealth of the civilization of the conquered populations of the Iberian Peninsula and the advantage of assimilating themselves, almost naturally, to the Hispanic-Roman culture. Paradoxically, the Visigoths thus turned from being invader-victors into being invaders-defeated, who did not in fact alter the previous civilization with their own tribal customs, as threatened at the beginning of the conquest. This process continued to the point where the Visigothic kings assumed the custom of prefixing their Gothic name with the Roman *praenomen* Flavius, to indicate a sort of *imitatio* or *continuatio Imperii* that they sought to manifest toward the Roman civilization in a desire to realize a sort of ideal continuity with imperial Rome in the style of government they effected. In addition to using the imperial identifier of Flavius, the Visigothic kings also assumed the symbols of Roman imperial power. In time they also underwent a strong Byzantine influence both in their customs and in their royal symbologies.

In the opinion of historians, the Visigoths almost immediately abdicated their authoritarian, violent, and hard dominion of the Hispanic-Roman people and were assimilated into the Hispanic-Roman culture. An example of this assimilation was the wise decision made by the Visigothic kings to use the Latin language as the official language of the empire and to assume the corpus of Roman laws for the administration of power and continuing legislation of the kingdom. Also on the subject of language, a decent form of Latin became the everyday language of the cultured Visigoths and, in every case, the language they used with the Hispanic-Roman people. Another sign of their assimilation was the fact that, even though they professed Arian beliefs at the beginning of the conquest, they never, with the exception of some brief historical periods, persecuted the Catholic Church.

THE FLOURISHING VISIGOTHIC SPAIN INTO WHICH JULIAN OF TOLEDO WAS BORN

Nobody could have foreseen, then, that this empire, which was formed in a relatively short time, seemingly so strong from a military point of view and so well integrated into the Hispanic-Roman culture (because of the politically astute adhesion to the Catholic Christian religion enacted by its kings along with the adoption of the Latin language and Roman legislation for its government), would have been neither stable nor lasting. After little more than a century, starting in 711, it was swept away, practically without offering a real and effective resistance, in the wave of a new invasion of the Iberian Peninsula by the Arabs.

The Visigothic story, therefore, was brief, but with respect to the cultural, social, political, and religious dimensions, the period of domination was both intense and rich. It was, in fact, in the Visigothic epoch that Spain saw the development of the ideal of its political and religious unity, as well as its concrete realization, which was stimulated, shared, and assisted by the Spanish hierarchy of this period, represented by the greatest theological and political minds of the time.

The Spain of the fourth and fifth centuries had already produced men of culture, letters, and poetry of the first degree who were also particularly Christian in their character, for example, the poet Prudentius and the learned versifier of the Gospel, the presbyter Juvencus; but the Iberian Peninsula had also produced such figures in the pagan era: wise men and writers such as Seneca and Martial, or Roman emperors of broad political and intellectual views like Adrian and Trajan, who were without doubt culturally superior to many others.

This is why the Spain of the sixth and seventh centuries, from many points of view, including the artistic as well as the ecclesial and theological-juridical, is universally considered to be a golden age and a great intellectual light in the almost total obscurity of Europe, above all for the production of literary and theological works, almost all written by ecclesiastical hands.

So in Hispanic-Visigothic society a literary and theological culture of the highest level developed involving the upper classes of society, particularly the clergy, monks, and secular members of the aristocracy. In particular the Hispanic-Visigothic political-religious project experienced a great development of the praiseworthy ecclesial and episcopal custom of the convocation of the ecclesiastical (provincial or national) councils, partly because it was supported by the imperial power, which continued to increase in the following centuries and which is, undoubtedly, an expression of great ecclesial and cultural maturity. The bishops of the whole nation, the learned clergy, and the palatine secular nobility participated in these councils. Both civil and political decisions were reached during the councils, above all according to the suggestion of the king; but they also formulated important doctrinal and theological positions that summarized the Hispanic-Visigothic theological approach to the doctrine of the Christian faith, as first and foremost disciplinary in all the fields of the ecclesial life, particularly the liturgical and moral aspects.

During the Visigothic domination of Spain, literature, poetry, and the arts flourished; there was a great development of theological competence, which was expressed in a way tightly connected with the Christian faith in hundreds of works, some of which were very remarkable from the cultural and theological point of view and thus contributed to the conviction that the Church of Spain had assumed a role of primary doctrinal importance in the Western world. Furthermore, a new and culturally advanced society had been created along with a new church, whose vitality points to a theological and pastoral renaissance prior to that of the Carolingian era.

Thanks to the contribution of the church, a good deal of importance was given to education and pedagogical and cultural formation, which was substantially derived from the classical Roman model but was also open to the knowledge of the new *auctoritates*, that is, both the Latin and Greek fathers of the church, and to their pastoral praxis and theological ideas. Some of them, for example, Augustine and Gregory the Great, were not only well known and revered in Visigothic Spain, but were also considered doctrinal models to imitate and develop.

In this national educational project a strategic and farsighted importance was given to the theological and doctrinal formation of young people (both clergymen, as prescribed by some councils,[11] and secular, very often the Visigothic nobility). They, in fact, were to be the future perpetuators and developers of the model of society and church that was successful in the Iberian Peninsula during the Visigothic domination. The monastic and episcopal schools and, to a lesser extent, the secular schools gave a notable impulse to the cultural elevation of the new society that was born as a result of the barbarian invasion. But the pedagogic contribution extended also to the common, but less famous, parish or rural schools that sprang up by the hundreds in the towns and villages of the kingdom and were sensibly concerned with a basic education of the people, who were devoted to a large extent to agriculture and the breeding of livestock and were thus strangers to city life.

This Spain, which was so exuberant in culture and knowledge, liturgy and theology, and its new art (even if this was indebted to Roman and more elaborate Byzantine art)—this new society that had succeeded in integrating the invaders and turning them into lovers and defenders of *Mater Hispania*—is the Spain where Julian of Toledo was born and lived and where so many other illustrious figures of the Hispanic Church before him worked and sensitively contributed to the growth of that ideal of church, culture, and society. The greatest of these were Profuturus of Braga, Iustus of Urgel, Justinian of Valencia, Petrus of Lérida, Eutropius of Valencia, Apringius of Beja, Martinus of Braga, Licinianus of Cartagena, Leander of Seville, Iohannes of Bíclaro, Isidorus of Seville, Braulio of Saragossa, Eugenius II of Toledo, Ildephonse of Toledo, Fructuosus of Braga,

Taio of Saragossa and, last but certainly not least in terms of historical and theological importance, Iulianus of Toledo.

From these names we can deduce that, to a large extent, the intellectual and cultural dimension of the Iberian Peninsula was of Hispanic-Roman origin, not Visigothic. Indeed, in a certain sense one could say that if the ethnic group of the invaders had assumed as its principal tasks governing and the military defense of national unity, then it was the Hispanic-Romans, and above all the clerics, who had been entrusted with the task of thinking about and elaborating doctrines and sociocultural projects of great prominence.

The extraordinary pastoral and theological work of many of these learned and holy bishops, along with a farsighted imperial politics, aroused, for a certain period of time, the hope of building a national, political, and religious unity that would have brought peace, stability, and prosperity to all the members of the kingdom.

In this sociocultural situation, an ideal interpretation or a true theology of history was born in many authors, including Julian of Toledo. This ideal and national integration brought Isidore of Seville to express an extremely positive judgment on the Visigothic empire in his *Historia Gothorum: Gothorum antiquissimam esse gentem certum est.... Nulla, enim gens in orbe fuit, quae Romanum imperium adeo fatigaverit.* He formulated a hypothesis of historical change at a high level, almost an about-face in human history, in which chosen minds saw the realization of a theology of the history and a plan of the divine providence. Isidore affirmed in particular that the Visigoths were not to be regarded as invaders of Spain but, on the contrary, as heirs of the new Roman Empire, which was Christian. And if for many historical, political, and social reasons Rome had lost its central position in the world, then Spain, in all its splendor, was now ready, perhaps by divine will, to take up its role as point of reference and axis around which the new world and the new Christian Church could be born, develop, and revolve. The new world society would have been guaranteed by the Visigoths and by the Catholic Church, and would have preserved all of the good produced by the Roman Empire, projecting itself, so well equipped, into the future of history.

The Catholic Church of Spain as partner of the Visigothic empire

The enlightened Visigothic government considered the Catholic Church, almost from the beginning, as the ideal partner in government and in the development of the nation. The Visigothic empire recognized the objective, centuries-old experience of the church in many fields, which it would have been foolish not to take advantage of, and even more foolish to underestimate. The church was, in fact, experienced and cultured in many important fields: social, economic, and juridical, not to mention, of course, any strictly ecclesiastical affairs. The state was able, therefore, to consult and lean on the church with trust, while facing the many problems that the young empire was not able to face alone. It received advice, lessons, and in many cases a ready and suitable solution to the problem. The state would have been able to assimilate from the life of the Catholic Church principles and norms of a juridical, social, cultural, and, above all, religious nature, which were of great importance in the life of Hispanic-Visigothic society. Particularly striking is the importance that the new kingdom gave to education and the diffusion of culture. This politically wise choice was really drawn from the example of the Spanish Church, which had been engaged for centuries in furthering popular culture, as well as in the intellectual and cultural formation of the clergy.

The church, particularly through the pastoral and theological ministry of a cultured Hispanic-Visigothic ecclesiastical hierarchy, assumed an increasingly important role, even from the political point of view, which led the church not only to take an active part in the election of the king but also to crown him with a solemn liturgy presided over by the bishop of the royal city. During the tenure of Julian, the bishop of Toledo became a leading personage in the empire, especially in political terms, and assumed, with the consent of all the Hispanic-Visigothic bishops, the fundamental function of primate of Spain, that is, the undisputed head of all the local churches of Spain, somewhat analogous to the imperial power.

In view of all these signs of novelty and cultural growth, we can consider the Visigothic epoch, above all that of the sixth and seventh centuries, more as the beginning of a new civilization, and therefore

a true heralding of the medieval period, rather than as the melan-
cholic epilogue of late Christian antiquity.

THE ROLE OF THE CATHOLIC HIERARCHY IN THE
DEVELOPMENT OF THE VISIGOTHIC EMPIRE

We have seen that the Hispanic-Roman population ended up
accepting the new rule, particularly when they saw that the Visigoths
had converted to the Catholic Church and shared their Christian
faith. This was attributable not only to the decision of King Recared,
but also, and above all, to the constant, hard-working, and patient
activity of persuasion carried out by the chosen members of the
Spanish hierarchy.

The most cultured representatives of the Hispanic-Roman
Church became, in fact, promoters and supporters of the adherence
of the Visigoths to Catholicism, as can be seen, for example, in the
appreciation expressed toward the prominent learned saints and
brothers Leander and Isidore, bishops of Seville. According to their
judgment, the Visigothic empire had produced social and political
progress of such importance as to arouse a true love for the country
by all the members of the nation, as is attested by the enthusiastic
patriotism and effective collaboration with the Visigothic state of
many important characters, and of the whole Spanish hierarchy during the most important national councils in Spain.

This was probably due to the fact that the Spanish hierarchy
quickly understood that the dominant ideal of Visigothic politics (to
create national unity and an empire that involved all the peoples of
Spain) was also convenient and fitting for the organization and life of
the Christian faithful who lived in the territory of the empire.

Accordingly, the well-founded fear that the barbarians might
extinguish the Hispanic-Roman civilization in a violent and bloody
way was definitively averted, to a large extent thanks to the politics
and active mediation of the church. But undoubtedly the empire of
western Europe had faded away by now and been transformed into
the kingdoms of Italy, France, and Spain under the control of the barbarian invaders. Naturally, in Spain, as in other places, many barbarians occupied the most important positions in government
institutions (army, administration, etc.) and constituted, to a large

extent, the king's court. In Spain, however, there had arisen a new state that could have developed much further than it did and could have become a point of political-religious reference to the west of Rome if the historical conditions had been more favorable.

THE WEAKNESS OF THE HISPANIC-VISIGOTHIC EMPIRE

Historians agree that the Visigothic kingdom was characterized also by some critical weak points related to its imperial organization. These frailties not only prevented its expected development, but were absolutely decisive for the institutional crisis and the sudden and definitive collapse of the empire.

The first of these weak points was certainly that the Visigothic imperial circle, with a few exceptions, lacked a dynastic monarchy that could guarantee continuity within the empire and could decrease unrest and political intrigue. Such intrigue was particularly frequent among members of the Visigothic imperial court, that is, between the bishops and the magnates or the noble class of the kingdom, and was directed toward demonstrating a powerful influence in establishing the royal succession and electing the successor of the dead king. The absence of a right of succession to the throne brought with it a marked lack of continuity in the royal line and in government, along with continuous political uncertainty. Power games had long determined this regrettable situation: it was the Fourth Council of Toledo that ruled, under pressure of the magnates of the aristocracy who were evidently involved in the struggle for power, in favor of the principle of the eligibility of the king over that of dynastic succession.[12]

To this impediment one must add also the practical impossibility of creating a stable monarchy on account of the frequent violent deaths of Visigothic monarchs, through court conspiracies, popular uprisings, betrayals, and the plots of which Visigothic history is full and which Julian of Toledo witnessed, recorded, and, perhaps unwittingly, took part in.

A further fundamental weak and negative element of Visigothic imperial politics was its hostile attitude toward the ethnic group of the Jews, to the point where they became the object of very severe, if not cruel, legislation on the part of some kings and some of the national councils of Spain. Despite all the possible historical interpretations, this extreme negative attitude toward the Jews remains one of the darkest pages of Spanish history or, perhaps more precisely, is a black stain in the development of the social, political, and religious ideal of the Visigothic empire.

THE VISIGOTHIC HISPANIC ANTI-JUDAISM

The Jewish presence in Spain dates back to very early times.[13] Jews were first established in the Iberian Peninsula as a small minority, but with the passage of time the number of Jewish communities and their "*portentoso*"[14] development in Iberian society increased greatly. Hence, the problems in the relationship between Christians and Jews began. The Council of Elvira[15] made the first provisions[16] against the Jews in order to establish a clear distinction and carefully avoid any confusion between Christianity and Judaism.

At the time of the Visigothic invasion of the peninsula, the Jews of Spain, "superior in culture and astuteness"[17] to the invaders and perhaps also in their traditional, even legendary, spirit of adaptation to the most adverse of historical situations ever since biblical times, achieved a better position for themselves than that of the militarily defeated Hispanic-Roman Catholic population. It is clear that the invaders, perhaps because they were less prejudiced against the Jews, initially accorded them public office and many rights. It is certainly the case that at the beginning of the Visigothic domination a significant number of Jews were court officials, physicians, creditors of their Visigothic occupiers, tax collectors, landowners, and, in many cases, skilled businessmen. They became related through marriage to the Visigoths and also obtained permission to marry Christian women or to hold them as attendants or even as slaves.[18]

The culture of the Jews advanced greatly, particularly on the level of literature and science, to the point where they were able to call Spain their "second Jerusalem"[19] and themselves the protagonists of a new Jewish renaissance. However, their contact with Christians and Muslims also increased—at times it was polemical and violent; at others it was more peaceful. Periodically laws were enacted that were hostile to the Jews and even decrees of expulsion from Spanish soil.

This situation of relative tolerance and social integration of the Jews in the Hispanic-Visigothic empire lasted up until the time of King

Recared.[20] Along with the Visigothic people, Recared adhered to Catholicism, a change that led, henceforth, to a substantial alteration in the attitude of the Visigothic empire toward the Jews. A prohibition of Jewish proselytism was instituted, which eventually led to the forced conversion of Jews to Christianity or the separation of children from their Jewish parents so that they were obliged to receive a Christian education.[21] Marriage between Christians and Jews was prohibited by the Third Council of Toledo[22] with the same canon prohibiting Jews from keeping Christian slaves or holding public office (and therefore having power over Christians). Because of these legislative provisions, Jewish proselytism became difficult and the Jews went from being privileged to being barely tolerated and then, finally, being persecuted. This happened above all because the Jews remained the only religious ethnic group that opposed, de facto, the religious and political union of the Iberian Peninsula reached by Recared with the Catholic faith, and to the unification of the Hispanic-Roman people with the people of the Visigothic invaders. For these reasons the legislation against the Jews in Hispanic-Visigothic territory became more and more intolerant, up to the point where physical violence was cruelly and hatefully used.

In the first decades of the seventh century, the Visigothic kings, particularly King Sisebut,[23] enacted serious provisions against the Jews that were perhaps more directed to the defense of Christians from the Jews than specifically aimed at depriving them of their freedom. King Sisebut promulgated a wretched order by which all the Jews present in Toledo had to be forcibly baptized, on pain of their expulsion from the city and the consequent forfeiture of all of their goods. The result was sensational: around ninety thousand Jews were "converted" to the Christian faith, but, obviously, they never became convinced believers; rather, this unhappy provision multiplied hateful sacrileges. The Councils of Toledo inform us that not only did some of these "converts" turn back to Judaism, but they did so in a more convinced way than before, and with the great fervor of their proselytism they convinced some Christians to adhere to their faith, including even circumcision. Many Jews took refuge in France, however, or disappeared into the countryside.

It is very interesting to note that this exceedingly aggressive and violent attitude of the empire was criticized by the brightest and most open minds of the Spanish ecclesiastical hierarchy. Isidore of Seville, for instance, judged such provisions negatively in his *Chronicon*, identifying them as a product of the unenlightened zeal of the king. This means that in his opinion the Jewish conversions, though necessary, should not be obtained through violence but with "persuasion and reasoning."[24] Naturally, the expressions with which Isidore condemns the conduct of King Sisebut are not of total disapproval, as we would register today, but his criticism does show how an enlightened spirit and intelligence could render, even in his time, a severe and negative judgment of this way of addressing the relationships between Christians and Jews. At any rate, ever since the epoch of Sisebut, the Jewish ethnic group has been able to divide itself into three parts: sincerely converted Jews, those converted by force though remaining Judaic, and Jews that had not received baptism.[25]

With a more balanced judgment on the situation, the Fourth Council of Toledo, while it still prevented all Jews from assuming public offices or giving legal testimony and forced the children of Jews to be educated as Christians, positively decreed that the Christian faith should not be forcibly imposed[26] as it was in the time of King Sisebut.

Although, or perhaps because, they were a minority, however, the Jews of Spain were often a true obsession for the Visigothic kings and some of the ecclesiastical figures of Visigothic Spain. In particular, several of the Councils of Toledo passed a series of laws against them in an attempt to resolve the problem once and for all.

But, undoubtedly, as some historians acutely observe, the need to proclaim many times and put in writing in the acts of the councils the renewal and the validity of the previous laws against the Jews, and to add new measures, points out that, effectively, those laws and measures were fortunately not, in many cases and to a large extent, applied.[27] This is confirmed also by the fact that, despite all the legislation that came down from the Councils of Toledo, the Jews were never assimilated into Hispanic-Visigothic culture and society, and they succeeded in surviving in the Hispanic-Visigothic kingdom only with great difficulty. This was certainly due in part to their own legendary vitality but also to the less-than-perfect application of the severe laws promulgated against them.

The doctrinal polemic of Julian of Toledo with Talmudic Judaism

In this situation, Julian of Toledo, who was also, as we will see later, probably of Jewish descent, did not accept the typically severe religious zeal against the Jews that was directed toward their conversion. It is true that during the reign of Ervig he presided at the council that promulgated negative legislation against the Jews who attacked the Christian faith. But the fundamental attitude of Julian was certainly not one of anti-Judaism, nor were his writings anti-Judaic. None of his writings contains even a reference to the violence against and contempt for the Jews. One of his works, the *De comprobatione sextae aetatis*, as we will have the opportunity to see later, does seek to contest the Talmudic doctrine that teaches that the Messiah will come on the stroke of the sixth age of the world and usher in an epoch that, according to Jewish scholars, was still to come. This criticism, however, comes solely on the biblical and hermeneutic level, that is, the intellectual level. A polemic or doctrinal discussion like this one can certainly not be likened to an anti-Judaic or anti-Semitic attitude.

It is, rather, very probable that Julian of Toledo, in opposition to the current trend, maintained a good relationship with the Jews of Toledo. In this way it is hard to see how the fact that Julian put the first copy[28] of his main work, the *Prognosticum futuri saeculi*, into the hands of a Jewish dealer or merchant named Restitutus, for it to be delivered as soon as possible and intact to the recipient, Idalius, bishop of Barcelona, can be interpreted in a contrary sense, and even as an ironic element, almost a mockery.[29] Indeed, the task given to the Jewish dealer, as we will see later, was so delicate and personal that it is more than reasonable to think that Julian considered the Jewish messenger to be a man who enjoyed his trust, perhaps even as a servant—at the very least a person known and appreciated for his virtues and, therefore, one who had free access to the primate of Toledo.

Despite this positive evidence about the moderation of Julian toward the Hebrews of Toledo, the Seventeenth Council of Toledo, which was convoked by King Egica in 694, a few years after the death of Julian, contains the canon VIII: *De Judaeorum damnatione*, in which provisions are restated for the measures to be taken against Jews who are guilty of rebellion against the king and the empire (abduction of the children so that they could be educated as Christians, prohibition of mixed marriages, etc.). This repetition of legislation against the Jews in the Visigothic empire leads one to think, however, that, all things considered, those laws were largely ignored and that only a group of intransigents periodically brought them again to the attention of the Toledan councils.

This *modus procedendi* is, obviously, open to criticism, but above all it is the dreadful Visigothic repressions of the Jews[30] that were sometimes carried out that ought to be judged very negatively. The rather awkward and simplistic attempt to find a solution through the imposition of Christian proselytism is equally open to criticism. False conversions were its only result. As J. F. Rivera Recio tellingly says, "el bautismo que reciben es agua que resbala sobre los cuerpos sin penetrar en el corazón mosaicamente circuncidado."[31]

In reality, it seems that what was at stake was not so much the conversion of the Jews to the Christian faith as the desire of the Visigothic kingdom to be able to exercise power and control over the Jewish ethnic group, which was important for the Visigothic kingdom for both economic and political reasons.

Technically, however, we cannot say that the Visigothic attitude toward the Jews, however extreme it may have been, was racist or anti-Semitic. This important detail can fortunately be deduced from the fact that the doors were opened to public office for those Jews who converted to the Christian faith, and they were allowed to take up other activities in Hispanic-Visigothic society. Had there existed an absolute sociopolitical racism or an anti-Semitic attitude, not even a possible conversion to the Christian faith and an abnegation of their own religious faith would have been able to blot out their affiliation to the Jewish ethnic group; neither would it have been able to give them the social liberty that was clearly enjoyed by Jews who adhered to the Christian faith.

In any case, the final measures against the Jews taken by King Egica and the Seventeenth Council of Toledo came too late because, within a few years, the Arabs, who had Jewish support, conquered the cities of the kingdom one after another, provoking the miserable fall of the Hispanic-Visigothic empire.

THE KINGDOM OF TOLEDO: THE IMPERIAL CITY OF THE VISIGOTHIC EMPIRE (507–725)

Toledo was the imperial or royal city in which Julian of Toledo was born, lived, worked, and died. The information about his life furnished by the biographer Felix says nothing in particular about Julian's travels or various residences. He probably never lived outside of his beloved Toledo, spending the whole of his short existence there.

But Toledo had not always been the *urbs regia*. Though the Visigoths had the greatest power in the Iberian Peninsula, they had to share the territories with other peoples in the sixth century: the Swabians, who resided in Galicia; the Basques, who claimed the independence of the mountainous zones of northern Spain; the Byzantines, who still controlled large areas in the South of the peninsula. Toward the end of the sixth century, however, the Visigoths succeeded, both through military campaigns and by means of other political and religious initiatives, in completing the work of the reunification of the whole of Spain under solely Visigothic hegemony, albeit in a precarious equilibrium, as Julian himself says in his *Historia Wambae Regis*.

The winning and decisive strategic move of the Visigoths was, undoubtedly, the transfer of the royal capital from Toulouse to Toledo, at the very heart of the peninsula and perfectly equidistant from its natural borders. The author of this move was King Leovigild (568–586), as Isidore of Seville narrates. From that moment Toledo became the capital of the empire and the royal city of the Visigothic empire.

So, in the beautiful and fortified city of Toledo, which was situated on the river Tago and perched on a natural fortress surrounded by enclosing walls that made it resemble a Greek acropolis,[32] a true imperial court was born. Here even the Visigothic kings, who were little inclined to pomp, started to exercise a kind of *imitatio imperii* or followed the Byzantine example of making the figure of the king and the imperial court public (for example, dressing regally, sitting on the throne, minting coins that carried imperial effigies, etc.). King Leovigild also tried to overcome the religious obstacle that most certainly divided the Hispanic-Roman and Visigothic peoples, that is, the division between Catholic Hispanic-Romans and Arian Visigoths. His attempt was awkward and unsuccessful, however, owing to the resistance of the Catholic bishops, who obviously did not subscribe to the king's strange invitation to them to become Arian, that is, to adhere to and confess the Visigothic faith and religious creed.

Furthermore, events became tragic when Ermenegild, son of Leovigild, who had been named by his father as regent of the province of Baetica, converted to Catholicism under the influence of Leander, the bishop of Seville. This put Ermenegild in opposition to his father, who had conquered Seville and invited him to abnegate the Catholic faith. Ermenegild refused and was imprisoned. Subsequently, in mysterious circumstances, he was killed in Tarragona in 585. It seems entirely improbable that the principal instigator of the homicide had been his father. While Gregory the Great in his *Dialogi* regards Ermenegild as a martyr, the historian of the period, John of Bíclaro, instead condemns him as a traitor and a rebel.

On the military side of things, however, Leovigild had more success, conquering various cities and regions and reducing the power of the Byzantines to the southeastern corner of the peninsula; he did the same thing with the rebel population of northern Spain (the Basque region) and with the Swabians, from whom he removed domination over the northwest of the peninsula. Toward the second half of the sixth century, therefore, the territorial and social unity of the empire could be said to be more than worked out, thanks also to the king's presence at the center and the imperial court in the royal city.

In the first ecclesiastical organization of Spain, the metropolitan city had been set as Cartagena, chief town of the ecclesiastical province. Toledo was not considered until Cartagena was nearly destroyed, first by the Vandals in 425, and then by the Swabians in 443. After 554, Cartagena passed under the control of the Byzantines and therefore no longer belonged to the Visigothic ecclesiastical province. It was in those circumstances that Toledo effectively became the metropolitan see of the ecclesiastical province, though without having the right to it from a canonical point of view.[33]

Undoubtedly the process of assimilation of the Visigoths to the Hispanic-Roman culture coincided with the choice of Toledo as imperial city. This, perhaps, was due to the unusual geographical and topographical similarities shared by Rome and Toledo. Just as Rome was at the center of the empire, equidistant from its borders, so Toledo shared a similar geographically central position, being equidistant from the principal cities set at the cardinal points of the Iberian Peninsula; further, as Rome was set on seven hills and was crossed by a historic river, so Toledo was situated on seven hills and with a river, the Tago, at the foot of its mighty fortress. In addition, the Roman conquest had strengthened Toledo and given to the *urbs regia* great buildings of imperial grandeur, a sign of the esteem and importance that the city already had in the context of the Roman Empire. Finally, since Toledo had always suffered from a shortage of water, the Romans had built for its citizens a gigantic aqueduct that brought water into the city, though not up to the summit of the acropolis.

The Toledo in which Julian was born and grew up was a special city. Besides being capital of the Visigothic kingdom, Toledo was bustling with commercial life and was full of artisan experts in their workshops. Just as Cordoba was famous for the tanning and treatment of animal skins, so the artisans of Toledo specialized in the construction and forging of weapons, but they were also magnificent goldsmiths and silversmiths, as demonstrated, for example, by the splendid workmanship seen in the precious metal of the votive crowns belonging to the Visigothic kings that have survived to this day.[34]

As the center of the Hispanic-Visigothic imperial power, Toledo was a city visited by illustrious characters and foreign ambassadors, but one also characterized by dramatic events such as conspiracies and plots for the succession to the throne. The imperial city was often crossed by the triumphal parades of the kings with their armies, back from victorious military campaigns against the rebels, the Saracens, the Byzantines,[35] or the Basques. The outskirts of Toledo were characterized by the presence of various monasteries of monks and nuns, some of which had already produced personalities of great value to the Toledan Church. Among the most famous monuments of the imperial city was the basilica devoted to the Toledan martyr Leocadia, which was constructed by King Sisebut (621). This basilica was the destination of pilgrimages and the venue for various Hispanic-Visigothic councils and, up to the time of the Arabic invasion, was the pantheon for the burials of the kings and the archbishops of Toledo. The veneration of the martyr Leocadia particularly recalled the long period of persecution of the Christians of Toledo that had occurred under Diocletian and Maximus. Also on the outskirts of the city were great Roman ruins: the circus or theater, temples devoted to pagan gods, the *naumachiae* fed by the water of the Tago, and, above all, the farmable zones where peasants sought to support themselves by living off the land.

The society and economy of the Hispanic-Visigothic empire in the seventh century

Despite the sure social progress brought about by the political unification between invaders and the Hispanic-Roman population, it should not be forgotten that Visigothic society continued to practice slavery and class division within its population. Besides the aristocracy, it saw the existence of two separate groups: free men, who were the majority, and slaves, those who were not free. Social position depended on family lineage, possessions or wealth, or power derived from carrying out a public task or from a personal relationship with the king or his court. There was, therefore, a dominant noble and aristocratic caste that constituted the Palatine court. The aristocrats enjoyed various privileges and legal exemptions, often bestowed with little prudence by the king of the day (for example, exemptions from taxes, from judgment, from torture, etc.), and they had the right to their own guard and, above all, to elect the new king.

The rest of the population, on the other hand, was composed of free men, with rights and duties but entirely separate from the aristocracy. Those in an urban environment lived as dealers and artisans, while the majority of the people lived in the countryside, as tenant farmers to the nobility. Many of them were members of the Hispanic-Visigothic army that was assembled on the occasion of the military campaigns. King Wamba attempted wide-ranging reforms in this area, forcing all clergy, including bishops, to do military service so as to have an efficient army always ready to intervene in case of national emergency. However, these measures aroused from various camps opposition that, in the long run, must be regarded as an integral part of the general opposition to King Wamba that ultimately brought about his deposition.

Finally there were the slaves, who were deprived of freedom and rights and considered to be mere commodities. Generally speaking, slaves were enemies captured in war, people who had been in financial difficulties, or people who had committed a crime, and so on. They could be freed from slavery by following a legal procedure, but few succeeded in this endeavor. Slaves either worked the land or became domestic servants. In addition to the nobility and the king, the church itself also had slaves in its service, but it treated them with great moderation in comparison to other sectors of the society.

The economy of the Hispanic-Visigothic society was more or less the same as that of the Roman epoch and rested on two pillars: commerce and crafts and, above all, agriculture, regulated by norms that concerned the owners and the farmers. Agricultural products were also very similar to those of the Roman epoch and included, therefore, a reasonable production of cereals, fruit and vegetables, wheat, oil, and wine. Farming, however, was barely profitable because of the chronic shortage of water and frequent droughts, the scourge of the grasshopper invasions, and the use of outdated methods of cultivation. The forests provided an abundant source of firewood and materials for building and making furniture.

Hispanic-Visigothic society was particularly welcoming to the dealers of merchandise who came from outside the empire, particularly merchants of luxury goods such as perfume, fabrics, jewels, and precious stones. They were, generally, merchants who came from the east (Greece, Syria, Egypt, and, above all, Byzantium), but some of them were Jewish merchants. It is possible, though it is only conjecture, that one such Jewish merchant was Restitutus, to whom Julian himself turned, entrusting to him, as already mentioned, the delicate and precious task, during his journeys across the Iberian Peninsula, of delivering the first copy of the *Prognosticum futuri saeculi* to the bishop of Barcelona, who in the letter of reply to Julian publicly praised the Jewish merchant-traveler for having completed his office with care (but only, as we will see subsequently, after having initially passed an ignoble judgment on him).

The monetary system of the Visigothic empire was very similar to that of the Roman era, that is to say, founded upon the *solidus*, a gold coin that was the unit of currency, while the coin in day-to-day circulation was of a lesser value (half or one-third of a *solidus*). Generally there was an engraved motif or imperial inscription on the coins, while on some editions inscriptions of kings such as Leovigild were to be found.

Daily life in these times, both in the city and in the countryside, was particularly sober, if not difficult. One had no choice but to follow the cycle of the seasons. If autumn was characterized by the vintage, by euphoria for the new wine, by the harvest of olives, and by sowing crops, the following months, those of the rigid winters of the center of Spain, held both cities and countryside in the grip of cold. The long winter put a stop to both nature and human work. As is well known, during those harsh centuries some of today's comforts simply did not exist, and the day, particularly in the winter, drew to a close very early, in the first hours of the afternoon, at the setting of the pale winter sun. Most people did not have access to the unnatural and expensive means of providing illumination such as oil, animal fat, and candles.

The only occupation of the rural population during these harsh winters was breeding poultry or livestock, which scarcely provided enough money for the household. The only occasions on which they even considered the possibility of eating more was at the time of the festal meals over the Christmas period. The people would gather around the great fire in the farmyard on the cold nights of December to celebrate the birth of the Savior, or for the slaughter of the pig that, all being well, would provide food for the whole year. Another occasion for sober fun was the carnival period, prelude to the hard Lenten season that would culminate in the great feast of Easter, harbinger of the spring. When spring finally arrived it was as if everything had come to life anew: in the fields, in human beings, and in the animals. The earth was tilled again for agriculture, and in the warm summer months the harvest could finally be made, on which depended in part the survival of all through the following winter. In short, a natural cycle, but a "cycle" to which human beings seemed inexorably subjected.

THE SPANISH CHURCH BEFORE AND AFTER THE BARBARIAN INVASIONS

When the Visigoths reached and conquered the western part of the Roman Empire, particularly the southern part of Gallia and the whole Iberian Peninsula, the most common religion in these territories with the greatest number of followers was the Catholic Christian faith. The Church of Spain was already highly developed from the theological, doctrinal, and disciplinary point of view. A sign of this high level of development is the fact that the most ancient council for which we possess acts or canons is the council held in Elvira (the ancient Iliberri), a city of Hispania Baetica, in AD 300 or 303. In this council, as is well known, the decision was made to impose priestly celibacy on clergymen, a decision that subsequently progressively extended throughout the whole Latin Church. The same council also rigidly determined the differences between Christians and Jews.

In the same way, on the plane of ecclesiastical personalities, the Church of Spain of the fourth century was already at the cutting edge. An example of this is to be found in the fact that the bishop who presided over the famous Council of Nicaea, which condemned Arianism and formulated the christological dogmatic doctrine, was a Spanish bishop: Osius of Cordoba. The name of Osius is, in fact, the first one on the list of bishops who took part in that important council; it precedes the names of the bishops of the most ancient and venerable churches of the apostolic and subapostolic period, such as Alexandria, Antioch, and Jerusalem.

The Church of Spain then underwent a difficult internal struggle against the Priscillianist heresy, which, born and very widespread in Spain, was both an ascetic exaggeration and also a doctrinally antitrinitarian heresy and very close to Sabellianism. It confused the divine Persons of the Holy Trinity, but was also a christological heresy that resembled Apollinarism. After a long battle fought by a strong and united episcopate, the heresy was defeated in Iberian territory, thus demonstrating that the Hispanic-Roman Church possessed a great theological vitality.

The Germanic peoples who invaded Spain at the beginning of the fifth century were Christian, but had received from their first evangelizers a faith that was strongly contaminated by the Arian heresy. Having conquered Spain, they expressed the desire to make Arian Christianity the official imperial religion. In the whole of the west, after a struggle against that heresy, Arianism had almost completely disappeared and was therefore considered a problem that had been overcome by the dogmatic definitions made during important councils of the past, namely, Nicaea, Ephesus, and Chalcedon. The new diffusion of the Arian heresy brought about in Hispanic territory by the Visigothic conquerors placed it side by side with the orthodox Christian faith of the majority of the conquered people, who were, instead, Catholic Christians. And so a division was created between the two resident peoples in the peninsula, on the one hand, the Visigothic dominators, who professed an Arian Christian faith, and, on the other, the subjugated Hispanic-Romans, who were of the Roman Catholic faith.

It can be said that the conquerors were essentially tolerant toward the Catholic Church and it benefited from relative peace throughout a long period at the beginning of the Visigothic domination. The Catholic bishops were able, therefore, to gather in council, where they took note of the political situation and also prayed for the Arian king.

After a rather uncertain period, with the advent of the reign of Leovigild, the desire for national unity grew to the point that the king made this goal the objective principle of his imperial politics. Therefore, in order to promote the integration of the two populations, he began the process of repealing the law that had prohibited mixed marriages between Catholics and Arians. A series of victorious military campaigns against rebellious populations undoubtedly increased the popularity of this Visigothic monarchy. But it was, above all, the struggle against the Byzantine enclave and the conquest of the kingdom of the Swabians in Galicia, which hence became a Visigothic dominion, that helped the Hispanic-Roman people to see that the conquerors had now begun a stable and structured settling in the Iberian Peninsula and had truly founded an empire that was also of benefit to the Hispanic-Roman population. Arianism was the single obstacle to the completion of national unification.

Solutions were found for this problem as well, however, and within a few decades Arian Christianity, including its hierarchy, was absorbed and assimilated into the confession of the Catholic faith.[36] The Hispanic-Visigothic Church, therefore, became a national church, centralized and more closely united to the state, with Toledo as the religious and political capital.[37]

Its organization grew and was consolidated above all through the common use of councils that involved all the bishops and the local churches of Spain. The organization of the Spanish Church during the Visigothic period did not undergo substantial changes with respect to that established during the centuries of Roman domination. In that period the six civil provinces of Tarragona, Cartagena, Baetica, Lusitania, Galicia, and Narbonensis (called also *Septimania* or *Gallia gothica*) were confirmed as ecclesiastical provinces under the leadership of a bishop who treated as suffragan the other churches of his ecclesiastical province. The only change of significant import was the transfer of the metropolitan see of the ecclesiastical province of Cartagena (which had fallen under Byzantine control) to Toledo, which proved to be important and decisive in the political choice of the Visigothic kings to establish the capital of the empire at the center of Spain. This geographical transfer began a glorious chain of events that led the metropolitan Church of Toledo to be recognized by the Twelfth Council of Toledo (681) as the Primatial Church of the whole of Spain with its bishop as primate, giving him the right to consecrate bishops for every diocese of the kingdom.

Episcopal praxis foresaw that the bishop of a diocese would stay in the church that had been entrusted to him up to his death, that he would live in the urban center while also extending his jurisdiction to rural parishes, and that he would be chosen by the clergy and the people of the diocese. With the passage of time, and after the reign of Recared, the king's approval became essential for an episcopal election to be considered valid.

The local bishop had some very precise obligations as far as pastoral ministry was concerned and generally carried them out conscientiously, particularly in the area of the formation and education of the clergy. There was no lack, however, of contrary examples of moral laxity among both bishops and the rest of the clergy, particularly concerning the ecclesial prescriptions pertaining to priestly celibacy that were enacted by the Council of Elvira (around 300–303) and confirmed by all the subsequent Councils of Toledo.

The bishop had jurisdiction over the clergy on the questions that directly concerned the Christian faith, such as doctrinal deviations, superstitions, infanticides, and so on, and on the Jews. He could impose, through a court, punishments that included excommunication, public penance, imprisonment in the monastery, and exile, though he could not inflict bodily punishments, mutilations, or death sentences.

THE SPANISH LITURGY: HISPANIC-ROMAN AND HISPANIC-VISIGOTHIC OR MOZÁRABIC

A sensitive contribution to the attainment of political-social compactness and unity of religious faith of the Christians of Spain also came, without doubt, through the original form of the Hispanic-Visigothic liturgy.

A historical presentation of the Hispanic liturgy is not within the scope of this volume, but because of its intrinsic beauty, antiquity, and importance in the life of the Hispanic-Visigothic Church, along with the fact that among the merits of Julian of Toledo, he was, together with other Spanish fathers, an expert reformer of the Hispanic-Visigothic liturgy as well as the editor and creator of new liturgical prayers and renovator of ancient formulas, it seems to be opportune to devote a brief excursus to this ancient and venerable Christian rite, a precious pearl of the Hispanic-Visigothic tradition that reached its full maturity in the seventh century with its splendor so great as to be able to affirm that that same seventh century is to be considered the golden age of the Hispanic liturgy.

The Hispanic-Roman liturgical rite is truly the way in which the Spanish Church has celebrated the sacramental liturgical actions for about ten centuries. It is, therefore, the result of a centuries-old editorial itinerary, marked by sobriety and essentiality of the texts and liturgical actions, which stretches from the settlement of the first Christians in the Iberian Peninsula to the seventh century.

Such a tradition inherited historical liturgical forms that derived from the primitive celebration of the mysteries of the Christian faith during the apostolic period and, subsequently, as testified to, for example, by the martyr Justin, from the Church of Palestine of the middle of the second century. This does not exclude the fact that it was also influenced by the ancient and venerable Churches of Antioch and Alexandria, as well as those of Rome and Byzantium (much admired in the Visigothic epoch). The Hispanic rite developed, however, as autonomously as the Latin liturgical rite. Therefore it shares antiquity and honor with other Latin liturgical rites such as the Roman, Ambrosian, Gallican, and so on, but it has the great merit of having better preserved the original historical-salvific and strongly eschatological flavor of the texts and liturgical actions, as seen in the most archaic liturgical forms.

Essentially, the Hispanic eucharistic liturgy, with its sobriety and simplicity, closely reproduces the apostolic eucharistic gesture that began to be celebrated in Jerusalem after the death and resurrection of Jesus. To that simple eucharistic gesture were added, in time, some earlier ritual forms such as the proclamation of the Word of God, and prayers and liturgical invocations according to the time in which the liturgy was celebrated.

This ancient rite was preserved also during the Visigothic domination of the Iberian Peninsula and, from the fifth to the seventh centuries, even experienced development and was greatly enriched, above all thanks to the contribution of the great and scholarly bishops of the Visigothic Church. The rite was also preserved amid much difficulty during the Arabic domination, both in Toledo and in the north of Spain.

Subsequently, above all through the work of Pope Gregory VII and for reasons that are practically incomprehensible to us—that is, a politics of centralization of Roman pontifical power and the desire to impose uniformity on liturgical rites—an expansion of the Roman rite took place that was accepted also in Spain, especially in the kingdoms in Aragon and Castile, and so the Hispanic rite was in serious danger of being extirpated.

In Arab-occupied territories, however, such as Toledo, for example, the Hispanic rite survived and, for this reason, was often referred to as the Mozárabic rite, after the name by which the resident Christian believers were identified in the territories ruled by the Arabs. For the populations subjected to Arabic domination, the Mozárabic rite became, therefore, both the sign of the incarnation of their own faith and the sign of the cultural, religious, and national identity of their resistance to the invader, a true symbol of liberty and a perspective of liberation.

The fidelity to the rite proper in the Spanish Church brought about a new epoch of Christian martyrs in Spain and the birth of a spirituality of martyrdom that can be seen very strongly in liturgical texts. The archives of the cathedral churches and some parishes of Toledo, along with cultural centers and the libraries of abbeys and monasteries, preserved a part of the precious liturgical manuscripts of the Hispanic-Mozárabic liturgy, in this case the Missals and the Breviary.

After the Spanish reconquest of the territories under Arab rule took place in the eleventh century, the rite was again at risk of disappearing, just as was the architecture of the Visigothic churches, which was so close in its artistic expression to the liturgical texts. It was thanks to the Christians of Toledo, impassioned custodians of the liturgical tradition with which they had expressed their faith for centuries and that had kept them politically united in the most dramatic moments of the invasion and Arabic rule, that the rite, through a compromise, was vigorously maintained in six ancient parish churches of Toledo, while in the cathedral of the royal city and in the other parishes and churches of Spain the use of the Roman rite was continued. The great Catholic kings of the fourteenth and fifteenth centuries were also great supporters of the recovery of the religious and political symbolism of the Mozárabic rite, which was so tightly bound up with the ideal of the Catholic Christian empire of Visigothic Spain.

The notable decrease of believers in the ancient Toledan parishes and the difficulties faced by the clergy in understanding the ancient liturgical books led to the risk, once again, of a disappearance of the ancient and venerable rite. It was thanks to Cardinal Cisneros (1495–1517) and his patronage that the Mozárabic rite was submitted to an accurate revision that took as its starting point the ancient liturgical texts. From this revision a new printed edition of the Mozárabic Missal and Breviary was created for use in the surviving Toledan parishes and in a special chapel, dedicated to the *Corpus Christi*, and built by the same cardinal in the Cathedral of Toledo. In the early decades of the sixteenth century, there was a revival of the Hispanic-Mozárabic rite in Salamanca at the Talavera, or Savior's chapel.

Subsequently another extraordinary patron of the Spanish Church, the primate of Toledo Cardinal F. de Lorenzana (1772–1800),[38] edited a new, improved, and annotated edition of the Hispanic-Visigothic Missal. An authentic restoration of the rite took place in the monastic world, when the treasure of the Hispanic-Mozárabic liturgical books from the tenth and eleventh centuries was rediscovered, after centuries of lying forgotten in Spanish libraries and archives, in the monastic communities such as the Benedictines of Silos and that of St. Millán de la Cogolla, or exhumed from other archives or European libraries such as Paris, London, and Verona. Thanks to specific studies, such as that of Dom Marius Férotin, the ancient liturgical texts were revived.

Finally, the primate of Toledo, Cardinal González Martín (1972–1995), submitted the Hispanic-Mozárabic Missal to a new revision, with respect to the recommendations of the Second Vatican Council and in particular to the Constitution on the Sacred Liturgy *Sacrosanctum Concilium*. The constitution declared that "Holy Mother Church holds all lawfully acknowledged rites to be of equal right and dignity; that she wishes to preserve them in the future and to foster them in every way. The Council also desires that, where necessary, the rites be revised carefully in the light of sound tradition, and that they be given new vigor to meet the circumstances and needs of modern times" (§4). The purpose of the new revision of the Hispanic-Mozárabic rite was to get the most authentic text possible. It was also addressed to other churches, from Spain and further afield, that sought to experience the ancient rite or those with particular historical-religious interests. It is desirable for this praiseworthy historical rediscovery to extend beyond the Missal, to include the complete sacramental *Ritual*, the *Martirologium*, the *Sanctoral* and other liturgical books.

A new reference to the Hispanic-Mozárabic liturgy is to be found in the *Catechism of the Catholic Church*. The *Catechism*, citing *Sacrosanctum Concilium* §4, affirms at n. 1203: "The liturgical traditions or rites presently in use in the Church are the Latin (principally the Roman rite, but also the rites of certain local churches, such as the Ambrosian rite, or those of certain religious orders) and the Byzantine, Alexandrian or Coptic, Syriac, Armenian, Maronite and Chaldean rites. In faithful obedience to tradition, the sacred Council declares that Holy Mother Church holds all lawfully recognized rites to be of equal right and dignity, and that she wishes to preserve them in the future and to foster them in every way." In the Spanish edition of the *Catechism*, the reference to the historical and theological value of Hispanic-Mozárabic liturgy is more explicit: "Las tradiciones litúrgicas, o ritos, actualmente en uso en la Iglesia son el rito latino (principalmente el rito romano, pero también los ritos de algunas iglesias locales como el rito ambrosiano, el rito hispánico-visigótico o los de diversas órdenes religiosas) y los ritos bizantino, alejandrino o copto, siriaco, armenio, maronita y caldeo."

It is particularly worthy of note that a precious and solemn recognition of the value and venerable antiquity of the Mozárabic liturgy occurred during the Second Vatican Council, when the holy Eucharist was celebrated in the Basilica of St. Peter according to the Mozárabic rite in the presence of the council fathers. Furthermore, in 1992, the bishop of Rome, Pope John Paul II, on the occasion of the presentation of the new edition of the Mozárabic Missal, personally celebrated the holy Eucharist in the Vatican basilica according to the Mozárabic rite[39] on the solemnity of the Ascension, as a sign of homage to the venerable Church of Spain and as recognition of the historical and liturgical value of the Hispanic-Visigothic liturgy.

Today, the Hispanic-Mozárabic rite has only around two thousand faithful and six priests and its daily celebration in the Cathedral of Toledo is not well supported. However, the Archdiocese of Toledo, with the agreement of the Spanish Episcopal Conference, is undertaking a work of reevaluation and popularization of the Hispanic-Mozárabic liturgy,[40] focusing particularly on the eucharistic liturgy and on Hispanic-Visigothic liturgical chant (also called melodic or Eugenian chant), which is attributed to the predecessor of Julian of Toledo, the musicologist and bishop of Toledo, Eugene II. This praiseworthy work aims not only to increase the appreciation of the historical heritage of this venerable liturgy, so full of spirituality and theology, and to promote its renaissance in every liturgical-sacramental ambit, but particularly to encourage the participation of the faithful in the original liturgical Hispanic-Mozárabic celebration. Such participation, according to the *Praenotanda* (nn. 159–60) to the postconciliar edition of the Hispanic-Mozárabic Missal, must be encouraged not only within the historical ecclesial communities of Spain, which have inherited and jealously preserved the rite, but also in other Catholic communities provided that they are duly prepared.

Chapter II

THE LIFE AND WORKS OF JULIAN
OF TOLEDO (642–690)

THE HISTORICAL-BIOGRAPHICAL SOURCES OF THE LIFE
AND WORKS OF JULIAN OF TOLEDO

Julian of Toledo is considered the last of the great bishops of Visigothic Spain whose life and writings are known,[1] although only partially, and who had a religious, political, and, above all, theological influence in Spain and in western Christianity. According to some scholars, he was an "hombre de estado, Príncipe de la Iglesia y personalidad literaria,"[2] and therefore "was not an obscure provincial author....Educated in the royal capital, primate of Spain from 680 to 690, he knew both Isidore and Gregory well, but his debt to them does not obscure his originality,"[3] and we can consider him to be "el escritor mas fecundo de la escuela toledana."[4]

Others have emphasized Julian's talent as a skilled administrator of ecclesiastical power, in addition to his qualities as a theologian. For example, F. X. Murphy, in an excellent article, defines Julian as "in all probability, the ablest administrator as well as the most competent theologian among the Visigothic Bishops of Spain."[5] Even more radical and flattering is the judgment of Murphy when he describes Julian, for his wise methodological innovations in theological language pertaining to christological matters, as simply "the most competent seventh century theologian in the West."[6]

The only important and, above all, reliable historical-biographical source, because it is contemporary with Julian of Toledo, is the brief *Vita seu elogium*,[7] written only three years after Julian's death by the metropolitan bishop Felix, his second successor[8] to the episcopal

see of Toledo.[9] Felix, who would be the last metropolitan of Toledo in
the seventh century, lived very near Bishop Julian and was perhaps
also his disciple at the Episcopal School of Toledo, where Julian was
for some time "grammarian and preceptor,"[10] and Felix was certainly
his presbyter appointed as archpriest of the Cathedral of Toledo during Julian's episcopal ministry.[11]

Felix had been, therefore, a direct witness of the intense episcopal ministry of Julian, but also of his relationships with the imperial
Visigothic political power and with the papal see. Felix also knew
Julian of Toledo's abundant historical, poetic, liturgical, and theological literary production. He is, therefore, the most ancient biographer
referred to by all subsequent writers who have dealt with Julian of
Toledo and have tried to reconstruct his earthly story.[12] The *Chronicle*
of Isidorus Pacensis (754)[13] judges Felix as a good bishop, very prudent and serious in the exercise of his episcopal ministry.[14]

In the brief biography of Julian, written in the imperial city,
Bishop Felix shortly describes the most important stages of the life of
his predecessor, and particularly the qualities of his ministry; he also
furnishes us with a rather incomplete[15] but very precise list of the
works of Julian that he knew, along with brief but adequate descriptions of his writings. In the opinion of Hillgarth, the precision of the
description of the works probably depends on the fact that the list
seems to have been written while the biographer had the codices of
the works of Julian before his eyes,[16] deposited on a table in some
room of the episcopal atrium or in the rich library of the bishop's
palace in Toledo. Felix wrote only a few years after the death of the
great primate of Spain, and he browsed through the works of Julian,
briefly summarizing parts of the most remarkable contents of them.
The truly biographical part occupies the first part of Felix's short text.
The information that he supplies is judged by researchers to be a reliable, but very generic, compendium of the data about the life of
Julian and about the peculiarities of his character, centered, above all,
on three virtues: zeal, justice, and charity.[17]

Despite its brevity, Felix's biographical work is of fundamental
importance for reconstructing the essential parts of Julian of Toledo's
life and episcopal career in the bishopric and for getting to know
Julian's writings. The *Vita Juliani*,[18] in fact, is composed of twelve brief
chapters, half of which are dedicated to the list and brief description
of Julian's works. This detail is indicative of the importance that Felix

attributes to the literary production of the bishop-theologian Julian of Toledo, to provide a good framework for judging him.

There is no reason to doubt that the biography written by Bishop Felix was written in Toledo. With an evident attitude of benevolence toward Julian, it expresses the admiration and the consideration of the author for the personality and the pastoral ministry demonstrated by Julian in his decade of holding office in the Metropolitan Diocese of Toledo: a "panegírico entusiasta, pero digno de fe e inapreciable para medir la actividad literaria de Julián."[19] In the opinion of historians, therefore, the *Vita* is trustworthy, albeit sober in the details that we would now consider of great importance. In fact, the *Vita* completely lacks any news about Julian's family, the place and the precise date of his birth,[20] the particularities of his studies, and other important news, such as Julian's presidency of four national councils of Spain,[21] as well as the diatribe that opposed Julian to the Church in Rome[22] and his activity as a politician attentive to the developments of the internal politics of the Hispanic-Visigothic kingdom.[23]

Felix is rather inclined to introduce Julian under a benevolent and special light, omitting some details evidently considered inopportune by the biographer[24] (for example, Julian's probable Jewish ancestry). It is thus fully possible to share what a noteworthy expert on Julian[25] affirms: all those who have been interested in the work and the person of Julian of Toledo during the course of the centuries or who have treated of him have inevitably had to resort to the brief but substantial biography written by Bishop Felix.[26]

In addition to the biography written by Felix, we have some autobiographical notes of Julian, which are found, as we shall see, though rarely, in his works.

Another source of historical information on Julian, not contemporary but nonetheless worth quoting, is the eighth-century *Chronicle* written by Isidorus Pacensis, from which we learn the important news about the Jewish ancestry of Julian. He writes, in fact, in his *Chronicle*, also called the *Continuatio Hispana*:[27] Hic anno primo concilium duodecimum Toletanum in aera 719 triginta quinque episcoporum cum inaestimabili clero vel Christianorum collegio splendidissime colligit. In cujus tempore Julianus episcopus "ex traduce Judaeorum," ut flores rosarum de inter vepres spinarum productus, omnibus mundi partibus in doctrina Christi manet praeclarus, qui etiam a parentibus Christianis progenitus splendide in omni prudentia Toleto manet edoctus, ubi et postmodum in episcopatu exstitit decoratus.

The acts of the Twelfth, Thirteenth, Fourteenth, and Fifteenth Councils of Toledo, which were presided over and led by Julian, are also to be considered sources for knowing Julian more closely, since he is also the literary author of a large part of the councils' canons.

Lastly, in his *Liber de scriptoribus ecclesiasticis*, Sigebertus Gemblacensis, a Benedictine monk of the beginning of the twelfth century, briefly remembers, and finally without any confusion with Julian Pomerius: Julianus, Toleti Hispaniarum urbis episcopus, scripsit ad Idalium episcopum Barcinonae librum quem praetitulavit Prognosticon, id est Praescientiam futuri saeculi.[28]

The secular confusion between Julian of Toledo and Iulianus Pomerius

A final piece of introductory information concerns the confusion of identity that often occurred over the centuries with authors or the transcribers between Julian of Toledo and the monk and African abbot, *sed in Galliis florentem*[29] Julian Pomerius,[30] or between two persons of the same name (Julian), both of Toledo, to one of which was attributed not only the name of Pomerius but also the works of the true Julian of Toledo.[31] Or else, the same author has been erroneously and indifferently referred to as "Pomerius" and "of Toledo." Just when the confusion between the two Julians, of Toledo and Pomerius, began is unknown, but it is an established fact that some manuscript codices of the *Prognosticum*, from the ninth century onward, already confuse the two persons. Contributing to the interchange of persons was probably also the fact that Julian often quotes the writings of Julian Pomerius in his works.

As for the origin of the strange appellative "Pomerius" given to Julian of Toledo, J. Madoz gathers some hypotheses, without any of them being really convincing.[32]

A remote testimony of the confusion between Julian of Toledo and Julian Pomerius is found already in the *Adversus Elipandum*[33] of Alcuin of York (d. 802). Alcuin, in fact, identifies Julian of Toledo as author of the *Prognosticum futuri saeculi* or of the *Prognostica*, as he calls the eschatological work of Julian, though referring to him as "Iulianus Pomerius" and excusing him, in every case, from the adoptionist heresy that raged in Spain and of which Elipandus, bishop of Toledo, was a supporter.

Moreover, at the end of the eighth century, a letter of a certain Tusaredus or Tuseredus, probably a monk of Cordoba, addressed to Ascaricus, bishop of Astorga in the Asturies (northern Spain), distinguishes the true identity of Julian of Toledo from that of Julian Pomerius. The interesting text, which praises Julian of Toledo's *Antikeimenon*, a work of biblical exegesis devoted to the solution of the apparent contradictions of the biblical texts, affirms: Illi vero, qui contradicunt dicentes: nemo ascendit in coelum, nisi qui descendit de coelo filius hominis, legant librum "beati Juliani non Pomerii sed Toletani."[34] Evidently the attentive monk of Cordoba was already aware of the confusion between the two theologians and tried to correct it by warning his readers not to confuse the persons because of the homonym.[35]

In the twelfth century, Honorius Augustudunensis still confused the work of Julian Pomerius, *De vita contemplativa*, with the *Prognosticum futuri saeculi* of Julian of Toledo, saying that Julian Pomerius had written the *Prognosticos tres de futurae vitae contemplatione libros*.[36] As signaled by Flórez,[37] however, Pelayus or Pelagius (1101–1129), bishop of Oviedo, created a lot of confusion by mixing this time not only the titles of the works but also the names, referring even to a single personage: *beatus Iulianus Pomerius Toletanae sedis archiepiscopus*.

Besides, an eleventh-century manuscript catalogue of relics, compiled by the same Bishop Pelagius and preserved at Oviedo, says: sancti Juliani Pomerii qui arcam ipsam a Toleto Ovetum transtulit. The relics, however, are really those of St. Julian of Toledo and not of Julian Pomerius, who is never mentioned as a saint and anyway goes back to the fifth century. It was, in fact, the body of Julian of Toledo that incurred a transferal from Toledo to Oviedo at the beginning of the Arabic invasion of the Iberian Peninsula.[38]

Moreover, Rodrigo Jiménez de Rada, archbishop of Toledo at the beginning of the thirteenth century, in his *De rebus Hispaniae*[39] (otherwise called *Chronicon*, the ruling source of the history of Spain up to the fifteenth century), perpetuated the confusion in that he copied the famous passage of chapter 50 of the *Continuatio Hispana* or *Chronicon*, of Isidorus Pacensis,[40] which speaks of Julian of Toledo, but he introduced in the copied text, immediately after the name of Julian, the expression *dictus Pomerius*, a nickname that was evidently in common use in his time. Thus he continued to promote the many equivocations about the true identity of Julian of Toledo precisely in the medieval era and beyond: In cuius tempore iam Iulianus episcopus, "dictus Pomerius" ex traduce Iudeorum, ut flores rosarum...etc.

After two more centuries, the conflation of the names and the personages continues. In fact, in the *De scriptoribus ecclesiasticis*[41] of the prolific spiritual writer Benedictine abbot Ioannes Trithemius (d. 1516) we find not only that their names are still being equated but that their works have been confused as well, inasmuch as he attributes all the works of Julian Pomerius to Julian of Toledo and includes only the *Prognosticum* among those that the latter actually wrote.

From the *Notitiae Historicae* of Nicolas Antonio we finally know that the *Chronicon*[42] of the Pseudo Julianus added a third Julian to the already tangled story of the first two, and he underlines, ironically, *duobus non contentus.*[43]

The conflation of the two Julians still continued for centuries, if we just think of how even in the sixteenth century, erudite people and expert humanists such as the Jesuit P. Labbé[44] and G. Barthios continued to follow the wrong correction of Rodrigo Jiménez de Rada. And in his *De Scriptoribus Ecclesiasticis liber unus,*[45] at the end of the brief biography devoted to Julian of Toledo, Robert Bellarmine also speaks of "tres Iuliani Pomerii, unus Presbyter, alter Diaconus, et tertius Episcopus" (!).

Beginning in the eighteenth century, with the growth of the studies of medieval prosopography, however, these historical errors of identification have been entirely disproved and eliminated.[46]

The birth of Julian and his baptism in the Cathedral of Toledo

Julian was born, therefore, in the royal city of Toledo,[47] *caput Hispaniae,*[48] in approximately 642,[49] in full Visigothic kingdom. The month and the day of his birth are unknown. He was baptized in the Cathedral Church[50] of Toledo, the Church of Santa Maria,[51] probably in the period following Easter or after the solemnity of Pentecost,[52] the only period in which the baptistery of the Cathedral of Toledo was "open."[53] And the name *Iulianus*[54] was imposed upon him, a name of the typical "sonoridad romana"[55] and thus very different from the German-Visigothic names that resulted rather "disonantes"[56] in comparison to the sweetness of the Latin of the liturgical language. We know nothing about his family, though it is likely that he was not an only child and that his lineage was of those who lived in the center of the city. Such silence of information about his original family could be interpreted as meaningful and favorable to the hypothesis that Julian was of Jewish origin and thus of an origin unmentioned by his contemporary biographer, but which will subsequently be admitted by other authors.[57] We do not even have any information about Julian's physical appearance, nor do we know anything about the composition and the rank of his family in the Visigothic kingdom.

The question of the probable Jewish origin of Julian of Toledo

On this matter the tradition expresses itself in a double sense. According to an important source,[58] in fact, Julian was of Jewish descent, but his family was already Christian.[59] This was highly probable, because at the time there was a vast Jewish presence in Visigothic Spain.[60] Some problems were created by this situation, for example, involving conversion to the Christian faith,[61] not to mention the political plots in which it seems that various Jews (also baptized) took part, such as happened in the history of King Wamba.

Reasons of political and religious opportunity probably convinced Bishop Felix, Julian's contemporary biographer, to keep silent about his Jewish descent, while, as Murphy rightly notes, spreading the news about his Jewish descent must no longer have been a problem several decades later,[62] when other chronicles were written about him, such as the one quoted by Isidorus Pacensis.

Important contemporary authors, as well as such experts on the history of Toledo, the Visigothic empire, and the life of Julian as J. F. Rivera Recio and J. N. Hillgarth, do not see reasons to deny the Jewish origin of Julian. The historical information about it is very explicit, and Julian himself takes care to make known that his ancestors were detached from the Jewish religion in distant times and that his parents were, therefore, already Christians.[63] In the sixteenth century, the *Crónica General de España* of Ambrosio de Morales maintained that the authors of his time unanimously considered Julian to be of Jewish ethnicity.[64] Authors in subsequent centuries[65] did the same, perhaps placing excessive trust in the one testimony of Isidorus Pacensis[66] or in the *Chronicle* or *Continuatio Hispana* of 754.

Other authors suppose, instead, that Julian had been a *conversus*, that is, a convert to the Christian faith from Judaism, as a youth or an adult,[67] or that his parents were recent converts to the Christian faith,[68] with sincere fidelity and without hypocrisies or yielding to the violent anti-Jewish legislation of King Sisebut.[69]

Modern historical prosopography of Judaism considers Julian of Jewish descent and affirms that there were many others like him, especially among the princes of the church, who in the Visigothic era were opposed to the Jews and persecuted their ancient co-religionaries with the zeal typical of converts.[70] In addition to Isidorus Pacensis, in the eighth century,[71] another convert from Judaism in the Scholastic period, Paul of Burgos,[72] would confirm this traditional interpretation. Yet both Flórez[73] and Cardinal de Lorenzana[74] deny the Jewish descent of Julian.

Finally, we must also mention the classical objection of those who for various reasons maintain, instead, that Julian could not have been of Jewish stock. The first reason is the previously noted historical unreliability of Isidorus Pacensis's *Chronicle*, as shown in some passages of his work and maintained, for example, by E. Flórez. In second place is the difficulty, indeed great, that Julian could occupy such an important position as the metropolitan see of Toledo if he were of Jewish ethnicity:[75] beginning from the rule of King Recared, in fact, all Jews were excluded from public positions,[76] unless their Jewish lineage lay very distant in time—that is, unless their ancestors had already been Christians for several generations.[77]

The most critical position is probably that of U. Domínguez Del Val, who maintains that if Julian had been of Jewish descent he would not have been able to occupy such an important public position. He adds that an exception to this rule, as we have seen in place from the reign of Recared onward, "debe probarse positivamente."[78]

Education and pedagogic formation in the Visigothic kingdom

We know with certainty that Julian attended the Episcopal School of Toledo for some years, before becoming deacon and then presbyter of that diocese.

It is possible to think that all the adolescents of the Hispanic-Romans and Visigothic Catholic Christians living in the city who in general came from noble or high-ranking families received their formation and education in the Cathedral School.

Yet the majority of those who lived outside of the walled city did not have access to higher learning and had to be satisfied with the lower level of education they could receive in the environments of the rural parishes. Nonetheless, those who cultivated the earth and raised livestock did have a basic knowledge of mathematics and some juridical principles related to the purchase and sale of cereals, livestock, and so on. This means that they had a base culture sufficient to face the daily problems associated with the work of the fields or with the breeding of livestock, and also that Visigothic society had not provoked a sharp or deep cultural separation between the learned and the ignorant. A basic level of culture and Latin language, in fact, existed also in the rural zones, even if it was hardly comparable to the formation of the urban social elite.

In this way, an encyclopedic and vast work such as the *Etymologiae* of the great Isidore of Seville could be interpreted as an attempt by him to produce a synthesis of ancient and modern knowledge intended not just for learned souls but rather, as profit and practice, also for the great majority of the population without any level of higher education. The twenty books of the *Etymologiae*, in fact, contain all the knowledge of the time, but communicated through a methodology that often appeals to the memory and defines and orders reality starting from the meaning or etymology of the name of that same reality. Isidore undoubtedly gives maximum importance to the etymology, almost as if it were a guide to the discovery of the mysteries, and had an almost metaphysical value as a tool of knowledge.[79]

The work of Isidore contains, therefore, the classical subjects that constituted the liberal arts (the *trivium*: grammar, rhetoric, and dialectics; and the *quadrivium*: arithmetic, geometry, astronomy, and music) and that could also have been quite difficult for the reader or listener with an average cultural level. Yet a large part of the *Etymologiae* also contains an opening to the "modern" knowledge of Isidore's era, which contemplates all types of "science" and everyday reality, the knowledge that the farmer or the breeder or the housekeeper also acquired with their own eyes as they reaped the wheat, milked the cows, or pruned the vines. Isidore supplies the reader of—or, better, the listener to—his work with a key to interpreting their microcosm through accessible interpretative dimensions, such as through the explanations of medicine, classical cosmology, zoology in all its aspects, anthropology, botany in many of its manifestations, mineralogy, the ingenuous oceanography of the times, and, above all, what Isidore considers the teacher of humankind—history. Besides that, Isidore's encyclopedia is full of descriptive references related to the most various cosmic realities and human activities, such as construction, foods, shipbuilding, animal training, transportation, containers, masculine and feminine clothing, shoes, chess, ball games, metals, wars, gems, horse tack, and so on.

Thanks to the acts of the Toledan councils, and to their attitude of treating not only religious or theological matters but also, as is known, matters of social and political importance, we are able to know the probable pedagogic contents and the common subjects of teaching in the Cathedral School of Toledo. The Fourth Council of Toledo,[80] in fact, which was held in 633, decreed the importance of the education and learning of the cathedral schools.[81] There were probably two distinct levels of study[82] for adolescents (canons 24 and 25): an elementary level of education and a subsequent, or higher, level of studies.

The first level was a basic education geared toward the reading and understanding of texts, generally of a religious nature. Much care was taken to teach the correct pronunciation and accentuation of the words. To this purpose, the study of reading was practiced with great appeal to or use of the memory, which is particularly efficient and elastic in adolescents. The pupils repeated aloud, many times, what the magister taught them to pronounce. A parallel form of learning was that of song: to sing what was learned meant to add an incisive and strongly memorizable element, such as music, combined with the words. All of this simplified and favored the learning process. But, while in the pagan culture the pupils were made to memorize the classical texts (poetic and not), in the ecclesiastical schools the biblical texts were often used instead, especially the Psalms and the wisdom books, and in particular, the sequences of the proverbs, which were very useful for their conciseness and brevity. But the ecclesiastical schoolteachers were not above resorting to some pagan text taken from the classics that was particularly suitable for the mnemonic exercise.

This simplified mnemonic methodology also had some very practical motives: first of all, it avoided having to find and use expensive writing materials (tanned skins, parchments, quills, inks, special desks to hold the tanned skin firm in order to produce an orderly writing, etc.). All of this was beyond the reach of the pupils of the first scholastic level and also beyond the daily use of the schools of the time, especially for economic reasons. This same expensive apparatus of writing belonged, instead, to the *scriptoria* of the monasteries and the *curiae* or chancelleries of the kingdom or the ecclesiastical environments, where the work of the copyists took place. Using the writing tools of the time required special skill and experience. With inks, quills, and precious parchments the adolescents would certainly have only made a big mess. This is the simple reason why the rudiments of Latin grammar were taught to the pupils by exploiting, above all, their prodigious memory.

In addition to reading, however, the pupil also had to learn to write, which did not only mean forming the letters to make words. The student also had to learn the most common ways to abbreviate literary expressions (small tricks to save time and money), as well as numbers, and how to count. This was done through the use of a very ancient and economical, but not very practical (because "without memory"), writing material: the classical wax tablet, upon which the memorized words were engraved with an iron stylus, a residue of the Roman school that still persisted up to the sixth and seventh centuries.

The whole course of learning took place as an internship in the Cathedral Church. Once they had finished the first level, the students who chose to do so requested to continue their studies, passing on to a subsequent pedagogic level. In general, only those who were following an ecclesiastical career or, as the councils repeatedly recommended, those who were to be provided with a special formation were admitted to this higher level of education. Also among these, however, were those pupils directed toward becoming officials of the court or the kingdom, or those children of wealthy families or of noble origin who continued their studies for their own choice.

In the second level of studies the pupils were educated, first of all, in a serious in-depth examination of grammar, studying morphology and syntax, but also prosody, that is, the intonation, rhythm, and accentuation of the spoken language. Subsequently, they studied the liturgy and liturgical texts, and ecclesiastical music. Above all, they deepened their knowledge of Sacred Scripture, exercising in exegesis precisely the interpretative grammatical instruments they had studied and learned in the preceding years of study. The collections of theological and canonical texts, canonical regulations, and theological doctrines were documents subjected to close examination.

Subsequently the pupils were involved in learning rhetoric, poetics, and declamation, reading directly the codices of the classical literary works and those of the fathers of the church. In some schools, in-depth study of subjects that were only touched upon in the first cycle of studies, such as mathematics, music, and so on, took place. Special attention was given to preparing the candidate for public debate and for dialectical disputation, both actual as well as in a possible written work.

The entire formation process was directed toward preparing the candidate to be able to create a good catechesis, a convincing sermon, both persuasive and communicative, or an elegant prayer, using anthologies or *florilegia* of classical Latin texts or texts of the fathers, but also to undertake other pastoral activities. After the end of the long period of formation, the students finally proceeded to ordination to the diaconate at the age of twenty-five and priestly ordination at the age of thirty, but not before having passed many difficult intermediate examinations that were greatly feared by the candidates.

Julian's adolescence: His education and formation at the Cathedral School of Toledo

Prior to adolescence, Julian, probably because his parents, being of wealth, had already offered him as an oblate[83] at the Cathedral Church of Toledo while still a child, did his first studies at the Episcopal School of Toledo, which was situated near the metropolitan basilica.[84] From the words of the biographer Felix: *illic ab ipsis rudimentis infantiae enutritus*,[85] it seems highly probable that the Episcopal or Cathedral School was found near (*illic*) the residence of the bishop[86] and the cathedral, and that the general principle of the school, as well of the pedagogic guides that constituted the underlying structure, was that of simultaneously instilling in the pupils profane science as well as religious piety and knowledge.

The biographer Felix does not say anything about the period of time passed by Julian and by the other pupils in formation and education, but we know from other sources that the Church of Spain had long ago ensured that the clergy and other social classes would receive good instruction and education.

Already in the Second Council of Toledo (527), the first three canons specifically concern the formation and education of the clergy[87] in addition to loyalty to the bishop and the obligation of priestly celibacy. Subsequently, the Fourth Council of Toledo (633) greatly insisted upon the necessity of communal life among adolescents aspiring to the priestly ministry,[88] where, in a direct way, under the watchful guidance of lectors (that is, teachers) and of a wise and exemplary priest as the principal pedagogue, they attended to their formation in an environment dedicated to them.[89] The pedagogic formation was so strict that some pupils who were particularly spirited or disobedient to the educational plan were sent for correction and discipline to the monasteries surrounding Toledo, where they were subjected to an even more severe rule.[90]

Naturally Julian was not the only adolescent of Toledo to follow this basic scholastic plan. From Felix we know the name of a schoolmate of Julian who was probably involved in the same course of studies: the noble Goth Gudila. And the biographer Felix was himself probably a pupil of the same school, and, subsequently, of Julian himself, when the latter became, in turn, teacher at the Episcopal School.

In the years when Julian attended the Episcopal School of Toledo, it was directed by Bishop Eugene II,[91] as noted by the biographer Felix[92] and as Julian recalls in the third book of the *Prognosticum*, quoting his venerated teacher and preceptor in reference to the theological matter regarding the realism of the bodies of the risen ones at the end of time.[93] The eschatological content of such texts of Eugene mentioned by Julian leads one to believe that a theological dialogue occurred between Julian and his preceptor that continued after the basic formation and the formation as clergyman in the Cathedral School. It seems, therefore, that Eugene was no longer for Julian the revered *Praeceptor noster*[94] of his adolescence, "teologo e poeta, liturgista e musico"[95] for whom he certainly had a sacred respect, but a master of theology, of whom Julian felt himself to be, and indeed was, a disciple[96] as well as a partner in dialogue in his theological maturity.

In addition to Eugene II, in his humanistic and theological formation, Julian also benefited from the vast culture and the pedagogy of another great bishop of Toledo, Ildephonse, who had been his teacher in the Episcopal School. Julian later wrote a brief *Vita seu elogium* about Ildephonse when the former became bishop of Toledo.

The demanding pedagogy and the solid intellectual formation in use at the time[97] were probably moderated by the great affection that Bishops Eugene II and Ildephonse felt for their pupil[98] Julian. The result of this substantial youthful formation is verifiable in the cultural judgment expressed about Julian by Ioannes Tritemius, who defined him as "a very erudite man in the Sacred Scripture, sufficiently educated in the profane doctrines, with a clear and scholastic style."[99]

All that he had learned at the Episcopal School added to his desire for knowledge and his bright intelligence.

It is not difficult to imagine that Julian's adolescence was also the suitable time for receiving an introduction into the mysteries of faith, celebrated in the sacramental liturgy of the Cathedral Church of Toledo in which he probably often took part by acting in some liturgical function during the sacred services.

J. F. Rivera Recio quotes a curious medieval document, the eleventh-century *Diario*[100] of a student of the Swiss monastery of Reichenau, who describes with an abundance of detail the structure of an academic year and the life of the pupils of a monastic school. *Mutatis mutandis* this unique work could, according to the author, describe the ambience and the scholastic activity of the atrium of Toledo in the Episcopal School, with Julian himself and the pupils of the school as the main characters along with their pedagogues, particularly Eugene II and Ildephonse of Toledo.

According to the *Diario* of the student of the Swiss monastery, the scholastic year began, as it still does today, with the assembly of the noisy and happy students. After a few weeks of study, the pupils learned to read and to write. The fatigue of learning was accompanied by days of rest and long strolls in the surrounding areas, visiting monasteries and other monuments. Subsequently, the grammar of Donatus was studied, with the help of an older student charged with verifying the learning of the eight parts of the oration and the rules of their use. Punishments for scholastic breaches were frequent (deprivation of part of lunch or other sorts). The students spent the afternoons applying what they had learned in the morning lessons, and in the evening they would read a passage of Sacred Scripture. The next day they were to repeat that passage from memory. They then studied the second part of the grammar of Donatus, and they read and transcribed the Psalms. At the end of the winter, each student had read and transcribed the entire book of the Psalms. The pupils, having by now reached the second year of studies, could participate in the liturgy of the hours in the monastery choir or in the Cathedral Church on Sundays and feast days.

The third year of studies included the study of the classical and Christian poets, as well as classical prosody, especially that of Virgil. In the fourth year the more advanced pupils taught those who had just entered the school. At the end, examinations were taken in the subjects studied during the three preceding years. Having passed this examination, the student could then begin the study of rhetoric, using the works of Cassiodorus, Cicero, and Quintilian as textbooks. Such authors were commented on and used for oratorical compositions. History also was studied, using the works of Paulus Orosius, Eusebius of Caesarea, St. Jerome, and, more recently, St. Isidore, but also those of such pagan authors as Sallust and Livy. Subsequently the student began the study of dialectics, which rendered the pupils, by now true men of culture, capable of facing polemics and exercises of various kinds, bearing in mind the rules of Porfirius, Cassiodorus, and Boetius. The disputations were founded upon collections of texts and canons of the juridical anthologies, as well as upon the knowledge of some parts of the *Etymologiae* of St. Isidore of Seville.

At the end of the first three years, a dreaded general examination on the *trivium* concluded the first level of studies. The students could thus pass on to the higher level, that is, to the knowledge of mathematics and other similar subjects (such as geography, zoology, mineralogy, botany, and astronomy), which, together with music, constituted the *quadrivium*. At this point in the course of studies, at the age of about twenty, the students who were continuing toward an ecclesiastical career began the truly theological-dogmatic treatises.[101]

If this were, more or less, the *cursus studiorum* followed by Julian of Toledo, he undoubtedly had a solid and strict education and ecclesiastical and classical formation according to the prescriptions of the Fourth Council of Toledo. In comparison to other schools, however, it needs to be said that the Episcopal School of Toledo, from which Julian profited so highly, was experiencing a "peak" moment,[102] in that, as we have seen, his preceptor and master was a very learned personage of an elevated cultural, moral, and religious level—Eugene II,[103] first abbot of the monastery of Agali and then archbishop of Toledo, the best Latin poet of Visigothic Spain.

Therefore, when Eugene became archbishop of Toledo, he sustained the Episcopal School in many ways, first of all by directly participating in the formation of the students, especially of the clergymen, by teaching various subjects, above all, music,[104] in which he was very experienced, but also by endowing the already rich library of Toledo, thanks to the cultural level of his predecessors, with many other codices, in particular the works of the fathers of the church, written in Latin, and perhaps the works of the Eastern fathers, written in Greek.

Julian of Toledo: Hispanic-Roman or Visigothic?

Apart from the question of the more or less probable Jewish descent of Julian, another question is raised: whether Julian, who was born and integrated into the culture of the Iberian Peninsula, must be considered Hispanic-Roman or Visigothic. The question is not secondary, because the possible affiliation with one or the other culture provides a foundation for hypothesizing some information and favoring some additional explanations in order to understand the character, thought, pastoral action, and behavior of the theologian and bishop Julian of Toledo. Moreover, from a historical and social point of view, the Hispanic-Roman or Visigothic identity could be quite significant from the familial and social point of view as well as from an economic perspective, which may well shed light on possible privileges enjoyed by Julian.

After the Germanic peoples invaded the Iberian Peninsula, therefore, even though the invaders had by then been introduced and assimilated into Hispanic society, it is normal to ask if a public person of a certain importance was to be considered Hispanic-Roman, that is, a native of pre-Visigothic Spain, or the descendant of the invaders and conquerors, that is, Visigothic. But without official registry documents from that time, and when even the historical information contained in the chronicles or in the *De viris illustribus* is unable to provide an answer to the question, the only criterion that remains for establishing the descent of a person is to verify if his name, and/or its meaning, can be considered to be of Hispanic-Roman or Visigothic origin.[105]

In the case of Julian of Toledo, the name given to him in baptism, Iulianus, is certainly Latin and, on the basis of this criterion, he should certainly be considered of Hispanic-Roman descent. Nonetheless, this does not prevent him from probably having a distant Jewish heritage. If, in fact, he had been of Visigothic descent, some trace would have remained at least in his name, because during the whole time of their hegemony the conquerors never renounced their names. It suffices to scan the list of the Visigothic kings, bishops, or nobility of Spain between the sixth and seventh centuries, which frequently contains typical names of the conquerors, which are so difficult to render in Hispanic-Roman phonetics. A concrete example can be found in the brief *Vita* of Julian written by Felix. Speaking about Julian's adolescence, he quotes the young Gudila, whose name is obviously Visigothic, and who, as we will see, was a brotherly friend and colleague in the ecclesiastical career of the future primate of Spain, but who died prematurely while deacon of the Church of Toledo.[106]

Along with his name, therefore, the fact that Julian was baptized "in the principal Church of the city" of Toledo—that is, in the cathedral, as Felix narrates[107]—can also indicate that he belonged to a family of Toledan nobility and/or antiquity, and that his lineage had some relationships with the local bishop and religious connections with the Cathedral Church, that is, with the central fulcrum of the ecclesial life of Toledo.

The fact, then, that Julian subsequently was educated, as we have seen, in the Cathedral School and that, in the prescribed years, he followed the course of studies and the ministerial levels to the point of becoming presbyter and then metropolitan archbishop[108] of Toledo and primate of Spain can be considered confirmation of the affiliation of Julian's family with the Hispanic-Roman nobility, or, in any case, another sign that he had not been, in short, a *parvenu*, or that his family was of low social status.

The fervent young Christian Julian and the great friendship with the noble Visigothic Gudila

Julian's adolescence was characterized by a great friendship with his contemporary, the young noble Gudila, whose name, as we have said, betrays a likely Visigothic origin[109] and who was also probably a pupil at the Episcopal School of Toledo. We know nothing about Gudila's origins and personal history. The biographer Felix affirms that the two brotherly friends were bound by deep affection.[110] Julian's friendship with Gudila lasted for the entire period of studies at the Cathedral School, up to ordination as deacon and beyond, until Gudila's premature death. To show in a meaningful way the intensity of the friendship between the two, Felix, who evidently knew their life well, compares it to the friendship and the exemplary love that existed among the earliest Christian believers who belonged to the Church of Jerusalem and are exalted in the Acts of the Apostles (4:32).[111] A modern author likens the brotherly friendship between Julian and Gudila to the one between David and Jonathan in the Old

Testament, or to the one between Alipius and Augustine in the patristic period.[112]

During the course of studies, as Felix tells us, the two friends had
strongly shared a desire and a common ascetic aspiration: to experience and perhaps embrace the monastic life so as to enjoy contemplative quiet in some oasis of monastic spirituality on the outskirts of
Toledo.[113] Such enthusiasm may have been aroused by the diffusion
and popularity of monasticism in seventh-century Spain, or by the fact
that many of the great and saintly bishops of the period came from
monastic environments.[114] It may even have been inspired by the
direct example of the master and pedagogue of the two inseparable
friends, Bishop Eugene II, who was himself attracted by the monastic
life at a young age,[115] or still more by assiduous participation in liturgical services in a monastery in the proximity of Toledo.[116] The two
brotherly friends were evidently fascinated by the monastic and religious life in its classical form. It is not difficult to imagine the long discussions between the two friends about the pros and the cons of a
possible monastic choice, toward which they undoubtedly felt
attracted. This pious desire, however, did not last long and soon
waned as a result of unknown events. The abandoning of this desire
was probably determined by the appointment of both as clergymen
who, having already received the minor orders in 667,[117] were directed
toward the studies and the pastoral activity of the Diocese of Toledo.
According to Felix, the renouncing of the monastic life was decided
by Divine Providence (*aliter in superni numinis fuit judicio*),[118] that is, it
was by divine will that the pious desire for the contemplative life be
put aside in favor of belonging to the diocesan clergy of Toledo.
Evidently God had other projects in mind, for Julian in particular but
also for his great friend and brother Gudila. But, perhaps even more
simply, it may be that Felix did not know the true motive that led the
two young men to renounce their monastic aspirations.

The unsatisfied monastic desire of the two friends[119]

Julian's biographer, as we have seen, underlines the fact that
Julian and his friend Gudila, in the fullness of their youth, had a
strong desire to embrace the monastic life. But, because of events that
the biographer Felix identifies as providential, in the end both opted
for the priestly ministry and the pastoral life in service to God in the
Church of Toledo.

It seems important to underline that the monastic ideal had become very widespread in seventh-century Spain, starting from the initial foundations of the fifth century. One can say that every Iberian diocese was surrounded by several monastic foundations, both male and female, and that the number of monks was much greater than that of the diocesan clergy.[120] Some of these monasteries became very important for religious or political reasons and some of the monks and abbots were chosen and consecrated bishops (e.g., Eugene of Toledo and Ildephonse) or in other ways actively participated in the conciliar sessions of the Hispanic-Visigothic Church and often served as advisers of the king. The monastic foundations evolved around five religious rules: two attributed to St. Fructuosus of Braga;[121] one to St. Leander of Seville; one to his brother, St. Isidore; and one to John of Bíclaro. Female monasticism was also highly developed; in Toledo, for example, there were several female monasteries inside the walled city.[122]

The monastic religious movement flourished for some time in the land of Spain, but problems began when the monasteries became the destination for those whom ecclesiastical authorities obliged to public penitence or to withdrawal from worldly life. They were confined in the monastery in order to make worthy penitence. In an analogous way, as we have seen, the monasteries also became the place of punishment for those students who were expelled from the Episcopal Schools or for those clergymen who were insubordinate or suspected of heresy because of having consulted magicians and diviners, as well as for those who had participated in bloody revolts, who were stained with impurity, and the like. In short, in the common mentality, the monastery took on the character more of a jail than of a place in which the vocation to the holiness was to develop into perfection.[123]

In reality, monasteries were created as places of Christian fraternity where an austere and simple life was divided between prayer, work, and rest, according to a by then consolidated scheme. In particular, the western monasticism of the High Middle Ages was characterized by the love and care devoted to the religious and secular cultures, above all through the manufacturing and the copying of book codices. Some monks of every monastery, therefore, were trained for this purpose, and they were greatly appreciated for the care that they took with the calligraphic writing and the copying of the books. We owe it to these anonymous, patient monks that the works of the fathers, the Greek and Latin classics, and the collections of theological and dogmatic texts have reached us, partly, intact. The preservation and the transmission of the "literary joys"[124] of antiquity are owed to the work of copying that they carried out in the *scriptoria* with patience, artistic creativity, and technical ability.

This positive monastic ideal so briefly described helps us to understand why Julian and his Visigothic friend felt so attracted by the monastic life. But, as we know, their desire did not come to fulfillment, and they had to replace the contemplative peace of the monastery with the exercise of the priestly office in the service of the Lord and the people of God. Therefore, "they decided to be clergymen of the Church of Toledo."[125] Felix comments on this ministerial choice in a very positive way: "They were virtuously busy in instructing their charges, seeking their benefit; they served the Lord with zeal, being very active in obtaining the decorum of the house of the Lord."[126]

Various factors could have dissuaded the two great friends from entering the monastery. Perhaps, and mainly, the dialogue with their preceptor and teacher, Eugene II, could have convinced them that the monastery was not the right life for them, in that they would be able more effectively and usefully to serve Christ, their master, and his church by remaining as priests within the Church of Toledo in such a delicate historical moment as that of the Visigothic hegemony.

The ecclesiastical careers of Julian and Gudila

The two friends progressively ascended the various levels of training for their vocations as clergymen of the Church of Toledo, including the diaconate,[127] to which they may have been ordained in 669–670,[128] and then on to the priesthood, to which Julian was ordained some years later,[129] that is, upon completing the canonical age of thirty.[130] In these same years, beginning with the death of Ildephonse, Julian had the opportunity to make his intellectual and pastoral gifts count in the life of the diocese, occupying himself with prudence and dedication in carrying out the various ecclesiastical offices entrusted to him by the bishop and entering the Episcopal School, perhaps together with Gudila, where they probably eventually became established teachers.[131] Beyond this little information, we know nothing about the life of Julian in this period of priestly ministry before he was ordained bishop.

Around ten years after the ordination as deacon, probably toward the end of 679 or 680,[132] suddenly, and in a tragic way or at least prematurely,[133] Gudila, who had in the meantime become archdeacon of the Church of Toledo,[134] suddenly died on September 8.[135] This sad event must have struck the young, but already mature, priest Julian deeply. Gudila was buried in the suburban monastery of St. Felix,[136] near the small city of Caba.[137] In this regard, it is not difficult to imagine how often Julian went to pray at the grave of Gudila, raising prayers of supplication to God for his friend or offering, as priest or bishop of Toledo, the Eucharist for his companion of dreams and hopes, of enthusiasms and of a strong, common Christian spirituality.[138] Indeed, only death could have separated them.

Julian, therefore, continued alone along his ecclesiastical path that soon placed him on good terms with the political power of the monarchy as well. In approximately 673, Julian had already written the eulogistic *Historia Wambae*, about the Visigothic warrior king who had freed the kingdom from insurrections and betrayals. He would also become a personal friend of the palatine knight Ervig, of Byzantine origins, who rose to the throne a few months after Julian's election as bishop of Toledo, but, as we will see, in controversial and even mysterious circumstances that involved Archbishop Julian himself.

Julian's relationships with the ecclesiastical authorities were excellent, as is shown by his relationship with the bishop of Toledo, Quiricus, and the friendship that bound him to the bishop of the distant Barcelona, Idalius, to whom he dedicated his most important work, the *Prognosticum futuri saeculi*. In this period he was probably called *Primicerius*, or the palatine clergyman of the praetorian basilica of Saints Peter and Paul[139] in Toledo, an office to which all the inferior clergymen owed obedience. His main task must have been to guarantee the decorous execution of the liturgical music and the service of worship in the cathedral and in the other churches of the diocese, as well as to verify the state of the churches of the royal city and to send the *ostiarii* in the outlying parishes to notify them of the days of fasting. It was always up to the *Primicerius* to watch over the life and the behavior of the clergy and, if necessary, to correct it, or to inform the archbishop in cases where obedience was lacking. It was obviously a very important and delicate responsibility, which the *Primicerius* carried out as the coadjutor of the bishop, even if in the Diocese of Toledo the *Primicerius* was above all the superior, after the archbishop, of the praetorian clergy.[140]

The election and the consecration of
Julian as bishop of the episcopal see of Toledo

In subsequent years Julian still had the opportunity to show his intelligence, his natural talents, his love of the study and knowledge of Sacred Scripture and the fathers, as well as his skills of prudence and *savoir faire* in addressing the most delicate matters. He probably divided his life between his priestly duties and sharing in the life of the Episcopal School, where he held the delicate role of helping the students, that is, as a young teacher, who, in the meantime, perfected his biblical, liturgical, patristic, and canonical studies.[141] In all likelihood he had at his disposal the three books of the *Sententiae* of Isidore of Seville or the works of the great fathers of the church, especially Augustine and Gregory the Great, or even the precious canonical-theological collection (the *Hispana*) that already existed in Julian's time (and which he, as archbishop, would help expand in terms of documentary quantity and importance). The *Hispana* gathered the best of the acts of the ecumenical councils, the pontifical letters, and the acts of the Hispanic councils not only for practical use but also as evidence of the very high cultural level of the Church of Spain. It was regularly consulted by scholars, theologians, and canonists, as well as by the chancelleries of the kingdom. All these works had to be present in the well-stocked episcopal library and accessible to the young teacher of the Episcopal School.

Julian's charity toward the poor, so praised by the biographer Felix,[142] deserves particular mention as a dimension of perfection that would characterize him as priest and above all as bishop of Toledo.

On January 16, 680, only a few months after the death of Julian's friend Gudila, the metropolitan Quiricus also died, and Julian was chosen by King Wamba as bishop of Toledo and presented to the Spanish bishopric for episcopal ordination. His great religious and human qualities, as well as his decade-long pastoral and theological activity as priest, were determinative of his being chosen for this office. It is easy to imagine that the priest Julian was one of the most well-known and esteemed ecclesiastics of Toledo, for his culture and many other virtues that the biographer does not hesitate to enumerate.

Felix does not refer to any hesitancy on the part of the newly elected bishop, who must have thus gladly accepted the serious responsibility of governing the diocese of the royal city and rejoiced in the choice and in the preference shown him by King Wamba[143] upon having examined the possible candidates. Evidently King Wamba, already pleased by the historical account of his enterprises so elegantly and vigorously written by the priest Julian in his *Historia Wambae*, had seen in Julian the necessary requisites of a good archbishop: patriotism, religious zeal, and good literary personality. On January 29, 680, a Sunday, the young priest Julian, who at the time must have been only thirty-six or thirty-eight years old,[144] was ordained bishop of the *urbs regia* by the bishop of Játiva in the Cathedral of Toledo, dedicated to Santa Maria,[145] where he had been baptized and where he had received his first communion, where he had prayed and served the Lord in liturgical worship.

After sixty years of bishops coming from the monastic clergy, Toledo finally saw as their own archbishop a priest chosen from among the secular clergy of the royal city.[146] His election to the bishopric of Toledo also implied that he was bishop of the imperial Visigothic court residing in Toledo, and of a vast ecclesiastical province—that of Cartagena, which included around twenty suffragan dioceses of Toledo. It is completely possible to suppose that, as the new bishop, Julian would have had continuous contacts and frequent consultations with the bishops of the suffragan dioceses in order to have a common pastoral direction and full integration into the civil society. The suffragan bishops, for their part, showed themselves to be "obedient and reverent" to their metropolitan,[147] not least because their ordination, ministry, and office depended on him. As decreed by the sixth canon of the Twelfth Council of Toledo, the bishop of Toledo was also, as metropolitan, the examining and ordaining bishop of the vacant dioceses of all the ecclesiastical provinces of Spain, that is, of Cartagena, Tarragona, Narbona, Betica, Lusitania, and Galicia. Finally, he was the head of the provincial ecclesiastical organizations, such as the ecclesiastical court, and he was responsible, in the highest degree, for the observance of the ecclesiastical-canonical norms of the church promulgated by the councils and episcopal sessions of the Hispanic-Visigothic Church.

As the archbishop of Toledo, Julian himself had the faculty of summoning the bishops to council according to the canonical norms of the Church of Spain. By that time Toledo had been a metropolitan diocese for almost a whole century. But under the episcopate of Julian, already beginning from his first year in office, the diocese of

Toledo acquired an undisputed supremacy over the entire Hispanic-Visigothic bishopric, a supremacy that was legally ratified by the sixth canon of the Twelfth Council of Toledo, but also universally accepted by the ancient and venerable Church of Rome. In fact, Pope Leo II, inviting the bishops of Spain to embrace and to ratify, with a "simple and speedy acceptance,"[148] the christological doctrine of the Sixth Ecumenical Council of Constantinople (680–681), sent four letters to Toledo, one of which was personally addressed to the metropolitan archbishop of Toledo, Quiricus (though already dead for two years). This was a sign of the Church of Rome's recognition of the role of honor occupied by the see of Toledo within the Hispanic-Visigothic bishopric; the other three papal letters were sent to King Ervig, to the whole Spanish episcopacy, and to Count Simplicius, as representative of the nobility.[149]

From all this it is easy to understand how the election and ordination of Julian as archbishop of Toledo meant for him the assumption of serious responsibilities on both the religious and the civil level.

The main task of priests in the seventh century was to extend the pastoral ministry of the bishop to each of the individual components of the diocese, through the celebration of the Eucharist for and with the people, the preparation and the baptism of new believers, the reconciliation of penitents with God and Mother Church, the catechesis of the people of God and the blessing of the believers in all circumstances of the hard life of that century.[150] The great task of the bishop, then, who by ordination became united with the keeper of the apostolic succession, was to extend the fruits of the salvific work of our Lord Jesus Christ to the men and the women of his time. This he achieved through continuous Christian catechesis and the celebration of the mysteries of faith in the sacraments of the church, especially in the sacraments of confirmation and reconciliation as celebrated during the eucharistic liturgy, which thus allowed the public penitents to return in the bosom of the Christian community.

Despite all these manifold pastoral, administrative, judicial, and governmental tasks, Bishop Julian succeeded in finding the time to write many works, some particularly meaningful for history, grammar, biblical exegesis, and theology. Therefore, in addition to the episcopal magisterium that originated from his function as vicar of Christ, successor of the apostles and master of faith and morals, he also exercised a magisterium that we could define as scientific, that is, founded on his multiple competencies in subjects such as the exegesis of the Sacred Scripture, knowledge of the works of the fathers of the church, liturgy, and the formulation of theological doctrines. This work was particularly taxing for him from an intellectual point of view, and yet he succeeded in organizing his pastoral work and governance so well that he was able to devote himself to the study and the editing of his numerous literary works.

As bishop, Julian was responsible also for the formation and education of the clergy, ordaining new priests and deacons, receiving the religious profession of the numerous monks and nuns of the urban and suburban monasteries, consecrating new abbots, inaugurating new churches built according to the characteristics of the solid and sober Visigothic architecture and consecrating its small altars, and, in a special way, participating in and, in the case of Julian, presiding over some of the great conciliar sessions of the Church of Spain. This he did even without having the full right to do so, since he was not the most elderly bishop, as was the custom.[151] Evidently, his personality, his theological preparation, and his culture rendered Julian of Toledo an episcopal figure of a superior and very influential level.[152]

Julian was assisted in the exercise of his apostolic mission by the urban clergy of the royal city, whom today we call the presbyterate or presbyteral council, who surrounded him in the liturgical celebrations and constituted the college of elders in reference to him. This college was comprised of the archpriest, the archdeacon, and the *Primicerius* of the Diocese of Toledo.

The rural clergy, who resided in the small or medium-sized villages, developed an important mission of catechesis and delivery of the sacraments to the people, but they were certainly more disadvantaged than the urban clergy. The rural clergy had barely enough culture to practice a decent priestly ministry. Upon nomination, it was custom of the Church of Spain to give every rural priest the "official book," or *libellus*,[153] that contained all the norms that the priest had to follow on the liturgical and canonical levels and of which he had periodically to give an account.[154] The parishioners were to provide for the priest's sustenance. In a period in which there were yet no privileges of exemption of jurisdiction, the regular clergy also depended directly on the bishop, who had charge also of the elections of abbots and the course of religious life. Despite the fact that this hierarchical and ministerial structure was quite efficient, during the Visigothic period serious problems of simony and nepotism were not unknown among the bishops and clergy. Yet these problems were nonetheless always seriously addressed, together with other pastoral concerns about the diocesan and regular clergy, by the strict provisions of the national and provincial councils of Spain. In relation to this, it must be said that the bishops also possessed a judicial power that was exercised for limiting abuses such as the quarrels among presbyters, for evaluating the authentic faith of converted Jews, and so on. In more serious cases another court intervened, considering that the bishop did not have the power to impose death sentences.[155]

Finally, the bishop also had the responsibility and administrative authority for the temporal goods of the church. We do not have much information about the ecclesiastical patrimony of the Hispanic-Visigothic Church, but we do know that, in general, the churches and the basilicas, as well as the monasteries, had more than enough funds with which to administer their institutions and their properties and buildings. These monies came from private donations of the faithful and from numerous endowments, tributes, pastoral visits, and the like. Naturally, the Cathedral Church of Toledo had to have a conspicuous endowment, considering the antiquity[156] of the church of the royal city together with the norm, which was strictly observed and applied, of never disposing of ecclesiastical goods but rather accumulating them. To this we must add the fruits of the cultivations of the numerous landownerships, which were divided among the bishop, the clergy, and the churches, above all for the sustenance of worship. The donations and alms of the Sunday Mass were divided equally among the bishop and clergy.[157]

It is good to remember, however, that to be chosen bishop during Visigothic hegemony, and especially bishop of Toledo, the imperial city, did not mean only being the head of a diocese with all the related powers; this office had deep social and political implications. In fact, as J. F. Rivera Recio acutely observes, during Visigothic rule, the exercise of the episcopal office of all the Hispanic-Visigothic bishops, and, in particular, that of Toledo, was in some way more or less closely connected with the person of the king or with political events of great importance.[158] It is certainly not of secondary importance that the archbishop of Toledo himself was to anoint and consecrate the kings of the Hispanic-Visigothic empire, and to preside over the conciliar sessions of the bishops of all of Spain and to be the first to sign the important acts, or to surround himself with a true court of bishops (suffragans) who came and went from the episcopal palace. Undoubtedly the archbishop of Toledo enjoyed a very important religious and civil position to the point of being counted among the greatest landowners and masters of slaves of the whole Visigothic kingdom. The prelate of Toledo also had power over the judges, civil or secular, of the city,[159] and he oversaw their behavior. By definition, he was considered to be the protector of those who suffered injustice and oppression, or of those who were not able to receive justice from the secular power.

Let us not forget, lastly, that the bishops belonged to the imperial council, which was presided over by the king and addressed matters concerning serious crimes committed by the subjects or by bishops, abbots, and clergy. Such a crime might be high treason, as demonstrated by the case of Duke Paul, which involved various clerics of some churches of northern Spain. Julian showed himself to be a loyal and skilled executor of all these powers, increasing the prestige of the Church of Toledo to having primatial dignity over all the churches of Spain.

But Bishop Julian is remembered by his biographer also as a man of generosity[160] and charity[161] toward the poor and indigent. This trait was obviously not just a special characteristic of Julian but depended on the availability of funds in the Church of Toledo, to which Julian, as archbishop, had full access. The whole Visigothic Church, and particularly that of the *urbs regia*, was, therefore, an heir of the ancient custom, which went back to the Acts of the Apostles, of assisting the poor and the needy. For this purpose, funds were thus gathered in all the Hispanic-Visigothic dioceses.

According to ancient ecclesiastical tradition, however, a bishop was to be chosen by individual votes from the clergy and by the acceptance of the faithful. Such traditions in the seventh century were, evidently, in decline because of the decisive role that the king had assumed in the episcopal election. The king chose the bishop and instructed the ordaining bishop to consecrate him as bishop of a particular diocese of Spain. Evidently the dignity of the clergy suffered, because they felt deprived of such an important right, but the people[162] also felt deprived of a voice in the process by which they could freely express their opinion.

Bishop Julian, expert reformer in liturgical[163] and canonical matters

It is undoubtedly important to discuss Julian of Toledo as a reformer of the ancient Hispanic liturgy, because "the Lord's cult worthily performed was his obsession."[164] This means that also in the field of liturgy he pursued the same general ecclesiological intent of his primatial bishopric: that the unity of the Hispanic-Visigothic local churches may be expressed in a common liturgy. As J. Madoz appropriately says, "el testimónio de Felix induce to creer que Julián fué quien después de Eugenio e Ildefonso dió a la liturgia mozárabica su sello definitivo."[165] On the liturgical level, the desired result, which he obtained with a decisive will, was a profound unification of liturgical rites and texts[166] for all the churches of the kingdom, as a tangible sign of the unity of faith of the ancient and venerable Church of Spain. But, naturally, this work of reform had as its ultimate goal the recovery of the dignity of the liturgical celebrations and the zeal of the Christian cult in general. And given that Spanish liturgical literature from that era is the most abundant of all Christian centuries, it is quite interesting that the last general editors of books about the Mozárabic liturgy were in fact two archbishops of Toledo, Ildephonse and Julian, and that therefore the Mozárabic liturgies celebrated in the Cathedral of Toledo (in the admirable chapel of *Corpus Christi*) are fundamentally still celebrated with the Missal that Julian of Toledo revised and composed.

This historical information is known thanks to Julian's biographer, Bishop Felix, who affirms that Julian was author of a *Liber missarum,* a Missal of the Church of Toledo[167] that covered the whole liturgical year (*de toto circulo anni*). The Missal was divided into four sections, of which Julian preserved the completed parts, emended some parts that were evidently corrupted *amanuensium incuria,*[168] and completed other parts, adding some *ex novo.*[169] The same biographer informs us that Julian revised, emended, and completed the *Liber orationum de festivitatibus* of the Church of Toledo, a liturgical book that contained all the liturgical feasts of the local church.[170] Thus, we can definitely say that Julian of Toledo had an important role in the history of the Mozárabic liturgy, through the work of revision and correction, which was already begun by the bishops of Toledo Eugene II and Ildephonse but completed by Julian. It was in fact Julian, and not

Leander or Isidore of Seville, who was to produce and give the final form to the Toledan Missal and Breviary of the Visigothic period.

In the period of the Arabic domination, the Missal of Julian became the *Missale mixtum*.[171] It is very probable that the liturgical Mozárabic codices that have reached us contain the structure and the final editorial form given to them by the liturgist Julian of Toledo.[172] Also the *Liber orationum*, quoted by Felix as the work of Julian, may be interpreted this way. Contained in this book were the three prayers composed by Julian that were also contained in the Mozárabic Missal. These *orationes* were found by Flórez[173] in the *Apologeticum* or *Apologia contra Hostegitium* of Abbot Samson of Cordoba, who wrote in the second half of the ninth century.[174] In fact, Abbot Samson, who copied two of these prayers, explicitly attributed them to Julian of Toledo. The third prayer composed by Julian is the one found in the beginning of his *De comprobatione sextae aetatis*.

Naturally, apart from these exceptions, it is difficult, if not impossible, to determine whether the liturgical texts in the Missal had been modified or created *ex novo* by Julian, because, being liturgical texts, they are obviously anonymous.

During his episcopal ministry, Julian also gave a strong impulse to another type of literary codification, the canonical collection of the Visigothic Church, the so-called *Collectio Hispana*, which he knew from the text of Isidore of Seville. Julian was the author of a revision of the *Collectio* (a collection of juridical-theological canons), which held in great respect the texts of the earlier councils along with other important documents.[175]

Julian of Toledo, primate of Spain and president of four Toledan councils

Julian of Toledo is the last great man of the church of the Visigothic period, with a vast view of the social, political, and religious problems of his time. It is understandable, therefore, that he also revived the synodal tradition of the Hispanic-Visigothic Church that had fallen into disuse[176] for several decades in Iberian territory, and that he was responsible for ensuring that such councils, with the consent of all the Spanish bishops, were held in the local Church of Toledo. The reason for this decision was most likely the fact that the city of Toledo was also the capital of the Visigothic kingdom and the residence of the sovereign and his court. Toledo, therefore, became the center of political unity as well as of the religious unity of all the local churches of Spain.

The following important steps in this direction took place when the whole Spanish episcopacy recognized the supremacy of the metropolitan Church of Toledo over all the other churches of Spain.[177] This supremacy allowed the bishop of Toledo to elect, with the consent of the king,[178] and consecrate bishops in all the dioceses of Spain and of the province of Narbonne. Julian, who succeeded in obtaining this important recognition from all the bishops of Spain, was, therefore, the first bishop primate of the whole Iberian Peninsula, and great emphasis was placed on this office with the introduction of the custom according to which the bishop of Toledo was always the first one to sign the acts of the councils of Spain.

As an indication of the importance of the synodal dimension of ecclesial government to Julian despite his primacy over all the churches of Spain, it needs to be underlined that in the decade of Julian's episcopal ministry, even though he was not the most senior of the bishops of the Visigothic kingdom,[179] he had the burden and the honor of presiding over four of the eighteen national councils of Spain, the Twelfth through the Fifteenth Councils. Julian's four councils were held in 681, 683, 684 and, finally, in 688,[180] the very busy year in which he had the theological dialogue about the last things with Idalius, bishop of Barcelona, who was in Toledo precisely for the celebration of an important national council.

That work-intensive year was also the one in which Julian composed the *Prognosticum*. This, in fact, reveals a further level of primacy of Bishop Julian of Toledo. He was indeed the bishop who saw the greatest number of council celebrations during his episcopal ministry: a total of four, all of which were presided over by him,[181] as noted above. This means that Julian "was responsible for the revival of the Conciliar tradition in Spain"[182] and that he was appropriately equipped to enable these councils to contribute to the evident growth of the collegial dimension of the ecclesial government. It is in this context that we should interpret the fact that Julian knew the *Collectio Hispana* in the version of Isidore of Seville, which was the collection of the conciliar acts and other ecclesial documents, and that it was he himself who increased it (*collectio Juliana*). His, in fact, was "the last important review of the Spanish canonical collection,"[183] demonstrating his appreciation of the collegial decisions made together with the bishops of the preceding centuries, in both the East and the West, as of both pastoral and theological significance. Moreover, it needs to be added that, with his influential personality and theological culture, he was the principal animator of some important councils, and he intervened "in the discussion and solution of problems."[184] Oddly, his biographer does not mention Julian's important episcopal activities in relation to his presidency of four national councils of the Visigothic Church, and this silence is even more surprising when we consider that Felix was his immediate successor in the primatial see of Toledo. He must have directly witnessed the confidence and effectiveness with which Julian had presided over the conciliar sessions and how, in the most difficult moments, Julian had demonstrated all his courage and his theological ability. Nonetheless, all experts on Visigothic Spain recognize that, in areas of discipline, Julian "definitively held the primacy of the Toledan Church,"[185] despite his high esteem for the collective nature of the Spanish episcopacy.

Julian's energetic personality as the primate of Spain suggests that he was worried about the doctrinal, disciplinary, and political unity of the Hispanic-Visigothic Church. In fact, the Church of Spain of the seventh century showed itself to be the most richly endowed with high-level pastoral and theological personalities, and Julian of Toledo is certainly to be considered, on the pastoral and doctrinal level, one of the most significant and prominent personalities of the whole century. M. C. Díaz y Díaz, in one of the most qualified and classical patristic manuals of our times, defines Julian of Toledo as "presumably the greatest theologian of the VII century."[186] It can be hypothesized, therefore, that the intellectual and theological superiority of the Church of Spain and the ecclesial and political unity achieved in the time of Julian of Toledo probably indicated also the realistic desire of the Spanish Church for a kind of theological and pastoral self-sufficiency, perhaps in imitation of the Church of Constantinople, and of Constantinople's relation to the Church of the West, which, instead, gravitated around the Church of Rome.

The councils of the Visigothic Church and their political-religious dimension

It is necessary to remember that, in the Hispanic-Visigothic imperial society, the national councils, which gathered bishops from all of Spain to pronounce themselves on civil or ecclesiastical matters, "formed one of the columns of the state"[187] and very effectively represented the most expressive organ of ecclesial communion. According to J. F. Rivera Recio, the Toledan councils represented "the most remarkable institution of the Gothic Church and a notable juridical source, whose echo extends throughout the Middle Ages, penetrates into the modern age and has repercussions in the actual canon law."[188] In addition to being ecclesiastical synods that treated questions associated with the Christian faith, ethics, and ecclesiastical discipline, the councils were also truly political assemblies, convoked, inaugurated, and made public by the king. This characteristic of the councils of Spain was evidently recognized also by the Roman see, since when Pope Leo II wrote to the Spanish bishops to call a council to approve the acts of the Sixth Ecumenical Council, he also sent a letter to King Ervig, asking him to summon all the bishops, thus recognizing the Hispanic-Visigothic conciliar praxis.[189]

Undoubtedly the most characteristic note of the Toledan councils, at least beginning with the Fourth Council of Toledo (633), and one that stands out more clearly in the eyes of us moderns, is the intertwining relationship or the "intimate union"[190] between the monarchy and the entire bishopric of the Hispanic-Visigothic Church.[191] Yet, while the bishops participated in all the conciliar activity, the presence and the role of the king were determined and limited in a very clear way.

To the king belonged the task of summoning the council (*Principis seu Regis iussu*).[192] Although this may seem an abnormal privilege and an interference of the powers of government in the life of the church—unthinkable in our days—it was actually due, in part, to practical motives. Only the king was able to send heralds and messengers throughout the whole kingdom for a swift convocation of the participants of the council, or to declare approved the acts of a specific council. It is helpful, however, to recall that in the first centuries of the Christian era the convocation of a council by a king or an emperor was a very widespread practice, not only for the first councils of the Church of the East, but also of the Church of the West, of the lower empire, and of the kingdoms that arose following the barbarian invasions, such as the Visigothic one.[193] Another task of the king consisted in addressing the bishops in an inaugural speech, though this was not a custom typical of the Visigothic Church. With this discourse the king addressed the bishops with veneration and respect and gave them directives to follow in their discussions and deliberations.[194] The king participated only in the initial and preliminary phases of the council, however, and once he had delivered his introductory greeting and handed over the *Tomus* to the participants, he withdrew. He did not personally follow the debate in the main hall, nor did he supervise the editing of the texts that would constitute the final acts of the council. The custom of the emperor delivering the inaugural address to the bishops at the beginning of a council had already occurred in three ecumenical councils of Christian antiquity (Nicaea, Constantinople, and Chalcedon) and was not, therefore, a novelty introduced by the Hispanic-Visigothic Church.

In line with this inaugural presence of the king at the beginning of the council was the delivery of the so-called *Tomus*[195] to the bishops participating in the council. The *Tomus regius* was a royal writing that, as a custom of the Visigothic Church that dated from the Third Council of Toledo (589) and would last up to the last Council of Toledo, was handed over to the bishops and contained a sort of agenda or a series of recommendations related to the themes and problems that the bishops would treat in their conciliar works. The *Tomus* also proposed concrete solutions to the problems raised, which the bishops were urged to follow. It was opened and read only after the king had left the main hall of the council. The custom of handing over the *Tomus* was probably borrowed from Byzantine praxis, perhaps through the works of Leander of Seville, who had lived in Constantinople and had assimilated the customs of that imperial church. In Constantinople, in fact, the emperors not only summoned the council; they also usually proposed the discussion themes to the bishops. The delivery of the *Tomus* ended the presence of the king in the conciliar hall; his departure from the hall is, in fact, often recorded in the acts of the Toledan councils, from the twelfth onward. In any case, the conciliar acts of Toledo never recorded further interventions of the king in the assembly of bishops, which guaranteed the liberty and independence of the episcopal meetings of the kingdom.

The only exception occurred during the Third Council of Toledo, when King Recared remained in the hall after the council had begun, together with the queen and the court nobility, on the occasion of his solemn abnegation of the Arian heresy and of his adherence to Catholicism. He intervened several times during the festive and solemn conciliar session.

In the Visigothic environment, however, the delivery of the *Tomus* took on a particular characteristic: it manifested the harmony and the mutual help that state and church offered each other. Rather than an interference of civil power in the ecclesiastical environment, the delivery of the *Tomus* from the king meant a demonstration of the king's trust in the wisdom and intelligence of the bishops, and also that he "delegated" the bishops' council to treat those precise themes or matters.[196]

Nonetheless, despite his formal withdrawal from the conciliar hall, the king continued to participate in the works of the council by means of the presence in the hall of a part of the *Aula Regia*, that is, of his court. The participation of the *Aula Regia* in the works of the council must be understood as a representation of the king in the affairs of the council. Beginning from the Third and Fourth Councils of Toledo, the presence of the *Aula Regia* also meant broadening the participation in the councils beyond that of the bishops to include priests, deacons, and laypeople as well, who thus took part in the discussions of the council. And as of the Eighth Council of Toledo, the "laymen" of the *Aula Regia*, the powerful persons and the nobility of the court, enjoyed a greater level of participation. They could vote for the provisions and the deliberations of the council, and their names were listed among the signers at the end of the acts and the conciliar decrees.[197]

After the Seventeenth Council of Toledo, the last of the series whose acts have been transmitted to us, this common praxis was modified. It was thus established that in the first three days of every conciliar session only the strictly ecclesiastical problems or themes were to be discussed, and the laity were not to be admitted to these discussions and votes. Instead, they were admitted and had the right to intervene, vote, and sign in the subsequent days of the council, when, in addition to ecclesiastical issues, the assembly also treated civil or other kinds of problems indicated in the royal agenda of the works and themes to be addressed.

Finally, it was up to the king to confirm the conciliar acts once the synodal works were completed and the bishops had signed their names on the parchments at the end of the texts.[198] According to some, this decree of the king confirming the deliberations of the bishops underlined either the auxiliary functions of the state toward the church, for which the ecclesiastical norms established by the council became the "law" of the civil society through the publication of a decree of the king—*lex in confirmatione concilii.* Or it indicated a certain subordination of the bishops and of the councils to the power of the king, considering that the bishops were limited to signing, with their doctrinal and moral authority, the decisions that the king already had somehow communicated to them with the delivery of the *Tomus.* But perhaps this is another case of our modern mentality not allowing us completely to understand the harmony between state and church that was present already in the Eastern councils, when the Byzantine emperors confirmed and concretely made public the dogmatic doctrinal deliberations[199] of the bishops gathered in a council.

The bishops, for their part, often but not exaggeratedly[200] addressed political matters, providing the king with a solution that, in their opinion, appeared to be the most appropriate. The sovereign generally accepted these indications or decisions from the bishops, counting above all on the fact that the ecclesiastics were undoubtedly the most intellectual, elite, and culturally prepared sector of the Visigothic kingdom,[201] and that throughout the centuries the church had given ample proof of knowing how to treat in a collective way and to judge with wisdom and equilibrium the most difficult and thorny matters, even those not specifically ecclesiastical.

The king, therefore, transformed the bishops' deliberations in ecclesiastical, juridical, and political matters[202] into civil laws, imposing them upon his subjects. The relations between the king and the bishops and between the laity and ecclesiastics in the council show that all the components of society of the time took an active part in the councils and brought their effective contribution in addressing the real problems of the kingdom, in addition to the theological or canonical questions.

Despite appearances, however, these close relations between ecclesiastical and civil powers must not be interpreted as indicating that Hispanic-Visigothic society was, after all, a religious and political theocracy, ruled by the Visigothic kings and by the bishops, nor, even less, that it was the result of an excessive mixture of civil and religious power.[203] Rather, this intervention of the civil power in the religious realm and vice versa must be interpreted as a demonstration, undoubtedly very strong, of the ideal of national and political-religious unity of the whole Hispanic-Visigothic kingdom. This unity had recently been established by the adherence of the Visigothic monarchy to Catholicism, and this was thus expressed on the public level and in the general interest, or common good, of the nation. The result, not always reached in the right way, was that each of the powers helped the other in the elaboration of laws or in the realization of decrees. "The princes considered themselves as defenders of the Church,"[204] while the bishops of the churches of Spain, especially in the councils, entered into dialogue with the civil power in the interest of the nation and of the common good.

Owing to the preponderant presence of the ecclesiastical power within the kingdom, the ecclesiastical function became the pivot around which all the rest rotated, the monarchy and the palatine nobility as well as the Hispanic-Visigothic people. In fact, all were convinced that the ecclesiastical hierarchy could provide the state in legislative matters not only with its centuries-old experience but, above all, with the supernatural dimension that had by then so strongly bonded the social life of the Hispanic-Visigothic people. Besides, the church "found favor with all the people" because it had already given ample testimony of itself and of its ability to protect the Hispanic-Roman population, which had been conquered by the barbarian invaders. Moreover, the church had shown its superiority over the invaders by converting them to the Christian orthodox faith and thereby unifying or trying to unify, with some degree of success, the two races, Hispanic-Roman and Visigothic, into the one people of the Iberian Peninsula, who were governed by monarchs chosen from the Hispanic-Visigothic nobility and religiously assisted by a strong, unified national church. Put concisely, we could say that "harmony was constant in the Visigothic period, and if the altar helped the throne, this, in turn, protected the altar."[205] The national councils were, to a large extent, the appropriate instrument for obtaining this political-religious result of great historical value.

Consequently, it would be wrong to interpret this osmosis between faith and religious power, on the one side, and civil power, on the other, according to our contemporary criteria of sociology and political theology, because ever since the Enlightenment in the West, the separation and the opposition between civil and religious powers have often become more distinct, if not entirely absolute. What happened in Hispanic-Visigothic Spain in the sixth and seventh centuries was, rather, the demonstration of a close collaboration between the religious and civil powers as a result of the primordial event at the basis of such cooperation: the conversion of the king and the Visigothic people to the Catholic Christian religion.[206]

The ecclesiological and political importance of the eighteen Councils of Toledo

The Councils of Toledo, or assemblies of the bishops of the Visigothic Church, that took place before the fateful and dramatic year of 711 have been interpreted in many different ways throughout the centuries. From the evaluation of E. Flórez, who considered them to be exclusively ecclesiastical meetings gathered to address, in a collegial way, theological, canonical, liturgical, and disciplinary problems, interpretations have progressively broadened to understand these councils as a series of meetings with strong political overtones, and thus as mixed political-religious meetings. Some scholars view such meetings as the predecessors of the medieval courts, which likewise gathered clergy and nobility around the sovereign for the government of the kingdom.[207] The councils, which were held in Toledo with increasing frequency, were undoubtedly of great importance and authority for the life of the Church of Spain and for the Visigothic kingdom.[208] Held so often as to have evolved into a healthy ecclesial custom, the councils certainly led to the prestige that the Church of Toledo and all the churches of Spain achieved over the centuries, thanks above all to the acts of the councils, which testify to the high cultural and doctrinal level achieved by the Hispanic-Visigothic bishopric.

Modern historians of the Toledan councils, however, prefer to define them as "institutions in continuous evolution, which adapt themselves to the necessities and the conceptions of the society in which they occur."[209] In addition, while being local councils affecting Spain, they were designated as general and universal councils because of the importance of some theological-dogmatic contents that they treated and because of the important doctrinal documents that took their shape from those very meetings. Besides, one of the most important results achieved by these councils was the Spanish bishops' unanimous recognition of the special role that the archbishop and the Church of Toledo was to have in historical and religious matters in seventh-century Spain. Toledo transformed itself, therefore, into a city/church, a symbol of national (political and religious) unity, but also into the hub of the Christian religious unity of the local churches of Spain. This led to the recognition of the primatial role of the church and of the archbishop of Toledo, approved without objections from the whole Hispanic-Visigothic bishopric and, in fact, also by the Church of Rome. Under the leadership of Julian, the Church of Toledo thus came to have real primatial power of episcopal election and consecration in all the dioceses of Spain and of southern Gallia or the Narbonnese ecclesiastical province.[210]

Altogether eighteen councils were held in Toledo between the years 400 and 702, even if not all were of equal political-religious importance. This high number of conciliar meetings alone reveals the attitude of the Church of Spain toward synodal government. Some of these councils can be considered milestones: for example, the council in 589 witnessed the public adoption of the Catholic faith by King Recared and the nobility and the Visigothic people. The Twelfth Council sanctioned the primacy of the episcopal see of Toledo over all the churches of Spain.

The series of important councils began with the Fourth Council of Toledo, which was summoned by King Sisenand and presided over by the great Isidore of Seville in 633. The synodal custom of such ecclesiological importance for the Visigothic Church started with this council: the increased frequency of the episcopal meetings, but at the same time, a theme of political significance was for the first time inserted into the agenda of the conciliar works, such as the recognition of the legitimacy of the new king. An important matter of national magnitude was presented to the bishops gathered in the council, as they were asked to approve the procedure leading to the election of the new king, since the Visigothic monarchy was elective in nature and not dynastic. Another important point of this council (see chapter 4) was the determination of the procedure for holding a council session.

Therefore, while before this time long periods had elapsed between the councils of the Church of Spain,[211] beginning with the Fourth Council the synodal assemblies of the bishops of the Visigothic

Church became much more frequent, reaching a true record: four-teen councils held in as few as sixty-two years, or an average of a council every four or five years. The importance of these meetings was progressively acknowledged by the bishops of Spain, because the number of participants in the councils notably increased with each council, until they attracted up to seventy participating bishops representing just as many Hispanic-Visigothic churches.

The fact, then, that the synodal assemblies were developed in Toledo, the royal city, contributed significantly to the increased importance of the figure of its archbishop, to the point where he attained primatial dignity over all the churches of Spain. Beginning already in 610, with King Gundemar's decree and the recognition of the bishops of the ecclesiastical province, the bishop of Toledo had, in fact, taken on the nature of metropolitan bishop of that province. But the exercise of primacy over all the churches started with the Twelfth Council of Toledo, when the archbishop of the royal city, as we have seen, began to preside over the council and to be the first to sign its acts.

In the Twelfth Council of Toledo (681), which promulgated the primacy of the Church of Toledo over all the churches of the whole peninsula and of the Gallia Narbonnese, the most important problem was of a juridical-political nature. Radical healing (*sanatio in radice)* was required in the wake of the events that had led to King Wamba's deposition and to the election and royal consecration of the noble-man Ervig as king. Led by Julian, the bishops authenticated documents and events,[212] and order seemed to have returned. With his ascension to the throne thus legitimately and canonically recognized, Ervig took the first magnanimous step: a general amnesty for those people, above all members of the nobility, who were tainted, under King Wamba's reign, by political crimes, desertion from the military service (*de his his qui ad bellum non vadunt*), and neglected defense of the country.[213] The destiny of the Twelfth Council of Toledo was most singular: crowning and legitimizing two kings: an ecclesiastical one in the person of Archbishop Julian of Toledo; and a civil one in the legitimation of Ervig's ascent to the Visigothic throne.

In the Thirteenth Council of Toledo, held in the Church of Saints Peter and Paul in 683 according to the wish of the king, some provisions were taken, above all, pardon for the many people who had been deprived of citizenship for having deserted or escaped military service under the rule of Wamba or who had rebelled, together with

Duke Paul,[214] against the legitimate sovereign, or even those overly burdened with taxes. Accordingly, the first three canons of the council, inspired by feelings of piety and forgiveness, commanded the restitution of dignity to those people who had been slandered and condemned. Other questions of a political nature were also examined, as were ecclesiastical questions related to feasts and to the cult of saints, and the primacy of the metropolitan of Toledo was reaffirmed over all the churches of Spain.

The Fourteenth Council of Toledo (684) was almost entirely theological-doctrinal, summoned by a letter from Pope Leo II to the primate of Toledo, to the Spanish bishops, to the king, and to the palatine nobility. The pope asked for the approval of the christological doctrine of the Sixth Ecumenical Council, the Third Council of Constantinople (680–681). It was followed by an important doctrinal and disciplinary event that put at risk relations between the primate of Spain and the bishop of Rome. We will address this more amply later.

The Fifteenth Council of Toledo (688) again treated important christological doctrinal matters and the stormy relations between the primate of Toledo and the theologians of the Roman curia.

Therefore, the national Visigothic councils of Spain were called to discuss and to decide not only ecclesiastical matters but also secular questions and, often, state affairs[215] and political matters of general importance, as, for example, the legitimation of the election of the successor to the throne of the kingdom. They often functioned also as supreme courts to treat civil and juridical as well as ecclesiastical and liturgical matters.[216]

Julian of Toledo and the kings of Visigothic Spain

A chapter often suppressed by modern historians who have studied the episcopacy of Julian of Toledo concerns Julian's political attitude toward the Visigothic monarchy and toward power in general. Understandably, it concerns the delicate relationship between church and state in Visigothic Spain. As we have already mentioned, the relationship was balanced enough, for as much as our modern sensitivity can understand about the matter, but in some cases it was characterized by excesses on both sides.

Some scholars, in fact, have judged Julian's behavior as scheming, unconventional, and without scruples of any sort in some important historical events of the kingdom such as King Wamba's[217] deposition or the election of the new king, Ervig.[218] They blamed Julian for having taken advantage of the political confusion to acquire such power to the point of being able to affirm that, in fact, "he practically ruled Spain"[219] and that "Julian indeed was at this time the greatest power in the state, and seems to have completely governed the vacillating and often conscience-stricken Ervig."[220] In the end, with his unconventional and power-craving behavior, he would even have been greatly in favor of the fall or the end of the Visigothic empire. Other historians, however, have considered the attitude of some kings to be intrusive and, to say the least, high-handed in their interference in ecclesiastical questions, an interference from which, in each case, Julian knew how to defend himself very well.

Given the importance of the matter, it seems necessary somehow to clarify things, or at least, to summarize the historical research about these accusations against Julian and his episcopacy, because they threatened to project shadows and suspicion upon the completely opposite image that has instead been handed down about Julian of Toledo, and which indeed shines forth from his exegetical and theological works, as well as from Bishop Felix's biographical notes.

According to such tradition, which goes back to his contemporary biographer, Julian was a tireless shepherd, a friend of the poor, a benevolent bishop, a writer on spiritual matters, a great theologian and, we add, the father of Christian eschatology. It is, therefore, really difficult to reconcile these virtuous dimensions of Bishop Julian's pastoral and theological personality with the judgment (in many cases, however, doubtful) of some modern scholars that Julian "inserted himself more than necessary in the prickly problems of the struggle for royal power, and in the doctrinal justification of not a few actions of the king, inspired, more or less, by him."[221]

During his brief earthly existence, Julian had important relationships with several Visigothic kings: Wamba, Ervig, and, partially, the perfidious king Egica; this was most of all due to his close contact with the royal power as the archbishop of Toledo. Thus, one can initially conjecture that, because of these circumstances, Julian "apparently took a large part in the administration of the Visigothic kingdom under Wamba's successors, kings Erwig (680–687) and Egica (687–702)," but it is undoubtedly an exaggeration to make him the one responsible for everything, including the Arabic invasion in 711 and the fall of the Visigothic empire. Murphy is right when he affirms that "he has been pilloried by nineteenth century historians who accuse him of having played a principal part in the deposition of king Wamba (November, 680)."[222]

Julian of Toledo and King Wamba's deposition

Julian's first contacts with the warrior monarch Wamba, who was king from 672 to 680, go back to 673, when Julian, still a young priest, wrote the *Historia Wambae* for the reigning Visigothic king of the time, a realistic historical work and stylistically very original for the period. The *Historia* is a work laudatory of the monarch but not so much to be defined as a panegyric, with his author a panegyrist,[223] nor as an exaltation of the king in return for favors. As we will see, in his *Historia Wambae* there is more than a simple desire to draw attention from the king to himself. Julian, in fact, wrote this work because he saw in King Wamba a providential monarch sent by God to save the political and religious unity of his country, fighting against the rebels in the north of the peninsula and against the Saracen aggressions on the southern coasts of Spain. Julian, therefore, did not hesitate to accompany King Wamba in his military expedition against Duke Paul, a traitor and rebel who revolted against the Visigothic monarch, who had sent him to the province Narbonnese to put down a revolt, and who, instead, rebelled against his king and declared himself king of Narbonne.

Wamba was of Visigothic nobility, belonging to the court of King Recesvint, and he had married the king's daughter;[224] upon the death of Recesvint he was publicly proclaimed king.[225] He tried in many ways to refuse the serious task, but threatened to death by a noble member of the court, he had to surrender "more to the threats than to the prayers"[226] and accept the royal office, obtaining only a delay in the consecration so that it could be celebrated in Toledo and not in the place where the monarch had died. He was, therefore, crowned by Bishop Quiricus in Toledo, in the praetorian Church of Saints Peter and Paul in 672, in a sumptuous ceremony prescribed by the Visigothic liturgy in a mystical and prodigious atmosphere,[227] which Julian narrated in his *Historia*.[228] The king made his oath of fidelity, and the bishop anointed him with the royal unction. At the end of the crowning ceremony, the new king was presented to the rejoicing crowd.

Julian was a friend of Wamba and his biographer. The king, for his part, greatly esteemed the governing abilities, the theological science, and the vast culture of the young priest Julian, all qualities that made him emerge in the ecclesiastical panorama of Visigothic Spain of that century, and particularly in the Church of Toledo. One can, therefore, hypothesize that the election of Julian as bishop of the royal city was a totally natural choice for the king and very suitable for the kingdom.

Wamba's rule was treated favorably by historians not only because he had been chosen by popular consent but also because, in 675, he summoned the Council of Toledo, after eighteen years of a synodal vacuum, and, even more, because he determined that all the bishops were to gather annually for an examination of the religious situation of the kingdom.[229]

In addition, Wamba had superbly defended the empire from two serious dangers: both internal insurrections and external invasion attempts.[230] To do so he had completely reorganized the Visigothic army, which was practically nonexistent as a result of the carelessness of preceding kings, and he had turned it into an efficient war machine.

In an excellent way, and with the solemn blessing of the Visigothic Church,[231] he had brought an overwhelming victory over the enemies of the empire, in the north as well as in the south of the peninsula, and he completely reestablished the imperial military political order. The Hispanic-Visigoths, therefore, were indebted to him, and they loved and respected him as monarch and military leader. In addition to the military campaigns, Wamba was devoted also, and above all, to the reconstruction of public monuments and the expansion of the defensive walls in the imperial city of Toledo,[232] adorning it with monumental doors, each of them topped with a tower-chapel devoted to the martyr patron of Toledo, the virgin Leocadia, and decorated with poetic inscriptions, perhaps with the intellectual help of Julian of Toledo.[233]

It is thus possible to agree with the concise judgment expressed by F. X. Murphy, according to which Wamba was a good king, that is, "a man of military ability, a builder and a good legislator,"[234] in that he knew how to organize well the complex Visigothic secular hierarchy on the military, administrative, and judicial levels, through the participation of the dukes, counts, and judges of the kingdom.

But this positive judgment about his rule undoubtedly clashes with the historical data informing us, instead, that after only a few years of rule, Wamba was the object of a palace conspiracy, perhaps sponsored by the Spanish bishopric, and was deposed in quite an unusual way—if the historical information is reliable. Why, then, did the Hispanic-Visigothic bishopric, forgetting the valuable services rendered by the skilled warlike king in defense of the national unity of the country, support in such an obvious way the attempt, which proved successful, to dethrone him and make him politically ineffective? If this was due to the hunger for power and the greed of the pretender to the throne, the nobleman Ervig, it is difficult to understand the tolerant attitude, to say the least, of the Visigothic bishopric and, particularly, of the primate of Toledo, the very one who had sung the praises of the person[235] and the military enterprises of Wamba and who was the severe judge of the betrayals plotted against him.

Probably the relationships between the king and the archbishop of Toledo and the Spanish bishopric had begun to break down when Wamba, convinced by recent political events in the kingdom,[236] determined that it was necessary to have an army always ready for combat and the defense of the country. He decreed that, in the case of hostile invasion, military service would become obligatory for all men, even for those belonging to the nobility and the clergy. Any defection would be severely punished.[237]

The decree obviously did not meet with the approval of the bishops and was interpreted as an excessive interference of the king in the ecclesiastical affairs, which had always been respected by the preceding monarchs. Yet the concern of Wamba was real, and the provision was finalized for the good of everyone and not as a pretext to irritate the clergy. In reality, Wamba, resorting to an obligatory law for military service that also included the clergy, intended to remind the Visigothic people firmly of its native warlike virtues and its military duties, underlining a serious gap in the organization of the empire. He complained most of all about the lack of patriotism of the members of the empire, particularly of the clergy and of the nobility, who considered their own privileged condition more important than the defense of the country. We can indirectly deduce that the problem was real from the discourse of King Ervig at the beginning of the Twelfth Council of Toledo, when he, listing and recommending to the bishops the problems and the matters to be examined, criticized the laws of conscription of Wamba, informing us, however, that in fact half of the Hispanic-Visigothic people had suffered punishments for military desertion.[238] This means that half of the men of Spain had deserted its military duties and that the empire, without a trained and numerous army, was indeed in serious danger as intuited by King Wamba.

A second decree by Wamba, even more displeasing to the ecclesiastical hierarchy, forbade the bishops to withdraw money from the donations of the faithful in the churches of their dioceses, or to subtract from such donations for their own personal use on the pretext that they had lost their right to do so after thirty years had passed.[239]

One can add to this that Wamba, undoubtedly exceeding his authority, interfered in the ecclesiastical affairs to the point of ordering the consecration of some bishops without the due ecclesiastical authorization of the primate and of the Hispanic-Visigothic bishopric. He even created a new diocese *castrensis* or *pretoriana*[240] with a new bishop[241] in a suburb of Toledo, obviously arousing the opposition of Julian, who saw his own canonical jurisdiction in the royal city compromised and limited, because the king intended to extend such praxis to other small inhabited centers. In the light of these developments, it is easier to understand how relations between the ecclesiastical hierarchy and the king, which had been good up to 675,[242] quickly worsened, and why the decrees of Wamba and his behavior were regarded by the Twelfth Council of Toledo, the first one presided over by Julian, as an arrogant liberty (*pro tam insolenti hujusmodi disturbationis licentia*)[243] and his orders as unjust (*iniustis Wambae Principis jussionibus*).[244] Undoubtedly the language used by the council toward the king, who in the meantime had become a harmless monk—as we will see, though in circumstances to say the least doubtful—seems rather excessive and does not express, at least for some matters, a dispassionate historical judgment about the rule of Wamba.

On October 14, 680, a Sunday, toward the first hour of night,[245] only eight months after the election of Julian to the episcopal see of Toledo, things worsened.[246] In fact, a mysterious plot or palace conspiracy transpired, to which the bishops of Spain were probably not outsiders,[247] and which led to King Wamba's deposition and to the election of the nobleman Ervig as his successor.[248] What we have come to know is that King Wamba fell into a condition of unconsciousness (officially interpreted as being of natural origin but very probably obtained with some narcotizing potion, as suggested by an ancient chronicle) and that this made him fear for his very life. The alarm resounded in all Toledo by the ringing of bells.

Archbishop Julian was hurriedly called by a group of courtiers to the bedside of the king in the imperial palace to assist him spiritually, as if he were dying. He had been informed that the king "had repeatedly manifested during his life the firm wish to die in a penitent suit," for which reason Julian immediately imposed upon the king the penitential discipline that he normally prescribed to the dying,[249] whose external signs were a shaved head (*tonsura sacra*) and the obligation to wear a suit or a monastic habit with ritual cilice sprinkled with ash. The king was urgently brought, in a state of unconsciousness, to the praetorian basilica of Saints Peter and Paul, where the liturgical rite was held (the shaving of the head[250] and the clothing with the religious habit, cilice, ash). With this solemn and public act Julian of Toledo "with unconscious complicity"[251] signed his part in the intrigue astutely organized by the pretender to the throne, the nobleman Ervig. At the end of the penitential rite the king was brought back to his Toledan residence, where he was given some documents to sign, attesting that he, taking on the penitential condition, abdicated his role as king and named, instead, the nobleman Ervig, one of the noble courtiers, as the new sovereign.[252] Wamba, still under the effect of the soporific potion and surely in a state of mental confusion for having found himself dressed as a monk and with the tonsure, signed the documents, certainly against his will. He also signed another document, also by force, directed to the primate of Toledo in which the archbishop was urged to anoint the new king without any delay.[253] After this dramatic penitential act and the signing of the documents, however, the king awoke from his condition of mental confusion or of unconsciousness, and he found himself, tonsured and dressed with penitential habit, prevented from taking back his role as king because of the evident *poenitentiae susceptio.*[254]

It was probably at this point that Ervig showed to the nobility and the clerics gathered in the imperial palace the documents, signed by the king, by which Wamba named him as his successor and commissioned the archbishop of Toledo to celebrate, as soon as possible, his enthronement and public consecration. From the nobility and the clerics he received a first response of acceptance without protests, or, at least not so as to be recorded in the chronicles and to reach us. The following Sunday, October 21, 680, Julian consecrated Ervig as king of the Visigothic kingdom. Wamba, the dethroned king, totally recovered from the mental confusion into which he had probably been induced, took note of the situation, and humbly withdrew to a monastery in the proximity of Toledo to live an austere life of penitence as a monk. Evidently he did not have the strength or the desire, perhaps because of his venerable age (eighty years old), to gather the nobility faithful to him and instigate an offensive against the usurper. He preferred to retire from the political scene in a spirit of great humility.

However, the truthfulness of the information about the modality of the deposition, the end of his earthly life, and the burial of King Wamba is controversial.[255] Murphy believes, for instance, that the historical information according to which Wamba, after his deposition, would have entered the monastery and spent the last seven years of his life as a monk is lacking in historical truth and is, almost certainly, a literary invention.[256] A similar judgment is expressed by the same author about the truthfulness of the story related to the poisoning, through a drugging potion, of Wamba, because neither the Councils of Toledo nor the chronicles of the period speak of this important event, though it must have been, if true, quite sensational. Therefore, also in this case, it is probably only a legend. What is certain is that Wamba was truly deposed from the throne and no longer appeared on the Hispanic-Visigothic political scene up to the day of his death.

To understand better the astute plan of the usurper who had organized the conspiracy against Wamba, it needs to be specified that the penitential discipline to which the king had been submitted had consequences not only on the religious-ecclesial level, but also on the civil level. It was impossible for one who had undergone the penitence to hold public office, if, for some reason, he recovered from his illness. In the case of Wamba this meant that once he had received the penitential rite, even if he came out of his narcotized condition, he would no longer be able to be king. The moment the act had been completed, therefore, the conspiracy could be considered a success. This means that it had been prepared with the maximum care, and that the trap had been deployed perfectly against King Wamba and with good timing.[257]

If, as it seems, the king had been drugged, it was obviously not the bishops or Julian who administered the narcotic to him. The ones responsible were most likely emissaries of Ervig, if not Ervig himself. It is probable, however, that the bishops, and particularly the primate of Spain, were well informed about the conspiracy. But it is just as probable that they did not know when or how it would occur, nor that it was to end in such a violent and illegitimate way. In any case, we can say that, when all was said and done, they offered their assent to King Wamba's deposition and to the usurpation of Ervig in the form most appropriate for them, that is, in its canonical dimension during the Twelfth Council of Toledo. What really happened and what role was really played by Julian and the bishops of Spain in this dark plot cannot be reconstructed with certainty, and in all the particulars,[258] based on the historical documents currently in our possession.

In the following months of 681, the new king evidently felt the urgent need to justify himself before the nation and to legitimize his election with the guarantee of the authority of the church[259] and of the court nobility. This legitimization would help silence any opposition. To reach this goal Ervig summoned a council in the dead of winter (January 9, 681),[260] presided over by Julian, in the Basilica of Saints Peter and Paul. It comprised three metropolitan archbishops, twenty-one diocesan bishops, and various episcopal vicars, abbots, and palace nobility. It is not improbable that Ervig had hoped to thus silence also the remorse of his conscience, in addition to the murmuring that had spread throughout the kingdom about the way he had become king of the Visigoths, that is, with intrigue, deception, and the betrayal of his legitimate king.

At the beginning of the council, as was customary, King Ervig made his welcome address to the council fathers and delivered to them his *Tomus*, or agenda, of the conciliar works. Immediately afterward the king abandoned the episcopal meeting, as expected. The bishops and the other council participants then examined the writings signed by Wamba. They considered both the text and the signature authentic,[261] and at the same time recognized as legitimate the behavior of the one who had imposed the sacred tonsure and the penitential habit upon the king, who was sick or in mental confusion. According to J. F. Rivera Recio, an expert on the history of the Visigothic period, "Today, after the distance of so many years, it is felt impossible to declare an opinion about the authenticity of this documentation"[262] undersigned by the participants of the council. It is certain, however, that the bishops accepted the documents as authentic and that they approved what had been done to Wamba from the canonical-penitential point of view, thus confirming the election and the crowning of Ervig. Therefore they freed the Visigothic people from their oath of fidelity to the former king and obliged them to swear fidelity to the new king[263] so that he would be officially recognized by everyone.

Historians are inclined to the view that the account approved during the council was not entirely truthful,[264] because it gave an appearance of legality to what had been a real coup d'etat.[265] But chronicles already at the end of the ninth century, such as the Chronicle of Alphonse III,[266] king of the Asturies, also known as Chronicle of Sebastian of Salamanca,[267] supply us with a very crude version of the facts, introducing Ervig as the most responsible—and almost the only one responsible—for the deeds; he is introduced, in fact, as the "conocedor de las intrigas palaciegas" and as the one who "superba e astutamente" devised the dethronement of Wamba. The text then goes into detail, furnishing also the name of the drug prepared for the king: an infusion of a grass called the *spartum* or *spartus*, which immediately deprived him of memory. In the same chronicle, however, the author presents the archbishop of the *urbs regia* and the nobility who were faithful to Wamba quite differently, as being almost pious. According to the chronicle, they (the archbishop and the palace nobility), upon seeing the monarch spread out unconscious on his couch and moved by compassion, even if in disagreement with him on many things and particularly with his last legislation that forced all to enter military service in defense and protection of the country. So that he would not die in such an untidy way, they imposed upon him "the rite" of confession and penitence. Evidently they were well aware of what was happening, just as the bishops of the Twelfth Council of Toledo had certainly been well informed about how the events had probably occurred. The point is that, nonetheless, by both imposing the tonsure and the religious habit, and confirming the election of Ervig in the acts of the Twelfth Council of Toledo, the primate as well the bishops of Spain and the nobility had actually guaranteed the behavior of Ervig. By then everything had been completed: Ervig had already been crowned, and King Wamba would not have been able to return to his former position. Probably the behavior of the bishops was led by a defense of the ecclesiastical forum to the bitter end, but also by the *raison d'état*, to avoid an institutional crisis that could indeed have taken on troublesome proportions and consequences for the stability of the empire. We can conclude by saying that the bishops opted for the lesser evil. A debat-

able choice for us moderns, but evidently not so for the bishops of
Visigothic Spain.[268]

We can add that it is probable, therefore, that the bishops, to
avoid the nth regicide, the *morbus gothicum*[269] as Murphy ironically calls
it, and to avoid other violences in the kingdom, they accepted the
lesser evil of the conspiracy and the narcotization of the king, including the painful stratagem of imposing the *ordo poenitentiae*. This lesser
evil would have at least saved the kingdom from terrible bloodshed
and, perhaps, an internal war.

The judgment of modern historians about the modalities and
the effective results of this conspiracy is naturally very negative.[270] T.
González maintains, for example, that Ervig and all the fathers of the
Twelfth Council of Toledo "contribuyeron políticamente al
hundimiento de la España visigoda," because, seeking to preserve
their own status and their own privileges within the Hispanic-
Visigothic Christian society, they actually weakened the monarchy,
favoring the ascent to the throne of a plotter such as Ervig, who,
moreover, had also been a friend of Duke Paul, already disavowed,
defeated, and punished for his betrayal of Wamba and who was not of
Hispanic-Visigothic but of Byzantine origin. The archbishop of
Toledo was named as "the central figure in the case"[271] and he was considered a plotting traitor by some historians of the sixteenth and seventeenth centuries, such as J. Mariana[272] and the cardinal Caesar
Baronius in his *Annales ecclesiastici*,[273] as well as by those of the late
nineteenth and early twentieth centuries. Some of them, for example,
A. Hellfferich,[274] F. Dahn,[275] P. A Wengen,[276] F. Görres,[277] gave an
extremely and completely negative judgment of Julian's part in the
deposition of Wamba, while others, such as P. Gams,[278] rather attenuated the direct responsibilities of the archbishop of Toledo.

More recent historians have reviewed this harsh judgment, reliev-
ing Julian of at least the principal responsibility for the betrayal of King
Wamba and also questioning the reliability of the news related to
Wamba's narcotization. Thus, in two important articles, F. X. Murphy[279]
operated a substantial rehabilitation of many presumed protagonists,
even of Ervig[280] himself. But there is disagreement about this by just as
many other scholars.[281] Perhaps, according to the actual state of our
knowledge, we can accept the judgment made by M. C. Díaz y Díaz
about the role played by Julian in these circumstances, that "in one way
or another he participated in King Wamba's deposition and in the elec-

tion of Ervig, with whom he collaborated and of whom he was always a good friend."[282] Julian was probably unaware of being an accomplice[283] or not fully aware[284] of the maneuvers of the astute Ervig, who was, instead, practically the only one who organized and carried out the plot. But not being able to establish with certainty the responsibilities of everyone, we can conclude, together with J. N. Hillgarth, that "all that need be said here is that the charges remain non-proven."[285]

In any case, however, King Wamba's deposition is to be considered a morally and politically illegitimate action, if not a true coup d'etat.

For Christians today, these events are obviously difficult to understand and even unacceptable from the religious and moral point of view, which is ever more inclined to separate civil and religious power. But things were different in those times. Political power and the monarchy were in many ways intertwined, as we have seen, with the pastoral government of the bishops, just as the episcopal power often intromitted itself into political matters. It must be taken into account that the conception of power, in those times and also for many centuries to come, was unitary, in the sense that the two powers, civil and religious, were believed to originate from the one and only supreme authority of God and that they had to be thus directed toward the same objective. So for the civil or ecclesiastical rulers of the seventh century, the interlacing of the two powers had to seem completely normal, without the risk of such mixture turning into a theocracy.

Therefore, the king's actions and his behavior could have the nature of a sacred or religious action, and, likewise, the ecclesiastical power, addressed not only ecclesiastical themes and matters, according to its competency, but also temporal matters. For example, in the Councils of Toledo the bishops often legislated on civil matters, at the explicit request of the king, who, as was the custom, established the agenda of the works or the themes to be treated in the councils, even if he then abstained from taking part in the discussions and the votes.

Undoubtedly this depended on a general conception of the kingdom as a political-religious unity, for which the terrestrial society should be, and could be, an image of the celestial city.[286] Bearing in mind this overall conception certainly does not justify the possible involvement of the bishops in the fraudulent deposition of Wamba, but at least it offers a key of interpretation of the political and religious society that allows us to understand a little better the unscrupulous behavior of those involved in the political-religious drama that occurred in Toledo.

As for the role of Julian in the dethronement of Wamba, today's tendency is to consider it an "important detail in the relation between Church and state in Visigothic Spain. It has been assessed as one of the main events leading to the downfall of the Visigothic kingdom and to the Arabic invasion."[287] "But the fact of his friendship with Ervig, coupled with his conduct at the Twelfth Council of Toledo, oblige us to conclude that his connivance has been secured by the conspirators, either before or during the plot."[288] It is certainly surprising that Julian, so prudent and balanced, so caustic in judging Duke Paul's betrayal in his *Historia Wambae*, then allows himself to become involved in Ervig's disloyalty and perfidy. That the archbishop of Toledo was truly involved is proven by the fact that Julian played a decisive role in the conclusion of the deposition, in that it was he who concretely created Wamba's penitent condition, which removed every right he had to occupy a public position and, all the more so, the office of king. It was Julian of Toledo who accepted as authentic the document submitted him, in which King Wamba ordered the archbishop to crown and to consecrate, as soon as possible, the new king in the person of Ervig, who was really the traitor and the usurper of the crown. It is difficult to know if this involvement was unconscious or not.[289] "Julianus probably became involved in a conspiracy to overthrow King Wamba and crown his rival, Ervig, as ruler of Visigothic Spain in 680."[290] And the point is that King Wamba was deposed and Ervig was crowned king of the Visigothic empire in very dark circumstances.[291]

Julian of Toledo and King Ervig

We have mentioned the fact that King Ervig was neither Hispanic-Roman nor Visigothic. According to the Chronicle of Alphonse III, in fact, he was Byzantine,[292] the son of a certain Ardabast, who had been expelled from Greece by the emperor of the East in the time of the Visigothic king Chindasvint (642–653), who welcomed Ardabast in Spain with honor and gave him one of his relatives as a bride. Ervig was born from this marriage, and he reached an excellent social condition, to the point of becoming a count.[293] The passage of his family from the East to the West should be no great marvel, since Byzantines had been present in Spain for a long time, at least from the year 550, when Emperor Justinian I had sent his army, at the request of the Visigothic king Atanagild, and they were installed in the southern territory of the Iberian Peninsula. It was only with the kingdom of Suintila (621–631) that the Byzantines passed under Visigothic domination and were defeated and expelled. They were often the cause of division and conflict among the same Visigoths, as in King Wamba's deposition, when it was precisely the Byzantine count Ervig who usurped the throne from the legitimately elected King Wamba through a conspiracy organized by his faction. Ervig's partisans had for a long time opposed Wamba, and Julian perhaps had a part in the conspiracy.[294] At least, as archbishop of Toledo, Julian was the one who consecrated Count Ervig as king and presided over the Twelfth Council of Toledo, which conferred legitimacy upon Ervig's assumption of the throne.

Before becoming king, Count Ervig was already on good terms with Julian of Toledo. This is shown by the dedicatory letter written by Julian at the beginning of his last work *De divinis judiciis*, but it was also attested by Julian's biographer, Felix.[295] The chronicles subsequently speak about the quite close relation between Julian and Ervig on the occasion of King Wamba's deposition, as well as when Julian was convoked by Ervig and presided over the Twelfth Council of Toledo.

During his rule, Ervig ordered a revision of the code of Visigothic laws, which engendered bitterness toward the Jewish ethnic group present in the territory of the empire.[296] He also decided to attenuate the provisions taken by King Wamba toward the Hispanic-Romans (generally nobility and free men) who had been deprived of their civil rights (of the noble titles, of wealth, and of the faculty to testify) and had been enforced by King Wamba, under threat of severe consequences, to do military service and to desist from rebellions and insubordinations. Julian presided over that council and has been accused of being King Ervig's principal instigator in reproposing the anti-Jewish legislation of King Sisebut.[297] Murphy has sufficiently demonstrated that Julian could theoretically have been the instigator of this turn against the Jews. Nevertheless, it is unlikely that he actually was, since this possible fury toward the Jews would have been in total contradiction to what Julian had written in his works, which do not contain violent principles against Jews, as can be found in the Visigothic laws of Sisebut. And so the same author can affirm that in the *Historia Wambae Regis*: "he [Julian] is no more violent against them [the Jews] than he is against the others involved in the insurrection," because he considered them involved, just as others, even those belonging to the Christian clergy, in the betrayal of the country.[298] In the same way, Julian certainly showed himself polemical with the Jews in the *De comprobatione sextae aetatis*, but his anti-Jewish attitude was more on the intellectual and exegetical level about what had been done during the generations of the sacred history beginning from the creation and about the messianic doctrine than on any other level. His attitude toward the Jews was, in short, an intellectual and theological controversy, and not a political attitude. And, as Murphy rightly says, his way of being polemical against the Jews "is in the patristic tradition,"[299] which is founded on Sacred Scripture and the interpretation of salvation history. If, then, Julian says in the preface letter of the *De comprobatione sextae aetatis*[300] that he has written the work at the request of King Ervig, this probably means that the king had invited him to write but did not indicate the contents or the methodology of his work, in which the motivations to oppose the Jewish conceptions are found in the problems related to the messianic era. The motivations are, in short, exclusively biblical, theological, and intellectual in nature. In the end, it seems sensible to say, with Murphy, that concerning the Jews, Julian "was a man of his age," and that the anti-Jewish legislation, therefore, though condemnable, was part of the historical period in which he lived. But in any case it is very problematic to prove Julian's compliance with this legislation or, even more, his participation in its redaction.[301]

Beyond the limited information that is available to us, we do not know what other relations Julian of Toledo had established with King Ervig and with his successor, Egica. Julian certainly had dealings with the Visigothic kings on the occasion of the celebration of the Fourteenth and Fifteenth Councils of Toledo, both held respectively during the reign of the two mentioned kings but presided over by Julian as primate of Toledo. In these councils, it was undoubtedly Julian, and not the Visigothic monarchs, who was the absolute point of reference, as demonstrated by the *querelle* with Rome and its consequences.

Nineteenth-century historians[302] regard the rest of King Ervig's story as a progressive but inexorable approach to the general decadence of the empire, for which they hold Julian of Toledo and King Ervig responsible, above all for having dethroned King Wamba, the only one to have been able to restore military and political power to the Visigothic empire.

A strong indication in this direction was the rebellion of a certain Sisebut, the successor of Julian in the see of Toledo, against King Egica and a series of negative events that occurred during the rule of Egica, such as a great famine and a pestilential epidemic, which resulted in thousands of deaths. If we unite these events with the widespread phenomenon of the avoidance of the obligatory military service, which greatly weakened the power of the Visigothic empire already before Julian and during the rule of Ervig, there were undoubtedly negative social and political conditions to explain why the empire began to teeter on its foundations and to weaken to the point of miserably collapsing with the first assault of the Arabic invading army.

But the overall responsibility of the fall of the empire being attributed to Julian and Ervig has been greatly revised by subsequent historiography. In fact, as Murphy rightly observes, it should not be forgotten that after Julian and Ervig, the Visigothic empire still lasted for a quarter of a century. The next kings had some difficulty holding the empire together, but, more important, the Arabic invaders had such an efficient and strong military power that they were successful in all their attempts to conquer the world of that time. How could the Visigothic army and defense have been able to withstand them? It is impossible, therefore, to attribute the responsibility for the fall of an empire to only one king, such as Ervig, or to a single ecclesiastical person such as Julian of Toledo. Undoubtedly the legislation of his kingdom was excessively characterized as being concessive: under Ervig, in fact, the nobility who had not paid the tributes were reinstated, as were the rebels who had plotted against the state (all those whom King Wamba had, instead, fought and defeated, forcing them to offer their services to the state, including military service and the payment of tribute).

Moreover, this conclusion is valid for the historical judgment about Julian of Toledo. Murphy, after having underlined that Julian was, after Isidore, "the outstanding Visigothic Churchman of his era and a man of extreme spiritual integrity," and that "the Spanish Church, in honoring him as saint on her altars, concurs in this appraisal," concludes that "it is extremely difficult to think of such a man in connection with political perfidy and treason." So it is completely wrong "to place on his shoulders the responsibility for the downfall of the Visigothic kingdom,"[303] as the aforesaid nineteenth-century historians have done. The judgment of Mrs. Humphrey Ward about King Ervig seems more realistic; she affirms that "his own reign appears to have been little more than a series of efforts, more or less successful, to maintain by concessions to the powerful parties who had carried him to power, the scepter thus obtained."[304] She adds: "By the modification of the law of military service, by the atrocious laws against the Jews, and by the concentration of the whole power of the Church in the hands of the Metropolitan of Toledo, the stability and coherence of the Gothic state were sensibly shaken."[305] But there is no certainty or historical proof for the accusation that she makes against Julian, and that is, that "the primacy of Toledo was Julian's reward for his share in the conspiracy against Wamba."[306]

The anti-Judaic laws of the Twelfth Council of Toledo

A longtime friend of Julian, Ervig was greatly implicated in the decisions of the Twelfth Council of Toledo which he had summoned. Above all in his introductory discourse to the council fathers and in the *Tomus*, with a pressing request, expressed in a dramatic way (*Judaeorum pestem...exstirpate*),[307] he asked the council to enact a series of laws against the Jews.

Most of the twenty-eight anti-Judaic laws promulgated by the council were old laws that were resumed and confirmed. Twenty-six of these laws concerned Jews who had been converted (but only in name) and who had been baptized as Christians. As baptized they were obliged by the current legislation to make a profession of Christian faith. But, in reality, many of them "were still Jews at heart."[308] The old punishments of stoning and being burned alive were replaced by punishments that were not so cruel and bloody but were in any case very severe, such as the confiscation of goods, floggings, cutting of the hair, and even exile. The first two laws were created, instead, for and against the Jews who had not converted and were not baptized. They dealt with those who blasphemed against the Most Holy Trinity and who withdrew or subtracted their children from the grace of baptism. According to an important author of an entry devoted to Julian of Toledo, these two initial laws were the work of Ervig and the metropolitan of Toledo himself.[309] In the same entry, she affirms that modern writers have considered these anti-Judaic laws of the Twelfth Council of Toledo in particular as "the price paid by the usurper for the church's co-operation in the plot against Wamba."[310] Therefore, "it is at any rate impossible to exonerate Julian from a principal share in them." At the same time, these laws also represent, according to some, a stain difficult to remove from his episcopal activity that was in other ways so open and mature.

These indisputable judgments or inferences obviously do not rest on any historical documentary proof. If the anti-Judaic laws of the council are a reality, this is due to several factors, such as the political influence of the king on the council, the anti-Judaic spirit of the time, and the existence of the corpus of anti-Judaic laws of King Sisebut. But it remains only conjecture, and nothing else, that there had been a sort of a deal between Julian and Ervig, reproposing the laws in exchange for the endorsement, by Julian, of the conspiracy against Wamba.

Paradoxically, the anti-Judaic laws, of which King Ervig, Julian, and the entire Twelfth Council of Toledo were authors, showed themselves to be, on the contrary, the foreboding of a sort of historical nemesis.[311] Under King Egica's rule, in fact, a Jewish conspiracy was discovered that led to an alliance between the Jews of Spain and the invading Muslims, and which favored the fall of the Visigothic empire. A little more than twenty years after the death of Julian, in fact, the decisive battle of Guadalete against the Arabic invaders was lost, and the Hispanic-Visigothic empire was so shaken that it fell miserably not long after; and the dreams of national and ecclesial unity, and of political-imperial greatness, also fell with it.[312]

The primacy of the episcopal see of Toledo over all the churches of Spain: The ecclesiastical masterpiece of Bishop Julian of Toledo

A second important resolution of the Twelfth Council of Toledo concerned specifically the position of the metropolitan of Toledo in the ecclesial world of Visigothic Spain. The resolution, promulgated in canon 6[313] of the same council, in fact, contains the foundation of the primacy of the see of Toledo over all the churches of the Hispanic-Visigothic kingdom. It can be considered the ecclesiastical masterpiece of Julian, at the beginning of his episcopal ministry, or, as some maintain, "the special guerdon of Julian's compliance in the events of 680."[314] It is noteworthy that what the sixth canon of the Twelfth Council of Toledo established about the primacy of the episcopal see of Toledo was not a theme that had been inserted into the agenda of the conciliar works proposed by the monarch in his *Tomus* to the council fathers, but it was, instead, a "spontaneous decision of the bishopric."[315]

From the historical point of view, the importance of the Church of Toledo had grown in the last centuries and, especially, in comparison to the beginnings of the seventh century. The Church of Toledo was then in fact a local church or a diocese that belonged to the ecclesiastical province of Cartagena. The bishop of Cartagena was the metropolitan of all the churches of the province, including the local Church of Toledo. But Cartagena was always more under the Byzantine influence, and this was not pleasing to the Church of Toledo. In 612, therefore, with a decree of King Sisebut, Toledo detached itself from Cartagena and was constituted as the metropolitan see of the region of Carpetania. Just the title given by the council to the canon that addressed Toledo and its role in the ecclesiastical panorama of Spain allows us to understand how great the power of the archbishop of Toledo was about to become and what a leap the ecclesiastical history of Toledo was about to make: "The power of the general council is granted to the pontiff of Toledo, so that the bishops of a different province, with the consent of the princes, are ordained in the royal city" (De concessa Toletano pontifici generalis synodi potestate, ut episcopi alterius provinciae cum conniventia principum in urbe regia ordinentur).

With such a canon, therefore, the whole Hispanic-Visigothic bishopric showed itself in agreement with granting to the archbishop of Toledo, in accord with the imperial authority, the power in the imperial city to elect, examine, and ordain bishops of other ecclesiastical provinces to replace those who had died. The candidates were to be named by the king, as Lord over all the territory of the kingdom, and considered worthy by the archbishop of Toledo. The practical reason for such ample power granted to the archbishop of Toledo, which was almost parallel to that of the king, is indicated in the text of the canon as being connected with the existing difficulties associated with the election of the bishops in the various ecclesiastical provinces. Given the great distance that was necessary to cross in the vast imperial territory, a long period of time often passed before the news about the death of a bishop would reach the king and, consequently, the election and designation of the new bishop by the king, necessary according to the reigning praxis, could suffer unacceptable delays. This provision found its origin also in the fact that the bishop of a diocese of the Visigothic kingdom was involved in various offices, including those of an administrative and civil nature, in addition to liturgical and ecclesiastical ones, and therefore a diocese without a bishop would suffer also from the lack of these civil functions. Besides, the designated bishop had to be indicated to the affiliated metropolitan so that he would give his opinion about the suitability and canonical capability of the candidate. This series of tasks considerably increased the amount of time required for the election process, especially when to all these difficulties was added the eventual possibility of the king not being present in the royal city, in which case he had to be reached often far from Toledo to obtain his consent. Accordingly, therefore, the council made the solemn decision that the metropolitan of Toledo, in the name of the other metropolitans, could examine and consecrate bishops of other ecclesiastical provinces of Spain, as the successors to bishops who had died in the meantime.[316] In so doing, the archbishop of Toledo required the newly consecrated bishops to present themselves to their own metropolitan within three months of their ordination, in order to receive the responsibilities for the new episcopal see.[317] Those who failed to do so would be excommunicated, unless they were prevented from presenting themselves to their metropolitan by order of the king.[318]

With the accord reached in the council among all the bishops present, and with the general delegation and the faculties attributed to the archbishop of Toledo, the prestige of the Toledan see grew enormously, and indeed, it was transformed into a real primacy in the national ecclesiastical[319] government. Thus, the archbishop of Toledo acquired a real preeminence over all the bishops of the Hispanic-Visigothic kingdom. From then on he would be the one to preside over the national councils of Spain, no longer taking into consideration the ancient praxis according to which the council was presided over by the most elderly bishop, and it would always be him, the archbishop of Toledo, who put his signature first at the end of the conciliar acts. Finally, with the primacy, the archbishop of Toledo would become the official spokesman of the national Church of Spain, for matters of doctrine, in relation to other churches. The two *Apologetica* of Julian, solemnly approved by the Fourteenth and Fifteenth Councils of Toledo and containing a refined illustration of the christological dogma, would be compiled by Julian specifically bearing in mind this general representative function of the primate of Spain from the doctrinal point of view.

We do not know if the proposal of the general delegation of episcopal ordinations to the archbishop of Toledo was made by a metropolitan close to Julian, or if it had been somehow insinuated by the royal power. In any case, it appears to be objectively evident from this resolution of the Twelfth Council of Toledo that the archbishop intended to operate a centralization of the episcopal power concerning nominations of the new bishops of every province of Spain. In fact, according to the previous practice, going back all the way to antiquity, certainly more transparent and more oriented toward the participation of all the members of the church in the election of the bishop, the new shepherd was elected by the clergy and by the people, with the approval of the king, and he was ordained by the respective metropolitan together with the suffragan bishops. All this ecclesial procedure, of great historical value, was overlooked as the Church of Spain was centralized in Toledo; the primate of Toledo became its *Pontifex Maximus*, with a power without limits and without any control.[320] Objectively the motivation of the provision that led to the conferring of primacy on the archbishop of Toledo—that is, the delay in the *celeritas nuntiorum* in communicating the death of a bishop, owing to the *longe lateque diffuso tractu terrarum* that the news had to cross before reaching Toledo—would not seem to have been so urgent and important as to revolutionize such a solid and ancient canonical praxis. Evidently, behind this official and pastoral motivation was already a tendency toward centralization that hardly seems deniable.

Therefore, it is very probable that the true motivations reside in Julian's desire, which upon election became a true episcopal program to carry out, to maintain and obtain an ecclesial, as well as political and institutional, unity so strong and sure as to become, in the end, a centralized uniformity, parallel to the monarchic one. As some scholars maintain, the primacy of Toledo became a kind of symbol of the national Church of Spain and of national independence, especially since the primacy of the metropolitan Church of Toledo had been obtained without a consultation or a pronouncement from the Church of Rome on the subject. Julian's goal was, therefore, an "aggrandizement of the National Church and of Toledo as its head, bringing with it, as a necessary consequence, independence of all authority from without."[321] Likewise, it can be hypothesized that Julian had considered it the right moment to achieve overall unity of the churches of Spain, believing, perhaps erroneously, that the Germanic elements of Visigothic origin and the Hispanic-Roman characteristics could meld into a national unity,[322] in imitation of what had happened in the Byzantine Empire with the city of Constantinople. Perhaps in his clever and programmatic mind, Toledo had to become the new Constantinople or the Constantinople of the West, as a sort of Western patriarchate with all the consequences of greatness and parity with the other Christian churches, including Rome. The point is that the Spanish bishopric considered the decision of the council to be legitimate, as, for example, Idalius of Barcelona, of the ecclesiastical province of Tarragona, who, in his letter to Julian thanking him for sending a copy of the *Prognosticum futuri saeculi*, twice calls him bishop "of the primate see." Other documents refer to him as "the first one in the ecclesiastical hierarchy of Spain,"[323] comparing him directly to St. Peter, in the sense that if Peter was the first of the apostles, the bishop of Toledo is to be considered the first of the bishops of Spain.

Moreover, it is amazing that the other metropolitans of Spain—the archbishops of the other important ecclesiastical provinces, Tarragona, Braga, Santiago and Seville—did not offer any resistance to having a good part of their power and their episcopal prerogatives vanish, as a result of the recognition of the absolute primacy of the archbishop of the *urbs regia*. In truth, they seem subjugated rather by the decision of the council, though it is probable that there had been a debate during the council, and perhaps dissent had also been expressed. But, in the end, with a good dose of savoir faire, the proposal was approved and voted on favorably by the majority of the bishops present, thus becoming an official determination of the council in every respect. It can be significant, however—but this is only conjecture—that some manuscripts of the acts of the Twelfth Council of Toledo, as signaled in the editions of the conciliar texts, lack the words *atque Galliae* after the expression of the general consent of the gathered bishops: *Unde omnibus placuit pontificibus Hispaniae*. It is as if the ecclesiastical province of Gallia had accepted the directive only subsequently and therefore had been included only later among the provinces that accepted the deliberation of the council. The point is that after some years, during the Thirteenth Council of Toledo, the primacy of the archbishop of Toledo was quite solemnly confirmed,[324] together with all the other canons of the Twelfth Council, this being a sign that in the previous two years the new praxis had been consolidated.

The Bishops also condemned the institution of new dioceses made by Wamba, as well as the ordinations of bishops nominated by him.[325] All of this increased considerably the powers of the archbishop metropolitan of Toledo over the bishops of the whole of Spain. All the metropolitan bishops signed the acts of the council (two of them through their representatives), as did seventy-two bishops.

Undoubtedly such a complete result of conferring the primacy on the archdiocese of Toledo was made possible almost exclusively by the ingenious and strong intellectual and episcopal personality of Julian of Toledo and, perhaps, by the weakness of King Ervig[326] or, as the historians of the intrigue say, by the debt that the king had contracted with his longtime friend because of the conspiracy that led to the deposition of Wamba and to the crowning of Ervig. History tells us that the successors of Julian, having neither his temperament nor his strength as episcopal personalities, certainly did not make the primacy of Toledo stand out as he had. Besides, the Visigothic kingdom was on the point of vanishing, on account of the Arabic invasion, and the primacy of Toledo would not be mentioned for a long time.

In fact, events worsened when King Ervig, confirming his weakness, abdicated to his son-in-law, Egica, because of a serious illness. He requested "the penitence," that is, the tonsure and the religious habit of penitence. Julian himself was the one to repeat the celebration of the penitential rite that seven years before he had celebrated for King Wamba,[327] though certainly in less clear circumstances; and so Julian thus made a monk of Ervig. In the final months of 687, Ervig died. The new king, Egica, vengeful and despotic by nature, contributed even more to the fall of the Visigothic empire, mercilessly opposing the royal family and its privileges. He even summoned a council, the Sixteenth Council of Toledo, presided over by Julian, to settle the thorny dilemma created by two oaths he had made to Ervig: one, on the occasion of his marriage to the king's daughter, to protect the royal family; and the other, at Ervig's deathbed, to defend the people and guarantee justice. Since the two oaths seemed contradictory to him, he asked the council to make a pronouncement on the question. The council obviously put the common good in the first place above family affairs, but it also recommended that the king treat the royal family with justice, without any kind of revenge or prejudice. But King Egica, dissatisfied and taking advantage of the fact that Julian of Toledo had died in the meantime, convoked a council of the province of Tarragona to decree the forced life imprisonment of the queen, Ervig's widow, in a monastery. That Egica had committed a serious abuse by forcing the bishops to make such a pronouncement is shown by how a provincial council dared to contradict a national and plenary council of the Hispanic-Visigothic bishopric. The primate of Spain Julian certainly would never have permitted such a serious canonical offense.

It was only some centuries later, toward the end of the eleventh century, that the primacy of the archbishop of Toledo was again referred to in ecclesiastical documents. Surprisingly, however, in some pontifical documents, the Church of Rome, through Pope Urban II, referred to the primacy of Toledo turning to the archbishop of that episcopal see, the Cluniac monk Bernard de Sédirac (1050–1125), reminding him that primacy was given to Toledo as privilege of the Roman see (*privilegi nostri statuimus*). For some, this reference is to be interpreted as a strong and clear affirmation of the power of the Church of Rome,[328] which thus underlines that it is up to the Church of Rome to confer such a title; however, for others, based on ungenerous and unfounded historical judgment, especially for the second part of the sentence, the primacy "had been originally assumed independently of Rome and used in a spirit of hostility to her."[329]

The presumed anti-Judaism of Julian of Toledo

In some entries dedicated to Julian of Toledo in historical and theological dictionaries and encyclopedias, an uninhibited anti-Judaic attitude, typical of his time, is sometimes attributed to Julian, both in his episcopal ministry and in his political activity, as well as in his writings.

Hillgarth records this tendency when he affirms: "in the last century Paul à Wengen and Mrs. Humphrey Ward saw in Julian of Toledo the instigator of Ervig's legislation against the Jews." But as we have seen, "there is not direct proof of this charge,"[330] because it cannot be affirmed that the *De comprobatione sextae aetatis*, which undoubtedly is a polemical work against the biblical hermeneutics of the Hebrew interpreters, incited the violence toward and the persecution of the Jews. In his work, the objections of the Christian author Julian of Toledo are exclusively related to the messianic doctrine of Judaism that denied the messianic identity of Jesus,[331] because the sixth age of the world had not yet come. Julian objected and contested this affirmation with an exegetical, hermeneutical approach and, above all, with an extreme use of the mathematical calculation. The anti-Judaic polemic, therefore, is present in these works of Julian, but only on the intellectual level, as it serves above all to convince Christians rather than to convert Jews to Christ: "the aim of the work is to convince the Christian reader of the falsity of the Jews' claims,"[332] of their *manifestissima caecitas* in not recognizing the Messiah in Jesus of Nazareth.

In any case, the accusation of anti-judaism against Julian does not refer, naturally, to violent anti-Judaic action, but rather to the sharing of the anti-Judaic attitude of the century in which Julian lived, especially on the political level. In reality, Julian was not a *persecutor* of Jews, nor did he ever have a bad disposition toward them. To the contrary, it is probable that he had good relationships with some Jews of his time, at least with those belonging to the Jewish community of Toledo. If undoubtedly the seventh century of the Christian era was generally characterized by a heavy negative disposition toward the Jews and Judaism, particularly in Visigothic Spain, this attitude does not seem to be attributed to Julian of Toledo. Both in the life and in the works of Julian, in fact, there are many signs contrary to this presumed anti-Judaic attitude.

First of all, there is the historical information, quite well founded,[333] that Julian was born into a family that was Christian but of Jewish origin. As we have seen, the matter is still debated and, in effect, some scholars are more inclined to deny rather than to admit this Jewish ancestry of Julian.[334] Good sense suggests that if Julian indeed had Jewish ancestry, then it would be hard to understand his having a hostile attitude toward Judaism.

In the second place, we can find an important and clarifying sign of Julian of Toledo's attitude toward the Jews precisely in his main work, the *Prognosticum futuri saeculi,* and specifically in the letter written by Bishop Idalius to Julian. Idalius, in fact, thanks Julian in a letter for having dedicated the work to him and for having then sent a manuscript copy of the *Prognosticum* to him in Barcelona as the valuable result of their theological dialogue. After having praised the wise editing of the work, indeed, the aforesaid bishop of Barcelona appears rather surprised at the fact that Julian had sent him the treasured volume by means of a Jewish messenger, a *brutum animal,* as

Idalius unfortunately defines[335] the messenger. With such information, though unpleasant for the vulgar epithet attributed to the messenger, the bishop of Barcelona, nonetheless, renders a valuable service, informing us about the facts and even the name of the person, a Jew, to whom Julian entrusted the delicate charge of delivering the manuscript of the *Prognosticum* to the bishop of Barcelona, as Idalius writes: *quidam Iudaeus, nomine Restitutus*, a certain Jew named Restitutus.

In the rest of the letter Idalius repeats again his marvel that the precious volume of the *Prognosticum* had reached him by the hands of a person "extraneous to the faith." And here he offers us another service: he informs us, in fact, that Restitutus was not a Jew converted to Christianity, but a Jew who had maintained his Jewish religious identity, and who, therefore, was to be considered, according to the vision of the time, "extraneous to the Christian faith." Restitutus was probably on good terms with Julian and was perhaps a frequent traveler, maybe even a merchant. This would not be surprising, because during the reign of Egica Jews were allowed to possess slaves, in exchange for the promise of conversion to Christianity. Under his rule, Jews freely practiced their livelihood, devoting themselves to commerce, as, perhaps, in the case of Restitutus, the Jew who acted as intermediary between Julian and Idalius of Barcelona, carrying, according to Idalius, unaware of the treasure he transported, a copy of the *Prognosticum* along a road that he surely knew well enough to frequent it with assiduousness as a traveling dealer of other merchandise. The roads crossed by Restitutus had to be, in part, those built by the imperial Rome, first of all, for military use and then for commercial use. But in the seventh century, after the decline of the Roman Empire, the admirable and perfect Roman road system, initiated in the fourth century BC, reinstated in a grandiose way during the time of Augustus and improved in the following centuries, had been seriously compromised by carelessness and wear.

Finally, at the end of the letter, Idalius attributes, in any case, this strange story to Divine Providence, as he writes that everything that had happened had certainly been by the will of Christ. Idalius, in the end, redeems himself from the unwise and unhappy expressions used for qualifying Restitutus, claiming to want to thank the Jew Restitutus for having delivered to him intact the precious copy of the work of Julian, after the long journey.

The unflattering expressions, unforgivable for us today, which Bishop Idalius used to describe the Jew Restitutus, invite us to reflect and to draw some conclusions. Indeed, if Idalius was amazed that Julian had really entrusted the first fruit of his work to the hands of a Jew, it should not be at all surprising that Julian himself judged him instead to be a prudent and sure choice. Evidently, he totally trusted the person to whom he gave such a delicate task, as perhaps he had already done on other occasions, and this means that Julian had a good relationship with Restitutus. Murphy clearly underlines this personal attitude of Julian toward the Jews when he says, speaking of Restitutus, that "the one instance we possess of his personal dealing with a Jew finds him being chided for his kindness and trusting-nature by a fellow Bishop."[336] Perhaps Restitutus was a *famiglio* (servant) or an ancient acquaintance of the family of Julian. In reality we do not know who the one named Restitutus was, but he certainly had to have been an accustomed traveler or perhaps a merchant who covered with a certain regularity not only the considerable distance between Toledo (in the center of the Iberian Peninsula) and Barcelona (on the banks of the Mediterranean Sea), but also to the northeast of the Iberian Peninsula—a fatiguing trip of around seven hundred kilometers. He was, therefore, a trustworthy person and also an experienced traveler, with whom Julian was well acquainted. To travel in the times of Julian, in fact, was indeed a dangerous adventure, full of risks exposing the wayfarers to dangerous situations of every kind. But Restitutus evidently knew his craft and, in a reasonable amount of time, after some weeks of travel, he reached Barcelona with the precious volume to deliver to the bishop of the city, who was a colleague of Julian.

At last, it seems very meaningful and opportune to quote a source that is the expression of contemporary Jewish thought to see what it says about the presumed anti-Judaism of Julian of Toledo.

The entry *Julian of Toledo* contained in the *Jewish Encyclopedia*,[337] in fact, after having said rather generically, but in a true way, that Julian belongs to an anti-Jewish period of the history of the Western Church, underlines the fact that, contrary to the tendency of the time, Julian was, instead, a moderate, benevolent, and charitable bishop. At the end of the entry the author also quotes the "history" of Restitutus, as an evident sign of a benevolent attitude of the primate of Spain toward the Jews of Toledo and of an opening to dialogue with them and to meet with them. The conclusion made by the author of the encyclopedic entry is that, accordingly, negative attitudes, in an aggressive sense, toward Jews cannot be attributed to Julian of Toledo, considering that he entrusted with such an important object as the first manuscript copy (or at least one of the first manuscript copies) of his *Prognosticum* precisely to the Jew, Restitutus, in order for him to deliver it to Bishop Idalius in distant Barcelona.

Profile of the human, theological, and pastoral personality of Julian of Toledo

Julian of Toledo is, in order of time, the last of the great literary and theological figures of the Visigothic Church of Spain[338] that constitutes the flowering of the intellectual and theological movement, starting with St. Martin of Braga, at the end of the fourth century, and extending up to the conquest of Visigothic Spain by the Arabs.[339]

He was one of the best among the not very numerous theologians of the seventh century and "was certainly a scholar, for his time, of the first rank, a formidable theologian and a bishop not likely to allow the position of the Church in Spain or that of his own see of Toledo to be lightly challenged."[340] Julian also belonged to the extraordinary flowering of Spanish bishops of those centuries, along with Isidore of Seville,[341] Ildephonse of Toledo,[342] and Braulio of Saragossa; and he was "the strongest figure of the Visigothic bishopric as character as theologian as Prince of the Church."[343] Hillgarth, paraphrasing what the biographer Felix wrote, gives us a very positive spiritual portrait of him: "like so many other Spanish bishops he was noted for his almsgiving and for his life of prayer, as well as for his practical skill in affairs and in the solving of vexed liturgical problems."[344] And the biographer adds, on the ecclesiological level, Julian "is the portrait of a great bishop of the age, distinguished for his defence of the Church, ever watchful in ruling his flock, fearless in his attitude to the great, justly celebrated for his goodness to the poor, making himself the servant of his people."[345]

Within the movement of cultural rebirth that began in the Iberian Peninsula at the end of the fifth century and ended suddenly with the Arabic invasion (711) and the fall of the Visigothic empire, Julian of Toledo was, after Isidore of Seville, the most emerging personality, while as a writer and theologian treating doctrinal matters of great theological substance, he was certainly superior to the same great bishop of Seville.[346] Scholars of the seventh century patristic period of the Iberian Peninsula do not hesitate to define him "for some aspects, the greatest theologian of the Visigothic Fathers"[347] and to put him on the same level with the other great Spanish fathers. They praise him not only in matters of classical and theological culture, but they exalt him, even more than the *Ispaliensis* himself,[348] for the originality and the depth of his theological thought (known to us only from the few works that have survived), in addition to the boldness of character and firmness that he manifested in the guidance of the Primatial Church of Toledo and of the churches of Visigothic Spain.

In addition to Julian the person and his historical-ecclesial conscience, it is important to recall the frantic conciliar activity of the Spanish bishopric under his guidance (we have already mentioned that four of the eighteen Councils of Toledo were, in fact, presided over by him in the ten years of his bishopric) and the conviction with which he succeeded in attributing the role of primatial see of all of Spain to the Church of Toledo. The same can be said about the boldness of how he related to the church in Rome on the occasion of a theological controversy in which he showed himself to be "very above the Catholic hierarchy of his time,"[349] displaying a "healthy and robust"[350] knowledge of the patristic literature and having very refined theological criteria and method, also with respect to the classical christological definitions of the patristic period. We can say that the knowledge that Julian displayed in abundance, especially in theological matters, practically embraced all the erudition of his time. He was, in fact, an experienced liturgist and a liturgical reformer, an expert in canon law and at the same time a legislator, an experienced grammarian, a poet, an innovative historian, a great theologian, or better "un teólogo formidable,"[351] and even so convinced of his doctrinal knowledge as to resist resolutely the objections coming from the pontifical theologians of the Roman curia; but he was also an accomplished politician. He was, in short, as Hillgarth defines him, "un erudito, para su época, de primera categoría."[352]

Julian had a strong character, inclined to command, but he also knew how to be a wise man of great shrewdness and discretion, prudent and mature in judging, very charitable and able to moderate his severity with sweetness. The psychological portrait of his character that his biographer gives us is very flattering and grounded in reality: "excellent in the defense of all the Churches, sleepless in governing the subjects, full of zeal in the repression of the conceited, ready to sustain the humble, splendid in the exercise of his own authority."[353]

But Julian was also, and he showed it more than once, a skilled politician who knew how to move himself well in the difficult social situation and politics of Spain in the seventh century, when violent changes of the imperial political order occurred. According to modern historians, he was undoubtedly the most skilled administrator and the most competent theologian among the numerous bishops of Visigothic Spain[354] and the most capable administrator and competent expert of the seventh century in eschatological and christological matters. [355]

He was so convinced of the validity of his theological writings that he did not hesitate even a moment to protest with all of his theological reasons when Pope Benedict II and the Roman curia accused him of maintaining incorrect christological doctrine.[356] His strong and justified dialectical reaction, not at all diplomatic, was undoubtedly the sign of his intellectual boldness and his theological conviction, even if rather intemperate in language. His reactions were viewed as justified in the end by Rome, which in turn withdrew every accusation against him, and even approved and made public, also in the East, the valuable theological elaboration of the primate of Toledo in christological matters.

For this polemic with Rome and for the exercise of the primacy of the episcopal see of Toledo, Julian has strongly been criticized by various modern historians, both Catholics and Protestants. Some of them, in fact, interpreted the *querelle* with Rome as a real attempt at schism—an "exaggeration, without a doubt"[357]—while others, likewise exaggeratedly, saw his whole bishopric as an unbridled ambition for power and the primacy of the see of Toledo, for which Julian did not hesitate, in addition to rebelling against Rome, to plot politically and participate in the deposition of King Wamba, guilty, perhaps, of having offended the Spanish bishopric and the primate of Toledo.[358] But this double negative judgment by historians, reported by Hillgarth,[359] has been strongly revised by the publication of more recent and less presumptive studies[360] that have shown that the most serious accusations against Julian of Toledo were lacking in foundation. It remains true, however, that Julian knew how to move with a lot of prudence and circumspection in the difficult political environment of the imperial city, traversed by court intrigues and characterized also by very strong episodes of political violence.

Julian of Toledo was thus a notably outstanding personality of the Visigothic Church of Spain, "perhaps the most interesting among the Iberian authors of this period."[361] His theological preparation and his intellectual abilities are certainly to be considered above average[362] in the western European episcopal panorama. He was a true wise man,[363] who knew well Sacred Scripture, philosophy, history, poetry, grammar, and especially theology, which he learned from reading and studying the ecclesial documents of the canonical collections and the works of the fathers of the church.[364] In particular, his knowledge of patristic texts and their theological content and his ability, indeed admirable, to generate systematic and theological syntheses, certainly distinguish his preparation and intelligence with respect to other intellectuals of his century. The creation of his own personal method of study and theological research, which gave him a systematic approach, even if only initial, to the contents of Christian faith, as well as his dialogue abilities, manifold interests in the fields of liturgy, mysticism, history, philosophy, grammar, logic, philology, and so on, together with the decennial exercise of a strong episcopal ministry as primate of the bishops of the Iberian Peninsula and as defender of the churches of all of Spain, make Julian of Toledo a seventh-century person of notable ecclesial stature and theological depth and a precursor of the theological renaissance of the Carolingian period.

At the same time, the Christian and pastoral virtues and the talents of Bishop Julian cannot be overlooked. The sequence in which his biographer transmitted them to us, which we suppose was done with sincerity, is worth mentioning for the enthusiastic admiration conveyed for his pastoral ministry, even if it greatly resembles the literary and rhetorical canons of the time, as was customary in the *De viris illustribus*. According to Felix, in fact, Julian

> was ready to assist whoever was in the need, and his charity was so extraordinary *(exuberans)* that he never refused to give something to anyone who asked. And with such a way of proceeding he sought to be pleasing to God and to be useful to people.[365] He was full of the fear of God, exemplary in prudence, discreet in decisions, remarkable in discernment, extraordinarily devoted to giving alms, ever ready to have compassion on those who were miserable, prompt in the undoing of oppressors, discreet in action,

zealous in the affairs to be settled, righteous in emitting sentences, moderate in judgment, excellent in the defense of justice, praiseworthy in discussions, assiduous in prayer, admirable in the fulfillment of the divine praises. And in the case, as it occurred, of any difficulties in the divine offices, he showed himself most capable of resolving the problem, passionately exhorting the sacred praises, eminent in the defense of all the Churches, sleepless in governing the subjects, full of zeal in the repression of the conceited, ready to sustain the humble, splendid in the exercise of his own authority, rich in the desired good of humility, and, in general, distinguished for the total integrity of his customs....As equal to his illustrious predecessors in deserving merits, as in no way inferior to them in overall virtues.[366]

If this text of Felix seems too laudatory or panegyric in connection with the same episcopal family,[367] it is also true that contemporary scholars have not said less than the biographer Felix, even if in more abstract terms, emphasizing above all the theological and literary abilities of Julian, when they have affirmed, as J. Madoz does, that Julian was a "meaningful figure of the Visigothic Church, comparable only to Isidore of Seville, to whom he concedes the place in encyclopedic knowledge, but whom he exceeds in personal vigor and originality....Under certain aspects he is the greatest theologian of the Visigothic Fathers."[368] Or that Julian "is the last eminent churchman of West Gothic Spain, and, next to Isidore of Seville, perhaps the most eminent," though another scholar adds that "Julian's medieval reputation cannot indeed be compared with that of Isidore."[369] In a very similar tone, U. Domínguez Del Val has written instead that Julian is even superior to Isidore of Seville in doctrinal matters and as a writer.[370] Moreover, he was an expert in Sacred Scripture and in pagan literature, and his literary style was clear and scholastic in the exercise of logic and reasoning.

We conclude by making our own the summarizing judgment expressed by J. Madoz at the end of an important study of his on Julian and his work, in reference to Julian's theological, pastoral, and political personality. According to the prolific scholar of Spanish matters, therefore, Julian was free, in general, from the defects of the decadence, frequent in his epoch, vibrant and overwhelming in the anti-Judaic polemic, deep and mystically elevated in his reflections on the afterlife, enthusiastic and poetically ornate in his patriotic historical narrations, catechetic and familiar, finally, in the questions and answers of his Grammar. In sacred and profane erudition he is a worthy successor of Isidore. Disciple of Eugene, the poet, Julian is an exponent of the high-level to which the classical studies had reached in Spain in his times. The "Historia Wambae" and his "Ars grammatica" move us to presume he had a rhetorical formation that was not imparted in the other nations of the Latin world[371] [in the seventh century].

The death of Julian of Toledo and the cult of veneration[372]

Julian of Toledo died of natural causes,[373] probably in the episcopal building of Toledo, at the age of forty-eight (or forty-six),[374] on Sunday, March 6, of the year 690,[375] two years after the edition of the *Prognosticum* and after ten years[376] of episcopal ministry. No information has been handed down to us about the cause of his death, even if, having occurred at the end of the frigid Toledan winter, it could be imputed to its strong influence or fever with respiratory complications that the medicine and the pharmacopoeia of the seventh century were not able to cure.

Christian belief that death is the passage to eternal life was evident throughout Julian's life and especially in his activity as a theologian. This is shown by the text of the first book of the *Prognosticum*, which is wholly dedicated to the subject of death, its origin, and the Christian remedies to face it with great serenity and courage. His interest in the theme of death is confirmed also by the intense "thought toward death" in the *Oratio ad Deum*, which precedes the text of the *Prognosticum*, where Julian manifests his detachment from this world and an aching nostalgic desire for eternal life in the homeland of the heavenly Jerusalem.

It is probable that at his death a mortuary room was prepared in a hall of the episcopal building or in the cathedral, where so many times he had celebrated the sacred liturgies. Here the corpse of the primate was exhibited, dressed in the liturgical vestments and the episcopal insignias; in his hands, stiffened by death, probably was placed the cruet of the holy oil, sign of the priestly dignity of the primate, with which he had anointed so many bishops and two Visigothic kings;[377] on his breast, instead, was placed the book of the Gospel, sign of the *munus propheticum* that he had practiced during his pastoral and theological *magisterium* in the service of the Word of God.

It is just as likely that the corpse of Julian was honored by the visits of the king and of the palatine nobility, as well as by other bishops present in Toledo. Prayers of suffrage and psalmody were certainly recited by the bishops who had come for the occasion, by the clergy and by the people of Toledo. Even if we do not have any historical information about it, it is likely that the solemn funerals of the primate were celebrated with honors in the Cathedral of Toledo, in the presence of the king, the imperial court, and about ten concelebrating bishops, according to the prescribed formula of the Mozárabic liturgy. The body of Julian was interred with honors, after a long and sad procession through the streets of the royal city, in the church of the Toledan martyr Leocadia,[378] symbol of the Christian faith of Toledo and by then the customary place for the celebrations of many of the important national councils of Spain, but also a symbol of the Hispanic-Visigothic political and religious unity. The Basilica of Saint Leocadia had for a long time been the *pantheon* of the last metropolitans of Toledo, who, beside the mortal remains of the Toledan martyr, awaited the final resurrection of their bodies: Quiricus, Ildephonse, Eugenius.[379] The entombment of the corpse of Julian was preceded by the celebration of a second Holy Mass of suffrage and by the incensing of his body in token of the future glorification as work of the power of Christ. Finally, after having removed the book of the Gospel from the breast of the corpse and after having unveiled the face from the shroud that until then had covered it, holy chrism was sprinkled upon his mouth, as a sign of participation in the eternal life, and the body was at last entombed.[380]

The popular cult of Julian began shortly after his death, first in Toledo and then in the whole kingdom.[381] According to Hillgarth, Julian "received liturgical commemoration and cult by ca. 875, at the latest, when Usuardus included him in his Martyrologium."[382] In the Mozárabic calendars of Silos[383] (of the tenth and eleventh centuries), in addition to the already mentioned *Martyrologium* of Usuardus[384] and some Missals,[385] the liturgical feast devoted to St. Julian of Toledo was established for March 8. The error of the two days of discrepancy with respect to the date of his death (March 6) seems to be attributable to the publishers of both the *Missale mixtum* and the *Breviarium Gothico-Mozarabicum*, respectively printed in 1500 and 1502 and edited by Cardinal Ximenes de Cisneros. The liturgical feast was established on March 8, which then became the date that was also inserted in the *Martyrologium Romanum*. Currently, the Mozárabic calendar sets the feast of Bishop Julian on January 14, probably to prevent the liturgical feast of the bishop saint from occurring during the Lenten period.

With such veneration Julian of Toledo was recognized for his merit of having been a bishop full of charity, as well as courage in defending the liberty of the churches of Spain both from the royal power and from the ecclesiastical power, and to have been, in any case, one of the greatest doctors in the Church of Spain, and not just in the *urbs regia*. For many years his grave was the destination of pilgrimages, especially after Julian was included in the register of saints of the Mozárabic calendar. It was probably encouraged by the bishops of Toledo, Julian's successors, or perhaps it was due to the spontaneous spread of popular devotion. The first historical information about the cult of Julian, however, dates back to the second half of the ninth century (875, or even before, 858, according to Hillgarth).[386] This means that the birth and development of the liturgical veneration of the primate of Toledo was not weighed down by possible suspicion about his having a considerable part in the unjust deposition of the warrior king Wamba, nor was his veneration as saint damaged by his proud reaction to the doctrinal objections of the Roman theologians. On the contrary, the diffusion of the veneration toward Julian means, instead, that his decennial of bishopric was appreciated and judged in a positive way, above all because he had exercised it as a defender of the freedom of the church[387] against all interference and illegitimate intrusions. In just a few years the cult of veneration of Julian had extended throughout Spain, and Julian was recognized as a saint of the Hispanic-Visigothic people, as well as one of the greatest theologians in the Hispanic-Visigothic Church.

But beginning from the fateful year of 711, the year in which the royal city of Toledo surrendered to the Arabic invaders, the cult of Julian and the Toledan saints buried in the Basilica of Saint Leocadia was suddenly interrupted. The sepulchres of the great metropolitans of Toledo were probably still intact in the Basilica of Saint Leocadia perhaps until the year 754, but with the multiplication of sieges and political instability care was taken to transfer them to the north of the peninsula, to more secure places. The relics of the holy martyr Leocadia, and then the body of Ildephonse of Toledo, were brought to areas that were still Christian. Perhaps other bodies were also brought gradually to more appropriate places, but there remains no historical information about such transfers. There is news only in the Toledan breviary, which attests that the body of Julian was brought to the area of the city of Oviedo. According to a fairly well founded tradition, in the middle of the eighth century, perhaps to prevent the mortal remains of the venerable martyr Leocadia and of the holy bishops of Toledo buried in the basilica devoted to the holy martyr from being profaned during the Arabic invasion, they were moved to other places, obviously secret. The identity of the location was so well guarded that, with the passing of time, the memory of the site of the mortal remains of Julian of Toledo was lost.

A catalogue of relics preserved in the city of Oviedo and attached to a manuscript of the eleventh century compiled by Bishop Pelagius, seems to indicate that the mortal remains of Julian had been moved from Toledo to the city of Oviedo,[388] or, according to another tradition, to the surroundings of Oviedo. However, the manuscript erroneously identifies the mortal remains as belonging to St. Julian Pomerius. We have already discussed how the confusion and interchange between the two Julians (of Toledo and Pomerius) accompanied the figure of the bishop theologian of Toledo for centuries, even after his death. The text of the manuscript recites: "sancti Juliani Pomerii qui arcam ipsam a Toleto Ovetum transtulit." But since Julian Pomerius, abbot of Arles and tutor of St. Cesarius,[389] was never identified as saint, it is certain, by exclusion, that the Julian referred to by the manuscript of the catalogue of relics is actually Julian, the archbishop primate of Toledo.[390]

As for the second hypothesis of burial in the surroundings of Oviedo, some think that this gave rise to the name of a rural place, Santullano (an anomalous mixture of *Sanctus* and *Iulianus*), today one of the districts of Rivera, capital of the principality of the Asturies. In the thirteenth century, the Sanctuary of St. Millán of the Cogolla[391] is also mentioned in reference to relics of the saint bishop of Toledo.

To this date, however, the mortal remains of Julian of Toledo have never been found.

Conclusion

We have covered the principal stages of the life of Julian of Toledo, from his birth to his baptism, from his being a pupil in the Episcopal School of Toledo to being a clergyman, then a deacon, and then a priest of the metropolitan Church of Toledo. His human, intellectual, and pastoral value, noted and appreciated by King Wamba, earned him the ascent to the episcopal see of Toledo for ten intense years of pastoral ministry, during which Julian was a protagonist of important, if not decisive, political events for the history of the Hispanic-Visigothic kingdom; for example, the scabrous case of King Wamba's deposition, in which, as we have seen, Julian somehow had a role—even if he was not entirely aware and not as directly involved as others—as was maintained by some historians in the beginning of the last century.

Subsequently he was the protagonist of many important events: the crowning and consecration of Ervig as the new king of the Visigothic kingdom, and a second crowning, that of King Egica. But we must add his active presidency of four important national councils of Spain, the attainment of the primacy of the episcopal see of Toledo over all the other metropolitan churches of Spain, the strong theological-canonical *querelle* with the Church of Rome, from which he emerged with head held high, as well as the numerous pastoral, liturgical, canonical, and other aspects of the decade of his episcopal government. This series of events makes Julian of Toledo a leading figure in the panorama of the European church and the western theological context of the seventh century of the Christian era.

We reserve a special place for the intellectual dimension of Julian, with the great finesse of his literary formation and his abundant literary production of various sorts, in which he was a profound exegete of Sacred Scripture; a brilliant historian, grammarian, rhetorician, poet, philosopher, and polemicist; and, finally, a theologian with a complex and complete vision of the truths and mysteries of the Christian faith, which he was able to interconnect with intelligence through a solid reference to the texts of the Christian tradition. On the theological level he has the unusual privilege and chronological primacy to be the father of Christian eschatology, having been the first to write a true manual and thorough treatise of eschatology, the *Prognosticum futuri saeculi.*

For all these qualities, the episcopal and theological figure of Julian of Toledo significantly emerges in the Hispanic-Visigothic horizon of the seventh century as comparable only to the greatest representative of Christian Spain, but still belonging to the patristic period, Isidore of Seville. Even if Julian never equaled Isidore in his encyclopedic culture, he certainly surpassed him in depth and for the value of his thought and his method. According to Rivera Recio, the unusual personality of Julian of Toledo originated in his Jewish ancestry. He, in fact, knew how to unite in himself, and marvelously, "the excellent mental qualities of this race with the ardent and untamable temperament of the Hispanic race."[392]

THE WORKS ATTRIBUTED WITH CERTAINTY TO JULIAN OF TOLEDO

Julian of Toledo was undoubtedly a fertile writer, or better, a prolific polygraph, author of books about grammar, history, biblical exegesis, theology, liturgy, and so on. Just as rich was his way of expressing his thought in writing. His style varied depending on the type of work and its content; his style was dignified and elevated, vibrant in polemical discussions, and warm with patriotic enthusiasm in his historical contributions.[393] He is, therefore, one of the more important literary figures of the Hispanic-Visigothic Church of the seventh century and is at the top of the intellectual and literary development that had begun some centuries before in Spain with St. Martin of Braga and that reached its apex with Isidore of Seville, Eugenius II, and Ildephonse of Toledo.

The works attributed to Julian of Toledo are, for various reasons, very interesting—certainly not less than those of his predecessors, even the most illustrious and great.[394] If Julian was equal in erudition to such great personages, in the opinion of many he surpassed them for the originality of his theological method and for his doctrinal system.

The biographer Felix enumerates seventeen works that he attributes to Julian of Toledo,[395] and at the same time, he gives us a synthetic though sufficient description of them. Fortunately, the five most important works of the list,[396] that is, *Prognosticum futuri saeculi, Apologeticum de tribus capitulis, De comprobatione sextae aetatis, Antikeimenon,* and *Historia Wambae Regis,* have survived through the passing of the centuries, together with his *Ars grammatica,* more recently attributed to Julian, and have reached us today. Julian, therefore, followed the example and the tradition of the fathers of the church, who, as is known, were to a large extent bishops and, for this reason, also fertile writers. His activity as a writer, therefore, is certainly the most interesting and valid part of his existence, and to it he devoted great attention and importance.

Reading the annotated list of the works of Julian of Toledo furnished by his biographer, one has the impression that he, briefly citing them one after the other, had before his eyes the whole collection of the manuscripts of his predecessor, very probably by then an integral part of the rich episcopal library of Toledo, which Julian himself had developed with great effort during the decade of his apostolic mission, as did his illustrious predecessors, Eugenius II and Ildephonse of Toledo. With a few sentences, Felix succeeds in describing the importance and the content of the works. In addition to the four works edited in volume 115 of Corpus Christianorum, the critical edition of the *Antikeimenon* was planned for volume 116 of the same collection, but to date it has not been published. Prior to the critical edition of the Corpus Christianorum, the best edition of the *Prognosticum futuri saeculi, De comprobatione sextae aetatis,* and *Antikeimenon* was the one edited by various Spanish scholars for Cardinal F. De Lorenzana and published in 1785.[397] The text of the works of Julian of Toledo from this edition was then edited by J.-P. Migne in volume 96 of his *Patrologiae Cursus Completus, Series Latina.*

A case apart is the *Ars grammatica*, of which we possess a certain number of manuscripts that attribute it all to Julian of Toledo.[398] It concerns a Latin grammar written in the period of Visigothic Spain. The scholars are nearly all in agreement that it was probably written in Toledo in the year 685. Therefore the place and the date of composition would be entirely compatible with the possibility of attributing the work to Julian of Toledo. The biographer Felix, however, does not enumerate the *Ars grammatica* in the list of the works of Julian, and since he is considered a reliable and precise source, the *Ars grammatica* should be considered a series of scholastic notes, gathered during the lessons of Julian at the Episcopal School of Toledo by one or more of his disciples, and very probably revised by him to provide uniformity and homogeneity to the notes. In this case, then, even if the work was not written *ex professo* and directly by Julian, it could unquestionably be attributed to his paternity. Patristic examples of this kind were not lacking at the time, such as, for example, some works of Augustine that were notes or comments revised by the author to become a work of his. It was perhaps this characteristic of the work, being a revision based on the notes of disciples, that caused Felix to exclude it from his precise list of the works of Julian. During recent decades new studies on the *Ars grammatica* have produced a critical edition of the work, but they have not achieved certainty about attributing the work directly to Julian of Toledo.

In the volume of Corpus Christianorum dedicated to the works of Julian of Toledo, the publisher has thought well to include in the volume also the *Epistula ad Modoenum*, a brief poem, published *cura et studio* by B. Bischoff,[399] whose attribution to Julian of Toledo seems sure. This text in verses was probably part of the more ample *Liber Carminum diversorum* written by Julian, which Felix mentions in his list of the works of Julian,[400] but which is considered lost. In the brief text (just thirty verses) devoted to the unknown Bishop Modoenus, the author explicitly draws from classical metric poetry instead of rhythmic poetry, showing how the poetic form can blend itself with doctrinal and theological content.[401] The number of quotations from authors of the classical period that Julian included in this text, in comparison to its brevity, is considerable: from Socrates to Ennius, to Homer, Varro, Caesar, Symmachus,[402] and other authors. That Julian quoted all these classical authors probably means that he knew and was familiar with their works, perhaps through the teachings of his preceptor, the poet Eugenius II, but also that he then knew their names and had read many of their verses, abundantly distributed in the pages of the *Etymologiae* of Isidore of Seville.[403]

We can conclude that the catalogue of the works of Julian of Toledo that has reached us manifests a great variety of genre and interests cultivated by the author: historical, exegetical, polemical, patristic, theological, and dogmatic in what concerns the Christian faith and its development, but also classical, grammatical, rhetorical, and poetic on the level of appreciation and knowledge of the refined pagan culture. This variety of interests not only means that we are confronted with a man of vast and high culture for his times, but, above all, a man with an intelligence and a personality not at all common in the seventh century.

The Elogium Ildephonsi *(667)*

The biographer Felix does not mention[404] another text that, owing to an abundant manuscript tradition[405] and to the unanimous opinion of scholars,[406] is surely to be attributed to Julian: the brief *Elogium Ildephonsi*,[407] placed at the end of the *De viris illustribus* of Ildephonse of Toledo.[408]

This writing is a brief biography of the Toledan bishop-saint,[409] of whom Julian, in addition to being a disciple, was second successor to the episcopal see of Toledo, thirteen years after the pious death of Ildephonse. The *Elogium*, therefore, is a biography of a bishop of Toledo who was a contemporary of Julian, written by an eyewitness.

About the date of composition of the brief biographical writing, one can tend for the period in which Julian was deacon of the Church of Toledo, that is, in 667. Cardinal Caesar Baronius attributes the *Elogium* to a certain Deacon Julian[410] and, therefore, it is likely that the writing was composed by Julian of Toledo upon the death of Ildephonse (667), that is, when his ecclesiastical career in the metropolitan Church of Toledo had just begun.

Julian not only knew Ildephonse personally, but the latter, together with Bishop Eugenius II, was his teacher and mentor in the five or more years of Julian's education and formation at the Episcopal School of Toledo. Julian therefore had the opportunity to know Ildephonse well and to appreciate his didactic abilities and the depth of his theology. Subsequently, when Ildephonse became bishop of Toledo, Julian could not help but admire his pastoral ministry.

The biography of Ildephonse is written in a simple way, avoiding the inclusion of narration of prodigious and extraordinary events.[411] But in one passage Julian seems to emphasize or to exaggerate with exuberant tones that the eloquence of Ildephonse was so convincing and of such high value that it seemed as if it was not a man but God himself who spoke through him.[412]

The brief biography is accompanied by a list of the literary works of Ildephonse and is written as the continuation of the *De viris illustribus*, written by Ildephonse himself. In it, Ildephonse traced the biography or the religious portrait of various illustrious clerics, thirteen to be exact, seven of whom had been bishops of Toledo. The intent of the great bishop is clear: to exalt, above all, the religious, pastoral, and moral virtues, and secondarily, the intellectual qualities of the most important personages of the metropolitan Church of Toledo, especially its bishops. In the case of the *De viris illustribus* of Ildephonse he inaugurates, therefore, a new typology of illustrious man (*vir illustris*). He does not exalt the illustrious writer, the scholar and the intellectual, as does the *De viris illustribus* of Gennadius of Marseilles. Ildephonse prefers to indicate as a model and exemplar the personalities of religious men, morally exemplary and edifying, saints in their behavior, even if they did not leave behind writings and important or incisive works. We can, therefore, speak of the *De viris illustribus* of Ildephonse as the family book of the Toledan Hispanic-Visigothic bishopric, with the finality of transmitting to posterity the memory of the pastoral and virtuous personalities of the bishops of Toledo.

But, in turn, the *De viris illustribus* of Ildephonse must not be considered a completely original work. With his writing, in fact, Ildephonse tried to continue and advance a tradition of similar works bearing the same title, whose forerunners were Gennadius,[413] the learned priest of Marseilles of the second half of the fifth century and the great doctor of the church Isidore of Seville, who had given great importance to the Spanish personages in his thirty-three biographical sketches,[414] including that of his predecessor in the episcopal see of Seville and beloved brother, Bishop Leander of Seville. With his work, Ildephonse tried to fill and complete the *De viris illustribus* of Isidore of Seville. But even before Gennadius and Isidore, St. Jerome[415] had written a work with the same title, naturally characterizing it in a Christian way. In his time, however, Jerome also had a model work to inspire him and to imitate: the one compiled by the pagan historian Suetonius.[416]

We do not know the reason why the *editio critica* of the brief *Elogium Ildephonsi* was not included in the volume 115 of the Corpus Christianorum, Series Latina. The reason for the exclusion is not chronological. But the *Elogium Ildephonsi* is, as we have said, certainly a work of Julian of Toledo, even if it is not quoted in the list of his works catalogued by his biographer, Bishop Felix. Nor is the reason related to any doubt about the authorship of the work. The critical edition of the *Elogium* was published[417] only a few years before the volume of Corpus Christianorum devoted to the works of Julian of Toledo.

The Historia Wambae Regis,[418] seu Liber Historiae de eo quod Wambae principis tempore in Galliis extitit gestum *(672–673)*

The *Historia Wambae* is probably the first or one of the first literary works of Julian of Toledo[419] written in a historical and rhetorical genre.[420] It was the first work of Julian to be edited critically, and it was then added to the volume of the Corpus Christianorum, Series Latina that includes the critical edition of the *Prognosticum futuri saeculi.*[421]

In the opinion of Hillgarth, the historical work of Julian surpasses that of Isidore[422] and "testifies to the existence of a far higher type of classical culture in Spain in the 7th century than in France."[423] The first historical news of the work is from the biographer of Julian who speaks of it in these terms: "Conscripsit...librum historiae de eo quod Wambae principis tempore Galliis exstitit gestum."[424]

According to some researchers, it is one of the most valid and important of Julian's writings; the style and the literary form alone, in fact, would be enough to make it an extraordinary work for the century in which it was written.[425] In the seventh century, in fact, there were no contemporary models of history. Moreover, the *Historia Wambae* possesses great historiographic value, even if it was written with an unequivocal spirit of bias and evident Hispanic-Visigothic patriotism. In it the young deacon Julian—or perhaps he was already a priest of the Church of Toledo—makes himself a historiographer of the Visigothic kingdom and a "war reporter,"[426] narrating the ascent to the throne of the Visigothic nobleman Wamba and his victorious military campaigns against the rebellious people north of the Iberian Peninsula and the traitors of the kingdom.

Present both in the de Lorenzana edition[427] of the writings of Julian of Toledo and in the *Patrologia* of Migne,[428] the *Historia* also had an edition and a reduced version, the *Textus tudensis,*[429] by Bishop Luke of Tuy (thirteenth century), inserted into his *Chronicon mundi.*[430] This reduced version is present in the aforesaid editions and was often preferred and copied by subsequent historians.[431]

The critical edition of the *Historia Wambae* was published in 1910 by W. Levison.[432] With this edition, for the first time in the modern epoch, a work of Julian of Toledo received the attention of scholars in a critical way.[433] But sixty-six years were to pass before the other surviving works of Julian would be edited critically by J. N. Hillgarth, in 1976, in volume 115 of the Corpus Christianorum, Series Latina:[434] *Idalii Barcinonensis Episcopi epistulae, Prognosticum futuri saeculi, Apologeticum de tribus capitulis,* and *De comprobatione sextae aetatis.* The critical edition of the *Historia,* edited by Levison, was included in the volume of the Corpus Christianorum, with the addition of the *apparatus fontium,* together with the brief letter in verse, *Epistula ad*

Modoenum, edited *cura et studio* by B. Bischoff, but previously already published,[435] as mentioned earlier.

In 1941, an English translation of the *Historia* appeared as a master's thesis by Sister Theresa Joseph Powers.[436] In 1990, the *Historia* was translated into Spanish by P. R. Díaz y Díaz,[437] and, finally, in 2005 a new English translation of *Historia Wambae* was published, with an introduction and notes by Joaquín Martínez Pizarro.[438]

In his *Historia Wambae* Julian narrates, first of all, the royal consecration of the Visigothic king Wamba, which occurred in 672, in the Cathedral of Toledo, capital of the Visigothic kingdom,[439] at the hands of Bishop Quiricus, the immediate predecessor of Julian in the episcopal see of Toledo. Subsequently, the work is devoted to the narration of the facts related to the civil war or insurrection, which erupted immediately after King Wamba's crowning (673) in the region of the Pyrenees (Cantabria), as the work of the Basque people, and in the Septimania (the *Gallia Narbonnensis*), which was a territory of the Visigothic kingdom. The leaders of the revolts were respectively Ildericus, viscount of Nimes, with his rebels, among whom were some bishops and local abbots and some Jews,[440] and the nobleman Duke Paul, who had been sent by King Wamba to repress the revolt but who in turn rebelled against his king, in league with some nobility and clerics.[441] He proclaimed himself king of the East,[442] that is, of the region of Narbona and Tarragona, but he aspired to dethrone Wamba from the kingdom, uniting himself to other rebels, in a direct military challenge.

King Wamba, who had already undertaken a military campaign against the Basque people, was informed of the events in the region of Narbonne by a letter from the bishop of that city who had not succumbed to the usurper. The king, instead of returning to Toledo for fresh troops and to reorganize the army, decided to intervene immediately with the same troops and, forcing the march, he reached, in order, Barcelona, Gerona, Narbonne, and, finally, Nimes. In a few months, the Hispanic-Visigothic army, more capable militarily than the rebellious army and the Franks who had hastened to support them, and certainly more motivated in the attempt to recover the insurgent territories that threatened the unity of the empire, overthrew the rebellion decisively[443] and without strong resistance. The outrageous letter, reproduced at the beginning of the *Historia*, that Duke Paul sent to Wamba in an attempt to dissuade him from his intention and from the battle, claiming a presumed invincibility and impregnability of his troops, as well as of his fortresses, was in vain. Actually, the military power and the strategic organization of the Visigothic army had, in a short time, overcome the insurgents and rebels, and Wamba, after a powerful siege, entered victorious in Narbonne. Meanwhile, Duke Paul was sheltered in Nimes, another stronghold of the revolt, but Wamba also besieged that city and, exactly one year after his election as king, after only two days of siege, he conquered and triumphantly entered the city.[444]

The duke, who also attempted to come to terms with the winners by sending the bishop of Narbonne, Argebardus,[445] to implore pardon from the king, was accused and judged to have committed high treason, was degraded, denuded, and completely shaved in front of his troops, who surrendered to Wamba. Bishop Argebardus was, instead, forgiven by the king, also because he was opposed to Duke Paul, while for other rebels the punishment was an example.

All these events are recounted by Julian with a colorful and vivacious narration,[446] seeking in every way to illustrate the psychology of the historical personages, just as before him, the ancient historiographers Tacitus and Titus Livy had done, as well as Sallust, Virgil, and Ovid,[447] who succeeded, with their words, in animating the characters and making them express themselves in vibrant discourses, harangues,[448] and pleas, or through epistolary missives strongly dramatized in their style and content. The whole account is, moreover, characterized by great patriotic fervor[449] and by an explanatory and didactic intent to underline how history can be a teacher about life[450] and can educate minds.

The *Historia* is followed by two brief writings: the *Insultatio vilis storici in tyrannidem Galliae* and the *Iudicium in tyrannorum perfidia promulgatum*, which narrate, respectively, the strong reaction of the king toward the rebels and the effectiveness of his military campaign that again brought order to the Narbonnese region. These two writings follow the first part of the *Historia* in most of the manuscripts. The *Insultatio*[451] is a real exercise of patriotic rhetoric, sincerely felt by the author and compiled according to the classical styles of both Greek and Latin. One can certainly affirm that the *Historia* is a beautiful example "of history documented and conceived in the classical way, an admirable chapter of historiography in the seventh century, but also a high indicator of the Spanish culture of the epoch."[452]

In the *Judicium*, Julian shows himself to be the brightest writer and rhetorician of his time. The text narrates how Duke Paul and the other persons responsible for the revolt were arrested and condemned to hard punishment. The text also narrates how, upon his return to Toledo, the king entered the royal city with a triumphant march, accompanied by the troops, evidently imitating the ancient military customs of the Roman Empire. He went to the pretorian Basilica of Saints Peter and Paul, from which he had departed, receiving the liturgical benediction of the archbishop. The same Archbishop Quiricus received him then as the winner with the same liturgical solemnity, congratulating him for his victory but also thanking God for his assistance. Behind the retinue of the king and his victorious troops were the defeated enemies, placed on wagons dragged by camels (or sitting directly on the camels),[453] barefoot and dressed in pig skins, with hair and beards shaved and exposed to the mockery of the people. Duke Paul, bearing a mock leather crown on the head and also dressed in pig skins and completely shaved, was deprived of every asset, tried and sentenced to death for high treason, because he had sworn (and signed) fidelity to King Wamba on the day of his election. He was also condemned to ecclesiastical excommunication.[454] By the magnanimity of the illuminated king, both he and his followers, in the end, obtained royal pardon. In only six months, the strategist and commander Wamba had thus defeated two revolts in the north of the peninsula and restored order and discipline in the rebellious regions, capturing and punishing the persons responsible for the rebellions. The Visigothic people were undoubtedly satisfied with the military value of their new king and his reborn and unconquered army.

The work of Julian, if not really commissioned by the king, seems to be, however, an almost official history of a segment of the Visigothic dominion. Hillgarth does not exclude that the work "may possibly have been commissioned by the king and certainly bears the stamp of official history."[455]

The *Historia Wambae* seems also to possess a religious and theological meaning that goes beyond the reported historical events. In the historical narration, the young theologian Julian seems to surrender to the temptation to represent a sort of political-religious theory of the events that he narrates. He considers the kingdom and the Visigothic monarchy to be a providential element of history that, in his eyes, seems to belong directly to the divine plan, because the king is sincerely involved in the search for the stability of his kingdom and in the attainment of the maximum common good: the unity of the people of Spain. We can, therefore, hypothesize that Julian interpreted the historical events in a theological sense, forming the beginning of a theology of history that we will find again in other works of Julian, for example, in the *Prognosticum futuri saeculi*. To complete this interpretation, Julian used a certain type of exegesis and interpretation of history in a providential sense, to discover and to communicate the role of the monarchy and of the Visigothic empire in the universal plan of God.

This historiographic approach was certainly pleasing to the king, who appreciated the intelligence and culture of the young ecclesiastic Julian. It is not to be excluded that King Wamba's choice of Julian as successor of Quiricus to the episcopal see of Toledo depended, in part, on the proof of fidelity to the empire shown by Julian in his narration of the *Historia Wambae*.

From a literary point of view, the work presents some affinities, decidedly intentional, with the historical works of Sallust, Ovid, and Virgil,[456] and it is written in an elegant Latin, with biblical and classical resonances.[457] The choice to emulate classical historiography is probably due to the lack of works of contemporary history that could serve as models to the young author, but it is probably also a specific choice for the purpose of assimilating the history of the Visigothic empire to the great Roman imperial history. It is not possible to know with certainty if these references to classical historiography are directly intentional and reflect Julian's personal knowledge of the historical works of the quoted classical authors, or if they were used in an indirect way, that Julian drew on them through other writings such as those of Isidore of Seville. In any case, such references show the high cultural level of the young historiographer of the Visigothic Christian empire and his ability to give a didactic value to the events, above all to arouse in the younger generations the love for the country and the king, as well as a readiness to fight, even militarily, for the unity of the kingdom.[458] Scholars are in agreement that the *Historia Wambae* of Julian of Toledo is the principal and more original work of Visigothic historiography,[459] very different, therefore, from the often negligent imperial historiography of subsequent centuries.

The date of composition of the work is not certain, but it must evidently coincide with the end of the political events and the war, or shortly thereafter, that is, with Duke Paul's rebellion and the consequential war. Therefore, the work was most probably composed in the year 673. In any case, it was written before Julian became bishop of Toledo.

The history of the manuscripts of the *Historia Wambae* does not equal that of the most known work of Julian of Toledo, the *Prognosticum futuri saeculi,* since it was obviously known as a work of national history and thus diffused only in Spain.[460] Certainly the fame of Archbishop Julian[461] and his *Historia Wambae* was known by historians in the Christian North of Spain, where the Spanish reconquest against the Arabs had its first beginnings. The *Historia* was, in fact, used by the Asturian chronicles of the ninth century and by some historians of the thirteenth century,[462] but it was not diffused in the libraries of Europe as were other works of Julian of Toledo. The patriotism so present in the *Historia* of Julian was, therefore, an example to nourish the desire in young Spanish generations for the reconquest of freedom on Iberian soil. It was, therefore, not by chance that the brief *Epitome Ovetensis,* of 883,[463] otherwise called the *Chronicle of Albelda,* exalted the warlike qualities and the military triumph of King Wamba (above all for having reduced the Basque rebels, Duke Paul, and the rebels of Gallia to silence), seems to draw plentifully from and to depend on the *Historia Wambae* of Julian of Toledo.[464] The contemporary *Chronicle of Alphonse III*[465] seems to do the same. But the history of the manuscript of the historical work of Julian of Toledo limits itself, certainly, to the Hispanic-Visigothic territory.

The historiographic importance of the *Historia Wambae* consists in the fact that, thanks to the direct testimony of Julian, it is possible to reconstruct an important political and military episode of Visigothic Spain, but also a real social situation of Spain in the second half of the seventh century. According to the judgment of Rivera Recio, with his *Historia Wambae* Julian reached "a perfection never before acquired by any medieval writer."[466]

The Ars grammatica[467] *attributed to Julian of Toledo (680–687)*

The Greek origins of the grammatical works are found in Plato, Aristotle, and the Stoic philosophers. It was then such Latin authors as Suetonius, Varro, and Quintilian continued and mediated an adaptation of the Greek grammar to the Latin language, a work that would be passed on, with a notable pedagogic importance, to the medieval era.

In the early Middle Ages, grammar was considered such a stable basic discipline and propaedeutic of the first *Scholae* that it also had a decisive influence on the study of other disciplines. In particular, grammar was deemed important for the methodology of studies, emphasizing the progressive passage from grammar as *ratio bene legendi, scribendi et loquendi* to the more demanding dimension of grammar as a hermeneutical science or *scientia interpretandi.*

Julian of Toledo had learned the rudiments of grammar in the Episcopal School of Toledo and had drawn great advantage from it in the exercise of his function as reader of and commentator on the Sacred Scripture and in the editing of his *Historia Wambae.*[468] He had greatly cultivated the study of grammar, evidently considering it a basic and propaedeutic science with respect to the others, to such an extent that we can suppose he made it the subject of his teaching at the Episcopal School of Toledo. And it would be natural that this teaching experience would lead to the publication of an important work of Julian—the *Ars Grammatica,* discovered only in the eighteenth century in a manuscript of the Vatican Library and attributed to Julian of Toledo, even if with some important dissenters,[469] because "there are difficulties in the way of proving his [of Julian] authorship."[470]

If prior to 1922 only parts of the *Ars grammatica* had been critically edited,[471] we now possess major studies clarifying many aspects of the work, dating it back to precisely the period in which Julian lived and to the Toledan environment.[472] The principal objection to Julian's authorship of the work derives above all from the fact that it is not quoted in the detailed list of the works of Julian furnished by his biographer Felix. If it is true, however, that Felix did not cite the *Ars grammatica* in the annotated list of the works of Julian, it is just as true that all the manuscripts of the work attribute it to the bishop of Toledo,[473] and this is an incontrovertible fact that does not leave room for doubts.

Meanwhile, for others, the work not only has all the "síntomas españoles" to be attributed to Julian, but it is to be considered, in its importance for the study of medieval culture, equal to the *Etymologiae* of Isidore of Seville.[474] The *Ars grammatica* is in any case deemed a milestone along the road toward the construction of the Christian grammars of the Middle Ages.[475]

The manuscript tradition of the *Ars grammatica* numbers seven manuscripts[476] and a certain number of citations in the catalogues of the medieval libraries. It was published by Cardinal de Lorenzana in Rome, in 1797, as an appendix to the writings of the archbishop of Toledo, contained in the second of the three volumes devoted to the works of the Toledan fathers.[477]

Having certainly come from Visigothic Spain and from a School of Toledo,[478] probably the Episcopal School[479] of the time of Julian, the work is a collection, perhaps made by the author or by a very diligent student, or even by a member of Julian's entourage,[480] of the teachings related to grammar, rhetoric, and metrics that were taught, or that Julian himself had perhaps taught[481] for some years in the Episcopal School. According to some scholars, the most probable date of the work's composition is during the reign of Ervig (680–687), which thus coincides with the bishopric of Julian. Hillgarth identifies the date of composition as the year 685.[482] The reason for this conviction lies in the fact that one of the grammatical examples given in the text refers specifically to King Ervig.[483]

The *Ars grammatica* is naturally a profane work, comprising a vast series of examples and grammatical quotations of preceding works dealing with the Latin linguistic structure, drawn upon by the most important grammarians of antiquity. The most illustrious is certainly Aelius Donatus,[484] but the work also depends on the writings of Maximus Vittorinus, Pompeus, Audax, and Isidore of Seville, in addition to those of Catullus, Pacuvius, Terentius, Ennius, Lucretius, Plautus, Livy, Lucan, Oratio, Lucilius, Persius, Juvenal, and, above all, Virgil, who is quoted 224 times in the *Ars grammatica*.[485] The grammar attributed to Julian possesses a lot of characteristics borrowed from the other grammars, for example, the pedagogic and catechetic form of the dialogue between the Master and the Disciple, as the methodology of learning and formation (a method known already from Vittorinus and Audax[486] and perhaps for that reason imitated by Julian). But the *Ars grammatica* possesses also original characteristics such as the quotation of numerous grammatical examples derived from the works not just of classical Latin authors but also of Christian authors, often also Hispanic-Romans (for example, Juvencus, Prudentius, Sedulius, Ambrosius, and Eugenius II).[487]

The *Ars grammatica* attributed to Julian is, therefore, to be considered one of the most original grammars of the seventh century.

The originality and novelty of the work leads us to believe that with these works Julian wanted to be the initiator of a new way of conceiving grammar and rhetoric, without denying the past, and that his *Historia Wambae* and *Ars grammatica* "reflect a continuity of Isidorian interests, combined with new sources, employed in a new way."[488]

The work is divided into two books:[489] the first is devoted to the prosody and knowledge of metrics, while the second covers the rudiments of grammar.[490] Even if the *Ars grammatica* was not materially written by Julian, it is important in that it contains over 150 quotations of classical authors from a vast temporal range of literary classicism. This abundant use of classical texts, whose quotations often are not firsthand or direct, is certainly amazing for the cultural level of the seventh century and must be due to the city of Toledo, which, most of all because of its scholarly bishops, especially Julian, preserved and increased, to a high degree, the level of knowledge and culture, both classical and Christian, that was necessary for the formation or pedagogic education of the *alumni*.

Undoubtedly the author of the *Ars grammatica* was accustomed to and had familiarity with the numerous classical authors quoted, which denotes his high level of culture. The originality of the work, then, lies in the fact that Julian also introduces into his grammar numerous examples drawn from Sacred Scripture and from Latin Christian authors, which he considers just as worthy of note and equal, literarily, to the examples drawn from the pagan authors.[491] The Latin Christian authors referred to are evidently not so much the fathers of the church, who (except for some), as is well-known, were mostly authors of prose, but rather the Christian poets such as Prudentius, Dracontius, Ausonius, Sedulius, Ambrosius, and, naturally, Eugenius II of Toledo, whose verses are quoted ten times in the work. These particular quotations lead Murphy to opt for a sure attribution of the work to Julian.[492] Obviously Julian considered these authors suitable models of literary *Latinitas*, above all for what concerns the correction and embellishment of the literary sentence, and, therefore, on the same level as the classical writers.

These characteristics make the *Ars grammatica*, attributed to Julian of Toledo, a work that is both classical, because it continues the Greek-Roman tendency of the authors of literary classicism, and at the same time strongly innovative and modern. The author's skill in furnishing examples from the Bible as well as from Christian authors thus underlines the cultural and literary growth of the Christian faith and its ability to produce literary texts that can be proposed as grammatical models of knowledge and interpretation and that are, therefore, equal to the works of profane culture.

The *Ars grammatica* of Julian of Toledo thus represents a point of departure for the linguistic reflection that will develop during the Middle Ages in a speculative grammar that is suited for the interpretation of the language. And if a work of profane science such as a grammar does not perhaps directly interest theologians or historians, it will indeed be of great interest to scholars of philology, linguistics, and pedagogy. The point is that an experienced theologian such as Julian of Toledo did not disdain this dimension of the language. Rather, it seems that he had given it a strategic importance in the elaboration of an educational and formative program for his time.

This means that, with Julian of Toledo, Visigothic Christianity during the seventh century did not present itself as a closed system, deprived of cultural stimulus. On the contrary, it manifested an opening to the appreciation of the pagan culture and to the appreciation of the value of its own Christian literary talents, ready to advance in appreciating human writing and speaking in view of a general theory of interpretation in the service of the Word of God.[493]

The De comprobatione sextae aetatis mundi libri tres[494] *(686)*

The *De comprobatione sextae aetatis mundi adversus Judaeos cum oratione et epistola ad Dominum Ervigium regem*[495] (The demonstration of the sixth age of the world against the Jews with a prayer and a letter to King Ervig) is an original treatise, or rather a "cosmological-messianic speculation"[496] or even an "apologética anti-judaica"[497] written in 686,[498] by Julian of Toledo, at the request of the Visigothic king Ervig[499] for "atraer a la verdadera fe a los judíos que negaban la venida de Jesucristo."[500]

Therefore, it is a reproposal of the traditional subject of the centuries-old biblical and theological controversy between Jews and Christians about the end of time and the coming of the Messiah.[501] The biographer Felix gives special importance to this work of Julian, specifically describing parts of it with precision.[502] He thus informs us that the work is preceded by a prayer to God and by a dedication letter addressed to King Ervig. The work is divided into three books, of which Felix traces a brief description of the content. He evidently considers the work very important, equal to the *Prognosticum*, the only other work of Julian whose structure and content are described by Felix with a certain precision.

We can say, more specifically, that the work was written by Julian for contesting the Jewish doctrine, based on interpretations of the Babylonian Talmud, about the era, far in the future, according to Jewish thought, in which the Messiah is to appear. The purpose of this work was to convince and convert the wise Jewish people of the time to faith in Christ through the study and interpretation of Sacred Scripture. Julian thus sought to confute the polemical writings of Talmudic origin that circulated in his time in Latin.

The work begins with the presupposition that for the Jews "le Messie n'était encore venu,"[503] a secular conviction of Israel and a traditional argument in the dialectics between Christianity and Judaism. Based on this theological interpretation, Judaism maintained that the Messiah would have been born and appeared only after the sixth millennium after the creation of the world and humankind.[504] Obviously, Jewish theologians believed that date to be far in the future. With this interpretation they denied that Jesus of Nazareth was the Messiah and, accordingly, maintained that the Christian religion was not a religion founded on the mission of the Messiah.

It seems that, from a historical perspective, this Jewish hermeneutics had been devised to maintain a certain religious cohesion within the Jewish ethnic group, but in the work of Julian it is interpreted as being the fruit of proselytism in order for Christianity and Christians to appear to be blinded by a historical illusion. The work of Julian, therefore, was, on the one hand, finalized to contest the Jewish biblical hermeneutics and the diffusion of its conclusions. On the other hand, it was to attract the Jews to the true messianic faith with an appropriate exegesis of the text and with a precise mathematical calculation of biblical chronology.[505] If, in fact, as Julian tried to show, the Christ or the Messiah had already come to the world, then Jewish interpretation and messianic waiting were accordingly to be considered a failure.

In any case, the text of Julian, which we could define as apologetic in nature, was written in the overall context of the "Jewish question" that strongly characterized the social and political life of the Visigothic empire, as well as the church and the Christian people, for the entire seventh century. In particular, such opposition to the Jews was concretized, toward the end of the century, in a series of legislative provisions that the Visigothic imperial politics and the church enacted against them in the Twelfth and Thirteenth Councils of Toledo. Despite these provisions, however, we know that historically the Jewish minority continued to exist even in the most difficult situations, perhaps sustained by that unifying element, capable of providing cohesion and strength of resistance—the expectant waiting for the messianic era, which they, obstinately, believed to be far in the future.

The fact that the work had been commissioned by King Ervig was evidently more than chance. The request itself underscored the close bond between the king, holder of the imperial power, and the young ecclesiastic Julian, several years after having become head of the Church of Toledo. Julian perhaps sensed that the king's request and the anti-Judaic demonstration he was preparing in his work were a sort of mutual service between the church and the imperial authority. It was the latter, however, that would end up benefiting most, since the "history" narrated makes reference to the exaltation of the dominant political power, which silences any voice to the contrary, in this case, the Jewish one. As Hillgarth says, the *De comprobatione* seems to be, more than anything else, an "apologetic history in the interest of the visigothic monarchy, from which the Spanish Church was by now hardly separable."[506]

The same author remarks that the tone of the *De comprobatione*, perhaps too polemical, ends up becoming a disadvantage for the validity of the work in comparison to, for example, the clearly apologetic though milder tone of the *De fide catholica contra Judaeos* of Isidore of Seville, a work containing a greater number of references to the biblical texts and a strict adherence to the *mysteria vitae Jesu*. Besides, Julian's exegetic and hermeneutic choice to follow the Septuagint version of Sacred Scripture in reconstructing the biblical chronology to oppose the Jewish one was objectively to his disadvantage compared to the choice, likewise exegetic and hermeneutic, of the Venerable Bede to follow instead the Jewish Bible, thus placing himself on the same methodological level as the Jewish antagonist (the *hebraica veritas* that Christianity has never forgotten).[507]

Therefore, the work is certainly against the Jews,[508] but in a biblical, hermeneutic, and doctrinal way, and surely not in a racist sense. It cannot be said, therefore, that in writing the *De comprobatione* Julian was animated by an anti-Judaic[509] spirit. With his work, however, Julian

did have an active role in the polemic against the Jews that characterized his time.[510]

The biblical and hermeneutic doctrinal thesis contested by the
author, and which is placed at the center of the demonstration, is that,
according to Talmudic interpretations, Jesus Christ could not be the
expected Messiah, because the Messiah was to come, according to
complex cabalistic calculations, only at the conclusion of the sixth
millennium after the creation of the world. Since, according to the
Jewish calendar, which begins precisely with the creation of the world,
the sixth millennium has not yet ended, as a result Israel still awaits
the coming of the Messiah.[511]

In the three books of the work, Julian contests this Jewish interpretation related to the messianic era. In the first book he analyzes
and interprets the texts of the Old Testament, particularly the ancient
prophecies of Mic 4:1ff.; 5:2ff.; Mal 3:1ff., and especially Dan 9:22ff.,
which, having already been fulfilled, indicate that the Messiah has
already been born. From the interpretation of such Old Testament
passages, according to Julian, it is understood that the Messiah, promised by God through the prophets, has already come into the world.

In the second book the author interprets the texts of the New
Testament that explicitly point to Jesus Christ as the Messiah foretold
by the prophets of the ancient covenant, whose texts are interpreted
by the apostolic writers as indicating the events of the fullness of time,
and not following the calculation of years. Jesus, the Messiah, was in
fact born precisely in the fullness of times. It is, therefore, not the calculation of the years that counts, as the Jewish scholars maintain, but
rather the whole of the historical facts in which Jesus presents himself
as the true Messiah sent by God. The most interesting argument is the
following: in the times of Jesus, the Jews raised no objections against
the messiahship of Jesus, because they themselves were convinced that
precisely in that epoch the Messiah they awaited would have come.

Finally, in the third book, Julian tries to prove that the sixth age
of the world has already begun and is in full course. This depends on
the fact that he did not use the Jewish Talmudic method of the mathematical calculation of the sum of the years of biblical history, but
rather the sequence of the generations, according to the narration of
the Old Testament in the Greek version of the Septuagint. But the two
chronologies, the Talmudic one and that of the Septuagint, are obviously different. Julian believed that he must adhere to the authority of

the Septuagint biblical text, which in his opinion was greater than that of the Talmud, owing to the miraculous and inspired aura in which the tradition narrates that it was compiled.

Undoubtedly, in this work Julian demonstrates a deep and analytical knowledge of the whole of Sacred Scripture, but at the same time an uncommon dialectical ability to obtain desired conclusions by completing logical and hermeneutic passages of notable literary ability.

Therefore, in his opinion, it was the biblical characters and the events lived by them that constituted the *aetates* to calculate and that allowed for an overall calculation showing how everything is by now fulfilled so the event of the arrival of the Messiah of history could occur. The biblical characters taken into consideration and the events concerning them, therefore, constitute the generations, the sum of which shows that we are already in the sixth age of the world, that is, the messianic age. The six ages are divided thus: the first, from Adam to Noah; the second, from Noah to Abraham; the third, from Abraham to David; the fourth, from David to the Babylonian captivity; the fifth, from the Babylonian captivity to Jesus Christ; and, finally, the sixth, from Jesus Christ up to our days.

Based on this result, Julian addresses himself, in a very heartfelt patristic literary style, to the people of Israel as to a single person, inviting him to ascertain the exactness of the proposed calculation, inviting him to become convinced of his error, to wake up from the sleep in which he lies, to recover the lost and right road that leads to salvation: Israel will achieve all of this with the recognition that the Messiah and Son of God has already come. Evidently, according to Julian, the Jews have the full right to salvation and to be able to enter as part of the new form taken on by the people of God: the Christian church.

The objection that can be raised to this work is that Julian proceeds on an a priori and unilateral level, from the Christian point of view. This means that, in the text, it is a Christian author, and only him, that enumerates the Jewish convictions, not a Jewish author that sustains his convictions. The work, therefore, lacks the contradiction or the dialogue between wise men, which is, rather, characteristic of other works *contra Judaeos*. And when he enumerates the reasons of Judaism it is not always easy to perceive that they are contrary argumentations. The problem, in short, lies in the fact that we do not have here a true debate between a Christian and a Jew, as was the case with Justin's *Dialogue with the Jew Tryphon*. The literary form used by Justin was not a pure convention but the elaboration of true conversations and discussions held with wise Jews. But also in the case of a fictitious literary dialogue, such as the one between the Christian Origen and a wise pagan contained in Origen's *Contra Celsum*, the *par condicio* compelled the author to introduce in a sufficiently complete way the contrary objections from the other side, extracting them from works or writings of the adversary side. In the work of Julian, however, the Jews are not represented by any of their theologians or intellectuals, even contemporary with Julian. Rather, the author takes the Talmud as a synthesis or summa of the Jewish doctrine, without conceding anything to his intellectual adversaries. What is really open to criticism, therefore, is that the Jews in this work (and generally in the Visigothic legislation) correspond to an anonymous and collective entity, but deprived of the right personally to defend its own convictions. It is true that the literary expressions used by Julian are mild, though not deprived of polemic verve. But, fortunately, precisely in the conclusion of the work "el Apóstol se sobrepone al polemista,"[512] above all when, with grievous and yearning accentuations, the author personally turns to Israel, imitating the way in which the God of Abraham, on some occasions, turned to his people in the Old Testament, to reproach him and to invite him to return to the right road that would lead him to salvation.[513]

In addition to the numerous biblical texts, the sources that inspired Julian include the exegeses of the most important Latin fathers of the church: first of all Augustine, and then Tertullian, Ilarius, Cyprian, Jerome, Gregory the Great, and Isidore of Seville.[514] He also quotes some Greek fathers. Finally, it is possible that Julian had partial knowledge of the Jewish discussion about the interpretation of the Babylonian Talmud concerning the ages of the world.[515] In any case, the underlying argument of the *De comprobatione sextae aetatis* can be connected to other meaningful works, for example, the already mentioned *De fide catholica contra Judaeos* of Isidore of Seville or the *De perpetua virginitate sanctae Mariae* of Ildephonse of Toledo,[516] both of which pursue the same aim: to show, with the texts of Sacred Scripture, that Jesus is the Christ and that the Messiah has already come. Perhaps Julian achieves this aim in a more intellectual and theological way than the other two Spanish theologians, emphasizing better the value of the witnesses of the Christian messianic tradition. However, the three books constitute a testimony of how the Jewish problem was felt in the Christian medieval environment of Visigothic Spain.

Despite its objective value, the *De comprobatione* did not have a great diffusion outside the Spanish borders, and knowledge of it was limited to the Mozárabic authors of Toledo and Cordoba. The reason for this scarce diffusion, despite the uniqueness of the work, especially in the first book,[517] was probably that the writing was occasional in nature. It is important, in this sense, to note the testimony of Hillgarth about the limited number of manuscripts of the work found in the catalogues of the European medieval libraries. He concludes that, compared to the *Prognosticum*, which was extensively circulated in medieval libraries,[518] the *De comprobatione sextae aetatis* "appears to have been almost unknown in the Middle Ages."[519] Above all, inasmuch as it was directed to a single controversy (with the Jews), it was not of much interest to medieval authors.[520]

Nevertheless, it is significant that the *Apologeticum* written by Abbot Samson of Cordoba in the year 864 demonstrates knowledge of the works of Julian of Toledo, quoting in particular the *De comprobatione sextae aetatis*,[521] the *Prognosticum*[522] and, several times, the *Antikeimenon*,[523] in addition to some liturgical texts of the archbishop of Toledo. The nine overall citations of Julian made by Abbot Samson and the appellatives used to indicate him: "beatus," "sanctus," and "venerabilis doctor" show, as Hillgarth observes,[524] the esteem in which the Toledan theologian was held in the ninth century. The *De comprobatione sextae aetatis* was broadly used by the Christian knight Alvaro of Cordoba[525] as the biblical weapon against Bishop Bodo Eleazar, apostate of the Christian faith and convert to Judaism.[526]

Antikeimenon libri duo,[527] seu Liber de diversis
(On the contradictory texts) (680-690)

The *Antikeimenon* is a work of biblical apologetics, divided in two books, quoted in the list of the works of Julian furnished by the biographer Felix.[528] In it Julian of Toledo analyzes, comments on, tries to harmonize, and seeks a concordance of those texts of Sacred Scripture that appear, at first reading, contradictory. This follows the ancient patristic custom of seeking to harmonize the Sacred Scriptures based on the hermeneutical principle that God cannot contradict himself.

The work, which Julian baptized with a Greek name,[529] reveals a vast culture, an extensive and analytical knowledge of the Sacred Scriptures, and a "very acute intelligence"[530] in resolving apparently serious contradictions in the biblical texts. As such, the work must have been intended by Julian as a didactic tool to facilitate biblical studies, probably compiled for the clergymen of the Episcopal School of Toledo, so they would not be passive or mute in the face of the apparent contradictions of the scriptural texts but would rather possess the correct interpretations to solve the contradictions. Yet, at the same time, it had to be a "practical manual" to protect the Christian from many difficult investigations in the biblical field and to provide what was necessary to overcome the apparent contradictions of Sacred Scripture. The didactic purpose of the work is very likely, as also for the *Prognosticum futuri saeculi*,[531] which was probably also conceived as a practical manual, as Julian himself says in the introductory letter, for the great themes of death, purification of the soul, eschatological punishment, and heaven and hell. Therefore, with respect to the *Antikeimenon*, the pastoral concern of the bishop of Toledo and the intellectual concern of the teacher of theological doctrine at the Episcopal School of the royal city are evident: to avoid a resigned and embarrassing silence when faced with objections about the biblical texts and, together, to facilitate the work of the students in the investigation of biblical passages difficult to interpret, gathering them all together, according to a logical division, between the Old and New Testament.

The book, which has an exotic[532] name probably taken from the *Etymologiae*[533] of Isidore of Seville, was composed with the intent to fill a considerable didactic-methodological void through the use of a literal or allegorical exegesis, often more useful for harmonizing the biblical affirmations. The work required of Julian a careful and meticulous reading of the biblical text, from which he drew 221 scriptural passages that presented some objective difficulty in interpretation: 138 belonging to the Old Testament and 83 to the New. For each of these texts Julian presents the difficulty and the relative solution. In many cases he finds the solution in the works of tradition, that is, in the writings of the fathers of the church. In such cases he limits himself to transcribing the patristic solution; however, in cases in which problems related to the biblical text have not been resolved already by tradition, he himself addresses the difficulty and resolves it resorting to his hermeneutic science.[534]

The date of composition of the *Antikeimenon* is still uncertain, because the greatest part of the manuscript codices of the work appear without attributing its literary paternity. But ever since the edition of the *Apologia contra Hostegitium* of Abbot Samson of Cordoba[535] (810–890), in which he quotes some passages of the *Antikeimenon*, correctly attributing them to the *Beatus Iulianus*,[536] there have been no serious challenges to the attribution of the work to Julian of Toledo and to the period of his episcopal ministry. Another test in this direction is found at the end of the eighth century in a letter of a certain Tusaredus or Tuseredus, probably a monk of Cordoba, addressed to Ascaricus, bishop of Astorga, in the Asturies. The letter contains a double quotation of the *Antikeimenon* of Julian, whose identity is finally distinguished from that of Julian Pomerius. The interesting text says: "Illi vero, qui contradicunt dicentes: nemo ascendit in coelum, nisi qui descendit de coelo filius hominis, legant librum 'beati Juliani non Pomerii sed Toletani' qui vocitatur 'anticimena', qui patratus est de his rebus quae contraria in Scripturis resonant, sed non contraria ab his qui vigili sensu Scripturam, si mundam inquirunt, intelligenda sunt, sicut sunt pluraque istis latet; et tunc tacere studeant et non loqui quae nesciunt. Si 'anticimena' abest currant ad Agustinum et ipsum inquirant in libro homeliarum cata Jhoannem, et ipsum hunc locum audiant explorantem."[537]

From the ninth century there is a quotation of the *Antikeimenon* in a patristic anthology in manuscript 384 of the Abbey of Montecassino.[538]

The problem of the attribution or the paternity of the *Antikeimenon* increased more markedly in the eleventh century, when it was attributed, as a result of a misunderstanding, by the *Chronica Monasterii Casinensis* of Leo Marsicanus and Peter Diaconus to Abbot Bertarius[539] of Montecassino. In reality, the abbot had only ordered to have a copy of the work made, as was done in the *scriptoria* of the monasteries. The attribution to Julian was not questioned because of this misunderstanding, since already in the ninth century, as we have seen, there were important testimonies attributing the paternity of the work to Julian of Toledo.

The method of composition of the work is unique and very didactic,[540] almost scholastic. The text, in fact, proceeds with a dialectic between questions (*interrogationes*), which underline the interpretative difficulties, and answers (*responsiones*), which contain the solutions that the reader and disciple can appreciate and easily memorize. According to Murphy, the work "is not an unworthy forerunner of Abelard's 'Sic et Non,'"[541] which emphasizes the ampleness of the biblical science of Julian of Toledo.[542]

The sources on which Julian draws to compose many of his
responsiones include the fathers of the church: first of all, Augustine,
but then also Jerome, Origen, and Ambrose of Milan. The fact that
Julian quotes the *Homiliae in Ezechielem* of Gregory the Great, a work
almost unknown by the great Hispanic-Visigothic theologians,
deserves particular mention. This work probably had recently arrived
in Spain, thanks to the fatiguing trip to Rome undertaken by Taio of
Saragossa to obtain a copy of it to bring to Spain.[543]

As Hillgarth suggests,[544] the controversial meaning of the
Antikeimenon against the Judaism of the time is not to be excluded,
because a more ample argument, hermeneutical in nature, lies hidden behind the investigation of the harmony between the writings of
the Old and New Testament, precisely against the pretension of Judaism
to be the one and only authentic interpreter of the Old Testament. This
hypothesis is supported by the fact that Julian of Toledo also authored
the *De comprobatione sextae aetatis mundi adversus Judaeos,* in which he
intellectually and hermeneutically contests the biblical calculation
of the historical eras made by the wise Talmudists of Judaism and
proposes, instead, a chronology based on the writings of the New
Testament.

Unlike the case of other works of Julian, the diffusion of manuscripts of the *Antikeimenon* outside of Spain and in the European
libraries was quite notable[545] and the work was well known in medieval
Europe.

The Apologeticum Fidei[546] *(683–684)*

The so-called first *Apologeticum* of Julian of Toledo, quoted in the
intellectual biography of Julian: *quod Benedicto Romanae Urbis directum
est,*[547] is a lost work[548] of Julian of Toledo. But we know a lot of important things about it from the reactions it aroused in the curial and
papal Roman milieus, and because of the reactions to the contrary in
Hispanic-Visigothic milieus of the seventh century.[549]

The first *Apologeticum* contains, therefore, the writing that Julian
sent with promptness to Pope Benedict II,[550] in answer to the written
order of his predecessor, Leo II, who had passed away in the meantime (in July 683), to summon a council of all the bishops of the
Iberian Peninsula to be celebrated in the imperial city, in 680–681, in
order to undersign and ratify the christological definitions and the
anathemas of the Sixth Ecumenical Council,[551] Constantinople III,[552]

which had already been accepted and confirmed by the Church of Rome. The text of the conciliar acts also contained the condemnation of the pliable and unresolved attitude of Pope Honorius I to the christological heresies.[553] Pope Leo II desired that the important decisions of that ecumenical council be made known to the bishops of Spain, to the priests, and to the Christian people.[554] The historical reason for Pope Leo II's command was the fact that neither the bishops nor the delegates of the Hispanic-Visigothic bishopric had taken part in the ecumenical Council of Constantinople in 680.[555] The Spaniards had not even been present at the precedent general council.[556] Therefore, they had not have yet "received" as dogmatically defined and valid the text of the acts of the council, nor had they approved and undersigned them. This means that the important Hispanic-Visigothic bishopric had not recognized that council as ecumenical. It was thus necessary, in the opinion of the bishop of Rome, to also obtain the approval of the important church of the Catholic West in order for the text of the council really to be considered ecumenical. The fact that Pope Leo II had sent only a part of the acts of the council to the bishops probably means that the translation of the conciliar acts from Greek into Latin[557] was not finished yet. At the end of the letter, the pope promised the bishops that he would have their signed documents deposited on the grave of the apostle Peter[558] as a gesture of honor toward the Spanish bishopric and as a sign of universal doctrinal unity.

All this seemed to be within the normal ministry of the bishop of Rome and the episcopal ministry of the bishops of Spain. This concern of the Church of Rome toward the Hispanic-Visigothic Church shows the pontifical authority over the Church of Spain in the seventh century,[559] as the same Pope Leo II affirms when he writes that as unworthy as he may be of this ministry, he nonetheless carries out the function of the prince of the apostles.[560]

Julian of Toledo, in the beginning of his episcopal mandate (680), had already presided over conciliar meetings of the bishops of Spain (the Twelfth and Thirteenth Councils of Toledo).[561] Moreover, the Thirteenth Council had just finished when the *Notarius regionarius*,[562] named Peter, reached Toledo, bringing Pope Leo II's letters,[563] and other papal envoys came from Rome near the end of 683. There were at least four letters of Leo II respectively addressed to all the Spanish bishops, to Quiricus (who had died in the meantime), primate of Spain and immediate predecessor of Julian, to King Ervig, and to Count Simplicius in representation of the palatine nobility.[564] The king was entrusted particularly to make the decisions of the ecumenical council known to all the prelates, clergy, and the Christian people of Spain, and also to verify that all the bishops of Spain signed the approval of the acts of the council. Bishop Quiricus of Toledo had passed away at the beginning of 680 and already in his place for almost three years was Julian. But in Rome, where there was also a new pope, Benedict II, the news of the death of Quiricus evidently (and oddly) had not yet arrived, nor had the election and the consecration of the new archbishop of Toledo been communicated. How such a lack of correct and timely information of the changes was possible is still an unsolved mystery.[565]

Julian naturally adhered with enthusiasm to Pope Leo II's request, also because the arrival of the papal envoys and the important conciliar documents in Toledo had the flavor of a great event for the imperial city, for the whole Spanish bishopric as well as for the king. In Toledo, they had not received papal envoys or pontifical missives for many years. The last time was in 638, when the Sixth Council of Toledo had just ended. At that time things had not really been for the best, since the papal document sent by Pope Honorius I to the Spanish bishops accused them of negligence and pastoral "timidity" toward the Jews. Considering this papal accusation to be defamatory, Bishop Braulio of Saragossa had answered in the same tone,[566] on behalf of the Spanish bishops.

This time things seemed entirely different because the pope did not reproach anyone but rather asked for an authoritative dogmatic pronunciation by the Spanish bishopric, a sign of the importance attached to the christological doctrine of the two wills in Christ, which constituted an important part of the western Catholic world at that time.

Julian, however, realized that the king could not assemble the requested general council of the Visigothic bishopric for two reasons. First of all, because the Thirteenth Council of Toledo had just finished in the beginning of November 683, and the bishops were either on their way or had already returned to their episcopal sees, it did not seem possible or opportune to reconvene the *dispersos* to Toledo for a new council.[567] A new convocation would have subjected them, in fact, to a second uncomfortable trip to the center of Spain. In second place, in that year the Iberian Peninsula had already begun to suffer a particularly harsh and frigid winter, with freezing and abundant snowfalls (*nivium immensitate*),[568] which made travel very difficult, if not practically impossible owing to road conditions that were already difficult in normal times.

King Ervig, however, in agreement with Julian, given the importance of the papal order, assembled in Toledo, in 684, a council of the ecclesiastical province of Cartagena (the Fourteenth Council of Toledo), gathering all the suffragan dioceses of Toledo. He summoned also the representatives of the other five ecclesiastical metropolitan sees of Spain, who, upon conclusion of the council, would have signed the acts in the name of their ecclesiastical provinces and would have then brought the results of the council to the episcopal sees of origin. Other local synods would occur in those sees to study and act upon the text defined in Toledo. In this way, a unanimous pronunciation of all the Spanish bishops would be obtained in a single edict, as if a national council of the Visigothic Church had been materially gathered. That edict would be promulgated by the king throughout the imperial territory, and it would be sent to Rome, as requested by the pope.[569] The program seemed, therefore, well organized successively to examine and approve the acts of the Third Council of Constantinople in a reasonable amount of time.

Since Pope Leo II had died in the meantime, his successor, Pope Benedict II (684–685), who had been elected but not yet enthroned[570] in 683, pressed the *Notarius regionarius* Peter to return to Rome with the documents of the Spanish bishopric ratifying the acts of the ecumenical council, that is, the condemnation of monothelitism, which affirmed the presence of only one will in Christ.[571] Upon receiving this letter, the *Notarius* hastened to depart before the Fourteenth Council of Toledo had begun. Julian probably gave the *Notarius* a christological writing that was to introduce the Fourteenth Council of Toledo, in which he presented the point of view of the Church of Spain on the christological matter addressed by the ecumenical council.

Julian presided, therefore, over the Fourteenth Council of Toledo or Synod of the Province of Cartagena (November 684), during which the primate of Spain, the sixteen suffragan bishops, the representatives of the episcopal sees of Palencia and Valencia, and eight other representatives[572] or vicars of the other ecclesiastical provinces of Tarragona (Cyprianus), Narbonne (Suntfredus), Mérida (Stephanus), Braga (Iulianus), and Seville (Floresindus) studied thoroughly and critically, in an intense week of work, the acts of the Third Council of

Constantinople, the sixth ecumenical council, comparing them to the texts of the first four ecumenical councils: Nicaea, Constantinople, Ephesus, and Chalcedon. At the end of this analytical and comparative study, in addition to condemning monothelitism (unaware of Pope Benedict II's criticism of the writing of Julian that had in the meantime been sent to Rome by means of the *Notarius*, the first *Apologeticum*), they approved the conciliar acts sent by Pope Leo II, considering them from then on official acts of the Catholic Church to be inserted immediately in the Canonical Collection of Spain, after the acts of the Council of Chalcedon.[573] But during the council, Julian himself presented the bishops with a supplementary commentary and summary of orthodox Christian theological thought about the question of two wills in Christ,[574] as had been defined by the general Council of Constantinople. This synthesis, the fruit of the zeal of Julian and perhaps of his desire to show the intellectual and theological value of the bishopric of Spain, constitutes the structure of the *Apologeticum* that Julian had already sent the preceding year[575] to the pope. While the council was assembled in Toledo and had approved the synthesis of Julian, the *Apologeticum* was probably on its way to Rome, in the hands of the *Notarius* Peter and one or more Toledan clergymen[576] sent by Julian. In view of the time it took to travel[577] and deliver the official missives, it is understandable why Julian had sent his *Apologeticum* to Rome: to avoid a long delay in responding to the request of the pope to approve the acts of the ecumenical council and, at the same time, to demonstrate the christological faith of the churches of Spain. Thus, Rome, according to the thought of Julian, would have appreciated the promptness of the bishop of Toledo and his bishopric of Spain.

Anyway, the events are very difficult to reconstruct precisely, because the canons of the Fourteenth Council of Toledo do not appear absolutely clear on the subject. There are two possible interpretations: the approval of the acts of Constantinople was sent to Rome only after the end of the Fourteenth Council of Toledo, while Julian's *Apologeticum* was sent before the council had begun its work; or, as J. Madoz[578] maintains, the provincial councils were celebrated before and, therefore, the bishops' approval, together with the text of the *Apologeticum* of Julian, was sent to Rome before the Fourteenth Council of Toledo was held.

If, however, one seeks to reconstruct and date the events with more precision, for a better idea of the chronological succession of the facts, one can probably hypothesize, following Murphy,[579] that in the autumn of 684, before the Fourteenth Council of Toledo started, Julian had sent his christological synthesis to Rome, by means of the *Notarius* Peter and the Spanish delegation; around five months later, in March of 685, Pope Benedict II, shortly before dying, received the documents from Toledo and Julian's *Apologeticum*. The pope criticized the Christology and, above all, the (new or unusual) christological language used with mastery by Julian, and he orally communicated his criticisms to the *Notarius* Peter and to the Spanish delegation to be reported to the primate of Spain, especially the need to strengthen the writing with patristic testimonies. The Toledan delegation did not return to Toledo with these papal orders until the beginning of 686, around ten months later.

In any case, at the end of the work of the Fourteenth Council of Toledo, the doctrine of the Third Council of Constantinople was approved, but, as T. González[580] justly underlines, not only because the pope had requested it, but because the acts, analytically studied and assimilated by the Spanish bishops, had been found in agreement with the christological definitions of the preceding general councils and they were thus able to be signed with full trust by all the bishops and to be entered as part of the official collection of the magisterium texts of the Church of Spain.[581] There is no wonder, as justly observed by Madoz,[582] that the Spanish bishopric dedicated such scrupulous analysis to the conciliar acts. It must be remembered, in fact, that the doctrine about the infallibility of the pope and of the ecumenical councils was not entirely clear in the seventh century. Accordingly the Spanish bishops felt the serious responsibility of analyzing thoroughly the christological doctrine proposed in the acts, before pronouncing themselves. The desire to avoid exposing themselves to error justifies, therefore, the prudent zeal of the Spanish bishops, together with the desire that no definitions that were even slightly uncertain or directly heretical enter into their official collection of doctrinal texts. With this the Church of Spain showed itself to have a great awareness of being on a high level, intellectually and theologically, in comparison to the rest of the churches and to the bishops of the western Christianity of the seventh century.

In the objective general decadence, therefore, the Hispanic-Visigothic Church had not only preserved its national identity, but it felt active and able, as well as young, because the conversion of the Visigoths to Catholicism had happened only recently (relatively, in

589). It was strongly convinced of the validity of its political-religious unity, having in its past such characters of great cultural, intellectual, artistic, theological intelligence as the Iberian fathers. Besides, the extraordinary conciliar activity (especially in the royal city) of the Church of Spain showed the great maturity of its bishopric, for centuries accustomed to collegial work for the good of the state and the church; likewise, the existence, production, and continuous updating of a doctrinal and canonical collection of texts of sure reference for the whole Church of Spain rendered the structure of ecclesial life very organized and theologically founded. This gave the Church of Spain an underlying confidence and a boundless trust in its abilities.

On the basis of this theological awareness, it was therefore decided that the doctrine against monothelitism promulgated by the ecumenical council should occupy from then on the place following the Council of Calchedon[583] in the *Collectio Hispana* or *Codex Canonum*,[584] making it the fifth[585] ecumenical council after Nicaea, Constantinople, Ephesus, and Chalcedon[586] with equal doctrinal authority.

Not satisfied with merely approving the acts of the Third Council of Constantinople—that is, with just the adherence of the Hispanic-Visigothic bishopric to the christological doctrine of the ecumenical council—the bishops also attached extracts of the synthesis magisterially compiled by their primate that also contained an explanation and a theological commentary by the Church of Spain about the christological dogma defined in Constantinople. Such canons, from the eighth to the eleventh of the Fourteenth Council of Toledo, explicitly focus the attention on the christological dogma explained by Julian with techniques of a proven theologian,[587] as indicated by their titles: VIII. *Allocutio ad totius compagem Ecclesiae de duabus Christi naturis inseparabilibus et perfectis;* IX. *De duarum naturarum Christi voluntatibus et operibus;* X. *De haereticorum contentionibus evitandis: et ut non discutiantur quae summa sunt, sed credantur;* XI. *De communi omnium judicio quo responsa partis nostrae firmata sunt.* The text containing the *apologetica responsa defensionis nostrae*[588] was formally approved by all the bishops of the Fourteenth Council of Toledo, and the same council accorded the text the value of decretal letters.[589] It had been compiled by Julian of Toledo with great accuracy and probably coincides with the *Apologeticum fidei*, now lost, which Felix[590] refers to when introducing the list of the works of Julian.

Therefore, Julian had not been satisfied with just an answer and a generic adherence to the definitions of the ecumenical council. He had studied the acts of the council together with the bishops of Spain, and we can suppose also alone, and he had added some subtle specifications and observations that were christological in nature, in the style of his preferred authors, particularly Augustine and Leo the Great. This means that he added to the definition of Constantinople an abundance of fine distinctions and multiplication of examples concerning the matter of the divine will, presented with a relatively new (or unusual) language, whose content was, however, accessible in the works of the saintly fathers.

He evidently deemed it important to communicate to the Church of Rome not only an explicit adherence to the christological dogma of the ecumenical council, but also the point of view or the theological judgment of the learned Spanish Church.[591] Particularly Julian, in addition to the classical christological dogma, had quoted the formula *Voluntas genuit voluntatem sicut et sapientia sapientiam* or *Voluntas ex voluntate sicut et sapientia ex sapientia*, obviously referring not to the human psychological dimension of Jesus or to the dimension of finite reality, but to the eternal procession of the Son from the Father, to point out that in God, who is one essence, the will of the Son is also generated by the divine will of God the Father, as affirmed by all the great fathers of the church (Greek and Latin), and as claimed by the orthodox Christian faith.

A second christological interpretation of Julian, inserted into the *Apologeticum*, was proposed by him in quite an unusual and original way in its literary formulation. It was precisely such terminological originality that perplexed the Roman curial environments, because the christological formula used by Julian spoke of "three substances" present in Christ—the body, the soul, and the divinity. This truth was taught also, according to Julian, by the doctors and by the whole church. But the theological lexicon of Julian was, in any case, unique and unusual, considering that the christological definitions, from the time of the Council of Ephesus, had always used a binary language: two natures (human and divine) in the one Person of Christ. The theological language that described the existence of "three" substances in Christ seriously risked, for those who lacked sufficient knowledge about the categories used by Julian and about the reflection maintained by the primate of Spain, being considered at least suspicious, if not straight out heterodox.

The intention of Julian, evidently, adding these christological formulations to the text of Constantinople, was to show the theological sureness, the intellectual high level, and the interpretative skill of the Hispanic-Visigothic Church, in addition to defending at the same time the orthodoxy and the doctrinal autonomy of the primate of Spain and the Spanish bishops.

What happened subsequently, however, led to the fall of events. Both the declaration of the Spanish bishops and the text, in commentary form, of the *Apologeticum* compiled by Julian, which in his opinion so worthily represented the Church of Spain, were delivered to the *Notarius* Peter. In the meantime he had been pressed by the new pope, Benedict II,[592] to hasten his return to Rome and so he quickly completed (*festina perficere*) his mission in the Spanish Church;[593] Peter, therefore, left for Rome together with some envoys and delegates of the Church of Spain.

The Apologeticum de tribus capitulis *(686)*[594]

Once the unique christological formulations compiled by Julian reached Rome in the form of complete text of the first *Apologeticum*, by the same pontifical envoy Peter and the clergyman sent by the Spanish bishops, they were read and examined, probably by the experts of the Roman curia, and immediately aroused some suspicions. In reality, it can be said, with a certain approximation to the truth, that the christological assertions of Julian were notably misunderstood.[595] The Roman theologians criticized them vehemently and reported them to Pope Benedict II. He also probably suspected them of christological heresy. To justify such unfavorable judgment aroused by the writing of Julian in the Roman milieu, we must bear in mind how difficult it was for both Roman theologians and the envoy of the Church of Spain to understand and express such a complex subject as Christology. In particular, the Spanish envoy evidently did not know how properly to introduce the christological explanations of Julian, nor did he try to defend them. Or, as we know from the second *Apologeticum* of Julian, the unfavorable reception of the christological commentary of the primate of Spain was due to a superficial reading of the dense text of Julian, superficiality attributed to the Roman theologians, and perhaps also to the sovereign pontiff himself.

Moreover, it can be hypothesized that the proven theological ability[596] of Julian, for decades accustomed to treating difficult dogmatic formulas as well as other theological themes, must have made quite an impression and aroused suspicions (or perhaps a kind of envy) in the Roman theologians. Probably some of these fine distinctions were not understood, or they seemed suspicious to the eyes of the theologians of the Roman curia. But, besides this suspicious attitude toward the primate of Spain, perhaps the true cause of the conflict that from then on developed between Rome and Toledo was the great attention that for centuries had characterized the *modus operandi* of Roman theologians, who were very attentive to terminological or literary variations in theological texts or in the endless historical discussions; they were, therefore, ready to identify and to consider any novelty or divergence from the classical formulas as a sign or suspect of heterodoxy.[597]

The point is that the pontiff, in reply to the christological text of the Spanish bishopric, and especially of their primate, with a certain vehemence asked for explanations from them both. Yet—and this was indeed an unforgivable (but perhaps intentional) oversight—the pope did so orally, and not in writing, expressing his criticisms of the Toledan Christology to the same clergyman sent by the Hispanic-Visigothic Church, manifesting to him his aversion to the dogmatic propositions expressed by Julian and by the Spanish bishops, and ordering him to report to the primate and to all the Spanish bishops what he had heard. The pontiff, in any case, did not object to the Christology of Julian, nor did he contrast it with other christological propositions or definitions[598] involving his magisterium. He requested further clarification and, as we have said, more patristic testimonies. An open invitation for Julian, so "versed in patristic learning." The pontiff ordered the same clergyman to return, therefore, to Toledo and to report these observations to the bishops of the Church of Spain and to the primate. It is not difficult to imagine the state of mind of the poor clergyman, sullen for the bad reception of Julian's writing in Rome and perhaps more worried about what he had to report in Toledo and about the predictable reactions of his bishop, the fiery and proud nature of whose doctrine he well knew.

All this happened in Rome while the text of Julian, because of the above-mentioned tree-branched celebrations of the provincial councils of Spain, had by then spread throughout all the ecclesiastical regions of Spain as the decree of the Fourteenth Council of Toledo and was therefore considered to be representative of the official chris-

tological faith of all the Hispanic-Visigothic bishops. Conflict was
inevitable.

When the primate of Spain finally saw his envoys return and
learned about the Roman objections, he was certainly upset and felt
it necessary, at that point, to reply immediately to the suspicions and
accusations, even though only orally expressed, coming from Rome
with a new national council, the Fifteenth of Toledo, with the purpose
of defending once and for all the christological orthodoxy of the
Church of Spain, which had seriously been doubted by the Roman
insinuations. The occasion to convene the council occurred when
King Ervig died and his son-in-law Egica rose to the throne (687–701),
drawing all the bishops of Spain to celebrate a national council in
Toledo in May of 688.

From the acts of the Fifteenth Council of Toledo[599] we know that
the primate of Spain defended with firmness and steadiness the christological ideas as well the literary expressions he had used, and to
which Pope Benedict II had objected, and he complained explicitly
and publicly about the thoughtlessness of the Roman theologians and
of the pope in judging his christological doctrine.[600] An example of
such superficiality is how Benedict II had not put his observations in
writing for such a delicate and important subject as Christology, but
rather had only expressed them orally to the Spanish envoy, ordering
him to report them to the primate of Spain and the Visigothic bishops. Despite this objective critical note, which Julian communicated
to the entire assembly of sixty-one Spanish bishops, the text does not
seem to be radically "anti-Roman," because even as Julian protests the
integrity of his theological doctrine, he also points to the figure of
Pope Benedict II in a positive way, qualifying him as *beatae memoriae*, of
holy memory,[601] since he had died in the meantime. This means that
the Fifteenth Council of Toledo knew that Pope Benedict II was dead,
and the primate of the Spanish bishops was manifesting all his respect
for the successor of Peter.

He was not lacking in courage, however, when he criticized the
superficiality of the pope for not having compiled some written document in objection to the christological formulas of Julian and to
have read the text without the necessary diligence and care (*incaute*)[602]
for such important doctrine. The situation was undoubtedly worse for
the enormous delay[603] in the return of the envoy of the Spanish bishops to Toledo (only in 686), after a very difficult trip from Rome. Such

delay or, according to the bishops, such silence from Rome had been interpreted by them as an attitude of sufficiency or, worse, as a reproach or a sign of mistrust from the Roman see toward the Church of Spain. It seems, therefore, clear that when the envoy finally returned to Toledo and reported the criticisms of the Roman theologians and the orders of Benedict II to revise deeply what Julian had expressed in his first *Apologeticum*, the primate and the bishops of Spain considered it a true theological censorship[604] and an offense against and an attack on their legitimate doctrinal liberty[605] and their theological intelligence.

It must have indeed been humiliating, an "estigma bochornoso e infamante," as Rivera Recio[606] comments, for the primate of Spain to see himself accused of heterodoxy in front of the whole Spanish bishopric, and what's more, by the apostolic see of Rome—Julian, the champion of the theological faith of the Hispanic-Visigothic Church, the faithful disciple of Augustine and of so many other fathers of the church, the primate of all the churches of the Iberian Peninsula. Moreover, the Toledan envoy did not have any document from the Church of Rome stating clearly what was wrong in the Christology of Julian, but only a charge and an order, to transmit orally, by means of someone not particularly competent in the matter, to the Spanish bishops to revise their dogmatic exposition. Indeed unbelievable!

The Hispanic-Visigothic bishopric was very upset by this event and by the Roman attitude, and it quickly reacted by delegating[607] Julian to compose a further theological reply to the observations of the pope and the Roman curia. This reply became the second *Apologeticum* or *Apologeticum de tribus capitulis*[608] remembered by Felix,[609] and it is easy to imagine Julian quickly working on it and dedicating the maximum attention to what he wrote. In this text,[610] through numerous quotations of works of authoritative fathers of the church, Julian, with great intelligence and a skilled use of the Greek and Latin patristic sources,[611] "tratando de una doctrina muy complicada"[612] provided a basis for the expressions that he had used and that Rome had considered suspicious of heterodoxy. In conclusion to his rich and clear exposition, perhaps in some parts rather sarcastic, he launched strong words against the superficiality of the man (*vir ille*),[613] undoubtedly Pope Benedict II, who had done such a negligent and too rapid reading of the text (*incuriosa lectionis transcursione*),[614] and he cast "furious words against the ignorance of the Romans" [theologians].[615] To the pope, who seemed to have misunderstood in a psychological sense the christological language of Julian, especially concerning the formula *voluntas genuit voluntatem,* Julian answered that he had not used such methodology at all,[616] because his text spoke of the will from the point of view of the divine essence, and he concluded his reasoning by saying that he was well aware of distinguishing the operations that are strictly divine from those that are comparable to the human dimension.[617]

The compiled and approved text was then sent to the pope in the same year 686,[618] and by means of the same envoy, accompanied by other clergymen,[619] who thus covered the same road in the opposite direction, but this time with more promptness. Unfortunately the entire text of Julian has not survived to our day. What we do know of it is the broad abstract that, adhered to by all the Visigothic bishopric, was then included in the acts of the Fifteenth Council of Toledo (688).[620] It contains the justification, on the doctrinal level, of the expression used by Julian: *voluntas genuit voluntatem* and the original affirmation according to which in Christ there are three substances (the body, the soul, and the divinity). In particular, Julian defended this last affirmation not only patristically and theologically, but also from a grammatical point of view. As F. X. Murphy noted, Julian, "school master that he had been"[621] as well as author of works of grammar (the *Ars grammatica*) and rhetoric applied to history (the *Historia Wambae*), reminded the pope, leaning on the authority of Isidore of Seville and his *Etymologiae,* what a synecdoche was, that is, that rhetorical figure, of biblical and patristic use, which consists in the use of the figured sense of a word in place of another based on a relationship of contiguity. If the pope had perceived this literary figure in the formula of Julian, this would have avoided all suspicion of heterodoxy in his literary christological expression of the three substances in Christ.

The answer, evidently composed by Julian still on the wave of the emotional reaction to the observations of Benedict II and his curia, comprised eighteen brief chapters containing first of all the defense (*Apologeticum*) of the so-called obscure expressions used by Julian in the first *Apologeticum* and, subsequently, the doctrinal precisions justified with numerous authoritative quotations of the fathers of the church, leaving no doubt about the orthodoxy of Julian and the Visigothic bishopric in the formulation of the christological dogma. Julian devoted particular care to the clarification of the theological terminology used, well aware that his expressions would have been weighed and analyzed in an even more meticulous way by the Roman theologians. In the elaboration of his second *Apologeticum*, it is legitimate to think that Julian was greatly helped not only by his bright intelligence but also by the particular wealth of his library of manuscript codices, which he used in abundance.[622]

But the primate of Spain did not limit himself to this solid technical answer. Indeed, in the final part of the text, he rallied in a strong way against his critics, almost with the tone of a theological challenge launched against those whom he negatively qualified as *aemuli ignorantes*,[623] that is, the rival theologians, though ignorant imitators, of the Roman curia[624] of that time. The final text, says Madoz,[625] is an explosive account loaded with bitterness:[626] "But if now, after all this, they still dissent in anything from the dogmas of the fathers from whom these things have been culled, we shall not further contend with them; but adhering straightway to the footsteps of our ancestors, our response will be sublime for the lovers of truth, through the divine justice, even if it should be considered indocile by ignorant rivals."[627]

Therefore, it seems that, according to Julian, it was the Roman theologians who dissented from the dogmas of the fathers, as they accused of disobedience and insubordination the one who instead followed the truth of the ancient fathers. He spoke even more incisively, in our opinion, when he affirmed that "as we are not ashamed to sustain the things that are true, some are so perhaps ashamed to ignore the same truths" (sicut nos non pudebit quae sunt vera defendere, ita forsitan quosdam pudebit quae vera sunt ignorare).[628] Seemingly, on the theological-doctrinal level and that of intellectual pride, the Visigothic Church, presided over by Julian of Toledo, did not accept lessons from anyone for what concerned the confession of christological faith, the doctrinal orthodoxy of the Church of Spain, not even from the Church of Rome. In fact, just before pronouncing the words that aroused so much scandal for historians, Julian appeals precisely to the christological and conciliar definitions such as that of Chalcedon and affirms strongly—in our opinion even more harshly than in the final conclusion—in that he invokes the conciliar condemnation of the detractors of the truth: Jam vero si quis contra haec ulterius non instruendum, sed contrarium se huic redditae rationi praebuerit, damnationem praefati concilii sustinebit. The final conclusion, already mentioned above, is well known for its verbal strength and for the underlying intellectual superiority toward those who had objected to the confession of faith of the Church of Spain.

Julian of Toledo's courageous attitude toward the theologians of the Roman apostolic see, verging on arrogance[629] and aggressiveness, must not be considered unique by modern readers, as if it were only an extemporaneous emotional reaction of the primate of Toledo. He, in fact, must have known that something similar had already happened, just a few decades before, between the Church of Spain and the church in Rome, during the Sixth Council of Toledo, when Braulio, bishop of Saragossa, but in the name of all the bishops of Spain, reacted strongly, to say the least, to the unjust and false affirmations and to the negative judgment formulated by Pope Honorius I against the Spanish bishopric. Julian probably felt authorized by this historical precedent, but above all by the validity of his observations and reflections, to assume a similar attitude of verbal harshness, perhaps even stronger than that of Braulio upon receiving the letter of Pope Honorius I. With two conflicts with the Church of Rome in only fifty years, both substantially won by the Church of Toledo, the Church of Spain in the seventh century attained a level of great ecclesial importance in the West with exceptional theological and doctrinal preparation, showing no weakness or inferiority complexes, even toward the venerable and ancient Roman apostolic see. Julian and his contemporaries were well aware that no western church, including that of Rome, could be compared culturally with the Spain of his time.[630]

In the meantime, however, Pope Benedict II had died and was not able, therefore, to receive the sharp and very informed reply of Julian of Toledo and of the Fifteenth Council of Toledo, which likely would have fully satisfied him. He probably would have had the new text analyzed by his theologians with maximum care before making any pronouncements about it. But it is very difficult, if not impossible, to foresee how the Roman curia would have reacted to the strong declarations of Julian, especially to the expression *aemuli ignorantes.*

The successors of Pope Benedict, Popes John V and Conon, had such brief reigns that they were not able to address and resolve the christological question between the Visigothic Church and the Church of Rome.

The answer of Rome to the second *Apologeticum,* however, finally did arrive, even if, as usual, after a notable delay. It was a unique and unexpected answer. It happened, in fact, that the next pope, Sergius I,[631] elected toward the end of 687, decided first of all to attenuate the polemical tones and, subsequently, to favor a greater pacification of the souls and intellects. He, in fact, contrary to what might have been expected, did not react polemically and negatively to the second edition of Julian's *Apologeticum*, assimilated in part by the Fifteenth Council of Toledo. Moreover, even if we do not know what happened exactly, the chronicles narrate that Pope Sergius I unexpectedly called a Roman synod, which discussed the matter and approved the supplementary christological reasonings of Julian and of the Visigothic bishopric. The pope then sent a letter to Julian of Toledo in which he affirmed that everything he had written about Christology commenting on the definitions of the sixth ecumenical council was correct and exact from the doctrinal point of view, and he congratulated Julian for the acuteness of his theology. Lastly, the pope ordered the text of the second *Apologeticum* of Julian to be translated into Greek and to be sent to Constantinople, so that also in the East the recognition of the text of the acts of the sixth ecumenical council by the Hispanic-Visigothic bishopric would be known and appreciated.

The news about the wise intervention of the Pope Sergius I is found in the *Chronicon* or *Continuatio Hispana* of Isidorus Pacensis, who, writing most likely in Toledo several decades after the death of Julian, makes him a hero of the Church of Spain, praising him profusely:[632] "Ejus in tempore librum de tribus substantiis" (thus he called the second *Apologeticum*), "quem dudum Romam *sanctissimus Julianus* urbis regiae metropolitanus episcopus miserat, et minus caute tractando papa Romanus arcendum indixerat, ob id quod voluntas genuit voluntatem, ante biennium tandem scripserat veridicis testimoniis, in hoc concilio ad exactionem praefati principis Julianus episcopus per oracula majorum ea quae Romam transmiserat vera esse confirmans apologeticum facit; et Romam per suos legatos eclesiasticos viros presbyterum, diaconem, et subdiaconem eruditissimos, in omnibus et per omnia divinis Scripturis imbutos, iterum cum versibus acclamatoriis secundum quod et olim transmiserat de laude imperatoris mittit: quod Roma digne et pie recipit, et cunctis legendum indicit: atque summo imperatori satis acclamando: Laus tua, Deus, in fines terrae, cognitum facit. Qui et rescriptum domno Juliano per suprafatos legatos satis cum gratiarum actione honorifice remittit, et omnia quaecunque scripsit justa et pia esse depromit."[633]

According to Murphy,[634] the information contained in the chronicle is trustworthy because the author demonstrates knowledge of the documents and facts of the period related to the life of Julian. In addition, he quotes the canons of the councils and the writings of different Toledan fathers, as well as the inscriptions King Wamba had inscribed on the monuments and city wall of Toledo. The same reliability is attributed to the chronicle concerning the full rehabilitation of Julian by the Church of Rome.

It was undoubtedly providential that Rome decided not to undertake other interventions that brought up the matter raised by Benedict II. It is probable that if the Roman curia had instead decided to continue the *querelle* and had answered negatively also to the second *Apologeticum*, the diatribe would have taken on even harsher tones and would have provoked, if not a schism, certainly a significant laceration of the relationship between the Church of Spain, in absolute solidarity with its primate, and that of Rome. Indeed, it is not difficult to imagine that Julian, with his impulsive character and with the intellectual pride that characterized him, would not have backed down from a second possible negative reaction from the Church of Rome.

Knowledge of this story was still alive several centuries afterward, such that in the thirteenth century, Rodericus of Toledo,[635] successor of Julian on the Toledan episcopal see, would repeat and emphasize the same words of Isidorus Pacensis describing how the metropolitan of Toledo and the bishops of Spain opposed Rome successfully. The stormy event, therefore, had a certain historical resonance.[636] But, while historians such as Mariana and the cardinal Caesar Baronius[637] found fault[638] with the disdainful and haughty tone of the language used by Julian in the second *Apologeticum*, Flórez tried to excuse him from the accusation of being a schismatic by making an exegetical study of the text of the second *Apologeticum*, perhaps a little forced, that allowed him to exclude the possibility of a bishop of the Catholic Church having ever called the bishop of the Roman see,[639] no less than the pope himself, an "ignorant rival." Other historians and national researchers[640] tried to do the same, while other authors such as the authoritative Bollandists decided to simply pass in silence over the matter by then smoothed over by the centuries, preferring not to blow on the burning embers but rather to underline the good memory left by Julian and the veneration of him as a saint of the Catholic Church, since his name was written in the Mozárabic martyrologies. Others maintained that the matter had not been so dramatic and that, all things considered, it was only a series of interpretative misunderstandings, even if objectively the language used by Julian was to be considered bordering on arrogance. The disdainful words written by Julian, however, can be interpreted as the demonstration of the awareness that Julian and the Spanish bishopric had of their theological culture and of the intellectual level of the Church of Spain. At the most, therefore, it can be affirmed that Julian and the Spanish bishops "dejaron correr demasiado la pluma,"[641] as A. Veiga Valiña so generously wrote, but without wanting to question the doctrinal and disciplinary authority of the pope.

One can think, therefore, that Julian might have succeeded in vindicating his magisterial and theological prerogatives toward the Roman curia and the pope, but, at the same time, that he had all the right to distance himself and the Church of Spain from any suspicion of heresy, especially since it came from the intellectual incapacity (often called also "ignorance") expressed in rash theological judgment.[642]

It is easy to imagine the full satisfaction that must have reigned in Toledo and in all the ecclesiastical sees of Spain when they learned of the conclusion, so honorable for the primate and for the whole Church of Spain, of the event that had opposed the two churches on such a decisive and delicate matter as christological dogma. The prestige of Julian increased certainly beyond all proportion, as did the consideration of his value as theologian and his courage. He alone, even if with the decisive support of the whole Spanish bishopric, which made him even more resolute, had dared to contest a theological judgment of his christological theology, undoubtedly an unfair judgment expressed by the most feared and most authoritative curia of the Catholic world.

The true problem, however, is another, more difficult one to resolve: why the sudden change of attitude of Rome? Naturally, there is no written document admitting the error of the Church of Rome in evaluating the Hispanic-Visigothic Christology, nor had the Church of Spain ever demanded it. What, then, provoked this sudden, almost unilateral, conclusion of the *querelle*? It is not difficult to imagine that the primate of Spain had expected a reprimand from Rome after the second edition of the *Apologeticum*. Besides his perfect theological explanations, which, in fact, would have been approved, Julian's text also contained considerations and judgments expressed in such a truly offensive way that they could have provoked a strong reaction from Rome. It is probable that Julian was prepared to defend his position to the bitter end, leaning solidly on the sureness of his theology, of his doctrinal orthodoxy, and on the whole bishopric of Spain, but undoubtedly risking ecclesial isolation,[643] whose consequences had not perhaps been seriously and completely considered. Are we, perhaps, to think that Rome was intimidated by Julian's aggressive expressions toward the theologians? I believe that a similar hypothesis must also be discarded.

It is more probable to suppose that Pope Sergius I, made aware of the diatribe, had ordered his experts to review with more attention and serenity, and with less quibbling, Julian's writing and that, after a while, some anonymous theologian of the Roman curia, more wise and endowed with a greater theological sense than his predecessors or other curia theologians, explained to the pontiff that, all things considered, there was nothing heterodox in the *Apologeticum* of the primate of Spain, but that, on the contrary, his explanations could perhaps contribute to obtaining a better understanding of the mystery of Christ, using a new methodology and new language.

A second reason that probably led the pope to heal the *querelle* could have been the realization that there were no pontifical documents existing on the matter raised by his predecessor against the Toledan Christology, and, as it is known, *verba volant*. The existence of any written document would have perhaps forced Pope Sergius I to continue the diatribe. In any case, the good sense of the pope prevented the conflict from degenerating into a crisis that, not unlikely, given the character of the primate of Spain and the atmosphere in which the national councils of Spain were celebrated, could have indeed turned into something unpleasant from the ecclesial point of view. It was, therefore, the good sense and the temperance of Rome (and not the Arabic invasion) that attenuated the tones, recognizing the due appreciation of the primate of Spain and eliminating the reason for the dispute while respecting, nonetheless, the requirements of justice, and therefore substantially justifying Julian and his theology.[644] The pope probably realized that the solidarity of the Spanish bishops with their primate would not have withdrawn from further theological objections coming from Rome and that, doctrinally and canonically, those in Toledo were without a doubt right.

This attitude of the pope, in any case, must have seemed to be a reprimand or a lesson for those in the Roman curia who had expressed such unobjective, conceited, hasty, and rather arrogant judgment about the christological theology of the primate of Spain.

To this day, therefore, and since we lack documents related to the event, we cannot know what really happened beyond these hypotheses, but it is nevertheless very important to underline that the Church of Rome approved the christological doctrine exposed by the Spanish bishopric in the acts of the Fifteenth Council of Toledo. We are left with only the possibility of making some conjectures and for-mulating some hypotheses.

As for the Church of Toledo, we know that, in homage to its pri-mate, the text of the *Apologeticum de tribus capitulis* was reformulated into the symbol of faith of the Sixteenth Council of Toledo in 693, three years after the death of Julian, even though the same Toledan council considered it best to insert a comment on the text in the form of a gloss, to avoid all possible and further doctrinal misunderstanding.[645]

A century later, during the Council of Frankfurt in 794, to reject and condemn the adoptionist heresy spread throughout Spain the bishops cautiously distanced themselves from the affirmations of Julian of Toledo in christological matters.

The querelle *between Toledo and Rome in the judgment of historians*[646]

The seventh-century dispute that occurred between the Church of Spain and the Roman see about christological matters of maximum doctrinal importance was a confirmation of the historical data accord-ing to which the relationships between the two churches were not always easy,[647] and the diatribes between the primate of Spain, Julian of Toledo, and the Roman curia ended up resonating universally.[648]

The need to maintain respect for the doctrinal authority of the pope, together with the strong desire for autonomy by the Church of Spain (given its theological sureness and the intellectual pride of the Visigothic bishops, and, particularly, of their primate), was unable to find the right equilibrium. Julian has been accused by various histori-ans of having been excessively hostile to the papacy and even of hav-ing come a step away from provoking a schism in the Catholic Church, as if the primacy over the churches of Spain could constitute a title

important enough for a total disciplinary and doctrinal independence from the venerable Church in Rome and from its ministry.

We deem these accusations entirely exaggerated.[649] However, we
fully agree with what Hillgarth says on this subject: "the Spanish
Church was not nationalistic but it was proud—and legitimately so—
of its increasing number of Saints and Doctors of its chain of
Councils, its splendid Liturgy, its continuous cultivation of Latinity,
compared with what appeared to Spaniards the outer darkness of contemporary Gaul and Africa."[650] Fortunately, with the passing of time
and, especially in our times, the strongest accusations have decidedly
attenuated, in parallel with a more serene evaluation of the events
and the recognition by many historians of the objective validity of the
christological explanations of the primate of Toledo and their doctrinal validity. Today it is substantially believed that the fiery and ardent
temperament of Julian and his intellectual and theological confidence undoubtedly led him, on the one hand, to exaggerate the tone,
yet the objective correctness of his theological thought in christological matters was perhaps beyond the intellectual possibilities of the
Roman theologians of the time. This Roman *ignorantia* filled the
bishop of Toledo with indignation to the point of generating a vehement and decisive reaction. It must not be forgotten that Julian at the
time held the important role of primate of Spain, a role he had wisely
and patiently built up during the years of his episcopal government.
As primate of Spain he would not allow for his important role to be
frustrated by the incompetent accusations of the theologians of the
Roman curia. Knowing that his Christology was correct and in line
with the doctrine of the ancient ecumenical councils, Julian could not
tolerate being accused of heterodoxy in front of the bishops of the
ecclesiastical provinces of Spain who were under his primacy, nor
before the king or the Christian people of Spain.

The historians' judgment of this series of events and of Julian
and the Church of Spain oscillates, therefore, between explicit accusations by Protestant historians of schism, rebellion, and opposition to
the apostolic see of Rome, above all because of the disdainful expressions used in the text of the *Apologeticum de tribus capitulis*.[651] At the
other extreme, Julian was held to be innocent of all rebellion because
his invectives were not aimed at the pope, Benedict II, or at the theologians of the Roman curia, but rather at unspecified contemporary
Spanish critics of Julian ("the ignorant rivals").[652]

As is often the case, the truth is probably somewhere in the middle: as other scholars have proposed,[653] the primate of Toledo and the Spanish bishops had effectively been wounded by the unfounded accusations and calumnies about the lack of orthodoxy of their theological doctrines and, perhaps even more, by the accusation of theological incompetence. They could not accept such censorship. What happened was probably a series of misunderstandings or mutual errors that led to the conflict. The theologians of the Roman curia had probably been too careless and perhaps too superficial in the evaluation or, rather, underestimation of the fine and learned christological reasoning of Julian of Toledo; but the reaction of the Spanish bishopric and its primate was probably too fiery and impulsive, undoubtedly appearing too vulnerable.[654]

How are we to evaluate the apparently aggressive attitude of the Spanish Church and its primate? Certainly from the point of view of catholicity, there were indeed problems between Rome and Toledo.[655] In fact, though fully admitting the primacy of the ministry of the successor of Peter, the Spanish bishops did not accept his questioning of their doctrinal orthodoxy, nor did they accept the superficiality with which the Roman theologians transmitted their observations to the Spanish bishops about so delicate a subject, that is, orally (and not in writing, as was custom), through the envoy of the bishops. Accordingly they deemed it opportune to react.

But this rather schismatic or extremely nationalistic attitude, as several historians have observed, seems to involve a series of facts that are incontrovertible from a historical point of view, and about which most of the protagonists were well aware.

I believe that the Church of Spain was legitimately proud of being, in that century, a light in the dark, and of living a very vital pastoral, theological, and spiritual existence, thanks to its saintly bishops and its great theologians. Thus, the Visigothic Church was, and considered itself to be, a united church, whose bishops were accustomed to a collegial government of the church, to a continuous and efficient synodal attitude, as shown by the series of national and provincial Visigothic councils held in Toledo. It was a church, therefore, accustomed to the collegial work of *équipe* and to an elaborate pastoral and doctrinal ministry by its episcopal body, even with a strong presence of the king and imperial interference. We can share this strong but truthful judgment of Hillgarth: "Julian and his Spanish contemporaries saw no Church in the West that could be compared to that of Spain, not even Rome. Rome had Apostolic authority but when it came to the elucidation of involved theological questions Spanish Theologians might well prove more reliable than those of Rome."[656] We can also agree with the similar judgment of Madoz:

> La Iglesia española tenía conscientia de su posición privilegiada entre todas las del Ocidente en el siglo VII. Preservada, casi la única, de la decadencia general, sentía en su venas el latir de su juventud desde la reciente conversión de Recaredo, fomentada por una recia organización político-religiosa. Sus figuras prominentes en la letras, la cadena gloriosa de sus concilios, su legislación canónica y civil, llamada a ser oráculo de consulta de las escuelas medievales, todo ello creaba un ambiente de seguridad y confianza autónoma que respaldaba el criterio de sus decisiones.[657]

"Julián era hombre tan seguro de su competencia o su pericia en la exégesis doctrinal che, en otro momento y llegado el caso, no dudó en mantener con los teólogos romanos un agria polémica que ha llevado algún estudioso moderno a hablar de un grave amago de movimiento cismático en la Iglesia visigoda."[658]

Moreover, the Visigothic Church was also a church with its own ancient, rich, and splendid liturgical tradition, the so-called Mozárabic liturgy, as well as a glorious theological tradition. The Hispanic-Visigothic Church also had a unique religious architecture, with its own traditions, its own art, a magnificent liturgical musical tradition, and its own line of poetry, not to mention the ancient local feasts in honor and veneration of the saints produced by the same church. Additionally, the Spanish theological schools of thought showed themselves to also have a healthy attitude of respect and a great knowledge of the classical culture and of the *Latinitas*. No "anti-Roman complex," therefore, could touch a church with such cultural and theological roots. It was a church objectively aware of being a mature and responsible church, without preconstituted submissions, without inferiority complexes, aware of being an integral and lively part of the Catholic Church, with an intellectual role of primary importance.

Nevertheless, as Madoz rightly observes, it is true that even today we would not hesitate to censor an insolent local church and its bishop who behaved the way Julian and the Spanish bishops did toward the apostolic Roman see and its head, the pope.[659]

The relationship of the Hispanic-Visigothic Church with the Church of Rome[660]

It is without doubt difficult to find in the history of the Christian Church a national ecclesial conscience[661] of the same intensity as that which united the bishops and the churches of Visigothic Spain in the seventh century.

That the synodal sense of episcopal collegiality was very accented in the Spanish Church is shown by the *cadena gloriosa* of its national councils, and of the innumerable provincial councils, in which the bishops for centuries had addressed problems and made important decisions of every kind: doctrinal, disciplinary, educational, juridical, social, political, and so on—often, as we have seen, also with political dimensions. Such imperial interference is problematic for us moderns, yet it was not so during the seventh century. The results of this activity were quite positive in maintaining a continuous control of the ecclesial situation and of Hispanic-Visigothic society that was obtained with the recurrent conciliar activity. This allowed problems to be identified and resolved as they arose.

Nevertheless, as historians of the Spanish Church rightly affirm, this did not mean independence and absolute autonomy of the Hispanic-Visigothic Church in matters of the doctrine of faith or ecclesial discipline. All of the Spanish bishops, including their primate, recognized both the authority of the bishop of Rome and the supreme authority of the general and ecumenical councils of the Catholic Church, especially those of the ancient church. Some national councils of Spain attempted to align the Church of Spain with Catholic doctrine while maintaining the characteristics and ways typical of the Hispanic-Visigothic ecclesial conscience. Such attachment to the ecclesial *traditio* can be noted, for instance, in the affirmations of the Third Council of Toledo,[662] according to which all that had been forbidden, approved, and defined by the ancient councils also had to be forbidden, approved, and defined by the national councils of Spain.

The same attention is paid to the universal value of the synodal letters of the pope and to the recognition of the primacy of the pope and to the power of intervention of the Roman apostolic see in the matters of the local churches, including Spain. This was true even if the dogma of the pontifical infallibility was far from being affirmed by the Catholic Church. T. González quotes some examples of how the Spanish bishopric consulted the bishop of Rome for an authoritative opinion on several theological-liturgical subjects.[663] J. Orlandis[664] does the same, recalling a whole series of relations between the Church of Spain and the Church of Rome, as well as the explicit signs of adhesion of the Church of Spain to the faith of the Catholic Church, as shown by the symbols of faith recited at the beginning of the numerous councils, the liturgical homologation, and the existence of the *Collectio Hispana*, which gathered the acts of the councils of East and West and which, unique in its genre, also contained a *summa* of pontifical decrees. There was great respect for Rome and the faith of the Catholic Church, but because of the ever-tighter bond that developed between the Spanish Church and the Visigothic kingdom, the Church of Spain developed a highly nationalistic and autonomous sense of affiliation and faith.

For this reason, therefore, relations between the churches of Spain and Rome decreased and became more rare as the Hispanic-Visigothic Church seemed increasingly oriented to living a life notably focused internally, a conviction strengthened by the so-called theological-literary "renaissance" that the Iberian Peninsula enjoyed beginning in the sixth century. A very cordial period between the two churches occurred during the pontificate of Gregory the Great, who had friendly personal relationships with Leander of Seville,[665] to whom he dedicated the famous *Moralia in Job*. This detail sheds light on the respect the future bishop of Rome, one of the greatest, had for the churches of Spain, above all from a theological and doctrinal point of view. On the other hand, we know that bishops of Rome such as Leo, Zenon, and Ormisda had sometimes sent their delegates to Spain to address and resolve doctrinal and pastoral-disciplinary matters concerning that church.[666]

This kind of attachment to the *traditio* and to ecclesial communion with the Roman apostolic see can be seen also in the celebration of the national councils of Spain, as well as in the constant use that the Spanish Church made of the symbols of faith of Nicaea and

Constantinople, and in the declaration, often repeated during the Toledan councils, according to which the Church of Spain upheld the same doctrine as the first four ecumenical councils (Nicaea, Constantinople, Ephesus, and Chalcedon). This means that the bishops and the primate of Spain, in varying degrees, have always accepted the idea of the unity of the faith and the doctrine in force in the Catholic Church, as well as the sacramental liturgy, ethics, and so on.

Nevertheless, relations and communication between the Hispanic-Visigothic Church and the Church of Rome were not frequent, not only because in that era it was difficult to maintain timely contact,[667] but also because the frequent national councils allowed for most problems to be resolved autonomously and without resorting to Rome[668]—almost as a historical anticipation of the principle of subsidiarity that is so important for modern ecclesiology. This situation had created a legitimate pastoral, liturgical, and theological autonomy of the Hispanic-Visigothic Church, which depended on the contribution of the great pastoral and theological personalities of the Spanish bishopric, and of whom the same Spanish episcopal body was particularly aware and proud. Furthermore, the popes of the period, knowing of this pastoral and theological maturity of the Church of Spain, probably limited their interventions.

But the relations between the Church of Spain and the Church in Rome also gave rise to more serious problems and quite antagonistic attitudes on the part of both the Roman see and the Spanish bishops. This probably is attributable to various factors, the first of which is certainly of a political nature. The bond between the Spanish Church and the Visigothic monarchic imperial power was not viewed positively by the Church of Rome, primarily because of the attitude of opposition of the Visigothic empire toward the Byzantine imperial power, to whose politics Rome was subjected. On the other hand, the Hispanic-Visigothic empire was often in polemics with the Byzantines, especially with those who continued to occupy an important part of the territory of the Visigothic kingdom on the eastern coast of the Mediterranean Sea.

In second place, the compactness and theological-doctrinal, pastoral, and disciplinary unity of the local churches of Spain was visibly accentuated by the celebrations of the national councils. These regular councils sometimes rendered appeal to the arbitration of the Church of Rome superfluous, since the churches of Spain were able to face and resolve their problems by themselves. This autonomy, the fruit of lengthy and continuous pastoral and theological work, often innovative and ahead of its time, could give the impression of concealing a tendency toward autonomy in an absolute sense, as if the Hispanic-Visigothic Church could carry on alone. But reality was quite different.

Awareness of the ecclesial maturity of the Hispanic-Visigothic Church was a fundamental reality and was in evidence especially during the councils. The brief but intense formula of the Fourth Council of Toledo,[669] presided over by the great Isidore of Seville, is a perfect synthesis of this unitary and compact attitude of the Church of Spain: one faith, one church, one kingdom. This formula indicates an element of cohesion of extraordinary power in Hispanic-Visigothic Christianity that led the same council to take a further step toward the unity of faith by establishing a uniform and liturgical cult in the whole territory of the kingdom. "Y la razón suprema de esa unidad de culto non es otra, según declaran los obispos, sino que todos están ligados por el doble vínculo de profesar una misma fe y pertenecer a un mismo reino."[670] Yet, to judge the Spanish Church as nationalist, independent, and in opposition to Rome[671] would truly be an exaggeration, not to mention being too hasty and without a historical foundation.[672]

The precedent: the case of the letter of Honorius I to the Spanish bishops and the firm answer of Braulio of Saragossa

About fifty years before the friction between Toledo and Rome, which occurred in the time of Julian of Toledo, and precisely in January of 638 while the Spanish bishopric was celebrating the Sixth Council of Toledo, a letter from Pope Honorius I[673] arrived unexpectedly, which, utilizing an unusual, and hardly fitting, example drawn from the Book of Isaiah[674] (Isa 56:10), exhorted the bishops of Spain to defend the Christian faith and not to be mute "as dogs that do not know how to bark" in the face of the danger to Christian faith represented by the Jews, especially by their proselytism. The text of the letter of Honorius has not survived, but we know the content of it, at least partially, from the firm answer of the Spanish bishopric addressed to the same pope.

The Spanish bishops were amazed by this accusation of negligence or pastoral weakness made against them by the bishop of Rome concerning the problem of the Jews and their presence in the Visigothic kingdom. It was probably the result of suppositions drawn from false and unfounded[675] reports that had reached the papal rooms. The bewilderment of the bishops reflected the fact that, when the letter arrived, the Spanish bishops were involved in examining, among many other local pastoral problems, the general legislation of the Visigothic kingdom toward the Jews. Thus, the accusations of pastoral negligence made by the pope against the Spanish bishops were totally without foundation, and the pope himself had been completely misinformed on the matter. Braulio, the bishop of Saragossa, in the name of the Hispanic-Visigothic bishopric, responded to the pope with a letter[676] in which he reaffirmed, above all, the recognition of the primacy and the infallibility of the magisterium of the bishop of Rome. At the same time, he stated that the bishops of Spain considered the pope's letter as aimed at soliciting the bishops to devote themselves to their main pastoral task, which is the preaching of the gospel and the care of the faithful, and not as a pastoral instruction about the way to obtain the conversion of the Jews.

But the tone and the literary expressions used by Braulio in the answer were rather harsh and characterized by a "steadiness respectfully ironic"[677] that returned the accusations to the sender. In fact, refusing the reprimand of the pope, Braulio maintained that the Spanish bishops did not have any reason for reproach in their pastoral praxis and their attitude toward the Jews, the bishops themselves being convinced that the Jews' conversion, if there is to be any, must be obtained in an agreeable way, with meekness and mildness, as the apostle Paul[678] recommends. Moreover, Braulio wrote that the Spanish bishops do not accept being compared to and called "dogs that do not know how to bark."[679] That image, Braulio wrote to the pope with great decisiveness, on behalf of the bishops of all the ecclesiastical provinces of Spain (and of the Gallia Narbonese), "ad nos…nullo modo pertinent,"[680] does not apply to us at all. The Spanish bishops, in fact, were well aware of their pastoral duty: to preach the Word of God, to protect and to take care of the faithful, to chase away the wolves, and to frighten the thieves. They have always done their duty and, even more, they have made public and applied the norms, laws, and punishments against the Jews who have transgressed or have returned to the Jewish creed after having adhered to the Christian faith. As demonstration of this total pastoral commitment, Braulio attached the acts of the councils previously celebrated by the Visigothic bishopric to the reply, together with those of the last council, the Sixth of Toledo.

We do not know if the firm answer of Braulio of Saragossa aroused reactions in the papal milieu. There probably had not been enough time, since Pope Honorius had died in October of the same year.

Not possessing the text of the letter of Honorius I, we are not really able to understand what had been the pastoral concern of the pope. Perhaps he believed the false rumors that the pastoral praxis of the Spanish bishops was too weak, though, in any case, he had expressed an excessive preoccupation with exaggerated language (even if borrowed from the Sacred Scripture) about the qualification of the bishops of the ecclesiastical provinces of Spain.

The firm reply of Braulio was intended to convey that the Spanish bishops were aware of their pastoral duty and knew how to conduct themselves with respect to the problem raised by the pope. It was not meant primarily to show an independent, nationalistic attitude in opposition to Rome on the part of the Hispanic-Visigothic Church. Besides—and this is certainly the better part of the letter—Braulio underlined and reminded the pope that the pastoral line of forced conversion, with the use of violence, of the Jews (quite diffused in the Christianity affected by this problem) was an instrument to be rejected in the most resolute way, because of the apostolic teaching that instead calls for kindness, meekness, and mildness in the attempt to persuade and engage in the Christian faith. This was an innovative contribution that seemed to break with the very praxis until then followed in the Hispanic-Visigothic milieu,[681] and that emphasized once more the preparation and the intellectual depth of the Hispanic-Visigothic bishops of the seventh century.

The Spanish bishops, therefore, were not at all "asleep," as the pope seemed to imply, but rather they had done their duty, even if their pastoral praxis included new methodologies of dialogue, directly inspired by the gospel and by the apostles,[682] innovations that merited praise rather than the reprimand of the Roman pontiff. It seems certain, therefore, that the pope had made a blunder and that the Spanish bishops were right to vindicate their own pastoral orthodoxy.

To this significant episode we must add, moreover, that a few decades later, in 681, Pope Honorius was described, in the letters of Leo II to the Spanish bishopric, as an ignorant shepherd who, even if he had not fallen into the monothelite heresy, had at least been weak and passive in avoiding it or condemning it. I believe it impossible, therefore, not to share the judgment of Hillgarth: "The recent lapse into heresy of Pope Honorius I, and his posthumous condemnation, announced by Leo II in his letters to Spain (PL 84, cols. 144–49), can hardly have encouraged confidence in papal theology."[683]

The pious intention of Braulio concerning the "soft" method of treating the Jews, was not an invention of the moment but rather a pastoral praxis that had been decided by the Fourth Council of Toledo, which had urged not to force the Jews into conversion. The council was aware of the examples of the past, the rigidity and absolute severity of the laws of King Sisebut, and the excessive tolerance in the time of King Suintila, neither of which had led to good results.

The good and moderate intentions of Braulio and the Sixth Council of Toledo, however, gave way to the "reason of state" and to a reckless, to say the least, provision of the king, which the bishops unfortunately tolerated. The acts of the council that were celebrated in Toledo when the letter of Honorius I had arrived, inform us that the bishops had expressed a public thankfulness to God and to their sovereign, who had shown the intention to address the problem of the Jews by permitting only Catholic Christian believers[684] within the confines of the Visigothic kingdom and, therefore, announcing a general and perpetual decree of expulsion of the Jews.

The lost works of Julian of Toledo

The following works of Julian of Toledo have not survived:

A *Librum plurimarum epistolarum*,[685] that is, the rich (*plurimarum*) epistolary collection of Julian, which is expressly cited by Felix. As in the case of the epistolary of Eugene II, or that more abundant one of Braulio of Saragossa[686] and others of the epoch, it is probable that it contained the missives written by Julian in his elegant Latin to colleagues in the bishopric or to abbots, princes, and kings, probably rich in doctrine, spirituality, and reflections on ethics and on the relationships between state and church, and so on.

The *Liber sermonum*,[687] or homilies of the bishop of Toledo; probably a collection of liturgical homilies, or of circumstance, written by Julian, or, as Felix says, a brief work dealing with the claim of the house of God as a place of refuge and shelter.

The *Liber responsionum*,[688] with which Julian intended to preserve and defend the canons and laws existing in the Visigothic kingdom that prevented slaves of Christian faith from serving unfaithful Lords, meaning Jews and not Christians.

The *Liber carminum diversorum*,[689] which, according to the biographer Felix, contained hymns, epitaphs, and numerous epigrams for various circumstances, all composed by the bishop of Toledo. It is most unfortunate to be unable to appreciate the poetry of Julian of Toledo, learned at the school of Eugene II of Toledo and from the reading and study of so many classical authors.

The *Libellus de divinis judiciis*,[690] or rather, a collection of texts drawn from Sacred Scripture and devoted to Count Ervig (not yet king of the Visigothic) through an initial dedicatory letter.

The *Excerpta de libris Sancti Augustini*,[691] texts written by the doctor Augustine to contest a heretical Pelagian named Julian and collected together by Julian of Toledo; to this anthological work must be added the *Ex decade psalmorum beati Augustini*, a collection of psalmic comments of the doctor of the church. Both works are collections of texts of Augustine, Julian of Toledo's author of reference in all of his works. These intelligent collections of texts were finished in the pre-episcopal period of Julian's life. Hillgarth interprets this youthful interest of Julian in the Augustinian writings as an intelligent and remote preparation of the young theologian Julian for the edition of his future works, in which he had the opportunity to make ample use of the writings of Augustine. He, therefore, learning from the fathers, prepared the arsenal of the fundamental tools[692] and the textual authorities with which he would subsequently construct his works. The collections of patristic texts, as well as of pagan poets and historians, were therefore the intellectual undertaking of the young Julian of Toledo.

Another *Liber responsionum*,[693] which promoted the right to asylum inside the churches.

The *Liber missarum*,[694] already quoted, which contained all the texts of the eucharistic celebrations of the liturgical year according to the Mozárabic rite in use in the Church of Toledo. Julian tried to restore the Missal to its native beauty and purity.[695] In this work of arrangement he manifested also a great knowledge of the Roman liturgical texts as well as of many patristic texts that lent themselves to liturgical adaptation.[696] Julian was, therefore, after Eugene II and

Ildephonse, the one who contributed more than anyone else to the definitive development of the Mozárabic liturgy.

We have a confirmation of it in the *Letter of the Spanish Bishops*[697] (792–793), sent to the bishops of Gallia on the occasion of the adoptionist heresy, in which they, refusing the heresy of Elipandus and professing the orthodox christological doctrine, lean upon the authority of a series of fathers of the church who are named one after another: Ilarius, Ambrosius, Augustinus, Hieronymus, Fulgentius, Isidorus. But immediately after Isidorus, the bishops of Toledo are named: Eugenius, Ildephonse, and, finally, Julian. The learned bishops of Toledo are, therefore, added to the authority of the ancient fathers. Later in the same letter, the three Toledan bishops are named again for their important—and orthodox—contribution to the edition of christological and trinitarian liturgical texts.[698]

To this testimony we must add that of Abbot Samson, who, in his *Apologeticum,* used two very elaborate liturgical texts that he attributed to Julian, referring to him with great respect and veneration: *Doctor Iulianus*[699] and then *Sanctus Iulianus.*[700] Finally, at the beginning of the last century, Dom Férotin[701] discovered an *oratio* of Julian that commended forgiveness of the offenses received and is a further confirmation of Julian of Toledo's activity as editor of liturgical texts.

The *Liber orationum,*[702] or rather, a book that contained all the liturgical feasts of the local Church of Toledo,[703] updated, amended, and completed by Julian.

The *De remediis blasphemiae*[704] is quoted by the biographer Felix.[705] The text of this work, dedicated to a certain Abbot Adrianus, has been identified by both Dom Morin[706] and García Villada[707] with a *Tractatus,* whose manuscript, kept in the Casanatensis Library in Rome, does not contain any attribution of authorship. The *Tractatus* is devoted to the study of the condition of the souls after the bodily death, and it was edited by Cardinal Mai[708] and then inserted by J.-P. Migne into his *Patrologia Latina.*[709] The title of the *Tractatus* is indicative of its content and is, in part, similar to the title of book II of the *Prognosticum:* "Utrum animae de humanis corporibus exeuntes mox deducantur ad gloriam vel ad poenam, an expectent diem iudicii sine gloria et poena."

The attribution of the *Tractatus* to Julian of Toledo and its identification with his *De remediis blasphemiae* have been, however, doubted and denied, with serious reason by both Madoz[710] and Hillgarth.[711] The latter considers it prudent to continue to attribute the interesting

Tractatus to an anonymous author. Thus, the *De remediis blasphemiae* still remains a lost work of Julian of Toledo.

The works not attributed to Julian of Toledo

By now it seems certain that the following works are not attributable to Julian:

The *Commentarium in propheta Nahum.*[712] In the opinion of most scholars, this work, which is not in biographer Felix's list, is not attributable to Julian for reasons in the manuscript tradition and intrinsic to the text, thus for reasons of a literary nature and of style.[713]

The same can be said of other works erroneously attributed to Julian of Toledo:

The *Chronica regum Wisigotthorum,*[714] a brief list of the Visigothic kings up to King Witiza, who was raised to the throne in 697, that is, after Julian had been dead for seven years.

The *Carmina duo quae cum apologeticis P. Romanae Ecclesiae missa* sunt,[715] some poetic texts that Julian had supposedly addressed and sent to the pope on the occasion of sending the two *Apologetica.*

The *Quattuor Epitaphia,*[716] dedicated to Ildephonse of Toledo, to his predecessor the Archbishop Quiricus, to Gudila, his dear friend who had died at a young age and, finally, to King Wamba.

It is quite surprising that Bishop Julian, so occupied with pastoral ministry and in active participation in the tumultuous political life of Visigothic Spain, nonetheless always managed to find time to devote himself to study of the Sacred Scripture and the works of the fathers of the church and to writing his many literary, historical, and theological works. Evidently, Julian was accustomed to a heavy work load, but he obviously knew how to organize it in the best of ways, making wise use of the time at his disposal.[717]

CHAPTER III

THE *PROGNOSTICUM FUTURI SAECULI* (687–688): THE MOST ANCIENT SYSTEMATIC TREATISE ON CHRISTIAN ESCHATOLOGY

The *Prognosticum futuri saeculi* is a theological work devoted to Christian eschatology that was written by Julian, bishop of Toledo, in 688 c. In it we see one of the links of junction that in the early Middle Ages allows us to connect both the thought of classical works and the theology of the fathers of the church to culture and to medieval theology.

But the *Prognosticum* is not a common book of theology. Overcoming the rosiest expectations of its author, its diffusion in the medieval epoch was extensive. Without a doubt, the theological-systematic and eschatological specifications of Julian of Toledo in this work "ont nourri l'imagination medievale. Il n'ait guère de bibliotèque qui n'ait possedé, seul ou regroupé avec d'autres récits de visions, le Prognosticum Juliani."[1] According to another author, the *Prognosticum futuri saeculi* can be considered "a manual on the future life, which enjoyed immense influence in the Middle Ages."[2] And for its historical-theological importance, it can be included in the "tableau des principales sources auxquelle s'alimente le pensée de nos pères."[3]

In this sense, therefore, Julian's work is the first treatise of Christian eschatology in the form of a complete systematic synthesis and was above all other works considered to be the "manual insostituibile"[4] of eschatology for nearly the entire Middle Ages as well as for a good part of the history of Western Christian theology. Julian of Toledo is important for having been the first theologian to transmit to the medieval generation "la dogmatique des fins dernières" in a systematic form, gathering the best of the patristic tradition with regard to eschatological themes,[5] logically connecting them in a systematic way and adding a set of rational conclusions of remarkable meaning on the methodological and theological level.

The first historical account of Julian's editing of the *Prognosticum futuri saeculi* is in Felix's brief biography of Julian compiled only three years after his death. Felix affirms that Julian wrote "the book of the Prognostications of the future century devoted to Idalius, of blessed memory, having at the beginning a letter directed to him and a prayer."[6] The brief but complete description by Felix continues in the summary of the three books that compose the work ("in tribus libris habetur...opus discretum") and their content: "of which the first one treats of the origin of the human death; the second, of the souls of the dead ones, in that condition they are found before the resurrection of their bodies; the third one, of the final resurrection of the bodies."[7]

According to his biographer, the basic elements of Julian of Toledo's principal work are the following: the title of the work (*liber prognosticorum futuri saeculi*); the recipient of the work, who, in this case, was Idalius "of blessed memory," bishop of Barcelona, who was already dead by the time Felix wrote the biography of Julian; a dedicatory letter set at the beginning of the work and directed to the same Idalius; and, finally, the beautiful *oratio ad Deum* with which Julian recommends himself and his work to the Lord Jesus Christ and which immediately precedes the text of the three books of the *Prognosticum.*

Many scholars assert that the content of the works of Julian, in particular that of the *Prognosticum*, suggests that they are a chain of patristic texts concerning eschatology that the author has gathered in an intelligent way. This description is only partly true and is in reality too reductive. Even if the *Prognosticum* cannot be considered a completely original work because of its reference to the texts of the fathers of the church, it is not merely reducible to a simple anthology of patristic texts that can be likened to other patristic collections in existence at that time.

Julian's work has a logical internal structure. It derives from a theological project and is the result of a close theological dialogue that arranges the choice of the eschatological matters to be treated in a theological way. It is also a work that required dedicated editing and that uses a new methodology that, with help from the texts of the fathers of the church, considers the eschatological truths as a fundamental dimension of theology and of Christian anthropology. For every eschatological question considered, from death's origin to the contemplative vision of God by the souls separated from their bodies, Julian of Toledo is quite capable of finding, critically selecting, and introducing into his essay a precise reference to one or more works of the fathers of the church.[8] Along with this critical selection, he labels the passages with an explanatory and thematic headings and makes distinctions based on the quality of the reasoning and the deductions he makes through critical reflection on the theme being treated. Hillgarth remarks that, in addition to his scientific reasoning, Julian uses another, more pastoral and popular methodology that foresees the choice of rhetorically dramatic patristic passages.[9] This is shown, for example, in the treatment of St. Cyprian's *De mortalitate*, which reassures Christians who are afraid of death; or the story of the incredulity of the physician Gennadius about the survival of the soul after death, a doubt that brings with it serious anthropological and theological consequences if not dispelled through the story of the oneiric experience of the doubting subject; or other concrete episodes of life as related in the writings of Augustine (*Progn.* 1.15; 2.33.27). In short, along with the critical and demythologizing dimension of his reflections, Julian tries often to give an exemplary, illustrative, ascetic, and pastoral tone to the *Prognosticum* that is perhaps less appealing to the modern reader, but that, according to Hillgarth, was certainly more attractive in the time of Julian, who was "so intensely concerned with the Last Things." The *Prognosticum*, however, as we will have the opportunity to verify, is neither a book of visions related to the description of the afterlife nor a book that narrates a journey in the hereafter.

Therefore, the *Prognosticum* is a work undoubtedly geared toward theological, scientific, and pastoral purposes that seeks to produce a certain doctrine in eschatology (in this sense the work can be said to be "scientific"), and that uses all means, including rhetoric as an art or method of persuasion,[10] to disseminate the truths related to eschatological realities as they were taught by the fathers of the church and by the pastoral magisterium of the bishops of the seventh century. This means, as Hillgarth points out,[11] that the *Prognosticum* is very different from Julian's other works. For instance, it is very different from the ideological anti-Judaic controversy of his *De comprobatione sextae aetatis* and from the defensive character of the *Apologeticum* (unfortunately lost) and of the *Apologeticum de tribus capitulis*, which is strongly polemical against those from Rome who accused Julian of heterodoxy in christological matters. But the *Prognosticum* is also just as different from the *Antikeimenon*, which focused on the exegetical resolution of the apparent biblical contradictions. These works of Julian are written to learned and experienced readers of exegetical or dogmatic matters. Instead, the *Prognosticum* is theologically and pastorally aimed at resolving the problems of the faithful through a good and wise catechesis on eschatology. But the work is also intentionally directed to theologians, to propose to them a structured doctrinal eschatology compiled by Julian that resorts to the surest and most unassailable sources upon which all of theology is founded and nourished: the Sacred Scripture and the dogmatic Tradition of the church.

These are only some of the reasons why it would be too reductive to characterize the *Prognosticum* as simply a rich anthology of patristic texts concerning eschatological matters. Rather, it turns out to be a well-crafted theological system to benefit bishops, preachers, and parish priests engaged in the ongoing catechesis of their faithful. It is addressed also to nuns and monks, cultured laymen and laywomen who seek knowledge about matters of faith in order to have objects of meditation and spiritual reflection and to nourish and help their Christian faith develop and flourish.

The plan of the work shows the depth and the vastness of the theological vision of its author, who did not hesitate to treat the greatest themes of Christian eschatology (death, intermediate phase of survival of the souls, formality of the bodily resurrection, divine vision). First of all, it sweeps away the popular conviction that nothing can be said concerning eschatology in any great detail unless one appeals to mystical visions or to stories of journeys in the hereafter. Second, it shows that it is possible not only to speak of such realities but also to make them direct objects of study and to build a logical and rational system of the final realities that concern God, human beings, and the cosmos. Julian substantially completed this hermeneutical operation in a new way compared to the theological methodologies of the past. In addition, throughout his work he consistently tried to implement (with success) a literary style that would interest the faithful and the readers or listeners of his time. In fact, it did interest the medieval authors who devoted themselves to the vast works of philosophical-theological synthesis such as the *Sententiae* or the medieval *Summae*, for example,

Hugh of St. Victor and Peter Lombard, who used the *Prognosticum* for the construction of the eschatological section of their works.

In this bold approach to the central themes of Christian eschatology, Julian deliberately imitates the fathers of the church, who were not afraid to face matters of great theological and intellectual difficulty. They considered it important to build a series of dogmatic elements that would constitute the basis of the faith of the believers. To accomplish his purpose, Julian did not hesitate to employ the proper tools, such as his particular methodology, which allowed him to produce an organic treatment that was scientifically compiled.

For these reasons, it is preferable to define the *Prognosticum* not as merely a chain of patristic texts concerning eschatology, but as the first complete treatise on Christian eschatology written in the West at the end of the patristic epoch and at the beginning of the medieval theological and intellectual renaissance that would coalesce in the great philosophical-theological syntheses of Scholasticism. If the *Prognosticum* had been simply an anthological collection of patristic texts, one could not explain the immense success and the thousands of manuscript copies of the work in the libraries of Europe from the ninth to the twelfth centuries.[12] But above all one could not account for the great intellectual and theological influence that the *Prognosticum* had on medieval theology in structuring the scholastic treatise devoted to eschatology, or *De Novissimis*. (*De Novissimis* is the generic title/name of several treatises devoted to the last things in medieval theology.) It is reasonable to think that among the thousands of readers of the work of Julian of Toledo in the medieval epoch were the greatest theologians of the period: Alcuin, Bede,[13] Peter Lombard, Haymo of Halbertstadt, Burchard of Worms, and others, who preferred to use the work of Julian rather than other writings, because doctrinally it offered a valid and useful thematic synthesis of eschatology and because it fascinated medieval readers. The popularity of the *Prognosticum* was such that in the thirteenth century this work of Julian was translated into Anglo-Norman poetry,[14] which showed in an aesthetic way its deep and dogmatic content. The *Prognosticum*, therefore, must be considered "the first autonomous Christian eschatology."[15] Its extraordinary influence on subsequent theology shows that its approach to the elaboration of systematic theology was neither surpassed nor replaced by the Carolingian theologians who immediately followed, nor by the first theological syntheses that, in eschato-

logical matters, were not very creative but rather used the eschatological treatise compiled by Julian.

THE EXTRAORDINARY FORTUNE OF THE
PROGNOSTICUM: THE MANUSCRIPT QUESTION[16]

The editor of the valuable critical edition of the Latin text of the
Prognosticum futuri saeculi, analyzing the numerous manuscripts[17] of
the work that have come to us, reached the conclusion that originally
there existed two families of manuscripts of Julian's work.[18] Almost all
the manuscripts seem to be derived not from the first copy of the
Prognosticum sent by Julian to Idalius, bishop of Barcelona, but from a
second copy sent by *noster Iulianus* to Spassandus, bishop of
Complutum (today's Alcalá de Henares) from 683 to 693, a diocese
that belonged to the ecclesiastical province of Toledo and therefore
one under Julian's immediate jurisdiction. The date of delivery of the
work is not necessarily 688–689, that is, the date in which the
Prognosticum was probably written. But it seems obvious that the copy
to Bishop Spassandus was sent by Julian himself before March 6, 690,
that is, before the date of his death.[19]

The proof of this unusual manuscript derivation of the
Prognosticum can be seen in the fact that many of the more ancient
manuscripts of the work (ninth, tenth, and eleventh centuries) reproduce, in the beginning of the work, an inscription naming this mysterious Spassandus. This strange *incipit* is found in many manuscripts of
both families of codices and is probably due to the fact that this
solemn introduction was found already in the second copy or archetype of the *Prognosticum,* a copy that, as we have said, was the one
Julian sent to Bishop Spassandus.[20] The inscription was considered by
the faithful copyists to be an integral part of the work that was transmitted by the author himself, who evidently had dictated it to the first
or second amanuensis. This copy, addressed to Spassandus, would be
the origin of the chain of manuscripts of the *Prognosticum* up to the
eleventh century that was to spread throughout all Europe. If this
incipit is lacking in some codices, it was probably the result of the
uncertain evaluation of a copyist who decided to omit it.

Instead, the first copy of the *Prognosticum,* the one sent by Julian
to Idalius (at that time still without the letter of Idalius to Julian), did

not have the same fortune as the second copy sent to Spassandus. It was not circulated so widely, despite having been sent in turn from Idalius to Bishop Suntfredus (as was discovered by the letter that Idalius wrote him and that is contained in the critical edition of Hillgarth), and by him to other bishops of the ecclesiastical province of Narbonne. This interepiscopal diffusion toward the North of Spain and up to Barcelona and to the ecclesiastical province of Narbonne in Visigothic southern Gallia was not extensive enough that any Hispanic copy of the *Prognosticum* derived from the one sent by Julian to Idalius could have come to us.

Five codices were utilized for the critical edition of the *Prognosticum* in the Corpus Christianorum. Among the many manuscripts of the *Prognosticum*, two emerge above all as very reliable, that of the Abbey of St. Gallen (Switzerland) and that of the Abbey of Corbie (northern France).[21]

THE RECENTLY PUBLISHED EDITIONS
OF THE *PROGNOSTICUM*

Prior to the critical edition of the Corpus Christianorum edited by J. N. Hillgarth, the best printed edition of the *Prognosticum futuri saeculi* had been the one edited by some Spanish researchers for Cardinal de Lorenzana and published in 1785.[22] For this edition of the *Prognosticum*, however, they did not compare sixteenth-century editions of the work, preferring the edition of Douai (1564) to that of Lipsia (1536) and letting themselves be convinced that the former was more authentic because the latter possessed inaccuracies in the patristic quotations that had to be resolved by the editor. This choice reveals itself to be wrong, however, because as it appears from a careful reading of the manuscripts of the *Prognosticum*, Julian shows great accuracy in quoting the texts of the fathers.[23]

Subsequently the text of the *Prognosticum* and the other works of Julian of Toledo of the de Lorenzana edition were inserted by Migne in vol. 96 of his *Patrologiae Cursus Completus, Series Latina.*

PURPOSE AND CHARACTERISTICS OF THE *PROGNOSTICUM*

Like other works of Julian, for example, the *Antikeimenon*, the *Prognosticum* was probably conceived by its author as a practical manual.[24] He affirms in the introductory letter or *Praefatio* to the work, that the goal of the *Prognosticum* was to produce in the one who reads it, the best understanding of the great themes of eschatology, from the mystery of death to that of the situation of the soul after the death of the body (with the possibilities of eschatological purification, heaven, or hell). It is to this end that Julian gathered together in a small volume and concisely, the opinions and the most remarkable affirmations of Sacred Scripture and the fathers of the church on these eschatological themes.

Julian also seemed aware[25] that this was the first time in the history of Christian theology that this kind of work was produced with this didactic and practical purpose; he also knew himself to be the first Christian author to write it. His motivations for writing the *Prognosticum* are of a didactic-pastoral nature: it would have been too difficult for the ordinary faithful to go in search of so many biblical and patristic quotations that shed light on eschatological themes. So he decided personally to complete this work of *acceptio rerum* for the benefit of believers. This is also the reason for Bishop Idalius's approval. In his letter of thanks to Julian for having sent him the desired copy of the *Prognosticum*, Idalius exalts the "*brevitas*" of the work that he defines as "*studiosa*," or sought and realized through wise study and synthesis, in order to deepen the knowledge or the reasons for the Christian faith in eschatological matters. In such a way Julian could offer the light of biblical affirmations and of patristic intuitions to all of his readers and could disperse the doubts and illuminate the dark realities. It is not to be forgotten, however, that Julian composed the *Prognosticum* as a brief work because he knew the "praise" of *brevitas*, in a rhetorical sense, that had already been made by other illustrious intellectuals of the past, from Cicero[26] to Severinus Boethius, and hence he applied the methodological criterion of it to his work.

The aim of Julian was, therefore, to create an authoritative theological synthesis, supported by a system of biblical and patristic authorities (but also enriched with his reasoning) that appear especially in the titles of the chapters and in the connections of the quoted texts. Julian resorted so profusely to the patristic texts both to make his eschatology practically unassailable by being confirmed by so many patristic authorities and also to ensure its acceptability by the readership for which he intended it. It would certainly have been better if his volume had been accompanied by the reputation of its content: the best of the eschatological and doctrinal thought of fathers of the church, in a little space.

The practical aim soon transformed itself into an academic aim, in the sense that the work was destined also for the students of the Episcopal School of Toledo, who in their second course studied theological themes. Probably, therefore, the *Prognosticum* also assumed the role of a manual of theology written for clergy in formation.[27]

With this probable academic application, the *Prognosticum* finally assumed the role of a dogmatic[28] synthesis of eschatology, whose form was used by many subsequent theologians as the basis of their treatment on eschatology.[29] Concerning the originality of the *Prognosticum*, one needs to distinguish within the work, on the one hand, the ancient texts brought by the author that were already full of authority at the time when they were written and, on the other hand, the editorial work of Julian, who knew how to gather the texts and to connect them in order to achieve a doctrinal synthesis.

As to the question whether the *Prognosticum* can be defined as a dogmatic text, the matter is more complex.

THE *PROGNOSTICUM* AS A DOGMATIC WORK OF ESCHATOLOGY

Considering the titles of the three books of the *Prognosticum*, which are a contribution or an exclusive literary creation of Julian, one immediately realizes that one of the verbs often used by the author is the verb *credere* ("to believe"). The textual variations of the verb are different (*ita debere credi, credere, si credatur, oportet ut…credamus*). This continuous and explicit reference to the Christian faith, which is not only grammatical but directed to fundamental data in eschatological matters, assumes great significance and reveals in a deep way the intention of the author. In fact, Julian seems aware that if, prior to him, the fathers and theologians had not treated eschatological questions systematically but rather in an isolated way without worrying about forming a system of doctrinal truth, he realized that these reflections need to take on a synthetic and practical character in a new form (that of a *tractatus*). This would provide the readers not only with a valuable anthology of texts, well reasoned and ordered by an experienced hand, but also with a *corpus* of theological authorities who interact in the text in a collegial way, even if coming from different centuries and cultures, to constitute a doctrinal base. This is just what the *Prognosticum* would be for many centuries, both for believers and theologians and for researchers: a solid manual from which to draw the orthodox faith of the Catholic Church on eschatology. This is certainly one of the causes, as all the scholars have remarked, of the great dissemination of the *Prognosticum* from the ninth century to the end of the twelfth, when it became desirable to have some general theological syntheses. This extraordinary dissemination and enormous publishing success of the *Prognosticum* undoubtedly contributed to the influence of the work on the medieval theological schools and made the *Prognosticum* a dogmatic book and a fundamental milestone in the history of Christian eschatology well beyond the original intentions of its author.

In short, the *Prognosticum* has had to play the role historically of the book that contained the doctrine of the whole Church of Spain about eschatological realities. It was used as a sort of manual, a remarkable theoretical treatise: an "outstanding theoretical treatment of the whole Eschatology,"[30] of doctrinal catechism and mystagogy of a high level. This aspect denotes how much its author was concerned with pastoral interests alongside theological ones. The pastoral nature of the *Prognosticum* can be deduced from the fact that the work was personally composed by the primate of the churches of Spain, devoted and sent first of all to the bishops of Spain: Idalius of Barcelona, Spassandus, Suntfredus, and through him to the other bishops of the ecclesiastical province of Narbonne. The fact that the first recipients of the work were all bishops indicates that with his work Julian indeed intended to provide a pastoral and theological service to his episcopal colleagues so that, considering the doctrine that his work contained, they would in turn be able to transmit it to others. Through the bishops it is probable that the *Prognosticum* also spread among the presbyters in care of souls so that they in turn could make it and its contents known to the people of God, dispelling, as was hoped by the author, any doubts and superstitions, uncertainties and confusions, and making known to them the clarity and the reasonableness of eschatological realities found in the Christian faith. The believers would be nourished by solid doctrine on questions in which Christian people had always shown great interest.[31] It is not a coincidence, therefore, that when Julian wrote the *Prognosticum* he had already been bishop of Toledo for almost a decade and the primate of all Spain for several years. He represented the faith of all the Spanish churches, and he practiced, with a praiseworthy habit of collegial work together with his brothers in the episcopacy, a manifold magisterium for the faithful, above all during the councils of Toledo. As bishop he was also in the best situation to perceive the real needs of faith of the people of God.

We can legitimately suppose that the Hispanic-Visigothic bishopric appreciated the theological contributions of Julian, which were so tightly united to the pastoral concerns. Julian had already demonstrated that he knew how to interpret the role of bishop, sustaining with vigor in a bitter *querelle* with the Church of Rome the theological reasoning of the Spanish episcopacy in christological matters and reaffirming the legitimate autonomy of the Churches of Spain in treating pastoral and doctrinal problems. It is no surprise, therefore, that with the publication of the *Prognosticum* Julian desired again to demonstrate to the bishops and the faithful his magisterial function in matters of faith. This also helps us better to understand why Bishop Idalius, having read the *Prognosticum*, decided to send a copy of it to the bishop of Narbonne, so that he, after having appreciated it, could in turn make a gift of it to the bishops of the ecclesiastical province over which he presided, and so on. The close pastoral and intellectual bond that characterized the Spanish bishoprics of the seventh century clearly manifests itself in this communication or transmission of doctrine through the ascetic-dogmatic work written by their primate. Accordingly, from ecclesiastical province to ecclesiastical province the eschatological faith of the bishops of Spain was spread and taught to the people through a substantial doctrinal unity, realized in the pages of the *Prognosticum*.

Thus, the *Prognosticum* must not be considered a theological-intellectual exercise of a seventh-century bishop-theologian, but rather the expression of the common faith of the churches of Spain in the truths transmitted by the tradition. Julian synthesized it with a double magisterium: the first magisterium was derived from his position and from his episcopal ministry as vicar of Christ, successor to the apostles, master and authentic herald of the Christian faith; the second was the scientific magisterium, which came to him from his study and in-depth biblical, patristic, and theological-dogmatic knowledge and his vast culture. This personal scientific preparation undoubtedly brought an added value to his episcopal ministry and his theological magisterium, and it passed naturally through the writing of his works. As successor to the apostles, Julian had received the assignment to teach and to be the principle and the basis of the unity of faith of the faithful submitted to his care; but as primate of Spain he also had to be the basis of the unity and the doctrinally correct faith of his fellow bishops. One can well say, then, that the eschatology of the *Prognosticum* represents the eschatological faith of all the churches of Christian Spain as taught by their bishop primate. Julian appears as the last great theological and pastoral figure of seventh-century Visigothic Spain in whom is reflected the doctrine of the great theologians belonging to the patristic age and of the ecclesiastical writers who lived shortly before him.

But there is another important reason why Julian wrote his eschatological work, a reason that we can assume to be the silence or the void of the magisterium of the Catholic Church in eschatological matters. For some centuries in fact, the ecclesial magisterium had been entirely silent on the matter of eschatological doctrine. Julian's initiative in publishing his work can be interpreted, therefore, as indicating the concern of the Spanish episcopacy to fill this void in an autonomous way, and that it considered itself to have the abilities to elaborate, with the theological intelligence of the primate of Toledo, a corpus of eschatological doctrine that was gathered together and interconnected. Objectively we can say that any local or national church of this period could boast of having a doctrinal apparatus similar to that of the Hispanic-Visigothic Church of the sixth and seventh centuries.

The dialogic origin of the work shows even more the value of its final result, since it is the ultimate demonstration of the ecclesiological custom of the Spanish episcopacy to communicate and to discuss problems collegially and together find the solution and the suitable answers, even of a doctrinal nature, to pastoral, liturgical, and theological problems.

Beginning in the sixth century, dangerous heresies circulated in the Iberian Peninsula, more than anything else of a christological nature, such as Priscillianism. Strange theological conceptions were also being affirmed, however, that questioned the survival of the soul after death and that raised strong questions about the difficult matter related to the material identity of the bodies of the risen ones.[32] The magisterium of the Catholic Church had not yet produced dogmatic texts about these difficult questions. The composition of the *Prognosticum* seems, therefore, to be the answer to this silence, considering that the object of discussion between Julian and Idalius, at the origin of the second and third book of the *Prognosticum*, concerned precisely these two problems: the situation of the souls after death and the conditions of bodily resurrection. In short, it seems that it can be said that the eschatological problems debated in this period are treated scientifically, relative to the time, in the *Prognosticum* of Julian. Accordingly, the *Prognosticum futuri saeculi* can also be considered a "contextual" book for the theological problems of the time.

Although theology, beginning with Julian, constantly focused on eschatology and made meaningful doctrinal contributions, we must wait until the end of the thirteenth and the beginning of the fourteenth centuries for an important dogmatic intervention by the magisterium of the church in eschatological matters, which was sparked by the stormy question of the homilies preached by Pope John XXII in Avignon, and when his successor, Benedict XII, published the Dogmatic Constitution *Benedictus Deus* (1336), which put an end to the infinite discussions aroused by the intervention of the so-called heretical pope.

If what Hillgarth affirms is true, that is, that "in the Prognosticum it is impossible to discover the theology of Julian if we separate his theology from his sources,"[33] then the converse can also be understood. We would hardly have so complete and deep a treatment of eschatological matters if Julian, with his theological method, had not retrieved and systematized in a logical way the most important and authoritative affirmations of the fathers on the subject, and if he had not pondered them with an original and scientific rigor, to reach a satisfactory level of thematic completeness. Without Julian's work of synthesis, in short, the reflections and reasoning made by the fathers of the church would have been lost in their works, and they might not have had the powerful influence on theology and the magisterium of the following centuries that they did enjoy because of Julian's eschatological synthesis, which was accepted by the greatest Scholastic theologians.

Therefore, if it is true that Julian and his eschatology could not have existed without the fathers, it is also true that without Julian and his work, the eschatology of the fathers, because of its fragmentary nature, would not have exerted such a great influence on subsequent theology and on the ecclesiological dogma that started to assert itself only at the beginning of the fourteenth century on the trail left by the eschatology of Julian of Toledo.

Thus, the *Prognosticum* can be defined as a true historical-dogmatic treatise on the essential truths of Christian eschatology: origin and transformation of death in Christian death; the state of the souls surviving and subsisting after the bodily death and before the resurrection or recovery of their bodies; the condition of the risen ones in the eschatological world or definitive kingdom of God, up to the contemplative vision of the divine essence. All this has been achieved with the irreplaceable contribution of divinely revealed Scripture and through the systematization of the main eschatological affirmations of the fathers of the church, before whom Julian always referred to himself as a humble disciple, considering them to be true and inaccessible giants, and showing them, ever since the beginning of his career as shepherd and theologian, a boundless admiration.

Even if with a pinch of Iberian chauvinism, Cardinal Lorenzana, in the preface to the edition of the works of Toledan fathers,[34] intelligently says that if Julian of Toledo had done with the other fields of theology what he did with eschatology, that is, create a dogmatic synthesis, we would not have had to wait for the medieval syntheses such as those of Peter Lombard and the other Scholastics in order to have a *summa* of theological sentences. Unfortunately, owing to his brief earthly existence, Julian of Toledo did not have the time to undertake such a manifold theological synthesis. He did, however, succeed in writing important works that even today, from a distance of thirteen centuries, are appreciated and sought to be understood.

DEVELOPMENT OR EVOLUTION OF DOGMA IN THE *PROGNOSTICUM*?

We now come to the most delicate and important question. It could be formulated thus: Is the *Prognosticum* a work that contains an important theological development of eschatology or a true dogmatic evolution of it?

Some authors affirm without hesitation that the *Prognosticum* is an "original dogmatic synthesis."[35] Others say instead that "in the *Prognosticum* there is no evolution of the dogma."[36] The opinion of J. Madoz, however, is that Julian brought meaningful changes in the way of doing theology. Invoking the authority of J. de Ghellinck in matters of knowledge of medieval cultural institutions, Madoz says, "su labor de sistematización asociada a la de Isidoro de Sevilla y a la de Tajón de Zaragoza, imprime un verdadero progreso scientifico en la Teología, no superado por el mismo renacimiento carolingio."[37]

This requires clarification. From a certain point of view, precisely that of theological methodology, Hillgarth's affirmation is maintainable: in Julian's work there is no evolution of dogma, if by these words we mean the addition of new theological doctrine to those previously existing. This is not because Julian, with his methodology, was unable to make progress within his systematic synthesis of eschatology but, on the contrary, because in his work, as in all works of theology, there can be no dogmatic evolution in the strict sense of the term. Dogmatic evolution, in fact, denotes an unpredictable and unexpected growth of theological knowledge, a real new truth, a jump of so ample a meaning as to be inapplicable as such to the truths maintained by the theologian. Rather, dogmas, understood as strengthened, encoded, and crystallized truths, come from the affirmations of Sacred Scripture and Tradition that are universally interpreted by the church. The truth taught and proposed as the belief of the faithful owes its being, therefore, to divine revelation. Otherwise it is considered the fruit of human talent, or at least not revealed. Only divine revelation can produce an evolution of doctrinal truths, as, for instance, happened in the crucial passages from the faith and doctrine of the Old Testament to the faith and doctrine of the New Testament, from the monotheism of the ancient covenant to the monotheistic tripersonalism of the New Testament.

Insofar as it is possible to define the *Prognosticum* as a first systemization, in the scholastic sense, of Christian eschatological faith, it is at the same time possible to say that this work, coming after the first seven centuries of the church's history, had as its aim to summarize the thought of the patristic age and to use the well-defined patrimony of historical-dogmatic elements to point toward new developments.

The same thing can be said of the contribution made by the works of Isidore of Seville, Taio of Saragossa, Ildephonse of Toledo, true anticipators of the theological method that will develop enormously in the Scholastic epoch. If the contribution of Julian and of his *Prognosticum* is not dogmatic in a pure sense, it can nevertheless be defined as an inner dogmatic development of the theology that will lead to the production of a synthesis of the dogma of the last things. This means that he did not invent or add any theological or dogmatic truth to the eschatological doctrinal corpus of the church, but that for the first time, in an absolute way, it was presented in a systematized and organically structured way, allowing new starting points to be deduced from this system that would aid in obtaining a global vision of Christian eschatology.

To further clarify this reflection, we can quote §25 of *Lumen Gentium*, in which, as is well known, the Second Vatican Council teaches the truths pertaining to the magisterium of the bishops and the pope. At the end of the paragraph, it is written that when defining a point of doctrine the ordinary or extraordinary magisterium of the bishops and of the pope, even when they are pronouncing infallibly, does not produce a new and absolute truth but explains and develops the examined matter, which, in any case, has its origin in revelation, that is, in Sacred Scripture and Tradition. Accordingly, the dogmatic definitions cannot be interpreted as evolution, but as a development pronounced "in accordance with Revelation itself... which as written or orally handed down is transmitted in its entirety through the legitimate succession of Bishops and especially in care of the Roman Pontiff himself, and which under the guiding light of the Spirit of truth is religiously preserved and faithfully expounded in the Church" and that "the Roman Pontiff and the Bishops, in view of their office and the importance of the matter, by fitting means diligently strive to inquire properly into that revelation and to give apt expression to its contents; but a new public revelation they do not accept as pertaining to the divine deposit of faith."

In the case of the *Prognosticum*, the eschatological dogmatic synthesis of Julian is the result of the ordinary magisterium of two bishops in matters of faith and, subsequently, of Bishop Julian's scientific magisterium, acquired through the personal study and the comparison of the doctrines of his episcopal predecessors, namely, the fathers of the church. This means that Julian starts with the primordial unity of the faith as witnessed to by the fathers, to reach the unity of theology, produced by the gathering together, as teachers and doctors, of many church fathers who through Julian continue to teach eschatological doctrine together. Julian considered himself to have been taught by the fathers and therefore saw fit to teach, in turn, what he had received. This is the purest concept of tradition, beginning from 1 Cor 11:23; 15:3.

In short, in the transition from divine revelation to its dogmatic elaboration, Julian is found in the last stage, that of the first coding that is written in the form of a *summa* or of a historical-dogmatic *tractatus* of a synthesis containing eschatological doctrines. As such, the work of Julian reenters and represents one of the phases of producing dogma, in its theological and methodological development. He does not proceed *per via* of authority, however, as happens when one starts from dogmatic definitions of the magisterium. Rather he proceeds by way of the transmission of the ecclesial doctrine.[38]

The fathers themselves, those theological authorities who meet the Christian criteria of antiquity, universality, and unanimity,[39] are the ones who assure, by means of their doctrine and their consensus, that the eschatology contained *in nuce* in Sacred Scripture was presented by Julian, in a global and concise way, as a founded general-dogmatic formulation.

Julian undoubtedly used reasoning and argumentation to achieve what was dear to him: the first systematic synthesis of Christian eschatology. But precisely because it was the first synthesis to have been produced it was to be subject to improvements, corrections, and completions. Julian took the first step in this direction. It seems, therefore, that Julian and his *Prognosticum* accomplished what had been hoped for in the times of Vincent of Lérins, that is, a progress or a decisive development of eschatology. It has grown and changed without losing its identity. Therefore Julian achieved a work of extraordinary importance with regard to the content and the systematic writing of eschatological doctrine.

If a great part of the eschatological truths summarized by him still today constitute the eschatology of the Catholic Church, this means that he has had a decisive role in the formulation of those same truths. It also means that he has been the means of transmitting the doctrinal corpus of the fathers to subsequent theological elaborations: Carolingian, monastic, and Scholastic. Julian's intention was not to furnish examples of theological opinions but to offer an unas-sailable, sure, and stable doctrinal corpus, with a clear basis in revela-tion and in tradition. With the eschatology of Julian of Toledo, completely grounded in Sacred Scripture and the fathers, and with his added reasoning, we are thus faced with a classical case of *senten-tiae fidei proximae.*

It seems correct, therefore, to complete Hillgarth's undoubtedly true assertion, "in the *Prognosticum* there is not any theological dog-matic evolution," with the following expression: but there is undoubt-edly a development of the eschatological dogma, and the treatise of Julian of Toledo can be defined, in such sense, as the first historical-dogmatic treatise on Christian eschatology. Julian did not create *ex nihilo* a new doctrine (which would be an evolution of dogma), but rather he used the vast existing material to construct "a meaningful building." Nor did he ever intend to show his readers unknown things (*incognita*).[40]

The history of theology comforts us when it tells us that the eschatology elaborated by Julian was gradually to develop into the eschatology of the monastic and Scholastic Middle Ages. From here it came to be approved by the Catholic Christian magisterium, not only concerning the great distinction between the final eschatological phase and the intermediate eschatological phase but also concerning some doctrinal points about the theology of death, the purification of the soul, and the resurrection.

The original contribution of the *Prognosticum futuri saeculi* to Christian eschatology: the doctrine of purification in the afterlife

From the theological point of view the *Prognosticum*, besides being the first complete essay on eschatology in the history of the Western Christian theology, offers original eschatological formula-tions not found in a systematic way in the preceding centuries, either in the works of the fathers of the church or in the doctrinal docu-ments of the church. These formulations represent Julian's personal contribution to the dogmatic formulation of eschatology and demon-strate that the *Prognosticum* is not only an ordinate anthology of bibli-cal and patristic texts but a theological work upon which the author wanted to "leave his own personal imprint and thereby contribute to the evolution of Catholic eschatological doctrine."[41] Undoubtedly the most original contribution of the *Prognosticum* consists in the elaboration, to which the whole of book II is devoted, of the so-called intermediate eschatology. In it, in fact, the author, on the basis of the biblical and patristic data, developed a rich theory about the providential survival and subsistence of the soul from the dramatic moment of bodily death and up to the final event of the universal resurrection. About this situation of the soul Julian traces a network of logical, anthropological, and theological connections that, at the end of his work, show a complex and almost complete synthesis of the matters related to the condition of the soul separated from its body.

Many authors prior to him, ancient philosophers as well as Christian theologians, had already expressed themselves concerning the separated soul, but none of them had organized the theme of the condition of the soul after bodily death in a summarizing and comprehensive way, nor had they answered the many questions about the state of souls after death and before the resurrection. In particular, Julian felt the need to know if souls separated from bodies could already be in condition to live their eschatological outcome and in what way. There were many existing theories, but there was no doctrinal clarity on the matter—not even by the magisterium of the Catholic Church, which remained quite silent about the question. Julian, however, grounding himself on the liturgical ecclesial praxis of intercession for the deceased that had been an important feature of Christian life ever since the beginning of the third century, and interpreting the *lex orandi* as a sure indication of the *lex credendi*, decisively elaborated the whole book II of the *Prognosticum* (and some parts of book I), dedicating it completely to this theme. He thus succeeded in treating the matter, reasoning through the problem, and providing a satisfactory solution to the theme of the individual eschatology or eschatology of the souls.

Obviously, the value of the *Prognosticum* is not merely in having elaborated this wise distinction, which renders justice to the eschatology of the individual and of his/her soul, but in having logically and theologically connected this important theme to the essential one of the eschatological destiny of the community of human beings, and thus in the collective perspective of the universal judgment of God upon humanity and history, and of the final resurrection of the dead, which is constitutive of the eternal church.

Prior to Julian, no one had thought of formulating a treatise about the state and condition of the souls separated from the body, nor, in fact, did anyone ever think about uniting this theme to a subsequent treatise concerning the final resurrection, the universal judgment of God, and the destination of the whole cosmos (which is the subject of book III of the *Prognosticum*). Julian of Toledo successfully maintained these two phases of eschatology in a "maravilloso equilibrio entre los dos elementos de esa dualidad,"[42] that is, between an anthropological perspective, which gave due attention to the eschatological destiny of the single human being and his/her soul, and a collective perspective, or better, ecclesial perspective, which is developed, as it is known, throughout the Bible, and especially in the New Testament.

Concretely, the original contribution of Julian to the Christian eschatological doctrine consists in having elaborated an eschatological system that was an "evolución que muy lentamente coinduciría a la construcción de un Purgatorio."[43] It is probable that Julian was aware that with his theological reflections he was contributing to the birth of a new level of theological knowledge, superior to that of the preceding centuries, even if his eschatological vision benefited from the doctrine of the fathers. As we shall see better in the theological commentary, Julian succeeded in retrieving from Sacred Scripture the most convincing proof text for the intercession for the deceased: the Second Book of Maccabees. Yet he did not forget to underline an important methodological principle of theology by which, even if Sacred Scripture could not furnish a foundation for the construction of doctrine, the church could promote with its doctrinal authority, in this case on the liturgical level, the development of an innovative doctrine.

García Herrero maintains, moreover, that Julian achieved a theological rationalization based on which he reduced the four anthropological categories elaborated by Augustine as an "estructura dual duplicada,"[44] to three, in an eschatological sense of ethics and religious. Thus, while Augustine distinguished the post mortem condition of the dead in *boni, non valde boni, non valde mali*, and *mali* (good, not fully good, not fully bad, and bad), attributing the condition of otherworldly purification only to the *non valde boni*, and damnation as the only eschatological outcome for the *non valde mali* and the *mali*,

Julian sustained a threefold structure of the eschatology of the souls: that is, the *boni*, the *non valde boni*, and the *mali*, so as to be able to easily identify the condition of the *non valde boni* as a median condition or as a third state of souls, intermediate between beatitude and damnation. The *non valde boni* are, therefore, the souls of those who, in the most opportune ways foresaw by divine providence, can undergo a purification and become *boni* thanks to the work of suffrage of the church and the work of purification of God himself. Thanks to this concise work of Julian condensing the categories, this third possibility for the *non valde boni*, with respect to beatitude and damnation, thus became the basis of a doctrine that in the course of time would become the Christian purgatory.

This means that, according to Julian, not all the souls surviving bodily death immediately receive their eschatological destination upon departure from this world. Some of them are instead "detained" to be purified from their sins, that is, from those imperfections that prevent them from possessing perfect holiness.

Naturally, Julian does not refer to this situation of maturation or purification of the soul with the term *purgatory*, as will be done five hundred years later by theologians of the twelfth century.[45] He actually prefers the term *healing of the soul* (in our opinion, a more fitting expression also for contemporary eschatology), because these souls are subject to the care of the heavenly physician. But Julian does not disdain using also the term *ignis purgatorius*, purifying fire, because it conforms to the suggestion of some fathers (such as the two great ones, Augustine and Gregory the Great) and to the biblical testimony that sees in fire a symbol of purification.

More than on these images, however, Julian insists on the fact that this possibility of purification in the afterlife must be interpreted as a metahistorical extension of the providence of God and christological redemption, because God does not want to lose any of his own. Therefore, a last chance, a supplement of grace to obtain divine pardon for minor sins, is given to those who are imperfect. Julian, however, cautions one not to conceive of this fire, a symbol of purification, as the fire of damnation to which Jesus alludes in his preaching or eschatological discourses. Julian knows that the words of Jesus are always a performative and allegorical language. For Julian there can be no confusion, because purification leads to glory, while damnation is the eternal deprivation of the eschatological aim, or rather it is the anti-eschatology.

Insofar as Julian of Toledo is at the origin of the formulation of the ternary scheme of the eschatology of souls, not only can we attribute to him, at the end of the seventh century, "the clearest and most complete exposition of the Early Middle Ages about the future purgatory,"[46] but also, and above all, the beginning of a new methodological and theological development that will move the incipient medieval systematic theology from the substantially dualistic vision, in eschatological matters, that originated from the eschatological thought of the patristic period.

The genesis of the *Prognosticum*: THE THEOLOGICAL DIALOGUE BETWEEN JULIAN OF TOLEDO AND IDALIUS OF BARCELONA

The occasion that gave birth to the idea in the mind of Julian of writing the *Prognosticum* was the conclusion of an intimate mystical-theological dialogue between Julian himself and the bishop of Barcelona, Idalius, which occurred on Good Friday[47] of 687[48] in the rooms of the episcopal atrium[49] of Toledo.

The old bishop of Barcelona[50] had come to the royal city for the celebration of the Fifteenth Council of Toledo, which had been convoked by King Egica and over which Julian himself presided. The bishop's health had been precarious most of the time because he suffered from painful attacks of gout,[51] an incurable illness at the time, and it prevented him from traveling and participating as he would have liked in the important Hispanic-Visigothic episcopal meetings. He was therefore accustomed to sending deacons or archdeacons to represent him in the councils. But for the Fifteenth Council of Toledo, perhaps because of a significant improvement in his health, he made a heroic exception and submitted himself to a fatiguing journey of hundreds of kilometers on notably uncomfortable roads to reach Toledo, the see of the council.

Bishop Idalius was welcomed with brotherly affection and veneration by the archbishop of Toledo and was given hospitality in the episcopal palace, perhaps in a small apartment situated in the atrium. The day of the dialogue between the two bishops coincided with the most important day of the year from the point of view of the Christian calendar: Good Friday, the day of the universal redemption and of the

expiatory sacrifice of Jesus. As it is known, Good Friday is a day of liturgical silence during which the church abstains from the eucharistic
liturgy to highlight the historical redemptive sacrifice of the Lord in
his death and burial. Julian describes that memorable day spent with
the bishop of Barcelona with emotion and touching words in the dedicatory letter or preface of the *Prognosticum*, which was written to
Bishop Idalius. Julian remembers how his colleague and he had gone
to secluded places within the episcopal atrium better to experience
the great day of Good Friday, and how they had sat on little beds or
settees prepared for the occasion, wrapped in warm covers. With the
book of the Gospel in hand they recalled the Lord's passion, which
touched them to the point of tears. From this emotion a contemplative and mystical climate was born relating to the death of the Lord,
which made them enjoy the moments of this great spirituality and
awareness of the love of God.

Later, in this holy and mystical climate, starting perhaps somehow with the death and the permanency of Jesus in the sepulcher, the
two bishops began to question themselves about the state of the souls
between the event of their bodily death and the final event of the universal resurrection.[52] This was the true nucleus of the dialogue and
likewise, in the text of the *Prognosticum*, it was undoubtedly the most
important theological doctrine of the whole work. The dialogue began
as an eschatological discussion that brought the two dialogue partners
face to face with some of the related themes, such as the condition of
the souls without the body. Yet they did not find easy solutions or perfect accord, but rather they discovered in Sacred Scripture elements
that could clarify the issues and yield a satisfactory answer, or else they
searched their memories for passages in the works of the fathers that
could shed light on other possible solutions to the problems raised and
about which they had not reached an accord owing to the intrinsic difficulty of the themes. They thus passed the hours of that holy and austere day in continuous reference to Scripture and the patristic
Tradition without the support of the codices and manuscripts of the
works of the fathers, actual research into which would have consumed
much of the precious time shared between the two bishops.[53] This is
also the reason why Julian stresses that the quotations were retrieved
from the visual or intellectual memory of the two theologians.

It was at this point that Idalius persistently asked for the presence of a clerk or *notarius* who could fix in writing that which Julian

identified as the chapters[54] of a future work concerning those holy
and deep conversations, for fear that those intuitions and titles would
fall into forgetfulness. Julian does not tell us the name of the fortunate clerk called to so great a charge. It can be hypothesized that he
was one of the secretaries of the archbishop of Toledo or one of the
students of the second cycle of studies of the Episcopal School of
Toledo, already experienced in quickly writing notes on wax tablets
or, perhaps better, on some parchment sacrificed for the occasion.

Idalius finally succeeded in obtaining the promise from Julian
that as soon as he had the time, he would gather in a brief volume the
problems they had faced and the solutions they had found together
on that memorable day of dialogue. Idalius evidently considered valid
the content of the theological solutions he had elaborated together
with Julian, maintaining that they were worthy enough to be put into
writing for future use. The greatest worry at that point was methodological and didactic in nature. In fact, not wanting future readers to
be forced to procure the codices of the texts cited by Idalius and
Julian relating to the eschatological questions addressed, they agreed
that the work that Julian was to write would have to contain an anthological collection of the texts themselves, gathered together for the
convenience of the reader[55] and coordinated and logically situated in
the correct place. Additionally, Julian promised to treat all the most
important matters relating to another mystery of the faith, one that
could not be overlooked in the Christian eschatological vision: that of
the resurrection of the body, and this was to be in a second book of
the work.[56] Finally, the two bishops decided that it would have been
judicious if the two aforesaid books devoted to the state of the souls
after the death and to the resurrection were preceded by a further
thematic book devoted to human bodily death,[57] with the purpose of
clarifying the origin and meaning of death, and to try to root out the
fear of death from the mind of believers.

In such a way the theological triptych composed by the two bishops took on the nature of a true systematic treatise, in that it addressed
a whole section of the mysteries of faith and of the Christian creed.

The *Prognosticum* was actually written by Julian in a period of
time after the theological dialogue had occurred with Idalius. It is difficult to know precisely when Julian composed his work, but it is likely
that this happened in the months following the dialogue, between
Easter and autumn of 687/688. Julian recalls in the preface to the

Prognosticum that in those months the royal city of Toledo was empty, since the king (Egica) had departed for a military expedition, bringing with him not only the army but also part of the palatine court.[58] This situation of relative calm, with fewer audiences to be asked of the king and with fewer official appointments, probably allowed Julian the necessary time to concentrate and reflect upon the themes that he wanted to treat in his volume, besides satisfying the request of Bishop Idalius.[59] For the determination of the date of the work it can be useful to remember that the copy that Julian sent to Barcelona, to Bishop Idalius, though obviously not dated, informs us that Idalius was indeed in Barcelona and had been waiting several months for the copy of the work promised by Julian. Some months had passed, therefore (perhaps six or seven), after the Fifteenth Council of Toledo.

It is not difficult to visualize the archbishop of Toledo working in his scriptorium, the table laden with codices of patristic works, the Sacred Scriptures, the *Collectio Hispana*, all of which were continually pored over and consulted by the author in search of the passage or the correct biblical verse. It is an even more difficult enterprise if we recall that at that time neither the Bible nor the works of the fathers were divided into chapters, verses, or paragraphs. Finding a text was not a simple thing, which is the reason why in the episcopal or monastic schools great importance was given to the use of memory. One should not doubt, then—rather it is probable—that in the elaboration and editing of the text, Julian availed himself of one or more clerks or secretaries. The point is that in a few months, working briskly in the morning and in the afternoon, the logical structure of the chapters of the *Prognosticum*, divided into three books, was filled with authoritative texts from the Bible or from the fathers, along with the valid and convincing reasoning of the author. At the end of the work, Julian had compiled a useful collection of biblical and patristic texts on eschatological themes that had previously not existed and was logically connected to the themes enumerated by him. This compilation was strengthened by the addition of his reasoning, ability, and linguistic elegance. Above all, Julian had produced the first systematic treatise of Christian eschatology, and he was aware of this milestone and of being the first author to compose a work of monographic synthesis on eschatological matters.

The title of the work

We know with certainty the title that Julian, upon careful reflection, had personally decided to give to his work: *Prognosticum futuri saeculi*. It was a happy choice because the title, even if immediately comprehensible, also alludes to knowledge of a not-easily-accessible reality.

J. N. Hillgarth, editor of the critical edition of the *Prognosticum*, concludes that the term *Prognosticum* is preferable to the Greek version, *Prognosticon*.[60] All the ancient manuscripts,[61] in fact, contain at the beginning of the work the Latinized form *Prognosticum*, while only some later manuscripts, which are of lesser importance, bear the Greek term, though, in any case, always transliterated into Latin characters.[62]

We have firsthand testimonies attesting to the correctness of the Latinized title. First of all, it is found in the two letters of Idalius of Barcelona, the first addressed to Julian and the second to Bishop Suntfredus. In addition, the *Praefatio* of Julian and the *Vita Iuliani* written by Bishop Felix confirm the correctness of the title. Idalius and Julian, in mentioning the work, call it *Prognosticum*, while Felix uses a declined and plural title, but always Latinized: "librum prognosticorum futuri saeculi."[63]

The testimony of the letters written by Idalius to Julian to thank him on the occasion of the arrival in Barcelona of the first copy of the *Prognosticum*, which is dedicated to his colleague and sent to him by a messenger—whose name we know, the Jewish Restitutus—and to the Bishop Suntfredus, is objectively important. In the letter to Julian in fact, Idalius informs us that the title of the work, written at the beginning of the codex sent to him by Julian, is *Prognosticum futuri saeculi*. He gives us a further Latin translation of the first term of the title: *prae-scientia futuri saeculi* and says that he considers it very expressive and valid.[64] This remark means that the title of the work was not discussed by the two bishops on the occasion of their theological dialogue, but that it was personally chosen by Julian. Idalius speaks of it as if read for the first time, and he appears entirely in accord with its choice and its meaning. In the letter to Suntfredus, then, Idalius repeats the title of the work, without however giving a translation of it.[65]

The second direct attestation of the title of the work is found in the preface to the work written by Julian himself. In it the author says without any hesitation that the work's title is *Prognosticum futuri saeculi appelletur.*[66]

Contrary to what was proposed till now, the literary tradition has preferred giving to Julian's eschatological work the Grecizing title of *Prognosticon futuri saeculi.*[67] This was the case, for example, in the edition of the *Prognosticum* printed in Lipsia (1536) or in Douai (1564), from which the edition de Lorenzana (1785) was derived and inserted in the *Patrologia* of Migne.[68]

The Greek term *Prognosticon*, Latinized into *Prognosticum*, was the title of some works of Greek, Latin, and Arab authors who preceded Julian by many centuries and some who followed him, The term *Prognosticon* indicated foreknowledge, for example, in Hippocrates[69] in a medical sense; in Cicero[70] in a philosophical sense; in Avicenna[71] again in a medical sense. Likewise, many ancient, medieval, and modern astrological works bear the same name.

In the case of Julian, the meaning of the term is found in the *Etymologiae* of Isidore of Seville: "forecast of the course of an illness, so called by the verb praenoscere that means to know in advance or before."[72] For Julian this is really the most important meaning of the word: anticipated knowledge of the future realities. In such a sense it can be helpful to know that the term *Prognosticum* was used also in describing the content of a literary or theological work, such as in the information that Honorius Augustudunensis furnishes in his four books of the *De scriptoribus ecclesiasticis*,[73] in which he speaks of an author beloved by Julian, his namesake Julian Pomerius, who has so often been confused with him throughout the centuries. According to Honorius, therefore, Julian Pomerius wrote three *prognosticos* on the contemplation of the future realities, in his *De contemplatione.*

We can certainly suppose that Julian knew that the term *Prognosticum* was of Greek origin and that his decision to use a Greek term (as for other works of his) was probably determined not only by a vogue or intellectual mannerism of the time, but especially by the recognition of the expressive power of the Greek term, and perhaps by the reflection that saw in the Greek language the very root of the most ancient and cultured expressions of the Christian faith.

From the semiotics point of view, the title of the work personally chosen by Julian undoubtedly possesses a series of remarkable meanings. Certainly it is not a self-explanatory title, nor does it allude to a study of a science or of an art.[74] It is also, perhaps, a deliberately ambiguous title so as to attract the curiosity of the reader. But in reality, in the *Prognosticum* there is nothing to make one think about extraordinary revelations or, as Hillgarth says, "el contenido no es nada sensacional."[75] Julian intended more probably to allude to knowledge of a theological nature related to fundamental themes of the Christian faith, acquired with the intellectual rigor of its author. We are not able, however, to exclude the possibility of an aesthetic and literary or phonetic reason behind the choice of the title *Prognosticum*.

The title of the work comprises three words: the first, *Prognosticum* is, if we can say so, a "profane" or "pagan" word (considering that different *Prognostica* are attributed, as we have seen, to classical authors in both a medical and an astrological sense). The term makes one think about something esoteric, that is, written for the initiated or something mysterious: namely, the anticipated knowledge of things that are not easily accessible to everybody or to immediate perception. The selected term, therefore, probably had the purpose of attracting the attention and the curiosity of the frequenters of the medieval libraries. Probably the "rapid y brillante fortuna"[76] that the *Prognosticum* had from the ninth to the twelfth centuries in the Christian religious culture of Europe depended only in part on its title, which promised a significant increase of knowledge in the readers concerning such a difficult and dark subject as eschatology, above all as it related to the state of the souls after death or to the conditions of the future bodily resurrection. The dedicatee of the work, Bishop Idalius, in his letter thanking Julian for having sent him the manuscript codex, wrote that the term *Prognosticum futuri saeculi* could be translated in Latin as *Praescientia futuri saeculi*, meaning an anticipated knowledge of life, time, or the future world. The *Prognosticum*, however, does not have any of the characteristics typical of the books of prophecies, apocalypses, or esoteric visions that claimed to disclose the secrets of humanity, God, history, or the hereafter,[77] indicating with precision events, characters, and extreme situations of human history and divine intervention. On the contrary, the text of Julian potentially demythologizes an eschatology, or rather, a sensational apocalypse, and, as he himself says and as can be understood from reading the text, it is an argumentative and didactic science that has as a solid base the affirmations of Sacred Scripture and the intellectual and theological authority of the fathers of the church of the first six centuries of the

Christian era, with the addition of a series of conclusions of great interest achieved by applying the method of deduction.

If it is true that the *Prognosticum* satisfied the "curiosidad de los fieles sobre 'toutes sortes d'inaccesible problèmes,'"[78] then it is just as true that there is no trace of an exaggerated esotericism in the *Prognosticum*. Perhaps it is precisely for this reason—that is, for its solid methodological structure and for its contents, which did not feed popular beliefs or superstitions or cater to visionary and apocalyptic sensationalism—that it was so successful. Therefore, elaborating on these biblical-patristic foundations, Julian was able to draw objective and deep theological propositions to communicate to his readers, in a serious and reasonable way as well as in a didactic and catechetic-doctrinal way, clarifying the proposed matters without having the presumption of violating those mysteries that God has not deemed opportune for us to know on earth.

The other two words of the title, which are genitive singular, seem to resound with biblical language and are also notably mysterious because they allude simultaneously to an indefinite time (the *saeculum*), projected into the future, or to a world that is also in the future and that is, therefore, inaccessible. Or they refer to the life of the future, as Hillgarth suggests.[79] This second part of the title: *futuri saeculi*, can be considered, therefore, entirely "Christian"—that is, for centuries being part of the elementary lexicon of the faith. For example, the text of the creed that was recited at the opening of the Fifteenth Council of Toledo said: "exspectamus resurrectionem mortuorum, vitam futuri saeculi."[80] The *vita futuri saeculi* is, in a general sense, the eternal life promised by Christ to his believers. In the sense of theological investigation it indicates all the problems related to the existence of such a life or of the world following the earthly world, and it implicates a whole series of theological matters such as the survival and subsistence of the soul after bodily death, the state of the souls between death and resurrection, the real possibilities of the beatitude, purification, and damnation of the soul, and, finally, the problems related to the new heaven and the new earth where the risen ones will dwell and live.

Knowledge of the Greek language
at the time of Julian of Toledo

The term *Prognosticum*, used by Julian at the end of the seventh century in a culture that one can say was still entirely influenced by the Roman civilization, is derived from the Greek language. This raises the question about the knowledge and use of Greek in the early Middle Ages.[81] Certainly a considerable number of Greek words were known in the West and were used in medieval Latin. The reason for such knowledge depended on various factors. First of all, the schools of the ancient period produced some glossaries in bilingual form, Greek and Latin. An important example of such glossaries or Latin-Greek dictionaries includes the so-called *Philoxenus*, of which we possess an exemplary manuscript from the Carolingian period.[82] Another manuscript of the same work existed in France up to the sixteenth century at the Abbey of Saint Germain de Près and was used by Stephanus in the 1573 edition of his *Thesaurus Graece Linguae*. Thereafter nothing is known about the manuscript. There is, however, *e converso* a Greek-Latin glossary, called the "Glossary of Cyrill," in an uncial manuscript of the eighth century belonging to the library of Nicholas of Cusa and now located in London. According to some scholars of the dissemination of Greek in the medieval era, this glossary could be from the seventh century and, therefore, from Julian's period. Yet added to the question of the date is that of the origin of the glossary—that is, if it is to be considered Italic or from Gallia. It is not certain whether it belongs to the Byzantine area or to the Lombard area, and if it dates to the Merovingian or Carolingian epoch. Nonetheless, these four possibilities are geographically and temporally quite close to one another, and some of them are particularly close to the cultural area in which Julian lived and operated. Without intending to advance a concrete hypothesis, one could, nonetheless, presume that the intellectual curiosity of an exegete and theologian such as Julian would have brought him into contact with such a work as this "Glossary."

On the other hand, we must also remember that the fashion of using Greek terminology both in the writing and in the titling of works was common to authors such as Quintilian (first century AD), Lactantius (third century AD), Jerome (fourth century AD), and above all the Iberian Prudentius (fourth century AD), who gave Greek titles to almost all his works. Many of these writers were considered authors of reference in the medieval period, and thus models to imitate. Often, then, the corruption of words was such that it led to the belief there was a real *grecolatinum* in quite frequent use by intellectuals from the fifth to the seventh centuries.

Moreover, there was frequent use of the Greek language and Greek expressions in the technical language of the seven liberal arts, especially in rhetoric, astronomy, and music. Besides, many Greek words and different Greek expressions entered into the Latin language through the adoption of material objects, techniques, and arts or oriental models of behavior. Thus, for example, terms were added such as *analysis* in philosophy (Albertus Magnus was the first one to use this term), *astrolabe* or *astrolapsus*, and so on.

Bearing in mind that in the educational system of the early Middle Ages, the teaching of the seven liberal arts was a structural element of formation, one could draw some interesting conclusions from the fact that Julian, having attended a school of the early Middle Ages as well as an ecclesiastical school, would have somehow acquired enough knowledge of Greek, or at least of a basic Greek vocabulary, to be used in some of his works.

Western Christian theology has experienced the influence, and I would also say the charm, of the Greek language ever since its origins, and the use of the Greek language, especially of some phonemes, has become part of the theological lexical patrimony throughout the centuries. Likewise, many Greek words and specific terminologies have also been introduced into the medieval Latin dictionary. Among the many possible examples, W. Berschin cites the following: *anthropus* (with the end of the word by now Latinized) and the compound words *chiroteca, bibliotheca*; the words preceded by *arc, anti, pseudo*; and the terms *catholicon, dragmaticon, geronticon, gnotosolitos* (from *gnōthi seauton*), *metalogicon, Pantheon, Proslogion*. We have pointed out that almost all the works of Prudentius bear Greek names, and only one in Latin. These examples provoke emulation, and many authors, including Julian of Toledo, opted for the Greek forms of the titles of their works even though the works themselves were written in Latin characters: for example, the *Antikeimenon* and the *Prognosticum* of our author. We abstain from quoting the two *Apologetica* of Julian because it was a Greek term that was considered in common use and fully assimilated into the Latin dictionary of the educated.

In short, the learned, though somewhat improper, use of Greek terminology was a cultural tendency of the early Middle Ages that is not to be regarded as a mannerism or to be attributed to intellectual fashion. Rather, it was a characteristic of the creativity of the authors that consisted in adapting Greek words to Latin use because, according to them, the Greek language rendered the theological language more effective, precise, rich, and full of nuance, while also stimulating the reader (who also had to make an intellectual effort or do a little research to understand the meaning of the new words).[83]

DID JULIAN KNOW GREEK?

As we know from history and from literary documents, the ancient *romanitas* was to a large extent bilingual. This means that Latin and Greek were considered the expressive languages of the empire and, undoubtedly, were abundantly used for expressing the Christian faith, in liturgical texts as well as in theological works. Beginning from the end of the fourth century, however, it could no longer be supposed with certainty that Greek was known or that it was taught[84] in all of western Europe, even in the cultured class. This led to the need, which soon became absolute necessity, to possess translations from Greek to allow for access to literary works, particularly the theological works written in Greek by the great tradition of the schools of theology in Alexandria, Antioch, and so on. But there were naturally some praiseworthy exceptions. Among these was probably Julian of Toledo, who seemed to know Greek, even if it is difficult to establish to what degree or level he knew the language of the Athenians, and, above all, if he could read the Greek codices of the fathers of the church. Verification of this ability would undoubtedly constitute an element of further knowledge of *noster Iulianus*.

Julian of Toledo was the author of many important literary works that manifested his cultured and religious, intellectual and literary, spiritual and pastoral personality. His best contribution is probably the ability to elaborate theological syntheses and produce argumentative formulations and theological comments. Julian also composed christological texts of notable refinement and difficulty,[85] in which with self-possession and rare competence (for his environment and his time),[86] he used a language and new or at least unusual (for Western christological Latin theology) theological terms in order to explain the christological mystery better.[87] It is probable that in the formulation of such explications he drew upon Greek patristic theology, as shown by his second *Apologeticum*. Yet, according to many contemporary researchers, he was also the author, as we have seen, of an excellent *Ars grammatica*, which included many quotations of classical authors (as well as biblical and patristic authors). In that work Julian introduced an appreciation of the excellence of the Greek language, which, in our opinion, is of great significance. The text about the clarity of Greek with respect to all the other languages, as J. Madoz affirms,[88] was not composed by Julian but was taken from the writings of Isidore, who in turn drew from an affirmation of Augustine.[89] Undoubtedly Julian's decision to include in his grammar a text laudatory of the Greek language leads us to believe that he did not intend to limit himself, to a simple use of Greek, for example, only in the titles of his works, but that he was accustomed, as shown by some of his works, to drawing upon the thought of the fathers or of the Greek writers for the excellence of their thought expressed through their clear language, which Julian appreciated greatly.

Julian is also the author of a historical work, the *Historia Wambae*, which, in the opinion of many, is structured according to the historiographic methodology of the classical period, even if at the same time it shows itself to be an innovative and unique work in many respects.

Finally, it is not insignificant, even if it does not prove anything, that Julian had the intellectual taste to give a Greek title to two, or perhaps three, of his works: the *Prognosticum*, the *Antikeimenon*, and the double *Apologeticum* (this term actually is to be considered more as a very consolidated Latinization, rather than a Greek word). For some, this suffices to establish that Julian had some knowledge of the Greek language. The mere use of Greek in the titles of his works, however, does not seem to be a valid argument for establishing with certainty his knowledge of the Greek language.[90] This custom probably came to Julian from a dual source: first of all, it was commonly used by Latin writers, dating back to pagan antiquity.[91] Second, this choice could have matured in Julian as the result of his readings, for example, of the *Etymologiae* of Isidore of Seville or other works. In any case, the choice denotes a certain intellectual refinement, and it implies that the author devoted a certain attention to the choice of the titles of his works since he regarded the titles as important for their self-

explanatory force or for the initial impact of his writings on his readers. We note, along with Madoz,[92] that the biographer Felix underlines
the originality of the title for only one work of Julian, the *Liber de contrariis*, that is, the *Antikeimenon*,[93] overlooking the other two works of
Julian that bear a Greek title (or mixed Greek-Latin title): the
Prognosticum futuri saeculi[94] and the already Latinized *Apologeticum*.[95]
He evidently considered these two terms as already in use and part of
the common Latin lexicon among scholars.

To the considerations made thus far, however, we add a last
datum, a quotation previously mentioned, but particularly meaningful, if not decisive, for affirming Julian of Toledo's knowledge of
Greek. According to Hillgarth and Madoz,[96] in fact, the patristic quotation in *Prognosticum* III, 5 is, in reality, a rather free translation of a
homily of John Chrysostom, the *Homilia secunda de cruce et latrone*.
Since nothing is known about a complete Latin translation of this text
of Chrysostom, it can perhaps be traced back to the work of Julian,
who would have translated it for his use and inserted it in the text of
the *Prognosticum*. In this case it must be admitted that Julian had more
than an elementary knowledge of Greek. Madoz also analyzes other
works of Julian, searching for Greek patristic quotations of texts more
or less translated into Latin, or used indirectly by him.[97] But the conclusion at which he arrives concerning the quotation of the homily of
Chrysostom seems to leave no doubts: the translation from the Greek
language, he affirms, "es obra de St. Julián de Toledo."[98]

All these elements together, therefore, testify to Julian of Toledo's
knowledge of the Greek language. Julian, in fact, was of notable cultural, intellectual, and theological competence, a lover of Sacred
Scripture, but he also had a classical culture and great knowledge of the
theology of the fathers, both Greek and Latin, which he used extensively in all of his works. He was, moreover, bishop of a local church
in which his predecessors were illustrious for the high level of their
classical and theological culture as well as for their poetic art. Under
the guidance of Julian, the local Church of Toledo was to become the
primatial see of all the churches of Spain because of the doctrinal
splendor and the high cultural profile of his bishops. Moreover,
Julian's preeminence was by then undisputed, since as bishop he had
presided over and concluded four Spanish national councils and had
sustained, with notable courage and intellectual boldness and without
any obsequiousness, a *querelle* with the Roman curia and with the

bishop of Rome himself, from which, it can be said, Julian emerged victorious with head held high.

Accordingly, it is entirely possible to verify Julian's knowledge of the Greek language. It is testified to by the near certainty of some scholars not only that Julian's library possessed works of the Greek fathers in the original language, for instance, some writings of Epiphanius and Chrysostom,[99] but also that he could read these works, understand them, and eventually translate into Latin some parts of them to include in his works. On the other hand, Julian would not be the only one of the learned Hispanic-Visigothic bishops of the seventh century to manifest such a vast culture in comparison to the rest of Europe—possessing sufficient knowledge of Greek to read and to understand a patristic text. It is certain, for example, that Isidore of Seville, who had so much intellectual and theological influence on Julian, also knew Greek.[100] Thus, it makes little sense to deny that Julian of Toledo, so gifted culturally and not at all inferior to the great doctor of Seville, could likewise have a sufficient knowledge of the Greek language. The historical circumstances could confirm this hypothesis, considering that the southern Iberian coast facing the Mediterranean Sea had been, up to the sixth century, under Byzantine domination, and under the emperor Justinian such domination was renewed. If this culture had never been deeply grafted onto the Hispanic-Roman culture, it had certainly disseminated many Hellenistic elements in it.[101] Moreover, Byzantine influence "on Visigothic law, art and court ceremonial in the late 7th century"[102] has had an impact on the Hispanic liturgy.[103] Finally, the fact must not be underestimated that King Ervig, who was so attached to Julian, was of Byzantine ancestry and that his kingdom coincides almost exactly with Julian's episcopacy, and thus, precisely for this reason, the imperial city of Toledo could have experienced a strong influence by Byzantium.[104]

THE EDITION AND THE STRUCTURE OF THE *PROGNOSTICUM*

Together with Isidore of Seville and Taio of Saragossa, Julian of Toledo represents the beginning of a new theological methodology, in which the technique of the investigation leans on the double scriptural and patristic authorities, which are understood as complementary even if in a hierarchical order: first comes Sacred Scripture and then the theology of the fathers. As a qualified expert on classical culture, however, Julian does not disdain inserting into his texts some elements recalling, even if not explicitly but under the form of assonances, metaphoric allusions, allegorical dimensions, what he had learned from reading the classical texts. In short, he seemed to be aware of the theory of the complementarity between the classical and the Christian culture, as was shown by Origen or Augustine.

It is true that the *Prognosticum futuri saeculi* presents itself, at least apparently, in a literary form that was not unique.[105] In fact, at least in part, it is a collection or anthology of biblical and patristic texts. But it would be unjust, in any case, to say that the *Prognosticum* is only a collection or an anthology of patristic texts, because it is clear that those patristic texts that Julian quotes had never been selected, screened, and logically linked to form a doctrinal corpus. Julian made this choice and logically and theologically connected their more important affirmations with the biblical texts and his conclusions or logical reasoning. This is not a lesser way of doing theology but the inauguration of a new methodology that in the future would lead to more complex works such as the *Summae sententiarum* and the *Summae theologiae*[106] through which the thought of the fathers becomes a source of theological reasoning. Julian is the first one in his time to accord such great importance to the eschatological theme, at least with respect to contemporary authors, who gave, instead, a relative importance to this theme.[107] It is possible to maintain, therefore, that after the *Prognosticum*, the many works that would treat of eschatological themes would do so in dependence, consciously or not, on the system and the logical approach first compiled by Julian of Toledo.

The structure of the work presents itself, in fact, not as a collection of texts placed one after the other, nor as the fruit of the need to fight heresies. Rather, it takes on the form of a logical treatise, the first one devoted solely to the theme of eschatology in the entire history of Christian theology, even if, already from the beginning of the fifth century, summaries or manuals of the thought of the great doctors started to appear, which facilitated study for readers and researchers.[108] The *Prognosticum*, therefore, is one of the first examples of a new type of theological "treatise,"[109] a new methodological conception in which much doctrine is concentrated in the quotations but is expressed concisely also by an explanatory, dense, and summarizing title, the fruit of the intellectual effort of synthesis by the author, and of rational consideration. In this way, it can be supposed that works such as the *Prognosticum* and the *Sententiae* of Isidore of Seville and Taio of Saragossa represent a significant step forward in Western theological methodology, which becomes more and more reasoned, founded always on Sacred Scripture and on the fathers of the church. In the *Prognosticum*, in fact, and with a certain frequency, the author also intervenes in the body of the text to reason freely about the theme and to make connections among the numerous quotations, both intellectually and theologically, not only literarily.

Moreover—and this is particularly important—Julian thought that he could have said the same things that were found in the patristic texts, but he humbly preferred to let the authority of the fathers speak for themselves, placing them before himself and putting their doctrinal authority in direct light. Thus, there is a great deal of authoritative doctrine "in a small space."[110] It is as if Julian was obsessed by the problem of fitting a great amount of doctrine into a few pages of codex. Bishop Idalius greatly appreciated this editorial effort of Julian, and in his letter of thanks to Julian he congratulated the author and praised him for this *studiosa brevitas* of the work. The author probably considered the *brevitas* essential for reaching and satisfying more readers and not discouraging them with a voluminous treatise.[111] Julian probably considered this *brevitas* a didactic virtue, especially if, as is probable, the author also intended the *Prognosticum* for the pupils of the theological courses of the Episcopal School of Toledo. The students of the school would have certainly more appreciated a synthesis than a work of vast proportions.[112] As Hillgarth effectively says, in the *Prognosticum* there is "much learning in a small space."[113] He also reminds us that the writers of the Visigothic epoch frequently appeal to brevity, perhaps as an initial declaration intended to reassure the reader about the essentiality of the text.[114] In any case, the basic reason for this *brevitas* is to be understood in a widely pastoral[115] and didactic way.

The titles of the chapters are, undoubtedly, the most interesting part, methodologically speaking, of the work of Julian of Toledo, because they contain the author's theological synthesis and explication, in addition to the paraphrases of and the commentary on the biblical and patristic texts in the body of the work. The titles are substantially the theses reached by Julian on the basis of his biblical and patristic study of the matters that he posed and discussed with Idalius. Therefore they represent the synthesis of Julian's theology, as well as his original contribution to the field of eschatology. From the titles, the points of arrival of his investigation, he will start again in the inverse direction in the body of the text to place in evidence the contents retrieved from his sources. But, naturally, in the editorial disposition of the chapters and the books, the initial titles of the chapters become the points of departure that must be proved in the body of the text following the title. In reality, the hermeneutic process has already been completed by the author. He then didactically leads his readers through the same process, starting, however, from the synthesis (the titles) that he has already elaborated for them.

This leads us to suppose that in the long personal reflection after the theological dialogue, with which Julian was occupied for weeks, he put in writing the theological synthesis that he wanted, organizing the text in an admirable way, *per titula et capitula*. This was possible probably with the help of one or more scribes, who were certainly not lacking in the episcopal curia of Toledo, not only using the text of the Bible and the works of the fathers, but also the notes written by the *Notarius* during the dialogue with Bishop Idalius.

Making continual use of the above-described theological method, Julian saw his *Prognosticum* grow and develop to become, chapter after chapter and book after book, the theological manual of eschatology that we know. The final result was a brief, concise, essential text, just as its author desired, where there is objectively nothing superfluous, but everything is essentially connected to the treated themes, without the need to exceed either in the biblical quotations—which could certainly be more abundant than the ones cited[116]—or in the patristic quotations, for which Julian would have had only the embarrassment of the choice. Therefore, it contained "much learning in a little space," with sure and explicit references both to Sacred Scripture and to the doctrine of the fathers of the church. The *Prognosticum* is not to be considered a mere anthology of texts because of this concentration and thematic conciseness.[117] On the contrary, "it is one of the first of a new type of treatise,"[118] in which Julian becomes the author of a new eschatological theology, both because objectively there was no text of Christian eschatology before the *Prognosticum*, but also because the synthesis of Julian was composed with a methodology not much utilized at the time. The result of this new theological methodology is that, as Idalius wisely wrote to Julian,[119] doubts are dispersed, while the most difficult things to understand are illuminated. And if the truth emanates from the sentences of the fathers, a new and well-founded or very perfect synthesis is derived from the author's work of systematization.[120]

The *Prognosticum* is, therefore, a dogmatic work, ascetic as well, and it has the purpose of compiling, in a concise way, the most relevant eschatological data of the consolidated patristic tradition, which its author had assimilated very well, with the aim of systematizing it as a new doctrinal synthesis for the believers of his time.

Second, it seems important to mention the strongly anthropological, perhaps anthropocentric, approach of the three books that constitute the work. The eschatological questions are in fact addressed especially in relation to the human being. The interest in the human being pushes Julian to seek the truth about human death, its causes, and its origin, and to try to clarify the situation of the human soul after the physical death of the human being, with the separation of the soul from its historical body. In addition, the article of faith concerning the resurrection of the dead is treated in many of its aspects, sometimes in too much detail, against the background of the value of male and female corporeality, considered worthy by God himself of belonging to the renewed creation. Alongside this anthropological dimension of Julian's methodological approach must be added also the fundamental and strong christological and ecclesiological dimension of the work.

The first book of the *Prognosticum*, devoted to the problem of death, is entitled *de origine mortis humanae* and contains twenty-two brief chapters in which Julian faces the most burning questions related to the thorny thanatological matter. First of all, Julian tries to understand how and for what reason death entered the world. The answer is the traditional one considered by the fathers, contemplating the teaching of St. Paul, which affirms the dependence of death upon human sin. A series of chapters is then devoted to other matters: why death has been inflicted upon human beings; a curious etymology of the word *mors*; whether human beings were created as mortal or immortal (for this question Julian proposes an original solution); the distinction of the different kinds of death; the harshness of death; how its harshness can be transformed into goodness; why Christians do not fear, but rather, in a certain sense, desire death; how to prepare oneself for death and help the sick to die with Christian dignity; how to bury the corpses; how to help the deceased after their death; and so on.

The second book, which has a self-explanatory title: *de animabus defunctorum quomodo se habeant ante ultimam corporum resurrectionem*, contains thirty-seven chapters and can be considered the heart of Julian's work. It contains the nucleus of the theme that most interests him and that he intends to develop as much as possible: the so-called intermediate and vital condition of the souls of the deceased after their bodily death and before the final events of history. Julian confronts the problem of the so-called location or the places of afterlife. He does so with a notable critical spirit and a demythologizing orientation, offering a convincing intellectual solution; he then speaks of the admission of the souls to their metahistorical state, and subsequently he speaks of the souls regarding their state of perfection in comparison to the desire of holiness of God himself. Here he establishes the concrete possibility of the purification of the souls *post mortem* and of the vision of God (II, xi; xviiii–xxii). Of particular theological significance is his decisive affirmation in favor of a unitary anthropology when he says that the "defunctorum animae desiderent corpora sua recipere" (II, xi); a series of chapters affirms, instead, with the authority of the Bible and of the fathers, the extreme vitality (cognitive, volitive, affective, sensitive, etc.) of the souls of the dead (II, xv–xvi; xxiiii–xxxvii). Undoubtedly it is this insistence on the vitality of the souls separated from their bodies that is the most important anthropological and eschatological contribution of the *Prognosticum*, given the skepticism or agnosticism about the "life of the soul after death" that was already very widespread in Julian's time.

Finally, the third book, entitled *de ultima corporum resurrectione*, treats, in sixty-two chapters, a whole series of matters related to the final phase of eschatology. The questions are to a large extent in dogmatic and christological order, starting with the greatest matters related to the universal judgment and to the *parousia* of Christ the judge (III, i–xiiii); followed by the modalities of the resurrection and the nature or qualities of the risen bodies, but also many *quaestiunculae*, as Julian himself, calls them (III, xv–xxxi); then the modalities of the universal judgment (III, xxxii–xxxviii); and finally a whole series of problems related to the definitive retribution of the damned or the blessed ones, and of the cosmic consequences of the final events (III, xxxviiii–lxii).

Beyond the theological evaluation of the single themes, many of which Julian treats with a critical approach, it is important to underline that the *Prognosticum* has the great merit of recording and testifying how, already in the seventh century, it was taken for granted that the Christian eschatological doctrine must contemplate a double dimension or phase: an intermediate and a final phase, which are mutually complementary, and that this dual vision allows for the possibility of a progress of perfection in the souls of those who have left the world in a situation of substantial goodness, yet in need of maturation and additional purification.

But Julian goes beyond even this important theological achievement, because he consistently and successfully attempts to hold these two dimensions of eschatology tightly united and wisely balanced. This formulation seems to show the author's complex and integral theological vision. He knew well, in fact, that only in this way—that is, integrating the two anthropological aspects of soul and body and the double individual and collective dimension of eschatology—could he maintain fully intact the creative and redemptive plan of God. He knew well, that is, that God created human beings as a unity of soul and body, and as such redeemed them, but he knew also that God considered human beings in their double role of collective humanity and single human beings. This is perhaps the reason for the logical primacy of some realities over others. For this reason, God first of all redeems the human soul and gives it a metahistorical future, to make it participate with the body as well in the final and collective destiny of humanity in the resurrection of the body. This eschatological outlook has the great advantage of maintaining its connection with the historical salvific dimension, which is substantially collective, while it examines the metahistorical destiny of single individuals.

Therefore, the *Prognosticum* is a rational treatment of a series of themes of Christian faith, gathered under a logical-theological heading—that of eschatology—and addressed with the help of the Bible and patristic thought, but also by opening itself to the novelties of the *ratio* and of *argumentatio*, composing a corpus of eschatological truths. Before the *Prognosticum*, no one had furnished an overall theological perspective of eschatological character in so complete and balanced a way. The methodological and doctrinal structure of the work evidently had the intrinsic ability to guarantee itself. The history of theology confirms that the almost universal recognition of the soundness of the eschatological thought of Julian of Toledo, which occurred in the decisive centuries of the theological medieval systematizations of Scholasticism, constitutes the most valid recognition of the validity of his *Prognosticum*.

THE LITERARY, BIBLICAL, AND PATRISTIC SOURCES OF THE *PROGNOSTICUM*

"Well versed in patristic learning,"[121] Julian learned to love the fathers of the church through his formation at the monastery of St. Felix and at the Episcopal School of Toledo, under the direction and the intellectual enthusiasm conveyed to him by Bishops Eugenius II and Ildephonse of Toledo. But this initiation in the fathers would be the prelude to an ongoing and lasting contact that the mature deacon Julian would continue to have with the patristic sources, even in Greek, which was quite rare in the Western world at that time.

Julian's affection for the theology of the fathers is not to be interpreted as an indication of an underlying conservatism or of a lack of openness to the development of theological doctrine; nor as a sign of a static conception of theology, as if it were only to repeat and transmit what had already been said, once and for all, by the fathers of the church. On the contrary, Julian uses the fathers and their writings as authorities upon which to base the construction of a new theological synthesis and for the discovery of new ways of intellectual elaboration.

The many allusions or quotations that we find in his works, however, also involve the classical authors and their works: Virgil, Sallust, Livy, and many others, demonstrating his knowledge (whether direct or indirect is difficult to say) and love of classical culture.

The assiduous study of these two literary sources, so different from each other but so capable of expressing the desires, projects, and dreams of both humankind and divinity, is to be considered a constitutive reality of the character and the human, religious, and theological formation of Julian of Toledo. It can be said that he practically lived all his brief life in continuous contact with the texts of the writers of the past, pagans and Christians, as well as of the greatest ecclesiastical writers of his time.

According to Hillgarth, the literary sources of Julian of Toledo's works amount to around sixty, twenty-four of which are the works of those authors from whom he draws, even if more detailed studies of the *Antikeimenon* indicate that this number is destined to increase significantly.[122]

The most quoted Latin authors in the *Prognosticum* are Augustine,[123] Gregory the Great, Jerome, Isidore of Seville, Cyprian, Cassian, Hilary, Julian Pomerius, Orosius, Ambrose, Fulgentius of Ruspe, Abdias, and Eugenius II of Toledo. The Greek authors quoted in the work, however, though less numerous, are very meaningful: Athanasius, Origen, Cyril of Alexandria, Epiphanius, Eusebius of Caesarea, and John Chrysostom. According to Hillgarth, the Greek authors are almost all quoted from Latin translations,[124] with the exception, according to Madoz, of Chrysostom's *Homilia de cruce et latrone*, which, in his opinion, was freely translated by Julian himself. In any case, the greatest proportion of the quoted fathers are post-Nicene, while the pre-Nicene ones number only three: Origen, Cyprian, and Abdias.

Classical literary quotations are not lacking in the *Prognosticum*. Such is the case, for instance, of the quotations from Virgil identified by Madoz.[125] Hillgarth also identified a passage of Julian's *Praefatio* to the *Prognosticum* that clearly shows Virgilian influence.[126]

If it is certainly true that "the great authors of the Latin West of the century VI and VII were fundamentally authors of compilations and encyclopedists, rather than creators of new and original works,"[127] it needs to be said, however, that in the case of the *Prognosticum* this tendency is realized through a reasoned selection of the texts and, above all, through a critical reflection on the fundamental themes of the Christian eschatology found in them. The quotations, therefore, serve to structure the theses so as to form a system of theological *loci* eschatological in nature. With his *Prognosticum* Julian sought to establish the eschatological doctrine for the churches of Spain. That implies that the author already had an outline of the work he intended to undertake, and that he used his deep, often mnemonic knowledge of the fathers' writings to complete his work with authoritative quotations using a relatively new method. I say "relatively new," because to justify their theological and dogmatic theses, the ecclesiastical writers of the first five centuries leaned almost exclusively on the authority of Sacred Scripture, written under the inspiration of the Holy Spirit. Such doctrine could be considered a sufficient basis, both stable and universal, upon which to found the Christian faith. This methodology became widespread because the authors or the ecclesiastical writers were evidently not yet considered authorities or sources capable of constituting a homogeneous and stable tradition to place alongside Sacred Scripture for the purpose of expressing Christian theological doctrine.

But the method of Julian is relatively new precisely for this reason, because already halfway through the sixth century, the authority of the fathers of the church had become an ascertained fact, as shown, for example, by such a text as the *Confessio rectae fidei*[128] of the emperor Justinian (527–565), in which the author makes extensive use of patristic and conciliar references, together with scriptural texts, upon which to base the doctrine of the orthodox faith. This methodology, which attributes authority to the fathers of the church to be placed alongside that of Sacred Scripture, will set an example for so many subsequent works, and the *Prognosticum* will be among the first works in the West to acknowledge this new methodology. In any case, it is in this period that the fathers of the church, Latin and Greek, begin to be considered *doctores defensoresque Ecclesiae*, as Licinian of Carthage (d. 600) magnificently writes in a letter,[129] perhaps in 595, addressed to Gregory the Great. A similar thought, as Hillgarth suggests,[130] is present also in the dedication letter of the fifth book of the *Carmina*[131] that Venantius Fortunatus wrote to Bishop Martinus of the ecclesiastical province of Galizia. In this text the "new masters," that is, the fathers of the church such as Hilary, Gregory, Ambrose, and Augustine, are placed side by side with the greatest philosophers such as Plato, Aristotle, and others.

Julian of Toledo seems to have assimilated this idea and inherited this new methodological approach to producing a theological study, and he applied this new methodology to almost every chapter[132] of his *Prognosticum*, quoting one or more patristic authorities[133] to give a doctrinal basis to the title of the paragraph he composed in the form of a theological thesis. Therefore, he considered it both practical and valid to furnish his readers with a double series of data, biblical and patristic, upon which to base his demonstration of the final thesis.

The respect that Julian had for the fathers is absolute and, in fact, he often introduced authors such as Augustine, Gregory the Great, and Cyprian with honorary appellatives such as *Doctor egregius* and similar titles. The custom of quoting and leaning upon the authority of the greatest ecclesiastical writers would become widespread to the point that in 653, only seventeen years after the death of Isidore of Seville, the Eighth Council of Toledo would attribute to him the title of *Doctor*, accentuating, however, the fact that he belonged to the present time: "nostri quoque saeculi doctor egregius."[134] If Julian did not expressly quote Isidore of Seville in his works, except once,[135] it was probably because he considered him a contemporary and therefore not comparable to the fathers of the church, or—and perhaps this is a more interesting reason—because he considered him, as so many others of his time, his mentor, his adviser, one to be consulted daily for an etymology or a meaning or a *differentia*, for a concept or for a doctrine, especially if eschatological in nature. That there is no text of Isidore that Julian had not read and reread, and on which he had not somehow drawn for the editing of his works or to be delighted by for the clearness of the truth expressed by Isidore, always bearing in mind the spectacular praise offered by the Eighth Council of Toledo with the following words: "Nostri quoque saeculi doctor egregius, Ecclesiae catholicae novissimum decus, praecedentibus aetate postremus, doctrinae comparatione non infimus, et quod majus est in saeculorum fine doctissimus, atque cum reverentia nominandus Isidorus."[136]

It is clear that the intellectuals of the seventh century were aware that their own knowledge depended on that of previous authors and that it was subordinate to it. They had a true veneration for the ancient authors, considering them entirely superior to themselves. Julian expressed this attitude many times in the *Prognosticum* when he referred to the fathers of the church as the *Maiores*, whereas he and the other writers of his time were really and objectively to be considered the *Minores*.[137]

Therefore, one of the principal characteristics of the *Prognosticum futuri saeculi* as well as of other works of Julian, as also of many of the works written in the West by the authors of the sixth and seventh centuries and not only in Spain,[138] was to draw, in the editing of their works, from previous sources and authorities, above all with the purpose of justifying and proving the hypotheses and the resulting reasoning, and thus providing them with an absolutely authoritative, unassailable, stable, convincing, and lasting base.

It is not a lack of originality that is discernible in the dependence of Julian and other writers of his time on authors who had spoken and written about such themes before them. Rather, this dependence illustrates how much these authors valued the tradition and how they tried in every way to preserve it and to update it, with an almost sacred respect and with the desire to give a future to the fathers and to their works. They knew, therefore, how to select with great intelligence particularly meaningful texts from the earlier authors' writings that expressed broad agreement and great authority on the theme treated by a whole exegetical or theological tradition and that would have helped them to generate a complex and rich theological system. Julian expressly said in the *Prognosticum* that he would be able to demonstrate how he had expressed, in a nutshell, a theological hypothesis in the titles of the chapters of his work, but that he preferred to prove his hypothesis with the aid of the great doctors of the past, whom he calls, not by chance, *Maiores* (while, as we have already said, he qualified himself as belonging to the *Minores*). The fathers, in fact, "perfectly assimilated and made his own,"[139] were for him reliable witnesses of the doctrine they had received, elaborated, and developed, and then passed on. Besides, in the preface of the *Prognosticum*, almost as if wishing to stress that a great part of his work was of patristic origin, he affirmed: "in quo tamen non mea, sed majorum exempla doctrinamque reperies; et tamen si alicubi parum aliquid vox mea insonuit, non aliud quam quod in eorum libris legisse me memini, proprio stylo conscripsi."[140] According to Julian, therefore, intelligently furnishing a work with texts and quotations is not an operation without value or of scarce intelligence, but, on the contrary, is the demonstration of possessing a vast series of knowledge, often preserved mnemonically ("in eorum libris legisse me memini")[141] and very articulated, but above all the attestation of possessing a demonstrative method and of wanting to acknowledge a debt to the past. If, therefore, one can speak of an objective doctrinal dependence of Julian upon the fathers of the church, it is not to be understood in a passive and negative sense. It is, instead, a voluntary choice to appropriate the enormous wealth of the patristic heritage, and above all the consensus of the fathers, in order to advance theological knowledge for the present and the future.

Among all the fathers, Augustine is certainly the most frequently quoted by Julian and is thus the one with whose thought he was most intimately familiar. The second father in order of preference is Gregory the Great, very famous in Spain and celebrated by the Eighth Council of Toledo.[142]

Thus, the quotations that Julian includes in the *Prognosticum* are essentially of two types: those drawn from Sacred Scripture and those drawn from the patristic works or, sometimes, from contemporary authors in whom the author recognizes a greatness and an importance analogous to those of the ancient fathers.

The patristic quotations are often the same ones found in authors before Julian, but there is no reason to think that Julian had not personally read and studied the texts, perhaps having initially found them quoted in the works of Ildephonse of Toledo, Taio of Saragossa, Gregory the Great, Isidore of Seville, and others. Scholars believe that Julian's library must have been very well furnished with patristic literature, both Latin and Greek, if the *Prognosticum* contains lengthy quotations from Ambrose, Augustine, Cassian, Cyprian of Carthage, Eugenius II, Gregory the Great, Jerome, John Chrysostom, Julian Pomerius, and Origen. We are in debt to Julian for having made known to us the existence of some works by two authors that had been considered lost or were otherwise unknown, because he quoted some passages from them in his works: Julian quotes a passage from Eugenius II, from his work devoted to the Trinity,[143] and many passages from Julian Pomerius's important treatise *De animae natura dialogus*.

As emphasized by Hillgarth, Julian does not explicitly quote Isidore of Seville, although he has made use of his works, such as texts from the *Etymologiae*, the *Differentiarum libri*, and the *Sententiae*. The reason for this may be psychological: the strong bond that tied Julian to Isidore, considering the contemporary theologian as family for the churches of the Hispanic-Visigothic period.

In the *Prognosticum*, as we have mentioned, we also find some quotations from the Greek fathers: Athanasius,[144] Cyril of Alexandria,[145] Epiphanius of Salamina,[146] Eusebius of Caesarea,[147] John Chrysostom,[148] and the great Origen.[149] Some of these works are quoted indirectly,[150] but for others we must assume that Julian had Latin translations, which have survived, or more probably that he had enough knowledge of Greek to translate the passages that served him at that time to support his theological thesis.[151] Julian probably did not have to count

on his rich library alone. We know, in fact, that in the seventh century
in Toledo there were other well-furnished libraries and that it was not
unusual to lend the codices, as shown by a letter of Braulio of
Saragossa.[152] Moreover, in the seventh century there were a number of
anthologies of texts selected from the works of illustrious authors.
Julian's biographer informs us that when he was young, Julian had
gathered a selection of texts of Augustine in two collections of *sententiae* or *excerpta*[153] that would have served him in the following decades:
"Already he was amassing the arsenal of patristic learning he was to
put to such good use in later years."[154]

Like his theology, Julian of Toledo's pastoral activity was strongly
characterized by a deep bond with the fathers of the church and their
teaching. Julian was inspired by their pastoral method when, for
example, he promoted the formation and the education of the clergy
at the Episcopal School of Toledo, personally committing himself in
teaching, or when he gave priority in his pastoral ministry to the synodal dimension of the government of the church and of the churches
of Spain, summoning four times in the ten years of his ministry the
entire Spanish episcopacy or interacting with the imperial power to
seek the common good, even if it meant opposing the king. But Julian
was, above all, doctrinally very tied to the theological-doctrinal
achievements of the fathers, whose writings he appropriated "with
great personal sureness, fruit of an extraordinarily mature reflection
in theological field."[155]

Therefore, we can affirm that the *auctoritas* of Julian of Toledo
in eschatological matters really consists in the ability to make wise use
of the teachings of the fathers for the benefit of his readers and for
the development of eschatology. He became such a master of patristic
thought in eschatological matters as to be able to incorporate it
coherently into the theme being addressed. Thus, Julian prevented
the fathers from falling into obscurity, but at the same time he lifted
them from the context in which they had written their works as they
sought to furnish immediate answers in the historical-theological circumstances. In the patristic era, building an organic, orderly, and systematic synthesis of Christian doctrine was of lesser importance. Thus,
their numerous eschatological assertions were dispersed throughout
many works, and it would have been difficult for the common faithful, even the educated ones, to locate and synthesize even the most
relevant statements. Such an operation would have required time, a

deep knowledge of the subject matter, and a methodology of investigation and study that not all could have possessed. Preceded by others such as Isidore of Seville and Taio of Saragossa (to mention only those in the Hispanic-Visigothic circle), Julian had the idea of gathering the teachings of the fathers on one or more eschatological matters so as to offer those who were eager to know and to deepen their own faith a comprehensive synthesis of the solutions proposed by the fathers themselves for eschatological problems. As he explained in the *Prognosticum*: "This, therefore, seems to me the essence of the little question that I exposed, which even if I am unable to express in the same words with which the greatest have developed it, I nonetheless believe that it was defined in the same sense by the doctors, and even though I discover something of it, which they had defined, I prefer to follow their thought."[156]

THE MNEMONIC ABILITY OF JULIAN OF TOLEDO IN THE *PROGNOSTICUM*

In the *Prognosticum* Julian speaks often of memory, in both a positive and a negative sense, and he sometimes uses the verb "to remember" to indicate that he did not have before him the text he intended to quote but that he remembered that text, more or less—or at least he remembered the sense of it from having read it. What does this imply?

To us, great users of the printed word or of easily printable electronic pages, this statement can appear to lack a serious application to study. What we would think of a contemporary author who admits to having read in a certain theologian an important assertion but does not remember in what volume and on what page it can be found? We would accuse that scholar of approximation and of insufficient methodology. In Julian's time, however, memory was intensively utilized even in the elementary first level of studies, and for various reasons. First of all, writing material, being very expensive and usable only once, was at a premium; second, the use of quills and inks required a particular skill to avoid damage. The pupils of a school could not possess them, especially in the first years of their formation. Therefore the exercise of the abilities of memory compensated for the lack of possession of the parchments.

Evidently Julian preserved the use of memory as an adult as well, through techniques learned in his years in school. He looked upon this positively, although it sometimes betrayed the author, as can be noted in the text of the *Prognosticum*. In the *Praefatio*,[157] in fact, Julian reports a lack of memory with respect to the passage of Sacred Scripture that Bishop Idalius and he had read and meditated upon at the beginning of the day of theological dialogue that inspired the *Prognosticum*. Subsequently, however, in the same text, Julian states that during the theological dialogue with Bishop Idalius, they quoted the Catholic authorities "not with a continuous leafing through the books, but aloud, with the application of memory."

Another reference to memory in the *Praefatio* does not betray the author of the *Prognosticum*. Julian, in fact, with the great humility that characterizes him, discloses that his work does not contain *his* eschatological doctrine but that of the *Maiores*, that is, of the fathers, and if here and there the reader finds the thoughts of the author of the work, they are derived from what he remembers to have read in the books of the fathers: "in quo tamen non mea, sed majorum exempla doctrinamque reperies; et tamen si alicubi parum aliquid vox mea insonuit, non aliud quam quod in eorum libris legisse me memini, proprio stylo conscripsi."[158]

A suggestive but perhaps conjectural interpretation of this passage is found in a recent study by G. García Herrero, who contends that Julian was well aware that his work and his theology were contributing to the development of the eschatological doctrine of the Catholic Church, but that his humility caused him to hide this conviction behind the authority of the fathers. In fact, "en un tono engañosamente humilde"[159] he affirms that it is the doctrine of the *Maiores* (and therefore not his own) that is present in his work, even if he does not remember well (or pretends to not remember) the work from which has learned it. According to N. P. Stork, the use of memory is "the fundamental paradox in the composition of the Prognosticon," because in his work "Julian is remembering what he knows about the future, he recalls only those passages from his extensive reading that refer to future time and our fate in eternity. He blends Scriptural and Patristic authors in his quest to reveal the truth of our ultimate fate and inspire his readers to forsake sin."[160]

Still in the *Praefatio*, Julian makes another reference to memory, saying that having gained some calm as a result of the departure from

Toledo of the troops guided to battle by the king, he remembered his promise to Idalius to work on the written edition of the work projected with the bishop of Barcelona: "and so I happened to remember your command and my promise."[161] Finally, at the end of the *Praefatio* Julian makes a last reference to memory, saying that he had then finished the work and that it was due to two factors: argumentative distinction (*dinoscentia*) and memory (*recordatio*), a very elegant way of indicating the tools of his theology: the tradition and the organizational and penetrating ability, in a critical sense, that produce development and increase of knowledge.

In *Prognosticum* II, iiii, Julian says: "I remember having read about a distinction of the hells in the treatises of the blessed Augustine." It is a literary expression with which the author informs the reader that he did not have access, at that time, to the volume containing that text. As we have already said, Julian possessed an important and rich library, a rare and expensive thing in his times. The library of the bishop of Toledo had been founded before Julian, and it was already extensive at the time of Julian's last, more learned predecessors, Eugenius II and Ildephonse. Julian probably greatly enriched it with new acquisitions during his ten years as bishop, but the expression meant that the library did not contain everything and that Julian had thus read the quoted text of Augustine in another library or in a borrowed codex. In any case, it is evident from this text that the methodology of the writers of the seventh century relied on visual memory of the authors, which underlines the scarcity of resources at the disposal of seventh-century writers. They compensate for what is lacking with a developed exercise of memory, as well as with their intuition, ingeniousness, and intellectual ability.

Finally, in *Prognosticum* III, ii, alluding to a failure of his memory, Julian says: "I do not easily remember what I have read about it in some codices." Evidently this was another instance in which he was unable to recover that text in the codex where he had read it.

THE INTRODUCTORY LETTERS TO THE *PROGNOSTICUM*[162]

The letters of Idalius, Bishop of Barcelona

The letters of Idalius, bishop of Barcelona, to Julian, bishop of the primatial see of Toledo, and to Suntfredus, bishop of Narbonne, in southern Gallia, were transmitted together with the text of the *Prognosticum*, but not in most of the best codices.[163] The *editio princeps* of the letters of Idalius is that of the publisher Iohannes Cochlaeus. He published, in Lipsia (Leipzig), the two letters of Idalius in 1536, setting them at the end of the text of the *Prognosticum*.[164]

The *Prognosticum* edited by Cardinal de Lorenzana in 1785[165] contains the letters of Idalius to Julian and of Idalius to Bishop Suntfredus. The edition of Migne also contains the *Idalii responsio*, preceded by the letter-*praefatio* of Julian, but it lacks the letter of Idalius to Suntfredus. The latter is found, however, with the letter of Idalius to Julian, in the *appendix secunda*[166] to the works of Julian of Toledo in the same volume 96 of the Latin *Patrologia* of Migne,[167] reproducing the edition of Dom Luc D'Achery[168] (*ex Acherio, Specilegium*), monk of the Congregation of St. Maurus. His edition, in the opinion of Hillgarth, is not exempt from errors, and it was partially corrected subsequently by E. Flórez in *España Sagrada* in 1775.[169]

The letter of Idalius to Julian of Toledo

Since Idalius had received from the hand of the Jewish Restitutus the copy of the *Prognosticum* sent to him by Julian, it obviously did not contain his answer of thanks to the primate of Toledo. This means that the manuscript copy of the *Prognosticum* sent by Julian to Idalius contained only the letter-preface of Julian and the *Oratio ad Deum* of the author. When, then, Idalius's letter of congratulations and thanks, probably written in Barcelona in 689,[170] finally reached Julian, he evidently decided to attach it to subsequent manuscript copies of the *Prognosticum*. The same probably happened when Julian received a copy of the brief letter of Idalius to Suntfredus, in which he complied with Julian's intention expressed in the preface to the work, to make the work known to the bishops of the nearby ecclesiastical provinces. In any case, the reply letter to Julian was not delivered to Julian's Jewish messenger Restitutus; in fact, it was written some months later, when Restitutus had probably already left Barcelona.

It is likely that Idalius kept the codex of the *Prognosticum* for a certain period of time, reading and rereading it with satisfaction. But in the end, he ordered one or more copies to be distributed to the nearby bishops, the first one being Suntfredus, bishop of Narbonne.

The manuscript tradition of the letter of Idalius to Julian consists of two families of manuscripts,[171] by comparing which it has been possible to obtain a *textus emendatus* in which various errors have been corrected. The manuscript tradition of the letter of Idalius to Bishop Suntfredus, however, is less extensive.[172]

The letter of Idalius to Julian expresses the great respect that the bishops of Visigothic Spain, such as Idalius, had for the bishop of Toledo and the great regard they had for his theological thought, even if they were senior to him in age and in pastoral experience.[173] But, at the same time, the fact that it was probably Julian himself who wanted to insert the letter in the first copies of the *Prognosticum* means that the favorable judgment of Idalius, expressed so flatteringly in the missive, constituted for him a guarantee of the quality of his work, because Idalius was one of the most senior bishops of Spain and his testimony could be a very prestigious preface for many potential readers. In any case, it is very likely that the letter was quite pleasing to Julian, who decided to attach it to the future copies of the *Prognosticum*.

The letter is written in an elegant if somewhat emphatic Latin prose and includes some biblical quotations. It can be divided in three parts with an epilogue.

In the first part (1–31, according to the *divisio textus* established by Hillgarth in Corpus Christianorum, Series Latina vol. 115), after having precisely defined the identity of the recipient as the bishop of the primatial see of Toledo, Idalius expresses to his friend the anxiety that he experienced waiting for the work that Julian had promised to send him. This anxiety had brought him to think that God no longer wanted to hear his prayer because of his sinful state, and that Julian himself had forgotten his promise. But his trust and hope in God and in Julian's promise were, in the end, rewarded.

The second part of the letter (32–59) narrates the sudden arrival of Julian's messenger, Restitutus, who delivered the precious volume of the *Prognosticum* to Idalius. From the letter we know that Restitutus was accustomed to transporting "caduca mercimonia."[174] This probably means that he was a professional traveling merchant or a frequent carrier of merchandise from the coast of the Iberian Peninsula—that is, from the important harbors of Barcelona and Valencia, within the country, to Toledo, and vice versa. Therefore, he was not a *brutum animal*, as Idalius horribly called him, but a merchant who was quite well off and well acquainted with the Iberian road system. Besides, he probably also possessed a team of assistants or slaves who followed him in the journeys of his caravan. It is likely that in leaving Toledo with the precious task entrusted to him by Julian, he would have followed an itinerary that took him, via probably uncomfortable internal roads, to the shores of the Mediterranean Sea and from there, probably near Valencia, he would pick up the road Baetica (which to the south led to Andalusia) and then continue toward the north, along the coastal road (that is, the Via Augusta) in Cataluña, up to Barcelona.[175]

In the sequel to the letter, however, perhaps Idalius had realized that it was Restitutus who had delivered intact the desired codex from Julian, who must have respected him to entrust him with this task, so Idalius tried to balance his unfortunate judgment with a sincere thanks to the Jewish messenger and praise to God, whose secret plan he had intuited. But his thanks are extended also to Julian for the humility shown in entrusting his precious work to a merchant of "caduca mercimonia." It is also probable that Idalius gave Restitutus a generous gratuity as thanks.

Idalius then narrates how he immediately opened the codex and how he was, first of all, amazed by the title. But upon careful reflection, he approved it as the best possible; he also marveled at the brevity of the work, which he exalts as sign and fruit of the author's great talent and intelligence, but also as something that would be welcomed by the future readers of the work.

In the third and last part (60–84), Idalius says that he has eagerly read the whole codex. He writes a sort of "review," describing its division into three books and the overall contents of each of them. His impression, after this first reading, was completely positive, because he realized that the *Prognosticum* would have been able to dispel the reader's every doubt and to shed light on the mysterious realities that Julian had treated with so much wisdom. He emphasizes Julian's ability to appropriate the authority of the fathers to support his theological reasoning. The result is a very well-founded and reasonable synthesis.

In the epilogue (85–110), Idalius gives thanks to the Holy Trinity for having given so much wisdom to Julian, and he wishes for him that God will grant him a long life in which to educate his faithful up to the day in which he can enter the heavenly kingdom together with the saints.

The letter of Idalius to Suntfredus, bishop of Narbonne

The second letter of Idalius[176] is addressed to Suntfredus, bishop of Narbonne. Suntfredus[177] was the thirteenth bishop of the Narbonnese diocese in the last quarter of the seventh century. He personally took part in the Fifteenth Council of Toledo (688) and sent his representative to the Twelfth (683) and Thirteenth (684) Councils of Toledo. We know also that, upon the death of Suntfredus, the Diocese of Narbonne remained vacant for eight years, because the city was in the hands of the Saracens.

The letter of Idalius to Suntfredus is a very interesting missive from the point of view of the history and distribution of the *Prognosticum*, because it provides a probable account of the first journey completed by the first copy of the *Prognosticum*, sent by Julian to Idalius. In turn, Idalius had one or more copies of the *Prognosticum* made, probably in Barcelona, to be sent, first of all, to the bishop of Narbonne in southern Gallia, but also to other bishops. Judging from the manuscript history of the *Prognosticum*, this first distribution of Julian's work did not meet with great success, and it probably played itself out by the end of the eighth century.

From the letter of Idalius to Suntfredus we learn that he had sent the *Prognosticum* to Narbonne through a messenger of his, in answer to a pressing request of Suntfredus.[178] Evidently Suntfredus had learned, during a local council or through some contacts with other bishops returning from Toledo, that the primate had composed this work, and he expressed the desire to read it. Idalius adds an important notation, however: he hopes that Suntfredus, upon receiving the manuscript, would in turn make the work known, that is, would have copies made for the bishops of the Narbonnese ecclesiastical province over which he presided, so that they could enjoy its theological teaching as well as its depth and pastoral usefulness. Idalius characterizes Julian's teachings on eschatology as ancient, coming from the fathers, but also as new, proposed by the author with a new (*nova brevitas*) theological method. This means that Idalius hoped that further copies would be made from the one sent to the bishop of Narbonne, so that Julian's teaching could be spread to the other local churches. This datum, besides underlining the episcopal collegiality and the intense communication among the bishops of the Narbonne province, shows the existence of a praiseworthy custom of signaling or exchanging with their brothers in the episcopacy the works they regarded as useful for the spiritual and theological enrichment of the bishops and presbyters and, through them, of the Christian people.

Finally, Idalius invites Suntfredus and the bishops who will read the *Prognosticum* to praise and thank the Holy Trinity for protecting the author of the work that has given them superior knowledge. In particular, he asks Suntfredus to ask for prayers for himself, Idalius, so much in need of help and divine pardon.

THE LETTER-PREFACE OF JULIAN OF TOLEDO TO THE *PROGNOSTICUM*

R. Ceillier, presenting the *Prognosticum* as "des prognostiques, c'est à dire, de la consideration des choses futures,"[179] dwells first of all on Julian's introductory letter or *praefatio* of the work, which accompanied the first copy of the work to the bishop of Barcelona. Evidently the mystical atmosphere described by Julian in the dedicatory letter, when he spoke of that Good Friday as a memorable day not just for the liturgical reasons of the Easter Triduum, but also for theological reasons, must have greatly struck the eighteenth-century French ecclesiastical writer.

The details meticulously and opportunely remembered by Julian—the coincidence of Good Friday, the retreat in the remote and silent places of the episcopal palace, the two dialogue participants sitting on two small lounges wrapped by the warmth of the covers and thus in a comfortable position favorable to dialogue and reflection, the climate of contemplative silence, their souls moved to the point of forgetting the afflictions of the present (the attacks of gout for Idalius), the felicitous resort to a clerk who, by his writing, helped to avoid the loss of important thoughts about the destiny of the souls after death and about the condition of the risen ones—all of this shows how Julian's preface represents "a good specimen of Julian's style, and contains some interesting personal reminiscences."[180]

But in the introductory letter of Julian there is something else that deserves mention: the methodological and theological approach he used in realizing the work. In fact, he affirms that the main reason he composed this work full of biblical and patristic quotations was the desire to furnish readers with an easy way of learning the mysteries of the Christian faith, since they cannot be expected to obtain and study codices and manuscripts with a view to extracting the most significant thoughts on eschatology. Julian had made this work for them, and now he was ready to offer the result of his search to everyone.

From the *praefatio* we also know that the whole theological dialogue and the editing of the titles were finished on that same day (*eodem die*), an indication of the physical and intellectual ability of the two bishops to carry on and then to dictate sustained theological thinking.

The letter is notable from the stylistic and literary point of view. Julian confidently uses a linear and almost chronological prose that concentrates and amplifies the supernatural and spiritual meanings of the constitutive elements of that memorable day.

The dedication of the work to Bishop Idalius, therefore, is not only a historical testimony of the genesis of the work but the occasion to underscore its methodology and the theological contents. It was not rare in the culture of Visigothic Spain to dedicate literary works to more illustrious persons. For Julian of Toledo, then, it almost seems a well-rooted custom, considering that his biographer, Felix, informs us that Julian dedicated some of his more important works to kings, abbots, and bishops.[181] Such is the case of the *De comprobatione sextae aetatis* and of the lost *Libellus de divinis iudiciis*: these two works are dedicated to King Ervig.[182] The same Idalius, besides being the dedicatee of the *Prognosticum*, is also the dedicatee of the *Liber responsionum*. Finally, the still lost *De remediis blasphemiae* was dedicated by Julian to a certain Abbot Adrian.[183]

THE PROBABLE SECOND DEDICATION OF THE *PROGNOSTICUM* TO THE BISHOP SPASSANDUS[184]

Thus Julian dedicated the *Prognosticum* to Idalius and sent him a copy[185] of the work because it was from the theological dialogue with the bishop of Barcelona on Good Friday of 688 that the idea of composing the *Prognosticum* was born. It was customary in Visigothic Spain to dedicate works to a particular person;[186] but what is problematic in this case is how and if it were really possible for the same work to be dedicated to two different, but contemporary, people. And this is what seems to have happened with the *Prognosticum.*

As Hillgarth indicates,[187] there is probably a second recipient of the work of Julian, until now completely overlooked by scholars of the *Prognosticum.*[188] He was probably a contemporary of Idalius. Already in the preparatory phase of the critical edition of the *Prognosticum,* Hillgarth had indicated[189] that "many of earlier codices, incidentally, bear a hitherto unknown heading, which runs as follows: 'In nomine Domini nostri Iesu Christi...Utere feliciter Spassande papa iugiter per saecula longa.'"[190] Undoubtedly this text, which also serves as a solemn *incipit,* heading, and dedication of the work, refers to a real person, a contemporary of Julian and Idalius, named Spassandus. Who was Spassandus?

Spassandus[191] was probably the bishop of the Diocese of Complutum (the actual Alcalá de Henares)[192] from 686 to 693, in the ecclesiastical province of Toledo. He had taken part, and was a signing participant, of some of the councils of Toledo,[193] of which one (the Fifteenth) was presided over by Julian. Spassandus had probably already been a signer also of the acts of the Thirteenth Council of Toledo in 683,[194] as archdeacon taking the place of Cyprian, bishop of Tarragona. Whatever his identity, it is evident that the inscription inserted by the copyists at the beginning of many codices of the *Prognosticum* seems to be a solemn initial formula. In the first part it invokes Christ himself (*In nomine Domini nostri Iesu Christi*). This lets the readers know that they are at the beginning of a theological Christian work; then the title page quotes the title of the work of the author, while the second part invites, in imperative form, its recipient, Spassandus, to make good, long use of the work devoted to him (*Utere feliciter Spassande papa iugiter for saecula longa*). A literal translation of the formula could be: "Take advantage abundantly, o Bishop Spassandus, continuously for long ages."

According to Hillgarth[195] more than a few copyists, not under-standing the sequence of the words of the inscription, have simply preferred to omit it, preserving only the christological *incipit* followed by the title of the work; in some cases, the inscription was purged of personal references so as to constitute a generic expression ascribed to the single reader of the *Prognosticum: utere lector feliciter.* Since the inscription is found in the various series of manuscripts from which the *Prognosticum* spread throughout Europe[196] and which constitute the rich manuscript tradition of the work, it is possible that it was present in the archetype or first copy of the work, a copy of which was sent to Bishop Spassandus.

Hillgarth is convinced of it, and his hypothesis seems reasonable, given the constant intellectual dialogue among the bishop participants of the national council of Toledo of 688, or the manifold contacts of such a metropolitan as Julian with the suffragan bishops of the ecclesiastical province. Therefore, it could have happened in this way: Spassandus, having known (from fellow bishops or from Idalius) that Julian was about to publish or had just published in a manuscript codex the result of the theological dialogue he had had with Idalius, may have requested a copy of the codex directly from Julian, as soon as it had been completed. The coincidences from which this request could be deduced would be the simultaneous presence of Julian, Idalius, and Spassandus in the same place and on the same days: in Toledo in 687. It is likely, finally, that Julian accepted with pleasure the request of Spassandus, and that he had provided that cheerful dedication to him on the first page of the codex and then sent him one of the first manuscript copies of the *Prognosticum*, after the one sent to Idalius. This would justify the presence of the inscription (which is not a dedicatory letter as in the case of Idalius), which the copyists then transmitted in a more or less precise way. Perhaps—but this is only a conjecture—it was a dedication written by the author in his own handwriting. The informal, joyful, and confidential character of the dedication could suggest this hypothesis.

Finally, Hillgarth supposes that it is not impossible that Julian himself would have been responsible for the appointment of Spassandus as bishop of Complutum, a diocese that belonged to the ecclesiastical province of Toledo and was thus under the direct jurisdiction of the primate of Toledo. Julian, having evidently known Spassandus well, had a good impression of him and considered him fit to govern a diocese. It must be remembered that, according to a prescription of the Seventh Council of Toledo of 646, the bishops of the Toledan ecclesiastical province were obliged to have a pastoral visit with the primate almost once a month[197] and that, during this period, they also had to report to the court about the status of their diocese. Such a frequent stay in the royal city could have been a further motive for giving the codex of the *Prognosticum* to Bishop Spassandus, who had certainly become, by then, a close friend of Julian. He could also have received the manuscript copy of the *Prognosticum* directly from Julian on the occasion of one of his visits in the royal city.

JULIAN'S *ORATIO AD DEUM*

The *Oratio ad Deum* of Julian serves to introduce the reader to the proper religious attitude for understanding the matters treated in the *Prognosticum*. Such an attitude is the one aroused by faith, that is, by the Christian's belief in realities that are unseen. In this sense, in fact, the *Prognosticum* can be considered a book of faith, a faith that has not yet officially been turned into precious dogmatic truths of an eschatological nature,[198] but that is the current faith of the Christian believers of the seventh century. Julian had set for himself the goal of formulating a synthesis of such faith, so as to serve as the fundamental stage for gathering the different Christian beliefs on the important theme of death and the survival and the subsistence of the soul after death and before the final resurrection. The work of Julian is an element of theological development that provides a good service to the faith and to theologians, who, reading and studying the eschatological synthesis of Julian, will find a solid base of the eschatological Christian faith and the reasons for a further development and study of the matters treated by him.

Therefore, in the prayer Julian imagines himself to be a pilgrim, blind and sick, wandering through the desert of Idumea, who cries out to the Son of David to have pity on him. In fact, he needs the pardon of God because he is looking for his lost country, the eternal Jerusalem, and desires to contemplate its inhabitants, the saints of God.

The *incipit* of the prayer has an undeniable Jewish flavor and is inspired by Old Testament references to the desert and its crossing, to Idumea, to blindness and illness, and to the invocation of the Son of David. The author, in fact, declares that he feels like a blind and sick subject, wandering in the inhospitable desert of Idumea.[199] The author identifies with the human characters in the Psalms, such as the author of Psalm 62:1-3 (*Antiqua Vulgata*), the biblical text by which Julian seems to have been inspired in composing his *Oratio ad Deum*, because the whole psalm reflects a situation similar to that described by Julian. Like all those who find themselves in distressing situations, so too for Julian nothing remained except to invoke divine help. Just as the biblical characters cried out to their God, likewise Julian identified himself with one of them and also cried out (*ad te clamo*) to his Lord, called the Son of David, to obtain liberation and relief in view of reaching the final goal. In the text this final goal coincides, significantly, with the eternal Jerusalem. The biblical spirituality of a pious Jew thus becomes the attitude of the theologian who, treating of the future things, burns with the desire to possess them and to flee to the heavenly Jerusalem (*cupiens evolare*). From God he asks to recover from his blindness so that with new eyes he may reach the final goal without any impediment from enemies. For him, Christ is the only way to get there and to calm his uneasy heart (*anxium cor meum*).

Therefore, he places himself before the Master of Masters, offering him his work, well aware that what he has gathered and discovered is only what mortals can say about the future realities, while he knows that there are greater things but ones entirely hidden and inscrutable. His trust in Christ is total in that he recognizes him as the way that allows him to advance; as the truth that prevents him from stumbling; as the life that fills the future even if he still has to cross the threshold of death and thereafter to experience the judgment of God. The thought of death and its harshness compels him to ask for divine help and protection (*angelicis excubiis*).

But the consciousness of his own sins terrifies him and he feels lost. He fears being punished for the rashness shown in treating the future realities and for having erred in divulging the truth. He calls upon the blood of Christ and his cross to defend him. He understands that the only appropriate attitude before the future that awaits him is humility. He presents himself before his God as a poor man, mendicant but tenacious and insistent (*pauperem tuum, mendicantem et pulsantem*),[200] protesting his correctness as a theologian who has not arrogantly violated the mystery, but who humbly desires to know (*agnoscere cupientem*) what God wants us to know of the world to come.

Finally, the desire of the reward: knowledge of the future things is asked of God by the one who prays, both in this world with the eyes of faith, that he might happily enjoy it, and in the other world, where those things that the human senses ("eyes and ears," as the apostle Paul teaches) have never seen nor heard can be contemplated directly. It is significant that Julian insists, even in the final situation of human life, on underlining the value of earthly knowledge (*hic*), even if *cog-*

nitio vespertina in comparison to the endless value of the future knowledge (*illic*), or *cognitio matutina*, which no human text will ever be able
to describe.

THE ORIGINALITY OF JULIAN OF TOLEDO'S
THEOLOGICAL METHOD

The methodological structure of the *Prognosticum* is simple. It
consists of the enunciation of the thesis in the title of the chapter; the
demonstration of the thesis, often starting with the biblical sources
and completing it with a wise choice of patristic texts; the insertion of
reasonings in the body of the text or at the end of the chapter.

This methodological scheme means that the *Prognosticum* is a
studied and elaborated selection of fundamental eschatological data
of the faith of the Catholic Church in the seventh century. As we have
already said, the verb "to believe" is repeated throughout the text of
the *Prognosticum*. This means that the criterion that serves as point of
reference is the *fides ecclesiae* as witnessed by the fathers, in addition to
Sacred Scripture. If the Bible seems to have absolute authority as the
primary source from which all other truths are derived, the *consensus*
of the fathers represents for Julian the actualization of those same
truths grounded in the Christian faith and already submitted to theological elaboration.

It is not difficult, therefore, to imagine that Julian's work consisted in the patient exercise of retrieving and transcribing the patristic texts cited, resorting to his excellent visual and conceptual
memory, in addition to his rich library. But above all, the principal
work of the author probably consisted in the intelligent insertion of
the patristic texts within every paragraph of the three books in order
to construct with these patristic "stones," held together with the
cement of theological reasoning, an eschatological building.

The titles of the paragraphs are generally self-explanatory. The
elements of the work have been wisely connected and united by introductory sentences, reasonings, and conclusions. It was obviously not a
work of copy and paste, nor of only lining up other people's texts.
Organizing his work, in fact, Julian shows that he knows how to apply
his critical judgment[201] to the selected materials to the purpose of providing the doctrinal bases. Julian himself defines his work, with its log-

ically and systematically connected theological themes, as "*librorum formatio ordinate,*"[202] an orderly—that is, a systematic—collection of books. Yet he never fails to give credit, carefully citing the authors of the sources that he uses. The work of the final editor thus acquires a decisive importance for the explanatory value of the eschatological doctrine. One might say that it is as if Julian had organized an international seminar in which the fathers of the church, coming from different centuries and speaking different languages, were active participants. And Julian has the serious task of coordinating their various contributions to fashion for all Christian believers a corpus of stable, unassailable eschatological teachings.

This means that the work of Julian is the first historical example of a systematization of eschatological matters and texts in a single manuscript codex. He has, therefore, the merit of having practiced an original method in systematizing the convictions and the knowledge of his time, and of the patristic era. What Isidore of Seville had done in his *Etymologiae*, in an encyclopedic sense, but also in his *Sententiae*, the first examples of arrangement of the doctrines of the Christian faith, Julian of Toledo, his ideal disciple, has done producing the first system of Christian faith devoted to the eschatological question.

Then the humility that Julian manifests in the *Praefatio* of the *Prognosticum* when he declares that his work "tamen non mea, sed majorum exempla doctrinamque reperies,"[203] must go together with the objective methodological innovation that he produces with the *Prognosticum*, precisely because he has written it with his own method (*proprio stilo conscripsi*).[204]

At the same time, however, Julian has a clear understanding of the theological value of his work, when, still in the *Praefatio*, he first of all rejects the idea that his work contains esoteric themes: "Therefore, it has seemed right to me that this work be compiled not so much to reveal to the readers the things almost unknown."[205] In other words, not everything can be understood with respect to eschatology, but only what has been revealed on the subject or that the doctrinal tradition has discovered and materialized in its theological theses. Further, he delineates in the *Praefatio* the finality of his work: he has written it so that "the discourse about the future things, collected here in unity, might touch in a more intense way the minds of the mortals, because, here reunited, they could read them without effort, and, so their composed reason could bear fruit in due time, by the fact that they are offered food here without effort."[206]

As can be deduced from his words, the goal of the *Prognosticum* is entirely related to the faith of the believers, which must receive a reasonable and logical knowledge of the future things and nourishment of a didactic and doctrinal nature. Therefore, the whole eschatological doctrine is proposed in a way that does not require too much intellectual effort, but, through such didactic sagacity as the enunciation of the title, the brevity of the text, biblical quotations, patristic citations, and the reasoning of the author, it achieves the desired goal: a deepened knowledge of the mysteries of the Christian eschatological faith.

THE LATIN OF JULIAN

According to scholars, the literary style of Julian's works is superior to the decadent Latin of the period in which he lived: "une latinité assai élégante pour cette époque."[207] Probably this linguistic quality is derived from his close acquaintance with the learned Bishop Eugene II of Toledo, whose poetic and rhetoric skill are universally recognized, but also from Julian's own erudition, nourished by the reading of the Latin classics and the works of the fathers of the church, both Latin and Greek.

The important concern of the church in Visigothic Spain for the formation and the education of the clergy and of the laity who were to occupy important political and administrative roles in the kingdom certainly favored the survival, as well as a certain development, of the Latin language. Julian had expended much effort in this direction ever since he was presbyter and teacher at the Episcopal School. As is known, the *Ars grammatica*, a methodological foundation for the teaching of Latin, is attributed to Julian and probably originated during his stint as teacher at the Episcopal School of Toledo. He obviously composed this work convinced of the need for the Hispanic-Visigothic culture of his time to have "its" own Latin grammar.[208] Although Julian may have had sufficient knowledge of Greek, considering that in the titles of his works he does not avoid quoting Greek words, it is clear that in his works and in his pastoral ministry he always utilized the language of Rome.

The Latin of Julian is, however, the Latin of his time, which is obviously not the Latin of imperial Rome or the refined and literary language of Cicero. The Latin of the seventh century, especially in Spain, was a rather plain language, though it was still a world language, thanks to Christianity, which used it for its liturgy[209] as well as for its many documents.[210] Latin was also used by the chancellery of the Visigothic kingdom for documents of the court.[211] Jerome's Latin translation of the Bible from Hebrew and Greek undoubtedly brought an important re-appreciation of the Latin language in the Western Christian world. But the Latin of the sixth and seventh centuries, of Isidore of Seville as well as of Julian of Toledo, is not to be considered a language only for the erudite. Thus, despite the fact that it was a written language, it was not considered a dead language. For Isidore and Julian, in fact, the Latin of the seventh century was also the language used every day, a spoken language, therefore, but one that also served in a distinguished way for a profound theology of the authors of the period, when they decided to use it in a more articulated and complex way. Latin served also for poetic expressions, which, in Spain at that time, were not few nor were they to be underestimated, as they were characterized above all by a certain linguistic liberty that is often a sign of the vitality of the language and of its evolution.

Latin, in short, was the mother language that enabled Julian of Toledo and the other seventh-century scholar bishops to express their theological, historical, and liturgical thought with good results. According to Rivera Recio, in the writings of Julian "the Latin loses barbarity to achieve fluidity and clarity, a very natural quality of him [Julian] who was the author of an *Ars grammatica*."[212] Undoubtedly, however, written Latin was used with enough mastery by only a minority of Hispanic-Romans, those who had been educated in the episcopal or monastic schools, and had then continued in the use of the written language, nourishing themselves with readings of a certain level and with the aim of achieving clear intellectual communication.

It is indisputable that sixth- and seventh-century Spain has left us a notable quantity of written works. This probably means that their authors thought that they had a vast audience who could read Latin. While R. Menéndez Pidal's work on the origin of the Spanish language has not benefited from the new linguistic theories, his description of the place of Latin in the Visigothic kingdom does not seem to be without foundation. He says, in fact, that in the Visigothic court the

more learned spoke a scholastic Latin similar to that written by Julian,
Ildephonse, or Isidore. Those who had not completed particular studies undoubtedly spoke a vulgar Latin. But the plebs, or the peasants,
did not speak Latin.[213] They probably spoke a mixed vernacular in
numerous peninsular dialects, with many different inflections, perhaps also Latin, but that allowed them to communicate sufficiently,
though minimally.

The profound knowledge of Sacred Scripture in Latin and many
works of the fathers of the Western church, united to his educated literary style, accustomed ever since childhood to clear expression, thanks
precisely to his mastery of Latin, all make Julian of Toledo one of the
most remarkable writers of his century.[214] It should not be forgotten,
besides, that the Spain of these centuries was under the Visigothic
dominion, and that Latin was certainly not the language of the domi-
nating forces. It seems certain, however, that the Visigoths made an
uncommon effort to use the language of the conquered, to the point of
adopting it as the official language for the documents of the kingdom.
Naturally the linguistic uniformity of the Hellenistic or the Roman
Empire was only a historical memory at the time of Julian. In fact, there
were in these centuries linguistic differences that marked the diversity
of the political dominions, but perhaps this allowed for balancing the
overall tensions among the peoples of Europe. Only the Western
Christian Church preserved its Latin linguistic unity, which lasted for
the whole medieval period and beyond. And this was certainly a unifying factor also from the social-political point of view.

Spain, therefore, in the general sameness of all of Europe, possessed a vitality and intellectual activity of primary importance, also
from the linguistic point of view, which prefigured the so-called renaissance of the Carolingian epoch.[215]

The rich library of Julian of Toledo

Madoz concludes his excellent article on Julian of Toledo by saying that Julian's writings "revelan además la existentia de una gran biblioteca en la sede toledana."[216] Like Isidore of Seville, Julian must have
possessed a well-furnished library of several hundred manuscript codices
of various genres. Hillgarth, too, believes that Julian "had an excellent
library" and, even more importantly, "he knew how to use it."[217]

THE *PROGNOSTICUM FUTURI SAECULI* 231

The collection of codices in the episcopal residence of Toledo[218] was, therefore, extensive and had probably been formed during the episcopacy of the predecessors of Julian, particularly by such learned ones as Eugene II and Ildephonse, but it had also been notably enriched with other codices owing to the proximity of the Episcopal School. We can suppose that the episcopal library was situated in the atrium, on the ground floor of the episcopal palace, and that the places dedicated to the library or an adjacent scriptorium must also have been the privileged place for the composition of the *Prognosticum* and other works of Julian of Toledo.

The library certainly grew during Julian's tenure as bishop, with a notable quantity of precious and expensive manuscripts, and especially the works of the fathers of the church,[219] as well as those of ecclesiastical writers and classical works that Julian obviously knew how to put to good use. He probably had a well-furnished personal library that he probably merged with the episcopal one. That Julian was a bibliophile, therefore, is a given.

The possession of a personal library in those times was not common. A manuscript codex was very expensive; further, there were very few places (in general, only in the monastic environments) where it was possible to have good codices made—and truly competent copyists were rare. Julian, therefore, must have invested a huge patrimony in the purchase of manuscripts, and he must have been legitimately proud of his enviable collection of codices.

Undoubtedly the desire to own a library of codices derived from an appreciation of the works of the past, especially those of the fathers of the church, as a rich mine from which to draw wisdom and knowledge and also as a pastoral and apostolic resource. At the same time, reading the works of the fathers nurtured Julian's aspiration to assimilate the criteria used by the fathers for the development of theological doctrine. This idea of the development and the systematization of biblical and theological knowledge was at the basis of the edition of several works by Julian, especially the *Antikeimenon* and the *Prognosticum.*

The biographer Felix informs us, however, that Julian contributed to enriching the library of Toledo *ad utilitatem Ecclesiae* not only with his bibliographical acquisitions but also with the codices of his own works, which were arranged, perhaps by Julian himself, in beautiful order in the *armaria* of the episcopal library: "summam librorum ejus, quos per eum Deus ad utilitatem Ecclesiae suae deprompsit." According to Felix, it was the will of God that such a rich library of codices would be there in Toledo and that Julian would have enriched it with his own manuscripts. The biographer adds: "*istinc lector addisce*" ("Reader, learn from this!"). Learn, that is, what attitude of service to believers (*ad utilitatem ecclesiae*) has inspired the edition and composition of the writings of the fathers of the church and of the primate of Toledo.

We can surmise that the hundreds of manuscript codices of the episcopal library were written on parchment and contained the texts of Sacred Scripture in the Latin edition (*Vetus Latina* or that of St. Jerome, which had already existed for centuries). The *armaria* must not have been lacking such collections of canonical-theological texts as the *Collectio Hispana*, which were important in the series of national councils of Spain, nor the works of the greatest theologians of Toledo such as Eugene II and Ildephonse, as well as other learned bishops of venerable churches of the peninsula, such as the works of Isidore of Seville, Braulio, and Taio of Saragossa. Most of the manuscripts probably were copies of the works of the Greek and Latin fathers of the church: "Julian possessed a remarkable library, which may have included a few patristic texts in Greek."[220] And this is indeed interesting considering that we know with certainty, at least judging from the content of the catalogues of the medieval libraries, that the Ante-Nicene and Post-Nicene Greek Fathers were "faiblement représentés"[221] in the libraries of the period, as also in the following centuries.

To judge from the patristic citations made by Julian in his works, the authors whose works were present in Julian's library and in that of the Toledan Church included Origen, Eusebius of Caesarea, Epiphanius, John Chrysostom, Athanasius, Cyril of Alexandria, Tertullian, Cyprian, Hilary of Poitiers, Ambrose, Jerome, Cassian, and Julian Pomerius. In addition, works of Augustine and Gregory the Great must have been present in a great number, since they were the most quoted by Julian in his main writings such as the *Prognosticum* and were evidently held in high esteem by the authors of the sixth and seventh centuries. Julian's classical formation and the culture of his preceptor and predecessor, Eugene II, make it likely that the library also contained at least dozens of codices of profane Latin authors of the classical period (poets, historians, grammarians, and others) such as Virgil, Sallust, Livy, and so on. And it is not improbable to suppose that Julian had read, studied, and, above all, assimilated the works of all these authors.

THE CODEX-BOOK IN THE SEVENTH CENTURY

The volumes contained in libraries of the sixth and seventh centuries were in the form of codex-books made of parchment. Beginning in the second/third century AD, the codex-book replaced the roll of papyrus or parchment, which was bulky, fragile (especially if made of papyrus), and awkward to consult.

The codex had already been used by Greeks and Romans for accounting and for scholastic didactics. It consisted originally of two or more rectangular tablets of wood held together by metallic rings or by skin and covered with a fine wax layer. It was possible to write on this wax layer with a metallic stylus, after having heated the wax and canceled what had previously been written. The defect of this method was evidently the impossibility of "saving" what was written. To remedy this serious drawback, scribes began to produce codices made of several sheets of parchment. The parchment was chemically treated, though not always in the same way, but a rudimentary chemical treatment was required and very refined, laborious manual work, in order to obtain parchments of good quality. The folded up and cut skins were fixed to the tables of the copyists and only at the end of the work of transcribing were they sewn along the external edge and bound with a cover of wood or thicker skin slabs. Qualified personnel were required for the process of making a codex-book, such as skin selectors and tanners who used a refined technique and, above all, reliable and cultured copyists. Also needed were binders experienced in manufacturing parchment volumes, able to trim them as well as to cover them with a strong rigid cover to protect them from time and carelessness. All these steps involved a considerable amount of time.

Very widespread in the liturgical environment, the codices allowed for easier consultation and maneuvering in comparison to the rolls. Among the most remarkable examples of this epoch, the *Codex rossanensis* or *Codex purpureus*[222] deserves special mention.

In the early Middle Ages, books were usually of a religious and didactic nature or copies of classical works. They were copied and recopied, and sometimes, for economical reasons, anthologies of the texts or works of important authors were compiled. The amanuenses were generally monks, who carried out their anonymous and important labor with great patience in the *scriptoria* attached to the libraries of the monasteries. At the end of the eighth century, with the cultural rebirth promoted by Charlemagne, the capital script (uncial and semi-uncial) of Latin derivation was replaced with the *Carolina* writing, with its more elegant and rounded forms. Around 1100, Gothic characters were introduced, which, with their angular lines and very dense characters, displayed in narrow columns, allowed for a great quantity of text to be contained in a little space, though they were less easy to read.

In the seventh century the technique of copying was well established in the whole basin of the Mediterranean Sea, Asia Minor, continental Europe, the islands of the North, and the Middle East. It was made possible by *ateliers*, or specialized centers (usually monasteries), full of calligraphers and scribes, along with the collaboration of innumerable artisans for the production of support materials (lamb or sheep skins, well tanned chemically to avoid immediate deterioration caused by biological residues) and writing implements and products (inks, colors, tempers, calami). These artisans also handled seams, binding, and simple page ornamentation. The codex of the early Middle Ages was a sober handmade article and completely devoted to its practical use: reading and studying. The codex was generally of modest size, with small to middle-sized pages filled with dense text, so that no available writing space would be lost. The immediate goal in copying the codices was to provide a good level of legibility, while the more long-term purpose was the transmission of the culture through the preservation and renewal of the patrimony of the codices.

The codex of the Hispanic-Visigothic period upon which the works of Isidore of Seville or Julian were written followed the prescribed standard concerning the form and size, but was distinguished by the presence of lower-case Visigothic writing, perhaps like that found in the *Codex Seguntinus 150* (sec. XI) and in the codex of the *Vita Sancti Fulgentii* (sec. X). The *littera toletana* was probably the script in which many works of the period were written and copied. The most ancient manuscripts of the *Prognosticum* that have reached us, however, were written in uncial or semiuncial characters, in some cases with marginal notes or with additions made in Visigothic cursive.[223] Subsequently, the uncial and the semiuncial scripts were replaced by the easier lower-case Carolingian letters. But it cannot be excluded that the first copies of the *Prognosticum* were written in the *belles lettres Visigothiques* or in Visigothic cursive. It was, in fact, probably during the first half of the seventh century, that is, during the time of Isidore of Seville and Julian of Toledo, that Visigothic writing had begun to develop its own characteristics. Unfortunately, very few manuscripts from the period of the Visigothic domination have been preserved, that is, from the last half of the fifth century to the Arabic invasion in 711. We possess no original form of the official documents from the chancellery of the Visigothic kingdom. Some findings from the imperial chancellery would be of considerable help for paleographers to reconstruct the history and the unique forms of Visigothic writing.

But it is probable that the work of Julian of Toledo was also written in *minuscula cursiva*, especially those manuscript copies that made their way to northern Europe and that were the prelude to the great medieval dissemination of Julian's work in first Carolingian and then Gothic writing.

Finally, starting from the end of the seventh century, the practical codex-book progressively gave way to the great medieval codices, which were more manageable, yet large and heavy. They were written with big letters, often surrounded by drawings occupying a large part of the page, almost as if they were made to be seen more than to be read for their content.

THE LATIN BIBLICAL TEXT QUOTED BY JULIAN

According to John Trithemius, Julian of Toledo "was very erudite in the Sacred Scripture."[224] We can conjecture that Julian's acquaintance with the biblical text began at the Episcopal School of Toledo in the first cycle of his studies, and that it then continued with his participation in the liturgical celebrations in the Cathedral of Toledo and, again, during his second course of studies in the diocesan school. Later Julian became a commentator and an exegete of Sacred Scripture, besides being, as bishop, a preacher of the Word of God. Obviously Julian was an expert in the Latin text of Sacred Scripture and probably, as was the custom of his time, knew large parts of the Bible from memory.

The Bible used by Julian for his studies was probably the text of the *Vetus Latina*, that is, the grouping of the different forms[225] in which the Bible was read and studied before the dissemination of the *Vulgata* and also parallel to it. In addition to the *Vetus Latina,* Julian also used the *Vulgata* for his works, as, for example, in the edition of the *Prognosticum.* The *Vulgata* or *nova translatio,* though not without defects, had ever since the time of Augustine and then of Gregory the Great, found favor with the fathers of the Western church because, having been translated from the Hebrew language, it allowed them to draw from the *hebraïca veritas.* It was by then considered the official Bible of the Catholic Church. The term *nova* indicated that the Latin translation of Jerome was viewed as a turning point in comparison to the *vetus translatio* of the preceding centuries (the *Vetus Latina* included, in fact, almost all the translations from the Greek to the Latin of the biblical text from the third to the sixth centuries).

Julian never quotes the Bible in Greek or in Hebrew, and we know that he made some references to Sacred Scripture from memory, thus with a possibility for oversight (as occurred in *Prognosticum* III, xxiiii). His hermeneutics of Sacred Scripture was notably oriented toward a literal interpretation of the text,[226] even if he did not disdain allegorical and metaphorical interpretations.

THE INFLUENCE OF THE ESCHATOLOGY
OF THE *PROGNOSTICUM FUTURI SAECULI*
ON MEDIEVAL ESCHATOLOGY

Outside Spain, Julian of Toledo is known most of all as the author of the first systematic work of eschatology, the *Prognosticum futuri saeculi.* With this work, in fact, together with those of Isidore of Seville and Taio of Saragossa, he "marks a true scientific development in theology, not even surpassed by the Carolingian renaissance." [227] His other interesting works, in comparison to the *Prognosticum,* had a scarce manuscript tradition and, above all, very limited distribution. We have already underlined that the *Prognosticum* had an extraordinary circulation throughout the whole European continent, including the northern European islands. But from the cultural point of view, we can agree with the judgment formulated by Mrs. Humphrey Ward that: "the catastrophe of the Mussulman invasion, on which his life borders so closely, destroyed his work to a great extent and effaced the traces of his influence."[228] The Arabic invasion provoked, objectively, the loss of an enormous patrimony of codices in the Iberian territory from the seventh to the tenth century, which likely included the whole literary production of Julian and, therefore, also his main work, the *Prognosticum futuri saeculi*. This catastrophe would explain in part the reason why there are no Spanish manuscripts found among the codices of the works of Julian of Toledo that have survived from the eighth and ninth centuries. It is unfortunately a matter of fact that none of the first wave of the extraordinary transmission of the *Prognosticum* has reached us; "we possess today no manuscripts of the 'Prognosticum' of the seventh and eighth" centuries.[229]

According to Madoz,[230] the *Prognosticum*, because it was written by Julian of Toledo in a systematic form, has become one of the precursors of the works of systematization typical of medieval Scholastic theology, such as the *Sententiae* and the *Summae*. For Hillgarth as well, the works of Isidore of Seville, Taio of Saragossa, and Julian of Toledo are to be considered no less and without a doubt models "from which descended, in the course of time, the books of 'Sentences' and the 'Summae' of the twelfth and thirteenth centuries."[231] As J. de Ghellinck has also written,[232] Julian, Isidore, and Taio provided the first models or at least the first essays of systematic theology, prior to the works of Abelard and the *Sententiae* of Peter Lombard, which so greatly met the intellectual needs during the early Middle Ages[233] of Christianity. De Ghellinck maintains that, since the *Prognosticum* was so frequently present in the medieval libraries, there is no wonder that the *Sententiae* of Peter Lombard, a work he defines as essentially a compilation but that nonetheless became the point of reference and the text that most influenced the theological elaboration of the whole medieval Scholastic period in philosophical and theological matters, utilized Julian's compact and complete text of eschatology to elaborate the eschatological theses and the *de novissimis* questions of the book IV of his *Sententiae*. De Ghellinck considers this another indication of how the medieval libraries contribute to clarifying the process of elaboration of theological thought that they have constantly influenced through the centuries.[234]

Medieval Christianity thus recognized in Julian of Toledo a "considerable theological authority" of his time in eschatological matters. An unusual destiny for Julian of Toledo! Precisely he who had relied upon the greatest doctrinal authorities of the past such as Sacred Scripture and the works of the fathers of the church to elaborate his eschatological system, confessing frequently that he preferred "to give voice" to the fathers through their writings rather than to express his own thought, then became in turn an authority for the authors of the Scholastic period, upon whom they relied for elaborating a dogmatic theology of the last things.

Except for the long mention of Julian in the *Chronica* of Isidorus Pacensis or the *Continuatio Hispana* at the height of the eighth century, the theological influence of Julian of Toledo on subsequent centuries probably began with the mention of some texts of his inserted in a letter[235] in the collection of letters of the Christian knight Alvarus of Cordoba, around the year 860. In this epistle,[236] written by an anonymous bishop, two texts are quoted from the lost works of Julian. But it is already significant that the author of the letter referred to Julian with the greatest respect and great veneration, "in terms applied by Julian in his own day to a Doctor of the Church such as Augustine,"[237] that is, just as he himself liked to express when quoting authors whom he recognized as having intellectual superiority and absolute theological authority.

Also in the eighth century, knowledge about Julian and his *Prognosticum* was attributed to a certain Pirmenius, probably a Hispanic-Visigothic monk in exile in Germany. But Hillgarth expresses strong doubts about this episode, considering it a misunderstanding.[238]

Julian was subsequently quoted by Abbot Samson of Cordoba (864) with reverence and recognition of his theological value. In his *Apologeticum*, the abbot quoted some passages of the *Prognosticum*, the *Antikeimenon*, two prayers composed by Julian, and some beautiful *sententiae*,[239] for a total of nine quotations. But, more than the number of quotations, Abbot Samson referred to Julian with such highly honorable titles as "Beatus," "Egregius Doctor." The testimony of Abbot Samson of Cordoba, however, is the only quotation of the *Prognosticum* found in works composed in Spain in the ninth century, whereas the work of Julian was cited, still in Spain, toward the year 882, only in a catalogue of books.[240]

Then there are two important episcopal documents in which Julian is quoted in passing. The first is a letter[241] that the bishops of Spain addressed to those of Gallia in 792–793 in which they quoted three great metropolitans of Toledo, respectively, Eugene (II), Ildephonse, and Julian as dogmatic sources or authorities about the Mass *de cena Domini*. And this datum coincides with what we have said about Julian as an experienced liturgist, reformer, and composer of liturgical texts.

The second document is the *Epistola ad Alcuinum*[242] of Elipandus of Toledo,[243] written in 798. In it the heretical bishop looked for support for his heretical adoptionist doctrine and presumed that he could find it in the doctrinal and theological tradition of his undisputed and learned predecessors in the episcopal see of Toledo. Julian is quoted by Elipandus among the *Sanctorum patrum venerabilium* of the Toledan Church who gave their important contribution to the edition of the liturgical texts and the dogmatic formulations of the mystery of the incarnation.[244] Julian is regarded with veneration and legitimate pride as simply *noster Iulianus,*[245] as are the most important and more representative theologians of the seventh century and of the Hispanic-Visigothic Church, such as Isidore of Seville, cited immediately before Julian in the same letter. Both documents quote different brief dogmatic-liturgical texts from the works of the quoted authors. In the case of Julian, they were *excerpta* of lost works.

Later, Alcuin, the probable author of the *Epistula synodica* of the 794 Council of Frankfurt addressed to the bishops of Spain, quotes Julian of Toledo, together with Ildephonse and Eugene II of Toledo, reproducing the text written by the Spanish bishops in which the Toledan saint theologians were cited as *auctoritates.* He concluded, however, that, in any case, despite how great such doctors were, they were incomparable, for example, with the authority of Sacred Scripture, and with what is said in it of Christ as the only-begotten of the Father,[246] or with what the great doctors, for example, Gregory the Great, say. In the text that followed, Ildephonse of Toledo was mentioned, but it is clear that the reasoning of Alcuin can be applied also to the other two Toledan doctors, Eugene II and Julian. According to Alcuin, "si Hildefonsus vester in orationibus suis Christum adoptivum nominavit, noster vero Gregorius, pontifex Romanae sedis et clarissimus toto orbe doctor in suis orationibus semper eum unigenitum nominare non dubitabit."[247]

Almost to balance his previous, overly severe judgment about the Toledan doctors, because of an unequal comparison with the *Pontifex Romanae Sedis,* that is, with the scientific and papal authority of Gregory the Great, Alcuin wrote the *Adversus Elipandum*[248] in 799, a treatise against the heretical adoptionist doctrine. In it he explicitly said that there was nothing unorthodox or heretical in the works of

the Spanish fathers, especially of the Toledans, whom he has read and
to whom Elipandus, instead, turned for having some "patrons" to justify his doctrine. In this text Alcuin expressly quoted the *Prognosticum
futuri saeculi*, giving rise to some confusion because he attributed it to
Julian Pomerius (as so many others would do after him) and because
he changed the name of the work to *Prognostica*. But he declared positively that he had examined[249] the *Prognosticum*, evidently with a critical eye, and that he considered it affirmatively as an *ex sanctorum floribus
collecta*, an anthology of selected texts of the saint fathers. Certainly a
favorable judgment, even if not too enthusiastic, which from such a
critical and severe theologian as Alcuin could not have been expected.
He did declare, however, that he was unable to identify any element of
the heresy of Elipandus[250] in the work of Julian, and for him this is what
counted more in the context of his work. The *Prognosticum* is, according to Alcuin, a work exempt from error. To read a similar judgment
written by the pen of such a severe judge as Alcuin, and in a moment
of great theological emotionalism due to the spread of the adoptionist
heresy, generates a certain reassuring intellectual satisfaction about the
theological value of the work of Julian of Toledo.

Among the medieval authors who used the *Prognosticum* in their
works, there is also the monk Honorius Augustudunensis (twelfth century). His popular *Elucidarium*[251] was certainly a dogmatic work but with
a catechetical aim, as shown by the structure of the work, constructed
on the scheme of questions of the *Discipulus* and wise answers of the
Magister. The use of the *Prognosticum* seems to be abundant especially
in the third part, or *liber tertius*, of the work, which is devoted to eschatological matters. The work enjoyed great success throughout
medieval Europe and was also translated into various languages.

Therefore, in addition to the severe judge Alcuin, another theologian a few centuries afterward, Honorius, read and studied the
Prognosticum, considering it to be not merely an anthology of texts (as
did Alcuin), but a text of reference for elaborating a theological
scheme and furnishing a complete doctrine of eschatological matters.

The eschatology of Julian of Toledo was also known and broadly
used by the Benedictine monk of the monastery of Fulda, then
bishop, Haymo of Halberstadt (d. 853).[252] There is no doubt about the
influence of Julian and his *Prognosticum* on the *Haymonis Halber-
statensis Episcopi De Varietate Librorum sive de Amore Coelestis Patriae Libri
Tres*.[253]

The *Prognosticum* was known also by the canonist and theologian Burchard of Worms (d. 1025). He made abundant use of the titles and the content of Julian's work in the 110 chapters, entitled *De contemplatione*, of the twentieth volume of his *Decretorum libri viginti*.[254]

The *Prognosticum* was still amply used in the twelfth century by the French Benedictine monk Lambert, canon of St. Omer, in his extraordinary *Liber Floridus*,[255] written in 1120.[256] Hillgarth has demonstrated this in an interesting comparative study between the text of the *Prognosticum* and some textual passages of the *Liber Floridus*, concluding that not only did Lambert abundantly use the text of the *Prognosticum*, but he was also able to consult the text in two different manuscripts, both present at the library of the French Benedictine Abbey of St. Bertin, where he lived. The first manuscript[257] must have been a collection of *excerpta* of the *Prognosticum* produced in England.

In fact, the studies of E. M. Rayne[258] have demonstrated that these texts used by Lambert were the principal source for a homily in Old English, or Anglo-Saxon, of Ælfric,[259] Abbot of Eynsham (Oxfordshire, 955–1020). Ælfric "drew from his own compilation of excerpts from this work."[260] But since Lambert also used other textual extracts of the *Prognosticum* that were not in the manuscript of English origin, there must have been another manuscript copy of the *Prognosticum* in his monastery of St. Bertin, probably more complete and already attributed with certainty to Julian of Toledo (*Iuliani pronostica*)[261] in the catalogue of the library of the monastery, a work that was then lost.

In the works of both Lambert and Abbot Ælfric, therefore, we can identify another step in the distribution and theological influence of the *Prognosticum* on the writers and theologians of the twelfth century.

The influence of the *Prognosticum* on the Master of the Sentences, Peter Lombard, deserves special mention. We can affirm with considerable certainty that the *Prognosticum* was the principal theological source of the *Sententiae* of Peter Lombard for what concerned his eschatology.[262] In the *Sententiarum Libri IV*, particularly in book IV, the Master of all Masters of medieval Scholasticism not only explicitly quotes Julian of Toledo as an authority in eschatological matters, but continually recalls his thought, as can be noted specifically in the critical edition of the *Sententiae*.[263] In Index III: *Auctores et Scripta*, there are around thirty references to the thought and work of Julian in relation to the distinctions XLIII–L of book IV of the *Sentences*. Moreover,

Peter Lombard addresses the state of the souls after the bodily death especially in the distinctive XXI.

After having reached, undoubtedly, the apex of a vast distribution in the cultural and theological environments of the Middle Ages, the popularity of the *Prognosticum* and the specific interest for that type of work and its circulation began to decrease when the mendicant orders and the medieval universities took the place of the monks, monastic *scriptoria*, and the *Scholae* that were still, to a large extent, dependent on the monasteries.[264]

In the late Middle Ages, the *Prognosticum* was less appreciated and less widely circulated than in the preceding centuries. The manuscripts of the work continued to be present not only in the houses of study of the new religious orders and in the scholastic libraries but also elsewhere, for example, in the libraries of the Italian courts or of the scholars of the Renaissance. Undoubtedly by then, however, prevailing in the *Scholae* was the comprehensive systematic structure of the Master of the Sentences,[265] so work such as that of Julian of Toledo was less able to assume a place.

In the thirteenth century, the *Prognosticum futuri saeculi* of Julian of Toledo was translated, in the form of a freely adapted poem, into the Anglo-Norman language, which facilitated the spread of the eschatology of the *Prognosticum* to the Anglo-Saxon realm.[266]

Therefore we cannot but agree with Hillgarth when he says that "Julian might not be a Doctor of the Church, to be put on a level with Gregory the Great, but he had written at least one book that was to earn him the heart-felt, if not always articulate, gratitude of the Middle Ages."[267] A flattering judgment on the work of Julian was given also by the French secular historian J. Le Goff.[268] He was not a theologian, nor did he profess himself to be a Christian, but he was nevertheless able to understand, from his historical sensitivity, the importance of the work and the thought of Julian of Toledo, considering it to be a historical phase of exceptional meaning. Le Goff opportunely situates the work of Julian in the early Middle Ages, together with that of two other great Spanish bishops: Taio of Saragossa and Isidore of Seville, with whom, in his opinion, Julian forms a theological triad of notable importance. According to Le Goff, therefore, Julian not only no longer belonged to the epoch of the fathers,[269] but he was already considered and qualified as a theologian and his work appraised as "un véritable traité détaillé d'eschatologie…l'exposé le plus clair et le plus complet du haut Moyen Âge sur le futur Purgatoire."[270]

Le Goff, however, obviously does not appreciate the innovative characteristic of the work of Julian, above all on the level of methodology, or rather, he appears to not know it at all, thinking that Julian limited himself to repeating what had already been formulated by the eschatology of Augustine. We have already seen that the case was otherwise and that Julian's work was a kind of eschatological *summa* that then served as a basis for the treatment of the *de novissimis* by a major part of the most important theologians of medieval Scholasticism.

THE REASONS FOR SO MUCH SUCCESS OF THE *PROGNOSTICUM* IN THE MEDIEVAL EPOCH

As we have seen, the *Prognosticum futuri saeculi* had an extraordinary circulation in the Middle Ages and was the most known work on the *de novissimis*[271] throughout the medieval centuries. The work was particularly copied and read in the early Middle Ages, more than in the following centuries, and it was circulated to almost all the libraries of Europe between the tenth and twelfth centuries.[272] The Carolingian renaissance appreciated it notably, and Cistercian monasticism offered a good reception to the work of Julian, to the point of including the *Prognosticum* in the list of the books to be read in the regular Chapters or to be distributed to the monks[273] as theological-spiritual reading in the Abbeys of Cîteaux and Cluny.[274] According to F. Brunhölzl,[275] Julian is "le personnage le plus important dans la vie spirituelle de la seconde moitié du VIIe s. en Espagne" and, we add, also outside Spain in the following centuries, specifically from the ascetic-spiritual point of view.

From these details we can infer that the immense popularity of the work was due to the fact that the *Prognosticum* was considered a text of sure doctrine and of great spiritual elevation. The fact that some monasteries possessed two or three copies of it leads one to believe that it was a work in great demand for the study and the spiritual readings of the monks.[276]

There are several reasons why the *Prognosticum* had such wide circulation in the medieval epoch. First of all, the title of the work, *Prognosticum futuri saeculi*, could have contributed to the success and the distribution of the work. It is, in fact, an original or unusual title to indicate a work of theology and had certainly been studied, analyzed, pondered, and appreciated by the author himself before being selected and attributed to the work.[277] Both Idalius, in his letter to Julian, and the author himself, in the *Praefatio* to the *Prognosticum*, justify the exactness and the appropriateness of giving such a title to the work. They stress that the original intention of the dialogue between the two bishops, and then of the one who took care to put it in writing (that is, Julian himself), had been that of gathering, in an ordered way, the most important sentences of Sacred Scripture and the fathers of the church about the selected themes, and considering, in a logical and theological way, all the most important matters related to death, to the state of the souls between death and the resurrection of the body, and to the final resurrection and its formalities. So Idalius emphasized that the title of the work or the term *Prognosticum* could be understood, not inappropriately,[278] as *praescientia*, as foreknowledge of the future things or of the future life or of the future world. Evidently the author, attributing a certain importance to this meaning, had opted in the end for a title that could convey his intentions and also attract the curiosity of the reader, and, then, once the reading or the study of the work had begun, objectively arouse interest in the reader.

But I believe that the title of the work has a further meaning. It eliminates, in fact, every ambiguity, because it does not make any reference to a promise of revealing esoteric secrets or supernatural visions, nor to sensational[279] apocalyptic prophecies concerning the future or the afterlife. Beginning with its title, therefore, Julian's work was intended as an appeal to the knowledge, study, and in-depth analysis of the sources of theology in order to elaborate a theological system related to the eschatological condition of humanity and the cosmos. The term *Prognosticum*, therefore, is considered fitting to represent the work of Julian of Toledo because it is loaded with a meaning of *scientia* and doctrine guaranteeing the reader a grounded and reliable theological knowledge.

A second, already mentioned, reason for the immense success of the *Prognosticum* in Europe from the ninth to the twelfth centuries is the brevity or conciseness of the work, which was very appealing to readers and researchers, and thanks to which they could find in the work of Julian a complete abridged edition containing ample doctrine, which was otherwise difficult to access as a whole theological system. In short, a lot of doctrine in few pages of text.

From these two reasons follows a third and, perhaps, the most important explanatory reason for the wide distribution of the *Prognosticum* in medieval epoch—the fact that the work of Julian filled a void in eschatological matters. Prior to Julian, in fact, there was no summary or synthesis that contained the entire Christian eschatological doctrine. Nor was there an official doctrine of the magisterium of the church on the subject, apart from the simple but important eschatological assertions of the Christian creed, the Nicene-Constantinopolitan symbol of faith, about the resurrection, the second coming of Christ at the end of history, the universal judgment, and eternal life. Such truths required a more articulated explanation than what the creed contained and a thematic analytical exegesis of its components. Eschatological problems were popular and aroused the minds in the Middle Ages, but there was no work that had, before Julian, addressed the most important eschatological problems in their entirety. The work of Julian served this necessary function, elaborating the more important eschatological themes through a wise and intelligent use of the biblical and patristic sources, furnishing, with his added reasoning, a dense and useful synthesis of dogmatic truth on a subject that, while it aroused so much interest in the believers, theologians, and shepherds of the church of the seventh century, brought at the same time many uncertainties and doubts.

Only in this way can one explain why two centuries after the death of Julian, through its initial circulation thanks to the monks of northern Europe, the *Prognosticum* became in a short time one of the books most reproduced by the medieval copyists. As Hillgarth acutely observes, it was not, therefore, the title or the literary form of the work, but rather the theological content of the *Prognosticum* that decreed its European success. It supplied the Middle Ages with the possibility of filling a theological void about the last realities.[280] The work of Julian indeed responded in a new way to the most difficult matters of eschatology. It begins, in fact, with what could be interpreted as the great premise of the work: a substantial explanation about the origin of human death. In addressing this initial theme, Julian underlines the originality of the Christian intuition: establishing that death did not belong to the creative plan of God but that it entered into human history because of the dramatic event of the original sin. It is not, therefore, to be considered a natural phenomenon, to be accepted with resignation and without hope, because it has a cause and a reasonable explanation. And when the cause and explanation of a problem are known, in most cases it is possible to find the solution and one or more answers. From this premise the author passes boldly to the examination of a dozen other matters, of primary or secondary importance, as, for example, the immortality of the soul and its qualities, even after death; the intermediate condition of purification, a true theoretical conquest of the eschatological synthesis of Julian of Toledo; the respect with which it is necessary to treat the bodies of the dead; the dramatic questions about the possibility of damnation and its forms; and then, above all, the dogmatic questions and the answers to the major dogmatic themes of eschatology—the second coming of Christ, the final judgment, the resurrection of the body, the contemplation of the divine mystery without the body, and, finally, with the body. He then covers the less important questions, but nonetheless of popular and pastoral interest, about the conditions, properties, and possible necessities of the risen bodies in the future life and in the renewed world (food, clothes, knowledge, age, and so on). Julian's answers to these questions are generally characterized by moderation, avoiding morbid curiosity and following the internal coherence of his theological system.

Therefore, in spite of its brevity, the *Prognosticum* was able to answer most of the eschatological questions of its time and, above all, of the centuries following its publication. This praiseworthy merit undoubtedly constituted the main reason for its dissemination. On the other hand, the eschatological themes seem to be connatural to the human condition, which has always asked fundamental questions about the last things since the first human cultural and religious development. Who is not interested in such questions? Who is not interested in having concrete, well-founded, and certain answers on such difficult matters?

A further and last reason that contributed to the extraordinary European diffusion of the *Prognosticum* lies in the fact that this work was composed in Spain in the seventh century, which was certainly the country most intellectually, theologically, and culturally equipped to furnish such a remarkable work to the rest of Europe.[281] But if Spain undoubtedly was the ideal cradle for the origin of such a dogmatic treatise upon the last realities, the first transmission of the

Prognosticum toward Ireland and the Anglo-Saxon[282] countries was the second providential turning point for the work. From the northern islands, in fact, began a constant and, all things considered, fast chain of copying and distribution of the manuscripts of the *Prognosticum*, which through the libraries reached the monasteries of northern Italy. So, in a relatively short time, the *Prognosticum* was present in most of the libraries of the northern European monasteries under Celtic influence (Reichenau, St. Gallen, Bobbio, Fulda).[283] Beginning from the ninth century, France also had an important role in the diffusion of the *Prognosticum*.[284] In the tenth century the work had spread to other monasteries, in particular, those in Germany.[285] In the eleventh century, the English and Italian libraries were enriched by many copies of the *Prognosticum*, while in the twelfth century, a notable number of copies of the work of Julian of Toledo were produced in France and Germany.[286]

The conclusion that can be drawn from the significant number of manuscripts of the *Prognosticum* that reached us is that, according to an estimate very near to the reality, there were around fifteen hundred or two thousand manuscripts of the work[287] circulating in the medieval era. This was indeed an extraordinary number for such a work as the *Prognosticum*, which was originally created for an audience of readers certainly limited to the bishops of Visigothic Spain and, perhaps, to the students of the second course of studies of the Episcopal School of Toledo.

THE *PROGNOSTICUM FUTURI SAECULI* AS WORK
OF ANTI-APOCALYPTIC ESCHATOLOGY

Augustine was already convinced, as others before[288] and after him, that, in view of the great political-military upheavals (the barbarian invasions) happening all over the world, which would in a short time have brought the fall of the Roman Empire, the world had reached the final phase of its existence and soon the end of every terrestrial thing would come: "*Perit mundus, senescit mundus, deficit mundus.*"[289]

Gregory the Great had this conviction, expressed both in the *Dialogi* and in the *Moralia in Iob*, that the world had reached its eleventh hour,[290] that is, its end, and that there were already signs of this end, or of this new beginning. Two of these signs were especially evident, and opposite one to another: on the one hand, the malefic activity of the Antichrist already long at work in history;[291] and on the other hand, the Christian missionary development in northern Europe, sustained by Pope Gregory, a sign that was also meant to be apocalyptic in commitment of the church to prepare all people for the meeting with the Christ in the *parousia*, by then so near.[292]

This apocalyptic sensitivity, so developed in Gregory the Great and in the fathers of the church preceding him, does not seem to have been present theologically in such an obsessive way in the more representative authors of Visigothic Spain. The reason for this is not difficult to understand. In Spain the barbarian invasions were a reality, as in many other regions of Europe, but unlike these other places, the invasions had not generated in the Iberian Peninsula such an extreme perception of the signs of the end of all things. On the contrary, the invasion that concluded with the supremacy of the Visigoths had produced in Spain, politically, religiously, and pastorally, a much less dramatic vision of reality, and the beginning or the birth of a founded hope in a future formed of stability, political and religious unity, ecclesial expansion, and national safety. For instance, a representative protagonist of the Hispanic-Visigothic Church, Isidore of Seville, did not consider eschatological problems in such an extreme way in his works and probably not even in his pastoral office. Indeed, he had been witness to the birth of the new Hispanic-Visigothic state and of a new religious society after the conversion of the Visigoths to Catholicism (589). Isidore was pleased that the barbarian invaders had been assimilated into the Hispanic-Christian Catholic culture,[293] consequently starting a new unified state in which the church had found a central role and was actively involved.[294] Isidore had contributed to the birth of this new sociopolitical and religious project by writing his works, which were new and ready to be used as the cultural, universal, and encyclopedic guides of the new society, for example, the *Etymologiae* and the *Differentiae*. This probably meant that Isidore, along with the other ecclesiastical authors and the Hispanic-Visigothic bishops of the sixth and seventh centuries, did not believe history to be at its end but rather that it was close to a progressive and positive change of reality that would produce the constitution of a new imperial state, born to the west of Rome, that is, in Spain, and that this new reality would perhaps replace the role of the Roman Empire, which was by then far too decadent.

And if this "theology of history" that was spreading among the theologians and Hispanic-Visigothic writers of the seventh century had been realized in the ways and in the proportions foreseen by divine providence, the new city, the head or center of the new empire—in short, the "new" Rome—would have been Toledo. It would have been able to replace Rome, moving the axis of the empire to the west, and, perhaps, also replace Byzantium, in the East, presenting itself as the new ideological, political, and religious leader of the entire Christian world, both Latin and Greek. This providential vision of history of the Hispanic-Visigothic fathers appeared well rooted in reality and in historical events, but they did not imagine it in an apocalyptic sense, as if it were the realization of the kingdom of a thousand years of Christ with his own on earth. It was simply a change of key, anticipated by divine providence, which would have given a greater impulse to the role of the church in the building of the worldwide Christian society.

This unified vision of the political and religious reality, which was not an anticipation of the apocalypse, seems also to be present in the writings of Julian of Toledo. In fact, in the *Historia Wambae*, he maintains that the Hispanic-Visigothic empire, driven by its brave and courageous king, represents in contemporary world history the presence and the action of divine providence; and that King Wamba in particular is the providential king chosen and sent by God to save the political and religious unity of Spain, and with important universal consequences. The *Historia Wambae* seems therefore to have a religious and theological meaning beyond the historical events narrated by Julian. In it the young theologian Julian seems to surrender to the temptation to see the historical events as narrating a kind of political-religious theory, or better, a theology of history that seems even to belong to the general plan of God. The entire historical work of Julian intends to show that the king was sincerely engaged in the search for the stability of his kingdom and in the attainment of the maximum common good: the unity of the people of Spain. We can therefore hypothesize that Julian interpreted the historical events in a theological sense, building the beginning of a theology of history that we will find again also in other works of his, for example, in the *Prognosticum futuri saeculi*. In this work he seems on a number of occasions to main-

tain the conviction that history is objectively driven by God and that it
will infallibly reach its goal despite contrary realities that oppose it.

His eschatology is therefore characterized by a series of elements of optimism that lead him to conclude in advance that God will
reach the goal of a new heaven and a new earth and of new and risen
human beings. The whole book II of the *Prognosticum*, dedicated to
maintaining the active and dynamic survival of the soul after the bodily death, namely, that it is already a positive anthropological datum,
has its fulcrum in the theology of purification, beyond this world, of
the *non valde boni*, that is, a well developed theological way to interpret
the theology of history by God himself. Salvation is therefore almost
within everyone's reach, and this possibility is most highly appreciable
from the eschatological point of view because it shows the will of God
in bringing his plan of creation and redemption to its universal conclusion through an additional tool, which is the purification beyond
death that presents itself as the metahistorical extension of the christological redemption. Purgatory is therefore a supplementary and
positive element of hope and great optimism in the eschatological
and ecclesiological Christian view of Julian of Toledo. In fact, to
affirm the existence of the state of purification means, on the anthropological level, to underline the importance of the individual and the
divine and ecclesial concern for the destiny of the individual and the
survival of his/her soul after death. This fully opposes every chiliastic
or apocalyptic vision that is instead directed to the final and collective
dimension of humanity. The state of purification beyond physical
death means to show, on the ecclesiological level, the dogmatic conviction that the church still has a long earthly, historical, and missionary journey to accomplish, and that in this way, perhaps, still for
millennia to come, the church must continually develop a great triple
task: on the historical level, through preaching and the sacramental
actualization of the mystery of Christ; on the salvific level, through the
continuous conferral of the fruit of redemption on those redeemed;
and on the liturgical level, especially in the liturgy of intercession for
the dead, through maternal concern for the eschatological destiny of
individual sons and daughters who have passed to the afterlife. This
global engagement of the church, which also goes beyond human
death, means underlining that the salvific power of the earthly ecclesial action—in that it is totally derived from the Easter mystery of
Christ and centered on him, present in the liturgical life and in the

faith of the church—can even be decisive for the success of the universal plan of redemption of God for individual human beings, naturally not out of necessity, but by the desire of Christ to involve his entire ecclesial body in the building of the heavenly kingdom.

With the editing of the *Prognosticum*, therefore, the orientation of the thought and of the theology of the history of Julian proceeds in this eschatological direction of the historical engagement of the church. The *Prognosticum futuri saeculi* thus seems to be averse and immune to any apocalyptic "fibrillation," even though it is an eschatological work in the fullest meaning of the term, dealing with all the eschatological themes. The way in which Julian treats the themes of eschatology and of the apocalypse does not seem to arouse extreme and catastrophic tones, as did Cyprian or some of the pages of Augustine or Gregory the Great, theologians who were venerated as *Maiores* by Julian himself and who are abundantly quoted in the *Prognosticum*. In the work of Julian, therefore, everything is rationalized, often in a demythologizing way or with a tone of respect for those realities that are still divine secrets not yet revealed (for example, the date of the *parousia* or the location of the definitive eschatological condition: hell and heaven).

Naturally, to complete this interpretation, Julian uses a certain type of exegesis and interpretation of history in a providential sense in order to discover and to communicate the role of the monarchy and the Visigothic empire in the universal plan of God. But also in Julian, as already in Isidore of Seville, this vision is completely lacking in any apocalyptic extremism, because all the events are developed as functional and in view of the attainment of a goal, the reaching of which begins a plain dimension of history in which the collaboration between state and church becomes the winning formula for the construction of a new Christian society.

In a similar way, but more strongly focused on the theological and religious level, in the *De comprobatione sextae aetatis*, Julian is disposed to show, in this case to the wise Jews, that the messianic time has already been fulfilled, and that the world and history have already penetrated the sixth age or millennium since creation, and that therefore the new age, the eschatological age, has already entered the world. This is the reason why, according to him, the Talmudic calculations were wrong and it therefore does not correspond to the truth that the end of everything is so near due to the coming of the

Messiah. The Messiah, Julian insists, has already come, and human beings are to prepare themselves to live a new historical-religious reality. Thus, no fear of an imminent end of the world is justifiable.[295]

J. Fontaine, and even Hillgarth, have a contrary opinion and think that Julian puts more emphasis on the apocalyptic rather than on the eschatological dimension because of the dramatic events of which he was a witness: the plague, the invasion of the grasshoppers, the economic and political impoverishment of the young empire, the usurpations, the regicides, the persecution of the Jews, the increasing threat of the Arabs pressing at the borders of the kingdom, the Byzantine incursions, and so on. This series of negative events would have provoked in Julian a pessimistic reflection and the vision of "une Espagne noir," entirely opposed to the optimist vision of Isidore.[296] Such an interpretation, founded on the negative historical events, seems completely absent from the *Prognosticum*, which instead supports to the bitter end the most solid, unassailable, and stable eschatological hope. It seems rather that the *Prognosticum* as a whole wants to be precisely a speculative meditation or reflection on the fact that God will bring his goal to completion despite all negative and contrary aspects, both those coming from history and those derived from natural catastrophes. In this critical evaluation of history, Julian seems to echo Jesus' recommendation to his disciples: "So, if they say to you, 'Look! He is in the wilderness,' do not go out. If they say, 'Look! He is in the inner rooms,' do not believe it" (Matt 24:28); or when misfortunes or catastrophic events such as wars will happen, well, "the end is not yet" (Matt 24:6; Mark 13:7–9, 21). Naturally I do not exclude that in some places of the *Prognosticum* there may be a more intense accent, such as when at the end of book I Julian considers it useful to quote the catastrophic tones of Cyprian of Carthage. In this case, in fact, the reference is not to the dramatic historical events, but to the circumstances of the death of the individual who is invited by those examples to live a spirituality of separation from the world and from his body. Further, it cannot be denied that Idalius, in the letter of thanks to Julian, assumes very chiliastic tones when he claims at this point to be "at the end of the times or rather (to say with greater truth), almost at the consummation of the world." According to him, it is precisely for this reason that God granted Julian a special grace by which he warns all about the eschatological destinies that await us: "he has infused into the heart of Your Beatitude the gift of his grace."[297]

Obviously this is not the thought of Julian. When Idalius of Barcelona wrote these words, in fact, he was already very elderly and ill, and his dramatic vision of history could probably also take on the sense of a sort of personal *nunc dimittis.* Likewise, it is not certain if Bishop Quiricus was apocalyptic when in a letter to Ildephonse of Toledo he spoke, perhaps in a dramatic sense, of the *plenitudo temporum,* in which the Messiah had come, and of the fact that he is present "*in hoc novis-simo tempore saeculorum.*"[298] In my opinion, this is not the thought of Julian of Toledo. On the contrary, Julian writes his eschatological work as a positive and alternative proposal to any form of millenari-anism, and in order to silence with a solid doctrinal synthesis all the suppositions and the presumed prophecies concerning the end of the world that circulated abundantly in the visionary writings of the time.

Therefore, the tendency of some scholars to consider the *Prognosticum* a work with apocalyptic tones is not convincing. To exclude this perspective from the *Prognosticum* of Julian, it suffices to cite the important elaboration of the theology of the purification of the soul after bodily death offered by Julian in order to introduce into eschatological doctrine a supplementary element of hope and of great optimism.

The eschatology of Julian, therefore, is not at all catastrophist, but it is simply what it must be: an eschatology that is a "performative" reflection, a *prae-scientia* engaged in order to teach believers all the eschatological truths and prepare them for a progressive journey of salvation that will culminate, for each and all, in eternal life. Certainly, Julian invites the bishops and the believers who will read his work to take the eschatological truths seriously. He also invites them to con-vert and, in so doing, shows the meaning and the ascetic-spiritual effect that knowledge of last realities produces, and yet it is done with-out dramatizing too much and without reaching extreme tones.

Another element that seems to me decisive in excluding escha-tological extremism in the work of Julian is his continuous reference in the *Prognosticum* to the faith of the believers and theologians, espe-cially in the titles of the chapters and in the content of the work; this means that the *Prognosticum* appeals directly to the faith that Christians have in God and in his providence, and it invites them to conversion by setting before them the eschatological truths that are so great and decisive for the future of each human being. But it is above all the increased salvific possibility that is offered by the theology of the purification of souls—and which was inserted for the first time by

Julian in a doctrinal eschatological corpus—that gives a very optimistic sense to the *Prognosticum* from the historical-salvific point of
view. The discovery of a further possibility of eternal salvation is such
a gratifying novelty, generating optimism within the faithful, that it
enables them to regard negative events and setbacks, whether historical or not, with a concrete hope.

What we propose is, therefore, an interpretation, which until
now has not been widespread, of the genesis and the contents of
Julian's eschatological work. It maintains that Julian was motivated to
write the *Prognosticum* because of the disproportionate importance
devoted to apocalyptic themes by many commentators on Sacred
Scripture, some ecclesiastical writers of the patristic period, and the
bishops of his time. In his eyes, they seemed obsessed by the thought
of the end of everything.[299] Moreover, this exaggerated apocalyptic
atmosphere particularly insisted on the rapidity of the approach of
the end, as well as on the transitoriness and futility of the present
world that was destined to perish, in comparison to the world to come
that was about to succeed. Faced with this situation, Julian's peda-
gogic-theological intention was to remedy these excesses by satisfying
the eschatological curiosity of the faithful. He thus composed the
Prognosticum, which addressed the eschatological themes with great
seriousness, completeness, and moderation, and which distanced
itself from the obsession with calculating the time remaining before
the end of the world and from detailed descriptions of the characters
and the places of the apocalypse. We have already mentioned to this
regard that the *Prognosticum* in some instances even demythologizes
the excessive apocalyptic eschatology contained in the works of some
authors or held in popular belief. Through his recourse to Sacred
Scripture and to the patristic Tradition as unassailable sources, Julian
succeeded in writing a compendium of eschatology that distinguished
itself radically from the easier task of editing a collection of "revelations" in visionary or apocalyptic style. His Good Friday dialogue with
the bishop of Barcelona was centered exclusively on such eschatological problems, particularly the intermediate state of souls, and not on
the interpretation of the Book of Revelation or the date of the *parousia*. But in that same theological dialogue, Julian realized that, in
order to be removed from extremist speculation, the entire eschatological theme had to be treated according to a new and scientific
methodology so that the resulting eschatology would be a body of sys-

tematic teaching and not a series of unfounded suppositions or popular beliefs. What the Christian faithful needed were doctrinal certainties, well founded on the authority of the sources from which the doctrine would be drawn.

With his systematic eschatology, therefore, Julian sought to rationalize as much as possible—that is to say, to bring under the rational and relative understanding of theology—the mysteries concerning the final things. He realized that his synthesis distanced itself from popular belief as well as from apocalyptic theological speculations.[300] This could also explain why around the tenth century or the year 1000 the *Prognosticum* was so widely circulated. Evidently it was necessary for an anti-apocalyptic work such as the *Prognosticum* to moderate the apocalyptic fears, which were very popular but misguided,[301] with the elaboration of a serene and constructive eschatological and theological vision of human history and cosmic reality.[302]

THE *PROGNOSTICUM FUTURI SAECULI* AS THE ORIGIN OF SYSTEMATIC CHRISTIAN ESCHATOLOGY

From a theological point of view, the Middle Ages is considered the great period of philosophical-theological doctrinal syntheses.[303] The long patristic period had produced a vast corpus of theological literature, which did not, however, include general works of a systematic character or syntheses of theological thought. Beginning with the first attempts of the Spanish theological school in the sixth and seventh centuries, and continuing to the work of the Carolingian school in the eighth and ninth centuries, the authors of the time sought to fashion a complete theological and doctrinal system capable of summarizing and containing all or most of the possible aspects of philosophy and Christian theology. For example, they considered the epistemological structure of Christian theology, devoting treatises to the main themes of theology such as the mystery of the Triune God; the creation of the cosmos; the creation of human beings and of angels; the mysteries of the incarnation, death, and resurrection of the Son of God; the sacraments; Christian ethics even up to such eschatological themes as the end of the world, the conclusion of human history, and the plan of God for the cosmos and for humankind.

From a theological point of view, the Scholastic treatises on eschatology are typically characterized as being concise and speculative in a Scholastic sense.[304] In these treatises, a mentality of a metaphysical-speculative nature prevails over one that is substantially still historical and salvific, such as characterized the patristic age. This new formulation is certainly due to the gradual adaptation in theology of categories of thought of a philosophical nature, particularly Platonic categories at first, and subsequently and above all, Aristotelian.[305]

A typical characteristic of medieval eschatology is the attention given to the eschatological destiny of the individual person.[306] More than a collective eschatology, which was abundantly attested in the New Testament and in the patristic writings, in this epoch there was a preponderance of interest in the destiny of the individual. Yet the community or collective and final dimensions of eschatology were not neglected, especially when the themes depended closely on the christological data of the New Testament. For example, the theme of the resurrection of the dead at the end of time certainly was understood in a collective sense, meaning in a Pauline[307] sense, by such prominent Scholastics as Albert the Great, Thomas Aquinas, Bonaventure, Alexander of Hales, and others.

To get to know systematic medieval eschatology[308] it would theoretically be sufficient to examine carefully the numerous *de novissimis* produced by various medieval authors and usually placed at the end of their treatises, from the eschatological questions in the *De Sacramentis* of Hugh of St. Victor to book IV of the *Sententiae* of Peter Lombard,[309] all the way to the great Scholastic works of Albert the Great, Thomas Aquinas, Bonaventure, and so forth. By the time we finished analyzing these texts, we would have a notable and rich theological system of eschatology and an ample and more or less homogeneous range of the theological vision on the matter. But the verification of this substantial homogeneity of the treatises would give rise to a fundamental question concerning the common source from which the greatest authors of the Scholastic Middle Ages had probably drawn for the theological elaboration of their eschatological synthesis. In other words, who was the first author to formulate in a systematic way the corpus of doctrines relating to eschatology that would give way to ever more ample elaborations?

The answer to this question is very easy: the common historical and theological source of medieval eschatology was the *Prognosticum futuri saeculi* of Julian of Toledo.[310] In fact, besides being the most ancient treatise on Christian eschatology,[311] it was certainly also the main source of medieval eschatology. The work of Julian of Toledo has in fact assumed the role of *trait-d'union* between the patristic theological epoch and the monastic, Carolingian, and Scholastic Middle Ages with regard to eschatological matters, summarizing the patrimony of the biblical and patristic authorities and introducing them into the environment of rational and theological investigation typical of the Middle Ages. In-depth knowledge of the methodological structure and theological content of the work of Julian of Toledo can shed light on the way Catholic eschatology subsequently developed in one way rather than in another, and how it took on a nearly definitive structure beginning with the general theological systemizations of the Scholastic Middle Ages.

Naturally, this does not mean that every medieval author, especially of the Scholastic epoch, had directly read the work of Julian of Toledo and was inspired by it. We know that beginning with the thirteenth century the European distribution of the *Prognosticum* decreased notably and the work was consequently not known directly by many of the great medieval authors. If the *Prognosticum* is to be considered the source of the subsequent medieval eschatological synthesis,[312] it is due to the fact that Julian's eschatology was known and assimilated in its main lines by an important author, Peter Lombard, whose philosophical-theological work[313] was very important in influencing the development of the whole of Scholastic theology. In this way, the *Prognosticum* received a sort of official recognition in the historical development of medieval theology. Peter Lombard's assimilation of Julian's eschatological thought at times reached the point where he reproduced the same literary forms.

Besides the authors inspired by his eschatological system, Julian of Toledo had in the Middle Ages also an audience of thousands of anonymous readers of his work. Therefore, the dissemination of the *Prognosticum* in the Middle Ages was an extraordinary event: there was not a single monastery, *schola*, or great theologian between the ninth and twelfth century that did not possess one or more copies of the *Prognosticum*, read or study it, and was not considerably influenced by it, either theologically or ascetically and spiritually.

In conclusion, therefore, Catholic eschatology at the end of the seventh century, after the patristic period—and thanks to the first

work of Scholastic systematization[314] of the topic by Julian of Toledo—
already possessed a theological structure and an epistemological
structure. With such constitutive elements, this eschatology, which far
surpassed the rosiest hopes of its author, passed through the centuries
substantially intact. Even better, it was fully adopted by the majority of
theologians in the systematic elaboration of eschatology in the Middle
Ages and subsequent centuries. In its main lines, this eschatology has
become the common eschatology of the Catholic Church. It has been
approved and given proper regard by the theological magisterium of
the church itself, beginning with the sober documents of the thirteenth to fifteenth centuries and continuing up to the latest contemporary theological doctrine.[315]

Thus, Christian eschatology has a historical-theological structure that cannot be neglected by contemporary theologians, as does
unfortunately happen. In even more explicit terms, this means that
originality and historical continuity, on the level of methodology and
content, have become for Christian eschatology a criterion of reliability for the transmission of authentic theological doctrine. We
believe that this aspect is decidedly primary in the theological investigation itself and can serve as a serious evaluation and verification of
the most different theological hypotheses, in an ecumenical context
as well.

THE COMPLEX QUESTION OF THE MANUSCRIPTS
OF THE *PROGNOSTICUM FUTURI SAECULI* AND ITS
DISTRIBUTION IN MEDIEVAL EUROPE

J. N. Hillgarth, editor in 1976 of the critical edition of the
Prognosticum futuri saeculi, reveals that already in the preparatory
phase of the critical edition he had before him "an embarrassingly
large number of MSS" of the *Prognosticum*: there were 152 more or less
complete manuscripts and twenty-six manuscripts containing part of
the work,[316] of which at least twenty-three belonged to the ninth and
tenth centuries and twenty-six to the eleventh century. This unusual
abundance of ancient manuscripts[317] undoubtedly means that the
Prognosticum was a work of "enormous popularity" in the early Middle
Ages. This is also evidenced by the frequent presence of the work in
over one hundred catalogues of European libraries.[318]

Only two years after the defense of his doctoral thesis, "A Critical Edition of the 'Prognosticum futuri saeculi' of St. Julian of Toledo" (Cambridge, Queen's College, 1956), Hillgarth, in a new and important article on the matter,[319] indicated the existence of 153 almost complete manuscripts of the *Prognosticum* and twenty-three other manuscripts containing parts of the work. Among the complete manuscripts, around thirty were from the ninth century, ten from the tenth century, and twenty-six from the eleventh century. Consultation of library catalogues shows that, in almost all the libraries of Europe between the ninth and the twelfth century, the *Prognosticum* was present in two or three copies and, judging from the annotations of the librarians, it was frequently requested by readers. This is proof that those copies did not remain "unread on the shelves."[320] The *Prognosticum* thus enjoyed a circulation among the libraries of Europe that de Ghellinck does not hesitate to define a "succès enorme, étonnant."[321]

But only a few years later, in 1963,[322] Hillgarth announced the need to increase his list of complete manuscripts by ten and to increase by six the number of the catalogues of libraries that contained some reference to the *Prognosticum*.

Finally publishing the critical edition of the *Prognosticum* in 1976, Hillgarth disclosed that there were around fifty-two complete manuscripts of the work from before 1100. Only two of them,[323] however, were written with the "belles lettres Visigothiques," and only a fragment (of a total of twenty-four) could be considered of Spanish origin.[324] As he indicates in the important introduction to the critical edition of the *Prognosticum*, the most ancient manuscripts of the work were written in uncial or semiuncial characters, possibly with marginal notes or some additions in Visigothic cursive.[325] Subsequently, the uncial and semiuncial characters were replaced by the easier lower-case writing Carolina, which was perhaps also used as an exercise for young copyists.[326] The two most ancient manuscripts of the *Prognosticum* that have reached us and that are witnesses to its circulation in the northern isles date to between the eighth and the ninth centuries.[327]

The lack of Iberian manuscripts of the *Prognosticum* in the first two centuries after the death of Julian is not surprising. None of the ninth-century manuscripts is of Hispanic origin, but the manuscripts of the other works of Julian inserted in the edition of Hillgarth were mainly Iberian. This means that the *Prognosticum* was probably better known beyond Spanish borders than in Julian's own country and that the principal cause of this anomaly was not the rejection of the work but the consequence of the historical upheavals that happened in Spain with the Arabic invasion and domination. These events probably provoked the destruction of a great part of the literary patrimony preserved in the monastic and episcopal libraries of Hispanic-Visigothic Spain.

An exception could be the manuscript to which Hillgarth refers when speaking of a copy of the *Prognosticum* coming from Oviedo (Asturias, northern Spain) and datable to 882. According to the hypothesis, which Hillgarth himself calls a "mere speculation,"[328] it is possible that such a manuscript "was a copy made at Toledo" and was therefore a copy close to the original that could have been brought to Oviedo in the North of the Asturias just before the Arabic invasion, perhaps along with other writings of Julian together with the relics of the saint. Later, the priests of Merida would have provided for the transportation of these together with the apostle James's relics in Galicia.

Seeking the reason for this absence of manuscripts of the *Prognosticum* in the Iberian Peninsula, Hillgarth took up the suggestion of an Italian scholar who indicated that something similar was already happening with the works of Beatus of Lièbana, which, oddly, were not widely distributed in Castile. The reason for this mysterious absence was that perhaps the writings of Abbot Beatus, being too apocalyptic, were underappreciated in the Spanish Mozárabic context.[329] Naturally such a reason is not *sic et simpliciter* applicable to the history of the distribution of the *Prognosticum*.

As for the geographical itinerary of the *Prognosticum* in its European circulation, Hillgarth maintains[330] that the work of Julian followed the same journey as the works of Isidore of Seville, which were very widely distributed and, to a greater extent than the *Prognosticum*, were found in the libraries of the Middle Ages.[331] Beginning in the ninth century, Irish and Anglo-Saxon[332] Benedictine monks distributed the *Prognosticum* in the most important libraries under their influence. In the Carolingian period, knowledge of Julian's eschatology was spread via the French scriptoria. In addition, in the twelfth century, the Cistercian Order significantly contributed to the knowledge of the *Prognosticum*. [333]

In the second half of the thirteenth century, however, the distribution of the work decreased in parallel with the birth of the mendicant religious Orders and with the growth of universities. These two developments replaced the monastic theology and the episcopal and monastic schools that were until then the custodians of the culture, of the patrimony of the manuscript codices,[334] and of theological knowledge.

THE *EDITIO PRINCEPS INCUNABULUM* AND THE PUBLISHING HISTORY OF THE *PROGNOSTICUM FUTURI SAECULI*

Toward the end of the fifteenth century, in the period in which the use of the printing press was established, the *Prognosticum* abandoned the spartan and difficult layout of the medieval parchment codex and manuscript to become *incunabulum.* The *editio princeps* was probably printed in Milan (Italy) approximately in the year 1490,[335] and its *incipit* gives evidence of the usual, centuries-old confusion between Julian of Toledo and Julian Pomerius. The *incunabulum* is in octavo (18.3 x 11.2 cm.) and consists of thirty numbered pages (Ai...Eiv). The title page in fact reads: *Incipiŭt pronosticata Iulia/ni pomerii urbis toletane epis/copi de futuro saeculo. Eivv: Expliciŭt pronosticata Juliani pomerii.*[336] The *incunabulum* does not furnish information about the printer, the date of the edition, the publisher, or the manuscript used for the edition, but, according to Hillgarth,[337] it seems to have come from a copy that merged the two families of manuscripts.

Subsequently, during the difficult theological debate that arose from the Lutheran reform, two controversialist and polemical counter-reformists, Ioannes Dobeneck (called *Cochlaeus*)[338] in 1536, at Leipzig, and the Dominican friar Nicholaus Bugnee[339] in 1554, in Paris, thought about ways to use the *Prognosticum.* They promoted its printing and circulation as a theological work of Catholic origin capable of showing the antiquity and, therefore, the authenticity, supported by the texts of the fathers of the church, of Catholic eschatological doctrine, especially the doctrine about the life and the immediate eschatological destination of the souls after bodily death and about purgatory.

This series of reasons was naturally directed against the contestations, negations, and eschatological formulations of the Reformers (the *perversa dogmata*, as they were defined by Fr. Nicholaus Bugnee).[340] Never would Julian of Toledo have imagined that his *Prognosticum* would one day be exploited or used for such a controversial purpose.

The edition of Cochlaeus[341] carries the passage of the *De Scriptoribus Ecclesiasticis* of Ioannes Trithemius, purged of the misleading confusion of persons between Julian of Toledo and Julian Pomerius, whom Cochlaeus identifies as a Christian writer who lived in the fifth century.

The 1554 Parisian edition was edited by the Dominican friar Nicholaus Bugnee. The manuscript from which the edition drew was the one alluded to by Resendus in his letter to Bartholomeus Quevedo,[342] which had been stolen from him about ten years prior. He recognized it by the fact that the printed edition contained the same errors as the manuscript codex. As in historical romances, the publisher Nicholaus Bugnee narrates in the introductory letter to the archdeacon of the Diocese of Vannes that he had found by chance and in a bad state the manuscript of the *Prognosticum* (*fortuitu in cubiculo nostrum evertens reperi*).[343] Bugnee did not lose heart and succeeded in printing it by supplementing it with the insertion of texts to complete the parts lacking in the manuscript. Because of this, according to Hillgarth, the edition of Bugnee is irrelevant in the reconstruction of the original text. The de Lorenzana edition (1782–85) of the works of Julian knew and mentioned the Bugnee edition of the *Prognosticum* but did not use it. Not even Hillgarth used the edition of Bugnee, since it did not make valid textual contributions but rather contained different curious variants and omissions of entire chapters of book II.[344]

In 1564, in Douai (France), a new printed edition of the *Prognosticum*[345] was made by Boëtius Epo.[346] After centuries of equivocations, the editor definitively eliminated the confusion between the two Julians in the preface to the work, clearly distinguishing them as Julian of Toledo and Julian Pomerius, but he commits, in turn, another error. In fact, he attributes to Julian Pomerius the work *De comprobatione sextae aetatis*, which is instead certainly to be attributed to Julian of Toledo.

In 1575, Margarin de la Bigne[347] included the *Prognosticum* (edition of Douai) in the *Sacra Bibliotheca SS. Patrum*,[348] and this same edition was reproduced several times in subsequent collections of the works of the fathers.[349] In the second half of the seventeenth century, the *Prognosticum* and the other works of Julian were included in vol. 12 of the *Maxima Bibliotheca Veterum Patrum*.[350] After nearly a century, in 1782–85, the works of Julian, including the *Prognosticum*, were republished at the initiative of Cardinal de Lorenzana, then archbishop primate of Toledo, in vol. 2 of the works of the Toledan fathers:

Sanctorum Patrum Toletanorum quotquot extant opera, edited *cura et studio* of some Spanish scholars.[351] They compared the two different editions, that of Cochlaeus, or Lipsia, from 1536, and that of Boëtius Epo, or of Douai, from 1564, preferring the latter because, in their opinion, it was more precise in quoting Julian's patristic sources. In reality this was an erroneous evaluation,[352] not only because the edition of Cochlaeus (the manuscript from which he edited the *Prognosticum* having also been lost) seems, upon closer examination, to be more reliable, but above all because the manuscript from which the Boëtius Epo edition or that of Douai was edited belongs to a small group of manuscripts of lesser importance that date to the twelfth and thirteenth centuries.[353] According to Hillgarth, the edition of de Lorenzana, though prepared with care and diligence, cannot be compared to the great editions of Maurini or with the edition of the works of Isidore of Seville edited by Arévalo.[354]

Subsequently Abbé Migne undertook the bold enterprise of gathering *in unum* almost all the patristic texts, both Latin and Greek, putting the patristic works in a double edition at the disposal of scholars. And it was a grandiose work. Julian and his works (in the de Lorenzana edition) were incorporated into the extraordinary collection of Migne (vol. 96, cols. 445–818).

Lastly, the strong desire to return to the biblical and patristic sources expressed and manifested by both Protestant and Catholic theology at the beginning of the last century led to the progressive recovery of the origins of Christian theology after centuries of Scholasticism. Without overlooking the immense work of J.-P. Migne, which is still valid and in many cases still the edition most quoted for thousands of works not yet critically edited, the methodological and scientific requirements stimulated the birth of new collections of patristic texts that could furnish editions of great critical value. And also at this time the *Prognosticum* was subjected to a reevaluation of its biblical, patristic, and theological content, this time in a true, new, and more than satisfactory critical edition, based on a vast collection of codices of the work, giving rise, in 1976, after decades of hard and meticulous work,[355] to the critical edition, *cura et studio* by J. N. Hillgarth for the Corpus Christianorum, Series Latina, vol. 115.

THE CRITICAL EDITION OF THE *PROGNOSTICUM FUTURI SAECULI CURA ET STUDIO* BY J. N. HILLGARTH (1976)[356]

In 1999, on the occasion of J. N. Hillgarth's seventieth birthday and at the conclusion of his long academic career as an "inspiring scholar" and "exemplary teacher,"[357] the Institute of Medieval Studies of Toronto dedicated to him a miscellanea of studies in his honor with the collaboration of his former students.[358]

A man of great academic merits, Professor Hillgarth dedicated much of his intellectual strengths to the wise mentoring of many students who earned their doctorates by studying the historiography and the spirituality of Spain, as well as the relationships with Judaism and Islam in Spain in the early Middle Ages. He particularly inculcated in his students a love of the documentary dimension of study and of literary texts. More than other testimonies of the past that reach us through archaeology and other disciplines, texts serve as a *trait-d'union* to achieve an understanding of the institutions and the events of the Middle Ages. In this sense, Hillgarth is universally recognized as one of the greatest experts on the Middle Ages, especially the early Middle Ages and Visigothic historiography, as well as other medieval themes in which he developed a deep interest over many years: the history of the island of Majorca, where he resides for part of the year, and the works of the very prolific medieval Majorcan philosopher Ramon Llull.

Hillgarth's scholarship is shown by his rich bibliography,[359] which covers patristic Christianity to Scholasticism and both had and has a worldwide influence, above all in university environments concerned with studying the Middle Ages. Some of Hillgarth's works are now considered true classics and obligatory starting points for scholars seeking to delve into the historical interpretation of important events that have marked history and the European culture beginning with the early Middle Ages. This is the case, for instance, with Hillgarth's studies and publications about the conversion of the West—and, in particular, of the Visigothic empire—to the Catholic faith.

The work that Hillgarth has done to reconstruct the immense popularity and influence that Julian of Toledo and his *Prognosticum futuri saeculi* had in medieval Europe remains the true milestone of his scholarship. He has the great merit of having provided us with an excellent critical edition of this work (and of others) of the great bishop of Toledo, edited in vol. 115 of the Corpus Christianorum, Series Latina.

The work on a critical edition of the *Prognosticum* was begun by Hillgarth in the second half of the 1950s, upon completion of his doctoral thesis, "A Critical Edition of the 'Prognosticum futuri saeculi' of St. Julian of Toledo."[360] The edition of the *opera omnia* of Julian would have required a second volume to contain the long exegetical treatise written by Julian of Toledo and entitled *Antikeimenon libri duo* or *Liber de diversis*.[361] The critical edition was to be prepared *cura et studio* by the Spanish Dominican Adolfo Robles Sierra.[362] But his sudden death in 1997 prevented him from bringing the arduous work to completion, and so the *opera omnia* of Julian of Toledo is still waiting for the second volume.

Hillgarth's edition, vol. 1 of the *opera omnia* of Julian of Toledo contains seven works. Of them, five belong to the primate of Spain: the *Prognosticum futuri saeculi*, the *Apologeticum de tribus capitulis*, the *De comprobatione sextae aetatis*, the *Historia Wambae Regis*, and the *Epistula ad Modoenum*. The other two works are the two *Idalii Barcinonensis Episcopi Epistulae*, which are present in many manuscripts of the *Prognosticum*. Hillgarth has edited the critical edition of four of such works: the *Idalii Epistulae*, the *Prognosticum futuri saeculi*, the *Apologeticum de tribus capitulis*, and the *De comprobatione sextae aetatis*. The *Historia Wambae Regis* has been included in the volume *ad fidem editionis* of W. Levison,[363] while the brief *Epistula ad Modoenum* was edited *cura et studio* by B. Bischoff.[364] In the case of the *Historia Wambae Regis* and the *Epistula ad Modoenum*, Hillgarth introduced them into the volume having taken into consideration the corrections and the additions to the critical apparatus that had been made in the meantime. He has the merit of having gathered together the aforesaid works that form a true *corpus iulianeum*, upon which scholars can draw with confidence for a long time to come.

After this edition, two or three other works of Julian of Toledo are lacking, at least among those that have reached us: the quoted *Antikeimenon*, and the brief *Elogium Ildephonsi*, which was certainly written by Julian, as Hillgarth[365] maintains and had already critically edited;[366] and the *Ars grammatica*, widely attributed to Julian but still questioned by some scholars.

The critical edition of the *Prognosticum* was composed by Hillgarth with great care. He considered the analysis of a vast family of codices (over 170 by the end of his research), on the basis of which he established a very reliable text from the point of view of the science of paleography. The edition was the fruit of a patient work of comparison of two particularly reliable codices, even if with numerous possible textual variations. Hillgarth's intention is clearly expressed in the *Introduction* to the edition of the *Prognosticum*: "My aim has been to reproduce the text written by Julian not the texts of the current editions of the sources he employed. Since the greater part of the Prognosticum is taken verbatim from earlier authors it is difficult to avoid being influenced by the texts of the sources. It is largely for this reason that I have leaned heavily on the 'Praefatio', the only extensive section of the work where borrowing from earlier authors has not been demonstrated."[367]

It is this important distinction that Hillgarth makes between the text of Julian, which includes patristic sources, and the patristic texts themselves in the modern edition, that allows us to understand the difficulty met by the editor. He has justly pursued the aim of reproducing the text of Julian and not the single texts of the fathers, knowing that the final text, strictly speaking, is not of Julian. It is true, however, that a *lectio continua* of the work gives the impression of a studious interaction between the author and his sources, so that the text can be regarded as constituting a whole. This remark, at least for the *Prognosticum*, would perhaps have been able to inspire the decision of the editor not to insert an *index verborum* or lexicological list at the end of the work, as E. Ann Matter wished in the quoted review of Hillgarth's edition. It would have been greatly appreciated by contemporary researchers.

We have encountered an analogous difficulty in the English translation of the Latin text of the *Prognosticum*. After some translation attempts and careful reflection, we have reached the same conclusion as the editor and have come to the same conviction of having to make a similar choice: namely, to translate the text of Julian "as if it were *his* text." To have considered the modern editions of the patristic works quoted by Julian would have placed too much emphasis on his patristic *collage*, thus threatening to overlook the literary homogeneity of the texts that, thanks to the wise editing work of Julian of Toledo, was so successful.

THE CRITERIA OF TRANSLATION

It could seem a desperate enterprise to attempt to translate into a modern language a theological text from the seventh century that was written in Latin and is largely anthological. It is difficult enough to express or translate into another language the thought of only one author. Evidently then, difficulties increase greatly if the authors of the texts to be translated are thirty or more.

It was only the strong desire to make the eschatological thought of Julian of Toledo accessible to a wider public, thanks to the world-wide diffusion of the English language, and this thought alone, that allowed me to overcome the temporary crisis and reject the thought of renouncing the work of translation. Therefore, I decided to continue in my project, convinced of its intrinsic value and the goodness of its aim.

Concerning the criteria used in translating the *Prognosticum*, it is first of all necessary to say that it has been neither simple nor easy to express in a modern language the "composite" Latin of Julian. To succeed in this enterprise I had to be carefully attentive to ensuring that one would not feel "the differences" between the form of sentences of Julian and the patristic texts quoted by him. It was a basic necessity, in short, of literary homogeneity. After some trial translation attempts, however, and with a greater effort to adapt the text to the *intentio auctoris*, the resulting translations of the first chapters began to resemble the original one and were thus acceptable, even though it remained an attempt to transmit in a modern language theological ideas dating back more than thirteen hundred years, which were not to be compared for any reason to modern and contemporary eschatological theses. This would have been a serious error that would have jeopardized the historical and theological dimension of the work.

Therefore, I realized that, where the literary homogeneity was concerned, it put at risk the translation of the *Prognosticum*, which is itself for many reasons a quite different work from the other writings of Julian. The other texts of the *Prognosticum*, undoubtedly written by Julian, such as the *Praefatio* and the *Oratio ad Deum* did not help me in this direction. The *Praefatio* to the work, in fact, is written with emphasis in an elegant language, and is at times magnificent. The *Oratio ad Deum* is a heartfelt prayer to God by the author himself, written in a poetic language, in imitation of the biblical psalms of supplication and

request for divine help. But if these texts did not provide objective
help, there were, instead, the titles of the chapters of the *Prognosticum*
and the texts associated with the patristic quotations, which revealed to
me the true style to be adopted in translating. These texts, in fact,
express quite well the intentions and the theology of the author and,
paradoxically, the patristic quotations are interpreted as a commentary
to the titles and the reasoning of the author, not the contrary, as could
be deduced by a first reading of the work. I repeat: the patristic texts are
the commentary on the proposition or thesis articulated by the author
in the title of each chapter. In this way Julian undoubtedly succeeded in
rendering the Latin of the fathers of the church, who were chronologi-
cally and culturally very distant from him and from one another, in conformity with his Latin of the seventh century.

I realized, in short, that to obtain a translation compatible with
the original text it was necessary to complete the same effort done by
Julian. In a certain sense, he had done objectively something analogous in transmitting to his contemporaries the ancient texts, with the
immense advantage of having used the same Latin language.
Undoubtedly, however, the cultural mediation achieved by Julian had
to be a true mediation, and he succeeded with it. He had been the
mediator of his theses and had summoned a multitude of witnesses
(the fathers of the church) who confirmed it with their authority of
being *Maiores*.

I realized that the translation would also have had to express the
same intentions: to be a cultural mediation between the starting language and the target language. As the work proceeded, I realized that
this could also be done for the translation into a modern language
using the criterion of literary homogeneity to obtain a synthesis of
texts and styles.

Therefore, as much as possible, the translation was done in a literal way, almost *verbo e verbo* to render the thought of the author in the
best possible way. Naturally, because of this editorial choice, the translation asks of the benevolent reader an effort of understanding, above
all of the original theological ideas communicated with a terminology
that might seem unusual, or at least unusual for the modern language. But this effort is rewarded when the reader "enters" the text
through the mediation of the theological titles of the chapters.

When possible and in respect of the lexical constructions of
every language, the syntactic and grammatical structures of the text,

especially in the most complex or most remarkable parts, were always preserved.

I was attentive to the preservation and invariance of the semantic fields. This choice is really effective in giving homogeneity to the text so that the same terms were always maintained, almost in a "mono-terminology," to indicate the same semantic realities.

This did not prevent me, however, from trying to achieve a dynamic translation. This meant adapting the source language to the target language. The reason lies in the fact that in this perspective, the work, though preserving, as it was absolutely supposed to, the general and particular character of the theological work of thirteen centuries ago, acquires a dimension of objective comprehension through the new language in which it is, as it were, "poured out," thus overcoming the chronological gap that separates it from the historical present.

From a graphic point of view, the form of the text was maintained as it appears in Hillgarth's edition of the *Prognosticum* for the Corpus Christianorum.[368]

CHAPTER IV

A THEOLOGICAL COMMENTARY ON THE *PROGNOSTICUM FUTURI SAECULI* OF JULIAN OF TOLEDO

THE THEOLOGICAL AND ANTHROPOLOGICAL CHARACTERISTICS OF THE ESCHATOLOGY OF JULIAN OF TOLEDO

The purpose of this theological commentary is not to demonstrate how modern or up-to-date the eschatological thought of Julian of Toledo is. Such intentions are frequently found in authors who wish at all costs to actualize and modernize the message of a work written ages ago. Personally, I think that such an attempt is out of place and antihistorical. If anything, it should be to the contrary. The ancient work, in this case the *Prognosticum*, is what should be identified as the source from which the history of Christian eschatology began its theological development that then led to the elaboration of a doctrine in subsequent centuries.

The commentary we intend to make on the *Prognosticum futuri saeculi* concerns, rather, the desire to show how the author has succeeded, for the first time in the history of Christian theology and with significant intellectual effort, in connecting the different eschatological doctrines derived from Sacred Scripture and the fathers of the church, to form for the first time a theological system completely devoted to the eschatological dimension.

In so doing, Julian of Toledo has shown his originality in that he has chosen to build an eschatological system founded not so much on the events, realities, or themes of eschatology (the *eschata*, the last things), even though they are important elements of eschatology. Rather, he has founded his system on the subjects, both divine and human, who are at its origin and are also the historical protagonists, intermediaries, and final recipients of it. Thus we can say that Julian has constructed a real theological-dogmatic eschatology because he appeals to the principal mysteries of the Christian faith to elaborate essentially their eschatological dimension and nature. This is what happens in the explicit structure of the *Prognosticum*, which, upon careful and logical reading, appears to be composed of many different and complementary theological characteristics.

The eschatology elaborated by Julian of Toledo is in fact:

- A *trinitarian eschatology* in its origin, because it is to the three divine Persons that the double eschatological goal is attributed, that of creation and that of redemption.
- A *christological and pneumatological eschatology* because of the historicization of the eschatology of God upon humanity and the cosmos. God's Son and the Holy Spirit, with their historical missions, have come to complete in human history what was determined together with God the Father in the divine eternity concerning the elevation of the human creature to the supernatural state. Even if humanity had fallen in Adam, it was then redeemed or re-created. This means, according to the author, that without Christ and the Holy Spirit there would not have been any eschatology or final end to reach. The only discouraging truth that would have reigned over the human world would have been the certainty of having to die and remain forever in death, without any prospect of a continuing life.
- An *ecclesiological eschatology* in its historical and meta-historical dimension—that is, in the terrestrial church and in the heavenly church, because it is precisely in the church and for the church, animated by the Holy Spirit, that believers learn to know, nourished by the Word of God and the divine life communicated by the sacraments, with hope in the final end of human history produced by Christ and the Holy Spirit.
- A *strongly anthropological eschatology*, because the human being is always the recipient of the eschatology of God and is also the dialogical subject, fit for understanding the final goal.

The human being possesses characteristics that are spiritual
and bodily, willed intentionally by the creator, and that are
both included, by right, in the elaboration of the Christian
eschatology, wanted and realized by the Savior. The anthropological eschatology is presented by Julian in a double way: as
eschatology of the soul, compiled by him for the first time in
the history of Christian theology, but also as eschatology of the
body, more traditionally elaborated already beginning from
the New Testament. The author was thus inspired by the possibility of distinguishing two interconnected levels of the
eschatology of God: one being the survival of the soul after
death and its full experience of the eschatological results,
despite the fundamental absence of corporeality; and the
other being the plan, undoubtedly genial and divine, of recuperating the deceased corporeality in the perspective of the
final resurrection of the whole human being. The recovery of
the body in the final eschatology, the perspective of its eternal
duration with absolute characteristics of perfection (immortality, incorruptibility, absolute absence of limits) represents
one of the most captivating elements of the Christian faith
because its object is the integral redemption of the human
being, avoiding spiritualisms and/or materialisms of every
type. To this concrete human being God offers the possibility—rather, the certainty—of salvation and glorification,
which consist mainly in a series of relationships elevated and
transformed by the new condition of being risen and which
entails the vision of God and full communion with the angels
and the saints of all times. The impossible happens with the
conquest of the final end for the whole human being. The
unhoped-for becomes reality.

- Finally, a *cosmic eschatology*, because it concerns and involves
  the material dimension of the universe, which, belonging to
  the original plan of God, also enters with full rights into the
  resumption of the eschatological plan of God, owing to the
  missions of Christ and the Holy Spirit. Based on this inclusion of the cosmos in the final dimension of eschatology, the
  author can conclude his work of reconstructing the eschatology of God and humankind with a strong allusion to how
  the final goal of eschatology may actually be considered,

instead, as the beginning of a new history of relationships between God and human beings in a new world and in a new heaven.

Naturally the author does not remain silent about and does not exclude the possibility (which is not a certainty) of this complex dimension of God's eschatological proposal to humankind being refused. In this case the message that the *Prognosticum futuri saeculi* places before the eyes of the believing reader is the possibility, because of human responsibility, of what we could call an *anti-eschatology* occurring. Julian of Toledo proposes this possibility with the same performative language found in the eschatological preaching of Jesus, underlining the strong demarcation that exists between the *certainty* of redemption and the *possibility* of damnation. In addition to these main dogmatic themes, the *Prognosticum* includes other theological elements of notable value that we will try to point out during the commentary. But these main dogmatic dimensions of Christian eschatology—theological, anthropological, and cosmic—which Julian of Toledo presents in such a wisely interconnected way in the *Prognosticum futuri saeculi*, constitute, in our opinion, the very heart of every systematic theological elaboration of eschatological matters.

BOOK I: THE MYSTERY OF DEATH

The theology of death in the Prognosticum futuri saeculi *of Julian of Toledo*

Book I of the *Prognosticum*, devoted to the origin of human death, is not the direct result of the theological dialogue between Julian and Idalius about eschatological matters. The dialogue is rather at the origin of the whole publishing project of the *Prognosticum*, especially books II and III. The two bishops planned the project of these two books together, and they decided to precede them with an additional book devoted to the subject of death, but without having discussed its titles and contents, as they had done for the other themes. Book I, therefore, was compiled only by Julian using the same literary structure and "with a distinction of the titles similar to that of the other books."[1]

The reason why they had decided to place a book about death before the other two general eschatological themes was probably because of a pastoral problem mentioned by the two bishops in their conversation, most likely the fruit of their experiences as bishops. Evidently in Hispanic-Visigothic Christianity of the seventh century, believers had an excessive fear of death, or there was a certain diffusion of customs and beliefs about it that were not really Christian. Thus, it was necessary to clarify and/or correct the people's beliefs with the exposition of an appropriate doctrine. The two bishops believed that through an articulated reflection on death, particularly on the origin of death and on "Christian" death, which emphasized the paschal and christological meaning of death, this excess of fear could be attenuated and the practices of worship surrounding the dead regulated. Julian seems to allude to this problem in the preface of the *Prognosticum* when he says: "the reader's mind, terrified by an exaggerated fear of death, would be lifted up again by the hope of the heavenly joys."[2]

Therefore, Julian wrote book I in the months following his conversation with Idalius of Barcelona. The work begins with a basic question about the origin of human death, whether it is to be considered an element of nature or if, instead, it has a definite cause. Other themes related to human death are subsequently treated.

The origin or the "first time" of death (Prognosticum *I, i*)

Death has an origin. In the theology of death elaborated by Julian in the *Prognosticum* this is a fundamental truth, which he expresses with brevity, but in enough depth for the reader to remember it and understand that death cannot be attributed to the creative action of God. Death, therefore, is an element extraneous to the divine plan of creation of humanity and the cosmos, having entered human history in a precise moment in time and for a concrete cause.

Death made its appearance in the world because of the sin of the first man, as the apostle Paul teaches in his Letter to the Romans. The authoritative testimony of the apostle is judged by Julian as more than sufficient to begin his entire eschatological treatise and to base, specifically, a theology of the origin of human death in an original way in comparison to other religious visions or to other philosophical and cultural anthropologies that attribute death either to the divinity or to nature, considering it part of the "normal" or "natural" phenomena of life and terrestrial existence. According to Julian, however, death is unnatural, at least in its "first time"; it is an aggression against humanity that has a reason and a particular cause, knowledge of which may help people to understand the greatness and the magnanimity of the Creator, who did not foresee it at all for his creatures, and the pity and mercy of the Savior, who would come to transform death into an instrument of universal redemption.

The human being created exempt from death, but rightly become mortal (Prognosticum I, ii-iii)

On the basis of *De civitate dei* of Augustine, Julian introduces the two creatural subjects created by God: the angel and the human being. He clarifies, however, that God created them in different ways, and consequently they are very different creatures. Angels were created in such a way that even if they had sinned, they would not have undergone death, whereas human beings were created in such a way that if they had obeyed God, they would have been elevated to share divine immortality without the experience of death. But such finality depended on their behavior, for if they estranged themselves from God, bodily death would be the consequence, and it would be transmitted to their descendants. The result, Julian says, was a worsening of nature, because death brought with itself an inclination toward evil, bodily and spiritual corruptibility, pain, illness, and the disappointing experience of anthropological limits.

In the second place, in *Prognosticum* I, iii, still drawing on Augustine, Julian emphasizes how the human being, having been created free, had the power of *posse mori* and *posse non mori*, that is, the power to undergo death and the power to avoid death. But in both situations God wanted to avoid the irreparable, that is, sinning without the consequence of death as punishment, or, even worse, that the created human being would be mortal to the point of also being exposed to death without having sinned. The reasoning is quite complicated but it allows us to understand that even divine punishment is providential, in that it serves to avoid the worst.

Finally, the justness of the punishment of death is underlined. It was the consequence of not observing the divine precept, and thus in the bad use of liberty and the will that provoked the degeneration of

God's creation to the point of exposing it to the reality of the extinction of life.

From these considerations arises a theology of death that presents itself in an original way as an etiology of death founded upon Sacred Scripture and the reflections of Tradition.

The word death: *a creative etymology (*Prognosticum *I, iiii)*

Julian does not resist the temptation of using the method of hermeneutics and the knowledge of reality that were brought to the highest point by Isidore of Seville in his monumental *Etymologiae* and experienced and practiced in a grammatical and rhetorical way by the *grammaticus* Julian in the years of his teaching at the Episcopal School of Toledo. He does so to investigate why death is called "death," using a play on words between the terms *death* (in Latin, *mors*) and *bite* or *morsel* (in Latin, *morsus*), which unfortunately does not transfer into English. In Latin, however, it is phonetically quite effective: *mors a morsu*, death from a bite (or morsel). According to this methodology, knowledge of the etymology contributes to a further understanding of the reality. This called for resorting to the doctor of Seville, and the great Isidore does not delude him. With the phonetic creation of the assonances brought to the limit, Julian affirms that to indicate death the Latin word *mors* (death) is used because it refers to the *morsus* (bite) by the first parents from the fruit of the forbidden tree, which is the symbol of humankind being cast out from the divine plan. The bite to which Julian refers is the one, according to the Bible, of the fruit from the tree of knowledge of good and bad: "So she [Eve] took some of its fruit and ate it; and she also gave some to her husband, who was with her, and he ate it" (see Gen 3:6).

If for us such a cognitive methodology is almost deprived of sense, in the eyes of the ancient ones it appeared, instead, as a precious indication that often permitted reaching the heart of the problem and the root of things. Moreover, the Bible has a great regard for names (of things as well as of people), almost as if they render their very being. Therefore, death is called so because of the negative action of the first parents. The etymology may be ingenious or banal, but it is undoubtedly effective.

In this case, therefore, Julian is successful in making his readers understand that the responsibility for death, and even its name, is not of God but of the human being, who, disobeying, fell in sin, and the deadly weakening of its created being was the result of sin. We could define this etymological and phonetic analysis as a second proof of chapter I, in which Julian, relying on the authority of Paul, had already attributed to the human being the responsibility for the entry of death into the human world "for the first time."

There is death and death: the science of the distinction (Prognosticum *I, v*)

Following the Isidorian methodology, from the etymological approach Julian passes to the science of the distinction or the differences, which on a level different from etymology but just as effective, allows for order to be established in things. With this science of the distinction we are already on the level of a phenomenology of the problem of death.

Therefore death is not one and the same, but differs based on the circumstances of human life. Death, in short, is entirely related to the human condition. In a concise way—better still in a proverbial way so as to facilitate memorization—Julian proposes distinguishing death in three groups: unripe, immature, natural. It is unripe, as a fruit far from maturation, in the case of children. This kind of death has always aroused disturbance, perplexity, and deep questions in the human being, and it continues to do so. Why the death of children, always countersigned by a particular characteristic of innocence and vitality of their human condition in growth toward maturity? Why the death of children, so frequent even in the prenatal state or for newborns in the times when Julian wrote? The question is so profound as to justify the distinction of their death from other types of death, being especially compassionate and agonizing.

But death has another specific difference. It can also be immature, which is characteristic of a human life that has not yet reached its full maturation, as in the case of those who die in the prime of their years, that is, in youth. This is also an agonizing death because it occurs in the moment of the maximum physical, intellectual, and affective development of the human being and before reaching anthropological maturity.

Finally, death can be natural, as in the case of the elderly, meaning those who have consumed their charge of vital energy and are no longer able to arrest the physical deterioration of their body.

Apparently it seems that the adjective used by Julian (natural) indicates the normal conclusion of the biological and anthropological process of human life. But we must bear in mind what the author had written before, that death is the consequential punishment for the sin of disobedience toward the Creator and that it degenerates nature ("it changes nature for the worse"). Therefore, *naturalis* is applied to this nature changed for the worse, but not as a normal reality due to the creative action of God; human nature is degenerate, and for this reason it has become incapable of preserving and developing its vital energies—incapable, therefore, of stopping the physical deterioration or illness that mysteriously and without an easily identifiable reason leads to death. This is shown by the fact that even the elderly fear death and desire to escape it, because death is something unnatural; it is against the nature created by God for immortality. Human beings always bear within themselves the desire for infinity and eternity. But death is always also natural because we attribute it to the human nature, even if degenerated because of sin. The only consolation is that the elderly have lived a long and fruitful life, and therefore their bodily death is generally less agonizing and painful, for the one who dies as well as for those who are close at the time of death.

The distinction made between undegenerate nature, for which death is "against nature," and degenerate nature, for which death is "natural," is still maintained in the documents of the Second Vatican Council[3] and in the latest theological and dogmatic synthesis produced by the Catholic Church.[4] In both cases the texts affirm, with a certain solemnity, that the church "teaches" the doctrine according to which bodily death is not a creation of God and humans would have been exempt from it had they not sinned. The use of the verb "to teach" evidently wants to show that the church calls upon all its doctrinal authority to defend this thesis of theological anthropology.

The phenomenology of death (Prognosticum *I, vi*)

The *Prognosticum* begins its analysis of human death with a direct reference to the harshness of death, with consolation from the thought of Augustine. Death is harsh not only because of the separation from the earthly world and from dear ones, but mainly because of the separation within the human being of the soul from the body and vice versa. Therefore, in the anthropological thought proposed by Julian, the ideal unitary nature of the human being emerges, which leaves no space for any body-soul dualism in authentic Christian reflection. The human being is, therefore, the result of an admirable unity of bodily and spiritual elements, in perfect equilibrium and complementariness. A duality on equal terms, therefore, not a dualism. In *Prognosticum* I, xviii, he says that the human being and its created condition are evident in the "*manente adhuc complexu corporis et animae.*" It is when this unity of soul and body is seriously threatened by death that death acquires its harshness or bitterness, or, better yet, causes worry, because this progressive separation produces the awareness of an inner laceration against which the human being feels its own forces to be unequal. Death is, therefore, the phenomenon that lacerates the unity of the conscious spirit dwelling in and vitalizing its own body. According to the medical science or human psychology of the ancient world, which was still in favor at the time of Julian, when the tendency toward the separation between soul and body reaches its maximum, the loss of consciousness occurs. And this is considered the prelude of death.

Julian, following the thought of Augustine, affirms that in some cases a sudden death or a rapid death prevents the perception of this painful separation or worry, because it occurs so immediately that the subject has no time to perceive the bitterness of the separation. But these are obviously conjectures strongly conditioned by the science of the time. The fact is that during the centuries the conviction will spread within Christianity, both spiritually and pastorally, that sudden death is to be carefully avoided in that it prevents a serene and necessary preparation for death. The litany-like invocation present in some spiritual texts is absolutely clear: "*a subitanea morte, libera nos Domine.*" Yet Jesus, himself, the model and absolute example of humankind, experienced death after a long and excruciating agony. Christians must also think about their own death and prepare themselves for the event in the best of ways, as suggested by so many texts of Christian spirituality.

The spirituality of Christian death: death as expiatory penitence (Prognosticum *I, vii*)

Julian realizes that what he said about sudden death could impress or frighten the faithful. He therefore corrects or completes his thought by introducing the great theme of the experience of

human death as an occasion and element of purification or liberation
from sins. In the perspective of Christian faith, in fact, such an objective evil as death can become, providentially, an occasion for penitence, requesting and receiving divine pardon, but also for personal
merit. If the painful death, conceived as separation of the soul from
the body, which produces worry and anguish, is borne with resignation, piety, and faith, it can become the sign of worth and of pardon
of sins, as the result of the resigned and humble endurance of the suffering. In this Christian perspective, in fact, though death is always
considered a punishment and consequence of sin, it is lived in
another dimension, typical of Christianity, as penitence for sins. To
this end Julian looks for the patristic and biblical basis for this theory
and finds it in Gregory the Great's exegesis, with a lot of interpretative liberty, of an episode in the Old Testament (1 Kings 13) narrating
how a prophet of God is "killed but not devoured" by a lion because
of his disobedience toward God. In this strange sequence, "killed but
not devoured," the unattainable hermeneutics of the fathers of the
church and their immense ability to see and find some invisible points
of connection between the biblical texts and reality (so often a source
of amazement, wonder, and admiration) contain two separate elements: first of all, the punishment inflicted by disobedience (the
prophet's death) but, subsequently, also the remission of the sin (his
being "not devoured," meaning the pardon of the prophet's disobedience). The prophet's death had evidently expiated his sin of disobedience. In an analogous way, Julian says that Christian death, with
its anguish and worry, purifies the souls from the least or lightest sins
at the moment of abandoning their body.

One could think that with these considerations Julian intends to
theorize that the believer's purification, necessary for being admitted
to the divine kingdom, coincides with and is exclusively contained in
this final situation of the human death. This means that the harshness
of death would be able to purify everyone needing pardon and would
push him toward a final decision, as if it concerned a moral obligation. A careful reading of the text of the *Prognosticum* does not make
this possible providence of God a doctrinal and universal datum or a
moral obligation of the dying one. As is known, a quite similar theory
has been proposed in recent times about making a final decision for
God in the moment of death, which would extend to all human

beings the salvific adherence to God as the conclusion of every human existence.

The transforming power of the Christian faith: from the "bad" to the "good" death (Prognosticum I, viii)

With the decisive help of Augustine, Julian justifies one of the most extraordinary paradoxes of the Christian faith: the transformation of human death from negative punishment "evidently contrary to life" into a fitting instrument for reaching the future immortal life. This transformation depends on the power of faith in God, who has given so much grace to faith as to overturn the meaning of death itself. This is the reason why Julian, with a play on words so loved by the fathers, can affirm that "at the most for the good it is good."

It is to be noted how this brief chapter (whose literary paternity is of Julian) begins, in an unusual way, with death as the separation of the body from the soul (not vice versa, as it is usually described—the separation of the soul from the body). It seems that in this way the author wants to present death from the point of view of an objective phenomenology of what really happens. Effectively, as shown by experience, during the course of death it is the body that slowly, or suddenly separates itself from its spiritual dimension, which does not undergo suffering or illness, pain or cellular decay, aging or interruption of vital functions. Accordingly, this definition of death as the "separation of the body from the soul" would indeed seem more appropriate and more reflective of reality.

The usual objection: why do those redeemed from sin and death continue to die? (Prognosticum I, viiii)

In this chapter of the *Prognosticum* the didactic and pastoral dimension strongly emerges, united to the intention of its author, that is, a bishop of the seventh century anxious to provide an answer to the concerns of the faithful and to form a theologically prepared clergy.

Among the most common objections of Christians of all times is a radical question, formulated in strictly logical terms, but evidently much too human. Many ask themselves, and they asked themselves also in the times of Julian: If death comes from original sin and if this sin, by the merit of Christ, is forgiven and removed from us in baptism, then why do we continue to die? In other words, if the cause of death has been removed by the salvific action of Christ in the sacrament of baptism, why do we still experience the bitterness of death?

Julian responds to the objection by turning to Augustine and to another beloved author, Julian Pomerius, to affirm that death, the separation of the soul from the body, has been left by God to believers as a "test," even if original sin has objectively been eliminated from everyone thanks to the celebration of baptism, which actualizes the mystery of redemption for every human being. The hypothetical conclusion is not without reason. If in fact the resurrection of the body was concretely given together with baptism, then the life of faith and hope in the future rewards of earthly Christians would be superfluous, considering that, as risen, we would already be glorified.

Faith in future realities helps us, instead, to overcome the trials of life, including the terrible one of death, as it occurred in the life of the martyrs. The baptized will thus reach eternal life, but not without passing through the trial of death, which means abandoning earthly life in order to begin a new life of glory. This requires a very significant bodily metamorphosis that would not have any sense in the earthly world.

The mysterious "presences" at the bedside of the dying: the psychopomp *angels (*Prognosticum *I, x)*

Nothing is more agonizing and mysterious than the agony of someone dying and the anguish of the believer who lives this frightening experience. Death is, in fact, an unknown feared by all. Even the Lord Jesus Christ underwent the *tedium mortis,* and as the history of spirituality teaches us, the saints were afraid to face their death, considering themselves, with great humility, unworthy of the kingdom of God and strongly fearing a possible damnation.

They have also often been tempted by despair in the face of the strait or narrow passage of death. Divine providence, however, did not want anyone to die without sufficient help for their salvation. That is why, ever since the patristic age, a doctrine has been developed according to which a certain kind of angel is present to receive the soul as it is separated from the body and to lead it to its eschatological destiny, a doctrine founded upon the text of Luke 16:22, which narrates how the soul of the poor Lazarus was brought by angels to the bosom of Abraham, and upon the testimony of the New Testament about the guardian angels, which dates back to the preaching of Jesus. They are the so-called angels psychopomp, a Greek term that means "companion of the soul." Julian knows this patristic tradition through Augustine's *De cura pro mortuis gerenda*, and he also knows well the biblical texts of reference. According to Julian, this double testimony is enough foundation for a doctrine attributing the psychopomp angels to the providential initiative of God.

Naturally, apart from the admiration for the faith of the ancient ones and for the providential meaning of an angelic presence established by God to help human beings to live the most delicate moment of their earthly existence, we cannot fail to note how both Julian and Augustine make a simple literal exegesis, perhaps too literal, of the text of Luke 16:22, which renders the validity of the patristic interpretation problematic. Moreover, in the Hebrew thought-world the expression "was carried away by angels to the bosom of Abraham" indeed proves to be somewhat redundant, thus showing that the angels in this quote (as well as the bosom of Abraham) could be interpreted only as a (perhaps somewhat elaborate) figure of speech, as in the oriental style.

From the pastoral point of view, the doctrine about the psychopomp angels proves itself to be valid because it allowed the shepherds of the people of God to reassure the faithful about the moment of their death, inasmuch as at that moment they would not be lacking the help of the earthly church nor the fortifying and accompanying presence of the priest, nor the presence and help of the celestial church, represented precisely by the psychopomp angels. This double presence at the bedside of the dying shows God's care for every single human being who abandons the terrestrial scene.

At the same time, the doctrine about the angelic presence at the moment of death insinuates and presumes, profoundly and positively, the affirmation according to which the human soul survives death, which from a strictly anthropological point of view concerns mainly the bodily dimension of the human subject.

A further meaning of the doctrine about the psychopomp angels is related to the custom of depicting the afterlife as an unknown and mysterious place, about which, therefore, no human being knows much. Accordingly, someone is needed to lead the soul to its eschatological outcome. The presence of the psychopomp angel is thus rendered necessary, but of a relative and opportune necessity, because the deceased can enter the afterlife with an angelic guide who knows the right way to go to complete the mission entrusted to them regarding every human being.

The fear of bodily death (Prognosticum I, xi-xii)

The chapter is entirely devoted to the need to establish a hierarchy of value between earthly and eternal life. The text, drawing from Augustine's commentary of the Gospel of John, uses literary exaggeration to underline the contradictoriness of the faith of many believers who make superhuman efforts to preserve their own earthly life, or to increase their terrestrial existence by only a few years. But, basically, when they make these attempts, their "death is deferred, not avoided." Julian underlines the illogicality of many who, acting in this way, totally overlook the most important thing: the eternal health of their own soul and the goodness of their own future. Expressions such as "mankind struggles to avoid dying, and yet, destined to live forever, they do not labour to avoid sinning" show the paraenetic dimension of the text, which levers upon the opposition between an exaggerated interest or attachment to terrestrial things (the life that passes away), only because they are of the senses, and the disinterest in or indifference to spiritual things or eternal life (the lasting life), which is not visible but is very real. Yet, the author says, God does not ask of his faithful heavy things but light things to conquer, also by merit, eternal life.

At the end of the text, *more paulino*, the author involves himself with his readers and pronounces a global reproach with an exhortative function: "sluggish are we, so lukewarm about achieving eternal life." The paraenetic tone thus reaches a very high note.

Chapter xii takes into account the innumerable types of death that threaten every mortal in daily life. The conclusion is that it is better to adhere to the thought of death, above all making it a "good death" even if in the midst of many difficulties. The main point is that this death becomes a good death based on what follows it across the line of life.

Also in this text the didactic and strongly pastoral finality of the reflection is evident. The figure of Bishop Julian emerges in all his strength, caring about the eternal destiny of his children, entrusted to him by God. He therefore works to convince and to form the consciences of the faithful, aware of being an eschatological guide for them who must lead them to the life without end. Otherwise his very apostolic mission would risk failure.

In the context of this paraenesis, however, the theme of the instinctive aversion of humanity to bodily death emerges for the third time. Evidently human beings do not recognize it as part of their vital dimension, and they try to escape it in any possible way. This attachment to life, even to ephemeral and earthly life, this deep desire to resist the painful laceration, both interior and exterior, provoked by death, is a confirmation that the desire to be elevated to share in divine life and to the state of supernatural grace has remained nearly intact in the human being. At the same time, however, such innate fear of death is also a sign of the human fragility that uselessly fights against an enemy infinitely stronger. The unequal struggle would finish with the triumph of *Thanatos*, if Providence had not decreed and realized, in a radically new way, the salvation and the glorification of human beings.

The pastoral ministry of death (Prognosticum *I, xiii*)

Also in this case, Bishop Julian's pastoral concern for the faithful entrusted to his care emerges from the title and from the text of the chapter. He invites people not to delude themselves and to have more fear about the "death of the soul" or eternal perdition than about bodily death. Supporting himself with the commentary of Augustine on the Fourth Gospel, he instructs the faithful about the inevitability of bodily death: "Be it today, be it tomorrow, it is to be: the debt must be paid." One must not be contented with some temporal delay of death. Rather, one should avoid above all, with all possible might and with the help of divine grace, the "second death," which is exclusion from the divine world. Particularly meaningful is the teaching, which Julian makes his own, about the fact that, according to the quotation of Matthew 22:23, God is the God of the living, that is, of Abraham, Isaac, and Jacob, and not of the dead. This means that Jesus considers the patriarchs as living beings beyond death. In addition, Julian insinuates as obvious and presupposed the survival of the spiritual element of the human being, endowed with conscience and will, which we normally call the "soul." Julian invites believers, therefore, to follow the example of the biblical patriarchs to live beyond death. And to be even more concrete he quotes the teaching of Jesus: "He who believes in me, though he die, yet shall he live" (John 11:25), making an anthropological-philosophical exegesis of it, identifying "though he die" with bodily death and "yet shall he live," with the life of the soul that survives death and also subsists without the body, though desiring it.

The exhortation then becomes again theological when he alludes to the fact that this whole situation of separation between body and soul will last up until the universal resurrection at the end of time, when the human flesh, by the almighty will of God, shall no longer be subject to death, but shall live eternally without the perspective of death.

So Julian shows, already in book I of his work, clear ideas about the anthropological situation between death and the resurrection with the survival of the soul, insinuating in this dimension an extreme vitality of the soul, about which he will specify more in book II.

Christians do not fear death (Prognosticum I, xiiii)

The reason why Christians do not fear death, or should not fear it, is derived from their faith, which is radical and global, and embraces also the anthropological situation following death, with the separation of the body from the soul. Julian imitates the rhetorical fury of Paul in the Letter to the Philippians (Phil 1:19–24), relying on Augustine and especially on the *De mortalitate* of Cyprian of Carthage, who teaches that "he who fears death is not willing to go to Christ." This dimension of the eschatological future touches the core of Christian faith; this means, in consequence, that the Christian who truly believes in God and in the salvific work of redemption from sin and death accomplished by Christ ought not to be afraid of death. Rather, the Christian is to long for death, because it opens the way for a new and deeper communion with the Lord. To support this thought Julian offers the example of the old Simeon (Luke 2:22–38), who, having seen the advent of the Messiah, intoned his *Nunc dimittis, Domine* with no regret for earthly life, thus declaring himself ready to die. But then, to defend the thesis that there is no need to fear death, Julian uses rather stoic language, comparing the Christian to a ship that was saved from the storms of this world by death and was led to a calm port. In short, once the difficult moment of the internal and external laceration of the human being has been overcome, death becomes a positive reality as it leads to the experience of immortality.

It is evident that with this reasoning we are in the presence of a complete revolution of the theological meaning of bodily death.

From punishment for sin, and from a test of the believer's faith, it passes to a new interpretation: death becomes even desirable, *more paulino* or following the heroic fury of the martyrs, because it allows for passage to eternal life, otherwise not achievable in any other known way. The qualitative jump was enormous: from death as a sign of curse to the Christian death as a passage, though difficult and narrow, to the life beyond death. Naturally all this is based on the mystery of the death and resurrection of Christ. It was he who changed the connotation of death and transformed it from a negative and destructive reality of the human condition into a passage to eternal life. The eschatology of Julian of Toledo shows itself capable of reconstructing these interpretative passages related to human death, which leads to a real metamorphosis of it, and to transmit its revolutionary meaning.

The desirable death and reunion with loved ones: Apocalyptic language, destiny of the individual, Christian and ecclesiological personalism of death (Prognosticum *I, xv*)

The reflection upon death as desirable is disturbing for any cultural identity, even for Christianity. Only someone who has lived during the time of the Christian martyrs of the first centuries, as did Cyprian of Carthage, can speak of it with so much boldness. Therefore Julian tries, within the limits of a "normal" faith, to face the problem of death. The invitation he makes is no longer to desire death but, more simply, to moderate the fear of death, not to cancel it. This means that the heroic fury of the martyrs is not asked of all in the face of death.

The text begins with a series of strong but generic affirmations, all taken from Cyprian of Carthage and related to the proximity of the advent of the kingdom of God, to the world that grows old, and to the transient things that yield their place to the new. Undoubtedly it is a summary of the extreme eschatological attitude that was widespread in the era of the martyrs, when the end of all things was perceived to be drawing near. This idea contributed considerably to providing comfort and the necessary courage for individuals to face the extreme persecution of their times. The reasoning becomes progressively more dramatic when the quotations from Cyprian's *De mortalitate* describe the violent action of Satan, who battles with his darts and weapons against the church and the believers, and who has by then

infested the world, disseminating the totality of vices that progressively replaced the virtues. Faced with this dramatic situation, the
extreme pastoral invitation is to long to die in order to go more
quickly to Christ, escaping from Satan, since death is like a passage to
eternity.

In the end, the tone seems to become apocalyptic when reference is made to the world that staggers like a house that is about to
collapse, to the extremely dangerous situation of some sailors who
find themselves about to perish in the midst of the waves and try to
avoid shipwreck by seeking desperately for a port. The conditional
verb is used because the apocalyptic dimension used by Julian actually
intends to be applied, above all, to the human subject who experiences death and not, as is usual in the apocalyptic texts, to a worldly
situation of struggle against evil and of the chaos produced naturally
or by the assaults of Satan and his followers. In short, what is being
treated here is the eschatology (not apocalypse) of the single individual, which is described, however, using apocalyptic language.
Undoubtedly, effective apocalyptic language involves the readers,
touching them in the depth of their being and almost making them
feel like protagonists of those dramatic situations.

But if this reflection was still not enough to convince the
Christian that it is better to die than to live, Julian, still relying on
Cyprian's extraordinary vision of the theology of history, attenuates
the tone, moderates the upsetting and fearful descriptions, and introduces a final, invincible, and unassailable reason why the Christian
ought to long for death: to die means, in fact, to return to the country from which we are in exile; to die means to again embrace loved
ones, beginning with the patriarchs and moving on to one's own parents, children, brothers, sisters, friends, the whole crowd who awaits
us and desires to be reunited with us. This anthropological and social
motivation, which reestablishes the affective bonds in the afterlife,
probably seems to be more convincing than all the others previously
described, because it profoundly touches the feelings and the bonds
of friendship and blood that are established in the terrestrial life.

Therefore, the reason why death should not be feared also
entails a strong personalistic anthropological component, as well as a
strongly ecclesiological dimension, which is not to be overlooked and
which produces an intense desire to be reunited to loved ones, but in
the atmosphere of the heavenly church and with no more worries or

hindrances as in earthly life. So death becomes a docile instrument that, in the hands of God, is rendered capable of reuniting *in unum* the various historical levels of affiliation in the church in the last ecclesiological phase, the heavenly one. The heavenly church will thus embrace all the believers belonging to the terrestrial church in every century and who have never met, though they are part of the same community.

For what concerns, instead, the didactic use of the dramatically rhetorical descriptions of the end of the world, I would underline that similar eschatological representations, founded upon violent persecutions of believers, as testified to by history, or upon a careless attitude of Christians toward the evil of the world, expose themselves to severe criticism in the elaboration of an authentic theological eschatology founded on the preaching of Jesus. Even if, in fact, these attitudes are comprehensible for the first centuries of Christianity, they nonetheless risk leading to the conviction that, for Christians, death is a way out or an alibi that subtracts the believer from the historical duty of transforming the world.

Since a similar prophetic attitude, with strongly apocalyptic tones or frameworks, is found in the New Testament, there are no objections to be made, even though a very attentive hermeneutical discernment is necessary. We know, in fact, that for the most part the Word of God predicts dramatic, even horrifying events to come, so that believers will repent in order to prevent these events from happening and thereby prevail upon God to change his mind. But when the theologian becomes the apocalyptic interpreter of history, the danger is precisely that of an eschatological representation brought to the extreme, which, however, hardly contains an active invitation to believers calling them to be what the Gospel teaches us: "salt of the earth and light of the world."

The exemplifying paraenesis of the Shepherd (Prognosticum *I, xvi*)

The chapter is an exhortation, with a catechetical and ascetic aim, destined to underline, with the aid of a text of Cyprian of Carthage, the possible contradictions of the Christian faith.

While, on the one hand, we express in prayer to God the Father our desire to do his will, on the other hand, we are resistant when God calls us to him through death and we *unwillingly* obey his call, which instead should make us rejoice.

The exhortation is illustrated with the story of an experience of an anonymous colleague of Julian in the bishopric who, at the moment of death, saw beside him a supernatural figure, perhaps the Lord himself, who admonished and reproached him for his resistance to leave the world. From this story Julian derives the exhortation to advance trustingly in the difficult and harsh passage of death that leads, however, beyond the ephemeral terrestrial life. Thus, it is possible to pass from a theology of death to a spirituality of dying well, which exhorts believers not to fear death but to consider it a providential moment of passage from this world to the other real and imperishable world.

As can be seen, Julian's theological methodology does not preclude the edifying story that has the hermeneutical function of depicting the wrong attitude of many believers. It allows for an easy explanation of the matter, without the need for abstract language, and, moreover, being a story, it is easily memorized and transmitted.

How to conquer the fear of death (Prognosticum *I, xvii*)

According to Julian, the fear of death is a natural fact, and those who think, in a stoic way, that the Christian is not affected by this disturbance are simply presumptuous. The fear of death is actually so typical of the human condition that even Jesus was afraid of dying. But he taught us all the best way of dying with his prayer to the Father in the Garden of Gethsemane, resigning himself in the end to do the will of God as the best of all possible options.

Therefore the extremes are to be avoided: neither boldness in the face of death, because it would be useless and harmful arrogance; nor desperation, because our faith makes us understand that Christ, by the power of his salvific action, has transformed death into a functional reality for us to reach divine eternity.

Since we as baptized and disciples of Jesus participate in the being of Christ, we are to imitate Peter, who, though not wanting to die, allowed himself nonetheless to be led to death as an act of love, according to the very teachings of Jesus: "when you are old, you will stretch out your hands, and another will gird you and carry you where you do not wish to go" (John 21:18).

Preparation for death (Prognosticum I, xviii)

In this chapter the teachings about the theology and spirituality of Christian death become more intense. Julian strongly advocates the need to get ready for death through assiduous prayer. He imagines death as the beginning of a long journey through unknown areas whose outcome, whether of blessed life or of punishment, is unknown to us. It is therefore appropriate to prepare ourselves with personal prayers, and with the recital of prayers and psalmodies offered for us by our brothers and sisters in faith who remain on earth. It is to be noted that this does not refer to intercessory prayers for the dead, but rather to a kind of reserve of prayer ("pre-intercessions," one might say), which can help face the fateful parting. Evidently, in his reference to psalmody, Julian was probably thinking about the customary care for the dying persons in the pastoral ministry of his time.

The reason for this prudent prayer, both personal and done by others, lies in the fact that the moment of death can be dangerous, because of the diabolic traps that can occur in that moment, as Satan *is present and threatens.* Prayers and psalmody have the necessary power to chase away temptations and desperation, and to have full trust in the mercy of God.

In this chapter, and for the second time, Julian defines death as separation of the body from the soul, and not vice versa.

Pastoral prescription for the sepulchres and the care of the dead bodies: the body as temple of the Holy Spirit, the natural love for the body, and the future and christological destiny of the human body (Prognosticum I, xviiii)

The chapter underlines the importance and the Christian custom of honoring the bodies of the dead. The reason why such honor is to be rendered to the corpses is supernatural in a double sense: first of all, it has a highly pneumatological meaning in the theological vision of Julian. He knows, in fact, that after the ascension of Jesus, the church and its individual members are entrusted to the care of the Holy Spirit, whose aim is to lead them to eternal life. But this pneumatological dimension does not refer only to the spirit of the human being, as could be expected. After baptism, in fact, the Holy Spirit, Master of Christian life, used the bodies of believers *as organs and ves-*

sels of good works; therefore, the first reason for honoring those bodies, now dead, is that they were the abode of the Holy Spirit.

In second place, Sacred Scripture comes to our aid as it establishes an important unitary anthropological principle, through the text of the apostle Paul (Eph 5:29) according to which "no one hates his own flesh." Therefore, in the Christian conception of death there is no room for contempt of the bodily dimension nor for any dualism that favors the soul to the detriment of the body.

Moreover, Julian introduces a matter a fortiori based upon which he is led to the conviction about the care for the body of the dead. If, in fact, even non-Christians honor the bodies of the dead, then all the more so should those who believe in Christ honor them, because the body that is now honored will be the same one that our Lord Jesus Christ will raise up again on the last day of history to live in eternity.

Therefore, the Christian anthropological realism that values the human body in addition to the life of the soul eliminates at the root any temptation to reduce humanity to only one of its constitutive elements, that is, the spiritual soul. Julian praises, as a model, the Old Testament figure of Tobiah, who deserved much from God for his piety toward the dead who were deprived of an honorable burial of their body. If someone then wants certainty that the pious practice of burial and care of the body of the dead is according to the will of God, it is sufficient to consider the preaching of Jesus, who praises, and wants for her to be praised, the woman who anointed his limbs with precious ointment as a prefiguring of his burial (John 12:7; Mark 14:8; Matt 26:12). Finally, the Lord himself was buried honorably and his body was anointed with aromatic oils and balsam (John 19:38–42; Luke 23:50–55; Mark 16:1). In the end, Julian specifies that this care of the dead body is done not so much for an intrinsic value of the dead bodies, but to sustain and assure faith in the future resurrection of the same body, which is now honored in view of its glorification.

As we have already noted, it is no wonder that the theme of chapters xix–xx revolves around the grave in general (preparation of the tomb, burial in the church, burial in the church next to the grave of the martyr who guarantees his patronage to the deceased). The modern reader must understand that so much insistence upon this theme is derived from the fact that in the High Middle Ages the place of burial and the sepulchre itself were considered elements of primary importance. The choice of the burial place (in the ecclesial hall, near the grave of a martyr or a saint, in a monastery, and so on) became particularly important in proportion to the increase of faith in the resurrection of the flesh, in that the place selected with so much care would then be the eschatological place where the deceased would await the day of the resurrection of the body.[5]

Buried together with the martyrs waiting for the resurrection (Prognosticum *I, xx–xxi)*

In the past, many buildings of worship have been built upon the place of martyrdom of famous witnesses of the faith in Christ. Accordingly, quoting Augustine, Julian maintains that it is a benefit to be buried near the grave of a martyr. The advantage is evident: whoever goes to pray near the grave of a martyr also includes a prayer of suffrage for the dead ones buried near the martyr's tomb, recommending their souls to the patronage of the martyr and to divine mercy.

The protection of a martyr is an excellent thing and can promote or accelerate a possible path of maturation and purification of the soul of the deceased. This shows, in the intentions of Julian, the existence of a real, though mysterious, contact and of the relationships that really exist between the terrestrial church, which prays and implores for the dead, and the heavenly church, which is venerated in its martyrs, and the church needy of suffrages and prayer. This ecclesiological triad leads us to believe that Julian had an ecclesiological vision of ample breadth and knew the three phases or levels of the life of the church: on earth, in the phase of maturation or purification, and in heaven.

Naturally, the patronage of the martyr entails nothing magical, nothing that can change radically the eschatological outcome of a dead person without the presence of a consistent moral and religious basis. No intercession can change the damned into a saint. From this point of view it is useless to have illusions. The justice of God is sovereign. Thus, it is futile for believers to have themselves buried near a martyr if they are guilty of serious and unresolved sins and died without repentance. What counts, therefore, is not the place of burial, which risks being mythologized, but the life that is conducted on earth. This proves to be the decisive element for the configuration of the eschatological destiny following death.

The biblical and ecclesiological doctrine about the sacrifices to be offered to God for the purification of the dead (Prognosticum I, xxii).

In this chapter we find some elements of great importance for understanding the eschatology of Julian of Toledo. Quoting Augustine, he maintains that the Old Testament already contained the basis for the prayer and sacrifice offered for the dead (2 Macc 12:40–46).

This means that already in the time of the Maccabees (second century BC) the idea was popular in Israel that the subjective and spiritual element of the human being survives death and can somehow be helped by believers on earth. In the case of the narration contained in the Books of Maccabees, it can easily be deduced that prayers of suffrage were offered to God for the soldiers who had died in battle, but what was especially offered in their favor and in sight of their future resurrection was the great sacrifice of expiation (the *Kippur*). It was the most important sacrifice of the Jewish liturgy, celebrated in the Temple of Jerusalem, in the Holy of Holies itself, only once a year and exclusively by the high priest to obtain pardon from God for the sins of the people. The text of the Second Book of Maccabees, quoted by Julian, contains the testimony, unique in the whole Old Testament, according to which sacrifice was offered, instead, to obtain the pardon for the sins of believers who had died. We are thus in the presence of a biblical basis of primary importance that alone would suffice as foundation for the doctrine of suffrage for the dead, and, therefore, of the existence of the intermediate phase of survival of the souls after death and before the resurrection.

But to this fundamental proof is added the authority of the church, which in its most important liturgical actions (those that occur at the altar of the Lord, meaning the celebration of the Eucharist) recommends the dead to God and intercedes for them. The purpose of the eucharistic sacrifice offered in suffrage for the dead is to obtain God's bringing to perfection what he had begun in them, the work of their sanctification, completing what was lacking in their moral and religious perfection. Julian also speaks about the result of such intercessions: the prayers will be an additional thanks to God if they are offered to the Lord for those who are already in the glory (the *boni* or *valde boni*, meaning the just); the suffrages can, instead, bring favor upon the not so bad (*not valde mali*), meaning those who are in need of maturation or purification and who can hope for an increase of the forgiving grace of God that will make them just. But for the very bad (*mali* or *valde mali*), such suffrages are not of any benefit. In the case of the latter, prayers of suffrage only serve as a consoling act for the living, that they may keep on hoping for a good eschatological outcome for their dear ones.

So Julian teaches or gives some strong reasons for believers not to be afraid of death, showing the importance of prayer for the dead, which can help them improve their condition as separate souls in the state of maturation. The reason for this possible influence lies precisely in the fact that everyone, the living and the dead, belongs anyway to the church of Christ, in which an extraordinary internal communication is possible through the intercession and prayer of suffrage for the dead members of the people of God. Above all else, however, is the salvific will of God, which is so great as to provide for a maturation of human spiritual subjects even after their bodily death.

In conclusion, we can say that the theme of death is treated in the *Prognosticum* from mostly the historical salvific point of view, and certainly not in a theoretical or abstract sense. For Julian, it suffices to elaborate a doctrine that clarifies for believers the simple but fundamental certainty that death does not belong to the creative plan of God. It arrived unexpectedly when the divine plan was compromised by the bad use human beings made of their liberty and of their will.

Moreover, the human condition of sin and human death paradoxically become the providential occasion for God to elaborate a plan of redemption. Involving the double mission of the Son and of the Holy Spirit on earth, the divine plan has the goal of destroying the two formidable obstacles that sadden, in different ways, the heart of human beings and of God: sin and death. This plan of redemption, achieved once and for all in the paschal mystery of Christ, is in its phase of extension and expansion to all humankind, and it will terminate, through the simultaneous action of the Holy Spirit and the church, only at the end of time, when the last enemy of humanity, death, will finally be defeated.

But in the meantime, the power of Christ and the supreme intelligence of God have transformed death, making it become what by its nature it is not: a passage to eternal life. An added value in this plan of redemption is constituted by the discovery of a providential grace of God that provides for a supplement of sanctifying grace and an integrative path of purification of the soul to be given to a large part of the deceased, often produced by the insistent prayer of believers on earth to the benefit of the souls of the dead.

Therefore, it seems that the first theological elaboration of the doctrine of purification beyond this world is to be attributed to Julian of Toledo. It is contained in the last chapters of book I of the *Prognosticum*, which serve as a transition to book II, which expounds *ex professo* on the more general theological problems associated with the condition of the souls after the bodily death.

BOOK II: *POST MORTEM ANIMAE NON SUNT OTIOSAE*: THE INTERMEDIATE ESCHATOLOGY

The survival and the subsistence of the soul after death. The first theoretical systematization of the intermediate[6] phase in Christian eschatology.

Book II of the *Prognosticum* undoubtedly represents the most important nucleus of the eschatological work of Julian of Toledo and his original contribution, on the theological and historical level, to the theological-dogmatic development of Christian eschatology. Book II, in fact, treats an eschatological problem of great difficulty and depth, which can be summarized in this question: What is the condition of the souls of the dead after the bodily death and before the final resurrection?

This difficult theme was also the true subject of discussion in the theological dialogue between Julian and Bishop Idalius of Barcelona on Good Friday in the year 688. In that conversation the two bishops decided by mutual consent that this same theme would be treated by Julian in the edition of the written work, equipping it with the necessary scriptural and patristic texts to show its theological foundation as authentic Christian doctrine.

According to some, the theme of the intermediate phase between death and resurrection, that is, of the survival of the soul after death and of its eschatological condition, would also have been treated by Julian in an anti-heretical sense.[7] We know that, faced with the difficulties raised by the problem of the souls' condition between death and resurrection, the two bishops decided to turn not only to Sacred Scripture but also to the fathers of the church or the Catholic teachers, as Julian defines them in the preface to the *Prognosticum*,[8] with the purpose of obtaining answers that made sense and that could be united to the biblical texts related to the subject, in order to elaborate, finally, a complete theological treatise on the matter.

The editing work of the chapters of book II presupposes that Julian maintained, first of all and as the basis for his reasoning (and, correctly appraising it, as the starting point for Christian eschatology in general), the affirmation of the existence of the human soul created by God, but also the certainty of the survival and subsistence of the same soul after death. He, in fact, excludes a priori the opinions of various infidels according to whom the soul resolved into nothing after bodily death. This means that, after the experience of bodily death, the souls continue their existence without the body; they do not disappear into nothing, "sino que tienen una vida mas rica,"[9] which has nothing to do with an idle life or with insensitivity.

Julian's view is certainly inherited from the patristic position, but it becomes in turn, because systematized for the first time, the source of subsequent elaborations that will lead to the foundation of Catholic eschatological dogma about the intermediate phase of eschatology. As it is known, the anthropological and eschatological conception present still today in the official documents of the Catholic Church maintains the principle of the survival and subsistence of the soul after bodily death, showing dependence on the eschatological presentation of Julian of Toledo.

In fact, the "Letter on certain questions regarding Eschatology," published in 1979 by the Congregation for the Doctrine of the Faith, clearly says: "The Church affirms that a spiritual element survives and subsists after death, an element endowed with consciousness and will, so that the 'human self' subsists. To designate this element, the Church uses the word 'soul,' the accepted term in the usage of Scripture and Tradition" (no. 3).[10]

An analogous position, but more historically and biblically documented, is found in the document of the International Theological Commission entitled "Some Current Questions in Eschatology,"[11] which affirms that the whole Christian tradition, with no exceptions of great importance, has conceived, almost up to our days, the object of the eschatological hope as constituted by a double phase.[12] The first phase is indicated as precisely the survival and subsistence of the soul after the bodily death; the second phase is characterized by the conclusive events of the history of salvation (*parousia* of Christ, universal judgment, resurrection of the dead). Moreover, the important study document of the International Theological Commission contains some interesting theological-biblical affirmations about the existence within the Bible of an internal development of the idea of Sheol and its inhabitants, the *rephaim* (= the shadows), which, together with the New Testament affirmations about the soul surviving death, constitute a good attempt to reconstruct the Semitic, biblical, Hellenistic, and Christian thoughts related to the problem of the subsistence of a human element after bodily death.[13] To this must be added what no. 366 of the *Catechism of the Catholic Church* affirms about how the church "teaches" that the soul does not perish during its separation from the body and that it will again be united to the body during the final resurrection. The verb *teaches* is an evident sign of how the magisterium of the church intends to utilize all its doctrinal authority in this affirmation.

The title of chapter xv of book II of the *Prognosticum* alludes precisely to this survival and subsistence of the soul after death: *Quod non sit anima privata sensibus suis post mortem corporis.* The soul, after the death of the body, is not deprived of its faculties or senses. On the contrary, it is in full possession of its faculties, as attested by two biblical texts decisive about the matter, but also at the base of the formulation of authentic doctrine. First of all, Luke 16:24, in which the rich man cries out to the poor Lazarus that he is indescribably suffering in the fire (*cruciari se in flamma*), and, second, the words said by Jesus to the good thief: "*Hodie mecum eris in paradiso*" (Luke 23:43).

Julian then demonstrates the existence and survival of the soul after death through the use of an interesting text taken from the *Conlationes* of Cassian, which intends to confirm the intense spiritual activity of the souls after their separation from the body. According to the penetrating expressions of Cassian, "the souls are not idle after the separation from this body, neither can one believe that they do not feel anything." In this way, he openly shows that "the souls of the departed not only are not deprived of their faculties, but that they are not even without their feelings, such as hope and sorrow, joy and fear, and that they already are beginning to taste beforehand something of what is reserved for them at the last judgment."

By these abstract terms, Julian alludes to the survival of the soul, in that it does not undergo the assault of death as does the body, but precisely that it survives. Yet his theological reasoning goes beyond to mean that the soul subsists, having the power "to be" without the completion of its body, and thus having its own life and existence, which is not reduced to idleness or to sleep as souls waiting for future events (*animae non sunt otiosae*); but rather, the life of the soul becomes even more intense (*vivacius subsistere*). This, however, is not a definitive condition for the souls. It will remain up until the universal resurrection when the souls will take back or will be dressed again with their bodies in a glorious way.

Julian, still availing himself of the writings of Cassian, subsequently offers two other proofs for the survival and subsistence of the soul. The first proof is of a rational nature, while the second refers to the primary source of theology, that is, to Sacred Scripture.

In the first line of reasoning he maintains that it is impossible that the soul, which is in the image and likeness of God, once relieved of "the burden of the body with which it is oppressed in this world is laid aside, becomes insensible" or loses its faculties, precisely because the soul "contains in itself all the power of reason and that it makes the dumb and senseless matter of the flesh sensitive through participation in itself." Moreover, "it is absolutely then consequent, and conforming to the order of reason," that the soul, by then no longer held back nor weakened by the "grossness of the flesh," that is, by the limits and the historical-earthly conditions, experiences "its intellectual capacities better than ever, and received in a purer and finer condition" than before.

Julian could be accused, and through him also Cassian, of trying to introduce in the reflection on the soul a sort of dualism or Platonism that intends to exalt the spiritual dimension of the human being to the detriment of the material and bodily dimension, which would instead be despised. Actually, more than to a radically opposing dualism between soul and body, his reference here is to a realistic consideration of the terrestrial life as the human being is currently forced to live it, that is, as a painful experience of weakness, mortality, corruptibility, marked almost completely by a series of limits.

The actual condition of human life leads to the objective and intelligent belief that this terrestrial life, so characterized by limits and weakness, cannot be the human life as it was planned in the project of the Creator. It is, instead, the result of the degeneration of humanity due to the sin of the origins, and it must therefore be considered a degeneration violently introduced in the human condition. Julian has already affirmed in book I of the *Prognosticum* that sin changed nature for the worse. From this ascertainment is born the consideration of human life on earth as a life in exile, away from the eternal homeland. God did not want humanity to be exiled; rather, it was his desire to give humankind a life of perfect communion with himself. This project, which failed because of sin, again became real in the mission of the Savior. God intends once again to give humankind that ancient finality, raising humanity to share in divine life already beginning in this terrestrial life.[14] This is made possible by the providential and objective reality according to which the soul is not subject to death but survives and subsists, and thus is ontologically able to live the eschatological outcome, even without the body.

The second proof is drawn from Sacred Scripture and is a series of elements of convenience. First of all, three Pauline texts are quoted: "my desire is to depart and be with Christ, for that is far better" (Phil 1:23). "While we are at home in the body we are away from the Lord" (2 Cor 5:6), and, "Yes, we do have confidence, and we would rather be away from the body and at home with the Lord. So whether we are at home or away, we make it our aim to please him" (2 Cor 5:8–9). These texts maintain that it is a good thing to die, or to not have the body, if this means, as is true, that it is possible to enter into deeper communion with the Lord and in an immediate way, that is, immediately after death. Therefore, there is no doubt that in the Christian conception, terrestrial and bodily life must be considered of lesser importance in comparison to the heavenly dwelling and life. The Pauline texts lose a certain aura of dualism because of the important finality that is intended to reach, with or without the body: communion with Christ and remaining in his grace.

Moreover, *Prognosticum* II, xxxiii, maintains, in a very strong way, the survival and the subsistence of the soul after death. The chapter begins by quoting another text of Cassian[15] that gives ample space to the biblical proofs of the active state of the soul after death. The quotations of Sacred Scripture range from the Old to the New Testament and are manifold (Dan 3:86; Ps 150:6; Rev 6:9ff.; Matt 22:31–32; Heb 11:16). Julian uses them to demonstrate, through a literal exegesis, the survival of the soul after death and the possession of its faculties.

The second part of the chapter is entirely occupied by a text of Augustine, who, like many fathers of the church, attributes a particular "proof" of the vivacity or survival of the soul after death to an edifying story or, rather, to a historical fact or episode—in this case related to the skepticism of a certain doctor Gennadius of Carthage about the survival of the soul after death. The story is completely centered on the doubts and dreams of Gennadius, by which he convinces himself in the end that the soul really does survive after the deposition of its own body. The dreamlike experiences of Gennadius are able to dispel every doubt about the survival of the human soul after death.

Naturally, a relevant methodological problem arises here: what value can we today give to these edifying stories, entirely subjective and without any historical confirmation, which the fathers instead considered to be true proofs? In fact, they are not even inspired texts of the Bible narrating apparitions or dreams, but human accounts of dreams narrated by Augustine himself. Modern methodology precludes a priori, and rightly so, these experiences from having any validity. The same can be said of possible mystical experiences. In Christian eschatology, therefore, mystical or dream-related experiences do not constitute proof or the basis of eschatological doctrine.

This can be considered, therefore, a weak point of patristic methodology, in general, and of the *Prognosticum* in particular. Fortunately, the number of edifying stories used by Julian as proof of doctrinal truth is not great.

The most important contribution made by the second book of the *Prognosticum* to Christian eschatology is undoubtedly its being the first systematization of the theological doctrine about the state of purification of the souls. This doctrine is founded by Julian, as usual, upon that of fathers, and, in particular, on the works of Augustine and the *Dialogi* of Gregory the Great, which speak at length about the purifying fire and the state of the souls and their relationship with the members of the terrestrial church. Through Julian and his work this can be considered a true doctrine on purgatory, meaning the possibility of the souls being purified *post mortem* by divine grace obtained through the prayer of the living. This optimistic doctrine will become so popular as to arouse real religious enthusiasm.

The discovery that christological redemption has the power, through the Holy Spirit and the church, to cross the border of the

death of individuals so that they may be purified from religious and
moral imperfections not forgiven in the terrestrial life, introduced an
element of great salvific optimism in medieval Christianity. But certainly the most interesting aspect of the doctrine is that it was elaborated by Julian, as Hillgarth notes,[16] five hundred years before that
twelfth century, in which the contemporary and secular historiography of the Middle Ages situates the so-called *naissance du purgatoire*,[17]
as a projection in the afterlife of the social state of the middle class.

The question of the relative beatitude and the absolute beatitude

The eschatology of Julian admits a difference between the contemplation of God, or beatific vision, of the soul without the body and
the contemplation of God, or beatific vision, of the whole human
being, soul and body, after the final resurrection.

For Julian, therefore, one thing is the happiness of the souls that
contemplate God without the body, and another, more perfect, will be
the happiness of the whole redeemed and glorified human being (soul
and body) that will contemplate God. There is undoubtedly a logic in
this analysis, as is expressed, for example, in *Prognosticum* III, x, when
Julian affirms "quod ante resurrectionem corporum non sic videatur
Deus a sanctis spiritibus defunctorum, sicut post resurrectionem vide-
bitur." This does not mean that the souls, in their state or condition of
life separated from the body, cannot have a beatific vision of the divinity, but that this beatific vision is undoubtedly present and that it will be
even more perfect as the human condition will be more perfect. Now
there is no doubt that the human being, risen and glorified in the soul
and in the body, is more perfect than the state or beatific condition of
only the soul, for as marvelously happy as it may be in its blessed condition after the bodily death. Yet it is precisely the soul itself, in fact, that
longs to have its own body back, because in this lies its perfection and
its perfect joy. It desires that its body may also enjoy the full happiness
that comes from the contemplation of God.

It seems possible, therefore, that in eternal life there will be a
"perfecting of the perfection," when also the glorified body will enjoy
the divine vision. Julian seems to allude to this also when, in
Prognosticum II, lv, speaking about the angelic contemplation of the
divine mystery to which the contemplation of God by the blessed is
assimilated, he affirms that "similes ergo tunc angelis erimus, quia
sicut illi nunc vident, ita nos Deum post resurrectionem videbimus,"

we will be similar to the angels because as they now contemplate God, we will also see him after the resurrection.

*Two paradises: the distinction (*Prognosticum *II, i)*

The distinction that Julian explains, basing himself on the authority of the master of differences, Isidore of Seville, has the purpose of clarifying the substantial difference that exists between the history of creation, with its terrestrial paradise, and the history of redemption, with its celestial or supernatural paradise as the final end to be reached. The consequences of this distinction are of the maximum importance for eschatology.

The interest of the author converges, naturally, on the second or definitive paradise, the final goal of God and humanity, where the souls of the blessed are immediately transferred upon going out of the body. Obviously theirs is a condition of great joy, but also of waiting for future events, because the soul, though able to subsist alone, is objectively deprived of the completion of itself that is its body, and it simply and naturally desires it, while in a supernatural way it desires that its body may also contemplate God. Therefore, it desires the restoration of the body by the One who had first given it to the soul: God himself.

In the anthropological realism typical of the eschatology of Julian of Toledo, the future event to which he refers is, therefore, that the souls "expectant receptionem corporum suorum." This clarification, made at the beginning of book II, dedicated precisely to the situation of the souls between bodily death and resurrection, is of exceptional importance because it accounts for the structure itself of the created human being, which is both spiritual and material. Julian does not surrender, therefore, to the temptation of extreme spiritualism, which is a dualism of opposition between soul and body. He seems instead to have clear ideas about the eschatological destiny of the human being and about the spiritual and bodily constitution of humanity as being willed by God. The authorities that fortify this anthropological eschatology include, besides the quoted Isidore of Seville, also Julian Pomerius, in the most often quoted but now lost *De animae natura dialogus,* and above all Sacred Scripture, with two separate texts: 2 Cor 12:2, where Paul narrates the (his?) rapture to the third heaven but without the body, which means that it is possible to ascend to the supernatural condition without the body; and Luke

23:43, where Jesus, promising the good thief entry into paradise on the same day of his death, proving *without any ambiguity* that this paradise, meaning the kingdom of God, is entered upon leaving the body, *sine ullo temporis intervallo*, with no temporal delay compared to the moment of death. This is what the Christian must believe: *quod ita debere credi*. In Julian's completely literal exegesis and in the absence, in his mind, of problematic questions about time, the words said by Jesus to the good thief indicate a very precise temporal dimension— today, and this does not allow for any temporal delay.

This means that in the mysterious heavenly equivalence to the "earthly today," about which we know nothing, the good thief will enter into the eternity of heaven promised him by the Savior of humankind. And Julian concludes his demonstration with an expression just as precise, with respect to the temporal dimension, which shows that the paradisiacal eschatological condition begins immediately after death: *sine ullo temporis intervallo*.

Is a location of heaven possible? (Prognosticum, *II, ii–iii*): *a model of demythologization of eschatology in the* Prognosticum futuri saeculi

One of the strongest criticisms made by modern and contemporary theologians to the eschatology and the theologians of the last centuries concerns the fact that they had insisted excessively, and often almost morbidly, upon the research of the material, physical, topographical, or geographical dimensions of some eschatological themes, as, for example, the description of the infernal punishments and the location of the eschatological states; in short, the curious search for the "where" and the "how," not to mention also the "when," concerning such eschatological realities as heaven, hell, purgatory, and so on. From these aspects, in the opinion of several theologians, eschatology rightly needed to be purified and demythologized, naturally in a moderate sense.

It is thus a pleasant surprise to discover in the eschatology of Julian of Toledo an interesting attitude in this same direction, that of a moderate demythologization of eschatology. The value of this critical attitude increases considerably if we think about how it occurred in a time far in the past compared to the scientific hermeneutics of contemporary theology.

In the *Prognosticum*, therefore, Julian demythologizes often and, even more frequently, decosmologizes or dematerializes some eschatological themes. In short, without renouncing the eschatological doctrine contained in images and metaphors that he also quotes in abundance, Julian successfully situates the material dimension of eschatological data on a secondary level, while always placing the more profound theological meaning in the foreground.

In *Prognosticum* II, ii, for instance, Julian criticizes in an intellectual and very effective way, judging it vain, the search for the geographical and topographical location of heaven. In the title of the chapter, perhaps somewhat maliciously, he attracts the attention of the reader by mentioning the location of heaven, but only apparently, as the readers themselves soon discover: *ubi sit paradisus*, where heaven is found, precisely that heaven in which the souls of the blessed, once gone out from their bodies, finally rest. In the body of the chapter, however, the expected revelation about the location is submitted to a strong downscaling of a biblical, rational, and theological nature. Starting with the Pauline experience narrated in 2 Cor 12:2, in which the apostle says that he climbed to "the third heaven," Julian, calling upon the authority of Augustine, excludes the possibility of any geographical or cosmic location of this "third heaven" or paradise, and he lists the first three "heavens" (bodily, spiritual, and mental) as symbols or conditions of human understanding. The third heaven, therefore, is the mental heaven, which corresponds to the situation of contemplation, by which we have access to secret and hidden things that are entirely beyond the capacity of the actual bodily and earthly senses. Therefore, it is useless and vain, if not even foolish, to seek while on earth or starting from the terrestrial condition things that cannot be deciphered, as is the case with heaven.

In second place, what wipes away every attempt to locate the celestial paradise is the fact that in this condition of the "third heaven" the very *ipsam Dei substantiam Verbumque Deum*, the divine substance and God the Word, is contemplated, seen, and felt, *in caritate Spiritus Sancti*. This affirmation is so laden with intellectual meaning and so dense with Christian theological meaning (such as a solemn trinitarian formula), to admit that the eschatology of Julian of Toledo excludes the blessed ones having only an *inchoatio vitae aeternae*. For them, instead, the contemplative vision is not only *inchoative*, but it coincides with the fullness of the contemplative beatitude of the souls.

Julian later affirms, in *Prognosticum* II, xxxvii, that the saints and martyrs, and thus not only the martyrs, see "God and Christ" immediately
after their souls go out of the body, just as, on the contrary and in a
parallel way, the damned are immediately in a condition of deprivation of the eternal goods, which constitutes the infernal damnation (*a
die exitus sui ignis reprobos exurat*).[18]

Therefore, it is necessary to overcome the old conceptions
related to the celestial paradise and not surrender to the temptation
of topographical and figurative representations that tend toward
materialization. What believers intend for paradise, in fact, is something else, as has been amply shown. Accordingly, says Julian, it is
opportune to change the name of the Christian heaven or to modify
it to avoid confusion and to make its oneness and the originality
emerge. Thus, it would be more fitting to refer to the true paradise
with a new name: *paradisus paradisorum*, the paradise of the paradises.

Another example of demythologization is present in *Prognosticum*
II, iii, which investigates the apparently mysterious meaning of the
expression "the bosom of Abraham," which occurs in only one
important biblical text of the New Testament, Luke 16:22–23. Faced
with the most varied interpretations of the expression "bosom of
Abraham," Julian quite simply chooses the one proposed by Ambrose,
Augustine, and Gregory the Great, which is also very near to the original biblical meaning of the expression. The phrase "bosom of
Abraham" is a way to indicate a positive eschatological situation,
meaning the abode of the just in the Jewish afterlife. The just are the
descendants of Abraham, so the expression means "in the company of
Abraham" or "with Abraham," referring to being reunited with the
patriarch, the father of those who believe and the progenitor of the
"history" of Israel.

Though not aware that the expression was used by rabbis to indicate the afterlife of the just and that Jesus had probably learned the
expression during his religious and rabbinic formation, Julian
reaches the same meaning, distancing himself from any other, fanciful interpretation.

Two hells? (Prognosticum *II, iiii*)

This chapter faces the difficult problem of the conception of the
afterlife, and of the afterlife, punitive or not, before the coming of
Christ—therefore in the Old Testament. That the matter is difficult

Julian clarifies with a humble declaration of "learned ignorance" from Augustine, which he makes his own: "as for hell, brothers, up till now we are not experts neither me nor you." Consequently, all the various explanations offered about the difficult theme are debatable.

For what concerns the Old Testament "*inferi*," according to Julian, who follows Augustine, all those who lived before Christ were destined to only one dimension of existence, the infernal one, which was a dwelling or abode common to both the just and unjust, but not in a diversified way.

But the situation changes considerably after the coming of Christ, which is at the origin of Julian's need to use again the method of the differences. If two hells or *inferi* exist, one must be on earth, coinciding with the terrestrial life, while the second would correspond to the punitive afterlife. In any case, Christ was sent by God to destroy both of these *inferi*.

According to another opinion, which seems rather similar to the conception and development within Judaism of the biblical theme of Sheol, though still characterized as debatable, hell could have two levels, a lower one that is punitive, and an upper one that is neither punitive nor positive but is able to give peace to whoever is there. The proof of this difference would reside in the text of Luke 16:19–30, where Lazarus is located above with Abraham, while the bad rich man is located below, among the torments.

Whatever the truth may be, it is sure that Christ descended to hell, but to the upper one, where the souls of the just of the Old Testament resided, to draw them out of that abode and to introduce them into the kingdom of God.

In any case, also in this chapter Julian takes for granted the survival of the soul after bodily death, and the immediate retribution of the soul, in such a way that these two aspects, survival and retribution, become closely united in the anthropology of Julian.

Even if the eschatology of Julian of Toledo does not seem to have yet reached the formulation of the existence of a personal or particular judgment of God of the human soul right after the bodily death (though in the *Oratio ad Deum* he seems to allude to it[19]) he undoubtedly appears to presuppose it because he describes the consequences of it, in the punitive sense or as purification or beatitude. This means that even if, naturally, the technical expression "particular judgment" is not present in the text of the *Prognosticum*, the indication according to which the eschatological retribution from God the judge is immediate and begins as soon as the terrestrial life of the human being finishes is not absent. If there is a reward, this implies that the divine judge evaluates the human condition from a moral and religious point of view. The final eschatological destination of the soul is based on such an evaluation actually occurring.

In this sense, it is not insignificant that in the Mozárabic liturgy, of which Julian, as we know from his biographer Felix of Toledo, was reformer and editor of the final literary and theological form, the idea of a second judgment of Christ is present. This could fortify the idea of a particular or personal[20] judgment already present, implicitly, in the theological reasoning of Julian.

Hell, an etymology (Prognosticum II, v)

Julian has already used the simple method of knowledge based on the etymology of a word when he was speaking of the meaning of the word *death*. It is no surprise, therefore, that also the word *hell* does not escape this analytical tool of knowledge. Julian thus explains that, by analogy with material things, if what is heavy is below all other things, then also the inferior spiritual dimensions are weighty, heavy, and sad and thus tend downward. They are *infra*, therefore, "under." Accordingly, the souls that are in the "lower" hell, like the bad rich man of Luke 16, live a situation of eschatological punishment.

With a second etymology, this time of the Greek word *Hadēs*, equivalent to "hell," Julian explains that it means an absolute lack of pleasant sounds, an oppressive silence, therefore more a psychological state similar, but contrary, to what Jesus described as weeping and gnashing of teeth.

Hell is not material (Prognosticum II, vi)

This chapter is an example of eschatological demythologization. Drawing support from Augustine, Julian excludes every material dimension from hell, preferring to view it as a spiritual dimension.

Moreover, and this is indeed noteworthy, he invites his readers to be critical of those who affirm the contrary. They, in fact, use poetic images in excess. This does not mean that Julian despises poetry, but rather that he does not consider it the ideal literary form to treat of such a difficult matter as eschatology, which is so easily exposed to ambiguities.

We wonder how Julian of Toledo would have evaluated such a poetic and eschatological work as that of Dante Alighieri. He probably would have exalted the literary and poetic value of the *Divina Comoedia*, but he might have criticized the eschatological vision as excessively descriptive and material.

The true theologian, Julian says, must not deviate from the authority of the Sacred Scriptures, but must have faith in them, especially when treating particularly difficult matters. It follows that, in this case, the theologian Julian exhorts his readers, especially the lesser experts, to use a critical and scientific method before formulating a theological hypothesis. Every theological thesis, therefore, must be founded on a solid and authoritative basis. Otherwise it does not have any convincing value.

It is useless to seek hell underground (Prognosticum, *II, vii*)

In this case, Julian affirms an underground location of hell, not according to the ancient religions or pagan cultures, but based on the authority of Augustine. Julian says that the *inferi* are underground because "thus it fittingly appears to the spirit," by analogy (*rerum similitudines*) with the dead flesh that, contrary to the soul, is concealed underground. But it is evident that these assertions are of a symbolic and analogical nature, and that they, therefore, do not coincide with the reality, which in this as in so many other cases escapes our present knowledge.

This does not mean that one should take on an agnostic attitude as a principle, but one should consider with wisdom the possibility of a learned ignorance on such a difficult and delicate matter.

The immediate reward of the souls of the dead (Prognosticum, *II, viii*): *intermediate eschatology and the theology of purification of the souls*

This chapter is certainly one of the most important of the whole work of Julian of Toledo. In it, he not only reaffirms for the nth time the survival of the soul after death, but, above all, he maintains the conclusion of his eschatological result, and in a double way.

In the title of the chapter, Julian refers only to the souls of the blessed ones that, having left the body, draw near to Christ in heaven. In the body of the text, however, Julian draws from the famous reflection of the *Dialogi* of Gregory the Great to show an important difference between the destiny of the souls of the blessed and that of the other souls not immediately received in heaven. These souls, in fact, live a particular condition of survival, because they have been judged not ready to enter in the kingdom of God, having "had something less with respect to perfect justice." For this reason, therefore, they must undergo a temporal delay (*dilationis damno*)[21] of their eschatological reward.

In these important words we cannot see anything but the salvific dimension brought to its ultimate degree, because divine providence, offering the further possibility of reaching salvation through the purification of the soul, achieves the result of not excluding many souls from the eschatological destiny of glory, which otherwise would have been lost forever. Instead, by means of the "damage of delay," God is able to bring souls to the right condition for obtaining perfect beatitude. This interval of maturation or purification happens through a punishment, in the state of separation of the soul from its body. Even if Julian does not yet use the technical term *purgatory* to indicate this extraordinary chance offered by divine mercy and providence, we can nonetheless say that his words contain the very substance and essence of it.

As for the souls of the just, there is no doubt that they have an immediate destiny of glory after their bodily death and are received into the heavenly abodes. Gregory the Great, however, does not hesitate to consider the abandonment of the body by the soul as a liberating factor. He, in fact, describes the body with a Platonic and dualistic terminology, brought to the limits of contempt, as *huius carnis claustra*, a jail of this flesh. This cultural and philosophical dependence greatly damages the general reflection.

According to Julian, Sacred Scripture is naturally the foundation for this doctrine, and in particular the mysterious words of Jesus: "Wherever the corpse is, there the vultures will gather" (Matt 24:28). The dead body is identified in an unusual way with Christ, while the vultures are the souls of the just. This is an allegorical exegesis in the extreme sense, especially for what concerns the identification of the characters, but also for its overall meaning. Other scriptural texts are quoted with more conviction, such as Phil 1:23, where Paul affirms, in a mystical rush, his desire for death in order to be with Christ immediately, and, with great realism, the text of 2 Cor 5:1, where Paul affirms that while our terrestrial abode, meaning the body, dissolves, God prepares for us an eternal abode in heaven.

In this chapter, therefore, as well as in *Prognosticum* II, i, Julian propounds his doctrine of the immediacy of the divine reward of the souls based on the merits accumulated by the human subjects in their terrestrial life. Therefore, according to this formulation, the eschatological condition of beatitude begins *statim post mortem*, immediately after death, and it concerns the souls separated in the meantime from the bodies that have undergone death. For Julian, the souls deserving of the celestial heaven are immediately transferred after having gone out of the body (*statim ut a corpore exeunt*).

This means that in the seventh century, Hispanic-Visigothic theology clearly affirmed the reward of human beings immediately after death, and that it was not necessary to await the end of time to know the eschatological outcome of the terrestrial existence of human beings.

The attention given to the single person denotes a very evolved theological and anthropological vision in contrast to other approaches that concern exclusively the collective dimension of eschatology.

The theory of the "receptacles" (Prognosticum II, ix)

The belief according to which the souls of the dead, once gone out of the body, are assembled in determinate secret places (*receptacula*) where they await the final judgment belongs to the collective vision of eschatology, which was very widespread in the patristic period. Julian mentions it in this brief chapter, perhaps in more of a documentary way. Objectively he does not seem to give a lot of importance to this question.

As we have seen in the previous chapter, there is no doubt that Julian strongly upholds the individual eschatology or the intermediate state of the souls, which holds that the eschatological results occur already after the death of the individual. The presence of the "receptacles" seems to be a digression with respect to the previous certainties, as if it meant a situation of waiting for final judgment.

Such a formulation, however, does not exclude the collective dimension of eschatology and the final judgment. In any case, thanks to the quotation of Augustine, Julian insinuates that those souls, though kept in the *receptacula*, already feel or have a foreboding of their final outcome, if it will be eternal rest or eternal punishment.

The theology of the "healing" of the souls (Prognosticum *II, x*)

After the conclusions of *Prognosticum* II, viii, the most important assertion made in this chapter, taken from the thought of Julian Pomerius, is that the souls of those who were not perfect are purified with *poenis medicinalibus*, with medicinal punishments.

There is no doubt that this is a technical affirmation of the intermediate state of maturation, or better yet, of the healing of the souls, considering that the adjective *medicinalibus* refers to a process of recovery that is obtained by taking the appropriate medicines, even if they are unpleasant. Such pharmacological care is inflicted by the divine physician as a therapy, painful but effective, that will bring the souls, once perfectly purified from their evil, to fully enjoy the heavenly beatitude.

What was said about the text of *Prognosticum* II, viii, is valid also, and even more so, for the assertions of this tenth chapter. Also in this case, even if the technical word *purgatory* is absent from the text, the substance of it is nonetheless present, formulated in the use of a very convincing manifold image that expresses trust and hope: the divine physician, the medicinal care, the positive recovery from illness.

Julian does not use a language that is excessively descriptive or inclined to underlining the suffering of this *dilationis damnus*. For instance, he does not refer to the theme of the purifying fire. Probably, and rightly so, he believes that the term *fire* could give rise to misunderstandings on the part of the readers, accustomed to thinking of fire as a punitive element in an infernal sense. On the contrary, the expression "medicinal punishments" leads us to think that the author intended to abstain from any attempt to materialize the mysterious state of the souls. In fact, no detail is given about the content of these mysterious medicines that are used with wise skill by the divine physician.

The second important thing that Julian underlines is the power that the terrestrial church has to supplicate God (*ecclesia pro eis "hic" efficaciter supplicante*) in an effective way for those who have gone out of this world without perfect holiness but who are not at all reprobates. The liturgy of suffrage for the dead finds its full validity in this affirmation. This means that, through this intercession with God and for the dead, it is totally clear that a moral and religious progress of the soul is possible after its death, the fruit of the work of God, not the church. Julian thus establishes a limit to the power of the terrestrial church (*hic*). It can only intercede with God for the dead; it has no other powers with which to influence the condition of the dead.

The final affirmation of the chapter shows itself to be of equal importance, as it maintains that, even when the human body will be raised up and will enjoy immortality, this will not constitute a reduction or diminution of beatitude. This means that Julian does not consider the human body to be a negative element that can decrease the beatitude, but rather an element of anthropological enhancement. Evidently Julian contests any spiritualism that would exalt only the spirit to the detriment of the body. Julian dissociates himself from the negative consideration of the body, as could have been understood from the thought of Gregory the Great, quoted in *Prognosticum* II, viii, when he says: *huius carnis claustra.* According to Julian, the body is considered instead to be a positive element, created and willed by God and then recreated by the same Lord as an essential component of the glorified human being. Since it has been redeemed, it has been made fit to be elevated to share in the divine life.

The restitution of the glorified body improves the already present vision of God (Prognosticum *II, xi*)

Careful theological and anthropological analysis leads Julian to establish an objective difference between the vision of God that the souls will have before the bodily resurrection and the one that the whole human being, soul and glorified body, will have afterward. The guiding principle is always both theological and anthropological: if recuperating the body means, for the human being, a complete perfecting (according to the creative and redemptive plan of God), then so also will the beatific vision be an improvement of its fullness.

The beatitude already enjoyed by the souls of the just is, therefore, true and full. But the vision of the unchangeable essence of God by the souls separated from their bodies is not comparable to the vision enjoyed by the angels in terms of quality and perfection. Indeed, having been created by God to be the head of the body, the soul desires to be reunited with its corporeality. Until this reuniting occurs, meaning until the body, no longer *psychic* but having become *pneumatic* (according to the difference or, better, the dialectics between the psychic and pneumatic body intuited by Paul in 1 Cor 15:44 as a result of the transformation caused by the resurrection), becomes again associated with the soul, the vision of the unchangeable essence of God cannot be said to be perfect. What for the soul had been a weight (the defective terrestrial body) will then, and only then, be transformed into an element of glory. The terrestrial body, in fact, because degenerated by original sin, has been defined by Julian, through his patristic sources, as a *sarcina gravis*,[22] a heavy weight. And the soul hopes for its liberation, esteeming the body, while it also desires to be liberated from it.

From his overall reasoning an important theological and anthropological consideration emerges—that the future body will be the terrestrial body itself, but greatly transformed. To this effect, therefore, every soul will receive its own body (not another body). This means that the human body continues to be, even in the eschatological dimension, the principle of individuation of the human subject, as is also the soul, for other reasons. At the same time, however, Julian affirms that it will be a new body, never possessed before, because structurally characterized by dimensions absolutely desirable though completely absent from the terrestrial body: immortality, incorruptibility, eternity, limitlessness.

The mystery of the descent of Christ into Sheol (Prognosticum *II, xii*)

Julian shows how the just ones of the Old Testament benefited in a special way from the universal salvific intervention of Christ. In fact, not only did the Lord open the doors of heaven to all through his sacrifice of death and burial, but just when he was bitterly experiencing human death, he personally wanted to descend into the kingdom of the dead that detained, even if in a serene way, the just of the Old Testament.

In short, Christ wanted to attend to the eschatological outcome of the members of his people who had significantly believed in his advent and had contributed to the arrival of the Messiah. Thus they were freed from that jail (1 Pet 3:19). Otherwise, those souls would have remained in the kingdom of the shadows up until the second advent of Christ, that is, until the end of time. The descent of Christ into hell is, therefore, the demonstration of the love and care of God for the souls separated from their bodies and for their eschatological destiny.

There remains a historical and salvific difference between the outcome for the just ones before and after the coming of Christ: for believers in Christ, as soon as they die or go out of the body, if just they are led to God's kingdom; but the just of the Old Testament underwent a notable delay in the realization of their eschatological destiny, a delay that coincides with the historical times of the history of salvation. But in the end, the liberator of all also involved them in his salvific and glorifying action.

The immediate and symmetric reward of saints and sinners (Prognosticum II, xiii)

Since Sacred Scripture (Luke 16:22; 23:43) attests that the just ones immediately receive their heavenly reward, so it consequently follows that "it is necessary to believe" (*oportet ut…credamus*) also in the immediate recompense of the unjust, by the symmetry and justice that characterize divine judgment. According to Julian, who bases himself on the authority of Gregory the Great, it is a matter of faith. This "necessity" is due to the "internal justice" of the immediate reward, which touches indifferently all the dead at the moment of their death.

The eternity of hell (Prognosticum II, xiiii)

The difficult question of the eternity of hell is faced by Julian without reference to problematic anthropological and psychological questions, as occurs in contemporary eschatology, but exclusively basing himself on the perpetuity of divine judgment. The biblical text invoked (Eccl 11:3) is of a symbolic but very effective nature, showing the immutability of the eschatological situation of the soul as it is determined at the moment of death: blessed or damned.

It can seem to be a reasoning that is harsh and excessively severe, but, according to Julian, any affirmation to the contrary would incur the serious risk of relativizing not only what is said regarding damnation but the whole doctrinal structure of eschatology and the seriousness of human liberty.

The vitality of the soul after separation from the body
(Prognosticum II, xv)

This chapter, one of the most beautiful and central of the whole *Prognosticum*, intends to reaffirm what has already been said—that is, that the souls not only "are not idle after the separation from this body," but that they enjoy an accentuated level of sensitivity, due to their manifold faculties, which can finally be exploited to the full extent of their power. This is said against the skeptics and the infidels who spoke of the soul being reduced to nothing after the death of the body. The souls, therefore, suffer if punished or enjoy if rewarded, as shown by the biblical cases of the New Testament (the bad rich man of Luke 16:23–24 and the good thief of Luke 23:43). But then the discourse takes on a highly psychological nature when Julian enumerates among the characteristics of the soul deprived of the body also hope, sadness, joy, and fear. In addition, according to Julian, the souls already experience in advance their eschatological destiny, which will be openly manifested in the final judgment and with the final resurrection of the dead.

Julian subsequently provides a theological anthropological reason for the immortality and vitality of the souls after the death of the body. The characteristics of the soul subsist, in fact, because it is *illam pretiosorem hominis portionem*, the most precious part of the human being. It is in the soul that we are most similar to God, meaning that reality which comprises our being in the image and likeness of God (Gen 1:26). Besides, from the point of view of anthropological analysis, there are other fundamental reasons that enable us to consider the soul as subsisting more vivaciously after the death of the body than when it was in the terrestrial life: first of all, the fact that it contains in itself every strength of reason. This means that, according to Julian, the soul is the center of rationality, the first quality that distinguishes the human from every other being. With this strength, in fact, the soul governs its own body, which otherwise, without it, would be mute and insensitive (as occurs precisely when the body, by death, is separated from the soul).

Therefore, its faculties not only remain in the condition of separation, but they live a better situation than what was experienced in the terrestrial life, when the material and transitory dimension of the terrestrial realities somehow held back its extraordinary abilities of knowledge and vitality.

In second place, relying on Sacred Scripture and the authority of the apostle Paul (Phil 1:23; 2 Cor 5:6, 8–9), Julian emphasizes an extraordinary quality of the soul, which demonstrates more than anything else what its vitality after death entails: the quality of being capable, even without the body, of a communion with the Lord, superior to what was possible while on earth. The terrestrial life after original sin, in fact, is qualified by the apostle as an "exile" that keeps us "away from the Lord," while the soul, by itself (meaning in its eschatological condition) can establish strong bonds of communion with the divinity and enter into an exponential dynamism of knowledge of God—this also superior to what can be experienced on earth.

The resemblance between soul and body (Prognosticum *II, xvi*)

This chapter serves as preparation to the one that follows, and it rests upon the psychological considerations of Augustine, which involve the dream-related sphere of the human being. Such reflections lead to the conclusion that the soul, by this resemblance, though unbodily is similar to the body and can experience heavenly rest or beatitude, as well as infernal torments. It is obviously an anthropological argument greatly influenced by the philosophical currents of the time, which raises more than a few difficulties of interpretation.

The incorporeal soul feels the torment of the bodily fire (Prognosticum *II, xvii*)

This chapter relies on the thought of Gregory the Great, and it is composed of two arguments that justify the thesis. The first one is rational in that it maintains the compatibility between corporeal materiality (for example, that of fire) and the soul, a compatibility that occurs already in the fact that in the terrestrial life the soul is kept by the body, by its materiality. Yet the reasoning of the argument, as it develops, does not seem to be particularly effective.

The second argument is drawn from Sacred Scripture and is, therefore, a matter of greater authority. The biblical text is interpreted in a very literal way. Nevertheless, the interpretation is more convincing than the preceding argument: if the Lord in the parable of Luke 16:23–24 presents to us the rich man as suffering in the flames, "what wise man would ever deny that the souls of the damned can be tormented by fire?"

It is interesting to note how the two proofs present in the chapter are quoted, together with the name of Julian (*et hoc etiam Iulianus*) in the *Supplementum* to the *Summa Theologiae* of Thomas Aquinas (q. 70, a. 3, *Respondeo*).

The one and only infernal fire punishes in a diversified way (Prognosticum *II, xviii*)

Based on the authority of Gregory the Great, Julian ventures into a naturalistic analogy of the fire of Geenna. The naturalistic image refers to the sun, which radiates in a constant way but with a diversified human perception. Likewise, the fire of Geenna has the same intensity, but it is perceived by the souls differently, based on the gravity of their punishment.

More convincing is what he says about the subjectivity of the sinners, which is at the origin of the diversity of punishment.

The theology of Purgatory (Prognosticum *II, xix–xxiii*)

For the third time Julian affirms the existence of the *post mortem* state of purification of the defective souls. Augustine and Gregory the Great are the main patristic authorities on whom he relies for the foundation of faith in the existence of a state of purification after bodily death. From Augustine he derives the idea that the purification of the soul can happen in the terrestrial life as well as after death. But the purification after death occurs through a fire, which is more painful "than anything a man can suffer in this life."

Whereas in the tenth chapter Julian did not refer to fire as an instrument of purification of the souls, choosing to speak, more opportunely, of the medicinal punishments prescribed by the divine physician, he now, instead, because of the undisputed authority of Augustine and Gregory, makes use of this image of fire, which, however, expresses the same idea of purification, though not without the possibility of misunderstanding.

There is no doubt that the interpretation of purification as a process of healing the soul through the medicinal care prescribed by the divine physician is much more effective than the description of the purification in a punitive sense, as we find in this chapter, in dependence on the writings of Augustine and Gregory the Great.

The formulation of Gregory is more technical and circumstantial, as he affirms that it is a part of Christian faith: "It is to be believed that before the final judgment, there is a purifying fire for light sins." Examples of light sins are listed: "persistent idle talk, unrestrained laughter or the sin of worry for family affairs," and so on.

The biblical foundation of the doctrine is taken from Matt 12:32, with a very (too much so) liberal exegesis of the text, and from the famous text of 1 Cor 3:5–15, quoted by many authors of the patristic period, in which Paul speaks about the one who builds (that is, evangelizes) with wood, hay, and straw and who is then saved "through fire." This situation is attributed, with a hardly convincing leap of logic, to the future purification after death, even if Gregory admits that what was said by Paul can be referred to the tribulations of the terrestrial life.

From this general formulation, Julian passes, in chapter xx, to the distinctions related to the nature of fire, affirming that there are two types of eschatological fire. One is a fire through which eternal salvation is obtained, of which Paul speaks (1 Cor 3:15), while the other is the fire reserved for the punishment of the damned and which finds its basis in the words of the eschatological discourse of Jesus (Matt 25:41, 46).

Chapter xxi clarifies the "when" of the purification. It will certainly occur before the final judgment, for a series of reasons that all stem from God's desire for no one to arrive at the final judgment, which will be the last and most rigorous, in a state of sin so as to receive eternal punishment. Therefore, it is not enough to be baptized. It is necessary to be justified in and by Christ, and this justification is obtained also with a purification, on earth or after death, or with both purifications, but always before it is too late, meaning before the eschatological judgment. It seems that, according to Julian of Toledo, the historical-salvific principle according to which God desires the salvation of all and in all possible ways, is the main axis of theological reasoning.

Regarding the "duration" of the purification, Julian clarifies that, just as the infernal punishments are not the same for everyone but are differentiated based on the state of sin of each, likewise, in an analogous way, purification is not one and the same for everyone, nor does it "last" as long for everyone in the same way, though it will not last beyond the universal resurrection.

Julian insists on the temporal difference as an element of distinction in the purifications. We know how much this formulation is contested by modern theologians because it obstinately attributes terrestrial temporality to the afterlife. Thus, we can say that this analysis of the temporality emerges as a weak point of the doctrine about the state of purification, formulated by Julian up to this point with considerable equilibrium.

In spite of everything, however, it is clear that, according to Julian of Toledo, the state of purification is to be considered a positive fact, an element of salvation and divine grace and never a punitive situation. Rather, it manifests the endless desire of God to save as many human beings as possible. Or better still, simply everyone.

Finally, chapter xxiii emphasizes an affirmation frequently made in the text of the *Prognosticum* that the death of the flesh, as well as the tribulations of human life, belongs to, and represents some elements of, the system of purification devised by God for imperfect human beings, through which even if with a painful punishment, they might by saved forever.

The mutual relationships between the souls of the deceased and their knowledge of reality (Prognosticum *II, xxiiii*)

The souls living in the afterlife recognize one another reciprocally. Luke 16 shows this with its characters, good and bad, conversing among themselves: the bad rich man and Abraham, and the silent "poor Lazarus." Following Augustine, Julian believes that this mutual knowledge has repercussions, both negative and positive, on the condition of the damned and the blessed, as it might increase and extend their condition of joy or punishment.

In the blessed something sublime also happens: they recognize even those whom they had never seen before, such as the saintly fathers, whom they had never personally known but whom they had known through the study of their precious writings. This reasoning, which could seem to be an ecclesial and intellectual one of mutual knowledge, is then embraced by an absolutely theological argument: since the blessed souls know God with the same clarity, then in God himself, who knows everything, they know everything and everyone.

Praying for everyone (also for the damned)? (Prognosticum II, xxv)

This question is of great psychological importance in eschatology because it takes into consideration the affective or other kinds of bonds typical of earthly life. Will such interpersonal relationships, be they affective or of blood, have repercussions in the eternal life?

Julian's answer, drawing from Augustine, is that we can pray for everyone, enemies included, as long as we are in the terrestrial life, that they may be converted and live, but we cannot pray for those whose eschatological and negative judgment has already been established, because it is irreversible. The reason is presented very effectively: the damned are not prayed for in heaven, for the same reason that the devil and his angels are not prayed for on earth, since they are already destined to eternal hell.

Moreover, the just, both when alive and even more so as deceased, do not feel compassion for the unjust, since they conform themselves to divine justice and it is impossible for them to desire anything that God does not want. This attitude could be extended also to the consideration of their loved ones. A great pain would perhaps seize the blessed souls in seeing their own dear ones damned, but their desire to be conformed to the will of God would nonetheless prevail. It is totally comprehensible how difficult it would be, psychologically, to defend this thesis.

The ecclesial communion between the heavenly church and the terrestrial church (Prognosticum II, xxvi)

This chapter begins with an argument a fortiori personally written by Julian without resort to patristic texts: if one of the damned, such as the bad rich man of Luke 16:23, worries about the eternal destiny of his dear ones and asks Abraham to warn his own so that they may change their life and avoid the eternal torture, all the more so, Julian says, do the holy souls worry, pray, and intercede for their dear ones as much as they are allowed to by God.

This shows, first of all, that the souls do not lose their faculties, especially that of love and memory of their dear ones. In second place, this dialogue of prayers and communion of prayer characterize the life of the church on the double level of both heaven and earth.

Therefore, "the crowd of pious faithful recommends itself every day to the chosen souls." Julian thus demonstrates a very mature ecclesiology, precisely for eschatological reasons, which he expresses showing the connection between the two levels of church.

The ending of the chapter is autobiographical, as Julian humbly claims that what he has written represents his solution to the question posed: "even if I am unable to express in the same words with which the greatest have developed it, I nonetheless believe that it was defined in the same sense by the doctors, and even though I discover something of it, which they had defined, I prefer to follow their sentence."

The joy and sadness of the souls, as well as the worry and care for the living (Prognosticum *II, xxvii*)

Julian maintains the thesis that the dead have great vitality. In fact, they worry about the destiny of the living ones (Luke 16), without knowing anything else about them, just as we the living take care of the eschatological destiny of our dear ones who have died, even if we do not know anything about their outcome and their eschatological life. This is shown by the ecclesial liturgical praxis of the suffrage by which the church contributes considerably to the attainment of the final goal for many souls.

Experience instead shows the care of the dead for the living. Julian, like Augustine and many other fathers of the church, quotes by way of example the story of a parent who appears in a dream to his son indicating to him where a certain document is kept that will free him from being accused unjustly of not having paid off a debt.

We have already observed how the resort to dreams, and to other existential situations, is used in a didactic way, that is, as an example to be remembered that fixes a certain truth in the experience and in the memory. But it can become a demonstration or a confirmation of the ability of souls having a conscious life to communicate with the living, even if separated from their bodies.

As has already been shown, this resort to dreams is certainly a problematic aspect of the methodology of some part of the *Prognosticum.*

The ecclesiology of the mystical body applied to eschatology
(Prognosticum, II, xxviii)

Julian faces the delicate theme of eschatology concerning the fullness, or lack of fullness, of beatitude of those who have overcome death and have been declared worthy of the blessed life.

In the title of the chapter, Julian, involving people from both the Old Testament (patriarchs and prophets) and the New Testament (the apostles), affirms that their joy or heavenly beatitude is not complete because they grieve for our sins, and until they know that we are completely free from sin they will not be fully happy. From the eschatological point of view, it is a serious declaration that arouses perplexity because it theorizes a deferral or a delay of perfect beatitude of those whom even the church has declared blessed and saints.

But what Julian said makes deep theological and ecclesiological sense. It can essentially be traced back to a psychological aspect and to a charitable and ecclesiological sensitivity, without thus compromising the truth of the beatitude of the saints. Even more opportunely, it can be traced back to the fact that everyone, blessed and *viatores*, belongs to the church and that the state of the church's members is strongly marked by the solidarity and concern that the blessed limbs of the body of Christ have for the state of the other limbs of the same mystical body.

This reasoning touches high moments in the course of the chapter. For what concerns the biblical personages of the Old Testament, the discourse is repeated and confirmed with the quotation of a text of Origen. The great Alexandrian cites the Letter to the Hebrews, which makes an interesting assertion according to which the remarkable characters of the Old Testament have achieved the promise only through the facts and the characters of the New Testament. Accordingly Abraham, Isaac, and Jacob waited for a long time before reaching eternal beatitude. Up to this point the discourse, however risky, can still stand. We would now expect the same declaration about the apostles, as indicated by the title of the chapter. Instead, they are not cited as biblical characters who do not yet have perfect beatitude. In their place a very meaningful textual sequence is proposed that, instead of making reference to the apostles, turns into a more compelling and comprehensive discourse that concerns the whole church—the ecclesiology of the church as the body of Christ as proposed by Paul in the First Letter to the Corinthians.

According to Julian, as long as even one of the members of the ecclesial body of Christ has not reached the final end, there will not be, and there cannot be, a full beatitude for those members who have already been redeemed and are safe. This ecclesiological theme, which appeals to the desire of God that all be introduced as members of the body of which Christ is the transcendent head, is enriched, then, with the quotation of the famous prophetic vision of the dry bones of Ezekiel 37. In the text of the prophecy, all the bones, as well as the flesh, skin, and nerves of that boundless mass "must be restored to their place." In an analogous way, the blessed ones are truly blessed, and this is certainly not questioned, but "it will then be truly full gladness when none of the members of the body will be missing." In fact, the ecclesial body of Christ is not perfect if it lacks even one of its members. And this applies for the blessed, for us, when we shall be blessed, and even for the Lord and Savior, who is head of the whole body: even for him there will not be perfect gladness "as long as he sees that his body is lacking some of its members."

It is impossible not to note Julian's intellectual effort as he expands the problem of the beatitude of the single ones to a broader vision that, in a very meaningful way, ends up embracing the whole redemptive plan of God. Situating the particular eschatological problematic within the universal perspective of salvation shows the high degree of knowledge and theological speculation of Julian of Toledo and his all-embracing vision of eschatology as a fundamental hermeneutics that succeeds in leading him toward an anticipated knowledge (*prognosticum, prae-scientia*) of the final result of the plan of creation and redemption—what we could call, in conclusion, the eschatology of God himself. According to this divine eschatology, any loss or failure of humanity (the damned) cannot be qualified except as an anti-eschatology.

Therefore, this is how Julian succeeds in formulating a risky thesis of eschatology. Relying on Pauline ecclesiology, he is able to overcome the dangerous contradictions between relative beatitude and perfect beatitude, and he treats the matter not as if he were dealing with a *refrigerium interim*, as occurred in the beginning of Christian eschatological reflection,[23] but he introduces it within the overall theological and anthropological problem of the final end.

The degree of knowledge of the dead (Prognosticum II, xxviiii)

On this difficult matter, the *prae-scientia* of Julian succeeds in formulating some hypotheses: three to be precise. But all the hypotheses are preceded by an initial assertion, derived from Augustine: the dead do not know the actions of the living ones on earth. They, however, can come to such knowledge in three ways.

The first one is the possible communication of the "newly" dead with those who have been dead longer. To the latter it is granted to communicate what God allows them to make known. The second way of knowledge about earthly things can come to the dead from the angels. According to the patristic angelology and, in particular, that of Dionysius the Pseudo-Areopagite, angels are the last layer of incorporeal spirits in the hierarchical descending ladder that goes from God to the human beings. Therefore, they are closer to earth and to knowledge of what happens in human history. Julian, however, does not rely so much on this patristic doctrine as on a biblical quotation, the usual one of Luke 16:22, a true gold mine for patristic eschatology, which narrates how the poor Lazarus died and "was carried away by the angels to be with Abraham." This means that angels know human events and they interact with them according to what is prescribed to them by the will of God. Finally, the third hypothesis is that the souls of the dead can be endowed with a special knowledge of human and earthly facts by the Holy Spirit himself. Such infused knowledge can concern the past, the present, or the future, like that of the prophets, but it is always conditioned by the divine will.

Thus, this thesis on the gnoseology of the dead establishes yet another testimony for the survival of the souls "endowed with conscience and will," meaning that they are vital and capable of knowledge and communication.

The apparitions of the dead (Prognosticum II, xxx)

According to Julian, the apparitions of the dead are possible, but absolutely in a passive sense, not an active sense. This means that they appear to human beings not by their initiative, but exclusively by the will of God or by divine permission. They can be sent from there to here, and vice versa, while human beings can also be taken up from here to there (for example, the apostle Paul, who was taken up to the third heaven, according to 2 Cor 12:2). To provide foundation for the thesis, Julian refers to biblical examples: the dead prophet Samuel, who appears to King Saul (1 Kgs 28:5), and especially the dead Moses, who appears, together with Elijah, beside Jesus who converses with them (Matt 17:1–8).

Julian realizes that this theme is very delicate and must be treated with a lot of sobriety, because an excessive expansion of it can negatively influence Christian religiosity. He prefers, therefore, to limit the thesis to what is essential, exclusively attributing to God the possibility to send, in exceptional cases, the dead to bring announcements or messages to the human world.

Again on the knowledge of the souls: the special knowledge of the holy souls (Prognosticum *II, xxxi*)

Julian returns to the theme treated in chapter xxix to deny, in principle, any possibility of knowledge of the souls concerning earthly life, as well as any possibility of knowledge of the living about the life in the hereafter. Such impossibility is due to the different manner of knowledge based on the difference of the kind of existence (bodily for earthly human beings and spiritual for the dead).

But Julian proposes a new element, which represents a general exception: the holy souls, having access to the beatific vision of the Lord, know all things in the vision of God and they contemplate them in his knowledge, such that in no way can there be something outside that they ignore. Obviously, this does not occur to those who are deprived of the vision of God. They do not know anything, and they live in the most absolute obscurity about the knowledge of earthly events.

Uncertainties and doubts about the knowledge of the soul before and after the christological event (Prognosticum *II, xxxii*)

The chronology of the christological events also has consequences in the afterlife. So if in Luke 16:23–31 the bad rich man saw Abraham, this happened before the Easter mystery of Jesus. But Julian asks himself if, after Christ descended into Sheol and brought the just of the Old Testament into the heavenly kingdom, something had changed or if the saints can keep on seeing the damned and vice versa.

The answer is found in the thought of Gregory the Great, according to whom before the final judgment the damned see only some of the just, while the saints always see the damned in their torture, and this vision does not decrease their beatitude in any way, because they contemplate all this in the light of their vision of the Creator.

The theological reasoning is not without its weaknesses, and it almost seems that Julian follows a literal exegesis of the biblical text too closely. Nonetheless, he does succeed in providing some explanation about the difficult matter.

The crucial problem of intermediate eschatology: the life of the soul after death (Prognosticum II, xxxiii)

Julian finds himself faced with the main problem that eschatology has to demonstrate against those who do not accept it by Christian faith: the survival and the life of the soul after the death of the body. He does not cite those who contest this fundamental anthropological truth by which death does not touch the existence, survival, and subsistence of the soul. Julian, however, realizes that the problem is not to be addressed in the philosophical sense but according to the method already experienced by Julian of the double authority by which to sustain doctrine: the biblical tradition and the theological-doctrinal tradition of the church.

For what concerns the Bible he is able to furnish some quotations that range from the Book of Daniel and the Psalms, to the Apocalypse of John, the Gospel of Matthew, and the Letter to the Hebrews, all of which attest, in a generic or more consistent way, that after death the "self" of human beings or the human spiritual subject subsists, endowed with conscience, will, memory, and other faculties.

For what then concerns the theological tradition, the doctrine is "fortified" with a text of Augustine that narrates an edifying fact: the conversion of the pious physician Gennadius of Carthage. He was a good Christian but somewhat skeptical as to the existence of the soul after death. So, to disperse his doubts and so that his story, common to so many others, would become the occasion of edifying adherence to the Christian truth, the Lord himself appears to Gennadius twice. The Lord, with the didactics of a true master of logic, places before Gennadius the fact of the existence of the soul and its knowledge, memory, and senses through an incontestable and unassailable demonstration. The result of the teaching is that Gennadius acquires full awareness of the important value of the survival and subsistence of the soul after death. Finally, the Lord gives the pious physician a lesson that will serve for all those who have the same doubts: "when you will be dead, while your bodily eyes shall be wholly inactive, there shall be in you a life by which you shall still live, and a faculty of perception by which you shall still perceive. Beware, therefore, after this of having doubts on the persistence of human life after death."

The story is truly edifying, but it arouses again the methodological problem already mentioned of how to evaluate the presumption of patristic theology that claims to derive theological and doctrinal teaching from someone's dream or story, real or fictitious.

It is not to challenge the pedagogic function and the very effective didactics of the story, but it is possible, instead, to object to the fact that it recognizes in the edifying story also a hermeneutic function or value, almost a demonstration of a theological truth. Accordingly, the demonstrative and theological value of the edifying narrated episode decreases considerably. It becomes complicated to accept from these demonstrations that during dreams the senses and the human consciousness can be conceived as a demonstration or a confirmation of the possibility of a conscious life and ability to communicate for the soul separated from the body in the afterlife.

The soul has a certain bodily resemblance, from which it derives its sensitivity for the pleasing or sad things (Prognosticum II, xxxiiii)

This theme also has a notable meaning in the eschatology of Julian of Toledo in that its treatment and the acknowledgment that the soul has a dimension that is not absolutely spiritual somehow allow us to realize that this bodily resemblance of the soul is what permits us to speak about the sensitive punishments or about joy and beatitude for the souls that have gone out of the body. But, obviously, the matter is very difficult to explain.

The beatitude of the first and second "stole" (Prognosticum II, xxxv)

The question about the qualities of the souls separated from the bodies becomes intense because it refers, as in this case, to the eternal reward. Julian introduces a difference between the objective state of beatitude of the souls after their exit from the body, but before the bodily resurrection, and the condition of beatitude that will be at the end of time, when the souls will take back their corporeality, which in the meantime will have been glorified.

The first phase of beatitude, following the example of the language used in the book of the Apocalypse, is called "the first stole," or "white robe" (Rev 6:11) in the actual translations of the Bible, and it indicates the "joy of the spirit" and "the rest." The second phase of beatitude is called the "second stole" (or the second vestment), and it is what the soul will receive at the end of time that will make them exult with full joy for the immortality of the soul and, then, also of the body.

The interpretation is obviously symbolic, but it refers to an eschatological sequence that undoubtedly raises a question: whether the beatitude of the souls is unchangeable and eternal to the point of not undergoing variations of any kind at the moment of being reunified with its body. Julian believes that this reunification for the glory of both elements that constitute the human person will bring a supplement of incomparable joy, just as, on the natural level, the reunification itself of soul and body will bring an increase of happiness.

Therefore, according to Julian, the white robe, or the first vestment, referred to in Rev 6:11 is the situation of rest, comfort, and joy following bodily death. Subsequently, a second vestment will follow, that of exultation, which will be delivered during the bodily resurrection. It will make the attainment of beatitude and immortality more explicit in the soul and in the body.

The overall interpretation of Julian shows itself to be quite moderate, because it follows closely the differences and distinctions between the first and second vestments that are found in the book of the Apocalypse and, especially, because Julian does not extend his exegesis and his opinion to make a theological doctrine of it.

It is helpful to remember how seven centuries later the same quoted text of the Apocalypse, in its rigid and extensive interpretation by the "heretical" pope John XXII, made a true theological upheaval in the Western Catholic Church.[24]

The simple, immense vision of God is the eschatological reward
(Prognosticum *II, xxxvi*)

The context of the assertions about the vision of God after death is that of the exhortation to martyrdom by Cyprian of Carthage. The promise of the divine vision is explicitly affirmed for all those whom God will deem worthy to receive it as gift. Therefore, after a Christian life and a holy death it is possible "to look upon God and Christ!"

The recommendation of Julian is that "we must be certain that, after death, we shall not be at all defrauded of the vision of God, but we shall enjoy it with gladness if we will have lived operating according to his approval." This means that eternal life is not "only" immortality, incorruptibility, eternity, or something immense or superior to the human condition, but it coincides with the intimate and experiential knowledge of the profound mystery of the transcendence itself of God the Father, of the ineffable mystery of the God made man, Jesus Christ, and of the Holy Spirit. Thus, and this is the most important for Christian eschatology, the ultimate goal, meaning the only reality that can satisfy the restless human heart, is the divine Persons and not "things."

Not only the martyrs but all the saints reign with Christ
(Prognosticum *II, xxxvii*)

Julian establishes a principle of eschatological equity when, basing himself on Augustine, he affirms that not only the souls of the martyrs (as asserted by the rigorous theologians of the first centuries, for example Tertullian, and even by Augustine himself) but also those of the pious or the "simple" saints reign already now, meaning before the resurrection of the body, with Christ in heaven and do not need other purification. The martyrs are therefore "the part for the whole," for which besides them all the other blessed reign from now on with Christ. What it means to reign with Christ can be understood only by reading the beatitudes recounted in the Gospel of Matthew (5:1–12) or in some chapters of the Book of the Apocalypse (Rev 20–21).

The fact that the "simple" saints already belong to the kingdom of God means that they have reached the perfect dimension of the church, that is, the church of the living and the dead. And this is a very precious ecclesiological dimension of Julian's eschatology, because, although he speaks about the destiny of single souls, he does not overlook the communitarian and ecclesial dimension (preferred terms for the more anonymous and generic "collective dimension") of eschatology.

Further, the terrestrial church admits this reign of the saints with Christ, because the church mentions their names during the liturgy, in which she proclaims the absolute royalty of Christ himself and in the very moment in which there is the maximum communion of the body of Christ with its head, in the celebration of Eucharist. "Though not with their bodies yet, their souls nevertheless *already* reign with him." They are, however, waiting for an event that will make them extremely joyful: the resurrection of their body and its reunification with their soul.

And while one could think, also legitimately, that this event of the resurrection of the flesh could lead to an increase in their happiness, Julian is quite happy to overcome this perspective, with the help of a text of Augustine's *De civitate Dei*. In this text the holy doctor actually speaks about the fact that the souls, waiting for the resurrection of their bodies, cry out their desire to God and "they desire that this beatitude be doubled," that the beatitude they already live with their soul be extended also to their body. But God asks them to be patient for still a little (Rev 6:11) while the mysterious "thousand years" elapse, which is repeatedly, though critically, spoken about in the book of the Apocalypse (Rev 20).

BOOK III: HUMAN CORPOREALITY HAS
AN ETERNAL DESTINY

The theology of the resurrection: the anthropological realism of the resurrection of the human body and Christology as the source and cause of the resurrection in the eschatology of Julian of Toledo

Book III of the *Prognosticum* is the lengthiest of the entire work. Indeed, it consists of sixty-two chapters devoted to the most different matters associated with the mystery of the final resurrection of the dead.

Before beginning the treatment of what Julian himself calls *quaestiunculae*, however, he shows how the doctrine related to the resurrection is actually founded on Christology and its mysteries still to be revealed, first among which is the *parousia* of Christ at the end of time, with all that is related to it, especially the universal judgment. The book, in fact, begins with the matters associated with the *parousia* of Christ. Julian then undertakes a healthy work of demythologization or theological moderation, as in the previous books of his work, about questions that for centuries had been turned into mysterious enigmas: for example, the theme of the valley of Jehoshaphat, or the valley of judgment; the time of the universal judgment; the judgment itself in its modalities; the destiny of Satan; the modalities of the *parousia* and the resurrection; the qualities of the risen bodies; the immediateness (*ictus oculi*) of the action of resurrection; and the realistic characteristics of the risen. He contests the *fabulae* about the resurrection, taking on a position of prudent eschatological silence about the corporeality of the damned, defending the female corporeality from absurd mistakes and sexual discrimination and other *fabulae*, but also defending the right to the resurrection of the aborted fetuses, of those deformed and those devoured by animals or destroyed by fire, and so on.

In addition to these interesting but minor chapters, he also treats a whole series of secondary matters that, as we shall see, actually end up damaging the theological structure of the *Prognosticum*, dispersing it in the search for the best solution to the *quaestiunculae*.

In any case, by the end of the text, the reader has the impression that a basic anthropological and theological principle has driven Julian in his investigation: the respect for and importance of the bodily dimension of the created and redeemed human being. As if he had understood that not only does the human being love his flesh and desire a glorious future for it, but that also God "*diliget carnem, tot modis sibi proximam, etsi infirmam*" (see Matt 26:41), God will love the flesh of the human being in many ways close to him, even though weak, as Tertullian had affirmed in an extraordinarily deep way in his *De resurrectione carnis.*[25]

The ignorance of the date of the parousia (Prognosticum III, i)

Book III of the *Prognosticum* opens with an explicit reference to the final christological mystery: the second coming of Christ, at the end of time, for the resurrection of the dead and the universal judgment of humanity, and above all to declare the old creation and its history closed. Afterward, the eternal kingdom of God with humanity in a transformed cosmos will be inaugurated in a universal way.

Therefore, while the title of the chapter and the beginning of the text make direct reference to Christ's final judgment upon humanity, in the body of the chapter the subject instead becomes personally christological and related to the mystery of the date or of the "necessary ignorance" about the date of the *parousia*. This date, according to Julian, is unknown to human beings, according to the will of God. This affirmation comes from the famous text of Mark 13:32, which seems also to proclaim the ignorance of the Son, in addition to that of the angels and human beings, about the prophetic date.

The Gospel text quoted (Mark 13:32) has been a true *crux interpretum* for exegetes and theologians of every century; its content has provoked the most extreme interpretations, and has also produced heretical christological visions such as that of Arius. Nevertheless, it has also prompted exegetical contortions for its intrinsic and objective interpretative difficulty. Julian chooses the moderate interpretative approach, which certainly does not attribute ignorance to Christ, but rather expresses the idea in terms of the Lord's unwillingness to reveal the date of the *parousia*. This means that even though he knew, Christ did not want to reveal the date of his coming. The reason for this reservation is not mentioned, but it probably involves the need for a conscious learned ignorance of the theologian. The ending of the text is inspired by the writings of Isidore of Seville, and it repeats the same interpretation, as if God wanted to preserve *in pectore suo* this eschatological decision.

In any case, it is interesting that Julian opens the discourse on the final resurrection of humanity with a direct reference to Christology. This shows an intent to dematerialize or demythologize the eschatological discourse about the judgment and the resurrection, in order to focus it upon the one who is the cause and produces these universal events, and who will preside over the universal judgment. According to Julian, in fact, since Christ is God the Savior, he is also for this reason God the judge of the living and the dead, in addition to being the one who has the power to snatch their corporeality away from death.

The "place" of the judgment: demythologization of the "valley of Jehoshaphat" (Prognosticum III, ii)

In this chapter Julian faces a secondary question though one particularly full of mystery that has fascinated many interpreters of Sacred Scripture: the place where the judgment will happen.

He addresses the biblical question, centered on the text of Joel 4:1–2, and he asks, with help from the exegesis of Jerome, if the name valley of Jehoshaphat should be interpreted literally to indicate a precise geographical and topographical reality, though still mysterious, or if the expression is to be interpreted in a figurative way.

The choice he makes favors a literal interpretation, but in a symbolic sense. According to him, in fact, the expression "valley of Jehoshaphat" simply means "the Lord's judgment," and therefore it points to the action of God that will assemble the people of the past and the present and will judge them. Nothing else. Julian has thus eliminated the temptation of a mythical interpretation by proposing the most moderate interpretation.

The "time" of the judgment (Prognosticum III, iii)

Basing himself on the power of the profession and confession of the faith of the whole Catholic Church, Julian affirms that Christ's judgment of the living and of the dead will occur. It is a certainty of faith.

But this final time cannot be analyzed in a human way. The "time" of the judgment, therefore, is and remains a mystery hidden in God. This also means that it is totally useless to investigate it. Once again we are provided with a beautiful proof of the theologian Julian's sense of moderation and of his specific awareness of the need for a *docta ignorantia*, a learned ignorance, before the mysteries that have remained hidden from believers by divine will. Therefore, the futility of the investigation is not because the question is taboo. Rather, it is more important to become aware that, by the commitment and constancy of faith, one can actually accelerate the coming of that blessed time.

The christological modalities of the parousia (Prognosticum III, iiii)

The text is entirely Julian's, and in it he returns to the christological theme of the *parousia*, or the second coming of Christ. Julian maintains the faith of the church, which believes that Christ will come at the end of time, with all the saints to judge the human world. But Julian adds an interesting christological detail: Christ will come with the same aspect of the body with which he ascended to heaven. This identifies the Christ who was risen and ascended to heaven with the Christ of the future, yet, at the same time, it also emphasizes the anthropological realism by which one can legitimately think that Christ who ascended to heaven had never left his human nature and his glorious body.

The doctrine about the return of Christ has its basis in the eschatological description involving the whole universe and the angelic world, which is found in Matt 24:29–31. Nor could it lack the very ancient text of 1 Thess 4:16 and other texts of the Old Testament, which are, however, adapted to the theme of the *parousia.*

The parallel between the two Christs, that of Easter-Ascension and that of the *parousia,* continues, then, with another important difference: the Christ of the incarnation came incognito to be judged by human beings, while the Christ of the *parousia* will come openly to judge everyone. All will see him, and the sight of him will arouse much fear. Julian speaks of the *parousia* without going into detail and without trying to understand what is meant by "all will see him." He simply accepts the biblical affirmation that this appearance will fulfill in an instant the self-manifesting desire of God. About the feeling that the appearance of the Son of God will produce in human beings, Julian seems to refer both to a sentiment of terror and to a more moderate one of fear; the former probably applies to the unjust, while the latter seems more appropriate for the just.

The great sign of the cross will precede Christ the judge
(Prognosticum *III, v*)

The tradition according to which Christ will be preceded and accompanied by that great instrument of redemption that is the cross has a discriminating function of great pastoral importance. In fact, the cross that will appear in the sky will show that it is the true Christ and his true glorious advent, in comparison to the many Antichrists or false Christs who are to come and pretend to pass themselves off as the true Messiah. The believers will know how to recognize the true Messiah by this extraordinary sign. The biblical text at the base is Matt

24:30: Then "the stars will fall...when the sign of the Son of Man will appear in heaven"—that is, the cross, according to the patristic interpretation. In this case the exegetical interpreter on whom Julian draws is John Chrysostom. The cross of Christ will be resplendent more than the sun and the moon, and it will be carried by the angels and the archangels on their shoulders as the banner of redemption. It will precede the coming of Christ himself.

The reason for this apparition, in addition to being the sign of the true Messiah, is, in part, to confuse the crucifiers of Christ, who will finally see him appear even with his physical wounds, as announced by the Gospel of John: "They will look upon him whom they have pierced" (John 19:37).

In this text, there does not seem to be any anti-Jewish sentiment in an ethnic or racial sense. There is undoubtedly the blame, which comes from the New Testament itself, as well as from the whole Christian tradition, for the blindness and impiety of those who did not recognize in Jesus of Nazareth the Christ sent by God, even though they were more capable of doing so than anyone else, but handed him over to his crucifiers. It is undoubtedly a polemical note against the Jewish authorities of the time of Jesus, but it also looks to the period in which Julian lives, when the Jewish problem is still present in the Hispanic-Visigothic kingdom.

The destiny of Satan (Prognosticum III, vi)

The chapter combines various extremely meaningful elements. First of all, the destiny of Satan. It is obvious, according to Julian, that the glorious advent of Christ at the end of time will also constitute the signal of the defeat of Satan and his awkward attempts to nullify the act of redemption achieved by Jesus with his Easter mystery. Satan, Julian says simply, "will be brought away to be condemned." He simply leaves the scene, without any possibility of fighting to defend his terrestrial dominion. There is too much disproportion between his enormous strength and the almighty transcendence of Christ. What will happen next will be for his eternal sentence. No added descriptive detail is included in the affirmations of Julian. What must emerge above all is the triumph of Christ, not the description of the end of an enemy by now stripped of his offensive power.

In second place, Julian considers the state of mind of the human beings already risen ("who will already be found with the body when the Lord will come for the judgment") at the moment in which the defeat of Satan will happen. They will be stunned by the vision of these events to the point that this experience will be for them a purification, if there is still anything in them that needs to be purified.

The parousia *is one but diversified* (Prognosticum *III, vii*)

The text, which is entirely Julian's, has as its subject the vision of the glorious Christ at the end of time. The vision will be universal, but its beneficiaries will react in a diversified way. The just will see him as having a meek attitude toward them, and this will be a source of great joy. The unjust, however, will see him as dreadful and terrible, and for this they will suffer immensely. Julian also adds a logical note: this situation will be enduring, because the just will continue to fear Christ and receive his meek glance, while the unjust will continue to not fear him and to lie in their vices.

The vision of the glorious Christ will be ocular and bodily (Prognosticum *III, viii*)

The Christ of the *parousia* will be visible to all because he will manifest himself to humankind with his human nature, but the just will also see beyond his humanity; they will have access to his divinity, and this will be an immense joy for them.

The unjust will instead see only Christ's humanity; they will be deprived of the vision that would fill them with joy, because to see God is the greatest desire of the human being. They will be deprived of it because they did not see it, that is, recognize it in history.

The parousia *will be of the Son, not of God the Father* (Prognosticum *III, viiii*)

In his christological eschatology, Julian follows the text of John 5:22, which attributes the judgment to the Son, by the will of God the Father. Then he finds the fitting reasons for this divine revelation in the theology of Augustine. First of all, if the judgment will be made by the Son, this does not mean that the Father will not be the judge. Julian already knows the theological axiom according to which all that God does *ad extra* must be understood as common to the whole Holy Trinity (therefore the Father "will judge through the advent of the Son").

In second place, Christ will be the judge because he has the human form and nature, and it was that nature that was judged by human beings. Julian considers it right that he who had been judged, and besides that unjustly, be the one to judge human beings, but with the perfect divine justice and with human form.

The "when" of the parousia (Prognosticum III, x)

If in *Prognosticum* III, i, Julian had spoken of the lack of knowledge about the date of the *parousia*, especially with regard to Christ, he now devotes this chapter to the problem of the "when" of the *parousia* from the human perspective.

The principal assertion is that the time of the *parousia* is unknown to us not so much for a mysterious reason, but essentially because it is not an event that belongs directly to human history. It concerns Christ and the events that he still has to complete at the end of the world, in order to close history and to inaugurate the absolute novelty of the kingdom of God. Accordingly, the *parousia* is the event that determines the end of an eschaton and the beginning of a new eschatological era. In any case, the judgment that Christ will come to make will concern those still alive on earth and, naturally, also all the deceased.

The final tribunal of history (Prognosticum III, xi)

Playing on the double meaning of the term *see*, meaning both the dwelling of God in the saints and at the same time the throne upon which God sits as sign of power, Julian indicates that Christ will not be alone in that event but will share his universal judicial act at the end of time with the apostles, as shown by the words of Jesus in Matt 19:28. Moreover, in the text of Matthew, Jesus makes an important allusion to the fact that the apostles' participation in the universal judgment will happen "in the new creation," which is a very evident way to refer to a totally unknown situation in comparison to the terrestrial dimension.

This means, first of all, that Christ will communicate his eschatological and divine power to the apostles and will not keep it for himself. This is undoubtedly an important sign of the degree of participation in the divine life that Christ has obtained from his Father for his disciples. Therefore, the judgment upon history, which would seem to be

an exclusive prerogative of God, will actually be shared with the group
of faithful disciples. In second place, the novelty of the setting of the
judgment leads us to understand that it will occur not only in an
unknown place but also in a way that is not given for us here on earth
to know.

Not only the historical apostles, but all the just will judge
(Prognosticum *III, xii-xiii*)

Julian clarifies, first of all, that not only the apostles but all the just
will take part in the divine judgment. The reason lies in the numero-
logical meaning of the collective name of the disciples: the Twelve. This
number, in fact, points to the totality of a whole, which thus expands
beyond its meaning as a composite number.

Besides, the author adds how Matthias, not Paul, replaced Judas
Iscariot as the twelfth of the apostolic group, and yet Paul was not at
all excluded from being called and from considering himself an
"apostle by the will of Jesus Christ." The concept of apostle is very
broad and foresees being extended to all the perfect.

Julian, in short, tries to render his readers and those who will
receive his teachings knowledgeable about the active role of the saints
in the final conclusion of history, together with their Lord.

The fact of the final resurrection of the bodies
(Prognosticum *III, xiiii*)

The resurrection, Julian of Toledo teaches, is an essential and
fundamental given of Christian faith, which concerns every Christian,
and no one, therefore, must doubt it.

The resurrection of all the dead, which will happen at the end of
time, however, will not be a natural event nor a historical event born
from within human experience. Instead, it can be traced back to a personal action of Christ, which will occur in a way recalling creation, that
is, with only the Word of God. The resurrection will be, therefore, a new
creation and the foundation of a new heaven and a new earth, where
new human beings will live, those resuscitated by Christ.

The text of John 5:25, 28–29, which is a solemn revelation of
Jesus, foresees, however, a double outcome of the resurrection based
on the evaluation of everyone's earthly life. This means that judgment

and resurrection coincide in the events or actions of Christ, but they are diversified in the anthropological outcome they produce.

The apocalyptic framework of the judgment and the resurrection (Prognosticum III, xv)

This chapter is characterized by a description of the judgment and the resurrection in apocalyptic literary terms. The sound of the trumpet of the universal judgment undoubtedly indicates that something is about to happen, and this sound, and the image it implies, serves only to draw attention to the event that is about to occur and that concerns the created universe. It does not seem that Julian, with the help of Jerome, seeks hidden meanings associated with the trumpet sounded by the seventh angel of the Apocalypse. He gives these things an explanatory value, very effective and easy to remember.

Therefore, the sound of the trumpet points to the action of God that will resuscitate the bodies of all the dead. They will get their own bodies back, but while in the terrestrial life they had a corruptible body, as testified by their bodily death, they will now have an incorruptible body. Incorruptibility is, therefore, the sign of the new human being of the new creation.

The image of the resurrection is very effective; it is described as occurring *ictu oculi*, in the wink of an eye (1 Cor 15:52), which excludes temporal and progressive passages, as if the divine omnipotence needed a sequence of consecutive actions. This might be to indicate the facility of execution and the speed of the divine operation, which are obviously beyond the range of the human being for what concerns the practical formalities of how the resurrection will happen. These two characteristics show, therefore, that it is not a fatiguing and laborious action but an instant action of the marvelous divine power. This allows Julian to classify as a *fabulam*, a fable or a legend, any theory about the resurrection that makes reference to different levels of resurrection, by which there would be those who are raised up first and those who are raised up later.

The final, and aesthetically very delicate, poetic image of the light feather, of the straw thread, and of the thin dry leaf that are raised by a gust of wind is both didactic and able to explain the ease of the magnificent event that will happen by divine will. Thus, a glance from God will suffice for the dead to be raised.

The difference between universal resurrection and glorious transformation (Prognosticum III, xvi)

Basing himself on the Pauline sequence that indicates the resurrection of all the dead but reserves the transformation only to believers (1 Cor 15:52), Julian explains that the resurrection will be general and will include the just and the unjust, while the transformation, which is access to the glorification of the eternal beatitude, will be granted only to the just.

Therefore, the final phase of eschatology will entail not only the resurrection but also another event that will mark the beginning of the glorification of the just. Such transformation shows the passage from terrestrial to risen corporeality, which will finally be characterized by immortality and incorruptibility. Those who are raised will thus be able to participate in divine life.

The judgment that coincides with the resurrection will evidently create the final eschatological situation characterized by an elevation of the just to the supernatural state.

The realism of the risen body (Prognosticum III xvii)

Christian eschatology sees in the risen body the beginning of the new and definitive creation of God. But elements of continuity exist between the previous divine creation and the one that is the result of christological redemption. One of these elements of continuity is found in the persistence of the bodily dimension of the human being. Therefore, according to Julian, the Christian faith is not an extreme spiritualist anthropology that abolishes the body or reduces it to an ethereal form. It is necessary to exercise critical vigilance and to refuse any theory of those who *fabulantur*, who tell fables about the risen having an ethereal or aerial body. With the help of his venerated preceptor, Eugene of Toledo, Julian affirms, instead, that the body of the risen will be the one in which they had lived, the flesh "in which we are and we live." The risen, therefore, will not be angels, who are by definition deprived of body, but human beings in every way. Therefore, the creative plan of God, which intends the human being to be made of body and spirit, is confirmed and finally brought to its perfect fulfillment.

The spirituality of the risen body (Prognosticum *III, xviii*)

The distinction between animal (*psychikon*) body and spiritual (*pneumatikon*) body is present in the Pauline writings (1 Cor 15:44) and indicates respectively the terrestrial dimension of corporeality, which is subject to corruptibility and death, and the glorious dimension, which has its origin in the resurrection and will not be subject to any corruption or to death. But, Julian affirms, even if we call the risen bodies spiritual, this does not mean that they will be spirit, just as the terrestrial animal body is certainly not a soul. He offers no further explanation. Perhaps in this case the *studiosa brevitas* of Julian of Toledo shows itself to be rather excessive.

The qualities of the risen bodies (Prognosticum *III, xviiii*)

The author has already clarified that the resurrection is universal (III, xvi). He now adds that all the risen bodies will be incorruptible and immortal, even those of the unjust. The difference between just and unjust is not for this reason annulled. In fact, the risen unjust will be destined to the exclusion from glory, while the risen just will inherit the reward of glory.

Finally, an inner distinction: if it is true that all the risen bodies will be incorruptible and immortal, nevertheless the bodies of the unjust will feel pain from the torments they will undergo. And the torment will not be mitigated (but it will not destroy them), despite their incorruptibility and immortality.

Quaestiunculae *about the resurrection and the risen ones* (Prognosticum *III, xx-xxxi*)

A series of particular questions related to the resurrection begins with chapter xx. Julian does not withdraw from the attempt to find an answer to the many questions that have been raised throughout centuries concerning the future event of the resurrection. The primate of Toledo has already proven himself in the exercise of critical vigilance as well as in an interpretative moderation that has brought him either to theological silence, respectful of the mystery, or to some form of demythologization of some fanciful interpretations. With the same attitude he now addresses the *quaestiunculae* related to the risen bodies.

Stature and age of the risen ones (*Prognosticum* III, xx)

The guiding principle for answering the question about the age of the risen ones is anthropological in nature. This means that the bodily identity possessed in youth, approximately at the age of thirty, will be the point of reference in the resurrection. This is the principle suggested by the citation of both Eph 4:13 and the reflections of the fathers of the church. Therefore, whoever dies in old age or dies before developing to bodily maturity will be raised again with their own body looking young and mature.

The reason why the risen ones will all be thirty years old is not, therefore, an imitation of the age of Jesus or otherwise. The reason lies in the fact that the resurrection reinstates human nature in its most perfect situation, and thus both the weakness of old age and the immaturity of adolescence or any other age are excluded. The same reasoning applies to stature: each will be raised again in the stature they would have had at their perfect age of youth.

As can be seen, it is without a doubt a secondary theme, it is true, but the way in which it is treated, meaning with the authority of Sacred Scripture and of Augustine and Julian Pomerius, is correct. Christ, in fact, is the model of the risen ones. But good theological sense is used to allow a moderate answer to emerge, deprived of oddness about possible mutations or metamorphoses of the human nature that would render it an unrecognizable reality.

Tall or short, thin or fat? (*Prognosticum* III, xxi)

The question of the height and bodily weight of the risen ones is certainly a secondary eschatological theme, but Julian addresses it, again with good sense and moderation, without letting himself go to bizarre and fanciful hypotheses. He affirms that human logic would lead us to think that the stature of the risen ones will be equal and uniform for everybody, and that bodily weight will be, in any case, perfect, meaning correct.

Julian adds, however, that as in the work of creation God wanted diversity in aspect to be a characteristic of identity and personality, so likewise it can be hypothesized that the risen ones will also have a bodily difference, and anything that had been lacking in the stature or weight of the bodily dimension will be added in God's work of re-creation. In short, God does not like uniformity, which is synonymous with a lack of variety and originality. Rather, God loves diversity, as indicated by

Wis 11:20: "Sed omnia in mensura et numero et pondere disposuisti," "but thou hast arranged all things by measure and number and weight."

The bodily perfection of the risen ones excludes every defect
(*Prognosticum* III, xxii)

If, as it is believed, the bodies will rise again without any corruption, then this excludes also every deformity in the body of the risen ones. This assertion, which seems superfluous to us, must actually have been greatly appreciated in the times of Julian, since there were many deforming illnesses that disfigured the bodies already in infancy and childhood.

An added value of the risen bodies will be, for the martyrs, that the scars of the wounds or lacerations suffered for their testimony of faith will remain visible. In this case, however, these scars or lacerations will not constitute an imperfection but rather will be valued as signs of the beauty and splendor of their heroic virtue in that they contributed to leading the martyr to eternal glory.

No reflection about the risen body of the damned
(*Prognosticum* III, xxiii)

With a desolate reflection, Julian affirms that the whole discourse about the stature, age, and beauty of the bodies of the blessed does not have any value or is of no use for what concerns the risen bodies of the damned. Of them *nihil fit*, nothing is said and nothing can be investigated, or anyway, it would be entirely superfluous and useless, because their condition will be what Jesus pronounced in the Gospel: gnashing of teeth, eternal and incessant weeping. And where there is eternal sadness and solitude nothing about the qualities of the body matters.

Paradoxically, the very lack of any description related to the risen bodies of the damned renders the exhortation of Julian particularly effective. The situation of damnation is so negative that it could be said to be an overturned ineffability. The readers of the *Prognosticum* will learn from these considerations to fear even more, if necessary, the perspective of damnation. The language used by Julian is evidently, like that of Jesus, performative and effecting responsibility.

Taking on this position, Julian thus abstains from any description of the corporeality of the damned as well as of their torments.

This choice is not the result of an agnostic position of the author, but rather indicates the most relevant reason for the miserable state of the damned, who will forever be deprived of any glory. This is, for Julian, rightly so, the true damnation: the loss of eternal salvation and of the relationship with God. Faced with such an absolutely negative reality, even the bodily deformity or the most cruel and severe material punishment would be little in comparison.

The sexuality of the risen: defense of female corporeality and femininity (*Prognosticum* III, xxiiii)

The matter faced in this chapter would seem at first sight to be a useless *curiositas*, but when one reads the text, the author's strongly demythologizing intention is clear as he seeks to discredit some fanciful and pseudo-theological opinions about women.

Julian begins by saying that many authors, including most of the ones studied by him, considered the female sex to be defective, which would mean that women will be raised up as males. This oddness, the fruit of insipid reflections, is vigorously contested by Julian. He maintains, instead, that, since God is the creator, founder, and savior of both sexes, so also in the new creation, which will be inaugurated by the resurrection, he will make it so that everyone will be of their own sex. Julian founds this eschatological truth on Matt 22:28–30. He commits a pardonable *lapsus memoriae*, however, when quoting the Gospel story, as he attributes to the woman who had been the wife of seven husbands (and who in the story is dead like them), and not to the Sadducees, the devious question asked of Jesus to trip him up about the theme of the resurrection.

In any case, the quotation suggests to Julian that in the risen life sexuality will not be abolished, but if anything it will be the conjugal relationships and, above all, the carnal lust that will be abolished and disappear. To fortify the reasoning Julian quotes also the assertion of the Book of Genesis according to which man and woman were naked, meaning that they displayed their sexuality without problems, and they did not suffer any disturbance from it.

In the end, Julian offers an Augustinian sentence, indeed liberating, about the concept of woman in the Christian anthropology prior to and contemporary with Julian: "the female sex is not a sin, but it is precisely nature." In fact, in the risen life it will be free from the need for mating as well as from the difficulties and pains of childbirth.

The revered preceptor of Julian, Eugene II of Toledo, allows the author to conclude the matter of the sexuality of the risen ones in a perfect way with the exaltation of the bodily aesthetics, saying: "So great and such is the beauty of the glorified body that, though delighting the sight, nevertheless the heart in no way induces to vice."

Such a favorable attitude of Julian of Toledo toward women could be praised, and greatly, being considered entirely current and modern. But as was said in the beginning of our commentary, this would be totally antihistorical and deprived of sense. Rather to be praised are Julian's intelligence and freedom from cultural conditionings as he was able to evaluate reality especially in the light of divine revelation and to refuse any attitude of contempt toward the creative work of God.

Eating and drinking as risen (*Prognosticum* III, xxv)

Eating and drinking in the current terrestrial life are two necessities that come from the fragility and the weakness of the human body, as well as from the need to renew physiological force. In the final analysis, eating and drinking are a repetitive way of keeping death and the corruption of the body away. But when the glorious body, foreign to death and corruption, will take the place of the terrestrial body, there will no longer be any need to eat and drink. Of course, it is true that the risen Jesus ate, and we even know what he ate, a question that had exercised the patristic ingeniousness.[26] But he ate not out of necessity nor to extinguish a weakness of his flesh but, on the contrary, to confirm his disciples in the faith about the historicity and truth of his bodily resurrection, in addition to lingering on pleasantly with them in a convivial way, as he had done so many times during his historical life—a way, that of conviviality, evidently greatly loved by Jesus. The fact that Jesus ate, therefore, means that he was lacking not the possibility of eating but rather the need to do so.

The garments of the risen ones (*Prognosticum* III, xxvi)

The curiosity as to whether or not the risen will be dressed with particular clothes receives a substantially negative answer. There will be no need, in fact, for garments of any kind for the risen ones in the new creation, and for two reasons. First, for a natural reason, in that they will have no need to cover themselves for protection from the cold and from its consequences, so pernicious on the earth, because their bodies will be incorruptible and immortal. Therefore, they will not feel warm or cold, nor will they be harmed by variations in temperature. The second reason is of a moral nature, in the sense that there will be no sin there that can contaminate the soul upon seeing men and women deprived of garments, as instead happens in terrestrial life due to carnal lust.

Yet if, for a motive unknown to us but that could theoretically be of an aesthetical nature, in the new world there were to be garments for the bodies of the risen ones, they would be of the same characteristic as the bodies, thus incorruptible, or they would be as those foreseen by the prophet Isaiah (Isa 61:10: "garments of salvation and robes of righteousness"). So the risen ones could be dressed in virtue or symbolically dressed in dimensions of holiness. Or, they might even more probably be dressed in their own garments, as in the case of the risen Christ, who wore, precisely, his own clothes.

The embryos and their right to the final resurrection
(*Prognosticum* III, xxvii)

The problem of embryos is raised correctly, even if Julian declares not to want to debate the matter, because it is of great theological difficulty and also because it somehow lies beyond the realm of eschatology. Nevertheless, his raising the question is indicative of Julian's high anthropological and pastoral sensibility, especially at his time, when the interruptions of pregnancy and the neonatal deaths occurred very frequently owing to a substantial lack of preventive, medical, pharmacological, and gynecological knowledge.

Julian wisely affirms that the fetus aborted from the womb of the mother is in fact a living being. "When a human being begins to live in the mother's womb, it is to be believed in truth that from that moment he/she can also die, and so whoever has life can also die, and then be restored in the time of the resurrection." If the fetus can live and die, this means that it is a human being in all effects and, accordingly, will be involved in the event of the final resurrection as all other human beings. He/she, therefore, will rise again not as a fetus or premature but rather in a fitting age, at the age he/she would have reached if he/she had kept on living in the maternal womb, had been born, and had grown up as a normal human being. The final resurrection, by providential divine disposition, therefore, will integrate what is lacking in the nature of the fetuses, meaning the years of bodily growth and the development of all of their limbs up to full maturity. How this will occur is entirely unknown and obviously concerns the omnipotence of God, who desires that all human beings reach full human maturity and participate in divine life. So God performs this integration in a universal and optimal way.

Another discourse is the one related to the eternal salvation of the risen fetuses as adult human beings. The problem arises mainly because they die in the condition of original sin and without the salvific contact with the redeemer Jesus Christ that occurs in the sacrament of baptism. But about this problem, Julian is silent.

Again on the bodily deformities (*Prognosticum* III, xxviii)

Malformed beings in the maternal womb, for reasons Julian declares to ignore (to a large extent for genetic reasons or for biological degeneration, as we would say today), also have the right to the resurrection, even those whose very human identity is seriously questioned as they are born with characteristics of abnormal deformity. Accordingly, they will rise again in a perfect physical integrity that will include the exact number of limbs and whatever limbs were superfluous or lacking will be eliminated or restored.

The eschatological destiny of those devoured or mutilated (*Prognosticum* III, xxviiii)

By whatever kind of dissolution of the flesh someone has died (Julian lists a series of extreme examples), nothing will prevent the power of God from restoring the flesh intact to the spirit that animated it right from the start, by the will of the Creator, and that will also constitute, in the case of the risen ones, an element of identification of the human subject. Naturally Julian does not mention any scientific question. Rather, the problem is addressed and resolved by appealing to the omnipotence of God. What seems impossible to human beings for many, if not infinite, reasons, such as how to raise up someone who had been devoured and digested by beasts, is instead not a problem for the omnipotence of God.

Quoting Gregory the Great, Julian relates the classical and exemplary case of a man being devoured by a carnivore, devoured in turn by a feline, which died after a short time. The example serves for underlining to the reader the objective difficulty in being able to find again the bodily subject of the man devoured in this triple passage. How will he be able to rise again with his flesh? Julian answers, with the help of the father of the church himself, relying on the limited physiological knowledge of the time and emphasizing, first of all, the fact that a mix of relatively simple elements is required to obtain human conception. Yet the simple mix that leads to conception produces endless variations in bones, nerves, muscles, skin, hair, fingernails, and so on. If God, through the natural laws established by him, is able to perform this miracle of diversified growth, all the more so will he have no difficulty in resuscitating someone who has been devoured by beasts or burned, perhaps also incinerated by the flames of a fire.

The invalid, the mutilated, the crippled, and the resurrection (*Prognosticum* III, xxx)

The reflection until now has exalted the omnipotence of the Creator in the event of the resurrection of all human beings, whatever their physical state was during their death. God is, in fact, able to recreate the personal perfection of every human body, even the most devastated. Accordingly, the reasoning can be expanded to other extreme cases: the invalidity, deformity, and bodily monstrosity, so frequent in the centuries when medicine and prevention were scarce. Therefore, those bodies that had been deprived, because of natural errors or other causes, of the harmony and the proportions of some bodily parts, by defect or in excess, and, above all, deprived of some beauty of the human body that derives from this harmony, just as the Creator had willed, these human beings, in the resurrection, will bear no sign of imperfection or disproportion. They will simply be perfect in their own corporeality, by then evolved to the supernatural state.

The last *quaestiuncula*: the risen body is restored even in its smallest realities (*Prognosticum* III, xxxi)

The desire not to leave unresolved any matter related to the bodily resurrection impels Julian to address a subject we would define as banal and deprived of sense. The question is the following: during the bodily resurrection, what will happen to the hair so often cut, and to the fingernails, so many times trimmed in the course of earthly life?

The answer should be that those bodily parts will be restored to their place, as Julian has already said about a body's lacking limbs. But in this case the logical reasoning does not work: fingernails and hair cannot return to their place without provoking a serious drawback,

which is easy to imagine. We would have immoderate lengths of these
bodily elements and this would be indecorous and entirely unaes-
thetic. The solution is found in the sense that all this bodily material
will be restored to the single corporeality, but as a whole, as described
by the beautiful example that Julian uses: when a clay vase is molded
again by the potter, all of its parts return to the original mass of clay
from which another vase will be formed. But the part of the clay that
was the handle of the vase certainly does not return again as the handle. There is no need for it to do so. And likewise it will also be for the
parts of the human body subject to being cut or trimmed.

As can be observed, the reasoning of Julian in this series of secondary matters, but excluding the single proposed cases, always seeks
to insist particularly on the fact that the material body of the human
being will have a future. This will happen because it reenters perfectly
in the eschatological plan of God, from the point of view of creation
as well as from the even more founded one of redemption, which
depends on the risen corporeality of Jesus and upon the desire of God
to raise the human being, soul and body, ever since the beginning, to
the sharing of divine life. The body, therefore, will enjoy, together
with the soul, all the perfections typical of the spirit, but it will also
enjoy a definitive perfection not known upon earth, which God has
prepared for the new world and the new creation. The latter will be
inhabited by humankind finally made perfect, and therefore new,
final human beings, and the body as well as the soul will be fully realized, but in an atmosphere entirely different from the earthly one,
because human beings will be by then alive in incorruptibility and
immortality.

If Julian expounds upon the *quaestiunculae*, he undoubtedly
does so for anthropological reasons and to dispel doubts and uncertainties of the faith of Christian believers. It cannot be denied, however, that this insistence is in the end detrimental to the depth of the
theological framework, as it disperses the reflection upon the resurrection into a thousand rivulets of truth. It would certainly have been
more fitting for the intelligence of the theologian, and above all for
the expert of Christology that he was, if he had placed greater emphasis, at least more than he did in his work, on the relationship between
the Christology of the resurrection and theological and eschatological anthropology. This would have allowed him to elaborate a broader
eschatological anthropology that might have prevented him from

being dispersed in what he himself calls *quaestiunculae*. Evidently the requests for explanation by the faithful about these particular matters were so numerous and pressing for an answer that Bishop Julian did not know how to avoid this didactic task.

The resurrection for the "second death" (Prognosticum *III, xxxii*)

The universality of the salvific plan of God achieved through the mission of his Son foresees all humanity being removed from death and being resuscitated, even those who freely refuse salvation. This means that Julian distinguishes between the objective redemption and its refusal, which is something personal and subjective. In the unfortunate case of the latter, however, the resuscitated dead are destined to be excluded from glory. Instead, their destiny as risen ones is to be united "to the devil and his angels."

The author then declares that it is entirely useless to inquire about the condition of their bodies, that is, of their physical features, their physical incorruptibility, and so on, because these realities, though present, will not lead back to glory. Julian concludes with a reflection on the general condition of these risen ones, which is totally miserable, in that their existence is characterized by unhappiness, by a pain that tortures without killing, by an existential corruptibility that Sacred Scripture describes with a name that arouses fear: the second death. Julian's reflection does not go further, because this theme of the eternal damnation of those who refused redemption is very difficult to address, almost covered by an impenetrable, mysterious dimension.

The judgment of God and questions about the fire of damnation (Prognosticum *III, xxxiii-xxxxiiii*)

Julian devotes eleven consecutive chapters to the final judgment of God. First of all, he distinguishes two orders of human subjects comprised of two groupings (chapter xxxii): those who will judge, or will be judged, but who nonetheless will reign with Christ (the perfect and the chosen); and those who instead will be judged negatively, either for having been found "outside of the church," meaning not on

the main road of salvation that God has placed in the church, or for
not having observed the precept of charity.

This judgment will be the cause of the separation of the just and
unjust (chapters xxxiii–xxxiiii), and such separation will again involve
the action of the angels as collaborators of Christ the judge (chapter
xxxv). They will be given the task of separation, just as they had been
charged with the ministry of accompanying the soul to its eschatological condition (the psychopomp angels of *Prognosticum* I, x). With this
angelic function Julian evidently implies the universal involvement of
the creatures (be they angels or human beings) on the occasion of
this final event of history. All take part: God, the angels, and humanity. This description is founded on biblical texts, mostly drawn from
the eschatological discourses of Jesus in the Gospel of Matthew or
from the Psalms.

Julian attributes notable importance to the identification of the
mysterious books referred to in the Book of Revelation (Rev 20:12),
books that will be opened after the just have been separated from the
unjust (chapter xxxvi). As an experienced exegete and with the aid of
the interpretation of Augustine, Julian identifies those books as the
story of the life of the individuals, even if the interpretation changes
depending on whether he speaks "of the books" or "of the book," an
addition made in the biblical text. By divine virtue, therefore, written
in those symbolic books, which are like "God's memory," are the lives
of all human beings and what they have done, good or evil. Once this
narration of the lives of each and every one has been completed, the
final eschatological state of the risen ones will begin.

Chapter xxxviii affirms with decision, based on three consecutive texts of the Apocalypse, the definitive defeat of evil and its per-
sonification, both singular and collective: Satan and his own. This
implies not only the positive dimension of the end of the history of
salvation with the annihilation of the enemy, but also the carrying out
of divine justice toward the one who, according to Sacred Scripture,
is mainly responsible for the miserable condition of the human being
after sin and who "had seduced them." All this represents the end, on
the hamartological side, of the theology of history, which has wisely
been led by God up to the decisive point of the reestablishment of the
universal equilibrium, even with or despite "the permission of the
evil." Satan and his own, that is, "the author of death and the infernal
punishments" will no longer harm God or the church or human

beings. Evil, meaning "death and hell," the great unsolved question of humanity, especially if added to the creative and redemptive plan of God, will no longer exist; it will be destroyed in the "pool of fire," the evident symbol of annihilation. The utopia of a human society without the presence of evil becomes a definitive reality.

Another book is quoted in chapter xxxviiii: the book of life, in which the names of those redeemed are written. Julian penetrates the inaccessible forest of the doctrine of predestination to salvation (or to perdition), invoking the "prescience of God" as the reality by which he has always known all the redeemed. Cautiously Julian does not venture in some calculation or percentage of the redeemed. Rather, following the Apocalypse, he seems to indicate that those who will not be written in the book of eternal life will be a minority, considering that God has always desired for all humankind to be glorified and share in his divine life.

Chapters xxxx–xxxxiii treat in an intelligent way the matters associated with the so-called infernal fire or punishment. About the possibility of damnation Julian does not look for esoteric details in biblical revelation to disclose about this mysterious element to arouse fear. He recalls, above all, the biblical images according to which the risen bodies of the damned will burn in fire, without being destroyed by the fire, contradictory to the usual characteristic of fire destroying what it burns. To show that this is possible, Julian turns to Augustine to sustain a psychological argument: just as the soul suffers but does not die, likewise, in an analogous way, it will be possible for the material body to suffer the torments without being destroyed by them. The reasoning works perfectly, even if it is, in any case, part of a rather descriptive section from an eschatological point of view.

As for the conditions of the punishment of fire, Julian follows a dialectical reasoning according to which the souls, having lived in the human body—that is, although they were incorporeal—had in any case been confined within the material body. This is enough for Julian to affirm that it is then possible for the souls also to suffer together with their bodies, because the future fire of damnation is a material fire that affects also the spiritual dimension.

The attention devoted by the author to divine justice produces the conviction that in damnation there is a gradualness of punishment corresponding to the difference, greater or smaller, of the guilt of each subject. Accordingly, for those who die in the state of original sin but without personal sins, the punishment will be "mild" (*mitissima*), while for all other sinners there will be a punishment that corresponds to the gravity of the sin committed in earthly life and never expiated. Therefore, God's judgment of the unjust is not undiversified and without an inner logic, but occurs accounting for the characteristics proper to each human subject.

Chapter xxxxiii gives Julian the opportunity to show once again that he is not animated by curiosity in explaining his eschatological doctrine. He thus deems it necessary to assume an attitude contrary (*contra illos*) to those who seek to understand the nature of this fire and where it can be found. Rather, according to Julian, if the *Maiores* had desisted from this inquiry, it means that it does not belong to the theological earthly science to know more about it. The quotation from Augustine, according to which "no man" is able to debate about that fire, "except perhaps the one to whom the divine Spirit manifests it," shows the limit of theological gnoseology and its terrestrial methodology. Undoubtedly a good example of theological humility but also of theological common sense.

Finally, in chapter xxxxiiii, following the biblical exposition about the judgment of God, Julian makes a logical-chronological order of it: first the unjust will be judged and only subsequently the chosen. According to Julian, this succession shows that the most important reality, that is, the glory of the chosen, will have a preeminence and a nature of absolute importance. This is why it is mentioned last.

*The last christological change and the charity of the Lord Jesus Christ (*Prognosticum III, xxxxv and l*)

In the change of the appearance of Christ, at the end of the universal judgment, from that of a humiliated servant to the Lord of glory, showing his divinity in all its splendor, Julian sees the definitive conclusion of the christological mission of redemption. If his own will see him in his divine identity, this means that he, their head, has brought them with himself as his body to deliver them, since they are his kingdom, to his Father. In this way the glorious condition of Christ, in communion with his Father and the Holy Spirit, which they can experience, will become their habitual condition of life. The evident christological and trinitarian dimension of this reflection shows how for Julian the eschatology of the chosen ones especially turns into a communion of human and divine subjects: of the members of the body of Christ with their head, and in profound relationship with the other divine Persons of the Trinity. The chosen will thus be admitted to the contemplation of the very mystery of the triune God.

This situation of anthropological perfection deriving from participation in the divine life is, so to say, improved even more by the realization of a promise of the historical Jesus (Luke 12:37). In that promise Jesus alluded to the situation of complete eternal happiness expressed in the fact that Christ himself will entertain his own in a convivial way and even pass among them during the eternal banquet of peace, serving them—that is, satiating them with the reward of himself. Therefore, according to Julian, heaven is not a static condition of intellectual contemplation, nor is it a place in the cosmos. Above all, it is an experience and an interpersonal and intimate communion among divine and human persons, as expressed by the idea of the eternal banquet, in which the relationships between God and human beings are best expressed by their dimension of communion: eating and drinking together.

The farewell to the old world and the inauguration of the new earth and the new heaven (Prognosticum *III, xxxxvi-xxxxviiii*)

In these chapters of the eschatology of Julian of Toledo, the initial phase of the new history of the relationships between God and human beings starts to appear on the horizon: a new world and a new heaven. The old world no longer has meaning and is submitted to a complete metamorphosis. Julian evidently stands at a distance from the apocalyptic idea that the end of time will bring the destruction of the old universe. Once again, he operates a demythologization of eschatology. Rather, according to Julian, instead of destruction, the divine economy foresees a metamorphosis in which the new world will be characterized by a series of elements in logical correlation with the dimensions of immortality and incorruptibility of the risen ones; while the old characteristics, logically correlated to mortal and corruptible human beings, will be eliminated. The reasoning is therefore one of appropriateness: to new human beings corresponds the need for a new world and a new heaven. This means that Christian eschatology accounts for the "very human" dimension of eternal life. Human beings will not lose their characteristics of "inhabitants of a world." They will not reside in the air or in a spiritual condition. They will have a world, a new world, but a physical world in which to live their perfect and eternal condition as risen ones, that is, in possession of their characteristic physical dimension brought to perfection by the resurrection.

Naturally not all the risen, by the fact of being so, will have a part in the new creation, which will be inhabited by only the saints (chapter xxxxviii). This means that the better metamorphosis of the human body that will become immortal, incorruptible, and without limits for the glory will not happen for those who were excluded or who excluded themselves from this final end.

Finally, a *quaestiuncula* directed *contra eos qui dicunt*, against those who interpreted the eschatological data so as to raise materially absurd questions. In this case they asked where the chosen ones would be as risen while the previous heaven and earth were shaken by the metamorphosis. Julian, relying on the sagacious mind of Augustine, answers that they will be either set in elevated places (far away from the fire) or where it pleases them to be, or even better, staying where they are, but by divine virtue, they will not be damaged by any element of conflagration. God has already done something similar in the episode narrated in the Book of Daniel, when three men remained unharmed in the burning furnace. In short, Julian seems to say that it is entirely foolish to ask such questions.

The gnoseological difference of the risen ones (Prognosticum *III, li*)

In this very brief but intense chapter, Julian pushes himself toward elements of eschatological knowledge at the limits of human possibilities, but, instead of turning to an esoteric knowledge or to dark reasons, he addresses the problem from the point of view of the relationships, existing or not, between the risen ones and Christ. The distinction between the possibility of the righteous and the unrighteous having knowledge revolves around the use of two adverbs of place that become christological adverbs: thus, those who are "outside" the kingdom of God and of the relationship with Christ do not know what happens "inside," while those who are "inside," meaning in the joy of the Lord, borrow from him a knowledge of all things. Once again, the answer comes not from an extrinsic dimension but from the eschatological and interpersonal relationship between Christ and the redeemed ones.

The celestial world: the condition of the blessed
(Prognosticum III, li-lxii)

The last ten chapters of this third book are devoted to the eschatological interpretation of the heavenly beatitude as it will be lived by the risen ones. In this way, Julian once again manifests the underlying anthropocentrism of his *Prognosticum*, written for believers who aspire to eternal life.

The risen body can ascend to heaven by divine virtue
(*Prognosticum* III, lii)

This section, devoted to the new world and new humanity, begins with the clear affirmation about the reality of the risen body, which will be the body "in which we now live" (III, lii) as had already been said by the Council of Toledo of AD 675. Besides, Julian knows and explicitly quotes the anti-Platonic polemic of Augustine because Platonism denied an eschatological future to the body. The reason given by Julian, availing himself of the answer of Augustine, is that even if perhaps from a natural point of view, the terrestrial corporeality would not be capable of ascending to the heavenly dimension, nevertheless, once risen and endowed with immortality by divine virtue, it will be able to ascend and live in a heavenly abode. This new, revolutionary possibility by which human beings can rise with their body to the divine world is entirely unsettling for any dualistic thought. But Julian resolves the difficulty by referring to the salvific and elevating action of God. Yet Jesus had revealed the divine intention of the Father in sending the Son: "I desire that where I am, they also be with me" (John 17:24). In these words there is a strong reference to the theology of the mystical body, a true ecclesiological datum for Julian. He, in fact, makes all his eschatology depend on such an ecclesiology, which closely links the destiny of the body with the destiny of its head. From these considerations emerges Julian's refusal of an eschatology that is only spiritual and marginalizes the human body from the eschatological future.

Connected to this great argument, Julian addresses a *quaestiun-cula* (chapter liii) related to the movements or bodily displacements of the risen bodies, associating himself with the prudence and discretion of Augustine. The only possible answer to this question is that the movements or displacements of the risen bodies in the new world to come will be appropriate and perfectly suitable to the body as well as to the spirit in that everything is perfect in the divine dimension. Nothing more can be said nor must be said, for reasons of intellectual honesty and because of Julian of Toledo's by then customary "learned ignorance," which prevents any methodological excess of curiosity.

The modality of the vision of God (*Prognosticum* III, liii)

The question raised may seem superfluous: in the heavenly beatitude, will we see God with bodily eyes, as we have them on earth? Julian, by means of Augustine, answers that, as difficult as it is to face such a question, the possibilities are either that we will see God with these eyes strengthened by the resurrection to the point of becoming capable, as also the mind, to see incorporeal reality (as is the extremely spiritual reality of God), or that a spiritual vision will also be added— that is, of our spirit. But it is just as possible that God will be seen with the spirit inside of us, in others, and in the new world itself—in short, everywhere.

The answer to the question, in any case, presupposes a transformation of the visual abilities both of the body and of the human spirit, inasmuch as belonging to the new world, the divine one, requires a change also in the gnoseological process of the human being, which will substantially be altered. The discretion, however, and the sobriety of the hypotheses become obligatory since these modalities are enfolded in the divine mystery.

The knowledge of God in the world to come (*Prognosticum* III, liiii)

To the previous considerations, however, and basing himself on some texts of the New Testament, Julian adds that it is possible to understand what the future modality of knowledge or vision of God will be. It will probably be like that of the angels and, in any case, it must be conceived as a reward for a life of faith in God. Therefore, it will not be a natural development of the capacity for knowledge but rather a gift of grace. The scholastics, as is known, call this new capacity for knowledge *lumen gloriae*, which is infinitely superior to earthly knowledge. As for the face of God, whose vision is promised in the Johannine epistolary (1 John 3:2), Julian specifies that by "face" we are to understand a manifestation of God and not a specific part of him. The language of John evidently is to be so interpreted. Yet Julian does not say how this angelic knowledge taken on by the risen ones will be. What is sure is that it will be different, and quite so, from earthly knowledge, which is entirely analogical, confused, and like a mirror image (1 Cor 13:12). Julian probably knows the reflections of Augustine about it, but for reasons of brevity, he is unable to include them in his work.

The blessed ones are free beings (*Prognosticum* III, lvi)

What is maintained in this chapter is a very original anthropological reflection. Though it does happen that the world to come is conceived or imagined as being a static situation of religious uniformity, the vision of the afterlife proposed by Julian is very dynamic and open to recognizing the role of individuals and their free will. His reflection is, therefore, founded on the idea of freedom. While the freedom of human beings on earth is relative because the inclination, or even subjection, to sin prevents them from reaching moral and religious perfection, in the new world this freedom will instead be full because, being so near to God, the blessed ones become exempt from any inclination to evil. The risen nature, therefore, changes for the better. It is freed from sin and from death in order to be free to adhere to God with all its strength, yet preserving the integrity of its own freedom.

Memory and forgetfulness in the world to come (*Prognosticum* III, lvii)

This typically human aspect of memory and forgetfulness is surprisingly included in the reflection on the life of the world to come, showing how the interest for the human being is always at the center of Julian's treatise. His insistence on the anthropological and psychological aspects of eschatology, and not on the topography of heaven or the description of the infernal punishments, clarifies the truly theological and anthropological approach of the primate of Toledo's eschatology, which obviously has no room for satisfying mere curiosity, while it does give ample space to matters that appear to be new because connected with a future transformation. Evidently the line

that the author follows is to try to understand what will remain and
what will change of the earthly habits or customs in the new world.

In the case of these two typically human realities, memory and
forgetfulness, Julian affirms that the blessed will not have memory
(meaning that they will be forgetful) of the evil or the negative situations through which they had painfully passed, yet they will have,
instead, memory or knowledge of the good past realities and also of
the damnation of the unjust.

Harmony of the differences (*Prognosticum* III, lviii)

The starting point of this chapter is that in the kingdom of God
there will be no uniformity, but the honors and the glories will be
diversified. Also in this case, the praise of differences applied to the
new world allows for understanding anthropological variety as being
willed by God. Thus, in the new world, the typically earthly attitude
called envy will not occur between the inferior and the superior.
Rather, the differences will be part of a general harmony that will contain everything and all; and everyone will have his or her own role
without desiring to be more, because what each one is must be considered a gift received from divine providence, to which each will thus
be completely conformed.

The vital and joyful prayer of praise of the blessed ones (*Prognosticum* III, lviiii)

Earthly prayer, even if done with faith, carries within itself a
dimension of sacrifice. It is often characterized by aridity, boredom,
and lack of enthusiasm. It is often mechanical, without soul, tied
down by schedules, times, and moments to which human beings must
adapt themselves, often not without difficulty and not without the risk
of neglect. Inconsistency is probably the most diffused defect of
earthly prayer, as is also the serious risk of praying with the voice without a corresponding moral and religious life. The experienced
Bishop Julian evidently knows these problems, because of common
practice in the monastic and ecclesiastical environments of his time.

To provide an understanding of the novelty of the new world or
of the eternal church, Julian thus shows that the above-mentioned
defects associated with prayer will all disappear in the activity of praise
of the blessed ones, as is emphasized in the New Testament. For a
start, the prayer of the eschatological future will not be fatiguing; it

will cost neither work nor sacrifice of sleep or of the mind. The unceasing prayer of praise to God will be pleasant and vital, comparable to the language of the divine Persons and the angelic court, considered as an acquired virtue whose great reward will be having a close relationship with God himself, who has given that virtue.

Eternal life is endless (*Prognosticum* III, lx)

The main difference between the earthly life of faith and the experience of God beyond history will consist precisely in the fact that the latter will be without interruption. Faith, as we know, can languish, decrease, disappear, or be put in crisis by events and psychological processes. The vision or experience of God will not be subject to these drawbacks. In particular, the vision of Christ will fulfill every human desire, and even overcome them, because he is the fullness of the truths about humanity, and all things will be finally explained in him.

God gives himself to the blessed (*Prognosticum* III, lxi)

The eschatological reflection of Julian of Toledo reaches its peak in the exposition of what will constitute the eschatological reward of the blessed ones. It does not consist in the possession of material reality or in the dominion over other beings, nor is it described as entering a material paradise, but it is the full satisfaction of what human beings really desire and what is able to quiet their restless heart: the intimate knowledge of God himself, of the divine transcendence that is at the root of all created reality.

God meets this innate desire of the human being but goes beyond any human expectation, in that he proposes himself as the absolute recompense, to be enjoyed by human beings in a perfect sharing of being or full participation in the divine life of the three Persons of the Holy Trinity. The utopia of every century and of every human civilization, the impossible taboo to be violated, the unreachable destination, the unattainable dream, the peak impossible to reach, offers himself to them in all his infinite presence.

This is for Julian the goal of the whole history of creation and redemption: the entry of humanity into the divine world to share in the infinite vital being of the triune God and to partake of his infinite divine perfections.

The end without an end is the beginning that will never end
(*Prognosticum* III, lxii)

Having reached the end of his eschatological reflection, Julian of Toledo affirms that human beings will find all their fullness and their realization upon entering the intimate life of God. The first effect of such insertion will be the fullness of communion with the risen Christ. After the lengthy ecclesial experience of faith and the sacraments as ways of assimilation to Christ, the Christification of humanity will then finally become complete and perfect, with no more need of any salvific mediation. This will make the blessed ones perfect, who will thus reach the very peak of their happiness, participating in the feast without end or the Saturday without Vespers, as Julian quotes from Augustine. Saturday without Vespers means that such happiness will never set and it will introduce us into the endless Sunday, where the new and definitive church of Christ will become for all of its members rest, knowledge, vision, love, and praise of God. Such elements of beatitude will interlace themselves to form the sublime modality of the new existence in the new heaven and the new earth. This will be the end without an end: to enter forever as part of the kingdom of God that will never end.

But if this is the attainment of the goal of the human being, at the same time that it is achieved, it becomes the beginning of a new creation where God and humanity, and other creatures, will live in perfect communion and in an endless and new history about which nothing can yet be said.

This means that the end, which is also the beginning, will also constitute the fulfillment of the eschatology of God, in addition to that of humanity.

LETTERS OF IDALIUS OF BARCELONA

BEGINNING OF THE LETTER OF IDALIUS,
BISHOP OF BARCELONA, TO IULIANUS,
BISHOP OF THE PRIMATIAL SEE OF TOLEDO

Idalius, bishop of the see of Barcelona to the most holy, and for me among all the others, illustrious Lord Iulianus, bishop of the primatial see of Toledo

Frightened by the reminiscence of my sins and always bewildered by the memory of great faults, I thought that the divine ears were completely hardened to my cries, since I had not received the work you had promised.

For this reason, I was shaken first from various disturbances, then also deprived of the good outcome of a desired opportunity, and (as it usually happens) overwhelmed by forgetfulness, wavering in my suggestions after having greeted each other, I had not presented my requests to Your Holiness; nevertheless I was confident in the oracle of our Savior and Redeemer with which he had reanimated the disciples, saying: "if two of you agree on earth to ask something, my Father who is in heaven will grant it to you" [Matt 18:19].

Trusting with full confidence in your promise, I was convinced in my innermost being that the truth could not lie in any way, nor could the lover and disciple of truth be slave to lies. I awaited what was promised by Your Holiness, having placed great hope in the Lord Jesus Christ: I prayed, nevertheless, sincerely and often even if not every day, so that he himself who is present everywhere would inspire your heart and finally ensure the realization of our desires.

Now, therefore, since the Lord has remembered me and has heeded my vows, when he brought your holy work to perfection, he filled my mouth with joy and my tongue with exultation, and he has enriched me with the completion of your work. I will say, therefore, to him, with the words of exultation of the spirit of his prophet: "blessed be God, blessed be the Lord, from day to day" [Ps 68:20].[1]

And indeed, here comes a certain Jew, named Restitutus, almost without the light of intelligence, for so to say an animal, transporting a matter conforming to the light, that is, the book that, with learned synthesis, not only from the sentences of the ancient and saintly fathers, but also under the inspiration and the teaching of Christ, with effort and particular application, you have brought to completion, and that the wisdom of Your Holiness took care to send to our ineptitude, and he presented it to me with both hands. The book that, out of desire to know it, I snatched rather than received, I most rapidly opened, and I confess to have been astonished upon seeing the title, because Your Holiness had thought to entrust the cause of such and so precious merchandise to a carrier so untrustworthy and outside the faith.

But immediately, made aware by that reason for which a treasure is entrusted to earthen vessels, before to you, I gave thanks to the aforesaid Jew because he had delivered intact what he had received, considering that you had perhaps acted for a change of the right hand of the Most High, so that he who was accustomed to transporting transient merchandise might be well disposed to the divine and eternal mysteries. I intuited, nevertheless, in this task the humility of your holy and refined heart, which renders thanks to God, by whose gift it comes to you, how much of what is beautiful, splendid, and pure is present in your words, returns considerable and excellent, certainly rejecting the vain glory, and [your humble heart] strives to show to the gaze of those who see the work of so little account as to decide to entrust it to a rather despicable carrier.

Therefore, observing the style of the aforesaid codex and having considered its title, I was not able to find any other name more profoundly suitable for this work than the one it seems to have at the beginning of the volume. In fact it is called *Prognosticum futuri saeculi*, which in Latin can also be said, not inappropriately, *praescientia futuri saeculi*.

In this work, for as much as it seems that the first book, in a certain way, wants to arouse harshness and fear in the sinners, the two subsequent books, nevertheless, lift the hearts of believers in Christ to

---

1. Ps 68:19 NRSV: "Blessed be the Lord, who daily bears us up."

a great confidence, because of the hope in the future resurrection and the kingdom that Christ has promised to give to his faithful. Moreover, avidly reading the remaining part of the whole codex, I found what the Lord Jesus Christ says in the Gospels: "every scribe who has become a disciple of the kingdom of heaven is like a household owner who draws from his treasure things both new and old" [Matt 13:52].

In fact, doubts are clearly dispersed and the things difficult to understand are illuminated, while the decrees of the ancient fathers and the proofs of the new synthesis of your science are exposed most fruitfully. Therefore, from their writings emanates the truth, while from your work has come a new and true synthesis.

Thus, whatever they truthfully, honestly, and soberly understood concerning the truths about God, you have in common together with them, to whose knowledge the teaching of the Lord has led.

Nonetheless he has also approved of your concern, because, having seen your pressing desire to know, he has clarified their statements and united them with an exposition of them that is accessible to the idlers and to the indolent. Therefore, even if, by the concession of Christ, it was they who furnished the material, nevertheless, the whole of it will be ascribed to your labor. In fact, even gold, for as much as it preserves the splendor of its origin and its nature, rightly exalts the talent of the artist when it is later skillfully transformed into forms and a variety of figures and is appropriately refined.

Moved by all of this, I would like to find the proper words to praise the effectiveness of the talent that the divine grace has conferred on your heart and the intense study with which you have clearly labored at the mysteries of Christ, and since I feel unable to do so, if I were not aware that this would displease you, I would like to ask others to praise you.

It remains, therefore, that I do what the soul of Your Holiness desires. And so my insignificance recedes, while the whole church is with me, as an ornament to which our weakness gave the news of your work. To the immense and ineffable Trinity it raises an abundance of thanks, not as much as it ought to but as much as it is able to offer, because at the end of time or, rather (to say more truthfully), almost at the consummation of the world, he has infused into the heart of Your Beatitude the gift of his grace together with the desire to accomplish this holy work. And he has lavished upon you the gift of a clear and harmonious word by which you may heal the hearts of those who err by instilling fear into them, and vivify abundantly those devoted to good works by confirming them in holy actions with the hope of the heavenly kingdom.

We pray therefore the great mercy of the divine majesty that he may prolong the years of your life and thus preserve you in the episcopal service of his church, so that you may enlighten the faithful; and thus grant an overabundance of the gift of his graces which he has infused into your heart, so that the Catholic people may be enabled to accomplish every good action through Your Holiness's zealous works and teachings, and may he grant you, for the holy constancy of your work, after a very long span of life, forgiveness of your faults and remission of your sins, so that you may possess the heavenly kingdoms together with his saints and his chosen ones.

[END OF THE LETTER OF IDALIUS, BISHOP OF BARCELONA, TO IULIANUS, BISHOP OF THE PRIMATIAL SEE OF TOLEDO]

BEGINNING OF THE LETTER OF IDALIUS TO SUNTFREDUS

Idalius, bishop of Barcelona, to the most holy and, for me among all the others, illustrious Lord Suntfredus, bishop of the first see of Narbona
The excellent work that, not only with great effort but also with the deepest dedication, in an admirable new synthesis of writings from the books of the ancient and catholic fathers, your brother my lord Iulianus, bishop of the primatial see of Toledo, wanted to gather in a single volume called *Prognosticum futuri saeculi*, and that he took care to send to our insufficiency, and that Your Beatitude, with praiseworthy obstinacy, ardently asked of us, I, being in this little city (over which I unworthily preside) and devoted to Your Holiness, offer with both hands through my fellow servant and send it to the see of your holy sublimity, so that from its knowledge the prelates of your whole province, participating in your joy, may ascertain with what gift of immense light the supreme divinity has enriched your above-mentioned brother to enlighten the church; and together they may bless the Lord God of Heaven, by whose benevolence your same brother deserved to receive this gift.

Therefore, may they offer to the divine Trinity the libations of their prayers, that he may protect with his grace the author of this work for his great efforts, and that the divine indulgence may cancel the sins of our perversity, in that our sloth was concerned to give them the knowledge through which their heart may overflow with spiritual fruit.

I also pray, my lord and fellow countryman, that you command me to approach to the power of the divinity with assiduous supplications, to cancel my guilt, so that I, who am crushed by so many troubles, may be worthy to be lifted up by the help of your prayer. Thus, may you enjoy possessing without end the grace of our Lord Jesus Christ.

[END OF LETTER OF IDALIUS TO SUNTFREDUS]

JULIAN OF TOLEDO

Prognosticum futuri saeculi

Foreknowledge of the World to Come

PREFACE TO THE BOOKS OF THE *FOREKNOWLEDGE OF THE WORLD TO COME* OF ST. JULIAN, BISHOP OF THE SEE OF TOLEDO

Julian, unworthy bishop of the Toledan chair, to the most holy and, among all the others, most intimate to me, Lord Idalius, bishop of the see of Barcelona

Who, with the obvious exception of the Redeemer of all, would be capable of finding the right words to talk about that most memorable day of the famous feast on which, this year, being together in the royal city, with joyful transport of hearts, we participated in the celebration of the passion of the Lord?

It then happened that, desiring convenient tranquillity for such a great feast, we secretly made our way into a more secluded place. There we were both welcomed by separate beds with covers, where, to be flooded by divine passion we took the Sacred Scripture in hand while we were illumined by eternal light. We read in lasting tranquillity. Then we scrutinized the secret things of the passion of the Lord, joining together the harmonies of the Gospels. But when we came to an admirable passage of the text, which now I am unable to recall to the mind, we were shaken, we groaned, we sighed. A certain sublime joy was born in our minds and suddenly we were raised to the highest point of contemplation. Our flowing tears deterred our attempt to read; a common anguish induced us to abandon the book and wait to be made productive by the sole gift of a reciprocal discussion.

Who could ever put in writing, or who would ever be able to recount with a fitting voice, what divine flavor touched our souls, what sweetness of supreme charity infused itself into our mortal minds? In fact, you were then (I confess it, my lord and most holy brother) writhing with the pain of gout, but much more elevated by the hope of divine contemplation.

I believe that all your tormenting pain was dispersed, when between us that divine dialogue started to occur. Then I experienced perfectly "how good and pleasant it is when brothers dwell in unity!" [Ps 133:1], when that ointment of the Holy Spirit, which from our head was poured upon the hem of his garment (which perhaps we then were), and it purified us with the fire of a quest both great and necessary.

Thus, invited to these banquets of victuals, we started to ask ourselves what the condition of the souls of the dead would be before that last resurrection of the body; such that we would know, through our reciprocal discussion, what we would be after this life, in a way that, reflecting upon this condition sincerely and with ardor, we might flee more certainly from the present things, the more avidly we would know the future things because of our investigation of them.

From this situation some *quaestiunculae* (small questions) have come to the light that, for their contradictoriness, touched our minds in a major way. Nevertheless, though unable to put together an optimal solution for them or a definition of concise meaning, our minds were equally lifted up, because whatever would be debated about the matter, it would have to be noted in writing; so that what reason required, and what was derived as defined by the thought of the Catholic masters, would express for us the thought of the sacred reading: this would be done not with a continuous leafing through the books, but viva voce, with the application of memory.

Then, if I err not, having called the scribe at your pressing request, I gathered together, in the same day and in your presence, with the greatest possible brevity, the chapters concerning the aforesaid *quaestiunculae*.

But impatient, as is usual in the things that concern God, the mind of Your Holiness pushed, with a very gentle, familiar command, the forces of my weakness and obliged me, with a precept consequent on [our] inseparable communion, so that these same [questions], which had previously been discussed, and which had received your approval, would be listed in the definition of the titles, as soon as I was aware that some free time had been given to me by the gift of God, and I would gather them together in one complete and concise volume. I would show, with their appropriate teaching, what the authority of the ancient fathers had understood in this regard; so that, however, in investigating these questions, the great number of books would not weary the soul thirsting for knowledge, but this concise collection might quench the manifold thirst of the reader. Moreover, it was also decided by us, in an exchange of mutual charity, to annotate as many as possible of the themes and *quaestiunculae* that we had gathered concerning the final resurrection of the body, and that I would take care to annotate them, with a style similar to that of the titles.

Moreover, we deemed that these two books would also be accompanied by the book "that saddens the heart," so that the first book, which would precede these two aforesaid books, would treat the death of the body, that it would be similarly structured with a listing of the titles, and that the reader's mind, terrified by an extreme fear of death, would be lifted up again by the hope of heavenly joys; and so by the investigation of the subsequent books, it has been underscored what and how great the enjoyment of the eternal beatitude, after the deposition or the recovery of this body, would be for the holy souls. Thus, you yourself know, together with me, all the things that we have treated and established in that unforgettable day.

Subsequently, since the departure of the glorious prince for war from the royal city had also brought about the removal of the turbulent units of the troops along with him, as I believe was the case, the agitation of our mind started to clear up after the storms with mild breezes, and so I came to remember your command and my promise.

Therefore I carried out, certainly not as I should have, but, in any case, as I was able, what I had promised. The first book treats the origin of human death; the second concerns the situation of the souls of the dead before the resurrection of their bodies; the third treats the future resurrection. Having established that everything would be contained in a single volume in three books, we gave it the title *Prognosticum futuri saeculi* with regard to its better and more extensive part. Nevertheless, you will find in it not my own teaching but the topics and the doctrine of the ancient fathers; and if in some places my voice does resound a little, I have written, in my own style, nothing else but what I remembered reading in their books. And if here I have said otherwise than what I should have said and have corrupted their teachings by arranging the things differently from how they should have been, may charity, which bears and tolerates everything, forgive me, as I admit to doing so; and moreover, may it obtain, in your holy mind, what the perception of our weakness less wisely prepared, may the help of your wisdom correct, reveal, and prepare it; and above all, may our prayers obtain from the Lord that whatever guilt I may have imprudently committed in this work, he may command that it be canceled by the merit of the loving blood of our Lord Jesus Christ, our Savior.

Therefore, it has seemed right to me that this work be compiled not so much to reveal to readers things almost unknown to them, since I do not doubt that I obtained knowledge of many of these things from the volumes of many books; but, rather, so that the discourse about these matters, unified here into a single collection, might touch in a more intense way the minds of mortals, because they could read this material without effort in such a collection, and, thus being offered food gratuitously, their composed reason could bear fruit in due time.

May this orderly collection of books with the contents gathered in them suffice for our mind to recognize itself in this faithful reproduction. If we, in fact, would meditate with a careful reflection on what we will be in the future, I believe that we would rarely, or never, sin. Thus, in fact, it is written: "Son, in all you do, remember the end of your life, and then you will never sin" [Sir 7:36].

Having brought to completion, therefore, those things that had been premised by discernment and memory, this I desire, for this I long, that the offered form of these books, whether it pleases you or displeases you, be clothed in a better garment from the exercise of your criticism, and that the outcome of your judgment be publicly known.

[END OF PREFACE]

Prayer to God by Julian himself

Dwelling, blind and ill, in the desert of Idumea, I cry to you, Son of David, to have mercy on me. I seek, in fact, Jerusalem, my eternal homeland; I desire to see its inhabitants, but I cannot find the guides with which to pass over there.

You, therefore, who have deigned to show yourself to me as the Way, reach out your hand to me, so that, no longer blind but seeing, I may arrive there without being impeded by brigands.

You are, in fact, the only Way, and such is the way that the brigand does not possess. Behold my restless heart, which, sighing at great length to you for the return to its homeland, is filled with an immense preparedness for the future realities: longing that, before the break of day, it may already contemplate in this world the joys of its future beatitude.

Investigating, in fact, to the best of my abilities, what enjoyment the souls of the dead experience after the death of this body, and also what glorification awaits them after they are reunited to their bodies, I have collected in this work the structure of the questions for as much as I have been able to derive from the discussions of the ancient fathers.

But even these things have been said for as much as can be said by mortals; nonetheless it was not possible to say all those things that necessarily treat of the future, because the paths of your judgments are inscrutable.

Nevertheless, desiring to fly away to the bosom of that fatherland of which so many things have been said, I ask that I may advance through you, who are the Way, in you, who are the Truth, that I may not stumble, that I may reach you, who are the Life. From you, therefore, who are the Way of the supreme happiness, do not separate me for any reason, may no impediment distance me; but, advancing toward you when I am near death, may I not suffer from brigands, and, once I am dead, not fear the accuser.

At the moment of my death protect me with angelic shields, and, called to you, may I be consoled by the tender mercy extended to me, so that, coming to you without hindrance, I may see what treasures are laid up in Jerusalem.

Immediately, immediately, Lord, it is enough, because dimmed to this point by the darkness of sins, I am lost. So that what I myself prepare as a remedy for myself and my brothers may not be an obstacle for anyone, I entreat you, by the glorious power of your sacred blood and the invincible and venerable sign of your cross, that I may not be accused as reckless for these actions of mine, that I may not go to ruin as one in error, that I may not be held worthy of being subjected to judgment and punished with those who speak a lot from their own hearts and not from your spirit. Here I am, Lord, I, your poor man, mendicant and knocking at your door, who does not arrogantly define unknown things but is humbly desirous to know those things that can be known.

Feed me, therefore, on all the promises of your grace, which, even if they cannot be experienced with the senses, are nonetheless believed to be fulfilled with the true firmness of faith, so that you may give that joy that no one can describe with the pen, "what no eye has seen, nor ear heard, nor the heart of man conceived" [1 Cor 2:9], to me, wretched as I am, that I may happily enjoy it here, while there I may contemplate it with a fuller clarity.

[END OF THE PRAYER]

BEGINNING OF THE CHAPTERS OF THE FIRST BOOK, ON THE ORIGIN OF HUMAN DEATH

[END OF THE CHAPTERS OF THE FIRST BOOK]

THE THREE BOOKS OF THE
FOREKNOWLEDGE OF THE WORLD TO COME

BEGINNING OF THE (FIRST) BOOK
ON THE ORIGIN OF HUMAN DEATH

I How death first entered the world.

The apostle Paul teaches that because of the sin of the first human being it happened that death has entered the world: "Just as through one person," he says, "sin entered the world, and through sin, death, and thus death came to all, inasmuch as all sinned" [Rom 5:12].

II Why God, after having created the angels immortal, threatened human beings with death if they sinned.

Death reaches human beings as a layer of sin. "It is not to be believed that God made mankind in the same way in which he made the angels, in such a condition that, even though they had sinned, they could no longer die. He had so made them that if they fulfill the obligations of obedience, an angelic immortality and a blessed eternity might ensue without the intervention of death; but if they disobeyed, death should strike them with just sentence."[1]

Therefore the first sinners "were so punished with death, that whatsoever sprang from their stock should also be subject to the same punishment. For nothing else could be born of them than that which they themselves had been. Their nature was deteriorated in proportion to the greatness of the condemnation of their sin, so that what existed as punishment in those who first sinned, became a natural consequence in others who would be born."[2]

III The condition of human beings as they were created and the punishment of death, to which they were justly condemned after their sin.

The first human being was created in such a condition of nature as to be absolutely capable of immortality and mortality: not immortal to the point that, also sinning, he would not have been able to die;

not mortal to the point that, also not wanting to sin, he would have been submitted to death. He was endowed with free will, so that by right he who did not want to sin, though capable of doing so, would have been blessed; or he who sinned, though having been able to avoid it, without necessity but by his own will would have been miserable. And since something cannot be said to be right or sinful without the observance of, or the failure to comply with, the precept of someone, the man who was established in paradise received the precept for which he had in his nature the power not to die and the power to die: if he had been found obedient for the fulfillment of the vital precept, he would have become immortal, so much so as no longer to be able to die; if he had been found disobedient for his transgression, he would have begun to be mortal such that he could not avoid death. This seems to me the reason why the first human being received the precept and why the punishment inflicted upon the sinner because of his transgression is just.[3]

IIII Why it is called death.

"It is called death, because it is bitter, or it is called this way because of the bite taken by the first human being.[4] In fact when the progenitor of the human kind, disobeying, touched the forbidden tree, through the bite he fell into death."[5] Precisely for this reason, from the morsel death itself takes its name.[6]

V The three kinds of bodily death.

"There are three kinds of death: unripe, immature, natural. Unripe is that of children, immature that of the youth, normal, or rather natural, that of the elderly."[7]

VI The death of the flesh is harsh, yet the dying often do not experience its unpleasantness.

"For what concerns the bodily death, that is, the separation of the soul from the body suffered by those who are at the point of death, it is not good for anyone. In fact, for as long as it endures, it possesses a bitter taste, and the force itself is against nature, eradicating what in the living had been joined and united, until the consciousness disappears entirely, that consciousness which was inherent in the very union of soul and flesh; sometimes a stroke of the body or a sudden separation of the soul impedes the feeling of unpleasantness by preventing it with swiftness."[8]

VII It often happens that through a harsh death of the flesh the soul is freed from sin.

"However it happens in the dying, if the loss of consciousness accompanied by a painful sensation is piously and faithfully borne, it increases the merit of patience but does not eliminate the meaning of punishment. Since death is doubtlessly the punishment of those born from the descent of the first man, yet if it be endured for righteousness' sake, it becomes the glory of those who are born again; and though death be the reward of sin, it sometimes ensures that nothing be awarded to sin."[9] Similarly, therefore, the blessed Gregory says: "It is written: 'from whatever death the just man is stricken, his soul will be at rest' [Wis 4:7]. So, for the chosen who tend toward perpetual life, what obstacle is there if they die harshly in a short time? Indeed, it is perhaps sometimes a guilt of theirs, albeit minimal, that must be eliminated by the same death....In fact, because the man of God sent against Samaria disobeyed by eating during his journey, he was slain by a lion along the way. But immediately, in the same text it is written that 'the lion stood beside the ass, and did not eat the dead man's body' [1 Kgs 13:28]. This shows that the sin of disobedience was forgiven, because the same lion that dared to kill a living being did not dare to touch one that had been killed. In fact, he who had the boldness to kill did not take the liberty to eat the carcass of the one killed."[10] So it is to be believed that "in most cases the very fear of even the slightest guilt purifies the souls of the just when they abandon the body."[11] "In fact as the souls of the chosen ones exit from life, they are terrified by an excessive fear, not knowing if they are heading toward the prize or toward torment. Some chosen ones are purified of their lesser sins in the moment of their death; while others rejoice in the moment of their death, contemplating the eternal goods."[12]

VIII Death is not a good thing, and yet for the good it is good.

Death, by which the body is separated from the soul, is generally good for those who are good, since through it one passes to future immortality. "Not because death, which before was an evil, has become something good, but because God granted so much grace to faith that death, obviously the opposite of life, became the instrument through which one passes over to life."[13]

VIIII Against those people who say: If the sin of the first human being is forgiven in baptism, why does death also await the baptized?

Care is to be taken by those who ask why people suffer death when their offenses are forgiven by the grace of baptism. In fact those who talk this way usually do so with witty propositions: "The death that affected the first human being originated from the evil of disobedience, and therefore, by that original sin, death has become the condition of everyone. Then why are we, whose original sin is forgiven in baptism, submitted to the tortures of this death?"[14] These objections are responded to by a well-known reasoning. Thus, in fact, the eminent doctor Augustine says accordingly: "The reason for the separation of the soul from the body, though its connection with sin was removed, is that if the immortality of the body followed immediately upon the sacrament of regeneration, faith itself would be thereby weakened since faith is really faith when it waits in hope for what is not yet seen in reality. And at least in adulthood the fear of death was overcome by the vigor and struggle of faith. This was especially conspicuous in the holy martyrs, who could have had no victory, no glory, to whom there could not even have been any conflict, if, after the *lavacrum* of regeneration, already as saints they could not suffer bodily death. Who would not, then, in company with the infants presented for baptism, run to the grace of Christ, so that he might not be dismissed from the body? And thus faith would not be tested with an unseen reward; nor would it even be seeking and receiving an immediate recompense of its works. But now, by the greater and more admirable grace of the Savior, the punishment of sin is turned to the service of righteousness."[15] Concerning this subject Julian Pomerius also says: "Therefore those regenerated cannot pass to eternal beatitude without the death of the flesh, because all the good that the sacraments effect in the regenerated does not belong to the present life, but to the future. And particularly, if whoever saves himself does so in hope, and hope does not belong to the temporal life but rather to eternal life, the reborn in Christ will not be saved by just any hope, if they want to be reborn in Christ not to obtain eternal beatitude, which is not seen, and for which hope watches, but to possess without end this visible life: and thus they could not even be regarded as faithful, because they would not have faith in things unseen and they would become lovers of the life of this world and tepid toward obtaining the unseen goods."[16]

X When believers die, angels are nearby, and their souls are received by these angels to be led to God.

It must be said that when the souls are separated from the body at the moment of death, angels are present to receive the souls of the just as they exit from the body and to introduce them into the abodes of the pious. Thus, when the rich man and poor Lazarus are mentioned in the Gospel, it is written accordingly: "It happened that the poor man died and he was carried away by angels to the bosom of Abraham" [Luke 16:22]. This assertion firmly confirms that in the moment of the separation of the holy souls as they leave the body, the care of the angels is always present. In fact St. Augustine, too, discussing the opinion that the dead know what the living do, adds to the debate about the question by saying: "If the Angels could not be present in the places of both the dead and the living, the Lord Jesus would not have said: 'It happened, then, that the poor man died and was carried away by angels in the bosom of Abraham' [Luke 16:22]. They could thus be now here, now there, since they conducted from here to there the one God wanted."[17] Similarly the same doctor says in the books on the Trinity of God: "Whoever, then, is renewed day by day by making progress in the knowledge of God, and in righteousness and holiness of truth, transfers the love from temporal things to eternal things....Whoever shall be found on the last day of this life in such progress and growth, holding faith in the mediator, is to be led to God, whom he has worshipped, and to be brought to perfection by him; he shall be welcomed by the holy angels, and so shall receive at the end of time an incorruptible body, not for punishment but for glory."[18]

XI The fear of bodily death.

"Everyone fears death of the flesh, few fear death of the soul. All are preoccupied with avoiding the coming of death of the flesh, which, sooner or later, certainly must come. And for this they weary themselves. Destined to die, humankind struggles to avoid dying, and yet, destined to live forever, they do not labor to avoid sinning. And when they struggle to avoid death, they labor in vain; in fact, the most they obtain is that death is deferred, not avoided; if rather they refrain from sinning, their toil will cease, and they shall live forever. Oh, that we could incite humankind, ourselves included, to be lovers of ever-lasting life at least as much as they are lovers of the life that passes away! Placed under the peril of death, what will one not do? When the sword was hanging over their head, human beings have abandoned anything belonging to them, just to live. Who would not do so to avoid being stricken? And yet after having lost everything, they were struck anyway. Who, in order to live, has not been willing to lose even their livelihood, preferring a mendicant life to a sudden death? Who has had it said to them: Set to sea if you would escape with your life, and has delayed doing so? Who has had it said to them: Set to work if you would preserve your life, and has continued a sluggard? It is but little that God requires of us, that we may live forever, and we neglect to obey him. God does not say to you: Lose all that you have, that you may live for a short time oppressed with toil, but rather: Give to the poor of what you have, that you may live always securely and without effort. The lovers of the temporal life, who possess it neither when nor as long as they want, are our accusers, and we do not accuse ourselves in turn, so sluggish are we, so lukewarm about achieving that eternal life that will be ours if we wish it and will be imperishable when we have it; but this death that we fear, notwithstanding all our reluctance, will yet be ours to possess."[19]

XII The particular fear that makes everyone wonder which is more bearable: to dread several kinds of death while still alive, or to endure the one that actually occurs?

"What does it matter," the blessed Augustine says, "the kind of death that puts an end to this life, when he who has died once is not forced to die anymore? There being innumerable kinds of death that threaten every mortal in daily life, as long as it remains uncertain in what way it will come, I would ask whether it is not better to suffer one in dying, than to fear all while living. Nor am I unaware that one chooses more readily to live for a long time in fear of many deaths, rather than to not fear some, dying only once. But one thing is what car-nal instinct, timorous, flees for weakness, and another what diligently enucleated reflection shows. A death that was preceded by a good life is not to be considered a bad death. Nothing, in fact, renders death bad except what follows death. They who are destined to die, then, need not be concerned about what will happen to make them die, but where they will be forced to go upon dying. Since, therefore, Christians are well aware that the death of the poor and pious Lazarus, whose sores the dogs licked, was far better than the death of the wicked rich man, who lay in purple and in fine linen, what horrible kind of death could bring harm to the deceased who lived a good life?"[20]

XIII How to console those who fear bodily death.

"What is this death? The dereliction of the body, the laying down of a heavy burden: but if man does not carry other burdens, what makes him fall into Gehenna? Of that real death then did the Lord say: 'Whoever keeps my word shall never see death' [John 8:51]. Let us not be frightened of the former death, but let us fear the latter. What is more grievous is that many, excessively fearing the first, have fallen into the second. It has been said to some: 'Adore idols; for if you do it not, you shall be put to death'; or, as Nebuchadnezzar said: 'If you do not, you shall be thrown into the furnace of flaming fire.' Many feared and adored: not wanting to die, they died. Through fear of the death that cannot be escaped, they fell into the death that could have easily been avoided, had they not unfortunately been afraid of that which is inevitable. Man, you were born, you will die. Where shall you go to escape death? What will you do to avoid it? Your Lord deigned himself to die willingly in order to console you in your inevitable death. When you see that Christ died, can you disdain to die? Therefore, you must die; there is no way to avoid it. Be it today, be it tomorrow, it is to be: the debt must be paid. What, then, does a man gain by fearing, fleeing, hiding himself from discovery by his enemy? Is he able to avoid dying? Or does he only die later? He does not obtain liberation from the debt, but only a deferment. Put it off as long as you please, the thing so delayed will come at last. Let us fear that death,"[21] the second one, which follows this first death of the flesh. "Let us keep, then, God's word in faith, as those who are yet to attain to sight, when the liberty we receive has reached its fullness."[22] "Concerning their fathers, long ago dead, the Lord gave this answer to the Jews: 'I am the God of Abraham, the God of Isaac, and the God of Jacob. He is not the God of the dead, but of the living' [Matt

22:32]."[23] "If, therefore, they live, let us labor so as to live, that after death we may be able to live with them."[24] This in fact is exactly what the Lord says: "Whoever believes in me, even if he dies, will live" [John 11:25], that is to say "'whosoever believes in me,' even though temporarily dead in the flesh, 'will live' in the soul, until he will be raised up and his flesh will never die again."[25]

XIIII Christians ought not to fear bodily death because the just one lives by faith.

As the blessed Cyprian, doctor and martyr, says in this regard: "He who fears death is not willing to go to Christ: and he who is not willing to go to Christ does not believe that he is about to reign with Christ. For it is written: 'The one who is righteous will live by faith' [Rom 1:17]. If you are just, and live by faith, if you truly believe in God, why, since you are about to be with Christ and are secure in the Lord's promise, do you not embrace the assurance that you are called to Christ, and rejoice that you are freed from the devil? Certainly, Simeon, that just man who was truly just and observed the commandments of God with a full faith, having been divinely given the oracle that he would not die before having seen the Christ, when the newborn Christ had come to the temple with his mother, acknowledged in spirit that the Christ was born, concerning whom it had previously been foretold to him; and when he had seen him, he knew that he would soon die. Therefore, rejoicing about his now approaching death and secure in his imminent summons, he received the child into his arms; and blessing the Lord, he exclaimed: 'Now, Master, you may let your servant go in peace, according to your word, for my eyes have seen your salvation' [Luke 2:29–30], assuredly proving and bearing witness that the servants of God then had peace, then free, then tranquil repose, when, withdrawn from these whirlwinds of the world, we attain the harbor of our home and eternal security, when having accomplished this death we come to immortality. That is our peace, that our sure tranquillity, that is the steadfast, abiding, and perpetual security."[26]

XV The considerations by which fear of death can be tempered, such that we should embrace rather than fear the day of our calling, and a great number of beloved persons awaits us there.

The previously quoted doctor says: "The Kingdom of God, beloved brethren, is beginning to be at hand; the reward of life, and the rejoicing of eternal salvation, and the perpetual gladness and the lost possession of paradise are now coming, with the passing away of the world; already heavenly things are following the earthly ones, and great things the small ones, and eternal things the ones that pass. What room is there here for anxiety and solicitude? Who, in the midst of these things, is trembling and sad, except he who is without hope and faith?"[27] Likewise, the same doctor adds: "what else in the world is done daily if not a battle against the devil, whose darts and weapons are battled against in constant conflicts? Our warfare is with avarice, with immodesty, with anger, with ambition; our diligent and toilsome wrestling with carnal vices, with enticements of the world. The mind of humanity is besieged, and in every quarter invested with the onslaughts of the devil, scarcely in each point meets the attack, scarcely resists it. If avarice is prostrated, lust springs up. If lust is overcome, ambition takes its place. If ambition is despised, anger exasperates, pride puffs up, drunkenness entices, envy breaks concord, jealousy cuts friendship; you are constrained to curse, which the divine law forbids; you are compelled to swear, which is not lawful. The soul suffers daily many persecutions, the heart is oppressed by many dangers, and yet it prefers to stay here at length among the swords of the devil, when it would be more appealing and desirable to go more quickly by death to meet Christ who comes, to Christ who instructs us: 'Amen, amen, I say to you, you will weep and mourn, while the world rejoices; you will grieve, but your grief shall be turned into joy' [John 16:20]. Who does not desire to be without sadness? Who would not hasten to attain joy? When our sadness shall be turned into joy, the Lord himself again declares: 'I will see you again, and your heart shall rejoice; and your joy no man shall take from you' [John 16:22]. Since to see Christ is to rejoice, and since our joy cannot be if not that of one who sees Christ, what blindness of the soul or what folly it is to love the afflictions and punishments and tears of the world, rather than hastening to the joy that can never be taken away! But this happens because faith is lacking, because no one believes to be true the things promised by God, though he is true, whose words to believers are eternal and unchangeable. If someone grave and praiseworthy should promise you something, you would assuredly have faith in the one who promises, and would not think that you

should be cheated and deceived by him whom you knew to be steadfast in his words and deeds. Now God is speaking with you, and you,
unfaithful, waver unbelievingly? God promises immortality and eternity to whoever leaves this world, and you doubt? This is not to know
God at all; this is to offend Christ, the teacher of believers, with the
sin of incredulity; for one established in the church this is not having
faith in the house of faith. How great the advantage of leaving this
world is shown to us by Christ himself, the teacher of our salvation
and of our good works, who, when his disciples were saddened
because he announced that he was soon to depart, spoke to them saying: 'If you loved me, you would surely rejoice because I go to the
Father' [John 14:28]; thereby teaching and showing that when the
dear ones whom we love depart from the world, we should rejoice
rather than grieve. Remembering this truth, the blessed apostle Paul
in one of his epistles says: 'To me to live is Christ, and to die is gain'
[Phil 1:21]. Considering it the greatest gain no longer to be held by
the snares of this world, to become free from every concupiscence
and vice of the flesh, but taken away from anguishing troubles, and
freed from the venomous jaws of the devil, to go at the call of Christ
to the joy of eternal salvation...."[28] "If therefore we believe in Christ,
let us have faith in his words and promises; and since we shall not die
eternally, let us come with glad sureness to Christ, with whom we shall
conquer and reign forever. While in the meantime we die, we are passing over to immortality by death; nor can eternal life follow unless it
should befall us to depart from this life. That is not an ending, but a
transit and, this journey of time being traversed, a passage to eternity.
Who would not hasten to better things? Who would not crave to be
changed and renewed into the likeness of Christ, and to the dignity of
heavenly grace?"[29] Likewise: "Whoever is going to the throne of Christ,
and to the glory of the heavenly kingdoms, ought not to mourn or
lament, but rather, in accordance with the Lord's promise, in accordance with his faith in the truth, to rejoice in this departure and passage."[30] Still: "To wish to remain at length in the world is for the one
whom the world delights, whom this age invites, flattering and deceiv-
ing by the enticements of earthly pleasure. Moreover, since the world
hates the Christian, why do you love that which hates you and why do
you not rather follow Christ, who both redeemed you and loves
you?"[31] Likewise: "With a sound mind, with a firm faith, with a robust
virtue, let us be prepared for whatever be the will of God; with the fear

of death laid aside, let us think about the immortality that follows. By
this let us show ourselves to be who we are, not grieving over the
departure of those dear to us, and when the day of our definitive summons shall arrive, let us go without delay and without resistance to
meet the Lord who calls us. What the servants of God should always
do must be done all the more so now as the world falls into ruin and
is besieged by the storms of evil that rage, in order that we who see
that terrible things have begun and know that still more terrible
things are imminent, may regard it as the greatest advantage to depart
from it as quickly as possible. If in your house the walls are shaking
with age, the roofs above you tremble, the house is already dilapi-
dated, and old age threatens the imminent ruin with an immediate
destruction of its structure, would you not escape at great speed? If,
when you are sailing, an angry and raging tempest, violently aroused
by the waves, foretold the coming shipwreck, would you not quickly
seek the harbor? The world is vacillating and falling down and witnesses to its ruin not now by its age, but by the end of things. And do
you not give God thanks, do you not congratulate yourself, that you
are removed from it by an earlier departure and delivered from the
shipwrecks and disasters that are imminent?"[32] And again: "Let us
embrace the day that assigns everyone to their abode, and restores us
to paradise and to the kingdom, snatching us up hence and freeing
us from the age-old ties. Who after having been in exile does not hasten to return to their native land? Who, navigating toward his dear
ones, would not eagerly desire a prosperous gale, that he might
sooner embrace those dear to him? We regard paradise as our homeland; we already begin to consider the patriarchs as our parents. Why
do we not hasten and run, that we may behold our homeland, that we
may greet our parents? A great number of our dear ones await us
there, a dense crowd of parents, brothers, and children is longing for
us, already assured of their own safety, and still solicitous for our salvation. What great joy for them and for us to attain to their presence
and their embrace, what pleasure there is in the heavenly kingdom,
without fear of death, and what lofty and perpetual happiness with an
eternity of living. There the glorious choir of the apostles, there the
host of the rejoicing prophets, there the innumerable multitude of
the martyrs....Let us draw near to them with an eager desire to be with
them soon, so that it may happen that we meet Christ soon. May God
behold this our eager desire; may the Christ look upon this purpose

of our mind and faith; he who will give the greater rewards of his love to those whose desire for him was greatest."[33]

XVI How contrary our will is to the Lord's prayer when we daily pray that God's will be done, and yet at the same time we do not want to pass over to him, because of the persistent fear of death, as in the story of the brother who was afraid to leave this world and to whom Christ appeared and rebuked him.

To this regard is the thought of the quoted doctor. He says, in fact: "We ought to remember that we should do not our own will but that of God, in accordance with what our Lord bids daily to pray. How preposterous and absurd it is, that while we ask that the will of God be done, when God calls us and summons us from this world, we do not immediately obey his will! We struggle and resist; like obstinate servants we are led to the presence of the Lord with sadness and grief, departing from this world forced by necessity, without the assent of the will. We insist on being crowned with rewards and honored with heavenly recompense by him to whom we come unwillingly. Why, then, do we pray and ask that the kingdom of heaven come, if earthly captivity delights us? Why with frequently repeated prayers do we entreat and beg that the day of his kingdom may hasten, if our greater desires and stronger wishes are to serve the devil here, rather than to reign with Christ? Finally, that the signs of divine providence may be more evidently manifest, proving that the Lord, prescient of the future, takes counsel for the true salvation of his own, when one of our colleagues and brethren in the priesthood, near to him struck by infirmity and worried about the approaching, prays for his departure, near to the one who prays and who is already just about to die is a youth, venerable in honour and majesty, lofty in stature and shining in aspect, and on whom, as he stood by him, the human glance could scarcely look with fleshly eyes, except for the one about to depart from the world who could already behold him as such. And he, not without a certain indignation of soul and voice, rebuked him, and said: 'You fear suffering, you do not wish to depart, what shall I do with you?' The voice was of one rebuking and warning, one who, worried about what follows, and sure about the departure, does not consent to the present desire, but looks to the future."[34]

XVII Let us not be overcome by despair when we are disturbed by the imminence of death.

Some often say: "Perhaps the soul of the Christian is not to be troubled by imminent death?" Those people who say these things receive a suitable reply. The firmest Christians, if there are any, are those who are not disturbed even by an imminent death; but are they perhaps more solid than Christ? What great fool can affirm this? For what reason therefore was he disturbed, if not that he has consoled the sick in his body, that is, in his church, by freely taking their infirmity upon himself; so that if some of his own who are still disturbed by imminent death look upon him, for as much as they feel the weight of their guilt, they are not swallowed by a death worse than desperation? Then how much goodness are we to expect and hope from sharing in his divinity, the divinity whose restlessness reassures us and infirmity strengthens us? In fact even the blessed apostle Peter, when the Lord told him: "When you grow old, you will stretch out your hands, and someone else will dress you and lead you where you do not want to go" [John 21:18],[35] what else did he want if not, freed from the body, to be with Christ? "Yet were it only possible, he had a desire for eternal life without the hassle of death; the hassle of death to which he was led unwillingly...and he left this weakness of infirmity behind by which no one wants to die, so natural that not even old age was able to take it away from the blessed Peter, to whom it was said: 'When you shall be old,' someone else will lead you 'where you do not want to go.'"[36] "But however great be the grievousness of death, it ought to be overcome by the power of that love which is felt for him who, being our life, was willing to endure even death on our behalf. For if there were no grievousness in death, even of the smallest kind, the glory of the martyrs would not be so great."[37]

XVIII At the time of their calling, all need to devote themselves frequently to prayer and need to be helped by the brethren's assiduous recitations of prayers and other texts.

When the last hour decreed for the end of our earthly life is imminent, continuous prayer ought to help us. In fact, if in this world we prepare ourselves to go to unknown or distant places, we recommend ourselves to the prayers of the brethren, and upon

departure we shed plentiful tears, asking the Lord to hasten with
calm travel companions. And if we do these things so carefully
among the known things of the world, while the union of the body
and the soul remains, how much more carefully should we do them
at the moment of our end, when we pass into that region where, the
body having been separated from the soul, we come to such
unknown things of which we do not have any knowledge here while
we are living, if after death the blessed life welcomes us or if, once we
have left the body, we are carried off to torture? In fact since the devil
tries to tie the end of our life with his drawstrings, if really in the
moment of leaving the body we are armed with the pious prayers of
the brethren and the assiduous offices of psalmody, he is always
chased afar, and he dares not enter the divine camps to cause harm
where he hears the name of the Lord resound from the mouths of
those who sing faithfully. In fact we read about some who are freed
from the devil who is present and threatens in the hour of their transition, through the brotherly prayers and the frequency of the
psalmody. Therefore there is no doubt that when the pious faithful
and the true Christians pass from this life, if they are helped by the
assiduous and frequent prayer of the brethren, not even the fero-
cious attack of malignant spirits dares touch them.

XVIIII The preparation of the tomb and the care of the corpses are duly imposed upon believers.[38]

Although "care of the corpse, preparation of the tomb, pomp of
obsequies are more comfort for the living than help for the dead,"[39]
nevertheless "the bodies of the departed are not to be despised and
flung aside, especially those of the just and faithful, whose bodies were
holily utilized by the Spirit as organs and vessels of good works. If, in
fact, a paternal garment and ring, and whatever such like, are more
dear to the descendants because the affection toward their parents is
greater, are the bodies all the more in no way to be spurned, which in
truth we wear more familiarly and intimately than any other garment?"[40] So for the human body, "whatever is bestowed on it is no aid
for salvation, but an office of humanity, according to the affection by
which 'no one hates his own flesh' [Eph 5:29]. Whence it is fitting that
care be taken, as much as possible, for the flesh of one's neighbor,
when the one who bore it is gone. And if those who do not believe in

the resurrection of the flesh do these things, how much more are they to be done by those who do believe; that so, an office of this kind bestowed upon a body, dead but yet to rise again and to remain in eternity, may also be in some way a testimony of the same faith?"[41] "Whence also the corpses of the ancient just were cared for with dutiful piety, their funeral rites celebrated, and their burial provided [Gen 23; 25:9–19; 47:30]: and they themselves while living, gave charge to their sons to bury or even transfer their bodies [Gen 47:30]. Tobias also was commended, by witness of an angel, for having buried the dead, he obtained favor with God [Tob 12:12]. Also the Lord himself, who would be raised on the third day, preaches and commends to be preached the good work of the pious woman who poured precious ointment over his limbs, that she did this for his burial. And the Gospel praiseworthily remembers those who, having removed his body from the cross, diligently and honourably took care to cover it and lay it in the sepulchre. In truth, these testimonies do not teach us that there be some meaning in the dead bodies, but signify that the providence of God, to whom such practices of piety are also pleasing, takes care even for the bodies of the dead to assure faith in the resurrection."[42]

XX Whether it benefits the dead for their bodies to be buried in churches.

"When someone is buried near the sepulchres of the martyrs, this alone already benefits the departed, because the survivor commending him to the patronage of the martyr increases the strength of the prayer."[43] Thus, "when the mind recollects where the body of a very dear person lies buried, and encounters a place bearing the name of a venerable martyr, the affection of the one who remembers and prays entrusts the beloved soul to the same martyr. And when this affection for the dearest departed is demonstrated by the faithful, there is no doubt that it benefits them who, while living in the body, merited that they shall benefit from such things after this life."[44]

XXI The dead who are entombed in the church greatly benefit from the belief that they are helped by the patronage of the martyr near whom they are buried.

Most believers, because of their aforesaid faith, make provisions for their own bodies or for those of their dear ones to be buried near the memorials of martyrs. I do not retain unfruitful what one believes or useless what is faithfully hoped for from divine help,[45] unless the guilt of those who are buried in the churches be so insoluble as to not allow them to be helped after death even by sacrifices offered to God. And therefore if that faith is believed of merit that fills whoever prays to God for his beloved dead who are buried in the places of the martyrs, how much more is the fruit of hope achieved by that faith that procures a salutary place for his own corpse while he is still alive? Indeed, St. Augustine answers thus to the bishop Paulinus, who consulted him about the question: "Since a faithful mother desired to bury the body of her departed faithful son in the basilica of a martyr, if she really believed that his soul would be aided by the merits of the martyr, because she thus believed, some supplication was made, and this benefited, and how it benefited. And since she returns in her spirit to this same sepulchre, and in her prayers more and more commends her son, it is not the place that aids the spirit of the departed, but, by the memory of the place, the living affection of the mother. For at once, both the one who commends and the one commended to, not unprofitably touch the religious mind of the one who prays."[46] These holy words are of Augustine, by which it is believed that the faith of the living who piously arrange to bury the bodies of their dear ones near the memorials of martyrs is not vain, even though we have learned, by many other reasons and examples from antiquity, that those who live impiously up to their own end are disgracefully buried in churches.[47] "In fact, if the merit whereby these things may benefit them are not verified in this life, it is vain to ask for life after this one. As in fact what is done to benefit them after the life of the body is merited in the life that each conducts in the body."[48]

XXII The sacrifices that are offered for the faithful departed.

"In the books of Maccabees we read of a sacrifice offered for the dead. Yet, even if such a thing could not be found at all in the ancient

Scriptures, great is the authority of the universal church that shines forth in this custom, by which the recommendation of the dead has its place in the prayers of the priest offered to the Lord God on his altar. In fact, when sacrifice is offered to God for the departed souls, it is a thanksgiving for the very good ones, propitiation for the not so bad, while for the very bad, even if the sacrifices are of no benefit to the dead, the act is nevertheless consolation for the living. To which nevertheless they benefit, or toward a full remission or at least for the damnation to be more tolerable."[49]

[END OF THE CHAPTERS OF THE FIRST BOOK]

BEGINNING OF THE CHAPTERS
OF THE SECOND BOOK,
ON THE SOULS OF THE DEAD:
HOW THEY ARE BEFORE THE FINAL
RESURRECTION OF THE BODY

XII   After the descent of Christ into hell, the souls of the elect are not kept in those places where the souls of the patriarchs had previously been kept, but they immediately go to heaven.

XIII   As the souls of the saints go to heaven upon leaving the body, likewise those of the sinners are delivered to hell.

XIIII   Those who have been hurled into hell will remain there perpetually.

XV   The soul, after the separation from the body, is not deprived of its faculties.

XVI   The soul possesses a resemblance to the body, and in the same bodily likeness it feels rest and bears the torments.

XVII   Whether one can believe that the soul, being incorporeal, is tormented with a material fire.

XVIII   There is only one fire of Gehenna, but it does not torment sinners in only one way.

XVIIII   It is believed that after death there is a purifying fire.

XX   One is the purifying fire, by which most are believed to be saved, and another is that fire in which the impious, by the judgment of Christ, will be immersed.

XXI   The souls of the dead suffer the purifying fire not after, but before the final judgment.

XXII   Whether it is to be believed that those who shall be saved through the purifying fire are tormented up until the time of the resurrection or afterward.

XXIII   The death of the flesh belongs to the tribulation of the purifying fire.

XXIIII   Whether the souls of the dead can mutually recognize one another after the death of the flesh and, at the same time, whether they mutually have knowledge there of those whom they have not seen in this life.

XXV   Whether the souls of the blessed dare to pray for those whom they believe to be assigned to hell.

XXVI   Whether the souls of the dead pray for the salvation of their living dear ones.

[END OF THE CHAPTERS OF THE SECOND BOOK]

BEGINNING OF THE SECOND BOOK,
ON THE SOULS OF THE DEAD: HOW THEY ARE
BEFORE THE FINAL RESURRECTION OF THE BODY

I The different paradises.

"One thing is the earthly paradise where the life of the first human beings was corporally born; another is the heavenly one where the souls of the blessed are immediately transferred as soon as they leave the body, and rejoicing for the merited happiness, they wait to have again their own bodies."[1] About this paradise Julian Pomerius said: "The souls of the just going out of the body seem to be conducted or to go to paradise, where the apostle [2 Cor 12:2] is said to have been abducted, with the mind but without the body."[2] In the same way, after other things he says: "This suffices concerning the heavenly paradise and the fact that the holy souls are sent there immediately, by the gift of God, as soon as they have departed their bodies. That this is to be believed is confirmed by the authority of our Lord Jesus Christ, who, when he said to the thief, 'today you will be with me in paradise' [Luke 23:43], proved without any ambiguity that the heavenly paradise welcomes the blessed souls gone out of their bodies, without any temporal interval."[3]

II Where paradise is, in which the souls of the
blessed rest once they leave the body.

We read in blessed Augustine, when he explains with great clarity those words of the apostle Paul with which the same apostle recalls having been abducted to the third heaven [see 2 Cor 12:2], that the paradise to which the apostle was abducted, and in which the souls of the blessed who have departed their bodies abide, is situated in the third heaven. The same author defines as material the first heaven, spiritual the second, mental the third, to which one ascends through the contemplation of the mind, and he thus affirms: "If we correctly understand the first heaven, by this general name every material thing is included that is above the waters and on the earth; the second one then is understood with a corporal similitude, what is discerned by the spirit, as that from which Peter, in ecstasy, was presented a dish full of animals to eat [Acts 10:10–11]. The third one then, which is seen with the mind, contains things so secret and hidden and entirely unattainable by the bodily senses, and pure things, such that the things that are in that heaven, and the same substance of God and God the Word through which all things were made, can be seen and heard ineffably in the charity of the Holy Spirit: it is not arbitrarily that we think that the apostle was abducted and taken there and that probably it is the best paradise of all, and so to speak, the paradise of paradises."[4]

III The meaning of the bosom of Abraham, where the souls of the blessed are received.

I do not question that the "bosom of Abraham" means rest of the father or the secret of rest or even paradise, as it is defined by the assertions of many doctors, since among others, Ambrose, Augustine, and Gregory have taught more appropriately that the bosom of so great a patriarch meant nothing other than the patriarch himself.[5]

IIII The different hells.

I remember having read about a distinction of the hells in the treatises of the blessed Augustine, in which he openly says that there are two hells, believing that there is a hell on earth and another hell below the earth, according to the word of the Psalmist, who confides in God: "You have delivered my soul from the depths of Sheol" [Ps 86:13].[6] In fact "for these two hells the Son of God was sent, to free from both. To this hell he was sent by being born, to that by dying."[7] And again he says: "As for hell, brothers, up till now we are not experts neither me nor you; and perhaps there will be another way that will not pass through hell; but these things are uncertain. Since the Scripture says the truth, and cannot be contradicted, from the expression 'you have delivered my soul from the depths of Sheol' we understand that there are two hells, one upper and one lower. In fact how can there be a lower hell if not because there is an upper hell?"[8] Likewise the same most holy doctor proposes another opinion for the fact that "in the same hell there is a lower part, where that rich man suffered inhumanely, and a higher part of hell in which Abraham rejoiced with Lazarus, also where all the saints were before the coming of Christ." Thus, in faith, the quoted doctor says "perhaps in the same hell there is a lower part where the ungodly are thrust who have greatly sinned. For we cannot define sufficiently whether Abraham was not in some particular place in hell. For the Lord had not yet come to hell that he might rescue from thence the souls of all the saints who had gone before, and yet Abraham was there in rest. And when that rich man was in torments in hell, he lifted up his eyes upon seeing Abraham. He could not have seen him by lifting up his eyes, unless the one was above, the other below. And what did Abraham answer unto him, when he said, 'Father Abraham, send Lazarus to dip the tip of his finger in water and cool my tongue, for I am suffering torment in these flames. My child,' he says, 'remember that you received what was good during your lifetime while Lazarus likewise received what was bad; but now he is comforted here, whereas you are tormented. Moreover, between us and you a great chasm is established to prevent anyone from crossing who might wish to go from our side to yours or from your side to ours' [Luke 16:24]. Therefore, two hells probably exist, one in which the souls of the just were at rest, and in the other the souls of the ungodly are tormented."[9]

V Why it is called hell.

"Hell is called *infernus* in Latin[10] because it is found below. Just as with bodies, if they have an order on the basis of their weight, the lower are the heavier, likewise in the dimension of the spirit the lower things are the sadder. In the Greek language, the origin of the name that designates hell refers to the fact that they do not have anything pleasant that can be heard to resound."[11]

VI How hell is and whether it is material.

As the blessed Augustine says, "certainly the reality of hell exists, but I believe that it is spiritual and not material. Those who affirm that hell can be explained in this life or that it does not exist after death are not to be listened to. In fact, it would seem to be interpreted somehow with poetic images: we are not to recede from the authority of the divine Scriptures, which alone is to be believed on this matter."[12]

VII Why it is believed that hell is underground.

"Justly one asks why it is said that hell is situated under the ground if it is not a material place, or why it is called hell if it is not situated underground,"[13] as St. Augustine says. Since the same doctor says accordingly: "Therefore one says or one believes that hell is situated underground because thus it fittingly appears to the spirit, with that similarity with corporeal things, such that the souls of the dead who deserved hell sinned for love of the flesh, be shown through those similarities with corporeal things that it is appropriate for the same dead flesh to be sealed underground."[14]

VIII As soon as they depart the body, the souls of the blessed go to Christ in heaven.

We read that the blessed Gregory responded this way to Peter, who questioned him on these things: "We cannot affirm this thing for all the just, nor can we deny it: for the souls of some just are not immediately gathered in the kingdom of heaven and they are held back still in some abodes. What else is understood in this punishment that comes from the delay if not that they had something less with respect to perfect justice? And nevertheless it is of a clearer evidence of light that the souls of the perfect just ones, as soon as they exit the prison of this flesh, are welcomed in the celestial sees. He who is the truth affirms this when he says: 'Wherever the corpse is, there the vultures will gather' [Matt 24:28], for where our Saviour is bodily present, there, without doubt, the souls of the just also gather. And Paul desires to be dissolved and to be with Christ [see Phil 1:23]. He, therefore, who doubts not that Christ is in heaven, cannot deny that Paul's soul is in heaven. The same apostle says about the dissolution of his body and the dwelling in heaven: 'For we know that if the earthly tent we live in is destroyed, we have a building from God, a house not made with hands, eternal in the heavens' [2 Cor 5:1]."[15]

VIIII The souls of the dead are detained in some abodes.

"During the time that is interposed between human death and the final resurrection, the souls are detained in hidden abodes in proportion to how each of them is worthy of either rest or tribulation for how each behaved living in the flesh."[16]

*X Even though the souls that have achieved something less
than perfect holiness and depart from this life in this condition
can one day obtain the kingdom with the saints,
they are anyway not immediately situated in the
heavenly kingdom upon leaving the body.*

Julian Pomerius says: "Since the church effectively pleads here
for those spirits that leave this world with not such perfect holiness as
to be able to go immediately to paradise after the deposition of their
own bodies, and do not live so badly and reprehensibly or persevere
in their own crimes so much as to deserve to be damned with the devil
and his angels, once they are purified with healing punishments,
when their bodies attain blessed immortality and they participate in
the heavenly kingdom, they will remain there without anything to
detract from their beatitude."[17]

*XI Before the resurrection of the body God is not seen
by the holy spirits of the dead as he will be seen after
the resurrection, and how the souls of the dead
now desire to have their bodies once again.*

In this respect blessed Augustine says: "But what need do the
spirits of the dead have to take back their own bodies in the resurrection, if they can obtain supreme beatitude without their body? It is an
objection that could upset some, but it is too difficult a matter to be
perfectly treated in this book. Nevertheless it is not owed at all to
doubt that the human mind, even when it is abducted away from the
senses of the flesh or when, after death, having departed the body, it
is no longer subject to the images of the body, cannot see the
unchangeable essence of God as the holy angels see it. And this can
happen for some other hidden cause or because there is innate in the
soul a kind of natural desire to govern the body. This desire somehow
constrains the soul to reach with all of its strength toward that highest
heaven until it is now reunited to the body so that its desire to govern
the body is satisfied. If, on the contrary, the body is of such nature that
it is difficult and tiresome to govern it as it is, this flesh that corrupts
itself and weighs down the soul—as the result of the propagation of
sin—all the more the mind is deterred from that vision of the highest

heavens. Thus it was necessary that the soul be torn from the senses of the same flesh so that it could be shown how to reach it.[18] Therefore, when the soul, made identical to the angels, takes back its body which is no longer animal[19] but spiritual because of the transformation to come, it will attain the perfection of its nature, obedient and dominant, enlivened and enlivening with such an ineffable facility that what was once a weight will become its glory."[20]

XII After the descent of Christ into hell, the souls of the elect are not kept in those places where the souls of the patriarchs had previously been kept, but they immediately go to heaven.

If he who had opened the doors of paradise to humankind through his death had not descended, the ancient patriarchs would not have been conducted to the kingdom until the advent of the Lord, even though they had lived justly. In fact, there is no doubt that the places of hell, although peaceful, nevertheless detained them, even after they had lived in justice. Instead, "after the advent of the mediator who was to come in this world," as blessed Gregory says, "we are conducted to the kingdom immediately upon leaving the body, and we obtain without delay what the ancient patriarchs deserved but received with much delay."[21]

XIII As the souls of the saints go to heaven upon leaving the body, likewise those of the sinners are delivered to hell.

"If we believe, by the attestation of Sacred Scripture, that the souls of the saints are in heaven, it is also necessary to believe that the souls of the iniquitous are, on all accounts, in hell, because for the retribution of internal justice by which the just are already glorified, it is also necessary that the unjust be tormented on all accounts. In fact, just as the beatitude gladdens the chosen, so it is necessary to believe that from the day of their death the fire burns the reprobates."[22]

XIIII Those who have been hurled into hell will remain there perpetually.

In the book of Solomon it is written: "Whether a tree falls to the south or to the north, in the place where the tree falls, there it will lie"

[Eccl 11:3], because in the moment when a human being falls, the saint or the malignant spirit receives the soul that goes out of the closed place of the body and will detain it forever with himself without any change, such that if it is raised to heaven it will not descend into torture, nor, if dipped in the eternal tortures, will it climb again to the prize of heaven.[23]

XV The soul, after the separation from the body, is not deprived of its faculties.

In the works of Cassian we read that "the souls are not idle after the separation from this body, nor do they not feel anything,"[24] since the rich man in hell cries out to the poor Lazarus that he was suffering in the flame [Luke 16:24]; and that from the cross the Lord told the thief: "Truly, I tell you, today you will be with me in paradise" [Luke 23:43]. For the Lord would certainly never have promised him this, if he had not known that his soul after being separated from the flesh would either have been deprived of perception, or have been dissolved into nothing. For it was not his flesh but his soul that was to enter paradise with Christ.[25] "These things said," as the same doctor says, "it is clearly shown that the souls of the departed not only are not deprived of their faculties, but that they are not even without their feelings, such as hope and sorrow, joy and fear, and that they already are beginning to taste beforehand something of what is reserved for them at the last judgment. Nor, as some unfaithful maintain, are they dissolved into nothing after their departure from this life, but rather they live more vivaciously, and are even more earnest in waiting on the praises of God. Is it not, perhaps, true that it is beyond every stupidity, not to say fatuity, and even insanity to have the slightest suspicion that the most precious part of the human individual, in which, according to the blessed apostle, lies the image and likeness of God, becomes insensible once the burden of the body with which it is oppressed in this world is laid aside, when it contains in itself all the power of reason and that it makes the dumb and senseless matter of the flesh sensitive through participation in itself? It follows then absolutely, and conforms to the order of reason itself, that when the mind has put off the grossness of the flesh with which it is now weighed down, it will restore its intellectual capacities better than ever, and receive them in a purer and finer condition than it lost them. The blessed apostle, in fact, knows that it is so true what we say that he actually desires to be separated from this flesh, that by this separation he might be rendered more strongly capable of being united to the Lord, saying: 'my desire is to depart and be with Christ, for that is far better' [Phil 1:23]. 'Even though we know that while we are at home in the body we are away from the Lord' [2 Cor 5:6]. 'Yes, we do have confidence, and we would rather be away from the body and at home with the Lord. So, whether we are at home or away, we make it our aim to please him' [2 Cor 5:8–9]. Proclaiming thus aloud that the soul, while it abides in this flesh, is in reality in exile far away from the Lord and separated from Christ, he trusts with all his faith that his separation or departure from this flesh, is instead proximity to Christ."[26]

XVI The soul possesses a resemblance to the body, and in the same bodily likeness it feels rest and bears the torments.

This is the thought of the eminent doctor Augustine on why the human soul has a likeness with the body. He says in fact: "Whoever affirms that the soul cannot have a likeness with a body or even with the limbs of a body, should say that it is not the soul that in a dream sees itself walking or sitting down, going and returning here and there, walking or flying; but nothing of this can happen without it having a certain likeness with a body. Consequently, if it also brings into hell such a likeness—which is not bodily but something similar to a body— it seems that it would likewise be found also in places that are not physical but similar to physical ones, both in rest and in torments."[27]

XVII Whether one can believe that the soul, being incorporeal, is tormented with a material fire.

"If the human soul, though incorporeal, can be detained in a living body, why after death could it not equally be prey to a material fire? We say that the spirit is possessed by the flame, in the sense that the fire, seen and perceived, constitutes a torment. It feels in fact the effect of fire upon seeing it and, when it sees itself burning in the flame, it burns. It so happens that a bodily substance, as is the fire, can burn an incorporeal one as the soul, when the invisible pain and burning are derived from the visible fire, as through a corporeal fire the incorporeal mind is tormented by an incorporeal fire. After all, from the sayings of the Gospel we can deduce that the soul suffers from fire not only because it sees it, but also because it experiences it. The voice of the truth, in fact, tells us that the rich man, upon death, was thrown into hell, and that his soul, prey to the flames, pushed him to beg Abraham, saying: 'Send Lazarus to dip the tip of his finger in water and cool my tongue; for I am in agony in these flames' [Luke 16:24]. Since, therefore, the truth shows us the rich sinner tormented by the flames, what wise man would ever deny that the souls of the damned can be tormented from fire?"[28]

XVIII There is only one fire of Gehenna, but it does not torment sinners in only one way.

"Without a doubt there is only one fire of Gehenna, but it does not torment all sinners in a unique way. Since as much as is required by each one's guilt, so much so is the punishment felt there. In fact, just as in this world many people live under only one sun, yet nonetheless they do not feel the burning of the same sun in an identical way, because it burns more one and less another; likewise there, in the one and only fire there is not only one way to burn, because just as there is a diversity of bodies here, likewise there is a diversity of sinners there, such that all have the one fire, and nevertheless it burns individuals differently."[29]

XVIIII It is believed that after death there is a purifying fire.

We know that there is a purifying fire after death, as defined by the writings of many commentators. Among them the eminent doctor Augustine, although he affirms that this can already happen to the believers in this life, he nevertheless believes that it is also possible after death to expiate some light sins, showing that this same purifying fire, now despised and considered by some as nothing, is in reality more painful "than anything a man can suffer in this life."[30] About this purifying fire, Gregory also affirms: "It is to be believed that before the final judgment, there is a purifying fire for light sins, as the truth says that 'whoever speaks against the Holy Spirit will not be forgiven, either in this age or in the age to come' [Matt 12:32]. In this expression it is given to understand that some sins can be expiated in this life, while others, instead, must be expiated in the future world. In fact, what seems to be denied for the one, subsequent understand-

ing shows is granted for others.[31] Nevertheless, as I previously maintained, it is to be believed that this can happen for the small and least
sins, as for instance: persistent idle talk, unrestrained laugh, or the sin
of worry for family affairs, things that are hardly practiced without
guilt, or by those who know how they must keep far from sin, or by the
error of ignorance about things that are not serious; all these things
also continue to be a weight after death, if while they are still present
in this life they are not totally remitted. Likewise Paul, when he says
that Christ is the foundation, adds: 'Now if anyone builds on the foundation with gold, silver, precious stones, wood, hay, straw…the fire will
test what sort of work each has done. If what has been built on the
foundation survives, the builder will receive a reward. If the work is
burned, the builder will suffer loss; the builder will be saved, but only
as through fire' [1 Cor 3:12, 13, 15]. Although this can be understood
about the fire of the tribulation as applied to us in this life, nevertheless if anyone interprets these things about the fire of future purification, he must carefully consider that he [Paul] said that by fire can be
saved whoever builds on this foundation not with iron, bronze, or
lead, that is, with the greatest and therefore more serious and thus by
then unforgivable sins; but with wood, hay, and straw, that is, the least
and lightest sins, which fire easily consumes. Yet, we must know that
no purification will occur in the future world, not even for the least
sins, if, during this life one did not commit oneself to good works in
order to obtain it in the other."[32]

XX One is the purifying fire, by which most are believed to be saved, and another is that fire in which the impious, by the judgment of Christ, will be immersed.

From the distinction made by the blessed Augustine we have
learned that one is the fire about which, according to the judgment
of the Lord, it shall be said to the impious: "depart from me into the
eternal fire" [Matt 25:41], and another is what is properly called purifying fire, destined for those who shall become saved through it. In
fact, nobody will be saved through the fire that is destined for the
impious, as it has been written: "And these will go away into eternal
punishment" [Matt 25:46]. Rather, through the fire that makes one
acceptable and purifies, certain salvation is promised. In fact, according to what the aforesaid doctor affirms: "But if we were to interpret

in this passage [of Corinthians] that fire of which the Lord shall say to
those on his left, 'depart from me into the eternal fire' [Matt 25:41],
so as to believe that among them there are those who build on the
foundation with wood, hay, stubble, and that they, through virtue of
the good foundation, will be freed from the fire after a time in proportion to their evil merit, what then are we to think about those on
the right, to whom it is said, 'come, you that are blessed by my Father,
inherit the kingdom prepared for you' [Matt 25:34], if not that they
are those who have built on the foundation with gold, silver, and precious stones? But if the fire of which it was said, 'but only as through
fire' [1 Cor 3:15], is to be interpreted this way, then both—that is to
say, both those on the right as well as those on the left—are to be cast
into it. For that fire is to try both, since it is said, for 'the day will disclose it, because it will be revealed with fire, and the fire will test what
sort of work each has done' [1 Cor 3:13]. If, therefore, the fire shall
try both, 'if what has been built on the foundation survives,' that is, if
the superstructure is not consumed by the fire, 'the builder will
receive a reward. If the work is burned, the builder will suffer loss' [1
Cor 3:14–15]; certainly that fire is not the eternal fire. For into this
fire only those on the left hand will be cast, and that with final and
everlasting damnation; but that fire proves those on the right hand.
Yet some of them it so proves that it does not burn and consume the
structure that is found to have been built by them on Christ as the
foundation; while it proves others in another way, so as to burn what
they have built up and thus cause them to suffer loss, while they themselves are saved because they have retained Christ, who was laid as
their sure foundation with an eminent love. But if they are saved, then
certainly they will stand at the right hand, and will hear with the rest,
'come, you that are blessed by my Father, inherit the kingdom prepared for you' [Matt 25:34]. And not at the left hand, where those will
be who will not be saved, and will then hear 'you that are accursed,
depart from me into the eternal fire' [Matt 25:41]. In fact from that
fire no one will be saved, because they all will go away into eternal
punishment, 'where their worm never dies, and the fire is never
quenched' [Mark 9:48]."[33]

XXI *The souls of the dead suffer the purifying fire not after, but before the final judgment.*

Concerning the reason for which the purifying punishments will be realized before the final judgment, St. Augustine, proposing a certain opinion, says: "For our part, we recognize that even in this life some punishments are purifying. But temporary punishments are suffered by some in this life only, by others after death, by others both now and then; but nevertheless before that last most rigorous judgment; yet among those who must suffer temporary punishments after death, not all fall into everlasting pains which are to follow that judgment. For to some, what is not remitted in this world is remitted in the next, that is, in order that they not be punished with the eternal punishment of the world to come."[34] Whereby, and after other considerations, the same doctor says: "Whoever, therefore, desires to escape eternal punishments, let him not only be baptized, but also justified in Christ, and so let him really pass from the devil to Christ. And we dare to think that any purifying pains will be before that final and dreadful judgment."[35] Therefore, confirmed by the thought of such a great doctor, we believe that this purifying fire acts here before the final judgment and that it precedes the fire in which all the impious, by judgment of Christ, will be thrown.

XXII *Whether it is to be believed that those who shall be saved through the purifying fire are tormented up until the time of the resurrection or afterward.*

It is my opinion that just as not all the reprobates thrown into the eternal fire are damned to only one kind of torment, likewise all those who are believed to be saved through the purifying punishments shall not sustain only one identical punishment of the souls for the same length of time. Therefore, what for the reprobates is established by the distinction of the punishments is determined, for those who are to be saved through fire, by the measure of time. But, for them the torment of the purifying fire will last longer or less according to how much they loved more or less the transient goods here. About this, in his books, the blessed Augustine, treating the purifying punishments, among other things, says: "And it is not unlikely that something of the same kind may take place even after this life, and it is a matter that may be inquired into, and either ascertained or left unknown, whether some believers be saved as soon as possible or later, through a kind of purifying fire, and in proportion to how they have loved with more or less intensity the goods that perish. This cannot, however, be the case of any of those of whom it is said, that 'none of these will inherit the kingdom of God' [1 Cor 6:10; Gal 5:21], unless after suitable repentance their sins be forgiven them. When I say 'suitable,' I mean that they are not to be unfruitful in almsgiving."[36]

XXIII The death of the flesh belongs to the tribulation of the purifying fire.

The eminent doctor Augustine, treating the purifying punishments, says: "Even the death of the flesh itself, which was contracted from the perpetuation of the first sin, can be a part of this tribulation, because each experiences the time that follows it in relation to the edifice constructed by each. The persecutions, too, from which the martyrs were crowned and which all Christians can suffer, try, as does the fire, both edifices: consuming some together with their builders if Christ is not found in them as their foundation, while consuming others without their builders if Christ is found in them. In fact, they are saved, even though with a punishment; but the persecutions do not consume the other edifices, because they find them made as to remain forever."[37]

XXIIII Whether the souls of the dead can mutually recognize one another after the death of the flesh and, at the same time, whether they mutually have knowledge there of those whom they have not seen in this life.

That the souls of the dead gone out of their bodies can recognize one another is attested by the evangelist when he says: "The poor man died and was carried away by the angels to be with Abraham. The rich man also died and was buried. In Hades, where he was being tormented, he looked up and saw Abraham far away with Lazarus by his side. He called out, 'Father Abraham, have mercy on me, and send Lazarus to dip the tip of his finger in water and cool my tongue; for I am in agony in these flames'" [Luke 16:22–24]. Here is how the soul of the rich man recognized the spirit of poor Lazarus. From this, without a doubt, we can deduce that in that place the souls of the dead mutually recognize one another. In fact, "the good" are able "to recognize the good and the wicked their own kind." "If in fact"—as St. Gregory affirms—"Abraham had not recognized Lazarus, in no way would he have been able to speak to the rich man situated in the torments about his late repentance, reminding him that Lazarus had received evil things in his life. And if the bad did not recognize the bad, the rich man situated in the torments would not have remembered his brothers who were still alive. Is it in fact possible for one who was concerned to plead for those absent not to know the ones present? In this it is also shown that the good can recognize the bad, and the bad the good. For the rich man was known by Abraham when it was said: 'Remember that during your lifetime you received your good things' [Luke 16:25]. And the chosen one, Lazarus, was also known by the rich reprobate, whom he called by name, praying that he be sent to him: 'Send Lazarus to dip the tip of his finger in water and cool my tongue' [Luke 16:24]. It is evident that this mutual knowledge increases in both the measure of the remuneration, such that the good enjoy all the more to see those rejoicing together whom they loved; and the bad, while they are tormented together with those whom they loved in the terrestrial life, despising God, not only suffer for their own but also for their punishment. Moreover, something wonderful happens in the chosen ones, because not only do they recognize those whom they had met in the world, but they also recognize as familiar and known those whom they had never seen. For example, when, in that eternal heritage, they shall see the ancient fathers, they shall not be unknown to them by sight, because they have always known them through their writings. In fact, since in that place all behold God with the same clarity, what is there that they know not when they know him who knows everything?"[38]

XXV Whether the souls of the blessed dare to pray for those whom they believe to be assigned to hell.

"They pray for their enemies," as St. Gregory affirms, "in the time when their hearts can be converted to fruitful penitence and, through this conversion, they can be saved. What else, in fact, can be implored for their enemies if not what the apostle says: 'God may perhaps grant that they will repent and come to know the truth, and that they may escape from the snare of the devil, having been held captive by him to do his will'? [2 Tim 2:25–26]. And how can they pray for those who in no way can be converted from their iniquity and brought to do the works of justice? Therefore the reason why those condemned to the eternal fire are not prayed for up there is the same reason why the devil and his angels assigned to the eternal torture are not prayed for. Can there be any other reason why holy people do not pray for those who die in infidelity and impiety, knowing them to be already destined to eternal punishment, if not to avoid that the merit of their prayer be canceled in the presence of the just judge? For if even the righteous, while still alive, take no compassion upon those who are dead and damned for their sins, although they are aware of incurring themselves in some guilt liable of judgment, since they are still in the weakness of the flesh, with how much more severity shall they behold the torments of the damned, when they shall be freed of all vice or corruption, and shall be more nearly and intimately united to true justice? For their minds are so fully united to the most righteous judge, that the strength of this union will absorb them in such a way as that it will not be possible for them by any means to like what does not accord with the requirements of the inner norm."[39]

XXVI Whether the souls of the dead pray for the salvation of their living dear ones.

If the rich man immersed in hell implores Abraham for his brothers that they be admonished and not fall into the places of torment, why should it be believed that the souls of the just, and especially those established in peace, are not concerned about their dear survivors? They can, in fact, pray for the salvation of the living, for as much as it is granted them by the Lord; in fact, they can certainly remember those whom they have loved while they were in this world: they have not lost the sensitivity that unites the living with the living, but it is to be believed that they have an even freer one, there where they cannot be weighed down by the bodily burden. According to the divine word, in fact, "a perishable body weighs down the soul" [Wis 9:15]; thus the soul, which now is weighed down by the body, once freed from the body, becomes more free. Therefore, after the death of the body, an integral sensitivity and a perfect memory belong to the soul. So the soul that avails itself there with certainty of the function of memory, remembers the sweetness of the dearest ones. Thus, remembering those whom it loved in the world, it can recommend them to Christ with prayers; after all, the prayers of the souls of the faithful do not ask for anything else than that their desires be granted. I affirm this even though in the custom of the faithful it is of common use in this field, when they recommend themselves to those who are about to die and they desire to be remembered by them. In this way, the friendship of the dear survivors was entrusted to the martyrs, when they were dying; in this way, the crowd of pious faithful recommends itself every day to the chosen souls, called away from this world, and asks them to remember them always. Nor in fact would the faith of the living ask this of the deceased, if they were not convinced that these, after death, could in some way assist them. But since the concern of such great authority does not go beyond, the outcome of the request is often verified since what many living ask of the dying to be done to them, they obtain without suffering delay. This, therefore, seems to me the essence of the little question that I put forward, which even if I am unable to express in the same words with which the greatest have developed it, I nonetheless believe that it was defined in the same sense by the doctors, and even though I discover something of that which they had defined, I prefer to follow their thought.

XXVII Whether the souls of the dead can become sad or glad over the salvation of their living dear ones, and whether they are touched by any sadness or worry about the living.

"If there were no care of the dead for the living,"[40] certainly that rich man who was tortured in hell would not have been worried for his brothers, saying to Abraham: "Then, father, I beg you to send him to my father's house, for I have five brothers, that he may warn them, so that they will not also come into this place of torment" [Luke 16:27–28]. And therefore, the dead can care for the living, even if they do not know what we do in the present, just as we the living care for the dead, though we do not know what they are doing. If in fact the living were not to care for the dead, we would not pray to the Lord particularly for them, offering sacrifices frequently. Teaching this and other similar things in his volumes, St. Augustine proposes only one example, which in no mediocre way is worthy of admiration: "We heard tell of a certain person of whom was demanded payment of a

debt, showing his deceased father's caution money, a debt that the
father had paid unknown to the son, whereupon the man began to be
very sorrowful and to marvel that his father while dying did not tell
him what he owed, when he also made his will. While he was in such
anxiety, his father appeared to him in a dream and made known to
him where the receipt was located that canceled the caution money.
When the young man had found and showed the document, he not
only rebutted the wrongful claim of a false debt, but also got back his
father's note of hand which the father had not got back when the
money was paid. This could lead one to believe that the soul of that
man cared for his son and that he came to him while he was sleeping,
teaching him what he did not know, to relieve him of a great trouble."[41]

XXVIII The patriarchs, the prophets, the apostles, and all the souls of the dead who have already passed to the blessed life ardently wait for us to rejoice with them, and their gladness is not perfect as long as they grieve for our errors.

About these things the doctor Origen, in his doctrines, so
teaches: "Since not even the saints, departing this life, immediately
obtain the complete rewards for their merits; but they also wait for us,
though hesitant, though idle. For them there is no perfect gladness as
long as they are distressed for our errors and cry for our sins. You will
not perhaps believe me who speaks to you; in fact, who am I to have
the audacity to confirm the meaning of such a great doctrine? But I
call upon a witness of these things, one whom you cannot doubt: he
is, in fact, the apostle Paul, 'a teacher of the Gentiles in faith and
truth' [1 Tim 2:7]. Writing then to the Hebrews, and having enumerated all the holy fathers who were justified by faith, he adds, after all
these things, this as well: 'Yet all these, though they were commended
because of their faith, did not receive what was promised since God
had provided something better for us, so that they would not without
us be made perfect' [Heb 11:39–40]. You see, therefore, that
Abraham still waits to obtain the realities that are perfect. Isaac and
Jacob also wait, and all the prophets wait for us, so that they may
receive perfect beatitude with us. For this reason, therefore, the mystery of the judgment deferred to the last day is preserved; in fact one
is the body that waits to be justified; one is the body of which is said to
rise again at the judgment. 'As it is, there are many parts, yet one

body. The eye cannot say to the hand, "I have no need of you," nor again the head to the feet, "I have no need of you'" [1 Cor 12:20–21]. Even if the eye is healthy, and it is not disturbed for what concerns the sight, if the other members fail, what gladness will it be for the eye? Or what perfection can there ever be if there are no hands, if the feet fail or the other members are not present? Because even if there is some eminent glory in the eye, it consists especially in the fact that it is the guide of the body or that it is not deprived of the functions of the other members. I think then that this is also taught us by the vision of the prophet Ezekiel when he says that bone must be rejoined to bone, and joint to joint, and nerves and veins and skin, and the single members must be restored to their place. In the end, see what the prophet adds: 'These bones,' he says; he did not say: these are all the human beings; but he said: 'These bones are the whole house of Israel' [Ezek 37:11]. Therefore you will have gladness leaving this life if you will have been holy. But it will then be truly full gladness when none of the members of the body will be missing. Since you also will wait for others, just as you have been awaited. If to you, who are a member, it does not seem perfect gladness if another member is missing, how much more does our Lord and Savior, who is the Head [see 1 Cor 11:3] of the whole body, not consider it perfect gladness for him as long as he sees that his Body is lacking some of its members."[42]

XXVIIII Whether the dead can know what the living do.

"It must be confessed," as the blessed Augustine says, "that without doubt the dead do not know what the living are doing here in the moment in which it happens, but subsequently they hear of it from those who, dying, hence go to meet them, and certainly not everything but what they are allowed to reveal, therefore also to remember these things, and to those which it is shown as opportune to know. The dead are also able to know from the angels, who are present to the things that happen here, of what he to whom all things are subject, judges that everyone must know. In fact, if the angels could not be present in the places of both the living and the dead, the Lord Jesus would not have said: 'The poor man died and was carried away by the angels to be with Abraham' [Luke 16:22]. Even the souls of the dead can know some things that happen here, when the Spirit of God reveals them, and it is necessary that they should know not only things present or past, but also future things that are necessary to know. Just as the prophets, unlike other people, while they were living here, not even they knew all things, but only what God's providence judged opportune to reveal to them."[43]

XXX Whether the dead can visibly appear to the eyes of the living.

Also about this, the aforesaid doctor affirms: "That some can be sent from the dead to the living as also, on the contrary, Paul, from the living, was rapt into paradise, is testified by the Sacred Scripture. In fact the prophet Samuel, even though dead, foretold the future to the living king Saul [1 Kgs 28:15].[44] Although some believe that it was not Samuel, who could have been evoked with magic arts, but that some spirit, prone to such evil actions, was introduced under his aspect. Nevertheless the book of Ecclesiasticus, which is said to have been written by Jesus son of Sirach, and that because of the language it manifests a certain similarity with that of Solomon, in the praise of the fathers, it confirms that Samuel even when dead did prophesy [Sir 46:24].[45] But, if this book of the Hebrews is not to be trusted because not in their canon, what shall we say about Moses who in Deuteronomy is certainly declared dead [Deut 24:5], while in the Gospel we read that he appeared to the living, together with Elijah, who is not dead?"[46]

XXXI Only the souls of the saints, and not those of the impious, will know what can be done by the living.

Without a doubt it is to be believed that just as the living are not able to participate in the happenings of the dead, likewise the matters of the living are not known by the dead. Nevertheless, we suppose that the souls of the saints do not perceive in any way this lack of knowledge, in that they know all things in the vision of God and they contemplate them in his knowledge. So also the blessed Gregory in the books of Moralia, in that passage where he seems to draw from the words of Job his well-known testimony, says: "Their children come to honor, and they do not know it; they are brought low, and it goes unnoticed" [Job 14:21], defining it this way: "For as they who are still living know nothing of the souls of the dead, in what place they are held; so the dead do not know how those who survive them live their life in the flesh. Because the life of the spirit is, in fact, very different from that of the flesh; and as the bodily one and the incorporeal one belong to different genera, likewise the modalities of knowledge are also distinct. This, however, has no value for the holy souls, because if they see in themselves the splendor of the almighty God, in no way can we suppose that there be anything they do not know. But because carnal persons bestow their chief affection on their children, blessed Job declares that they are hereafter ignorant of what they loved here with all their heart, so that whether their sons be in honor or dishonor they know not, whereas their care for these was always preying upon their minds."[47]

XXXII Whether after the advent of the mediator in hell, by which the way to heaven was opened for the saints, the good can see the bad in pain and the bad can see the good established in rest.

From the testimony of the evangelist we learn that while the rich man died and was immersed in hell, Lazarus was placed to rest in the "bosom of Abraham"; and the rich man, though in hell, could see Abraham and the poor Lazarus, while Abraham saw that rich man placed in the torments. We know that these things happened before the descent of Christ into hell. After all, when our Lord and Savior, dying for us all, descended with only the soul into hell, he opened the doors of the heavenly paradise to the patriarchs, who were confined in underground places. And since he snatched them from hell and placed them in the heavenly region, we ask ourselves, not without reason, in what way Abraham and the other saints, from the heavenly paradise where they were placed after the resurrection of Christ, could see the souls of the impious who are in hell; how could they do so from that place from which they were drawn after the death of Christ? Since it seems that it is I who pose such a question, myself being so occupied by various concerns, wherever I have read I have not easily found an answer. About this theme, I remember to have read something only in the *Homilies* of Pope Gregory, in which he affirms: "It must be believed that, before the last judgment, the impious see some just ones in peace, and thereby seeing them and ascertaining their joy, they are tormented not only by their own sentence, but also by the happiness of the just. The chosen ones, then, always observe the

damned in torture, and their joy increases, since they see the evil from
which they have mercifully escaped, and they direct all the more
thanks to their redeemer, seeing in the others the punishments that
they themselves could have suffered, if they had been abandoned.
The sight of the punishment of the impious does not obscure the
light of such beatitude in the just ones, because it is by then impossible to have compassion for the damned; thus without a doubt such a
sight cannot decrease their happiness. Why then should we marvel if
while the blessed see the torments of the impious, this becomes for
them an increment of joy, just as when in painting a background of
black color is first placed so that the white or the red may be seen
more clearly?…And although their joys suffice for them to enjoy fully,
without a doubt they nonetheless always observe the punishments of
the impious; because for those who see the light of their creator, in
the creature there is nothing that they cannot see."[48]

XXXIII Against those who say that after death there is no life of the soul.

Cassian says: "there are many who though they are dead in the
body yet bless God in the spirit, and praise him, according to this:
'Spirits and souls of the just, bless the Lord, and every spirit praise the
Lord' [see Dan 3:86; Ps 150:6]. And in the Apocalypse, the souls of
those who are slain are not only said to praise God but to address him
also [Rev 6:9ff.]. In the Gospel itself the Lord says with still greater clarity to the Sadducees: 'And as for the resurrection of the dead, have you
not read what was said to you by God, "I am the God of Abraham, the
God of Isaac, and the God of Jacob?" He is God not of the dead, but
of the living' [Matt 22:31]. About this the apostle says: 'Therefore God
is not ashamed to be called their God; indeed, he has prepared a city
for them' [Heb 11:16]."[49] The blessed Augustine and the other doctors
have also affirmed it in many passages and in numerous works. I want
briefly to recall an example of the aforesaid Augustine, which strengthens the reasoning. He reports that it is attested that "in Carthage"
there was a brother, a certain Gennadius, a physician "very well known
and very dear to him," "very generous," who outdid himself with untir-
ing mercy and well-disposed mind "in the care of the poor." This
Gennadius, however, "doubted…as to whether there was any life after
death. For as much, therefore, as God would in no wise abandon a

man so merciful in his disposition and conduct, there appeared to him in sleep a youth of remarkable appearance and good looking, who said to him: 'Follow me.' Following him, he came to a city where he began to hear, on the right hand, sounds of a melody so exquisitely sweet as to surpass anything he had ever heard. When he inquired what it was, the youth said: 'It is the hymns of the blessed and the holy.' I do not remember well what he himself reported to have seen on the left hand. He awoke; the dream vanished, and he thought of it as only a dream. The following night, however, the same youth appeared to Gennadius for the second time and asked whether he recognized him, to which he replied that he knew him well. Thereupon he asked him where he had become acquainted with him. There also his memory failed him not as to the proper reply: he narrated the whole vision, and the hymns of the saints that, under his guidance, he had been taken to hear, with all the readiness natural to recollection of some very recent experience. On this the youth inquired whether it was in sleep or when awake that he had seen what he had just narrated. He answered: 'In sleep.' The youth then said: 'You remember it well; it is true that you saw these things in sleep, but I would have you know that even now you are seeing in sleep.' Hearing this, he trusted, and in his reply declared that he believed it. Then he who taught the man added and said: 'Where now is your body?' He answered: 'In my bedroom, in bed.' 'Do you know,' said the youth, 'that your eyes in this body of yours are now bound and closed, and at rest, and that with these eyes you are seeing nothing?' He answered: 'I know it.' 'What, then,' said the youth, 'are the eyes with which you see me?' He, unable to discover what to answer to this, was silent. While he hesitated, the youth disclosed to him what he was endeavoring to teach him by these questions, and forthwith said: 'As while you are asleep and lying on your bed these eyes of your body are now unemployed and doing nothing, and yet you have eyes with which you behold me, and enjoy this vision, likewise when you will be dead, while your bodily eyes shall be wholly inactive, there shall be in you a life by which you shall still live, and a faculty of perception by which you shall still perceive. Beware, therefore, after this of having doubts on the persistence of human life after death.' This truthful man says that all doubts as to this matter were thus removed from him."[50]

XXXIIII Against those for whom it seems too little that the soul
after the death of the flesh, in a certain bodily resemblance,
sees delightful things or feels sad things, and that the delightful
or sad things seen there are more evident than the ones
that can be seen here by the soul in a dream.

"Once the souls have left their bodies, those realities by which
the souls are afflicted in good or in evil are not considered to be bodily but are similar to the bodily, since souls appear to themselves
under forms similar to their bodies; nevertheless those realities are
real and real is the joy or the pain produced by a spiritual substance.
Also in dreams, in fact, there is a big difference between dreams of
delightful things or of sad things. That is why in reality some are sad
waking up from dreams in which they had enjoyed some goods that
they had desired, while in other occasions, waking up from dreams in
which they had been troubled and oppressed by serious terrors and
torments, they were afraid to go to sleep to not renew the same bad
dreams. Now of course it must not be doubted that those that are
called punishments of hell are more intense and for this reason they
are perceived with more intense pain. In fact, those people who have
been removed from the senses of the body have subsequently said to
have found themselves in stronger experience than that of a dream,
although, naturally, it was less intense than how it would have been if
they had been totally dead."[51]

XXXV What reward the souls of the dead are believed to have
before the final time of the resurrection.

The souls of the blessed, as soon as they depart from the abode
of this body, and until they reach the time of the final resurrection,
benefit only from the joy of the spirit, as John attests concerning the
souls of those killed for the cause of the Word of God, saying: "They
were each given a white robe" [Rev 6:11]. Thus the first vestment that
the soul receives after the death of the flesh is one of rest and joy; the
second vestment will be that for which, once reunited with the body,
it will exult for the immortality of the soul and the body.[52]

XXXVI After the abandonment of this body, God is immediately seen by the holy souls.

The blessed Cyprian, illustrious doctor and extraordinary martyr, writing to Fortunate on the exhortation to martyrdom, among other things, says: "What dignity it is, and what security, to go gladly from hence, to depart gloriously between afflictions and tribulations; in a moment to close the eyes with which human beings and the world are looked upon, and at once to open them to look upon God and Christ! Of such a blessed departure how great is the swiftness! You will be suddenly taken away from earth, to be placed in the heavenly kingdom. It behooves us to embrace these things in our mind and consideration, to meditate on these things day and night."[53] Instructed by the exhortation of such a great doctor we must be certain that, after death, we shall not be at all deprived of the vision of God, but we shall enjoy it with gladness if we will have lived operating according to his approval.

XXXVII Even the souls of the saints already reign with Christ in heaven.[54]

St. Augustine, eager to teach with absolute certainty that not only the souls of the martyrs, but also those of the faithful chosen ones, reign now already with Christ in heaven, proposes the proof of the Apocalypse of John, in which it is read that the souls of those who had been slain for their witness to Jesus and for the Word of God— that is, those souls of the martyrs who have not yet been reunited with their bodies—reign "with Christ for a thousand years" [Rev 20:4]. But the same doctor, in order to avoid advancing the conviction that only the souls of the martyrs and not those of other faithful reign with Christ, adds: "The souls of the faithful departed, therefore, are not separated from the church, which is even now the kingdom of Christ; otherwise they would not be remembered at the altar of God in communion with the body of Christ. Nor would it be of any help for them to resort to baptism in danger in order to avoid departing this life without it; nor would it benefit them to resort to reconciliation, if by chance someone is separated by that body for a penitence or for a bad conscience. Why are these things done, if not because the faithful, also deceased, are his members? Though not with their bodies yet,

their souls nevertheless already reign with him." Now, even daily, they
desire that this beatitude be doubled, which they will then receive,
and their desires are almost made words of supplication with which
they beg God, that they may receive the resurrection of their deceased
bodies. Great, in truth, is their cry and great their desire. In fact,
everyone, the less he invokes it, the less he desires it, and he turns
instead with a greater voice to the ears of God, all the more he
expands himself fully in the desire of him. If in fact their cry did not
express desire, the prophet would not have said: "your ear heard the
desires of their hearts" [see Ps 9:38].[55] To these holy souls the white
vestments have already been individually delivered, meaning that
same heavenly beatitude in which they now exult, full of joy. To these
it was said: "Rest a little longer, until the number both of their fellow
servants and of their brothers and sisters will be complete" [Rev 6:11].
To say therefore to the souls that desire it, "wait a little longer," means
for them to aspire to the Lord, with the relief of consolation, in the
ardor of the holy desire of his very presence. Nevertheless, the kingdom of their souls, as we have already said, from now on is with him,
"while these thousand years pass by. For this reason in the same book,
and even elsewhere, it is read: 'Blessed are the dead who from now on
die in the Lord. Yes, says the Spirit, they will rest from their labors, for
their deeds follow them' [Rev 14:13]. Therefore the church now
reigns first of all with Christ in the living and in the dead. 'For to this
end,' as the apostle says, 'Christ died and lived again, so that he might
be Lord of both the dead and the living' [Rom 14:9]. He has mentioned therefore the souls of the martyrs only, because they, who actually fought for the truth till death, reign in a special way. Nevertheless,
taking the part for the whole, we understand that all the other
deceased also belong to the church, which is the kingdom of Christ."[56]

[END OF THE CHAPTERS OF THE SECOND BOOK]

BEGINNING OF THE CHAPTERS OF THE THIRD BOOK, ON THE FINAL RESURRECTION OF THE BODY

XIII   It is not to be believed that only the twelve apostles will sit on the above-mentioned twelve seats, but the whole number of perfect ones who will be subdivided by Christ into numbers of twelve.

XIIII   The final resurrection of the human body.

XV   When the seventh angel sounds the trumpet, the resurrection of the dead will occur in a wink.

XVI   The resurrection concerns all human beings, while the transformation concerns only the saints.

XVII   It is not an ethereal body that rises, but the flesh that we bear, without any corruption.

XVIII   How we believe that we will then have spiritual bodies, when our future bodies are truly admitted not as spirits but as bodies.

XVIIII   The property of the bodies that will be in the resurrection.

XX   In what age or stature will be those who rise, whether elderly, young, or children.

XXI   Whether the statures and the shapes of the bodies that rise again will be identical or different, and if in the resurrection the thin ones will preserve the same thinness and the fat ones the same fatness.

XXII   The bodies of the saints will rise again without any deformity.

XXIII   Concerning the bodies of the reprobates, it is superfluous to investigate in what size of the body or in what age they will be risen.

XXIIII   Men and women rise again in their own sex.

XXV   No trouble of food or drinks worries those who rise again.

XXVI   Our nature does not need bodily garments.

XXVII   About the aborted fetuses, and why one ought to consider that from the moment a human being begins to live in the mother's womb, then he or she is related to the final resurrection.

XXXXIIII The reward of the chosen follows after the damnation of the impious.

XXXXV Once the judgment has been completed, the servant aspect with which Christ exercised judgment will pass away, and then Christ will deliver the kingdom to God and Father.

XXXXVI The conflagration of fire by which, it is said, this world will perish.

XXXXVII Once the judgment has been completed, the new heaven and the new earth will begin to exist.

XXXXVIII Not all who rise again will be in the new heaven and new earth, but only the saints.

XXXXVIIII Against those who say that if after judgment has been passed the conflagration of the world will take place, where then can the saints be so as not to be reached by the flame of fire?

L The reward and the kingdom of the saints when Christ, after having girded himself, upon passing will serve his own.

LI Then the wicked will not know what happens in the joy of the blessed, while the good will know what happens in the punishment of the miserable.

LII Then we can be led to and live in heaven with this body in which we now live.

LIII Whether we will then have more refined movements of the body, and whether they will be identical to those that we seem to have now.

LIIII Whether God then is seen through these bodily eyes, with which we there see the sun and the moon.

LV Then we will see God with that vision with which the angels now see him.

LVI In the life in which they cannot sin, all the saints will exercise free will more steadily than in this life.

LVII Then we will have forgetfulness and memory in an equal way.

[END OF THE CHAPTERS OF THE THIRD BOOK]

BEGINNING OF THE CHAPTERS OF THE THIRD BOOK, ON THE FINAL RESURRECTION OF THE BODY

I No human being will know the time and the day of the judgment.

The Lord wanted the time or the day of judgment to be unknown to us. We read, in fact, that to the disciples who questioned him about the last day, asking him: "what will be the sign of your coming and of the end of the age?" [Matt 24:3; Mark 13:4], the Lord himself answered: "But about that day or hour no one knows, neither the angels in heaven, nor the Son, but only the Father" [Mark 13:32; see Matt 24:36]. Although he claims not to know the same thing, it cannot be judged that the Son himself knew not, but that, although knowing it, he did not want to say so to the others. "In fact, when the same Lord through the prophet says: 'For the day of vengeance was in my heart' [Isa 63:4], he thus indicates that he knows it, but that he does not intend to reveal it to all."[1]

II Whether it can be believed that there is a particular place where judgment will be made by God.

I do not easily remember what I have read about it in some codes: from the prophet Joel we have learned that in the time of judgment all the peoples will be judged by the Lord in the valley of *Jehoshaphat.* So, in fact, the same holy prophet says: "For then, in those days and at that time, when I will have restored the prisoners of Judah and Jerusalem, I will gather all the nations and bring them down to the valley of Jehoshaphat, and I will enter into judgment with them there" [Joel 3:1]. But let us listen to how Jerome interprets these words, so that the reader may better know from his words this place of Jehoshaphat where it is said that judgment will be passed, whether it is to be understood literally or figuratively. In fact the same blessed Jerome says: "[the term] Jehoshaphat is to be understood as judgment of the Lord."[2] This is, therefore, what he says: "When I will have compassion on them, that is, on those who will be recognized by the confession of my name, then I will conduct all of my enemies into the valley of Jehoshaphat, that is, in the valley of judgment." Moreover, "all the peoples" either designates all the incredulous nations, or indicates all the demons, because this is how the doctor himself continues in the same treatise: "These people, that is, those whom he calls incredulous nations, or demons, will not be judged on the mountains, nor in the plains, but in the depths of the underground, such that the very place of judgment will also be immediately for punishment."[3]

III No one will know for how many days such future judgment will endure.

"That Christ will come from heaven to judge the living and the dead is maintained by the whole church of God in the confession and profession [of faith]," as the blessed Augustine says, "we call it the final day of judgment, that is to say, the last time. In truth, it is uncertain for how many days the future judgment will endure."[4]

IIII On the terror of the coming of Christ. He will come for judgment and will pass judgment in the same way he was judged.

When the world will have come to its end, Christ, the Son of God, will come for judgment with all the saints in the same bodily aspect with which he ascended to heaven. Because of him, in fact, who comes from heaven for the judgment, according to what he himself said in the Gospel: "the powers of heaven will be shaken. Then the sign of the Son of Man will appear in heaven, and then all the tribes of the earth will mourn, and they will see 'the Son of Man coming on the clouds of heaven' with power and great glory. And he will send out his angels with a loud trumpet call, and they will gather his elect from the four winds, from one end of heaven to the other" [Matt 24:29–31]. Also the apostle Paul so speaks about the coming of his judgment: "For the Lord himself, with a cry of command, with the archangel's call and with the sound of God's trumpet, will descend from heaven" [1 Thess 4:16], [while] the psalmist proclaims: "before him is a devouring fire, and a mighty tempest all around him" [Ps 50:3]: because the same who once came incognito to be judged will then come visibly to judge everybody.[5] Having thus reunited all of his saints, he will come from heaven, according to what Isaiah affirms: "The Lord enters into judgment with the elders and princes of his people" [Isa 3:14]. Therefore, he will certainly come dreadful and striking much fear in the day of his judgment, when, with the angels and the archangels,[6] the thrones and the dominations and the other virtues, with the skies and the earth inflamed, all the elements moved in terror to obey him, he will be seen in the glory of majesty.

V *Christ will come to judge, preceded by his cross, and the same cross will be carried on the shoulders of angels, while Christ will come down from heaven.*

John Chrysostom,[7] in specifically examining and analyzing this problem, thus affirms: "We see in what way Christ will come with his cross: it is necessary in fact to expound upon this fact. He says: 'if they say, Christ is in the inner rooms, do not believe it. He is in the desert, do not go out there' [Matt 24:26], speaking about the second manifestation of his glory due to the false messiahs and the false prophets, due to the Antichrist, so that someone, prevented by error, does not run into a false Christ. Since the Antichrist will precede the coming of Christ the Savior, for this reason it is necessary to attentively prevent someone who is looking for the shepherd from running into the wolf. Therefore, I tell you this in advance, so that from this you may distinguish the coming of the true shepherd. He gave this sign: this in reality was his will, that his first coming be verified in a hidden way and that he looked for what was lost; yet the second coming will not happen like this, as he simply said: 'Just as lightning comes from the east and is seen as far as the west, so will the coming of the Son of Man be' [Matt 24:27]. He will suddenly appear to everyone, and he will not be missed by the one who asks if the Christ be here or there. This way, in fact, just as when the lightning flashes we need not ask ourselves if there has been lightning, likewise when the revelation of his presence shines we will not be impelled to ask if the Christ has come. But since we wonder whether he will come with the cross (I have not forgotten in fact the promise to treat this theme), listen therefore to what follows. He said, 'when he will come, the sun will be darkened, and the moon will not give its light' [Matt 24:29]. The eminence of the splendor of Christ will be so great that even the brightest lights of the sky will be dimmed before the brightness of the divine light. Then 'the stars will fall...when the sign of the Son of Man will appear in heaven.' Have you considered how great is the force of the sign, that is, of the cross? 'The sun will be darkened, and the moon will not give its light'

[Matt 24:29–30]. Instead, the cross will shine and, the heavenly bodies having dimmed and the stars fallen, it alone will radiate light, so that you learn that the cross is brighter than the moon and the sun, whose splendor it will overcome, illuminated by the divine brightness. And as the army precedes the king who enters the city, raising the royal insignias and banners, and announces the entrance of the king by rattling their weapons, so also will the army of angels and archangels precede the descent of the Lord from the heavens; and carrying on their noble shoulders that triumphant banner, they will announce to the astounded lands the divine entrance of the King of heaven" [Matt 24:30].[8] Similarly, the same doctor, after other things, continues: "But the reason why the cross will appear and why the Lord will come preceded by its manifestation is evident: so that those people who have crucified the Lord of majesty may learn the intention of their iniquity. In fact, by this sign the shameless impiety of the Jews is blamed. And since for this reason he will come with the cross, listen to him as he declares in the Gospel: 'and all the tribes of the earth will mourn' [Matt 24:30] seeing the same cross as their accuser and, while it accuses them, they will be aware, but too late, of their sin, and in vain they will recognize their cruel blindness. Why do you marvel, therefore, if he comes bearing the cross, given that he will then also show his wounds? 'They will look,' it is said, 'upon him whom they have pierced' [John 19:37; see Zech 12:10]."

VI The terror and the horror from the vision of the devil, when he will be taken to be led to judgment.

"When the devil will be brought away to be condemned, many of the chosen, who will already be found with the body when the Lord will come for the judgment, will shake from fear seeing that the impious one is punished with such a serious sentence. For this terror they will be purified, since if in them anything of sin still remains from the body, they will be purified by the same terror with which they see the devil condemned. What Job says derives from this: 'When he will rise, the angels will be afraid, and, petrified, they will be purified' [Job 41:17],[9] thus intending like angels also each of the saints and the chosen."

VII Christ, coming for the judgment, will show himself to be gentle with the just and terrible with the unjust.

When the Redeemer of humankind appears, he will be gentle with the just and terrible with the unjust. In fact, he whom the chosen will trustingly see as gentle will be seen by the ungodly as dreadful and terrible. Yet, for this reason, the chosen will not see him as terrible, because they do not cease even now to consider the fear of him. And therefore the ungodly will look at him as terrible because even now they hold in so little account the fear of him in the last judgment and, what is still worse, they lie, as it were, without fear, in their vices.[10]

VIII The just and the unjust will see with the eyes of the body the Christ, who, in the flesh, is coming to judge.

When Christ, the Son of God, comes to pass judgment, all the just and unjust will see his humanity in the same way. The unjust, nevertheless, will not see his divinity since only the just were promised to see it. That the unjust would not see his divinity then was attested to by Isaiah, who says: "the ungodly is carried away so that he does not see the majesty of the Lord" [Isa 26:10]. From this it clearly follows that "anyway the ungodly will then see the humanity of Christ, in which he was judged, so that they grieve about it; certainly they will not see his divinity, so that they may not have joy from it. In fact, those to whom the divinity is shown are certainly shown so that they may have joy from it."[11]

VIIII Why it is to be believed that not the Father but only the Son will come to pass judgment.

About this theme the blessed Augustine says: "The Father will not come to judge the living and the dead, nor however will the Father be separated from his Son. In what sense will he not come? For it is not he that will appear in the judgment. 'They shall look on him whom they have pierced' [John 19:37]. He will appear in that same human form in which he appeared when he was submitted to the judgment: what was judged will judge. It was judged unjustly, but it will judge rightly."[12] "Since therefore in the books of the prophets one reads that God will come to pass judgment, even though there is no distinction indicated about him, on the basis of the judgment only the Christ is to be understood; since even if the Father will judge, he will judge through the coming of the Son of Man. In fact, he 'will not judge anyone' with the manifestation of his presence, 'but he has given all judgment to the Son' [John 5:22]; since he who will manifest himself as man to judge was judged as man."[13]

X The question of "when" Christ will come down from heaven to judge the living and the dead is not a concern of this life.

We believe, consequently, that it does not concern this present life "when" Christ the judge, coming down from the skies, will appear plainly to all. In fact, according to the well-founded doctrine of the blessed Augustine, "what we confess as the future event regarding Christ, that is, that he will come from heaven to judge the living and the dead, does not concern our life that we live here, since it does not concern the things that he has done, but the realities that are to be done at the end of the world. Regarding this the apostle, continuing, added: 'When Christ your life appears, then you also will appear with him in glory' [Col 3:4]."[14] When, therefore, he comes, he will judge the living and the dead, because both the just, still living, and the deceased, rightly called the dead, will anyway be judged by him: "or rather we intend as living those who here have not yet died, and whom his coming will find still living in this flesh; and as dead those who, before his coming, have departed from the body or are on the verge of departing from it."[15]

XI The judges' seats.

We call "seats" what the Greeks call "thrones";[16] the Greeks, in fact, call seats "thrones." The saints, then, for as much as they themselves are seats of God, according to what is written: "the soul of the just is seat of wisdom" [see Wis 7],[17] will nevertheless have some seats upon which they will sit with Christ the judge, according to what the same truth says: "Truly I tell you, at the renewal of all things, when the Son of Man is seated on the throne of his glory, you who have followed me will also sit on twelve thrones, judging the twelve tribes of Israel" [Matt 19:28].[18]

XII Those who will sit with the Lord to judge.

It is clearer than day that all the saints who have departed the world in a perfect way will judge the others, sitting with the Lord. Therefore, what is read in the divine writings will then be fulfilled: "The man of God is known in the city gates, taking his seat among the elders of the land" [Prov 31:23].[19]

XIII It is not to be believed that only the twelve apostles will sit on the above-mentioned twelve seats, but the whole number of perfect ones who will be subdivided by Christ into numbers of twelve.

Concerning this, St. Augustine thus says in his treatises: "in fact since the Lord has said that his disciples will sit on twelve thrones, we ought not to suppose that only twelve men will judge together with him. For with the number twelve is meant, in a certain sense, the multitude of all those who will judge, since the two parts of the number seven indicate the totality of a whole; these two parts, meaning three and four, multiplied one with another, result in twelve, three times four, in fact, and four times three makes twelve. Another meaning can be found in the number twelve, which is toward this end. Otherwise, since we read that the apostle Matthias was selected [see Acts 1:26] in place of Judas the traitor, the apostle Paul [see 1 Cor 15:10], who worked more than all the others, would not have a place to sit in judgment; and yet he clearly demonstrates that he belongs to the number of the judges, together with the other saints, when he says: 'Do you not know that we are to judge angels?' [1 Cor 6:3]. The same observation regarding the number twelve is to be made with respect to those who are to be judged. It was said: 'judging the twelve tribes of Israel' [Matt 19:28], but not for this will the tribe of Levi, which is the thirteenth, not be judged by them; that is, they will judge only that people and not also the other peoples. Since then it was said: 'at the renewal of all things' [Matt 19:28], without a doubt it was understood to mean the resurrection of the dead. So then our flesh will be regenerated through incorruptibility, as our soul has been regenerated through faith."[20]

XIIII The final resurrection of the human body.

"Anyone who is really a Christian must in no way doubt that the flesh of all mankind, of those who have been born and will be born, and of those who have died and will die, will rise again, since the Lord says: 'In truth, in truth I tell you: the moment has come, and it is this, in which the dead who are in their graves will hear his voice and will come out—those who have done good, to the resurrection of life, and those who have done evil, to the resurrection of condemnation' [see John 5:25–28, 29)."[21]

XV When the seventh angel sounds the trumpet,
the resurrection of the dead will occur in a wink.

The blessed Jerome, commenting in his letter to Minervius[22] on the opinions of some who had disputed about the resurrection, thus affirms: "We are addressing why the apostle has written [1 Cor 15:52; see 1 Thess 4:15] that the dead will rise to *the last trumpet.* If, in fact, it is said that it is the last, this certainly means that others have preceded it. In the Apocalypse of John [see Rev 8—11] seven angels are described with trumpets, and when each of them plays, or rather the first one, the second, the third, the fourth, the fifth, and the sixth, it becomes apparent what each has done. At the sound of the last, that is, of the seventh, who will play the trumpet with a ringing sound, the dead will resuscitate, taking back as incorruptible the bodies that they had before as corruptible." Concerning what the apostle affirms about the resurrection of the dead, that is, that all the dead will rise in a wink to the sound of the last trumpet, the previously mentioned doctor says: "The resurrection of the dead will happen with so much speed that the living, whom the time of the consummation will find in their bodies, will not succeed in preceding the dead, who will rise from the underworld. In fact, when he says: the universal resurrection will happen in an instant, in the wink of an eye and in a moment, he excludes all the foolishness about a first and a second resurrection, as if one should believe that some will be the first to be raised and others last." Therefore he subsequently says: "We are to understand this in the same way that we understand that a light feather, a piece of straw, or a thin and dried leaf are lifted aloft by a gust of wind and a puff and are brought high from the earth; likewise, by a glance or a movement of God the bodies of the dead will move, ready at the arrival of the judge."

XVI The resurrection concerns all human beings, while the transformation concerns only the saints.

Here, the apostle says: "For the trumpet will sound, and the dead will be raised incorruptible, and we will be transformed" [1 Cor 15:52]. But just because there is a general resurrection of all the good and bad, it is not to be believed that there is a common transformation for all the just. In fact, according to what has been attested to by the blessed Augustine,[23] Jerome,[24] Julian Pomerius[25] and others, the resurrection will be the same for all the good and the evil; yet the transformation will be granted only to the just, which certainly involves the glorification of eternal beatitude.

XVII It is not an ethereal body that rises, but the flesh that we bear, without any corruption.

In no way are we to listen to those who make up stories about not knowing which kind of body will rise ethereal rather than of flesh. Instead, according to the truth of sacred history, everyone will rise in this body in which they live. In fact, not to mention the others, I briefly reproduce here the words of our excellent preceptor Eugene, bishop of the see of Toledo: "We profess," he says, "in all truth the resurrection of the flesh, and not, as those who rave, that we will rise in an ethereal or some other flesh, but in this one in which we are and we live, in which also each will deserve to receive either the crown for right behavior or the punishment for wicked actions."[26]

XVIII How we believe that we will then have spiritual bodies, when our future bodies are truly admitted not as spirits but as bodies.

"The bodies of the saints will rise again without any defect, without any deformity, as well as without corruption, weariness, deficiency. In them there will be as much readiness as happiness. By the fact that they are called spiritual, without any doubt, however, the future bodies will not be spirit. But just as the body is called now animal, though the body is certainly not soul, so then the body will be spiritual, and nevertheless the body will not be spirit."[27]

XVIIII The property of the bodies that will be in the resurrection.

As Julian Pomerius affirms: "The condition of their bodies that the condemned or the blessed will receive will be equally incorruptible and immortal; but the places and the merits they themselves will receive will be incomparably different and separate from one to the other. Thus the apostle affirms: 'We will all certainly rise again, but we will not all be transformed' [1 Cor 15:51].[28] What is meant by 'we will all rise again' is that there will be only one resurrection of all mankind, such that all the bodies of mankind, granted only one incorruptibility and immortality, can be eternally either in punishment or in reward. Therefore, it is to be believed that they will all rise together; but the impious will be sent to torture, the sinners to final judgment, while the saints are sent to the reward. The bodies of the condemned, however, will not be so immortal and incorruptible as if, unable to be corrupted or die, they could not feel any sensation of pain; but, since they have been situated in the eternal torments, the great pain neither weakens as it torments, nor destroys them; and for this reason the immortal flesh lives together with its condemned soul, in such a way as to feel; and it feels, to suffer, and undergoes pain, because it receives the things worthy of its merits."[29]

XX In what age or stature will be those who rise,
whether elderly, young, or children.

The most blessed Augustine, wanting to answer all those who obstinately and in various ways debated this problem, says: "If we were to say that even the taller bodies are to be reduced to the size of the body of the Lord, a large part of the body of such would be lost, while he himself promised that not even a hair would be lost. It remains, therefore, that everyone will get back their own bodily measure that they had in youth, even if they had died old, or the one they would have had, if they had died earlier. And furthermore, with respect to what the apostle recalls about 'the measure that suits the full maturity of Christ' [Eph 4:13],[30] we can interpret what was said in that the bodies of the dead will rise again in a form that is neither inferior nor superior to that of their juvenile aspect, but in the age and strength that we know that Christ had reached in this life (in fact, even the most learned of our time have determined that indeed youth occurs until around thirty years, which when it is limited by its own duration, beginning from that moment one declines from the strain of increased and senile age). Therefore we interpret that what the apostle said is not to be understood as the dimension of the body or the measure of stature but 'in the measure that suits the full maturity of Christ'[31] [Eph 4:13]. All therefore will rise again in the body as large as they were, or as they would have been, in juvenile age; therefore there will be no difficulty even if the form of the body is infantile or aged, in a condition in which no deficiency of the body nor of the mind will remain."[32] "For which," the aforesaid doctor subsequently adds, "if anyone claims that each will rise again in that bodily form in which they died, it is not necessary to oppose them with a laborious reply."[33] I will not overlook what Julian Pomerius also said concerning the subject: "Reasonably," he said, "about the age I do not believe that there is any problem, because whether babies are deprived of life in the maternal womb, or when they are already born, it is believed that they will rise again in that form that they would have reached if they had lived, advancing in years; since if the resurrection restores nature, nothing can come short of the perfection of nature."[34] This, the aforesaid doctor adds, also happens for those who die in advanced age, and he says: "Also he who will die in advanced or even decrepit age, will rise again in the age in which he was young, since every weakness of old age is eliminated by then. Or, if it corresponds more to that blessed time in which all the saints, without any defect to their beatitude, will be destined to live, if a diversity of ages may exist there, it will be such as not to imply any impediment or dishonour to those who reign without end."[35] And similarly he adds: "What we have said about age, the same can be understood about stature."[36]

XXI Whether the statures and the shapes of the bodies that rise again will be identical or different, and if in the resurrection the thin ones will preserve the same thinness and the fat ones the same fatness.

Concerning the stature with which in general the bodies will rise again, the most blessed Augustine, in a clear dissertation declaring his opinion, affirms: "It is not logical that the risen individuals have a different stature because they had different ones while alive, or that the thin ones will be resurrected with the same thinness and the fat ones with the same fatness. But if it is in the plan of the Creator that in everyone's aspect a characteristic identity and a recognizable similarity are preserved, and that, on the contrary, to the other elements of body an equal wholeness is restored, then the material constitution of everyone will be modified in such a way that nothing perishes, and every lacking thing is compensated by him who could create what he wanted even from nothing. If then in the risen bodies there will be reasonable diversity, such as happens to the voices with which a song is performed, this will concern in everyone the physical structure of their body so as to assign the body to the angelic hosts, without provoking any disadvantage to their sensitivity."[37]

XXII The bodies of the saints will rise again without any deformity.

"The bodies of all the saints will rise again," overflowing with every happiness and glory of immortality, and as they will be "without any corruption, lack, weariness, so they will be also without any deformity; in whose bodies," as St. Augustine affirms, "there will be as much swiftness as happiness."[38] The same doctor teaches that the "scars" may be visible in the bodies of the martyrs, but he believes that this will happen without showing any deformity. "In those bodies, in fact," as the same eminent doctor affirms, "there will be no deformity but beauty and in the body a great splendor will shine, even if not of the body but of the virtue."[39]

XXIII Concerning the bodies of the reprobates, it is superfluous to investigate in what size of the body or in what age they will be risen.

It is totally useless investigating whether the ungodly will be of identical or different stature, since in those who will remain forever distant from the blessed light and from the beauty of the eternal house, stature is not sought, which usually turns to honor, according to what a certain wise man says: "The beauty of bodies is uselessly sought where there will be screeching of teeth, eternal and incessant weeping" [Matt 13:42, 50; 22:13; 24:51; 25:30].[40]

XXIIII Men and women rise again in their own sex.

Most believe, by the fact that the apostle affirms: "Until all of us come unto him, to the measure of perfect man" [Eph 4:13],[41] that all women will rise again as masculine, since man was made from mud, while woman was made from the side of man [Gen 2:21; 3:19].[42] We, however, informed by the teaching of the Catholic masters, believe and consider this, that the Almighty God, who created, founded, and sought to redeem both the one and the other sex, will also reinstate them in the resurrection. Christ the Lord, in fact, tempted by the woman who had lost seven husbands and who asked him to which of her husbands she would have been given back when she herself was dead, answered: "in the resurrection, neither do the women bring husbands, nor the men wives" [see Matt 22:28–30; Luke 20:33–35].[43] From these most holy words it appears clearly evident that gender will not be extinguished there but only the marriage relation, nor will the nature of the flesh have to change, but its concupiscence shall have been extinguished. In fact, the blessed Augustine, facing this problem in his treatises, affirms: "It seems to me that those reason better who do not doubt at all that both genders will rise again. For there will be no sensual passion, which is the cause of disorder. In fact, before they sinned, man and woman were naked, and they were not disturbed. Therefore, the imperfections will be subtracted from those bodies, while the nature will be preserved. In fact, the female sex is not a sin, but is precisely nature, which will then be without a doubt free from carnal intercourse and from childbirth."[44] Having assimilated these reasons from the aforesaid doctor, it will happen as our holy preceptor Eugene teaches: "As great and such is the beauty of the glorified body that, though delighting the sight, nevertheless the heart in no way induces to vice."[45]

XXV No trouble of food or drinks worries those who rise again.

As long as our nature, being corruptible, is subjected to this body, it suffers the need for food and drinks that are given as a sort of medicine for extinguishing the weakness due to corruption and mortality. But once the resurrection of the body has occurred, there will no longer be any need to consume food or drinks, necessity that in this life is attributed to corruption. Indeed, the life that will come after this one will enjoy incorruptibility and immortality. And, in fact, in conformity to what Julian Pomerius affirms: "Having depleted every corruption and mortality, there will be no infirmity of the flesh but nature. Here, then, where flesh can die, it needs to be nourished with food and drinks so as not to succumb to death; in the other life, however, where it cannot die, the need for nourishment will not be felt, because hunger or thirst cannot destroy what is immortal."[46] If one objects to the contrary, saying that it is narrated that the Lord after the resurrection had eaten with his disciples [Luke 24:41–43; John 21:13], and from this his example believes that the risen ones will also eat, the same doctor answers: "Our Lord certainly ate, yet not out of necessity, but out of will; surely not to provide for the weakness of his flesh, but to show those who doubted that he was risen in a true flesh. In fact, if he had been a spirit, as it was then supposed, he would not have been able to consume any carnal food; and so he ate, both to confirm their faith that was starting to waver, and also to show them that he lacked not the possibility but the necessity of eating."[47]

XXVI Our nature does not need bodily garments.

I do not doubt that from the thought of many doctors it has been affirmed that in the glory of that final resurrection garments are not necessary to the bodies, because there will be no illness by which the incorruptible and immortal flesh can be killed, nor will there be any sin by which the soul may be forced to contaminate itself; thus our ancient fathers maintain that those who believe in these things, that is, those who affirm that the risen need clothes, do not believe in all the so-called future goods. And nevertheless, even if clothes happen to be there, as they allege as a reason, the incorruptible bodies will certainly use incorruptible clothes. Similarly Julian Pomerius says: "If our flesh is transformed not in kind, but in quality, and does not become spirit but spiritual, it will not need bodily things; then either there will be no clothes in the resurrection, or if there will be, it is to be believed that they will be totally incorruptible clothes for incorruptible bodies, and the saints will dress in such a way that no concern about themselves can endanger their future happiness; or perhaps the future garments will be of the kind in which the Prophet rejoices to be dressed again, in the image of the church, and he says: 'for he has clothed me with the garments of salvation, he has covered me with the robe of righteousness' [Isa 61:10],"[48] the same doctor referring the term "garments of salvation" to the flesh, and the term "robe of righteousness" rather to the soul. The same doctor thus continues: "If it is so and if it is granted that the risen ones will use garments, neither will they be identical, as it is read, to those that were of the Israelites, because even though for forty years they were preserved by divine will, they were nonetheless then consumed by natural old age; nor will they be identical to those in which Moses and Elias were seen on the mountain with the Lord, or the holy angels, whose clothes then dissolved into nothing from which they had temporarily originated; but perhaps they will be those in which the risen Lord appeared dressed; however, these were not temporarily assumed so that they could be seen by humans, but they were his own. If there will be garments in heaven, whatever or of whatever nature they may be, they will be spiritual for spiritual bodies; and so, although those spiritual [bodies] will not be nude, nevertheless, they will not need material garments."[49] This is what Julian Pomerius teaches. The evident definition of all the many other doctors, according to which the clear thought of our preceptor is invoked,[50] adds this: "Since in the glory of the future resurrection, where there will be no ugliness of the holy bodies nor any adversity of pain or fatigue, it will not be necessary to use garments for those for whom 'Christ is all and in all' [Col 3:11]."[51]

XXVII About the aborted fetuses, and why one ought to consider that from the moment a human being begins to live in the mother's womb, then he or she is related to the final resurrection.

If it can be known with certainty "when a human being begins to live in the mother's womb," it is to be believed in truth that from that moment he or she can also die, and so whoever has life can also die and can then be restored at the time of the resurrection. The blessed Augustine, in fact, not so much debating this matter but proposing it, among other things, thus affirms: "From the time that a human being begins to live, from that moment he or she can also die. I cannot imagine, in truth, that he who is dead, wherever he happened to finish the life, is not related to the resurrection of the dead."[52] Julian Pomerius also says: "Certainly also those who are expelled by the uterus will be resuscitated as if they had lived, and they will not be judged, but punished; because, being damned according to the condemnation of Adam, they had not been freed from the severity of the sentence. And nevertheless, whether the infants are deprived of life in the uterus or upon birth, it is believed that they will rise again with the age that, if they had lived, they would have reached during the course of the years; because if the resurrection restores the nature, nothing can be lacking in the perfection of nature."[53]

XXVIII How it is believed that those who are born with a greater or less number of limbs, or those who are born with two heads and one body or with two bodies and one head or other kinds of monstrosity, will be raised.

Regarding this question, the blessed Augustine thus says: "Nor, in fact is it to be denied that deformed beings who are born and live, even if they die quickly, will be raised, nor is it to be believed that they will be raised in that condition rather than with a restored nature without defects. Far be it from me to maintain that the creature recently born in the East with a double set of limbs, as faithful brothers have reported to me after having seen him and about which the presbyter Jerome,[54] of blessed memory, has left a written account, far be it from me, I say, to think that he will be raised again a single double man, and not rather two, as it would have happened if twins had been born. So, in the resurrection all the single newborns, who, considered in themselves are defined as deformed because they have come to the light with something more or less or with some serious deformity, will be restored to the image of human nature; in this way the single souls will have their single bodies, but without everything together with which they had been born, and provided, each for themselves, with their own limbs, so as to guarantee the full integrity of the human body."[55] Also Julian Pomerius, following the affirmation of the aforesaid doctor, affirms: "This I seem to understand, and that is, that our flesh, whether it is born with a lesser or greater number of limbs, will rise again with the usual and coherent limbs for its integrity, because both in those that have less, and in those that have more, there is a defect that here appears without a doubt contrary to nature, but that, in the future renewal of our body, it is believed that it will be eliminated, along with the corruptibility and mortality; so that the nature of our flesh rises again integral in all of its parts, according to its perfect form, without any diminution or addition of limbs. Also the bodies, whether two are born with only one head, or only one body with two heads, though for us, and especially for me, it is not clear how these things can happen, nevertheless, since I am certain, I affirm, without any ambiguity, that the two bodies will rise again with their respective heads if in them two souls were generated, since it cannot be denied that the individual soul will receive in an immortal way its own body which it had lost; or if only one soul is generated, whether it was generated in only one body with two heads, or in two bodies with only one head, it will receive only one body. And therefore the nature of our flesh, whether losing what is superfluous, or receiving what is lacking, reestablished in its fullness, without any corruption as well as without any illness, will be united to its spirit in an immortal way."[56]

XXVIIII *Those who are devoured here by beasts, or are mutilated from various lacerations, will obtain the integrity of their body in the resurrection.*

St. Augustine says: "The terrestrial matter from which the flesh of the mortals has been created does not perish in front of God; but in whatever dust or ash it is dissolved, in whatever exhalation or wind it becomes volatilized, into whatever substance of other bodies or other elements it is transformed, to whatever food of whatever animal, even of human beings, it is reduced and has been changed into flesh, it will return, in an instant, to that human soul that animated it from the beginning, such that it became a human being, grew and lived."[57] Blessed Gregory, making a similar proposal and discussing this matter in his treatises, affirms: "Some are often accustomed to objecting with this weak question: the wolf ate the flesh of a human being, the lion devoured the wolf; then, dying, the lion returned to dust; when that dust will be resuscitated, how can the human flesh be distinguished from that of the wolf or of the lion? To these what else can we answer if not that they must first reflect upon how they came into this world, and then they will discover in what nature they will rise again? Certainly you, O human who speaks, were once foam of blood in the womb of the mother; here you were a small and liquid agglomeration that originated from the seed of the father and from the blood of the mother. Do tell me, I beg you, if you know it, how did that humor of the seed harden into bones, how did the liquid stay in the marrows, how did it consolidate into nerves, how did it grow into flesh, how was

it stretched into skin, how was it distinguished into hairs and fingernails, such that the hairs are softer than the flesh and the fingernails
more tender than the bones, but harder than the flesh? If, therefore,
such and so many realities derive from only one seed and distinct in
kind, and nevertheless they remain united in only one form, what is
so odd if the almighty God, in the resurrection of the dead, will be
able to distinguish the flesh of mankind from the flesh of beasts, so
that that same and only dust will not rise again in that it is the dust of
the wolf or of the lion, and nevertheless it will rise again in that it was
the dust of mankind?"[58]

XXX Those who have departed this life as cripples will be resurrected with all their limbs.

If someone, invalid in the body, departs this life maimed or crip-
pled, there is no doubt that they can be reinstated in the due integrity
of the limbs at the moment of the resurrection; just as anything that
illness deformed in them or the cruelty of others mutilated, so will the
beauty of immortality transform it in order for it not to be seen here
as deformed nor as things unnecessary, nor dishonorable, nor dimin-
ished. In this way, in fact, does the blessed Augustine say: "Thin or fat,
they need not fear being here what they would not have wanted to be
even in the world if they could have helped it. All the beauty of the
body consists in the proportion of the parts, together with a certain
softness of its color. Where, then, there is no proportion of the parts,
something is not pleasant because it is deformed or because it is lacking or because it is exaggerated. Consequently, there will be no deformity, which is produced by the disproportion of the parts, there where
the realities that are deformed will be amended, and what is less than
appropriate will be brought to perfection by something that the
Creator knows, and what is greater than appropriate will be eliminated, except for the integrity of the matter."[59] Therefore, instructed
by the wise exposition of this doctor, we believe that also those whom
we have seen with our own eyes as having six fingers on the hands or
six toes on the feet, will not rise again with this deformity, once the
integrity of the body is saved; they will be with the number of fingers
that maintains the proportion of the bodily parts. I say the proportion
of the bodily parts, just as it occurs in the natural order of being born,
such that everyone has two eyes, two ears, five fingers on each hand,

and five toes on each foot, without adding or removing anything that brings deformity to the parts, so as to make us believe that nothing of the body can go lost. St. Augustine, in fact, says: "I did not say this because I believe that for any body a connatural part will be lost; but only what was born in a deformed way."[60]

XXXI Whether it is believable that in the resurrection all that had been taken from the fingernails and from our hairs, by cutting or dissection, will be restored.

About this the most blessed Augustine says: "Therefore the same earthly material, which becomes a corpse when the soul departs, in the resurrection will not be restored as those things that dissolve and are transformed into so many other things and other kinds and forms, even though they return to the body from which they were separated, it is necessary that they also be rejoined with the parts of the body in which they were situated. After all, if to the hair of the head is restored what a frequent cut subtracted, if to the nails what so many times had been clipped away, this lack of form appears excessive and inconvenient to those who think and do not believe in the resurrection of the flesh."[61] Therefore, as the same doctor says in another one of his works: "If the hair so many times shortened and the nails so many times clipped were to be restored to their places in a disorderly fashion, then they would not be restored; yet, nevertheless, they shall not be lost for those who will rise again; because, respecting the proportion of the parts, they shall be rejoined to the same flesh with the mutation of the matter so that here [that is, in the afterworld] any part of the body may be constituted in it. Though what the Lord says: 'But not a hair of your head will perish' [Luke 21:18], can be much more adequately understood as having been said not of the length but of the number of hairs; for in another place he says this: 'And even the hairs of your head are all counted' [Matt 10:30; see Luke 12:7]."[62] The same doctor, using for this question a similitude, says: "What, then, should I answer about the hair and the nails? Once it is understood that nothing of the body will perish, such that in the body there is nothing irregular, it is at the same time understood that all the parts that would have produced an excessive irregular greatness shall be joined to the same whole, not in those zones in which the form of the limbs is disfigured. As if one makes a vessel with the clay that, reduced again in clay, was reconstructed anew, it would not be necessary for that part of the clay that made up the handle to return to be handle, or for the part that had constituted the base to return to be the base, provided, nevertheless, that all of it return to all, that is, that all the clay, without any part of it being lost, returns to be the vessel."[63] This way, therefore, the same doctor affirms: "It does not concern the reinstatement of the body that hairs return to hairs and nails to nails, or if anything of them be perished, changed into flesh and other parts of the body, the providence of the maker taking care that there be nothing inappropriate."[64]

XXXII How those who have not been separated from the masses in perdition will be raised.

The most blessed Augustine affirms: "All those who have not been freed from that mass of perdition caused by the sin of the first human being, by the action of the only mediator between God and mankind, they too will rise again, each with their own flesh, but to be punished together with the devil and his angels. What need is there to tire ourselves so much researching if they will rise again with the vices and the deformities of their bodies, they who acted in such a way as to fill their limbs with vices and deformities? Neither, certainly, should the search for their physical features or beauty tire us in that their damnation will be certain and eternal. Nor should it agitate us in what way they shall have an incorruptible body, if it can be subject to suffering, or how it shall be corruptible, if it shall not be subject to death. Life is not true life if it is not that in which one lives happily; nor true incorruptibility if not when physical health is not altered by any pain. When, instead, it does not allow the unhappy one to die, or, as it were, death itself does not die, and when the pain without end does not kill, but torments, and such corruption does not have an end, this is what the Sacred Scriptures calls second death."[65]

XXXIII The order of the future judgment.

As we have said that there are some who shall sit with Christ as judges, so it is to be believed that there are others who shall be judged by the host of those who are seated. In fact, two differences or orders of humankind are gathered in the judgment, that is, those who are chosen and those who are reprobates, which, nevertheless, are divided into four. One is the order of the perfect ones who judge together with the Lord, of whom Christ says: "you will also sit on twelve thrones" [Matt 19:28]. These are not judged and they reign. The other order, then, is that of the chosen, to whom it shall be said: "I was hungry and you gave me food" [Matt 25:35]. These are judged and they reign. In the same way there are two orders of reprobates; the one being those who were found outside of the church. These shall not be judged and are lost; about whom also the Psalmist says: "the wicked will not stand in the judgment" [Ps 1:5]. The other order of reprobates is also of those who shall be judged and are lost, to whom it shall be said: "I was hungry and you gave me no food" [Matt 25:42]. "Depart from me, you accursed, into the eternal fire" [Matt 25:41].[66]

XXXIIII The separation of the good and the evil.

Here is what the Psalmist says: "He summons the heavens above and the earth to the judgment of his people" [Ps 50:4].[67] What is it that he says with "the judgment of his people" "if not, through a judgment, to separate the good from the evil, as the lambs from the goats?"[68] In fact, he shall then have the lambs placed on his right and the goats, instead, on his left.

XXXV This separation of the good from the evil occurs through the angelic ministry.

It is to be believed that the separation of the good from the evil, that is, the division, can be carried out through the angels. In fact, when the Psalmist says: "He summons the heavens above and the earth to the judgment of his people" [Ps 50:4], "the judgment of his people" refers to the separation of the good from the evil, and immediately, in fact, he adds: "Gather to him his faithful ones" [Ps 50:5].[69] To whom is it said: "Gather to him his faithful ones," if not especially to the angels? This, in fact, is what St. Augustine says about this text: "Then the discourse is turned to the angels, the Prophet having said: 'Gather to him his faithful ones.' Truly, in fact, such a great task can be accomplished through the angelic ministry."[70]

XXXVI Once the good have been separated on the right side and the evil on the left, the books are opened, that is, the consciences of the individuals.

Therefore, the good having been separated from the evil through the angelic ministry, in the presence of the chosen who are on the right and the reprobates on the left, the books shall then be opened, that is, the consciences of the individuals. In fact, the apostle John says: "And I saw the dead, great and small, standing before the throne, and the books were opened. Also another book was opened, the book of life. And the dead were judged according to their works, as recorded in the books" [Rev 20:12]. It is evident that what is intended by books is all the saints of the New and Old Testaments, in whose lives, as if they were books, we learn how we must live. In this book, then, about which he says: "Also another book was opened, the book of life" [Rev 20:12], which is the life of everyone, it is known, somehow by divine virtue, what good someone has done or has not done.[71] According to what St. Augustine says: "If that book was materially evaluated, who would be able to esteem the greatness or the length of it? And how much time would be required to read a book in which all the lives of humankind have been written? Perhaps there shall be as many angels as there shall be human beings, and everyone shall hear their life narrated by the angel assigned to them? Therefore, there shall not be only one book for all, but one for each. This Scripture, in truth, intending to mean that there is only one book, says: 'Also another book was opened.' Thus a certain divine power must be intended by which it will happen that all the good and bad works of everyone will be recalled by their memory and will be examined with admirable readiness by an evaluation of the intellect, such that the awareness shall accuse or excuse the conscience and each and everyone shall be judged at the same time. This divine power has certainly taken the name of book. In it, indeed, it is read, in a certain sense, all that under its action is recalled."[72] Then the Lord will remind his chosen ones what he had foretold in the Gospel, thus announcing: "Come, you that are blessed by my Father, inherit the kingdom prepared for you from the foundation of the world; for I was hungry and you gave me food, I was thirsty and you gave me something to drink, I was a stranger and you welcomed me, I was naked and you gave me clothing, I was sick and you took care of me,

I was in prison and you visited me" [Matt 25:34–36]. And he will reproach the reprobates who stand on his left side for not having done those things, reminding them, rather, that the ones who stand on his right have done those things. Once these two discourses of our Lord Jesus Christ have been completed, one with which the good works they have done are mentioned to the chosen ones, the other with which those things that they did not do are imputed to the reprobates, "these will go away"—as the Truth confirms—"into eternal punishment, but the righteous into eternal life" [Matt 25:46].

XXXVII *The just will not be afraid to listen to the punishment.*

Therefore, once the Lord has judged the impious and has sent them to the eternal fire, telling them: "depart from me into the eternal fire prepared for the devil and his angels" [Matt 25:41], the just, who have already been placed on the right side, shall not be intimidated at all in hearing this condemnation. In fact, by "hearing this condemnation" the eternal fire is meant, which is inflicted by the Lord; from which then, O Christ, with perpetual mercy, free us, and associate us with you, our head, as coreigning.[73]

XXXVIII *The ruinous fall of the devil and the perdition of the impious.*

With some allusions, the apostle St. John evidently wants to affirm the ruinous fall of the devil into the eternal fire. In fact, after having premised: "And the dead were judged according to their works" [Rev 20:12], he briefly adds in what way they will be judged: "Then Death and Hades," he says, "were thrown into the lake of fire" [Rev 20:14], wanting to designate the devil by these names, since he is the author of death and the infernal punishments, and at the same time the whole company of demons. This is, in fact, what he had previously said more evidently: "And the devil, who had seduced them, was thrown into the lake of fire and brimstone" [Rev 20:15].[74]

XXXVIIII What is that book about which the apostle John says: all those who shall not be found written then in the book of life shall be sent into the pool of fire.

About the resurrection St. John wrote in his Revelation, among other things, that those who shall not be found written in the book of life shall be sent into the lake of fire [see Rev 20:15]. Saying these things, he does not affirm that God suffers from amnesia, almost as if things unknown could be known from reading this book. "But this book," according to what St. Augustine says, "means the predestination of those to whom eternal life shall be given. Not that God ignores them and reads in this book to know them; but rather his very foreknowledge concerning them, which cannot err, is the book of life, in which they have been inscribed, that is, previously foreknown."[75]

XXXX The bodies of the impious shall remain in the fire, without being consumed.

St. Augustine, producing many and different kinds of examples, attests that it is known for certain that the bodies of the impious will burn in eternal fires without being consumed and that the combustion of the fires will not incinerate these same bodies, because they will burn in the eternal fire but cannot die. "What," the same doctor continues, "shall I show for the unbelievers to be convinced that human bodies, animated and living, not only cannot be dissolved by death, but can withstand even the torments of the eternal fires?"[76] "Likewise," after other things, he says: "the soul, whose presence vivifies and governs the body, can feel pain and cannot die; here, then, is found a reality that, though having sensibility to pain, is immortal. What we now know to happen in the souls of all will then also happen in the bodies of the damned."[77] And this being the way of things, he says: "why do they still demand examples from us by which we teach that it is not unusual for the bodies of humans that will be punished with an eternal punishment not to lose the soul in the fire and to burn without loss and to feel pain without end?"[78]

XXXXI How this future fire will burn the demons.

St. Augustine says: "Why could we not say that even the immaterial spirits, although in singular ways, though nonetheless truly, can be afflicted by the punishment of a bodily fire, if the spirits of humankind, which are themselves also certainly incorporeal, could be confined in bodily limbs and united indissolubly to their bodies?"[79] Similarly, the same doctor, after other things, says, "Gehenna, instead, which has been considered also as a lake of fire and brimstone [see Rev 20:9], will be a physical fire and will torment the bodies of the damned, that is to say, the material bodies of human beings and the immaterial ones of the demons, or just the human bodies, with their spirits, and the spirits of demons without a body, joined to the bodily fires, taking on the punishment, and not communicating life. Indeed, as the Truth has said, there will be only one fire both for the ones and for the others"[80] [see Matt 25:41].

XXXXII The variety of punishments in proportion to the diversity of fault.

"Punishment will be the mildest for those who, except for the original sin that they have contracted, will not have added other sins: while for all the rest who have added sin, the punishment will be more tolerable there the less the injustice will have been down here."[81] "In fact, it certainly cannot be denied that the eternal fire, too, based on the diversity of the faults, shall be lighter for some and more serious for others, whether its power and its ardor be different according to the punishment of each, or whether it be that it burns in the same way, but that it is not felt as the identical torment."[82]

XXXXIII Against those who seek in the most meticulous way what this future fire is and in what part of the world it can be found.

The knowledge of the contemporaries, compared to the science of the ancient fathers,[83] must be considered, if I shall not speak rashly, much less inadequately. Insofar as what the fathers and the scholars have claimed not to know, it would be very dangerous and superfluous, therefore, on our part, if anyone attempted to somehow define it; even the blessed Augustine, discussing this same future fire, seemed so to affirm. When, in fact, he spoke of the future damnation, saying: "therefore, those not written in the book of life having been judged and thrown into the eternal fire," he adds, "I think that no man, except perhaps the one to whom the divine Spirit manifests it, knows what type of fire it is and in what part of the world or of reality it will be found."[84]

XXXXIIII The reward of the chosen follows after the damnation of the impious.

The order of the Lord's words that relate to the promise by which we believe that Christ the Lord will give the kingdom to the saints and perennial torture to the reprobates presents itself in such a way that the condemnation of the impious comes first and is then followed by the reward of the chosen ones, as Christ the Lord forewarns: "And the impious will go away into eternal punishment, but the righteous into eternal life" [Matt 25:46]. In the Apocalypse, too, we read that this order is maintained, where it is clearly expressed. First, in fact, it refers us to the punishment of the devil and all his own, and it is said: "Then death and hell were thrown into the lake of fire" [Rev 20:14], and after that it is added about the future beatitude of the saints: "Then I saw a new heaven and a new earth" [Rev 21:1]. From these words it is given to understand that, for the right judgment of God, the sentence shall first be inflicted upon the sinners, and afterward, the eternal rewards shall be granted to the saints.[85]

XXXXV Once the judgment has been completed, the servant aspect with which Christ exercised judgment will pass away, and then Christ will deliver the kingdom to God and Father.

The servant aspect with which Christ will be seen making the judgment will disappear once the judgment is concluded, according to what has previously been written by the pen of the ancient fathers, an aspect that was shown precisely to complete the judgment. "That aspect," it was said, "shall pass, not in that it shall perish, but because it passes 'from the judgment to the kingdom.'" "Certainly the Lord, after the judgment, will change aspect for us," according to what the blessed Gregory says: "Because from the aspect of his humanity he raises us to the contemplation of his divinity. And his change of aspect means leading us to the contemplation of his splendor, because he whom we had seen with a human aspect in the judgment, we can see, after the judgment, also with that of the divinity."[86] Certainly, after the judgment he will hasten from here, and he will bring with himself the body of which he is the head, and he will offer the kingdom "to God and Father" [1 Cor 15:24]. And in which way, therefore, will he deliver the kingdom to God and Father, if not when he will manifest to his friends the vision of his divinity, in which he is one with the Father? And after he has led us, his members, to the vision and knowledge by which it is believed that he is equal with the Father and the Holy Spirit, then that aspect of God that cannot be seen by the reprobates will be completely seen by the chosen ones.

XXXXVI *The conflagration of fire by which, it is said, this world will perish.*

From the clear teaching of the ancient fathers it is determined that "once the judgment has been completed, then this sky and this earth will cease to exist, when a new heaven and a new earth will begin to exist. In fact, this world will pass away with a metamorphosis of things, not with a total destruction."[87] "Therefore, the form of this world will then pass away in the conflagration of all fires of the world, as the deluge happened with the flood of all the waters of the world. And so, as I have said, in that universal conflagration the properties of the corruptible elements that were appropriate for our corruptible bodies will disappear by being completely burned; and the same substance of being will have those properties that, for an extraordinary metamorphosis, are appropriate for immortal bodies, such that the world, clearly understood as renewed for the better, be adequately suited for mankind transformed for the better also in the flesh."[88]

XXXXVII *Once the judgment has been completed, the new heaven and the new earth will begin to exist.*

As the blessed Augustine says: "once the judgment has been completed and finished, then this heaven and this earth will cease to exist, when a new heaven and a new earth will begin to exist. In fact, this world will pass away with a metamorphosis of things, not for a total destruction."[89] Thus, the apostle also says: "'[For] the present form of this world is passing away' [1 Cor 7:31]; so the form passes away, not the nature."[90]

XXXXVIII Not all who rise again will be in the new heaven and new earth, but only the saints.

According to what we read in the codices of some authors, the sinners and the impious, though as risen are incorruptible and immortal, will nevertheless not be on the new earth, because they will be completely extraneous to the transformation of the saints. When, in fact, the apostle says: "We all, in truth, will rise again, but not all of us will be transformed" [1 Cor 15:51],[91] in general it suggests that there will be a future resurrection for everyone, while the transformation counts only for the glory of the saints.

XXXXVIIII Against those who say that if after judgment has been passed the conflagration of the world will take place, where then can the saints be so as not to be reached by the flame of fire?

The blessed Augustine so resolves this matter: "Perhaps someone," he says, "could ask: if, after the judgment has been concluded, this world will burn before it is replaced by a new heaven and a new earth, where will the saints be in the very moment of its conflagration, since they, having bodies, must be in some physical place? We can reply that they will be in the most elevated parts, where the flame of that fire will not reach, just as the wave of the deluge did not. In fact, their bodies will be such that they will be there, wherever they will want to be. But, rendered immortal and incorruptible, they will not be frightened by the blaze of that fire, if the corruptible and mortal bodies of the three men [Dan 3:23ff.] could remain unharmed in the burning furnace."[92]

L The reward and the kingdom of the saints when Christ, after having girded himself, upon passing will serve his own.

The reward of the blessed is the vision of God, which will give us ineffable joy. This reward is what I believe the prophet referred to when he said: "What no eye has seen, nor ear heard, nor the human heart conceived, what God has prepared for those who love him" [1 Cor 2:9; see Isa 64:4]. Even Truth itself, substituting for the reward the manifestation of his vision and promising it to his friends, says: "Whoever loves me, observes my commandments, and whoever loves me will be loved by my Father and I will also love him and will reveal myself to him" [John 14:21].[93] And in fact, according to the words of the same holy truth, he will then gird himself, and he will place us at table and, passing, he will serve us [see Luke 12:37]. "He will gird himself, therefore," as the blessed Gregory says, "that is, he prepares himself for the reward. He will place us at table, that is, he makes us relive in eternal peace; in fact, being seated in the kingdom means for us to be in peace. And passing, the Lord will then serve us, in that he satisfies us with the splendor of his light. What is said: *passes*, means that the Lord almost passes from the judgment to the kingdom."[94]

LI Then the wicked will not know what happens in the joy of the blessed, while the good will know what happens in the punishment of the miserable.

"Those who will be in the torments will not have knowledge of what happens inside, in the joy of the Lord; however, those who will be in that joy will have awareness of what happens in the darkness outside. For this it was said"[95] by the Prophet about the saints: "And they shall go out and see the corpses of the people who have rebelled against me" [Isa 66:24]. But what he said: "they shall go out," means "almost as a science,"[96] that is to say, "because it shall not be hidden to them even those things that happen entirely outside of them. If in fact the prophets could know these events even if they had not yet happened, for as little a way, in their mortal minds since God was present; how then shall the immortal saints not know what has already happened, since God shall be all in all? [see 1 Cor 15:28]."[97]

LII Then we can be led to and live in heaven with this body in which we now live.

St. Augustine, appropriately disputing against the Platonists, who claim that the human body cannot ascend to heaven, explains this, and shows with excellent examples of reasoning, that our bodies, becoming immortal after the resurrection, can have an abode in heaven.[98] In fact, certainly "after the resurrection, the saints were promised ascension into heaven in the flesh; Christ, in fact, said to the Father: 'I desire that where I am, they also be with me' [John 17:24].[99] If, in fact, we are members of the head, and one in himself and in us is Christ, undoubtedly, wherever he ascends, we will also ascend."[100]

LIII Whether we will then have more refined movements of the body, and whether they will be identical to those that we seem to have now.

About the movements of the body, St. Augustine, afraid to furnish a definitive teaching, thus says: "I dare not determine what the movements of such bodies will be there, because I am unable to imagine it; nevertheless both movement and stillness, as well as the semblances, whatever they may be, will be appropriate, since whatever will be inopportune will not be there at all. Certainly wherever the spirit will want, the body will be there immediately; and the spirit will not want anything that may be inopportune for the spirit and for the body."[101]

LIIII Whether God then is seen through these bodily eyes, with which we there see the sun and the moon.

St. Augustine, perspicaciously disputing whether we will be able to see God through our bodily eyes in the future life, says: "Therefore, when I am asked what these eyes will do in that spiritual body, I do not say what I already see, but I say what I believe in, according to what I read in the Psalm: 'I have believed and for this I have spoken' [Ps 116:10].[102] I say, therefore: they will see God in this body; nevertheless it is not a small matter if they will see him through the body, as through it we now see the sun, the moon, the stars, the earth, and the things that are found upon it. It is, in fact, hard to affirm that the saints will then have such bodies as not to be able to close or open the eyes when they want; besides, it is even more difficult to maintain that whoever shall close their eyes there shall not see God. Far be it, therefore, from saying that those saints will not see God in that life with the eyes closed, since they will always see him with the spirit. But, rather, the question is whether the saints will see God through these eyes of the body when they hold them open, if in fact also those same spiritual eyes in the spiritual body will have their power, such as we now have them—without a doubt God cannot be seen through them. Their power will be much different, therefore, if through them that incorporeal nature will be seen that is not contained in space but is all everywhere. For which" according to what the same doctor says, "it can happen, and it is very believable, that we shall then see the bodies belonging to a world of a new heaven and a new earth, such that in the most limpid clarity, through the bodies that we shall possess and that we shall perceive, wherever the eyes shall turn, we shall see God, who is present everywhere and who also governs all material things,"[103] not as the intellects now recognize the invisible realities of God in the things that are created, as in a mirror, in a confused and partial way, where the faith by which we believe has more value in us than the kinds of bodily realities that we distinguish through the eyes of the body.[104] But as soon as we recognize the human beings in the midst of whom we live, as existing and through their vital movements, we do not believe them to live, but we ascertain it, and even if we cannot see their life without the bodies, nevertheless we distinguish it in them without equivocation through the bodies. In the same way, wherever we shall turn those spiritual lights of our bodies, we shall observe, also through the bodies, the incorporeal God, who sustains all things. Therefore, either God will be so seen through those eyes, such that they have, in their superiority, something similar to the mind with which the incorporeal nature will also be seen, which is, however, either difficult or impossible to demonstrate with some examples and with the testimonies of the Sacred Scriptures; or, and this is easier to understand, all of God will be so equally visible so as to be seen by the spirit of each of us in every one of us, he will be seen by one in the other, he will be seen in himself, he will be seen in the new heaven and in the new earth and in every creature that will then be there, he will also be seen through the bodies in each body, wherever the eyes of the spiritual body will be turned with an acute sight that reaches the object. Even our intentions will reciprocally be manifest. Then, in fact, the thought of the apostle will be fulfilled, who, after having said: "Therefore do not pronounce judgment before the time," added immediately: "before the Lord comes. He will bring to light the secrets of the darkness and will show the intentions of the hearts; then everyone will have his praise from God" [1 Cor 4:5].[105]

LV Then we will see God with that vision with which the angels now see him.

We read in the Gospel that Christ said: "'Take care that you do not despise one of these little ones; for, I tell you, in heaven their angels continually see the face of my Father in heaven' [Matt 18:10]. Thus, as they see him, so also will we see him. Yet we do not yet see him so. Therefore, the apostle says: 'For now we see in a mirror, dimly, but then we will see face to face' [1 Cor 13:12]. So this vision is reserved to us as a reward of faith; about this the apostle John says: 'When he is revealed, we will be like him, for we will see him as he is' [1 John 3:2]. God's face, however, must be intended as a manifestation of him, not as that determined part that we have in the body and that without a doubt we call with this name."[106] We will then be, therefore, similar to the angels because as they now see, so also we will see God after the resurrection.

LVI In the life in which they cannot sin, all the saints will exercise free will more steadily than in this life.

All of the doctors clearly indicate that in that life the capacity of free will shall be greater for us than down here. If, in fact, as someone says, most live with free will in this life, during which, even if they can avoid the sins, nevertheless they cannot be without sin, how shall they not be more free in the soul there where the blessed will be so united to God so as not in any way to be subject to sin? In fact, the more one is free, the more that person is absolved from sins. And thus in that blessed life they will all be even more free so they will not be able to sin. In fact, according to what seems to me, if we are promised equality with the angels, how then shall we not have the free will by which they eternally praise God? Nevertheless, what perhaps happens for the reprobates is probably uncertain; because according to the thought of one who is rather hesitant about the matter, "for those who shall be estranged from the life of the saints, I do not know if there can somehow be free will for those who, condemned to the eternal combustion of the vengeful flames, can have neither a free soul nor a free body."[107]

LVII Then we will have forgetfulness and memory in an equal way.

"For what concerns the intellectual knowledge, everyone will also remember their past evils, but on the level of the sensible experience no one will remember absolutely anything. In fact, even the best physician knows almost all the illnesses of the body, as they are known in the art of medicine; but he is oblivious of many of them as they can be known in the body, not having experienced them. Therefore, just as there are two kinds of knowledge of evils, one by which they are not unknown to the power of the mind, the other because they belong to the experience of the senses (one thing, in fact, is to know all the vices through the teaching of wisdom, another is to know them through a foolish life), likewise there are two ways to forget the evils; the wise person forgets in one way; while whoever has experienced and suffered forgets in another way; the former by ignoring knowledge, the latter by avoiding unhappiness. Based on this forgetfulness, which is put in second place, the saints will not be mindful of the past evils; in fact all will be deprived of them, such that they will be canceled completely from their senses. However, with the capacity of knowledge that will be great in them, not only will their past not be hidden, but also the eternal misfortune of the damned will not be hidden to them. Otherwise, if they will be oblivious of having been unhappy, how can they say with the Psalmist: 'I will sing without end the graces of the Lord' [Ps 89:2]?"[108]

LVIII The variety of the merits and rewards in which, nevertheless, no one will envy anyone.

As St. Augustine says, "who is able to think, and even more, to say what shall be the various degrees of honors"[109] and the glories that will be in that life? Yet, that they shall be there is not to be doubted. "And that blessed city shall have in itself a good also for the fact that no inferior being shall envy any superior being, as now the other angels do not envy the archangels; as no one will want to be what they have not received, even though they are linked by the most serene bond of harmony to the one who has received it, as not even in the body does the eye want to be what the finger is, although the harmonious structure of the whole flesh contains both the one and the other member. Thus, certainly, one will have a smaller gift than the other, in order to have this gift as well, to desire no more."[110]

LVIIII The saints will praise God tirelessly.

The praise with which they will honor God will not be tiring for the saints, because according to what the Prophet says of them: "they will not be troubled nor will they get tired" [see Isa 40:31]. Indeed, they will enjoy the beatitude of eternity: this will be the reward of beatitude for them, in that they will be devoted to the incessant exultation of praise. The Psalm, in fact, says: "Blessed are those who dwell in your house, Lord, they will praise you forever and ever" [Ps 84:5].[111] "Therefore, he who has given virtue will be the reward for virtue."[112]

LX We will see God without end and he is the fulfillment of our desires.

If, according to what the apostle says, "we will be with the Lord for ever" [1 Thess 4:17], it is also certain that we will see him without interruption. "Christ will then be the fulfillment of all our desires, he who will be contemplated without end, loved without satiety, praised without weariness. This gift and this love, this action will certainly be common to all, just like eternal life itself."[113]

LXI Then God himself will be our reward, and our virtuous desires will be satisfied in a marvelous way.

He who created us promised us that he would give us himself as reward, than which nothing is better. "What else is meant by what he said through the Prophet: 'I will be your God, and you shall be my people' [Lev 26:12], if not: 'I shall be the one by whom they shall be satiated; I shall be those things that are virtuously desired by humanity, the life and the well-being and the nourishment and the abundance and the glory and the honor and the peace and every other good'? Thus, in fact, what the apostle says is also correctly understood: 'so that God may be all in all' [1 Cor 15:28]."[114]

LXII *The end without end in which we will praise God infinitely.*

Christ, our end, rendering us perfect, will be at the same time solace and our praise; we will praise him forever and ever and, praising him without end, we will love him. "There," says the most holy doctor Augustine, "truly will be the supreme Sabbath without sunset, which the Lord commanded to observe in the beginning of the works of creation, where it is read: 'And on the seventh day God finished the work that he had done, and he rested on the seventh day from all the work that he had done. God blessed the seventh day and consecrated it, because on it he rested from every work he had done creating it' [Gen 2:2]. In fact, we ourselves will be the seventh day, when we will be filled and restored to his blessing and glorification.[115] There it will be fulfilled: 'Be still and know that I am God' [Ps 46:11]."[116] Then truly it "will be our Sabbath, which will not end with sunset, but rather, the day of the Lord or the eternal eighth day, which has been consecrated by the resurrection of Christ....There we will rest and we will see, we will see and we will love, we will love and we will praise. Here is what will be at the end without end! In fact, what else is our end, if not to reach the kingdom of which there is no end?"[117]

[END OF THE CHAPTERS OF THE THIRD BOOK]

[END OF THE PROGNOSTICUM OF SAINT JULIAN, BISHOP OF THE TOLEDAN SEE]

NOTES

CHAPTER I

1. In this brief presentation of the historical, social, and religious environment of Visigothic Spain in which Julian of Toledo was born and lived, the following studies were referenced from among the thousands possible: R. Aigrain, "La Spagna cristiana," in *Storia della Chiesa*, vol. 5, *San Gregorio Magno, gli stati barbarici e la conquista araba (590–757)* (Rome/Turin, 1980), 315–52; J. Fontaine, "Conversion et culture chez les Visigoths d'Espagne," in *Settimane di Studio*, XIV, *La conversione al cristianesimo nell'Europa dell'alto Medio Evo* (Spoleto, 1967), 87–147; *The Early Middle Ages to 1300*, ed. R. Crocker and D. Hiley (Oxford, 1990); J. N. Hillgarth, *Christianity and Paganism, 350–750: The Conversion of Western Europe* (Philadelphia, 1986); idem, "La conversión de los visigotos: notas críticas," *Analecta Sacra Tarraconensia* 34 (1961): 17–46; idem, "Historiography in Visigothic Spain," in *La storiografia altomedievale: Settimane di Studio del Centro Italiano di Studi sull'alto medioevo* 17 (Spoleto, 1970), 261–311; A. Momigliano, *The Conflict between Paganism and Christianity in the Fourth Century* (Oxford, 1963); J. O'Callaghan, *A History of Medieval Spain* (Ithaca, NY, 1975); J. Orlandis, *Historia de España: La España Visigótica* (Madrid, 1977); R. M. Pidal, *Historia de España: España visigoda* (Vol. III 1/3), Reedición (Madrid, 1985); M. Sotomayor et al., *Historia de la Iglesia en España, I, La Iglesia en la España romana y visigoda (siglos I al VIII)* (Madrid, 1979); J. Orlandis, *La vida en España en tiempo de los Godos* (Madrid, 1991); *Historia de la Iglesia en España*, ed. R. García Villoslada (Madrid, 1979).

2. After the sack of Rome in 410, the Ostrogoths built an empire that had its center in Italy with its imperial capital in Ravenna.

3. Brother-in-law and successor, as king of the Goths, of Alaric. He reigned from 410 to 415, the year in which he was murdered in Barcelona. In Narbonne he married Galla Placidia, sister of the emperor Honorius. While outwardly showing respect and admiration for the Roman tradition, in reality he was a firm opponent of the empire. His kingdom was reduced to the Iberian Peninsula.

4. Paulus Orosius, *Historiarum adversus paganos libri septem*, Corpus Scriptorum Ecclesiasticorum Latinorum 5, 280; see also PL 31, cols. 663–1174.

5. J. F. Rivera Recio (*San Julián arzobispo de Toledo [s. VII]: Epoca y personalidad* [Barcelona, 1944], 8) says, "El sibaritismo remilgado de los galo-romanos del siglo V no puede tolerar el color sebaceo que despiden las crines intonsas de los invasores, relucientes de grasas."

6. Hillgarth, "La conversión de los visigotos," 17.

7. The most important source for the birth and the development of the Visigothic Empire in Spain is the brief *Chronicon* of Abbot John of Bíclaro, who belonged to a noble Visigothic family. The *Chronicon* covers the period from 567 to 590, the date when he became bishop of Gerona, and, for some unknown reason, stopped writing his chronicle. The *Chronicon* continues that of the African bishop Victor of Tunnunna and was compiled according to the historiographic structure of imperial Rome. Naturally, he gives a lot of importance to the events of the Visigothic kingdom.

8. Hillgarth, *Christianity and Paganism, 350–750;* idem, "La conversión de los visigotos."

9. J. Orlandis, *La Iglesia en la España visigótica y medieval* (Pamplona, 1976), 40–58.

10. This prohibition was already a few centuries old, dating back to a law of the western emperor Valentinian I (321–375) and of eastern emperor Valens (328–378). The law prohibited mixed marriages between Romans and barbarians. This law was also inserted into the so-called *Breviary* of Alaric, which is in the *Lex Romana Visigothorum*, an important collection of Roman laws compiled during the reign of Alaric II, king of the Visigoths (484–507), but derived from the previous collections of Roman laws (those of Theodosius II, of the Roman jurist Gaius, etc.). Despite the fact that the Roman Empire disintegrated quickly, the corpus of its laws endured and they were taken up by the new dominators.

11. For example, the Fourth Council of Toledo ordered that priests must have thorough knowledge of the Sacred Scriptures and the canons, that is, the theological doctrine of the church: Ut sacerdotes Scripturarum sanctarum et canonum cognitionem habeant. Ignorantia mater cunctorum errorum maxime in sacerdotibus Dei vitanda est, qui docendi officium in populis susceperunt: sacerdotes enim legere sancta Scriptura admonet, Paulo apostolo dicente ad Timotheum: "Intende lectioni, exhortationi, doctrinae, semper permane in his." Sciant igitur sacerdotes Scripturas sanctas et canones, ut omne opus eorum in praedicatione et doctrina consistat, atque aedificent cunctos tam fidei scientia quam operum disciplina (PL 84, col. 374C).

12. See J. Orlandis Rovira, "El poder real y la sucessión al trono en la monarquía visigotica," *Estudios visigoticos*, vol. 3 (Rome/Madrid, 1962); see also idem, "La Iglesia visigoda y los problemas de la sucesión al trono en el

siglo VII," in *Le chiese nei regni dell'Europa occidentale e i loro rapporti con Roma sino all'800*, 2 vols., Settimane di studio del Centro italiano di studi sull'alto medioevo 7 (Spoleto, 1960).

13. This excludes the possibility of any truth in the many apocryphal texts that substantiate the claim of a Jewish presence in Spain before the Christian era; the trend of present historians is to recognize the presence of some Jewish communities in Iberian territory in the first century of the Christian era; see I. Vásquez, "Judíos," *Diccionario de Historia Eclesiástica de España* (Madrid, 1972–75), 3:1255–59, here 1255.

14. Ibid., 1255.

15. J. N. Hillgarth, "Elvira, Council of," *The New Catholic Encyclopaedia* (New York, 2003), 5:178.

16. The first of the councils of Spain, and the most ancient council from which we possess disciplinary canons. Convened at Elvira (the ancient Iliberri, Andalusia) in 300–303, it calls for the punishment of excommunication for the period of five years for any parents who gave their daughter in marriage to a Jew.

17. Rivera Recio, *San Julián arzobispo de Toledo*, 165.

18. Vásquez, "Judíos," 1255–59.

19. Ibid.

20. Son and heir of King Leovigild, he succeeded him as king of the Visigoths in 586. He was responsible for the very successful unification of the Hispanic-Roman people with the Visigothic people. His more significant unifying act, however, which was inspired by his mother and by St. Leander of Seville (elder brother of St. Isidore), was his adherence, and subsequently the adherence of all his people, to the Catholic faith, thus abandoning the Arian heresy. He died in Toledo in 601.

21. Vásquez, "Judíos," 1255.

22. Canon 14. The Third Council of Toledo was convoked by King Recared in 586.

23. He became king of the Visigoths in 612. He reduced the rebellious populations of the north of Spain (Basque and Asturias) to submission and reconquered from the Byzantines some territories of southern Spain. He enjoyed the pursuit of poetry and science and wrote poems in hexameters, as well as many letters and the *Vita Desideri Episcopi viennensis*. He died in 621.

24. Isidore, *Historia de Regibus Gothorum, Wandalorum et Suevorum*. This same conviction that coercive measures should not be used for the conversion of Jews can be found in the *Adversus Judaeos* of Isidore of Seville, written at the insistence of his sister Florentine. Isidore does not exclude, however, the use of measures of persuasion that he calls "more or less unpleasant" (ibid.). Canons 57–59 of the Fourth Council of Toledo (633) also recommend that conversion should not be undertaken against one's will.

25. Rivera Recio, *San Julián arzobispo de Toledo*, 166.

26. *Ergo non vi sed liberi arbitrii facultate ut convertantur suadendi sunt, non potius impellenti,* says canon 57 of the Fourth Council of Toledo (PL 84, cols. 0379D–0380).

27. Modern Jewish historiography adds another practical reason for the lack of success met by the attempt at the conversion of the Jews: the economic-social reason: "The Church never did succeed in converting all the Jews in the country. It was simply unable to keep an eye on all of them. The nobility, still devoutly Arian in their faith and wavering in their loyalty to the crown, needed the services of the Jews and gave them refuge on their estates" (Yitzhak Baer, *A History of the Jews in Christian Spain,* vol. 1 [Philadelphia, 1992], 21).

28. It is very probable that Idalius was the first one to receive the *Prognosticum* because Julian had to consider the bishop of Barcelona, in a certain sense, as coauthor of the work. The final result of the rich theological dialogue in eschatological matters between the two bishops, which took place in the royal city during a break in the celebration of the Fifteenth Council of Toledo (688), is, in fact, the thematic substratum from which have been written the three books that constitute the work of Julian.

29. For example, R. Gonzálvez Ruiz, "San Julián de Toledo en el contexto de su tiempo," *Anales Toledanos* 32 (1996): 7–21, here 14, where he quotes the historian who made this judgment.

30. Rivera Recio, *San Julián arzobispo de Toledo,* 168.

31. Ibid.

32. Ibid., 13.

33. For the history of the ascent of Toledo to the status of a metropolitan see, and for the important consequences of this event for the whole Iberian Peninsula, see J. F. Rivera Recio, "Encumbramiento de la sede toledana durante la dominación visigótica," *Hispania Sacra* 8 (1955): 1–32; see also D. Mansilla, "Orígines de la organización metropolitana en la Iglesia española, "*Hispania Sacra* 12 (1959): 255–90.

34. The splendid votive crowns, the Guarrazar, kept in the National Archaeological Museum of Spain (Madrid), and the treasure of Torredonjimeno, are two magnificent examples of the Visigothic art.

35. Rivera Recio, *San Julián arzobispo de Toledo,* 7–15, 27–28.

36. Orlandis, *La Iglesia en la España visigotica y medieval,* 73–75.

37. L. Duchesne, *Origines du culte chrétien: étude sur la liturgie latine avant Charlemagne* (Paris, 1908), 40–41.

38. L. Sierra, "Lorenzana, Francisco Antonio de," *Diccionario Eclesiástico de España,* vol. 2, cols. 1346–48.

39. Precisely, May 28.

40. See, for example, the Insituto de Estudios Visigótico-Mozárabes of Toledo, founded in 1977, which publishes studies and works about the Hispanic-Visigothic and Hispanic-Arab culture and theology, liturgy, and so

on. See also the periodical *Cronica Mozárabe*, which in 2006 published an interesting article by the vicar-general of the Archdiocese of Toledo, Msgr. J. M. Ferrer Grenesche, "El legado de la Liturgía Hispano-Mozárabe," *Cronica Mozárabe* 65 (2006): 1–17. He is Mozárabe chaplain of the Cathedral of Toledo, professor of liturgy and author of numerous publications, including *Los santos del nuevo misal hispano-mozárabe* (Toledo, 1995); *Curso de liturgia hispano-mozárabe* (Toledo, 1995); "La eucharistía en el rito hispano-mozárabe," *Toletana, questiones de teología e Historia* 1 (1999): 59–88. I have personally had the opportunity to appreciate the exquisite gentleness, the passion, and the expertise of the vicar-general of the Archdiocese of Toledo, who is a convinced supporter of the liturgical "renaissance" of the Hispanic-Mozárabic liturgy.

CHAPTER II

1. J. N. Hillgarth, "El Prognosticon futuri saeculi de San Julián de Toledo," *Analecta Sacra Tarraconensia* 30 (1957): 5–61, here 5; idem, "St. Julian of Toledo in the Middles Ages," *Journal of the Warburg and Courtauld Institutes* 29 (1958): 7–26; R. Gonzálvez Ruiz, "San Julián de Toledo en el contexto de su tiempo," *Anales Toledanos* 32 (1996): 7–21.

2. J. Madoz, "San Julián de Toledo," *Estudios Eclesiásticos* 26 (1952): 39–69, here 39.

3. J. N. Hillgarth, "Eschatological and Political Concepts in the Seventh Century," in *Le septième siècle: changements et continuités: Actes du colloque bilatéral franco-britannique tenu au Warburg Institute les 8–9 juillet 1988* [The Seventh Century: Change and Continuity. Proceedings of a Joint French and British Colloquium Held at the Warburg Institute 8–9 July 1988], ed. Jacques Fontaine and J. N. Hillgarth (London, 1992), 212–31, here 226.

4. E. Cuevas, OSSa, and U. Domínguez Del Val, OSA, "San Julián de Toledo," in *Patrología Española*, 4th ed. (Madrid, 1956), 115*–22*. This can be found also in the appendix to the Spanish translation of *Patrology* of B. Altaner.

5. F. X. Murphy, "Julian of Toledo and the Condemnation of Monothelitism in Spain," in *Mélanges Joseph de Ghellinck, S.J.*, vol. 1, *Antiquité* (Gembloux, 1951), 361–73, here 361.

6. Ibid., 373.

7. *Vita Juliani auctore Felice Toletano etiam Episcopo*, ed. F. A. de Lorenzana, *SS.PP. Toletanorum quotquot extant opera* (Madrid, 1785). The work is present also in Migne, PL 96, cols. 444–52: *Sancti Juliani Toletani Episcopi vita seu elogium, Auctore Felice Toletano etiam Episcopo*, 1. Henceforth *Vita*, followed by the chapter number. See also *Biblioteca hagiographica Latina antiquae et mediae aetatis*, 2 vols. (Brussels, 1898–1901); Suppl. 2nd ed., ibid. 1911; here vol. 1:575 n. 4554; see

also *Acta Sanctorum, martii*, ed. J. Carnandet (Paris/Rome, 1865), *Vita Sancti Juliani et commentarius*, 1:780-86.

8. Julian also wrote, in his turn, a *Vita seu elogium* of his predecessor in the episcopal see of Toledo, the great Bishop Ildephonse. The biography is entitled *Beati Hildefonsi Elogium* and is identified in the Latin Migne as *Ex sancto Juliano in appendice ad librum de Viris illustribus ab ipso Hildefonso conscriptum.* Writing this little biography Julian continues the work of Ildephonse, himself author of the *De viris illustribus.* This work is a collection of biographies of the most important characters of the Spanish Church in the Visigothic era. If the three bishops have paid homage to their predecessors, this is more than the simple establishment of a custom. Rather, we are in possession of a direct testimony that allows us to obtain precious biographical and historical data, as well as showing a manifest awareness of the Toledan apostolic succession.

9. We know that Bishop Felix, before being metropolitan bishop of Toledo, was archpriest of the Church of Toledo and in this role participated in the Fourteenth and Fifteenth Councils of Toledo. He was then designated bishop of Seville. As a result of the deposition by King Egica of the intriguing Bishop Sisibert (693), Julian's immediate successor, who was accused of conspiracy and of high treason against the king, Felix was elected by the sixteenth national council as bishop of the imperial city and of the Metropolitan Diocese of Toledo. He was bishop of Toledo from 693 to 700. In the first years of his episcopate he wrote the short but very valuable *Vita seu elogium* on his predecessor, Julian. This work is a primary source, because it was written contemporaneously with the facts, and with direct knowledge of the life, personality, and works of Julian of Toledo. See Isidorus Pacensis, *Continuatio Hispana* 60; L. A. García Moreno, *Prosopographía del Reino Visigodo de Toledo* (Salamanca, 1974), 122 n. 253; E. Flórez, *España Sagrada*, 56 vols. (Madrid, 1750), 5:316–17.

10. Murphy, "Julian of Toledo and the Condemnation of Monothelitism in Spain," 361; Flórez, *España Sagrada*, 5:289–90, here 290. This author claims that Felix was not a disciple of Julian, because, if he were, he would have said so in the biography of Julian.

11. J. F. Rivera Recio, *San Julián arzobispo de Toledo (s. VII): Epoca y personalidad* (Barcelona, 1944), 132.

12. A. Veiga Valiña, *La doctrina escatológica de San Julián de Toledo* (Lugo, 1940), 12–13.

13. See T. A. [T. Arnold], "Isidorus (23) Pacensis," in *A Dictionary of Christian Biography*, ed. W. Smith, DCL, LLD, and H. Wace, BD (London, 1882), 3:313–15.

14. Felix is one of the first bishops of Spain who was "moved" from his see of Seville to that of Toledo. Until then, an episcopal assignment was considered the definitive placement of the bishop because he "married" his church and was faithful to her until death.

15. For example, in the list of the works of Julian there are two omissions; the short but beautiful *Vita Sancti Ildefonsi* and the *Ars grammatica*.

16. See Rivera Recio, *San Julián arzobispo de Toledo*, 207; the same remark is found also in Hillgarth, "El Prognosticon futuri saeculi de San Julián de Toledo," 7 n. 12.

17. See Rivera Recio, *San Julián arzobispo de Toledo*, 211.

18. The *Vita* was published by Cardinal de Lorenzana as an introduction to the works of Julian of Toledo; the short biographical work appears in PL 96, cols. 444–52 (see n. 7 above).

19. Madoz, "San Julián de Toledo," 39.

20. The silence of the biographer concerning these details has resulted in the silence of almost all authors on the same questions.

21. According to Hillgarth, *Sancti Iuliani Toletanae sedis episcopi opera*, vol. 1, Corpus Christianorum, Series Latina 115 (Turnhout, 1976), Introduction, IX (henceforth *Introduction*), this omission of the biographer is due to the fact that Felix follows "the usual pattern of the 'De viris' of St. Ildefonsus."

22. "Felix mentions Julian's relations with Rome only in passing" (Hillgarth, *Introduction*, IX).

23. It seems strange, but according to some scholars, "He [Felix] says nothing about his political activities." A. K. Ziegler, "Church and State in Visigothic Spain" (PhD diss., Catholic University of America, 1930), 117 n. 77.

24. This is perhaps the reason why the biographer Felix omits every allusion to the Jewish origin of Julian, while other sources mention it explicitly, as, for example, the *Chronica mozarabica* of 754.

25. Veiga Valiña, *La doctrina escatológica*, 14–15.

26. R. Ceillier, *Histoire générale des auteurs sacrés et ecclésiastiques, qui contient leur vie, le catalogue, la critique, le jugement, la chronologie, l'analyse & le dénombrement des différentes éditions de leurs ouvrages* (Paris, 1729–63), 17:733–39.

27. PL 96, col. 1260C; see the critical edition of T. Mommsen in *Monumenta Germaniae Historica, Chronica minora II* (Berlin, 1894), 349.

28. Sigebertus Gemblacensis, *De scriptoribus ecclesiasticis* LVI, in PL 160, col. 560A.

29. Nicolás Antonius, *Notitiae Historicae, Bibliotheca Hispana Vetus*, in PL 96, col. 428C.

30. Julian Pomerius was abbot of Arles and master of Caesarius of Arles; see Gennadius, *De scriptoribus ecclesiasticis* 98, PL 58, cols. 1117B–1118B; R.T.S. [R. Travers Smith], "Julianus (72) Pomerius," in *A Dictionary of Christian Biography*, 3:382. In the *Prognosticum*, Julian holds Julian Pomerius in very high esteem and quotes his thought and his important work on the human soul many times. It was probably the carelessness and lack of attention of some amanuensis, around the end of the eighth century, that led to the confusion of the two names and the attribution of the name *Pomerius* to the *noster Iulianus*.

31. Hillgarth ("El Prognosticon futuri saeculi de San Julián de

Toledo," 41) reports that in many catalogues of the medieval libraries the author of the *Prognosticum* was called Iulianus Pomerius.

32. Madoz, "San Julián de Toledo," 57–58.

33. Alcuinus, *Adversus Elipandum*, II, 8, in PL 101, col. 266B.

34. The text is in PL 99, col. 1238D.

35. Hillgarth, "El Prognosticon futuri saeculi de San Julián de Toledo," 41.

36. Evidently confusing the titles of the two respective works: Honorius Augustudunensis, *De scriptoribus ecclesiasticis*, III, 14, in PL 172, col. 223A.

37. Flórez, *España Sagrada*, 4:200.

38. See D. de Bruyne, "Le plus ancien catalogue des reliques d'Oviedo," *Analecta Bollandiana* 45 (1927): 93–96.

39. Rodrigo Jiménez de Rada, *De rebus Hispaniae*, in *SS.PP. Toletanorum quotquot extant opera* (Madrid, 1785), 3:13 (Corpus Patrum Toletanorum, 3, 77).

40. The already quoted text states: Hic anno primo concilium duodecimum Toletanum in aera 719 triginta quinque episcoporum cum inaestimabili clero vel Christianorum collegio splendidissime colligit. In cujus tempore Julianus episcopus ex traduce Judaeorum, ut flores rosarum de inter vepres spinarum productus, omnibus mundi partibus in doctrina Christi manet praeclarus, qui etiam a parentibus Christianis progenitus splendide in omni prudentia Toleto manet edoctus, ubi et postmodum in episcopatu exstitit decoratus.

41. Ioannes Trithemius, *De scriptoribus ecclesiasticis* (Cologne, 1546), 79.

42. N. 369.

43. Nicolás Antonius, *Notitiae Historicae, Bibliotheca Hispana Vetus*, in PL 96, cols. 427-444B, here col. 429B.

44. P. Labbé, *Sanctorum Patrum, Theologorum Scriptorumque Ecclesiasticorum Bibliotheca* (Paris, 1659).

45. R. Bellarminus, *De Scriptoribus Ecclesiasticis liber unus. Cum adiunctis indicibus undecim, & brevi Chronologia ab Orbe condito usque ad annum M. DC. XII*, in *Opera Omnia*, Vol. VI (Neapoli, 1862), 6:63.

46. See Flórez, *España Sagrada*, 5:300 and 508; Ambrosio de Morales, *Crónica General de España* (Alcalà de Henares, 1577), fol. 189; Nicolás Antonius, *Biblioteca Hispana Vetus* (Madrid, 1788), 1:413 (the edition was reprinted by J. P. Migne in his PL, vol. 96, cols. 427–44), and in the edition of the works of Julian of Toledo published by Cardinal de Lorenzana.

47. See M. C. Díaz y Díaz, "Scrittori della Penisola Iberica," in *Patrologia*, vol. 4, *Dal Concilio di Calcedonia (451) a Beda. I Padri Latini*, ed. Angelo Di Berardino (Genoa, 1996), 109–15; J. F. Rivera Recio, "Los arzobispos de Toledo en el siglo VII," *Anales Toledanos* 3 (1971): 181–217, here 205ff.; U. Domínguez Del Val, "Julián de Toledo," *Diccionario de Historia Eclesiástica de España* (Madrid, 1972), 2:1259–60. "Toledano de Toledo" is the emphatic title of the second chapter of the work, devoted entirely to Archbishop Julian, by his passionate scholar J. F. Rivera Recio (*San Julián arzobispo de Toledo*). This work fills a gap of some fifty years since the last research on Julian of Toledo.

In it the author renounces (pp. 4-5) the "erudición enfadosa" in favor of writing a work that is "vulgarizadora, quizá de alta vulgarización." However, the clear and often imaginative narrative of the learned author obviously required much study and "muchas horas pasadas sobre los documentos originales," so that it expresses in an obviously fictionalized but at the same time very realistic way the life, learning, and environment of Julian of Toledo. Well-deserved praise of the work of J. F. Rivera Recio is found in J. Madoz, SJ, *Segundo Decenio de Estudios sobre Patrística Española*, Estudios Onienses 5 (Madrid, 1951), 142–43. In 1991 the Estudio Teológico de San Ildefonso and the Seminario Conciliar di Toledo held a touching and solemn Sesión Académica en Memoria de Don Juan Francisco Rivera Recio, who was, by that time, deceased. Distingushed scholars emphasized the salient facts of his life and his passionate work as liturgist, archivist, and historian of the church and of the history of Toledo in particular. Suitable care was also given to the presentation of his rich scientific bibliography. The solemn Sesión was printed in a little volume published by the Estudio Toledano with the same title. For information on the scant biographical data on Julian provided by Bishop Felix, see also Veiga Valiña, *La doctrina escatológica*, 13; as well as Hillgarth, *Introduction*, VIII.

48. From the time of King Leovigild (568–586).

49. Gonzálvez Ruiz, "San Julián de Toledo en el contexto," 7; J. N. Hillgarth, "Towards a Critical Edition of the Works of St. Julian of Toledo," *Studia Patristica* 1 (1957): 37–43, here 37.

50. Rivera Recio (*San Julián arzobispo de Toledo*, 20) notes that the city of Toledo was Julian's only dwelling place for his whole life. Here he was born, baptized, and confirmed; and it was in this same royal city that he was educated, from his adolescence to the completion of his advanced studies. In Toledo he was ordained deacon, presbyter, and finally bishop, until his death. In particular, it was at the Cathedral of Toledo that Julian became Christian, and where he prayed and exercised his pastoral and episcopal ministry in the solemn atmosphere of the Mozárabic liturgy, which he had reformed and corrected, preaching the Word of God and celebrating sacramentally the fruits of redemption. Rivera Recio gives an interesting presentation of how the Cathedral of Toledo of the Visigothic epoch must have been, before it was subject to various building projects (pp. 20-21); see also Altaner, *Patrología Española*, 115*. See also *Benedictio super parvulum qui ad ministerium Dei in Ecclesia detonditur*, in *Liber Ordinum* 39, ed. Marius Férotin (Paris, 1904).

51. The baptism in the Cathedral of Toledo, which is dedicated to Santa Maria (Our Lady), is described by Felix in elegant prose: in ejusdem urbis principali ecclesia sacrosancti baptismatis fluentis est lotus (*Vita*, 1). See also J. F. Rivera Recio, "Giuliano di Toledo," *Bibliotheca Sanctorum* (Rome, 1965), vol. 2, cols. 1216–18, here 1216.

52. Rivera Recio, *San Julián arzobispo de Toledo*, 18.

53. For the rest of the liturgical year, as Rivera Recio opportunely reminds us, the baptistery was closed with the episcopal seal. He also presents (pp. 18–20 of the same work) the baptismal rite of the Visigothic epoch. This included the reception of the person to be baptized, carried by their godfather, who walked on a floor covered in goat hair (as a symbol of penitence), by the clergy at the door of the church. The priest took the person to be baptized into the baptistery and blew three times on the face to chase away unclean spirits in the name of the Holy Trinity. There then followed the sign of the cross on the newborn and the anointing of the mouth and the ears. In front of the baptismal pool, which had three descending steps symbolizing the triple renunciation of Satan, his works, and his orders, the child (through his godfather) underwent a dogmatic examination and was then immersed in the baptismal pool from which he reemerged trembling. The Mozárabic rite contained a single immersion in the baptismal water, in comparison with the three immersions used in other baptismal liturgy. The child, held in the godfather's right arm, received another sign of the cross, which was followed, as in the ancient liturgies, by the conferring of confirmation through the imposition of the celebrant's hands, holy unction, and the blessing of the bishop, thus strengthening the newly baptized with the gifts of the Holy Spirit. When the rite was finished, the bishop gave a catechesis to the adults who were present at the liturgy. Finally, the white garment was given, which was worn for the three days following the baptism and kept until death. The treatise *De cognitione baptismi* of Ildephonse of Toledo is very important for the appreciation of the structure of the Christian initiation in the Hispanic-Visigothic Church. See J. M. Hormaeche Basauri, *La Pastoral de iniciación cristiana en la España visigoda: Estudio sobre el 'De cognitione baptismi' de San Ildefonso de Toledo* (Toledo, 1983).

54. Such a name, evidently of Latin and Roman origin, clearly indicates membership in the aristocratic and illustrious *gens Julia*. The assigning of a Latin name probably indicates that Julian was Hispano-Roman by birth and not a Goth.

55. Rivera Recio, *San Julián arzobispo de Toledo*, 18.

56. Ibid.

57. *Ex traduce Iudaeorum*, according to the *Continuatio Isadoriana Hispana*, chap. 49, sixty years later (see T. Mommsen, ed., *Monumenta Germaniae Historica, Auctores Antiq., Chronica minora* II, 349; see n. 27 above). According to Gonzálvez Ruiz ("San Julián de Toledo en el contexto", 7), the greater number of historians agree on Julian's Jewish origins, because the events narrated in the *Continuatio Hispana* are so historically close to the life of Julian and, indeed, it was written soon after the life of Julian. The silence of Felix, the reliable contemporary biographer of Julian, on the Jewish origin of Julian can be linked to the fact that he does not give any information on his family. This is rather strange and leads one to think that he wanted to hide something.

Others, however, interpret the silence of the biographer as a demonstration that what was unknown to the contemporary biographer could be known by a subsequent historical *Chronica*. Proponents of this theory include E. Flórez, *España Sagrada;* Domínguez Del Val, "Julián de Toledo," 1259, while other authors consider the information provided by the *Continuatio* to be unreliable. Hillgarth is of this opinion (*Introduction*, VIII).

58. The *Chronicon* or *Mozárabic Chronica* of 754, of Isidore Pacensis of Beja—that is, the *Continuatio Hispana* (50)—highlights the fact that Julian is of Jewish descent, *ex traduce Iudaeorum,* but adds a hyperbolic image that is a disdainful slur against the Jewish ancestors of Julian although a favorable judgment of him: *ut flores rosarum deinter vepres spinarum productus.* Almost to lessen the severity of the judgment, he then adds: *etiam a parentibus Christianis progenitus.* See Rivera Recio, "Giuliano di Toledo," *Bibliotheca Sanctorum,* vol. 6, col. 1216.

59. This kind of information is found not only in historical entries but also in recently published theological entries devoted to Julian of Toledo and is accepted by most authors; for example, J. A. Fabricius, *Bibliotheca latina mediae et infimae aetatis,* vols. 3–4 (Florentiae, 1858); M. A. W. [Mrs. Humphrey Ward], "Julianus (63)," *A Dictionary of Christian Biography,* ed. W. Smith, DCL, LLD, and H. Wace, BD (London, 1882), 3:477–81; J. Forget, "Julien de Tolède, Saint," *Dictionnaire de Théologie Catholique* (Paris, 1903–50), vol. 8, cols. 1940–41; A. Robles Sierra, "Julien de Tolède (saint)," *Dictionnaire de Spiritualité* (Paris, 1974), vol. 8, cols. 1600–1602; M. Sehlmeyer, "Giuliano di Toledo," *Dizionario di Letteratura Cristiana Antica,* ed. S. Döpp and W. Geerlings; Italian edition ed. C. Noce (Rome, 2006), 447–48; T. F. Ruiz, "Julian of Toledo," *Dictionary of the Middle Ages* (New York, 1986), 7:181; J. Madoz, "San Julián de Toledo," *Estudios Eclesiásticos* 26 (1952): 39–69 ; idem, "Giuliano da Toledo, Santo," *Enciclopedia Cattolica* (Florence, 1954), vol. 6, cols. 747–48; Hillgarth, *Introduction,* VIII; idem, "Julian of Toledo," *New Catholic Encyclopedia,* rev. ed. (San Francisco, 2002), 8:50; *Patrología Española,* 115*; I. Gómez, "Julián de Toledo, San," *Gran Enciclopedia Rialp* (Madrid, 1973), 13:650–51; R. Collins, "Julian of Toledo," in *Key Figures in Medieval Europe: An Encyclopedia,* ed. Richard K. Emmerson and Sandra Clayton-Emmerson (New York, 2006), 387–88. According to M. C. Díaz y Díaz, the Jewish origins of Julian could explain "il suo energico appoggio alla persecuzione degli ebrei condotta [dal re] Ervigio" ("Scrittori della penisola iberica," 110).

60. F. X. Murphy, "Julian of Toledo and the Fall of the Visigothic Kingdom in Spain," *Speculum* 27 (1952): 1–27, here 5.

61. S. Katz, *The Jews in the Visigothic and Frankish Kingdom of Spain and Gaul* (Cambridge, MA, 1937), 15–22; P. Amón-Hernández, "La España Visigoda frente al problema de los judíos," *Ciencia Tomista* 14 (1967): 627–85.

62. Murphy, "Julian of Toledo and the Fall of the Visigothic Kingdom in Spain," 5.

63. Rivera Recio, *San Julián arzobispo de Toledo*, 17; Hillgarth, "Towards a Critical Edition," 37: "of Jewish descent, but of Christian parents"; idem, *Introduction*, VIII.

64. Ambrosio de Morales, *Crónica General de España*, vol. 3, book 12, chap. 58.

65. P. B. Gams, *Die Kirchengeschichte von Spanien* (Regensburg, 1874), vol. 2, part 2, 176; J. Forget supports the hypothesis of the Jewish descent of Julian, but emphasizes the fact that his parents were Christians: "de sang juif, mais né de parents chrétiens" ("Julien de Tolède [Saint]," col. 1940); J. de Mariana, *Historia General de España* (Barcelona, 1839), vol. 2, chap. 18, 79-80; Veiga Valiña, *La doctrina escatológica*, 4; Murphy, "Julian of Toledo and the Condemnation of Monothelitism in Spain," 361–73; Madoz, "San Julián de Toledo," 39–69.

66. Some authors do not trust the work of Isidore Pacensis; see, for example, *Patrología Española*, 115*: "el testimonio del Pacense es sospechoso." Long before Cuevas and Del Val (authors of the *Patrología Española*), Flórez expressed doubts concerning the reliability of Isidorus Pacensis.

67. See the entry "Pomerius Julian," *The New Schaff-Herzog Encyclopedia of Religious Knowledge* (Grand Rapids, 1949–50), 9:124.

68. This appears to be suggested by some recent interpretations: Sehlmeyer, "Giuliano di Toledo," 447–48.

69. Madoz, "San Julián de Toledo," 39.

70. M. Kayserling, "Julian of Toledo," *Jewish Encyclopedia*, on-line version, http://www.jewishencyclopedia.com/view.jsp?artid=717&letter=J&search=julian%20of%20toledo.

71. This is how Isidore Pacensis expresses himself in his *Epitome Imperatorum vel Arabum Ephemerides atque Hispaniae Chronographia*. This work can be considered the continuation of the *Chronica* of Isidore of Seville. See *Cont. Hisp.*, 50, in Mommsen, *Chron. Minora*, where the chronicler says that the parents of Julian were already converted to Christianity.

72. The rich and powerful Jew of Burgos (1351–1435), rabbi and scholar of rabbinic literature, converted to the Christian faith after studying the works of Thomas Aquinas. He became doctor in sacred theology in Paris, was an author, and in 1415 became archbishop of Burgos (Castilla and Leon). See I. Singer and M. Kayserling, "Paul de Burgos," *Jewish Encyclopedia*, on-line version, http://www.jewishencyclopedia.com/view.jsp?artid=115&letter=P&search=paul%20of%20burgos.

73. Flórez, *España Sagrada*, 5:293, §252.

74. PL 96, col. 446.

75. There are other examples of people of Jewish origin becoming bishops in Visigothic Spain. For example, Taio, a contemporary of Julian, who was bishop of Saragossa from 651 to 683. His austerity and severity, typical of converts, are often attributed to his Jewish origin. But, as with Julian, the

Jewish origins of Taio are disputed; see Díaz y Díaz, "Scrittori della penisola iberica," 107.

76. This was established at the very important Third Council of Toledo, held in 589. This council is the beginning of a series of Visigothic councils in Toledo, after the conversion to Catholicism of King Recared, the aristocracy, and the Visigoth people. Canon 14 of the council prohibits the Jews from assuming *officia publica*. This council is very important also because it introduced the recitation of the Niceno-Constantinopolitan Creed during Sunday liturgy and liturgical solemnities *secundum formam orientalium ecclesiarum*. This use will extend to the whole Latin Catholic Church. Finally, this council is important because it obliged the bishops to conserve and respect, over and above the acts of the ecumenical councils, the decrees of the bishops of Rome, recognizing, therefore, the magisterial value of the documents of the Roman see.

77. Veiga Valiña, *La doctrina escatológica*, 15. This could be the case with Julian, being of Jewish descent but having parents who were already Christians.

78. Domínguez Del Val, "Julián de Toledo," 1259.

79. J. Fontaine, *Isidore de Seville et la culture classique dans l'Espagne wisigothique*, 2 vols. (Paris, 1959), 2:1031; a third volume of *Notes complémentaires et supplément bibliographique* was published by Brepols in 1983.

80. The Fourth Council of Toledo, held in the Basilica of Santa Leocadia in 633, was presided over and animated by Isidore of Seville. Seventy-five important canons were promulgated, a fact that makes this National Council more important, on the disciplinary level, than all other Hispano-Visigothic councils. The council was convoked by King Sisenand and gathered approximately seventy metropolitans, bishops, and vicars. The acts of this council were inserted into the *Continuatio Hispana*. An interesting peculiarity is that some prayers of chapter 4, devoted to the *Ordo celebrandi Concilii*, were used during the celebration of the Second Vatican Council at the beginning of the general congregations. See G. Martínez, "Concilios Nacionales y Provinciales, Toledo IV, 633," *Diccionario de Historia Eclesiástica de España* (Madrid, 1972), 1:569.

81. Canon 25 of the Fourth Council of Toledo states explicitly: Ignorantia mater cunctorum errorum, maxime in sacerdotibus Dei vitanda est, qui docendi officium in populis susceperunt, sacerdotes enim legere sanctas Scripturas frequenter admonet Paulus apostolus dicens ad Timotheum: «Intende lectioni et exhortationi (I Tim. IV, 13). Doctores semper manere in his se sciant. Igitur sacerdotes Scripturas sanctas et canones meditentur, ut omne opus eorum in praedicatione divina et doctrina consistat, atque aedificent cunctos tam fidei scientia, quam operibus disciplina. And Canon 24 emphasizes the point, saying that: Quando presbyteri in parochiis ordinantur, libellum officialem a suo sacerdote accipiant ut ad ecclesias sibi deputatas instructi succedant, ne per ignorantiam etiam in ipsis divinis sacramentis offendant, ut

quando vel ad litanias, vel ad concilium venerint, rationem episcopo reddant, qualiter susceptum officium celebrent vel baptizent; see the acts of the Fourth Council of Toledo in PL 130, cols. 461–482D; here cols. 471D–472C.

82. For a presentation of the pedagogical structure in vogue in the episcopal schools at the time of Julian of Toledo, see Gonzálvez Ruiz, "San Julián de Toledo en el contexto," 8–9; see also P. Riché, "L'éducation à l'époque Wisigothique: les 'Institutionum disciplinae,'" *Anales Toledanos* 3 (1971): 171–80.

83. The *oblatus* condition of the adolescent Julian is presupposed by Rivera Recio, "Giuliano di Toledo," col. 1216.

84. According to Rivera Recio (*San Julián arzobispo de Toledo*, 29), the Episcopal School was situated in what was called the Atrium or House of the Church. It was a large, spacious building with a triple portico where the bishop and the greater part of the urban clergy of Toledo resided, and where the rooms of the school were situated. It is very probable that the rich library that had grown up in recent centuries (thanks to some learned bishops of Toledo) was located in these same rooms.

85. Felix, *Vita*, 1.

86. For an idea of what a school for adolescents in the seventh century was like, see P. Riché, *Éducation et culture dans l'occident barbare, VIe–VIIIe siècles* (Paris, 1962); L. Robles, "La cultura religiosa de la España Visigótica," *Escritos del Vedat* 5 (1975): 9–54.

87. See I. E. Alberca, "Toledo, Councils of," *New Catholic Encyclopedia*, 2nd ed. (New York, 2003), 14:99–101, here 99.

88. Canon 24 of the Fourth Council of Toledo explicitly stated: si qui in clero puberes aut adolescentes existunt, omnes in uno conclavi atrii commorentur. PL 84, col. 374B.

89. See Rivera Recio, *San Julián arzobispo de Toledo*, 29. The same council emphasized that adolescence is a delicate period in human life exposed to the dangers of temptation. The quoted canon 24 became a point of reference in treatises on Christian pedagogy.

90. Council IV of Toledo, canon 24, in PL 84, col. 374B.

91. The eyewitness account of the biographer Felix in the *incipit* of the *Vita* leaves no doubt: *Julianus discipulus Eugenii secundi*. It seems that Felix did not know that the first bishop of Toledo was a certain Eugene and that, therefore, this Eugene, successor of Eugene II, was Eugene III. It is possible, however, that Felix counts only the bishops of the Visigothic epoch; in this case the appellation "Eugene II" would be correct (Veiga Valiña, *La doctrina escatológica*, 15). The tutor of Julian, Eugene II, bishop of Toledo for about a decade (646–657), was previously a clergyman of the Toledan Church; then, perhaps in bizarre circumstances, he became a monk in a monastery in Saragossa. Subsequently he was archdeacon of Bishop Braulio of Saragossa. When Eugene I, bishop of Toledo, died, the Visigothic king Chindasvint named him bishop of the imperial city, in

spite of the remonstrations of Braulio, who wanted to keep him in Saragossa. He participated in many Councils of Toledo (from the Seventh to the Tenth) and was considered, both by his contemporaries and by those in posterity, to be the best Latin poet of the Spanish Visigothic epoch and was venerated as a saint. A fair few of his poetic compositions survive to this day. He also made a stylistic and doctrinal revision of the *Exameron* (the six days of creation) of Dracontius, a Christian poet of the fifth century, whose poems were very popular in the sixth and seventh centuries. His opuscule on the Holy Trinity, written, perhaps, against the Visigothic Arians, has been lost. He died in Toledo and was buried in the basilica of the Toledan martyr Saint Leocadia. Julian shows a true veneration toward him: see Ildephonse of Toledo, *De viris illustribus*, in PL 96, col. 204; F. de Lorenzana, *Patrum Toletanorum quotquot extant opera*, vol. 1 (Madrid, 1793); García Moreno, *Prosopographía del Reino Visigodo de Toledo*, 117–18 n. 248; J. F. Rivera Recio, "Eugenio II," in *Biblioteca Sanctorum* (Rome, 1965), vol. 5, col. 1964; J. Madoz, "Eugenio di Toledo," in *Enciclopedia Cattolica* (Florence, 1954), vol. 5, col. 804; G. Bardy, "Eugene II," *Catholicisme: Hier, aujourd'hui, demain*, ed. G. Jacquemet (Paris, 1948), vol. 4, col. 673; Forget, "Julien de Tolède (Saint)," col. 1940. The works of Eugene II have been edited by F. Vollmer together with the edition that the Toledan bishop made of some poetic works of Dracontius: *Fl. Merobaudis reliquiae, Blossii Aemilii Dracontii carmina, Eugenii Toletani episcopi carmina et epistulae, cum appendicula carminum spuriorum*, ed. Friedrich Vollmer in *Monumenta Germaniae Historica, Auctores Antiquissimi* 14 (Berlin, 1905). See also Rivera Recio, "Giuliano di Toledo," col. 1216; Hillgarth, *Introduction*, VIII. In 2006 the *opera omnia* (*carmina*, the *recensio* or *recognitio* of Dracontius's religious poems, and the letters) of Eugene II was edited by P. F. Alberto and published in vol. 114 of the Corpus Christianorum, Series Latina.

92. *Julianus, discipulus Eugenii secundi...et illic* [that is, in the principal Church of Toledo, the said Cathedral of Saint Maria] *ab ipsis rudimentis infantiae enutritus*; see Felix, *Vita*, 1.

93. *Prognosticum futuri saeculi*, III, 17. On this interesting quotation by Julian of a text of his master Eugene II (*aegregii praeceptoris nostri*), so favorable as to express a moderate but resolute realism and optimism about the resurrected body, see A. C. Vega, "De patrología española: Sobre el opúsculo 'De Sancta Trinitate' de san Eugenio II de Toledo (en torno a una cita de San Julián de Toledo en su 'Prognosticon' 3, 17)," *Boletín de la Real Accademia de la Historia* [Madrid], 166 (1970): 64.

94. Julian refers in this way to his venerated master Eugene II three times in *Prognosticum futuri saeculi* (III, 17, 24, and 26).

95. Rivera Recio, *San Julián arzobispo de Toledo*, 37.

96. Hillgarth, "St. Julian of Toledo in the Middles Ages," 7.

97. Education and intellectual formation in the seventh century, particularly in the ecclesiastical environment, were very rigorous; see Riché, *Éducation et culture*.

98. The young pupil Julian showed a particular intelligence, a solid personality, and a strong intellectual attitude. This provoked in his mentors the hope that he would one day be a clergyman in the Church of Toledo.

99. Ioannes Trithemius, *De scriptoribus ecclesiasticis*, 479.

100. Walafridus Strabo (= the Squinter), quoted in A. Messer, *Historia de la pedagogía*, Coll. *Labor* (Madrid, 1935), vol. 106–7, 109–24. Ample quotations of the "Diario" are in Rivera Recio, *San Julián arzobispo de Toledo*, 31–36.

101. It is plausible that, in the profoundly academic environment in which the students of the Episcopal School of Toledo lived, some works of Julian (a teacher at the school) were destined for the students of the theological course, including his *Ars grammatica*, his commentaries on the Sacred Scriptures, and, in particular, the *Prognosticum futuri saeculi*.

102. Gonzálvez Ruiz, "San Julián de Toledo en el contexto," 9.

103. See Veiga Valiña, *La doctrina escatológica*, 15. The author clarifies that he who is shown as Eugene II really should be called Eugene III, that is, the third bishop of Toledo with this name.

104. See Rivera Recio, *San Julián arzobispo de Toledo*, 35.

105. Gonzálvez Ruiz, "San Julián de Toledo en el contexto," 8.

106. It is probable that this was the Gudila who, as archdeacon, undersigned the acts of the Eleventh Council of Toledo: Gudila Ecclesiae Toletanae archidiaconus haec gesta synodica a nobis definita subscripsi. PL 84, col. 468A.

107. Felix, *Vita*, 1.

108. The term *archiepiscopus* was used very little or not at all in the seventh century. Only Isidore of Seville bore it as a title of great importance: Archiepiscopus Graeco vocabulo, quod sit summus episcoporum, tenet enim vicem apostolicam, et praesidet, tam metropolitanis quam episcopis caeteris. *Ethymologiae*, 340, 6; PL 82, col. 290D. So "archbishop" is an ecclesiastical and intermediate title between the "patriarch" and the "metropolitan bishop." Rivera Recio, *San Julián arzobispo de Toledo*, 125.

109. The name is rather frequently found in Christian antiquity beginning from the sixth century. A martyr saint bore this name (513–524), but Gudila is also known to be the name of the first king of the Goths (first century BC). See *Spain: A History*, ed. Raymond Carr (New York/Oxford, 2000); R. Collins, *Early Medieval Europe, 300–1000* (London, 1991); A. Konstam, *Atlas of Medieval Europe* (New York, 2000). Another Gudila at the time of Theodoric (493–526) was an envoy of the emperor with the job of verifying that imperial orders were observed in ecclesial synods.

110. Felix, *Vita*, 1: Et unitas in ambobus praefixa non duas animas, sed unam his inesse monstraret.

111. Felix describes still more intensely the bond of brotherly affection of the two friends: Tanta itaque erat inter eos adeptae unanimitatis communio, ut secundum Actuum apostolorum historiam in duobus corporibus

unum cor tantum putaretur et anima una (*Vita*, 1). Entirely unfounded is the rumor, however much widespread, according to which Julian undertook monastic life to become abbot of the Monastery of Agali. It is obvious that some authors confuse him with Ildephonse of Toledo and his monastic experience before becoming bishop of Toledo as successor of his uncle, Eugene II, himself also the abbot of Agali before becoming bishop of Toledo. For information on the deep friendship between the young Julian and his contemporary Gudila, see Gonzálvez Ruiz, "San Julián de Toledo en el contexto," 15.

112. Rivera Recio, *San Julián arzobispo de Toledo*, 40.

113. Felix, *Vita*, 1: quique divino afflante Spiritu theoreticae, id est, contemplativae quietis, delectati sunt perfrui bono, et monasticae institutionis constringi repagulo.

114. The great bishops—Eutropius of Valencia, Martinus of Braga, Pascasius of Dumio, Leander of Sevilla, Iohannes of Saragossa, perhaps the great Isidore of Seville, Eugenius II of Toledo, Ildephonse of Toledo, Fructuosus of Braga, Taio of Saragossa, Valerius of Bierzo, and others—were all monks.

115. Domínguez Del Val, "Julián de Toledo," 1259; see also Rivera Recio, "Los Arzobispos de Toledo," 190.

116. Some bishops of the Toledan Church perhaps came from the suburban monastery of St. Felix or Agali.

117. Domínguez Del Val, "Julián de Toledo," 1259; Madoz, "San Julián de Toledo," 40.

118. Felix, *Vita*, 3: Sed quia aliter in superni numinis fuit judicio, eorum est nihilominus frustrata devotio.

119. J. González Echegaray, "El monacato en la España nórdica en su confrontación con el paganismo (ss. VI–VII)," in *Semana de historia del monacato cántabro-astur-leonés* (Oviedo, 1982), 35–56.

120. Rivera Recio, *San Julián arzobispo de Toldeo*, chap. 4, "Monasterios y Monjes," 45–55, here 45.

121. J. Fernández Alonso, "Fruttuoso," *Bibliotheca Sanctorum* (Rome, 1965), vol. 5, cols. 1295–96.

122. Rivera Recio, *San Julián arzobispo de Toledo*, 111.

123. Ibid., 48.

124. Ibid. 54.

125. Ibid. 55.

126. Felix, *Vita*, 3: Erant enim in subditis docendis operosae virtutis, in profectu eorum desiderabiles, in servitute Dei ferventes, in desiderio decoris domus Domini strenui.

127. The diaconate, according to the ideals of the Second Council of Toledo, which was composed of eight bishops and presided over by Bishop Montanus (PL 84, col. 335B), could not be conferred before the candidate reached twenty-five years of age (the subdiaconate was not conferred before

the age of twenty). It was dependent on the renunciation of the married life and the judgment and evaluation of the bishop. The instruction of the Second Council of Toledo was confirmed by the Fourth Council, held in the same city in 633, with the participation of more than sixty bishops and presided over by Isidore of Seville. Canon 20, entitled *De numero annorum quo sacerdote et levitae ordinentur,* confirmed the previous canonical rule. This repetition was probably due to some abuses by which the diaconate had been conferred on adolescents or even children (*infantes et pueros,* says the conciliar text). Concerning the presbyterate, the same council fixed the canonical age at thirty years (*a triginta presbyteris ordinentur*). PL 84, col. 373BC.

128. Julian was ordained to the diaconate after the death of his second venerated master, Ildephonse of Toledo; see Felix, *Vita,* 4.

129. García Moreno, *Prosopographía del Reino Visigodo de Toledo,* n. 251, and in any case at the fateful age of thirty years, and therefore, toward 672, at the beginning of the reign of Wamba.

130. Also Hillgarth (*Introduction,* VIII) is of the same opinion.

131. "The friends seem to have become zealous teachers in the episcopal school of Toledo" (M. A. W. [Mrs. Humphrey Ward], "Julianus [63]," 477).

132. Felix, *Vita,* 3: sexto Idus Septembris funestae mortis eventu, anno octavo Wambanis principis sub digna confessione Dei clausit supremum curriculum.

133. See *Prognosticum,* I, V, where Julian indicates, among the three kinds of death, that of young people as immature: *immatura iuvenum.*

134. If this is the same Gudila, archdeacon of the Church of Toledo and participant in the Eleventh Council of Toledo in 675 (presided over by Bishop Quiricus). This could be deduced from the use of his name and from his signature on the acts of the council (PL 84, col. 468A). The office of archdeacon of the cathedral of Toledo was the third most important office in the Diocese of Toledo after that of prelate. The archdeacon exercised some important duties; see Rivera Recio, *San Julián arzobispo de Toledo,* 110. According to the same author, Julian was also among the presbyters who subscribed to the acts of the Eleventh Council of Toledo, but in his capacity as abbot of the monastery of the Church of Saint Michael. We know that Julian was never a monk or an abbot in the canonical sense; see Rivera Recio, *San Julián arzobispo de Toledo,* chap. 8, 109, and above all chap. 8, 111–12. In these pages the author assumes that Julian was (as presbyter) chaplain or spiritual director to the nuns of the monastery of St. Michael. For this ministry, occasionally, the presbyter assumed the title of abbot (but not of the monastery). And, in fact, in the acts of the Eleventh Council of Toledo, Julian was named as abbot of the monastery of the Church of St. Michael. Of such a monastery nothing is known. In short, the name of the presbyter Julian does not appear in the proper list of the abbots of monasteries, but in the list of the vicars of the bishops. It is possible, therefore, that the young presbyter Julian partici-

pated in the writing of the long and admirable formulation of trinitarian faith of the same council. According to Rivera Recio (*San Julián arzobispo de Toledo*, 111), a literary comparison between the admirable *regula fidei* of the council and the later writings of Julian would reveal many resemblances. According to Gonzálvez Ruiz, however, Julian took part in the council as "chierico di rango inferiore all'episcopato" (a cleric of inferior rank to bishop) ("San Julián de Toledo en el contexto," 15).

135. Strangely, both Rivera Recio ("Giuliano di Toledo," col. 1217) and Veiga Valiña (*La doctrina escatológica*), though quoting the *Vita* of Bishop Felix, seem intentionally to ignore the important fact of the premature death of Gudila, an event that probably had a great influence on the life of Julian, spurring him to dedicate his life to pastoral ministry in the Diocese of Toledo. Rivera Recio, however, does refer to the death of Gudila in "Los Arzobispos de Toledo en el siglo VII," 206–7; idem, *San Julián arzobispo de Toledo*, chaps 3, 4.

136. Felix, *Vita*, 3; see J. Á. Aparicio Bastardo, "Notas para la aproximación al estudio de las Iglesias de mozárabes en la urbe toledana," *Anaquel de Estudios Árabes* (1993): 10–24, here 12.

137. Felix, *Vita*, 3: in monasterio S. Felicis, quod est Cabensi in villula dedicatum. The place in which Gudila was buried is probably located in the environs of the hermitage of the Virgen del Valle; see Gonzálvez Ruiz, "San Julián de Toledo en el contexto," 9; Rivera Recio, *San Julián arzobispo de Toledo*, 113, where he also describes the simple and meaningful Visigothic rite of the accompanying of the soul and of the care of the body of the dead (with prayers, burial, etc.).

138. Into the "appendix secunda" of the volume of the *Patrologia Latina* that includes the works of Julian are also inserted a series of epitaphs attributed to Julian. This attribution is only a supposition, even if his contemporary biographer does speak of Julian as the author of epitaphs (Felix, *Vita*, 9). One of these epitaphs is devoted to his close friend Gudila. The intimate feeling between the two friends is expressed, undoubtedly, in an aesthetically admirable way: In sepulcro Gudilae archidiaconi Toletani. Gloria Toleti jacet hac sub mole sepultus / Gudila, pars animi dimidiumque mei. / Qui senis a tenera mores aetate tenebat, / Et ad diem octavam Martii hunc pentametrum sic legit: Cui, nisi simplicitas, nil juvenile fuit. Et juvenis fecit hic juvenile nihil. / Spiritus in sacro residebat pectore Christi, / Exprimit hunc totum, moribus, ore, manu. / Pauperibus cibus est, viduis solamen, ut aegris / Grata salus: miseris omnibus unus erat. / Mercaris meritis multis, bone Gudila, coelum: Nos desiderium lancinat usque tui. / Moerentesque vocamus eum, quem sustulit aether: Prosequimurque piis funera lacrymulis. Non violas, tenerasque rosas, non lilia cana / Spargimus ad tumulum, sed bona vota, tuum. / Nos ergo e supera prospecta candidus arce; / Teque amor, et moveat, Gudila, cura mei. Moenibus a patriis morbos averte, famemque, / Hostilesque minas, dogmata falsa, dolos. / Toleti ne temne preces, comitisque rogatus, / Qui tibi dat car-

men sat Julianus amans: /Ossaque Felicis tua sacra condit in aede, cujus mens superis est sociata choris. PL 96, cols. 815–16.

139. Rivera Recio, "Los Arzobispos de Toledo en el siglo VII," 206. See the *Benedictio ad consecrandum primiclericum*, in *Liber Ordinum* 53, ed. L. Férotin (Paris, 1904).

140. For this presentation of the figure of the *Primicerius*, see Rivera Recio, *San Julián arzobispo de Toledo*, 110–11.

141. Ibid., 58–59.

142. Felix, *Vita*, 5: Eleemosynis nimium deditus...in sustentatione humilium apparatus.

143. Murphy ("Julian of Toledo and the Fall of the Visigothic Kingdom," 20–21) ascribes the election of Julian to the episcopal see of Toledo not so much to his virtue as a politician as, more positively, to his intellectual ability as a theologian and a man of letters.

144. Probably owing to a mistake in calculation, Rivera Recio attributes to Julian the age of sixty at the time of his episcopal consecration. In reality, if the birth of Julian is datable to 642–644, then in 680 he would have been thirty-eight or thirty-six years old.

145. See Felix, *Vita*, 4.

146. Rivera Recio, *San Julián arzobispo de Toledo*, 114.

147. Ibid., 124.

148. Hillgarth, *Introduction*, IX.

149. A rich historical presentation of the event that led to a disagreement between the Church of Toledo and the Church of Rome can be found in Madoz, "San Julián de Toledo," 46–55.

150. See the tragic reports of the *Anales Toledanos* relating to the frightful famines that troubled Spain in these years leading people to eat dogs, cats, and even human flesh in order to survive (see the *Anales Toledanos*, quoted in Rivera Recio, *San Julián arzobispo de Toledo*, 131). In some cases the pangs of hunger were so strong that people ate poisonous mushrooms or soups made with the bark of trees and mud (see ibid., 132–33). The ingestion of these concoctions obviously provoked illnesses of every kind. This is the reason for which the country people, in particular the farmers, sought the church's blessing on the land, the sowing of seed and the harvest (wheat, fruit, olives, grapevines, etc.). This process of cultivation was, in fact, considered essential to survival, particularly in times of famine and pestilence. The Christian blessings, moreover, complemented the "agricultural" character of the Visigothic religion and of Visigothic worship. Therefore, even the invaders desired them. The pastoral ministry of the country people also provided for blessings to keep storms, as well as frost, fire, drought, and so on, at bay, Rivera Recio, *San Julián arzobispo de Toledo*, 130–31; see *Benedictio novarum falcium, vinearum, granorum, frugum, primitiarum, etc.*, in *Liber Ordinum*, 167–70. On the *Liber Ordinum*, see L. Férotin, *Le Liber Ordinum en*

usage dans l'Église wisigothique et mozarabe d'Espagne du cinquième au onzième siecle (Paris, 1904), reprint of the 1904 edition, and general bibliography on the Hispanic liturgy, prepared and presented by Anthony Ward, SM, and Cuthbert Johnson, OSB (Rome, 1996).

151. Madoz, "San Julián de Toledo," 41.

152. Veiga Valiña, *La doctrina escatológica*, 16.

153. See the accurate instruction of the Fourth Council of Toledo concerning the *libellus*: Quando presbyteres in parochias ordinantur, libellum officiale a sacerdote suo accipiant, ut ad ecclesias sibi deputatas instructi succedant, ne per ignorantiam etiam ipsis divinis sacramentis offendant, ita ut quando ad litanias vel ad concilium venerint, rationem episcopo suo reddant qualiter susceptum officium celebrant, vel baptizant. PL 84, col. 374BD.

154. In the Visigothic kingdom there also existed other kinds of churches, for example, churches *propriae*, of feudal origin, and "rectorates"; see Rivera Recio, *San Julián arzobispo de Toledo*, 119–21.

155. The Eleventh Council of Toledo contains some canonical and judicial rules of this kind.

156. Toledo was not as ancient as Constantinople, but like Constantinople it was the imperial city, which implied a series of advantages and privileges for the Church of Toledo and its archbishop, privileges that the other ecclesiastical provinces did not enjoy. The most important advantage was that of enjoying proximity to the crown and therefore royal favor, as well as being the center of the empire, where the most important political and administrative decisions were made.

157. For these interesting administrative notes, see Rivera Recio, *San Julián arzobispo de Toledo*, 122–23.

158. Ibid., 113.

159. Ibid., 123.

160. Felix, *Vita*, 5: Ut non esset cui in augustiis constituto non subvenire vellet.

161. Felix, *Vita*, 5: Unius charitatis exuberans.

162. Rivera Recio, *San Julián arzobispo de Toledo*, 115. He lists the impediments established by the Hispanic-Visigothic Church to the election and ordination of an archbishop. The candidate had to be examined, to this end, by a survey executed by a council of bishops to verify his canonical aptitude and his doctrinal orthodoxy. Among the impediments: guilt in crimes, public penitence, apostasy, polygamy, bodily mutilations, unknown origin or condition of slave, secular or military condition, ignorance, canonical age, or if he had been, or was, a rebel, or if he had been named bishop by his predecessor.

163. Concerning the decisive importance of Julian in the reform of the Mozárabic liturgy, see J. Janini, "Roma y Toledo," in *Nuevos estudios sobre la litúrgia mozárabe* (Toledo, 1965).

164. Rivera Recio, *San Julián arzobispo de Toledo*, 128.

165. Madoz, "San Julián de Toledo," 66. It also helps to remember that the letter of the Spanish bishops to the bishops of Gallia, sent on the occasion of the adoptionist heresy (792–793), cites Julian as author of the liturgical texts of the Spanish Church (together with Eugene and Ildephonse of Toledo). See *Monumenta Germaniae Historica, Concilia,* 2, 111f.

166. Díaz y Díaz, "Scrittori della penisola iberica," 110.

167. Also Hillgarth, *Introduction,* XIV, which emphasizes the important role played by Julian in the formation of the liturgy of the Church of Toledo, which will extend, subsequently, to all the churches of Spain.

168. *Inlatio* or *Praefatio,* in *Missale Mixtum.* PL 85, col. 85B.

169. Felix, *Vita,* 11: Item librum missarum de toto circulo anni, in quatuor partes divisum; in quibus aliquas vetustatis incuria vitiatas ac semi-plenas emendavit atque complevit, aliquas vero ex toto composuit. Domínguez Del Val, "Julián de Toledo," 1260; Gonzálvez Ruiz, "San Julián de Toledo en el contexto," 18.

170. Felix, *Vita,* 11: Item librum orationum de festivitatibus, quas Toletana Ecclesia per totum circulum anni est solita celebrare, partim stylo sui ingenii depromptum, partim etiam inolita antiquitate vitiatum, studiose correctum in unum congessit, atque Ecclesiae Dei usibus ob amorem reliquit sanctae religionis. See Flórez, *España Sagrada,* 5:253–54. L. Férotin, *Le Liber Mozarabicus Sacramentorum et les manuscrits mozarabes* (Paris, 1912), XVIff.; reprint of 1912 edition, and general bibliography on the Hispanic liturgy, prepared and presented by Anthony Ward, SM, and Cuthbert Johnson, OSB (Rome, 1995). See also M. C. Díaz y Díaz, *Index scriptorum Latinorum Medii Aevi Hispanorum* (Salamanca, 1968), 639; idem, "La fecha de implantación del oracional festivo visigótico," *Bolletín Arqueológico* [Tarragona], 113–30 (1971–72): 215–43.

171. PL 85, cols. 0109-1064.

172. This is what Rivera Recio (*San Julián arzobispo de Toledo,* 208) supposes; see also Domínguez Del Val, "Julián de Toledo," 1260. But Hillgarth ("El Prognosticon futuri saeculi de San Julián de Toledo," 3, nn. 10, 11) puts this in serious doubt, affirming that the attributions of authorship to Julian of a *Liber mozarabicus Sacramentorum* by Dom Férotin, and of the *Orationale* of Verona, by Porter, have no basis. We know only that Julian is author of some formularies of Holy Mass, as attest, indirectly, the heretical Bishop Elipandus of Toledo and, directly, the Abbot Samson of Cordoba.

173. Flórez, *España Sagrada,* vol. 11, appendix, 325–516.

174. The abbot Samson (810–890) was a remarkable character in the religious history of Cordoba of the ninth century. In 862 he was unjustly sentenced as a heretic by a Council of Cordoba that was manipulated by the bishop of Malaga, Hostegesis. In 864, during a voluntary exile in the south of Spain, Abbot Samson composed an *Apologeticum* in two books (a third book of the work may have existed, but it has not survived). In the first book he

expounded his doctrine, his story, and his behavior in opposition to the heretical doctrines of Bishop Hostegesis and other collaborationists with the caliphate of Cordoba. The second book, full of erudition and quotations of theological authority, is devoted to the analysis of the anthropomorphist doctrine of Hostegesis, which he vigorously contests while also ridiculing the heretical bishop for his grammatical ignorance and the blunders in his writing. The anthropomorphist heresy maintained by Hostegesis affirmed that God is a material and bodily being, situated in the very high celestial spheres; another doctrinal anthropomorphist error held that the divine *subtilitas* had allowed the Divine Word to become incarnate not in the womb of Mary but in her heart, a position completely at odds with orthodox doctrine on God and Christ. *Sanctorum Patrum Toletanorum, App.*, 2:139–265; M. C. Díaz y Díaz, "Sanson," *Diccionario de Historia eclesiástica de España* (Madrid, 1972), 4:2179.

175. See G. Martínez Díez, *La colección canónica Hispana*, vol. 1, Monumenta Hispaniae Sacra, Serie Canónica 1 (Madrid, 1966).

176. When Julian became bishop of Toledo, in 680, a good twenty-five years had in fact passed since the last National Council of the Visigothic kingdom (656). Julian himself had also listened to the satisfaction of the bishops and their thanks to God and to the king for the convocation of the Eleventh Provincial Council of Toledo, in 675, after eighteen years of synodal inactivity. Like the early church, the Spanish Church of this time considered collegial government to be the ideal way of facing problems and of making the most opportune decisions to improve and correct ecclesial and social life. See Rivera Recio, *San Julián arzobispo de Toledo*, 107; Hillgarth, *Introduction*, XIV.

177. Madoz, "Giuliano da Toledo, Santo," col. 747.

178. According to Hillgarth (*Introduction*, XIII), "the definite triumph of the See of Toledo was no doubt connected with Ervig's need for Julian's support in 681."

179. This historical account shows the prestige enjoyed by the bishop of the royal city among the bishops gathered in council. See Madoz, "Giuliano da Toledo, Santo," cols. 747–48; here 747; idem, "San Julián de Toledo," 41; Hillgarth, *Introduction*, XIV.

180. This presidency of the councils is interpreted as a demonstration of the great influence that Julian had on the whole Spanish Church. M. A. W. [Mrs. Humphrey Ward] ("Julianus [63]," 480) says, "of his literary and theological influence over the Spanish churchmen of his own day on both sides of the Pyrenees,...the whole history of the twelfth, thirteenth, fourteenth, and fifteenth councils of Toledo are a sufficient proof."

181. See Veiga Valiña, *La doctrina escatológica*, 18 n. 2, where he affirms that Eugene II participated in four councils (from the Seventh to the Tenth), as did Julian, but that he presided over only two, compared with the four presided over by Julian.

182. Hillgarth, *Introduction*, XIV.

183. Ibid., and n. 3, with important bibliographical references above all to the *Ordo de celebrando concilio*, which in its final Spanish version was partly the fruit of the editorial contribution of Julian.

184. Díaz y Díaz, "Scrittori della penisola iberica," 110.

185. Ibid.

186. Ibid., 109–10. The judgment is even more significant if we consider that this section of the text is devoted to the most important writers of the Iberian Peninsula, among whom emerge Isidore of Seville, Braulio of Saragossa, Ildephonse of Toledo, and Taio of Saragossa.

187. Gonzálvez Ruiz, "San Julián de Toledo en el contexto," 7–21, here 17.

188. Rivera Recio, *San Julián arzobispo de Toledo*, 148.

189. See Veiga Valiña, *La doctrina escatológica*, 16.

190. Ibid.

191. Ibid., 15–16. Veiga Valiña emphasizes that the church was intimately linked to the state and that the king, both publicly and privately, relied upon the church and the bishops since they were the most cultured and educated people of the whole Hispanic-Visigothic society and were able, therefore, to advise him on the theoretical and practical foundations of social life.

192. Even if there is no explicit juridical basis for this rule, it was the custom. It seems to be the result of the fact that the figure of the Catholic Christian king was the basis of political and religious unity of the Hispanic-Visigothic people, and that clerics were an integral part of this people. Veiga Valiña, *La doctrina escatológica*, 15.

193. G. Martínez Díez, "Los Concilios de Toledo," *Anales Toledanos* 3 (1971): 119–37, here 125–27; he reports the texts of the national councils related to the Visigothic, Frankish, and Swebian convocation. See Rivera Recio, *St. Julián arzobispo de Toledo*, 149. The very fact that Pope Leo II addressed a letter to King Ervig asking him to convoke a council, which subsequently met in 680 to approve the acts of the Sixth Ecumenical Council of Constantinople, clearly indicates that the practice of attributing the convocation of a council to the Christian king was indeed accepted in the Church of Rome. Veiga Valiña, *La doctrina escatológica*, 15.

194. Martínez Díez, "Los Concilios de Toledo," 127–28.

195. Ibid., 128 and 133.

196. Ibid., 136–37.

197. Ibid., 129–33.

198. Ibid.

199. Ibid., 134–35.

200. In reality, "legislations in civil matters" by bishops are relatively few; see Rivera Recio, *San Julián arzobispo de Toledo*, 149.

201. Veiga Valiña, *La doctrina escatológica*, 15–16.

202. Z. García Villada, "La Iglesia y la monarqía en la época visigoda," *Razón y Fe* 97 (1932): 79.

203. It should be remembered that the king periodically gathered his council of the kingdom, composed of all the components of the Visigothic people. The council discussed matters related to the kingdom, and appropriate decisions were made. This same council also had the important task of electing the new king. As Rivera Recio correctly notes, none of the Visigothic kings was ever elected by a council of bishops (*San Julián arzobispo de Toledo*, 149).

204. See ibid.

205. See ibid.

206. Martínez Díez, "Concilios Nacionales y Provinciales," 537.

207. Martínez Díez, "Los Concilios de Toledo," 119–37, here 132, with an ample bibliography in n. 2; see also idem, "Concilios Nacionales y Provinciales" and the entries related to all the Concilios de Toledo in *Diccionario de Historia Eclesiástica de España* (Madrid, 1973), 1:537–38 and 566–73.

208. Veiga Valiña, *La doctrina escatológica*, 17.

209. Martínez Díez, "Los Concilios de Toledo," 121.

210. Veiga Valiña, *La doctrina escatológica*, 18.

211. Martínez Díez, "Los Concilios de Toledo," 122.

212. M. A. W. [Mrs. Humphrey Ward], "Ervigius (1), Ervig, Ervich," *A Dictionary of Christian Biography*, ed. W. Smith, DCL, LLD, and H. Wace, BD (London, 1882), 186–88, here 186.

213. See Rivera Recio, *San Julián arzobispo de Toledo*, 146.

214. Council XII of Toledo, canon 9, in PL 84, col. 477A.

215. Alberca, "Toledo, Councils of," 99–101.

216. Veiga Valiña, *La doctrina escatológica*, 16.

217. Ibid., 17, according to which Julian "de una manera o de otra tuvo necessariamente que tomar parte" in the conspiracy against the old warrior king Wamba. See also S. Teillet, "La déposition de Wamba: Un coup d'état au VIIe siècle," in *De Tertullien aux Mozarabes: Mélanges offerts à Jacques Fontaine à l'occasion de son 70ᵉ anniversaire*, ed. L. Holtz and J.-C. Fredouille (Paris, 1992), 2:99–113.

218. Y. García López, "La cronología de la 'Historia Wambae,'" *Anales de Estudios Medievales* 23 (1993): 121–39.

219. According to M. A. W. [Mrs. Humphrey Ward], "Ervigius (1), Ervig, Ervich," 188: "Ervig seems to have come to power as the instrument of the vengeance of the church and nobility upon his predecessor, who had attacked the privileges and attempted to tame the excesses of both orders."

220. M. A. W. [Mrs. Humphrey Ward], "Julianus (63)," 480: "Under Wamba and before he became bishop, his influence appears to have been considerable, while under Ervig he practically ruled Spain, and his power remained undiminished under Egica."

221. Díaz y Díaz, "Scrittori della penisola iberica," 110.

222. Murphy, "Julian of Toledo and the Condemnation of Monothelitism in Spain," 361–73, here 361.

223. M. A. W. [Mrs. Humphrey Ward], "Julianus (63)," 477.

224. Murphy, "Julian of Toledo and the Fall of the Visigothic Kingdom in Spain," 2; M. A. W. [Mrs. Humphrey Ward], "Ervigius (1), Ervig, Ervich," 187.

225. As is well known, the Visigothic monarchy was not hereditary but elective: every king was elected by the aristocracy and the bishops; see Murphy, "Julian of Toledo and the Fall of the Visigothic Kingdom in Spain," 10.

226. Ibid., 8.

227. Julian narrates, in fact (*Historia*, chapter 4), that at the moment in which the oil touched the king's head, a column of smoke was formed from which a bee went out, a symbol of divine approval and a happy kingdom: see Rivera Recio, *San Julián arzobispo of Toledo*, 90. The extent to which this idea of the historian and patriot Julian was an illusion will be shown by the unhappy reign of Wamba and his dramatic deposition from the throne, in which Bishop Julian was also somehow involved.

228. *Historia*, chapter 4.

229. Rivera Recio, *San Julián arzobispo de Toledo*, 108.

230. Especially those of the Saracen pirates who invaded the coast of the south of Spain, the weakest front of the empire, which was also a dark premonition of the future Arabic invasion of the peninsula. Wamba had evidently realized what great danger the Saracen raids constituted and had fought an epic naval battle in which 270 Saracen ships had been destroyed. See M. Torres López, "El reino hispanovisigodo," in *Historia de España*, ed. R. Menéndez Pidal (Madrid, 1976–91), 3:103.

231. Rivera Recio, *San Julián arzobispo de Toledo*, 92–94. The author, with beautiful imagery, describes the solemn ceremony in which Julian was given the role of crucifer deacon. Carrying the Christian insignia, he leaves together with the whole army for the military campaign led by the king.

232. Much of the material necessary for the extension work of the walls of Toledo was taken from the pagan temples on the outskirts of the city, as well as from the circus and from other monuments of the Roman age.

233. Murphy, "Julian of Toledo and the Fall of the Visigothic Kingdom in Spain," 8. See the *Chronica* of Isidorus Pacensis, chap. 24, PL 96, cols. 1259–60; Rivera Recio, *San Julián arzobispo de Toledo*, 107.

234. Murphy, "Julian of Toledo and the Fall of the Visigothic Kingdom in Spain," 1.

235. At the beginning (chap. 2) of the *Historia Wambae*, written by Julian at the end of the military campaign conducted by the king in the north of the Iberian Peninsula, we find a paean devoted to his king, marked by the highest laudatory tone.

236. Besides the Basque and Narbonnese rebellion, the king also had to face the Saracen fleet, which threatened the empire from the sea; see Murphy, "Julian of Toledo and the Fall of the Visigothic Kingdom in Spain," 9.

237. See the *Leges Visigothorum*, IX, 2, 8 in *Monumenta Germaniae Historica, legum sect.* I, t. I. The punishment could consist of the payment of damages caused by enemies or, for senior clergy, exile. For the rest of the clergy and the laity, the penalty would be infamy (that is, the deprivation of the right to act as witness, and slavery). In the most serious cases the death penalty could be applied, along with the confiscation of all goods to compensate for the damages produced by the enemy as a result of the desertion of those being sentenced.

238. PL 84, col. 469A: ...dimidiam fere partem populi ignobilitati perpetuae subjugavit.

239. *Leges Visigothorum*, IV, 5, 6.

240. A few months after the deposition of Wamba and the election of Ervig as new king of the Visigoths, the Twelfth Council of Toledo expressed a very critical judgment on Wamba's conduct: PL 84, cols. 473–75. Subsequently, under the rule of Ervig, the new castrensian diocese was dissolved and its bishop was moved to another episcopal see.

241. Rivera Recio (*San Julián arzobispo de Toledo*, 114) emphasizes how much this pretentious desire of the king to create a bishop for a diocese or palatine church was in contrast to canonical discipline, and could be the origin of schisms and disputes among the bishops.

242. The date on which the Eleventh Council of Toledo and the Third Council of Braga were kept at his request. In the conciliar texts the conduct and the reforms of Wamba were praised by the bishops of Spain: see the acts of the Eleventh Council of Toledo in PL 84, cols. 451–68; Braga III in PL 84, cols. 585–92.

243. PL 84, cols. 473C–473D.

244. Pl 84, col. 473B: injustis Wambae principis jussionibus.

245. This specification, written when King Ervig was still ruling, is found in the *Laterculus Visigothorum*, in *Monumenta Germaniae Historica, Auctores Antiquissimi*, XIII, 468. In the following lines is King Ervig's panegyric. A description of events can be found in J. Orlandis, *Historia del reino visigodo español: Los Acontecimientos, Las Instituciones* (Madrid, 2003), 412ff.

246. A rather imaginative but fair presentation of events is in Gonzálvez Ruiz, "San Julián de Toledo en el contexto," 12; see also Rivera Recio, "Los arzobispos de Toledo en el siglo VII," 206–7: "inexplicablemente encontramos a Julián cómplice del destronamiento de Wamba." A more analytical presentation is in Rivera Recio, *San Julián arzobispo de Toledo*, 133–37; see also Hillgarth, *Introduction*, XI–XIII.

247. T. González, "La Iglesia desde la conversión de Recaredo hasta la invasion arabe," in *Historia de la Iglesia en España*, I, *La Iglesia en la España romana y visigoda (siglos I–VIII)*, ed. R. García Villoslada (Madrid, 1979), 400–727, here 474.

248. See the excellent presentation of the events in Rivera Recio, *San Julián arzobispo de Toledo*, 133–37.

249. Z. García Villada, *Historia eclesiástica de España* (Madrid, 1929); see also E. Amman, "Penitence," *Dictionnaire de Théologie Catholique* (Paris, 1903–50), vol. 12, cols. 833–35. Visigothic liturgy allowed a special rite, called the "order of penitence," for the dying who wished, as a sign of humility before God and before the faithful, to be included among public penitents. The rite did not require a public acknowledgment of sins, but, as with a profession or religious consecration, it meant that the person who received it could no longer carry out any kind of public civil appointments, but was wholly devoted to God and to penance.

250. It should be noted that besides the religious meaning of the sacred tonsure, this cutting of the hair was also considered a shameful sign of punishment and defeat, reserved for defeated enemies or traitors, as will be seen with Duke Paul and other rebels defeated by King Wamba.

251. Rivera Recio, *San Julián arzobispo de Toledo*, 134.

252. PL 84, cols. 471A–471B: Mox per scripturam definitionis suae hunc inclytum dominum nostrum Ervigium post se praeelegit regnaturum et sacerdotali benedictione ungendum.

253. The Twelfth Council of Toledo (PL 84, col. 471A–471C) contains the following summary of the events that led to the consecration of Ervig as king of the Visigoths: Etenim sub qua pace vel ordine serenissimus Ervigius princeps regni conscenderit culmen, regnandique per sacrosanctam unctionem susceperit potestatem, ostensa nos Scripturarum evidentia docet: in quibus et praecedentis Wambanis principis poenitentiae susceptio noscitur, et translatus regni honor in hujus nostri principis nomine derivatur. Idem enim Wamba princeps dum inevitabilis necessitudinis teneretur eventu, suscepto religionis debito cultu et venerabili tonsurae sacrae signaculo, mox per scripturam definitionis suae hunc inclytum dominum nostrum Ervigium post se praeelegit; aliam quoque informationem jam dicti viri in nomine honorabilis et sanctissimi fratris nostri Juliani Toletanae sedis episcopi, ubi eum speravit pariter et instruxit, ut sub omni diligentiae ordine jam dictum dominum nostrum Ervigium in regno ungere deberet, et sub omni diligentia unctionis ipsius celebritas fieret; in quibus Scripturis et subscriptio nobis ejusdem Wambani principis claruit, et omnis evidentia confirmationis earumdem Scripturarum sese manifeste monstravit.

254. On the historicity of this event, Murphy ("Julian of Toledo and the Fall of the Visigothic Kingdom," 20) expresses serious doubt.

255. Rivera Recio, *San Julián arzobispo de Toledo*, 135–36.

256. Murphy, "Julian of Toledo and the Fall of the Visigothic Kingdom," 19.

257. This is the explicitly severe judgment of Rivera Recio: "Todo aquello había sido una superchería y la consiguiente consacración real de Ervigio una tridora conjuración." The comment related to the role of Julian in this "mal affaire" of state is bitter: "Inexplicabilmente encontramos a Julián cóm-

plice del destronamiento de Wamba" ("Los arzobispos de Toledo en el siglo VII," 206).

258. M. A. W. [Mrs. Humphrey Ward], "Julianus (63)," 477.

259. Rivera Recio, "Los arzobispos de Toledo en el siglo VII," 206–7.

260. Even though the Fourth Council of Toledo indicated that a good date to celebrate a council would have been May 18, when the grass is green, everything is in the flush of life, and the temperature is mild, the date of the Twelfth Council coincides with a series of serious impediments typical of winter: frozen roads, mountains covered with snow, impassable mountain passes. All of this made the assignment of the royal heralds, who had the task of communicating the convocation of the council to the bishops, very arduous. Above all, however, it made extremely difficult the journeys of the bishops and their entourages who were coming to Toledo from all over the ecclesiastical province and indeed from dioceses in other parts of Spain.

261. For a possible presentation of events, see Rivera Recio, *St. Julián arzobispo de Toledo*, 143–47, who hypothesizes that the documents exhibited could be "diplomatically perfect but historically false" (p.145).

262. Rivera Recio, "Los arzobispos de Toledo en el siglo VII," 207.

263. The solemn text of the Twelfth Council of Toledo states: Et ideo soluta manus populi ab omni vinculo juramenti, quae praedicto viro Wambae dum regnum adhuc teneret alligata permansit, hunc solum serenissimum Ervigium principem obsequendum grato servitii famulatu sequatur et libera, quem et divinum judicium in regno praeelegit et decessor princeps successurum sibi instituit, et quod superest quem totius populi amabilitas exquisivit. Unde, his praecognitis atque praescitis, serviendum est sub Deo coeli praedicto principi nostro Ervigio regi cum pia devotione, obsequendum etiam promptissima voluntate, agendum et enitendum quidquid ejus saluti proficiat, quidquid genti vel utilitatibus patriae suae consulat: unde non erit jam deinceps aut ab anathematis sententia alienus, aut a divinae animadversionis ultione securus, quisquis superbe contra salutem ejus deinceps aut erexerit vocem aut commoverit caedem aut quamcunque exquisierit laedendi occasionem. PL 84, cols. 471C–471D.

264. González, "La Iglesia desde la conversión de Recaredo hasta la invasion arabe," 474.

265. See the harsh judgment of historians as reported by Hillgarth (*Introduction*, IX) according to which Julian had an "overmastering desire to assert the Primacy of Toledo and an unscrupulous readiness to aid Ervig to depose Wamba, who, on this theory, had offended the 'clerical party' by a law enforcing service in the army even on clerics, and had offended Julian in particular by dividing his See of Toledo."

266. *La Crónica de Alfonso III,* ed. Z. García Villada (Madrid, 1918), chap. 3, 56–57; see also idem, *Historia eclesiástica de España,* 2:99.

267. Published under the patronage of E. Flórez, *España Sagrada*, 13:464–69.

268. García Villada, *Historia eclesiástica de España*, 2:103.

269. Murphy, "Julian of Toledo and the Fall of the Visigothic Kingdom in Spain," 10. He recalls that up to King Witteric (who died in 610) ten Visigothic kings had been murdered (he significantly calls this regicide *morbus gothicum*), while only eight had died in their royal bed or in battle! Moreover, in the seventh century three kings were deposed, albeit in a nonviolent way: Suintila (612–631), Tulga (640–642), and Wamba (672–280).

270. Some, such as R. Ceillier, refute the possibility that the dark episode of Wamba's sudden illness can be attributed to a conspiracy. Ceillier speaks of it as of a natural event that, thanks to two key characters, Julian and Ervig, found a quick resolution and ensured the monarchic continuity of the Visigothic empire; see R. Ceillier, *Histoire générale des auteurs sacrés et ecclésiastiques*, 17:737–38.

271. Murphy, "Julian of Toledo and the Fall of the Visigothic Kingdom in Spain," 2: "…as Primate of Spain Julian has been harshly criticized by Catholic historians…as well as by German Protestant scholars." See also Hillgarth, "St. Julian of Toledo in the Middles Ages," 8.

272. J. de Mariana, *Historia de rebus Hispaniae* (Toledo, 1592), 278–80.

273. Caesar Baronius, *Annales ecclesiastici* (Mainz, 1601), vol. 8, cols. 735, 749, ad an. 685, nn. 5–7; ad an. 688, nn. 3–5.

274. A. Hellfferich, *Entstehung und Geschichte des Westgothenrechts* (Berlin, 1858), 90ff.; idem, *Westgothischen Arianismus* (Berlin, 1860), 77ff.

275. F. L. J. Dahn, *Die könige der Germanen*, 11 vols. (Leipzig, 1861–1911), 6:472ff. (1885).

276. P. à Wengen, *Julianus Erzbischof von Toledo: Seine Leben und seine Wirksamkeit, unter den Königen Erwig und Egica* (St. Gallen, 1891).

277. F. Görres, "Der Primas Julian von Toledo (680–690): Eine Kirchencultur, und literargeschichtliche Studie," *Zeitschrift für wissenschaftliche Theologie* 46 (1902–1903): 524–53.

278. Gams, *Die Kirchengeschichte von Spanien*, 2/2:166ff.

279. Murphy, "Julian of Toledo and the Condemnation of Monothelitism in Spain," 361–73; idem, "Julian of Toledo and the Fall of the Visigothic Kingdom in Spain," 1–27.

280. For example, M. A. W. [Mrs. Humphrey Ward], "Ervigius (1), Ervig, Ervich," 186: "What was Ervig's share in the plot cannot now be made out with certainty. The poison story, however, seems to be a legendary accretion of later times." The author asserts that rather than a potion it was an illness or an indisposition of the king that made him partially unconscious for a time; the conspirators obviously took advantage of the circumstances.

281. Regarding the "innocent until proven guilty" hypothesis of Murphy, Hillgarth states: "His picture of Julian as a passive bystander is not

convincing, nor his suggestion that Ervig may have been innocent" ("St. Julian of Toledo in the Middles Ages," 8 n. 13).

282. M. C. Díaz y Díaz, "Giuliano di Toledo," *Dizionario Patristico di Antichità Cristiane* (Casale Monferrato, 1983), vol. 2, cols. 1611–12.

283. This is the opinion of, for example, Rivera Recio, *San Julián arzobispo de Toledo*, 224.

284. According to Veiga Valiña (*La doctrina escatológica*, 17), Julian "de una manera o de otra tuvo necesariamente que tomar parte" in the events that led to the deposition of Wamba.

285. Hillgarth, "Towards a Critical Edition," 38.

286. R. Gonzálvez Ruiz, "San Julián de Toledo en el contexto," 13.

287. Murphy, "Julian of Toledo and the Fall of the Visigothic Kingdom in Spain," 1.

288. M. A. W. [Mrs. Humphrey Ward], "Julianus (63)," 477.

289. As held by Rivera Recio, *San Julián arzobispo de Toledo*, 136; the same author describes Julian as "ignaro della macchinazione" (Rivera Recio, "Giuliani di Toldo," *Bibliotheca Sanctorum*, vol. 6, cols. 1215–18; here 1217). Recently, J. Orlandis suggested that Julian looked favorably on the conspiracy, though he excluded his direct participation, since ancient sources remain silent on this point (J. Orlandis, *Historia del reino visigodo español* [Madrid, 1988], 417f.).

290. Ruiz, "Julian of Toledo," 181.

291. Madoz, "Giuliano da Toledo, Santo," col. 747.

292. Orlandis, *Historia del reino visigodo español*, 412ff.

293. *Crónica de Alfonso III*, chap. 3, ed. Z. García Villada.

294. The *Chronicle of Alphonse III*, 883, provides a detailed history of the deposition of Wamba and the career of Ervig, and of his Byzantine origin as related with the lineage of Chindasvint. As for the deposition of Wamba, the text expressly accuses Ervig of having drugged the king with an herb, which it refers to as *spartus*, while seemingly exonerating both Julian (newly appointed bishop of Toledo) and the aristocracy (the *optimates*) of any charge. According to the text, they were not party to the intrigue but acted in good faith. See *Crónica de Alfonso III*, 55.

295. Felix, *Vita*, 10: Item libellum de divinis judiciis, ex sacris voluminibus collectum, in cujus principio est epistola ad dominum Ervigium, comitatus sui tempore pro eodem libello directa.

296. The council incorporated in canon 9 the legislation against the Jews that had already been formulated by King Sisebut and was particularly severe.

297. Murphy, "Julian of Toledo and the Fall of the Visigothic Kingdom in Spain," 13.

298. Ibid.

299. Ibid.

300. Felix, *Vita*, 8.

301. Murphy, "Julian of Toledo and the Fall of the Visigothic Kingdom in Spain," 21.

302. Ibid., 19.

303. Ibid., 21.

304. M. A. W. [Mrs. Humphrey Ward], "Ervigius (1), Ervig, Ervich," 188.

305. Ibid.

306. Ibid.

307. The following order was pronounced by Ervig at the opening of the Twelfth Council of Toledo: Judaeorum pestem quae in novam semper recrudescit insaniam radicitus exstirpate: leges quoque quae in eorumdem Judaeorum perfidiam a nostra gloria noviter promulgatae sunt omni examinationis probitate percurrite, et tam eisdem legibus tenorem inconvulsum adjicite, quam pro eorumdem perfidorum excessibus complexas in unum sententias promulgate. PL 84, col. 468D.

308. M. A. W. [Mrs. Humphrey Ward], "Julianus (63)," 477.

309. Ibid.

310. Ibid.

311. Ibid., 481.

312. Ibid. The attitude of Ward seems entirely prejudiced and excessive, above all when she describes Julian, in an entirely univocal way, as "[t]he sombre figure of the intriguing and persecuting bishop" who through his behavior is held responsible for the assault of evil that destroyed the Hispanic-Visigothic ecclesiastical system.

313. PL 84, cols. 475C–476A.

314. M. A. W. [Mrs. Humphrey Ward], "Julianus (63)," 477.

315. See Rivera Recio, San Julián arzobispo de Toledo, chap. 12, "La primacía eclesíastica de Toledo," 151. The privilege of the Toledan see will be solemnly reaffirmed also in the following Council of Toledo, the thirteenth.

316. PL 84, cols. 475C–476A: Unde placuit omnibus pontificibus Hispaniae atque Galliae [in some manuscripts atque Galliae is missing], ut salvo privilegio uniuscujusque provinciae licitum maneat deinceps Toletano pontifici quoscunque regalis potestas elegerit et jam dicti Toletani episcopi judicium dignos esse probaverit, in quibuslibet provinciis in praecedentium sedium praeficere praesules, et decedentibus episcopis eligere successores.

317. PL 84, col. 476A.

318. Ibid.: excepto si regia jussione impeditum.

319. Rivera Recio, "Los arzobispos de Toledo en el siglo VII," 208.

320. Gams, Die Kirchengeschichte von Spanien, 2/2: 217.

321. M. A. W. [Mrs. Humphrey Ward], "Julianus (63)," 478.

322. Hellfferich, Westgothischen Arianismus, 73.

323. See Rivera Recio, San Julián arzobispo de Toledo, 158.

324. Perhaps in an exaggeratedly solemn way, considering that the expression used by the fathers calls into question the binding nature of the

resolutions made by the conciliar fathers: ea ipsa gesta, prout gesta sunt vel conscripta, omni temporum aeternitate valitura decernimus et omnimodae soliditatis vigore firmamus juxta ordinem capitulorum. PL 84, col. 495D.

325. The Twelfth Council of Toledo, canon 4, in PL 84, cols. 473B-475A.

326. King Ervig was easily influenced. He certainly did not possess the military temperament or governing ability of King Wamba. This can be seen from the increase of privileges of every kind that both the Hispanic-Visigothic aristocracy and the episcopate managed to extort from the king. Gonzálvez Ruiz ("San Julián de Toledo en el contexto," 14) quotes, for example, the fact that the bishops received from the king authority in the judicial arena. With this privilege they tried to check the numerous cases of corruption, usurpation, and extortion that were committed by corrupt judges. But undoubtedly they appropriated or heavily interfered with the judicial power.

327. See Rivera Recio, *San Julián arzobispo de Toledo*, 160–61.

328. A. C. Vega, "El Primado Romano y la Iglesia española en lo siete primeros siglos," *Ciudad de Dios* 155 (1943): 69–103; see also E. Magnin, *L'église visigothique* (Paris, 1912), 23–31; J. Madoz, "El Primado Romano en España en el ciclo isidoriano," *Revista española de Teología* 2 (1942): 229–55.

329. M. A. W. [Mrs. Humphrey Ward], "Julianus (63)," 478.

330. Hillgarth, *Introduction*, LXV; see Paul à Wengen, *Julianus Erzbischof von Toledo*, xvii n. 4; M. A. W. [Mrs. Humphrey Ward], "Julianus (63)," 477–78. R. Aigrain, in *Storia della Chiesa*, vol. 5, *San Gregorio Magno, gli stati barbarici e la conquista araba (590–757)* (Rome/Turin, 1980), 350 n. 122, emphasizes the excessive severity of the author of the entry in the *Dictionary of Christian Bibliography* in judging Julian of Toledo as a scheming bishop and persecutor of the Jews.

331. Hillgarth, *Introduction*, LXVI.

332. Ibid.

333. García Moreno, *Prosopographía del reino visigodo de Toledo*, n. 251.

334. For example, Domínguez Del Val, "Julián de Toledo," 1259–60, in addition to the aforementioned scholars.

335. The seriousness of the episode is weakened by Orlandis, *Historia del reino visigodo español*, 247.

336. Murphy, "Julian of Toledo and the Fall of the Visigothic Kingdom in Spain," 21.

337. Kayserling, "Julian of Toledo," online version, www.jewishencyclope dia.com/view.jsp?artid=717&letter=J&search=julian%20of%20toledo.

338. Madoz, "San Julián de Toledo," 39.

339. Veiga Valiña, *La doctrina escatológica*, 20.

340. Hillgarth, "St. Julian of Toledo in the Middles Ages," 8–9.

341. C. Codoñer Merino, *El De viris illustribus de Isidoro de Sevilla, estudio y ed. crítica* (Salamanca, 1964, 1972); J. Fontaine, *Culture et spiritualité en Espagne du IVe au VIIe siècle* (London, 1986).

342. J. Fontaine, "El De viris illustribus de San Ildefonso de Toledo," *Anales Toledanos* 3 (1971): 59–96.

343. This is the flattering judgment of J. Madoz, "Giuliano da Toledo, Santo," col. 747.

344. Hillgarth, *Introduction*, VIII–IX.

345. Ibid.; to complete the episcopal portrait, Hillgarth also quotes the brief poem "Versus ad Modoenum," which closes volume 115 of the Corpus Christianorum containing the works of Julian of Toledo, where Julian calls himself *Iulianus servorum domini servus.*

346. This flattering judgment is that of Domínguez Del Val, "Julián de Toledo," 1260.

347. See Madoz, *Segundo Decenio de Estudios sobre Patrística Española,* 142.

348. Ibid.

349. T. Stancati, "Giuliano di Toledo," *Lexicon–Dizionario dei Teologi* (Casale Monferrato, 1998), 579–80.

350. See Madoz, *Segundo Decenio de Estudios sobre Patrística Española,* 142.

351. Hillgarth, "El Prognosticon futuri saeculi de San Julián de Toledo," 8.

352. Ibid.

353. Felix, *Vita,* 5: In defensione omnium Ecclesiarum eximius, in regendis subditis pervigil, in comprimendis superbis erectus, in sustentatione humilium apparatus, debita auctoritate munificus.

354. So says Murphy, "Julian of Toledo and the Condemnation of Monothelitism in Spain," 361.

355. Hillgarth, "Towards a Critical Edition," 37.

356. "Pope Benedict II (684–685) found some of his ideas theologically unsound" (Ruiz, "Julian of Toledo," 181).

357. Domínguez Del Val, "Julián de Toledo," 1259; Hillgarth (*Introduction,* IX) reports the harsh judgment of historians on the political behavior of Julian. It should not be forgotten that the respect and recognition of the authority of Rome by the bishops of Spain was clearly affirmed by the Third Council of Toledo, which had ordered that, in addition to the acts of the ecumenical councils, the decrees of the bishops of Rome, too, should be preserved and respected, therefore recognizing the magisterial value and primary importance of the pronouncements of the apostolic see of Rome.

358. Hillgarth, "St. Julian of Toledo in the Middles Ages," 8–9.

359. Hillgarth, "El Prognosticon futuri saeculi de San Julián de Toledo," 2; see also idem, "Towards a Critical Edition," 37.

360. For example, Murphy, "Julian of Toledo and the Fall of the Visigothic Kingdom in Spain," 1–27; idem, "Julian of Toledo and the Condemnation of Monothelitism," 361–73.

361. G. D'onofrio, "Le origini del medioevo teologico (secoli VI–VII), vol. III, 3: Voci teologiche nelle regioni iberiche: dalla fine del regno visigoto

a Beato Libana," in *Storia della Teologia nel Medioevo*, vol. 1, *I princìpi* (Casale Monferrato, 1996), 83–89, here 84. The author affirms the *Antikeimenon* of Julian as the most noteworthy work of the bishop of Toledo. The *Prognosticum* is defined simply as "manualetto di escatologia elementare." While this unusual hierarchy of the importance of the works of Julian arouses wonder and is questionable, what the author affirms in speaking of the originality of the theological methodology of Julian can be shared, insofar as it can be shown to be "una prima forma di discussione critica dei dati raccolti nei testi sacri…segno, indubbiamente, di un passo in avanti verso l'elaborazione tecnica del metodo teologico medieval."

362. See the genuine and convincing affirmation of Forget, "Julien de Tolède (Saint)," col. 1940: "Parmi le rares théologiens du VIIe siècle, un des meilleurs."

363. Domínguez Del Val, "Julián de Toledo," 1260.

364. Ibid.

365. Felix, *Vita*, 5: …ut non esset cui in augustiis constituto non subvenire vellet; ita unius charitatis exuberans, ut non a se boni quidpiam cuique postulanti ex charitate praestare desisteret: sic denique se Deo charum maluit exhibere in omnibus, et praestabilem hominibus cunctis ostendere, ut et illi usquequaque placeret, et hominibus propter Deum, si fieri potest, devota satisfaceret mente.

366. Ibid.: Fuit enim vir timore Domini plenus, prudentia summus, consilio cautus, discretionis bono praecipuus, eleemosynis nimium deditus, in revelatione miserorum promptissimus, in suffectu oppressorum devotus, in interveniendo discretus, in negotiis dirimendis strenuus, in providendis judiciis aequus, in sententia parcus, in vindicatione justitiae singularis, in disceptatione laudabilis, in oratione jugis, in divinarum laudum exsolutione mirabilis. Quod si forsan in officiis divinis quidquam, ut solet, difficultatis occurreret, ad corrigendum facillimus, pro sacris luminibus vehementer admonitus, in defensione omnium Ecclesiarum eximius, in regendis subditis pervigil, in comprimendis superbis erectus, in sustentatione humilium apparatus, debita auctoritate munificus, amplectendae humilitatis bono opimus, ac generaliter universa morum probitate conspicuus.…Tanto nobilium praecedentium virorum dignis meritis coaequans, quanto ab eis in nullo virtutum corpore exstitit infimus.

367. Madoz, "San Julián de Toledo," 41.

368. Madoz, "Segundo Decenio de Estudios sobre Patrística Española," 142.

369. M. A. W. [Mrs. Humphrey Ward], "Julianus (63)," 477.

370. Domínguez Del Val, *Patrología Española*, 117*.

371. Madoz, "San Julián de Toledo," 69.

372. C. García Rodríguez, *El culto a los Santos en la España romana y visigoda* (Madrid, 1966).

373. The chronicles tell us nothing of the causes and circumstances of the death of Julian of Toledo. It is likely that he died of natural causes and that everything possible was done to save him, including calling for the best physicians of the imperial court, but evidently in vain. Julian died at the age of only forty-eight—a very young age according to current life expectancies, but old enough considering that the average life expectancy of the seventh century was around forty years. Rivera Recio (*San Julián arzobispo de Toledo*, 219–20) hypothesizes that Julian suffered a long illness and much agony.

374. Depending on whether we calculate his date of birth to be 642 or 644.

375. Felix informs us with unusual precision that Julian died *pridie nonas*, that is, on March 5 or 6 in the year 690. Many scholars, basing their judgment on this information from Felix, believe that the date is actually March 6, considering that the greater part of the manuscripts of the *Vita* include this expression, as do some books of prayer. Hence, E. Flórez believes that Julian died on March 6, 690, while other scholars, based on the liturgical-pastoral tradition of the diocese of Toledo, which keeps the memory of St. Julian on March 8 every year, consider this to be the true date of Julian's death. They think that the expression *pridie nonas* has, in reality, been misunderstood by copyists, and that the expression was originally *postridie nonas*, that is, the day after. See, e.g., Baronius, *Annales ecclesiastici*, 8:792; the Bollandist in *Acta Sanctorum*, vol. 6, part 1 (Anversa, 1715): *Martyrologium Usuardi Monachi*, 140; see the final *Observatio;* Mariana, *Historia General de España*, 2:80, Flórez, *España Sagrada*, 5:284.

376. The recording of the length of Julian's episcopal ministry is made solemnly by his biographer: Praesulatus autem honorem et sacerdotii dignitatem annis decem obtinuit, mense uno, diebus septem (Felix, *Vita*, 12).

377. See Rivera Recio, *San Julián arzobispo de Toledo*, 220. The author presents with feeling and, at the same time, with liturgical realism, the probable liturgical funeral rites of the Visigothic Church reserved to the primate of Spain.

378. The church was founded or restored by the Visigothic king Sisebut, a contemporary of Isidore of Seville; see Isidore, *Chronicon*, in PL 83, col. 1056A.

379. Rivera Recio, "Los arzobispos de Toledo en el siglo VII," 213.

380. The narrative pathos of Rivera Recio continues to the point of imagining the Latin inscription on the tombstone; see *San Julián arzobispo de Toledo*, 222.

381. Hillgarth, "El Prognosticon futuri saeculi de San Julián de Toledo," 8.

382. Hillgarth, *Introduction*, VIII n. 6.

383. See Férotin, *Liber Mozarabicus Sacramentorum*, 457.

384. Written around 875; see *Acta Sanctorum, Iunii*, vol. 6, part 1 (Anversa, 1715): *Martyrologium Usuardi Monachi*, 140; see B. de Gaiffier, "Les

notices hispaniques dans le Martyrologie d'Usuard," *Analecta Bollandiana* 55 (1937): 268–83.

385. For example, the Missals of St. Dominic of Silos located in the Bibliothèque Nationale de Paris, *Nouvelles Acquisitions* (n. 2194) and of Mont-St.-Remy (ibid., cod. lat. 823).

386. Hillgarth (*Introduction*, VIII n. 6) puts the date at 875; while the entry "Julian of Toledo" in *New Catholic Encyclopedia* (8:50) moves the date of the first testimony of a cult in Toledo to 858. The defining date quoted by Hillgarth is that of the death of the Benedictine monk Usuard, the author of the *Martyrologium*, written by order of Charles the Bald. The preface to the *Martyrologium* was written by him a short time before he died. Usuard was sent to Spain by his order to gather important relics and it is probably in this search that he came across the relics of Julian of Toledo and inserted him, therefore, into the *Martyrologium*. See de Gaiffier, "Les notices hispaniques dans le Martyrologie d'Usuard," 279. Other calendars and Missals of the period also include Julian. In the famous monastery of St. Millán de la Cogolla, one of the principal religious and spiritual centers of the Castile region, the existence of the relics of Julian of Toledo is recorded; see B. de Gaiffier, "Les reliques de l'abbaye de San Millán de la Cogolla au XIII siècle," *Analecta Bollandiana* 53 (1935): 90–96.

387. Hillgarth, "St. Julian of Toledo in the Middles Ages," 9.

388. See de Bruyne, "Le plus ancien catalogue," 95; Flórez, *España Sagrada*, 5:282ff.

389. Gennadius, *De scriptoribus ecclesiasticis*, 98, in PL 58, cols. 1117B–1118B.

390. See de Bruyne, "Le plus ancien catalogue," 93–96.

391. See de Gaiffier, "Les reliques de l'abbaye," 97.

392. See Rivera Recio, *San Julián arzobispo de Toledo*, 224.

393. Madoz, "Giuliano da Toledo, Santo," col. 748.

394. Hillgarth, "St. Julian of Toledo in the Middle Ages," 7.

395. Felix, *Vita*, 7–11.

396. Of these five important works of Julian, four were published in the critical edition in vol. 115 of the Corpus Christianorum, Series Latina, together with the brief poem "Versus ad Modoenum."

397. With the title *Sanctorum Patrum Toletanorum quotquot extant opera* (Madrid, 1785).

398. Hillgarth, *Introduction*, XV. See also C. H. Beeson, "The Ars Grammatica of Julian of Toledo," in *Miscellanea Francesco Ehrle*, Scritti di Storia e Paleografia (Rome, 1924), 1:50–70.

399. Corpus Christianorum, Series Latina, vol. 115, 257–60. The text was published at the end of the 1950s in *Hermes, Zeitschrift für klassische Philologie* 87 (1959): 251–52, and reprinted in *Mittelalterliche Studien*, I (Stuttgart, 1966), 293–94. The edition is based on two manuscripts.

400. Felix, *Vita*, 9: librum carminum diversorum, in quo sunt hymni, epitaphia, atque de diversis causis epigrammata numerosa. See also Hillgarth, *Introduction*, XV.

401. Díaz y Díaz, "Scrittori della Penisola Iberica," 113.

402. J. N. Hillgarth, "Las fuentes de san Julián de Toledo," *Anales Toledanos* 3 (1971): 98–99.

403. Ibid.

404. According to Rivera Recio (*San Ildefonso de Toledo: Biografía, época y posteridad* [Madrid/Toledo, 1985], 7), there are two reasons why Felix does not quote the *Elogium Ildephonsi* among the works of Julian. Either he considered it as a part and continuation of the *De viris illustribus* of the same Ildephonse, or, considering its brevity, he did not consider it a book or a real work of Julian. Veiga Valiña (*La doctrina escatológica*, 24) is also of this last opinion.

405. Madoz, "San Julián de Toledo," 60.

406. A number of manuscript codices from the ninth to the eleventh centuries attribute this brief biographical writing to Julian; see Rivera Recio, *San Ildefonso de Toledo*, 5 n. 3; Hillgarth, "El Prognosticon futuri saeculi de San Julián de Toledo," 5.

407. PL 96, cols. 43–44. See Rivera Recio, *San Ildefonso de Toledo*, 4–8.

408. Oddly, Julian, in giving the list of the works of Ildephonse, omits *De viris illustribus*, to which he himself will add the praise of Ildephonse.

409. Some later editions of the work have been embellished with some adventurous elements, for example, the escape of Ildephonse from his father's house, a classic of the hagiographic stories spanning several centuries; see J. Madoz, *San Ildefonso de Toledo a través de la pluma del Arcipreste de Talavera* (Madrid, 1943).

410. Baronius, *Annales Ecclesiastici*, vol. 8, years 657–80, 601.

411. There is also a "long" version of the *Elogium*, with a small addition where, as often happens in the biographies of the saints, the harsh opposition of the father to the monastic vocation of the principal character is relayed. Since this short *supplementum* suddenly dramatizes a text that is otherwise entirely ordinary, it is probable that the *supplementum* is an interpolation; see Rivera Recio, *San Ildefonso de Toledo*, 7–8.

412. PL 96, col. 43A: merito non homo, sed Deus, per hominem affatim eloqui crederetur.

413. The *De scriptoribus ecclesiasticis* or *De viris illustribus* of Gennadius (the text is in PL 58, cols. 1059–1120) was written by him to continue and complete the work of St. Jerome. The work of Gennadius is particularly important because it is a key source of fifth-century Christian literature, and also because of the very brief details that he gives us on some 101 authors. These details are, in some cases, the only information we possess. There are some obvious interpolations, however, including the autobiography of Gennadius himself that closes the work. The book is probably an imitation of

the *De viris illustribus* of Jerome, which finished in the same way. See *Patrologia*, vol. 4, *Dal Concilio di Calcedonia (451) a Beda: I Padri latini*, 276–79.

414. It is known that a "long" version (of some forty-six chapters) of the *De viris illustribus* of Isidore also exists, created by a fusion to the original in the ninth or tenth century in Spain. This edition had a wide circulation in its printed editions. For further information on the *De viris illustribus* of Isidore, see C. Codoñer Merino, *El de viris illustribus de Isidoro de Sevilla: estudio y ed. critica* (Salamanca, 1964); F. Bertini, "Isidoro e Ildefonso, continuatori di Gerolamo biografo," in *Gerolamo e la biografia letteraria* (Genoa, 1989), 105–22.

415. Written by Jerome in AD 392–393.

416. The Roman historian Gaius Suetonius Tranquillus (AD 75–160) was secretary to the imperial administration under Trajan. His principal work is the *De vita Caesarum*, the history of the first twelve emperors of Rome. His *De viris illustribus*, which comes to us in an incomplete form, is in five books, respectively devoted to poets, orators, historians, philosophers, and grammarians and rhetoricians of the imperial epoch (for example, Terence, Horace, Lucan, Pliny the Elder, and so on). Suetonius expressed harsh judgments against Christianity, which had just arrived in the eternal city, accusing it of fostering superstition (which was anything outside of the official Roman religion). As a result of this adverse attitude toward Christianity, the emperor Claudius expelled Christians from the Urbe in around AD 49.

417. J. Madoz has edited the *Elogium* in *San Ildefonso de Toledo a través de la pluma del Arcipreste de Talavera*; the critical edition was made *cura et studio* of U. Domínguez Del Val and was published in *Revista española de Teología* 31 (1971): 138–39. On this subject, see the review by E. Ann Matter of vol. 115 of the Corpus Christianorum in *Speculum* 55, no. 3 (1980): 624–25.

418. The complete title of the work is *Historia Wambae Regis Gothorum Toletani expeditione*. See *Clavis Patrum Latinorum qua in corpus christianorum edendum optimas quasque scriptorum recensiones a Tertulliano ad Bedam commode recludit Eligius Dekkers opera usus qua rem praeparavit et iuvit Aemilius Gaar † vindobonensis*. Editio tertia aucta et emendata (Steenbrugis, in Abbatia Sancti Petri, 1995); see also M. C. Díaz y Díaz, *Index scriptorum Latinorum Medii Aevi Hispanorum*, part 1, Filosofia y Letras, Tome XIII, núm. 1, Acta Salmaticensia (Salamanca, 1958). Ceillier (*Histoire générale des auteurs sacrés et ecclésiastiques*, 737–38) dwells on the fact that Wamba forced Duke Paul to return the stolen sacred vases and, above all, the precious votive gold crown that King Recared had placed on the grave of St. Felix of Girona and which the traitor had dared to put on his head (*Historia*, 26); see Rivera Recio, *St. Julián arzobispo de Toledo*, 102. On the historical work of Julian, see M. de Jong, "Adding Insult to Injury: Julian of Toledo and His Historia Wambae," in *The Visigoths: From the Migration Period to the Seventh Century. An Ethnographic Perspective*, ed. P. Heather (San Marino, 1999), 373–402; *The Story of Wamba: Julian of Toledo's Historia Wambae*

Regis, translated with an introduction and note by J. Martínez Pizarro (Washington, DC, 2005).

419. Hillgarth (*Introduction*, VIII) describes it as "one of his earlier works."

420. According to Madoz ("San Julián de Toledo," 42), it is a "notabílisima aparición de historia documentada y concebida al modo clásico, admirable capítulo de historiographía en el siglo VII."

421. W. Levison, *Historia Wambae* in *Monumenta Germaniae Historica, Scriptorum Rerum Merovingiarum,* 5 (Berlin, 1910), 486–535, reproduced in Corpus Christianorum, Series Latina, vol. 115, 213–55.

422. Hillgarth, "Las fuentes de san Julián de Toledo," 99.

423. M. A. W. [Mrs. Humphrey Ward], "Julian (63)," 480.

424. Felix, *Vita,* 7, 10.

425. M. A. W. [Mrs. Humphrey Ward], "Julianus (63)," 480. The affirmation can be shared on a historiographic level, but we are convinced that the most remarkable work of the literary and theological production of Julian of Toledo was the *Prognosticum futuri saeculi,* which, besides being the first systematic treatise of Christian eschatology, was also a widely circulated work in the Middle Ages and influenced Christian eschatology in a conclusive way.

426. Some historians think that Julian did not support the king and his army in the military campaign against Duke Paul and the other rebels of the North of Spain. This opinion is due to some confusion and geographical inaccuracies detectable in the *Historia*; but others think that the abundance of information contained in the work can derive only from a direct and personal participation of the author, in the stories that he narrates. See Gonzálvez Ruiz, "San Julián de Toledo en el contexto," 9–10.

427. *SS. PP. Toletanorum quotquot extant opera* (Madrid, 1785).

428. PL 96, cols. 761–808.

429. PL 96, cols. 763–797A; the *textus tudensis* is in PL 96, cols. 801–808C.

430. Madoz, "San Julián de Toledo," 42.

431. For example, the author of the *Chronica* of Silos (twelfth century), who in chapter 5 offers an *excerptum* of the *textus tudensis* (Flórez, *España Sagrada,* 17:264–65.

432. *Monumenta Germaniae Historica, Scriptores Rerum Merovingiarum* 5:500–535; the valuable introduction is pp. 486–99.

433. This remark is from Hillgarth, "St. Julian of Toledo in the Middle Ages," 7.

434. *Prognosticum futuri saeculi, Apologeticum de tribus capitulis, De comprobatione sextae aetatis mundi.*

435. B. Bischoff, "Ein Brief Julians von Toledo über Rhytmen, metrisches Dichtung und Prosa," *Hermes* 87 (1959): 251–52; reprinted in idem, *Mittelalterliche Studien* (Stuttgart, 1966), 1:286–98, with additions to the critical apparatus.

436. Sister Theresa Joseph Powers, "A Translation of Julian of Toledo's 'Historia Wambae regis' with Introduction and Notes," (MA thesis, Catholic University of America, 1941).

437. P. R. Díaz y Díaz, "Historia del Rey Wamba: Traducción y notas," *Florentia Iliberritana* 1 (1990): 89–114.

438. *The Story of Wamba*, trans. Joaquín Martínez Pizarro.

439. Toledo was the *urbs regia* (*Prognosticum, Praefatio Iuliani*) from the time of King Leovigild (568–586).

440. See Rivera Recio, *San Julián arzobispo de Toledo*, 168: he maintains that the sources attest the hostility of the Jews toward the country and that they gave their help to the conspirator Ildericus, viscount of Nimes.

441. Septimania is located in southern France or the province of Narbonne.

442. While he qualifies Wamba as king of "southern" Spain.

443. M. C. Díaz y Díaz moves the date of the *Historia Wambae* to 681: "progettato in epoca contemporanea agli avvenimenti, fu scritto solo nel 681, usando materiale di prima mano, forse degli stessi archivi regi" ("Scrittori della penisola iberica," 113). This dating seems unlikely since, among other things, in the first year of his ministry as archbishop of Toledo Julian was very busy, facing the crisis in the empire that resulted from the deposition of King Wamba and the celebration of the Twelfth Council of Toledo.

444. The triumphal entry of King Wamba into the city with his troops fully armed, with the rays of the sun amplified by their reflection on the armor and shields of the victorious soldiers, is described by Julian (*Historia*, 23); perhaps it reminded him of the triumphal entry of the army of the Maccabees into the city of Bethzechariah (1 Macc 6:39).

445. García Moreno, *Prosopographía del Reino Visigodo de Toledo*, 188–89 n. 529.

446. See, for example, *Historia* 1, 13–15. The presentation of King Wamba's military campaign made by Rivera Recio, *St. Julián arzobispo de Toledo*, chap. 7, 87–106, is even more detailed, colorful, and vivacious, using selected passages of the *Historia* of Julian while also imagining, with apparent realism, some details of which the author of the *Historia* does not speak.

447. Madoz, "San Julián de Toledo," 42.

448. For example, *Historia* 1, 9, where King Wamba pronounces fiery words against the Basque and Gallican rebels.

449. Rivera Recio: *San Julián arzobispo de Toledo*, 87.

450. Veiga Valiña, *La doctrina escatológica*, 24.

451. According to Hillgarth, in the *Insultatio* of the *Historia Wambae*, Julian utilizes the *Altercatio ecclesiae et synagogae*, the work of an anonymous author of the fifth century. See J. N. Hillgarth, "Historiography in Visigothic Spain," in *La storiografia altomedievale: Settimane di Studio del Centro Italiano di Studi sull'alto medioevo* 17 (Spoleto, 1970), 301f.

452. Madoz, "San Julián de Toledo," 42.

453. Rivera Recio, *San Julián arzobispo de Toledo*, 103.

454. Ibid., 104. He asserts that the remitted death penalty ought, however, to be replaced with a less definitive but equally terrible punishment that consisted in gouging out the eyes of the traitor. But the chronicle of Julian finishes without saying a word on whether the substitutive punishment was ever applied.

455. Hillgarth, *Introduction*, VIII.

456. See Murphy, "Julian of Toledo and the Fall of the Visigothic Kingdom in Spain," 7; J. Madoz, "Fuentes teológico-literarias de san Julián de Toledo," *Gregorianum* 33 (1952): 411.

457. Gonzálvez Ruiz, "San Julián de Toledo en el contexto," 11.

458. See, for example, *Historia* 1, 1, where Julian shows to the young people the virtue of glory, that is, the triumphant king.

459. Rivera Recio, *San Julián arzobispo de Toledo*, 87.

460. Hillgarth, "St. Julian of Toledo in the Middles Ages," 11.

461. See the praises of the primate of Toledo that are included in the *Continuatio Hispana*, ed. T. Mommsen, *Monumenta Germaniae Historica, Chronica minora* II, 349–50; it is likely that these authors also knew the brief *Vita* written by Bishop Felix, biographer of Julian.

462. See Hillgarth, *Introduction*, XIX.

463. T. Mommsen, ed., *Monumenta Germaniae Historica, Chronica minora*, II, 370–75, here 374.

464. Hillgarth, "St. Julian of Toledo in the Middles Ages," 12.

465. Edition of Garcia Villada, 54–55.

466. See Rivera Recio, *San Julián arzobispo de Toledo*, 211.

467. On the *Ars grammatica*, or better *Ars grammatica, poetica, rhetorica*, of Julian of Toledo, see Beeson, "Ars Grammatica of Julian of Toledo," 50–70; W. M. Lindsay, ed., *Julian of Toledo, De uitiis et figuris* (Oxford: Oxford University Press, 1922), 41, according to which a part of the *Ars grammatica* of Julian would be "nothing more than notes taken from Julian's lectures"; see also M. A. H. Maestre Yenes, *Ars Iuliani Toletani Episcopi: Una gramática latina de la España visigoda* (Toledo, 1973); S. Giannini, *Percorsi metalinguistici nell'Alto Medioevo: Giuliano di Toledo e la teoria della grammatica* (Milan, 1996); L. Munzi, "Note testuali all'Ars grammatica di Giuliano di Toledo," *Annali dell'Istituto Universitario Orientale di Napoli*, Sezione filologico-letteraria 1 (1979): 171–73; idem, "Cipriano in Giuliano Toletano Ars gramm. 197, 52–54 M.Y.," *Rivista di Filologia e d'Istruzione Classica* 108 (1980): 320–21; Madoz, *San Julián de Toledo*, 60–61. L. Munzi, "Ancora sul testo dell' Ars grammatica di Giuliano di Toledo," *Annali dell' Istituto Universitario Orientale di Napoli*, Sezione filologico-letteraria 2–3 (1980–81): 229–31.

468. Rivera Recio, *San Julián arzobispo de Toledo*, 61.

469. As we have seen, the biographer Felix does not know of the existence of this work and, therefore, he does not insert it into the list of the

works of Julian. But many modern authors do not particularly object to attributing the *Ars grammatica* to the literary paternity of Julian. Hillgarth thinks, however, that the critical edition of the *Grammatica* by C. H. Beeson (see n. 398 above) does not resolve "the question of authorship."

470. Hillgarth, "El Prognosticon futuri saeculi de San Julián de Toledo," 5; idem, "St. Julian of Toledo in the Middle Ages," 10; idem, "Las fuentes de san Julián de Toledo," 98; idem, *Introduction*, XV.

471. Lindsay, ed., *Julian of Toledo De uitiis et figuris.*

472. Maestre Yenes, ed., *Ars Iuliani Toletani episcopi;* see also L. Munzi, "Il *De partibus orationis* di Giuliano di Toledo," *AION (filol.)* 2–3 (1980–81): 153–228; idem, "Ancora sulle citazioni di Giuliano di Toledo (Ars grammatica e De partibus orationis)," *AION (filol.)* 2–3 (1980–81): 229–31.

473. See the considerations of Beeson, *Ars Grammatica of Julian of Toledo,* 50–60.

474. The comparison, which appears risky, comes in reality from a true expert in the subject, J. Madoz: "San Julián de Toledo," 60.

475. Bischoff, "Ein Brief Julians," 291.

476. See Hillgarth, "St. Julian of Toledo in the Middles Ages," 10 n. 22.

477. *SS. PP. Toletanorum quotquot extant opera* (Madrid, 1785).

478. Hillgarth ("Towards a Critical Edition," 39) states, "the work comes from the Visigothic Spain and no doubt from Toledo in the time of Julian."

479. Díaz y Díaz, "Scrittori della Penisola Iberica," 113.

480. This is the working hypothesis of Maestre Yenes, *Ars Juliani Toletani Episcopi.*

481. According to Murphy ("Julian of Toledo and the Fall of the Visigothic Kingdom in Spain," 7), the *Ars grammatica* is to be attributed without doubt to Julian and is "evidently the result of his years teaching grammar, rhetoric and metrics in Toledo."

482. Hillgarth, *Introduction*, XV.

483. The example is *Domni Ervigi regis (Ars grammatica,* 2, 36).

484. Elius Donatus, a Latin grammarian and rhetorician of the fourth century, was the most important grammarian of his epoch. He was of African origin. Among his pupils were Jerome and Rufinus; see A. M. Negri, ed., *Elio Donato: Ars grammatica maior* (Reggio Emilia, 1960); W. J. Chase, ed., *The ars minor of Donatus* (Madison, 1926).

485. See Hillgarth, *Introduction*, XVII.

486. Madoz, "San Julián de Toledo," 61.

487. Díaz y Díaz, "Scrittori della penisola iberica," 113.

488. Hillgarth, "Eschatological and Political Concepts in the Seventh Century," 226.

489. The *De uitiis et figures* edited by W. M. Lindsay could be the third book or the third part of the *Ars grammatica*; see Madoz, "San Julián de Toledo," 61.

490. Rivera Recio, *San Julián arzobispo de Toledo*, 63. According to Rivera Recio, over time the original order of the books has been reversed, so that the second book is in reality the first, and the first one, obviously, the second.

491. Giannini, *Percorsi metalinguistici.*

492. Murphy, "Julian of Toledo and the Fall of the Visigothic Kingdom in Spain," 7.

493. Lindsay, *Julian of Toledo, De uitiis et figuris;* Maestre Yenes, *Ars Juliani Toletani Episcopi;* Madoz, "San Julián de Toledo"; L. Holtz, "Edition et tradition des manuels grammaticaux antiques et médiévaux," *Revue des Études Latines* 52 (1974): 75–82; R. Stratti, "Venanzio Fortunato (e altre fonti) nell'Ars grammatica di Giuliano di Toledo," *Rivista di Filologia e d'Istruzione Classica* 110 (1982): 442–45; idem, "Ancora sulle citazioni di Giuliano di Toledo (Ars Grammatica et De partibus orationis)," *Rivista di Filologia e d'Istruzione Classica* 112 (1984): 196–99; Bischoff, "Ein Brief Julians," 247–56; Corpus Christianorum, Series Latina, vol. 115, 259–60; Z. Garcia Villada, "El 'libellus de remediis blasphemiae' de san Julián de Toledo," *Historia eclesiástica de España* (Madrid, 1933), 2/2:267–74.

494. Díaz y Díaz, *Index scriptorum Latinorum Medii Aevi Hispanorum*, nn. 266–68; Ceillier, *Histoire générale des auteurs sacrés et ecclésiastiques*, vol. 17, chap. 41: "S. Julien, Archevesque de Tolède," 733–39. The critical edition of the work is in Corpus Christianorum, Series Latina vol. 115, *Sancti Iuliani Toletanae sedis Episcopi opera, pars prima,* ed. J. N. Hillgarth (Turnholt, 1976), XVII, 141–212; on the manuscipt history and the editions of the work, see Hillgarth, *Introduction,* LXVI–LXX. See also J. Campos, "El *de comprobatione sextae aetatis libri tres* de San Julián de Toledo," *Helmatica* 18 (1967): 297–340; idem, "El *de comprobatione sextae aetatis libri tres* de San Julián de Toledo (Sus fuentes, dependencias y originalidad)," in *La Patrología toledano-visigoda* (Madrid, 1970), 245–59; Rivera Recio, "Los arzobispos de Toledo en el siglo VII," 211–12; A. Moreno Garcia and R. Pozas Garza, "Una controversia judeo-cristiana del S. VII: Julián de Toledo," *Helmatica* 53 (2002): 249–69.

495. The critical edition is in Corpus Christianorum, Series Latina, vol. 115, ed. Hillgarth, 141–212.

496. R. Guerreiro, "La imagen del judío en los textos hagiográficos y patrísticos. Siglos V al VIII," *Espacio, Tiempo y Forma*, Serie II, Historia Antigua 6 (1993): 543–50.

497. Madoz, "San Julián de Toledo," 45.

498. Julian himself points out this date in the text of the work; see PL 96, col. 584B, where he refers to the Spanish era, the year 724. From this date one must subtract thirty-eight years, from when the Spanish era was founded. This produces the true date of composition of the work, 686: Nunc autem acclamatur aeram esse 724. Detractis igitur triginta et octo annis, ex quo aera inventa est, usque ad nativitatem Christi, residui sunt 686 anni.

499. Julian dedicates the work to King Ervig with an introductory letter

to the "*inclyto et glorioso reverendo domino Ervigio regi Julianus servulus vester*," in Corpus Christianorum, Series Latina, vol. 115, 145–48.

500. Domínguez Del Val, *Patrología Española*, 118*.

501. Madoz, "San Julián de Toledo," 43.

502. Felix, *Vita*, 8.

503. Ceillier, *Histoire générale des auteurs sacrés et ecclésiastiques*, 736; he makes a brief but precise synthesis of the three books of the work.

504. The biblical text of reference for the temporal calculation of the ages of the world was Psalm 90:4: "For a thousand years in thy sight are but as yesterday when it is past." This calculation allowed both Christian and Jewish theology to establish the division of the history of the cosmos and humanity into six ages, corresponding to the days of creation as narrated in Genesis. The difference between the two perspectives is that the Jews calculated the ages not by generations, as had Iulius Africanus, Eusebius of Caesarea, Jerome, and Isidore of Seville in his *Chronicon* (PL 83, cols. 1017–82), but by thousands of years.

505. Forget, "Julien de Tolède (Saint)," cols. 1941–42.

506. Hillgarth, "Historiography in Visigothic Spain," 303.

507. For these important remarks, see Hillgarth, *Introduction*, XX n. 3, where he quotes the *Epistola ad Pleguinam de aetatibus saeculi* 16, ed. C. W. Jones, *Bedae opera de temporibus* (Cambridge MA, 1943), 314, 317.

508. The contemporary Jewish position on the attitude of the Spanish episcopate toward the Jews is summarized by Yitzhak Baer in these terms: "Isidore, Bishop of Seville, and Julian, Bishop of Toledo, wrote polemic works against Judaism. But the Jews too had books to strengthen their faith, preaching the messianic hope supported by eschatological computations, and telling tales of a king of the tribe of Judah holding sway somewhere in the East." Y. Baer, *A History of the Jews in Christian Spain*, vol. 1 (Philadelphia, 1992), 21.

509. In the text there is no lack, however, of expressions that accuse the Hispanic Jews of proselytism. For this reason, the Visigothic kings and some councils of Toledo took certain measures against the Jews.

510. G. Mathon, "Julien (Saint) évêque de Tolède," *Catholicisme: Hier, aujourd'hui, demain* (Paris, 1967), vol. 6, col. 1231; see also J. F. O'Callaghan, *A History of Medieval Spain* (Ithaca, NY, 1975), 88.

511. In the political-religious situation in which the Jews lived in Visigothic Spain, such an interpretation surely served to further the cohesion of the Jewish race; see Díaz y Díaz, "Scrittori della penisola iberica," 113.

512. A very opportune comment from Madoz, "San Julián de Toledo," 46.

513. In the following quotation we find the most yearning and heartfelt words of Julian: O quam dolendus est error tuus! Nulla enim te prophetalis historia juvat, nullus historicus ordo confirmat: jam signa tua non vides, jam non est propheta, nubibus enim mandavit, ne pluant super te pluviam; et adhuc dicis nasciturum esse Christum? Exspecto, inquies, qui jam olim venit

in mundum. Vere multum erras, multum desipis, multum stertis, graviter enim corruisti, o Israel; in iniquitatibus tuis collisus es, confractus es, conquassatus es. Viam perdidisti, viam ergo sequere, ut per viam venias ad salutem. Amen. *De comprobatione sextae aetatis* (Corpus Christianorum, Series Latina vol. 115, 202).

514. Concerning the influence of Isidore, we should bear in mind that he had spoken of the sixth age of the world, and Julian certainly knew his thoughts on this matter: *Residuum saeculi tempus humanae investigationis incertum est,* states Isidore in *Chronicon,* PL 83, col. 1056B; and, in the variants of *Isidoriana* of Arévalo (PL 81, col. 865) it is written: *Residuum sextae aetatis tempus Deo soli est cognitum.*

515. Babylonian Talmud, *Sanhedrin* 97a, b; Hillgarth, "St. Julian of Toledo in the Middle Ages," 11 n. 25.

516. Madoz, "San Julián de Toledo," 46.

517. Díaz y Díaz, "Scrittori della penisola iberica," 112.

518. Hillgarth, "El Prognosticon futuri saeculi de San Julián de Toledo," 7; idem, *Introduction,* XIX: "Only three surviving manuscripts of the De comprobatione are known to me"; idem, "Towards a Critical Edition," 41: "only two MSS are known to me"; see also Campos, "El *de comprobatione sextae aetatis libri tres* de San Julián de Toledo," 297–340; idem, "El *de comprobatione sextae aetatis libri tres* de San Julián de Toledo (Sus fuentes, dependencias y originalidad)," 245–59.

519. Hillgarth, "Towards a Critical Edition," 41.

520. Hillgarth, "St. Julian of Toledo in the Middle Ages," 10.

521. Quoted by Abbot Samson of Cordoba in his *Apologeticus,* II, Praefatio, 10; see Flórez, *España Sagrada,* 11:386.

522. Quoted by Abbot Samson in his *Apologeticus,* II, 20; see Flórez, *España Sagrada,* 11:467–68.

523. Samson of Cordoba, *Apologeticus,* II, 27; see Flórez, *España Sagrada,* 11:512.

524. See Hillgarth, "St. Julian of Toledo in the Middle Ages," 12 n. 35.

525. Alvaro of Cordoba (ninth century) was a secular Christian knight of Jewish origin and of notable intellectual capabilities, which he put to the service and defense of the Christian faith. He is the author of some works edited by Flórez in *España Sagrada* (vols. 10 and 12) and then inserted in PL 115, cols. 705–20; 121, cols. 397–566.

526. Bodo, bishop and deacon of the emperor of the Franks, Louis the Pious, converted to Judaism, assuming the name of Eleazar, and he married a Jewish woman. This had a role to play in provoking Arab opposition to the Christians of Spain. His correspondence with Alvaro of Cordoba, who converted, on the other hand, from Judaism to Christianity, is interesting because each of the two writers tries to convince the other to return to his previous religion. See A. Cabaniss, "Bodo-Eleazar: A Famous Jewish Convert," *Jewish*

Quarterly Review n.s. 43 (1953): 313–28. The letter of Alvaro of Cordoba that contains the quotations of the *De comprobatione sextae aetatis* of Julian di Toledo was written circa 840: see J. Madoz, *Epistolario de Alvaro de Cordoba* (Epistola 14, 2–6) (Madrid, 1947), 213–20; see Hillgarth, "St. Julian of Toledo in the Middles Ages," 12 n. 36.

527. The biographer Felix gives only the essential details of this work of Julian, but he does show its intention: the harmonization of seemingly contradictory aspects. He states the Greek title of the work and the division of the text into two books, the first regarding the Old Testament and the second regarding the New Testament: librum de contrariis, quod Graece Antikeimenon voluit titulo adnotari, qui in duobus divisus est libris: ex quibus primus dissertationes continet Veteris Testamenti, secundus Novi (*Vita*, 9). On the *Antikeimenon* of Julian of Toledo, see L. Galmés, "Tradición manuscrita y fuentes de los Antikeimenon II de San Julián de Toledo," *Studia Patristica* 3 (1961): 347–56; A. Robles, "Prolegómenos a la edición crítica del Antikeimenon de Julián de Toledo," *Analecta Sacra Tarraconiensa* 42 (1969): 111–42; idem, "Fuentes del Antikeimenon de Julián de Toledo," *Escritos del Vedat* 1 (1971): 59–135; Madoz, "San Julián de Toledo," 58-59. Unfortunately the planned critical edition of the *Antikeimenon, cura et studio* of Adolfo Robles Sierra, OP, which was due to occupy a second volume of the Corpus Christianorum, Series Latina devoted to the works of Julian of Toledo, has never come to fruition owing to the sudden death of the author in 1997. Until now, as far as I am aware no one has taken up this valuable work.

528. Felix, *Vita*, 9.

529. Madoz, "San Julián de Toledo," 59; Felix, *Vita*, 9: Item librum de contrariis, quod Graece Antikeimenon voluit titulo adnotari.

530. Veiga Valiña, *La doctrina escatológica*, 23.

531. Ut jam in perquisitione talium quaestionum, numerositas librorum quaerenti animae laboriosa non esset, sed multiplicem lectoris sitim haec collecta brevitas satiaret (*Prognosticum, Praefatio*, 63-65): "In investigating these questions, the great number of books would not be tiresome for the soul eager to know, but this concise collection could quench the manifold thirst of the reader."

532. Rivera Recio, *San Julián arzobispo de Toledo*, 197.

533. Madoz, "San Julián de Toledo," 59. Isidore of Seville, *Etimologiae*, 2, 31, 1.

534. To form an idea of the hermeneutic method of Julian and the biblical texts in question, see Rivera Recio, *San Julián arzobispo de Toledo*, 197–200.

535. Flórez, *España Sagrada*, vol. 11, appendix, 325–516.

536. *Apologia contra Hostegitium*, 1, 2, 27, 6; see Flórez, *España Sagrada*, 11:512.

537. PL 99, col. 1238D. In Migne, the letter of Ascaricus to Tusaredus is in PL 99, cols. 1231–1234A.

538. See E. Amelli, *Miscellanea Gerominiana* (Roma, 1920), 176–77.

539. *Monumenta Germaniae Historica, Scriptores*, 7:603.

540. G. D'onofrio, "Le origini del medioevo teologico (secoli VI–VII), vol. III, 3: Voci teologiche nelle regioni iberiche: dalla fine del regno visigoto a Beato Libana," 83–89. The author thinks that the *Antikeimenon* of Julian is the work "più degna di nota" del Vescovo di Toledo, "un passo avanti verso l'elaborazione tecnica del metodo teologico medievale" (p. 84). A similar remark is in Díaz y Díaz, "Scrittori della penisola iberica," 113. He thinks that Julian's methodology of *interrogatio* and *responsio* is "molto originale come andamento del metodo usato nei testi scolastici."

541. Murphy, "Julian of Toledo and the Fall of the Visigothic Kingdom in Spain," 7.

542. Hillgarth, "El Prognosticon futuri saeculi de San Julián de Toledo," 8.

543. See J. Madoz, "Tajón de Zaragoza y su viaje a Roma," in *Mélanges J. De Ghellinck* (Gembloux, 1951), 1:345–60.

544. Hillgarth, *Introduction*, XVIII.

545. "The *Antikeimena* exists in at least eighteen complete or fragmentary copies and was to be found in the papal library at Avignon" (Hillgarth, *Introduction*, XIX–XX). See also Galmés, "Tradición manuscrita y fuentes de los Antikeimenon," 347–56; Robles, "Prolegómenos a la edición critica del Antikeimenon," 111–42; idem, "Fuentes del Antikeimenon," 59–135.

546. This is the title that the biographer Felix attributes to the work of Julian (*Vita*, 8).

547. Ibid.

548. In the first half of the last century Z. García Villada believed he had found a fragment of the *Apologeticum* in the manuscript of Ripoll 49 fol. 137. But the manuscript, today preserved in the Archivo General de la Corona de Aragón (Barcelona) "ofrece una base tan exigua e incerta, que no creo pueda tomarse en consideración" (Madoz, "San Julián de Toledo," 50).

549. A good presentation of the facts is in R. Aigrain, *Storia della chiesa*, vol. 5, *San Gregorio Magno, Gli Stati barbarici e la conquista araba*, 347–50. See also Murphy, "Julian of Toledo and the Fall of the Visigothic Kingdom in Spain," 5–7; idem, "Julian of Toledo and the Condemnation of Monothelitism in Spain," 361–73; J. Orlandis, *La Iglesia en la España visigotica y medieval* (Pamplona, 1976), 73–75; see also Domínguez Del Val, "Julián de Toledo," 1259.

550. See T. R. Buchanan [T.R.B.], "Benedictus II," in *A Dictionary of Christian Biography*, ed. W. Smith, DCL, LLD, and H. Wace, BD (London, 1882), 1:311–12.

551. The acts of the sixth ecumenical council, which Pope Leo II sent to Spain, contained the dogmatic definition of the council, the *prosphonetic* acclamation and the imperial edict that universally promulgated the dogmatic definition of the bishops. In his letter to the Spanish bishops, the pope promised

to send subsequently the rest of the documents, as soon as they had been completely translated into Latin, if the Spanish bishops expressed the desire to have them (PL 96, col. 414; see also Rivera Recio, *San Julián arzobispo de Toledo*, 183). The text of the letter of Pope Leo II to the bishops of Spain is found in PL 84, col. 144C. In it Pope Leo says that the rest of the acts of the Third Council of Constantinople *necdum in nostrum eloquium examinate translate*. From this some deduce that Leo II's sending a text of the acts of the council translated from the Greek into Latin means that it was believed in Rome that the Spanish bishops were not able to read and understand Greek. But this does not seem to be a valid way to settle the matter, in the light of what happened in the time of Honorius I and his letter to the Spanish bishops, or the truly incredible oversight of sending one of the letters of Leo II to Bishop Quiricus, who had already been dead for two years. All of this demonstrates that the papal curia had little idea about the situation of the Spanish bishropic. One could also perhaps add to this series of oversights and errors the assumption that the Spanish bishops were not able to understand the Greek text of the council.

552. The council was convoked by the emperor Constantine IV Pogonato (= the Bearded), with the consent of Pope Agaton (677–681), and was celebrated in the imperial city from November 7, 680, to September 16, 681. For a presentation of the facts relating to relations between Rome and Toledo, see Rivera Recio, "Los arzobispos de Toledo en el siglo VII," 209–11; see also Veiga Valiña, *La doctrina escatológica*, 18–19; Murphy, "Julian of Toledo and the Condemnation of Monothelitism in Spain," 361–73.

553. In the acts of the Sixth Council of Constantinople, Pope Honorius I was clearly not accused of supporting the monothelite heresy or of having taught it, but rather of having been negligent at the beginning of the spread of the heresy. It was his duty, in fact, to intervene immediately in the debate and use his pontifical authority to eradicate the heresy, condemning it. In the Church of Toledo, Pope Honorius's condemnation contained in the acts of the ecumenical council must have made a certain impression, though it was probably not received with any amazement, since the same pope, only decades before, had made a strange diatribe against the Spanish Church, accusing the bishops of being "dogs incapable of barking" against the Jews. The Spanish bishops, as we will see later, were quick to defend themselves against the accusation of negligence and pastoral timidity, in a firm letter of protest written by Braulio of Saragossa on behalf of all the bishops of Spain.

554. Díaz y Díaz, "Scrittori della penisola iberica," 110.

555. G. Mathon justifies the absence of the Hispanic-Visigothic bishops at the Council of Constantinople by the fact that they had not been invited and states that, therefore, they were rather irritated and reluctant to approve the acts of that council; see "Julien (Saint) évêque de Tolède," 1230.

556. They had also been absent from the fifth ecumenical council, of 553, and had firmly refused to recognize its doctrine. Pope Leo II, with these letters, wanted to ensure that this situation was not repeated.

557. This has led to the assumption that Pope Leo II was convinced that the Hispanic-Visigothic bishops were not able to read and understand the Greek text of the conciliar acts. This deduction could be extended also to the unsolved question of whether Julian of Toledo, author of some works bearing a title or words of the title in Greek and who quotes in his works texts of the Greek fathers of the church, lacked the ability to read and understand a doctrinal text in Greek. See Madoz, "Fuentes teológico-literarias de San Julián de Toledo," 413.

558. Apud beati Petri apostolorum principis confessionem deponimus. PL 96, cols. 415B–C.

559. Madoz, *San Julián de Toledo,* 47.

560. Quia et nos, qui licet impares, vice tamen apostolorum principis fungimur. PL 96, col. 415B.

561. For a general outline of the councils of Toledo, from the first (400) to the last (1951), see G. Martínez, "Concilios Nacionales y Provinciales," 1:566–73, here 570.

562. This is what Julian calls him in the first chapter of the *Apologeticum de tribus capitulis.* This title indicates "a deacon or sub-deacon who is at the head of one of the seven 'regions'or wards of Rome."

563. The text of the four letters of Pope Leo II can be found in PL 96, cols. 411C–420D.

564. The participation of members of the aristocracy in the councils of Toledo was usual, as was the king's presence at some moments of their celebration. Therefore the modern reader should not be surprised if one of Pope Leo II's four letters was addressed to a member of the aristocracy of whom nothing is known.

565. See M. A. W. [Mrs. Humphrey Ward], "Julianus (63)," 477–81. See possible explanations, by various authors, on this omission or error, in the body of the article, p. 479.

566. With a prudent and euphemistic expression, J. F. Rivera Recio, narrating the firm answer of Braulio of Saragossa to Pope Onorius I, speaks of "respetuosa energía" on the part of the Spanish prelate.

567. M. A. W. [Mrs. Humphrey Ward], "Ervigius (1), Ervig, Ervich," 187.

568. The acts of the Fourteenth Council of Toledo recount, at the beginning of the synodal works, the factors that prevented the general council required by the pope from gathering. The reasons were twofold: the terrible and icy winter of the peninsula in that year and the fact that the bishops were already on the way back to their sees when the papal request arrived. De adversitate duplici qua non potunt generale concilium fieri....non solum tellus omnis hyemali stricta gelu glaciali nivium immensitate duruerat, sed et

tunc quando e vicino ex generali concilio nos absolutos jam esse constabat. Quo gemino obsistentis causae obice praepediti generaliter iterato tunc non quivimus aggregari, quos et vicina concilii absolutio propriis sedibus reddiderat imminutos et procellosi temporis adversitas non sinebat iterum adunari dispersos. PL 84, cols. 506C–D.

569. PL 84, cols. 505B–D.

570. For a detailed account of the events that led to the conflict between Rome and Toledo, see Rivera Recio, *San Julián arzobispo de Toledo*, 181–93. The author, who was canonical archivist of the Archdiocese of Toledo (he died in 1991), intentionally produced a popular book. It is clear that behind the simple narration of the facts lie meticulous historical research and a high level of erudition, which make this work even today the best complete biography of Julian of Toledo. Rivera Recio is the author also of numerous works of a precise historical character concerning the Visigothic Church, the Mozárabic liturgy, the bishops of Toledo, the Spanish Middle Ages, and so on. Praise for this unusual work is found in Madoz, *Segundo Decenio de Estudios sobre Patrística Española*, 142–43. Madoz gives a reconstruction of the facts in the same work (pp. 143–47), emphasizing that the personality of St. Julian was not such as to allow any suspicion of heterodoxy before the Church of Rome and that his prestige as a consummate theologian and primate of the Church of Spain could not be doubted.

571. Rivera Recio quotes an interesting fact: in the letters sent to Count Simplicius and to the primate of Spain, the pope had added, in his own hand, that the conciliar acts were carried by the *Notarius* Petrus together with a reliquary in the form of a cross or with a crucifix (the text says *venerabilem crucem*) and a key forged from the metal of the chains of St. Peter, a sign of the respect that the Church of Rome held for that of Toledo. See Rivera Recio, *San Julián arzobispo de Toledo*, 182; and PL 96, cols. 416, 418.

572. Among these bishops was Bishop Suntfredus, who, as we will see later, will be the recipient, as bishop of the province of Narbonne, of a letter from Idalius, bishop of Barcelona, in which he enclosed a copy of the *Prognosticum* of Julian recommending that the work be sent to the other bishops of the ecclesiastical province.

573. See the text of canons 5 and 7 in PL 84, cols. 505–10, here col. 507B–D.

574. The text is that of canons 8, 9, and 10 of the Fourteenth Council of Toledo; PL 84, cols. 508A–509A.

575. M. A. W. [Mrs. Humphrey Ward], "Julianus (63)," 479; see also U. Domínguez Del Val and E. Cuevas, "San Julián de Toledo," in B. Altaner, *Patrología Española*, Suplemento (Madrid, 1956), 115*–116*: "con el fin de no retardar demasiado la respuesta, compuso un Apologetico y lo envió a Roma." Hillgarth (*Introduction*, X) says that "not content with a simple acceptance of the doctrine enunciated by Constantinople, Julian, in the name of

the Spanish hierarchy, had already sent to Rome an explanation of the dogmas concerned, which was presumably identical with the 'Apologeticum
fidei', mentioned by Felix and now lost."

576. In the second *Apologeticum* (688), composed from the Fifteenth
Council of Toledo, Julian speaks rather of a single trustworthy clergyman to
whom Pope Benedict II reported his criticism of Julian's Christology. He was
probably the leader of a small group of clergymen sent to Rome by the primate of Toledo.

577. The long trip from Toledo to Rome could be made in two ways,
either over land or by sea, but in either case it was considered a risky venture.
The journey over land was very long (between 950 and 1,050 miles) and could
last five or six months, depending on the season, the weather, and the condition of the roads. The trip necessitated the crossing of the Pyrenees and other
Italian mountains found above Milan, from which the consular roads divided
in the direction of various destinations, with other passes to be overcome. The
trip by sea could last two or three weeks, but the crossing of the
Mediterranean, which was riddled with pirates, from Ostia to Cartagena or
Tarragona (or vice versa) was certainly more dangerous. The conditions of
the crossing were often very perilous, either because of forced delays while
waiting for calm and navigable seas, or because of frequent changes of route
owing to a lack of wind. Even in the Roman epoch the distance between
Tarragona and Ostia, the harbor of Rome, could be covered in about a week
in favorable conditions (Pliny the Elder, *Naturalis Historia*, 19.4). The first leg
of the journey from Toledo to Rome, before taking to the sea, was very
uncomfortable because the almost 250 miles from Toledo to Tarragona could
take about ten days, again depending on the season, the weather, and the condition of the roads. A simple look at the extraordinary *Tabula Peutingeriana* or
Itinerarium pinctum could discourage even the well-intentioned traveler,
because the journey was long and uncomfortable! The *Tabula Peutingeriana*,
dating from the twelfth century, is a copy of a map from the ancient world,
from west to the extreme east—that is, from Spain to India—drawn and
painted on a long (almost seven meters) roll of parchment separated into
twelve sections. This medieval artifact is kept in the National Library of
Vienna, although the first section (Spain, Morocco, Ireland, Britain) is missing. The origins of the map go back to the second or third century AD. It
underwent improvements and important changes beginning in the fourth
century. It is, above all, a map of the landmass, since owing to reasons of
graphic synthesis the seas are drastically reduced in the longitudinal
(west–east) sense. The map shows the roads (with the "service stations"), the
distances between places in Roman miles (but also in other numbering sys-
tems according to the country), the cities small and great, the rivers, the
mountains, the plains, the temples, the harbors, the thermal baths, and so on.
The map is of course approximate, but still of extraordinary historical value.

See E. Weber, *Tabula Peutingeriana*. Codex Vindobonensis 324 (Graz, 1976). For something even more extraordinary, an emblem of Roman pragmatism, see the *Itinerarium provinciarum Antonini Augusti*. It is a traveler's guide from the beginning of the third century AD that contains routes of journeys from northern to southern Italy (islands included), with distances shown in miles and includes lists of urban centers, "service stations," and so on. See the reprint of the classical text of O. Cuntz, *Itineraria Romana*, vol. 1, *Itineraria Antonini Augusti et Burdigalense* (Stuttgart, 1990).

578. Madoz, *El símbolo del concilio XVI de Toledo: su texto, sus fuentes, su valor teológico* (Madrid, 1946), 100.

579. One of the few authors who makes a real effort to reconstruct the tangled story is Murphy, "Julian of Toledo and the Condemnation of Monothelitism," 365 n. 15.

580. González, "La Iglesia desde la conversión de Recaredo hasta la invasion arabe," 400–727, esp. 689–97, here 695.

581. The insightful reasoning just mentioned perhaps represents a useful line of investigation for the understanding, at a distance of thirteen centuries, of the general ideal of Julian's primatial episcopate and particularly the ecclesiological vision of the primate and the Spanish bishopric in general. In fact, the approval of the conciliar acts of Constantinople by the Hispanic-Visigothic bishops and their decision to insert them after the acts of Chalcedon in the canonical collection of Spain, as if there were a doctrinal continuity, could be understood as an astute decision, as if the Spanish Church intentionally wanted to assume the role of primatial church of the Western world, opposite to the church of the Eastern world (Constantinople). This would also explain the zeal of Julian to add to the document of approval of the acts of the Council of Constantinople a christological exposition, parallel to the acts and highly theological. This important assumption will be clarified in another paragraph.

582. Madoz, "San Julián de Toledo," 47–48.

583. Post Chalcedonense igitur concilium haec debito honore, loco et ordine collocanda sunt. PL 84, col. 507D.

584. See canons 6 and 7 of the Fourteenth Council of Toledo (PL 84, col. 507D), which order that the acts of Constantinople III be inserted into the *Collectio Hispana* of the dogmatic canons, immediately after the texts of the ecumenical councils of Nicaea, Constantinople, Ephesus, and Chalcedon.

585. The fifth, not the sixth, therefore, because the Spanish Church still considered the fifth ecumenical council (that of the Three Chapters, of 553) as a council *non receptus*, that is, not yet studied in its acts and, therefore, neither accepted nor signed by the bishops of Spain.

586. See PL 84, cols. 505–10, in particular, cols. 507B–D. The list of the councils of the Fourteenth Council of Toledo does not mention the Second

Council of Constantinople, of 553, although in the letters of Leo II it is mentioned as ecumenical.

587. Madoz, "San Julián de Toledo," 48.

588. PL 84, col. 507A.

589. Domínguez Del Val, "Julián de Toledo," 1259; see canon 11 of the council, PL 84, col. 509A.

590. Felix, *Vita*, 8: Apologeticum fidei, quod Benedicto Romanae urbis papae directum est.

591. See Domínguez Del Val, "Julián de Toledo," 1259.

592. Pope Benedict II was elected in 683, was consecrated on June 26, 684, and died May 8, 685. He had to wait for more than a year for the imperial confirmation of his election and in the meantime he signed his acts as *Benedictus presbyter et in Dei nomine electus sanctae Sedis Apostolicae.*

593. See the text in PL 96, col. 424B.

594. The *editio critica* was edited by J. N. Hillgarth in Corpus Christianorum, Series Latina, vol. 115, 127–39.

595. Veiga Valiña, *La doctrina escatológica,* 19.

596. Rivera Recio, *San Julián arzobispo de Toledo,* 187; Madoz, "San Julián de Toledo," 50.

597. This hypothesis seems particularly convincing; see Rivera Recio, *San Julián arzobispo de Toledo,* 188.

598. Veiga Valiña, *La doctrina escatológica,* 19.

599. PL 84, cols. 509–526D, here col. 513.

600. At least this seems to be the sense of the following text: beatae memoriae Romanus papa Benedictus nos litterarum suarum significatione monuerat, quae tamen non in scriptis suis annotare curavit, sed homini nostro verbo renotanda injunxit...(ibid.). Veiga Valiña thinks, exaggeratedly, that in the writings of Julian "se tachaba de ignorante la Santa Sede" (*La doctrina escatológica,* 19). But to judge Julian of Toledo from this as guilty of rebellion against the Roman see and wanting to go down the road of doctrinal schism, as F. Görres ("Der Primas Julian von Toledo [680–690]: Eine Kirchencultur, und literargeschichtliche Studie," *Zeitschrift für wissenschaftliche Theologie* 46 [1902–3]: 524–53) thinks, seems to be going too far. Veiga Valiña concludes, paradoxically but also very pessimistically, that "gracias a la invasión saracena, desapareció el peligro de la ruptura con el Papado" and that if the (deadly) Arab invasion had not happened, there would have been instead almost certainly a schism of the Church of Spain. It would have preceded, in order of time, both the great Eastern schism of the eleventh century and the Western schism of the sixteenth century (*La doctrina escatológica,* 19). Earlier this was also the opinion of P. B. Gams (*Kirchengeschichte von Spanien,* 2/2:237–38). We judge entirely obsolete, and deprived of historical basis, such conclusions, which are pessimistic and conditioned by an interpretative a priori.

601. Rivera Recio (*San Julián arzobispo de Toledo*, 193) judges this expression sufficient to affirm decisively that the answer of Julian and the Spanish episcopate was not directed against the pope, whose authority the Spanish Church had always recognized, including in the national liturgy. The *j'accuse* of Julian was, rather, directed at the theologians of the Roman curia, who were regarded by him as "competitors or rivals" (*aemuli*), that is, lacking the necessary qualities of knowledge and intelligence (therefore, *ignorantes*). According to another hypothesis, Julian referred with those ardent words (*aemuli ignorantes*) to his Spanish antagonists and imitators who opposed him and also went against the Church of Spain; see, for example, M. Ménendez y Pelayo, *Historia de los heterodoxos españoles*, 2nd ed. (Madrid, 1917), vol. 2, chap. 1, p. 193.

602. PL 84, col. 513.

603. The text of Julian's speech to the plenary assembly of the bishops expressly states that two years had passed since he sent his first christological writing to Rome.

604. Domínguez Del Val, "Julián de Toledo," 1259.

605. Díaz y Díaz, "Scrittori della penisola iberica," 110.

606. That is a "marchio infamante" (brand of infamy); see Rivera Recio, *San Julián arzobispo de Toledo*, 188.

607. Veiga Valiña, *La doctrina escatológica*, 16.

608. For historical reasons that are difficult to put one's finger on, the title of the work is misleading ("confusing," says Hillgarth, *Introduction*, X) because the text has nothing to do with the dispute on the Three Chapters, which happened in the sixth century and, in any case, the treated points are not three but four.

609. Felix, *Vita*, 8, with an interesting addition: Apologeticum de tribus capitulis, de quibus Romanae urbis praesul frustra visus est dubitasse.

610. Murphy is convinced that the texts sent by Julian to Rome in subsequent years (683, 686, and 688) were three and not two, as was thought up to now; see Murphy, "Julian of Toledo and the Condemnation of Monothelitism in Spain," 361–73. But information from Felix and historical tradition seem to refer to only two texts: the *Apologeticum fidei*, in 684, and the *Apologeticum de tribus capitulis*, in 686. Murphy, in "Julian of Toledo and the Fall of the Visigothic Kingdom," briefly presenting the story of the opposition of Toledo to Rome, completely omits the final and judicious solution for which Pope Sergius I opted.

611. J. de Ghellinck (*Patristique et Moyen Age: Études d'histoire littéraire et doctrinale*, vol. 2, Museum Lessianum, Section Historique 6 [Gembloux, 1946], 276) summarizes clearly: "Julien de Tolède, qui a à sa disposition beaucoup de traités des Latins et Grecs, d'où il tire habilement et résolument la défense de son orthodoxie en christologie, un moment suspectée par Rome."

612. Hillgarth, "El Prognosticon futuri saeculi de San Julián de Toledo," 6.

613. PL 96, col. 526A.

614. Ibid.

615. Díaz y Díaz, "Scrittori della penisola iberica," 110.

616. PL 96, col. 527.

617. PL 96, col. 528.

618. Hillgarth, *Introduction*, X.

619. Three clergymen of the Church of Toledo were sent to Rome with the important task.

620. PL 84, cols. 513A–520A; 96, cols. 525–36. In the acts of the council, however, are mentioned two other chapters of the work of Julian that were not inserted in the acts and that, therefore, are considered lost. "The work is largely preserved in the Acts of the Fifteenth Council of Toledo (688)" (Hillgarth, *Introduction*, X, LXIII; see also LXIII–LXV).

621. Murphy, "Julian of Toledo and the Condemnation of Monothelitism," 369.

622. Díaz y Díaz, "Giuliano di Toledo," 1611–12, here 1611.

623. The text, vehement indeed, can be found in the last chapter (XVIII) of the *Apologeticum de tribus capitulis*; see PL 84, col. 520A

624. Domínguez Del Val ("Julián de Toledo," 1259) very generously qualifies these very strong words used by Julian as "frase incisiva."

625. Madoz, "San Julián de Toledo," 51.

626. *Apologeticum II*, in PL 96, col. 528C.

627. PL 84, cols. 519D–520A: Jam vero si post haec et ab ipsis dogmatibus Patrum quibus haec prolata sunt in quocunque dissentiunt, non jam cum illis est amplius contendendum; sed majorum directo calle inhaerentes vestigiis, erit per divinum judicium amatoribus veritatis responsio nostra sublimis, etiam si ab ignorantibus aemulis censeatur indocilis.

628. Translation of Murphy, in "Julian of Toledo and the Condemnation of Monothelitism," 370.

629. While Veiga Valiña (*La doctrina escatológica*, 19) says that with this text "se tachaba de ignorante a la santa Sede," Madoz ("San Julián de Toledo," 54) writes that "el tono de la respuesta es censurable pero no arguye una actitud fundamental de rebeldía."

630. Gonzálvez Ruiz, "San Julián de Toledo en el contexto," 16.

631. See J. Barmby [J.B-y], "Sergius (16)," in *A Dictionary of Christian Biography*, ed. W. Smith, DCL, LLD, and H. Wace, BD (London, 1882), 2:618–20.

632. The text of the *Chronicon* is in PL 96, col. 1261BC.

633. The testimony of Isidorus Pacensis is in PL 96, col. 1261BC. The text of the critical edition of the *Continuatio* published by T. Mommsen in 1894 (see *Monumenta Germaniae Historica, Auctore Antiquissimi*, 11:350 n. 55) contains some important differences that we will emphasize within square brackets: Eius in tempore librum de tribus substantiis, quem dudum Rome [instead of: Romam]

sanctissimus Iulianus urbis regie metropolitanus episcopus miserat [instead of: emiserat] et minus [the important: "caute" is missing] tractando papa Romanus arcendum indixerat ob eo [instead of: ob id], quod voluntas genuit voluntatem, ante biennio tandem scripserat, veridicis testimoniis in hunc [instead of: in hoc] concilium ad exaggerationem [instead of: exactionem] prefati principis Iulianus episcopus per oracula maiorum ea, que Rome transmiserat, vera esse confirmans, apologeticum facit et Rome [instead of: Romam] per suos legatos eclesiasticos viros presbiterem [instead of: presbiterum], diaconem et subdiaconem eruditissimos in omnia dei servos [instead of: in omnibus] et per omnia de divinis scripturis inbutos, iterum cum versos adclamatorios [instead of: cum versibus adclamatoriis], secundum quod et olim transmiserat, de laude imperatoris mittit, quod Roma digne et pie recipit et cunctis legendum indicit atque summo imperatori, satis adclamando; laus tua, deus, in fines terre! Cognitum facit. Qui et rescriptum domno Iuliano per supra fatos [instead of: suprafatos] legatos satis cum gratiarum hactione [instead of: actione] honorifice remittit et omnia quecumque scripsit iusta et pia esse depromit.

634. Murphy, "Julian of Toledo and the Condemnation of Monothelitism," 370 n. 37, 371.

635. See Rodrigo de Toledo, *De rebus Hispaniae*, III, 14.

636. Domínguez Del Val, "Julián de Toledo," 1259.

637. See Baronius, *Annales Ecclesiastici*, 8:748–50.

638. As with some modern authors. For example, the *Patrología Española*, 116*, speaks of "frases incisivas, molestas y hasta, si se quiere, irriverentes."

639. Flórez, *España Sagrada*, 6:298–99 (trat. 5, chap. 4).

640. Menéndez y Pelayo, *Historia de los heterodoxos españoles*, 2:193ff.

641. Veiga Valiña, *La doctrina escatológica*, 20; see Magnin, *L'Eglise visigothique*, 1:28, 31.

642. Hillgarth, "El Prognosticon futuri saeculi de San Julián de Toledo," 8.

643. Hillgarth, "Julian of Toledo," 50.

644. Rodrigo de Toledo, *De rebus Hispaniae*, III, 14.

645. The text of the Symbol (Creed) of the Sixteenth Council of Toledo is in PL 84, col. 534D.

646. A general outline of the different positions is to be found in Madoz, "San Julián de Toledo," 52–53. See also M. Strohm, "Der Konflikt zwischen Erzbischof Julian von Toledo und Papst Benedikt II: Ein Faktum von ökumenischer Bedeutung," *Annuarium Historiae Conciliorum* 15 (1983): 249–59.

647. Hillgarth, *Introduction*, IX.

648. This is the judgment of Domínguez Del Val, "Julián de Toledo," 1259–60.

649. The impoliteness of the literary expression of Julian related to the *aemuli ignorantes* is admitted also by Domínguez Del Val, "Julián de Toledo,"

1260. He denies, however, that this indicates insubordination toward papal authority. According to Del Val, Julian was angry, above all, with Roman theologians, not with the pope. The same sentiment is found in Rivera Recio, *San Julián arzobispo de Toledo*, 181–94.

650. Hillgarth, *Introduction*, XI.

651. For example, the Protestant historian F. Görres, author of a monographic study on Julian of Toledo (*Der Primas Julian von Toledo [680–690]*, 523–53) openly maintains that Julian and the Spanish bishops are to be considered guilty of rebellion against the Church of Rome. The Benedictine P. B. Gams expresses such a negative judgment on history and its Hispanic-Visigothic protagonists as to formulate a distorted theology of history, judging as providential for the unity of the Catholic Church the terrible Arab invasion of Spain that annihilated the empire and the Visigothic Church, and which, therefore, chased away the specter of a schism (*Kirchengeschichte von Spanien*, 2/2:237–38). As we have already seen, Veiga Valiña (*La doctrina escatológica*, 19) also supports this thesis. The thesis of Gams seems to reproduce the conviction of the historian Orosius, who maintained in his *Historia* that the barbarian invasions were to be interpreted as a punishment or divine intervention against the pagan world. Flórez, on the other hand, together with J. Tailhan, maintains that the invectives of Julian of Toledo were directed not at the pope but at his Spanish enemies. Menéndez y Pelayo (*Historia de los heterodoxos españoles* 2:193) is also in favor of this interpretation of the *aemuli ignorantes*. De la Fuente (*Historia eclesiástica de España*, 2:368–70) dismisses the accusation of schism against Julian. H. Leclercq (*L'Espagne chrétienne* [Paris, 1906], 352) rather thinks that the pope and the Roman curia were outrageously handled by Julian, while modern scholars such as E. Magnin (*La discipline de l'Église wisigothique au VIIe siècle* [Paris, 1912], 23–31), Z. García Villada (*Historia eclesiástica de España*, 2:1, 159–60), and M. Torres López (*Historia de España*, vol. 3, *España visigoda* [Madrid, 1940], 275) are inclined to lessen the importance of the facts and therefore the possibility of their leading to a separation or schism from Rome. For Madoz ("San Julián de Toledo," 54), Julian and the Spanish bishops never doubted the authority and the primacy of Rome, but certainly made known their opinions about them: "la respuesta es censurable pero non arguye una actitud fundamental de rebeldía." So also Murphy, "Julian of Toledo and the Fall of the Visigothic Kingdom in Spain," 6. M. A.W. [Mrs. Humphrey Ward] ("Julianus [63]," 481), however, used very harsh words concerning the attitude of Julian of Toledo toward the Roman see, qualifying his answer as "singular boldness, almost insolence."

652. This is the opinion of J. Tailhan, *Anonyme de Cordove* (Paris, 1885), 126ff.; see also Menéndez y Pelayo, *Historia de los heterodoxos españoles*, 1:200.

653. See Magnin, *L'église visigothique*, 1:28–31; González, "La Iglesia desde la conversión de Recaredo hasta la invasion arabe," 694–97.

654. Orlandis, *La iglesia en la España visigótica y medieval*, 73–75, here 74.

655. Ziegler ("Church and State in Visigothic Spain," 52) agrees.

656. Hillgarth, *Introduction*, XI.

657. Madoz, "San Julián de Toledo," 54.

658. G. García Herrero, "Notas sobre el papel del Prognosticum futuri saeculi de Julián de Toledo en la evolución de la idea medieval del purgatorio," *Antigüedad y cristianismo: Monografías históricas sobre la Antigüedad tardía* 23 (2006) (Ejemplar dedicado a: Espacio y tiempo en la percepción de la antigüedad tardía: homenaje al profesor Antonino González Blanco, "*In maturitate aetatis ad prudentiam*," ed. M. E. Conde Guerri, R. González Fernández, A. Egea Vivancos): 503–14, here 506.

659. Ibid., 505.

660. For the following considerations we have kept in mind the valuable study of González, "La Iglesia desde la conversión de Recaredo hasta la invasion arabe," 400–727, esp. 689–97.

661. González ("La Iglesia desde la conversión de Recaredo hasta la invasion arabe," 691) correctly clarifies that when we use expressions such as *National Church of Spain* (or *national council*), these words do not so much indicate a nationalistic or entirely independent dimension of the Hispanic-Visigothic Church, but rather the strong political bond that united the Hispanic-Visigothic people to the monarchy and held the structural and efficient organization of the ecclesiastical provinces of Spain together. Above all, these words indicate their awareness of having sufficient strength and intelligence to face and resolve the internal problems of the church and the state.

662. PL 84, cols. 341–51B.

663. For example, in 538, Bishop Profuturus of Braga consulted Pope Vigilius on liturgical questions; Leander of Cartagena questioned Gregory the Great, who was also his personal friend, on the problem of the single or triple immersion of the persons to be baptized in the baptismal font. For these examples, see González, "La Iglesia desde la conversión de Recaredo hasta la invasion arabe," 690.

664. Orlandis, *La iglesia en la España visigótica y medieval*, 63–75. He calls to mind a series of facts uniting the Church of Spain and the Church of Rome (pp. 64–66) as another explicit sign of the adherence of the Church of Spain to the faith of the Catholic Church: the symbols of faith recited at the beginning of the councils, the liturgical uniformity, the existence of the *Collectio Hispana*, which gathered acts of ecumenical councils of East and West, and, unique in its kind, contained a *summa* of pontifical decretals. This surely indicates that the Church of Spain had the maximum respect for the ancient and venerable Church of Rome and the faith of the Catholic Church. But, undoubtedly, because of the increasingly strong bond that developed between the Spanish Church and Visigothic kingdom, there grew up a strong national sense in the Church of Spain. Subsequently, contact between the churches of Spain and Rome became less frequent (pp. 66–69) and the

Church of Spain seemed geared toward living an autonomous life, strengthened by the extraordinary theological-literary renaissance.

665. The two were known in Constantinople when Gregory exercised the function of pontifical *apocrisarius* (official sent by the pope to the imperial court) in the imperial city.

666. González, "La Iglesia desde la conversión de Recaredo hasta la invasion arabe."

667. The efficient system of communication of the Roman era was by now but a memory. The road system, which was so important for strategic reasons in the imperial epoch, had gone to rack and ruin after the fall of the empire. This is why some of King Recared's letters to the pope received an answer only some years later; with Pope Gregory the Great apologizing to the monarch for the delay (of around one year) of his reply, which was due to the fact that he had not been able to find a ship that was sailing to Spain! We have already mentioned the delay of the letters of Pope Leo II to the bishops of Spain in the time of Julian of Toledo.

668. It is interesting to note that the national councils were also the courts to which any member of the faithful (laity, clergy, or bishops) could forward their request for justice. This is another reason for the historical scarcity of petitions *ad Petri sedem* coming from the Hispanic-Visigothic kingdom. For many questions there was no need to consult the pope. The judgment of the council was sufficient to resolve most questions and ecclesial problems; see González, "La Iglesia desde la conversión de Recaredo hasta la invasion arabe," 691.

669. Celebrated in 633.

670. This very effective expression, quoted in the study of González ("La Iglesia desde la conversión de Recaredo hasta la invasion arabe," 690) is from J. Orlandis, "Las relaciones intereclesiales en la Hispania visigótica," in *Historia de España*, vol. 3, *La España visigótica* (Madrid, 1977), 59–93; by the same author we have the definition of episcopal collegiality as "órgano de la 'communio'" (*La Iglesia en la España visigotica y medieval*, 77–88).

671. L. Duchesne, *Origines du culte chrétien: étude sur la liturgie latine avant Charlemagne* (Paris, 1908), 40–41; see González, "La Iglesia desde la conversión de Recaredo hasta la invasion arabe," 690.

672. While it is in part true that the Visigothic bishops did not always give their full assent to the authority of the pope, it is just as true that not only did links with Rome exist, but they were also marked by a sincere respect. For instance, a relationship of respect and friendship existed, as we have seen, between Gregory the Great and Leander of Seville. We know that King Recared, announcing his conversion to Catholicism to the bishop of Rome, defined the pope as the most powerful of all the bishops. Isidore of Seville gave the pope the title of "Head of all the Churches." Finally, it must also be noted that the scarcity of papal documents addressed to the Church of Spain

(only eight in our possession) indicates that papal interventions to the Church of Spain were considerably less frequent than those addressed to other churches. This fact could also be read as a sign of the popes' awareness of a special maturity possessed by the Church of Spain, which did not, therefore, have need of assiduous interventions.

673. The letter of Honorius is lost. We know of its existence and its contents thanks to Braulio of Saragossa's reply.

674. And not of Ezechiel, as maintained by the biblical experts who wrote the letter.

675. Braulio of Saragossa, *Epistola XXI eiusdem Braulionenis nomine Concilii VI Toletani scripta ad Honorium I*, in PL 80, col. 669B.

676. The integral text of the letter of Braulio in PL 80, cols. 667–70.

677. Díaz y Díaz, "Scrittori della penisola iberica," 95.

678. A *post scriptum*, in the name of all the bishops of Spain, invited the pope to meditate on the overly severe measures that he suggested using against the Jews (for example, the punishment with fire), because the gentle gospel of Christ is in total disagreement with them.

679. Whereas in the first part of his text Braulio corrects the letter of Pope Honorius from a biblical point of view, as we have seen, in the second part he firmly rejects the accusation of negligence toward the Spanish bishops. Since, says Braulio, the biblical quotation of the *Canes muti non valentes latrare* does not pertain to the Church of Spain and its bishops (*nullo modo pertinet*): Et licet nos horum quae in objurgationem nostri vestra sanctitas indebite protulit, pro hac duntaxat actione nihil omnino respectet, praecipue tamen illud non Ezechielis sed Isaiae testimonium, quanquam prophetae omnes uno proloquantur Spiritu: Canes muti non valentes latrare, ad nos, si beatitudo vestra dignatur considerare, ut praemisimus, nullo modo pertinet; quia gregis Domini custodiam, ipso inspirante, jugi vigilia peragentes, et lupos morsu et fures terremus latratu, illo in nobis non dormiente, neque dormitante, qui custodit Israel.

680. Braulio of Saragossa, *Epistola XXI eiusdem Braulionenis nomine Concilii VI Toletani scripta ad Honorium I*, in PL 80, col. 668D.

681. The Fourth Council of Toledo had, only a few years earlier (633), made strong provisions against the Jews, specified in ten canons (canons 57–66). These included the Jews' exclusion from public office; their exclusion from giving testimony; and a prohibition against their possessing Christian slaves; in addition, the prohibition of Christians from giving any kind of assistance to the Jews; the prohibition of former Jews having contact with still observant Jews; and, finally, the most terrible from a modern point of view, the separation of the children of Jews from their parents to prevent any contamination by the Jewish faith. PL 84, cols. 379D–381D.

682. See Rivera Recio, *San Julián arzobispo de Toledo*, 184.

683. Hillgarth, *Introduction*, XI.

684. The canon on the Jews in the acts of the Sixth Council of Toledo states: ...excellentissimus et Christianissimus princeps ardore fidei inflammatus, cum regni sui sacerdotibus praevaricationes et superstitiones eorum eradicare elegit funditus, nec sinit degere in regno suo eum qui non est catholicus, ob cujus fervorem fidei gratias omnipotenti Domino coelorum agimus, eo quod tam illustrem creaverit animam et sua repleverit sapientia, ipse quoque donet ei et in praesenti saeculo longaevam vitam, et in futuro gloriam aeternam. PL 130, col. 488B.

685. Felix, *Vita*, 9: Item librum plurimarum epistolarum.

686. See J. Madoz, *Epistolario de San Braulione de Zaragoza* (Madrid, 1941).

687. Felix, *Vita*, 9: Item librum sermonum, in quo est opusculum modicum de vindicatione domus Dei, et eorum qui ad eam confugiunt.

688. Felix, *Vita*, 7.

689. Felix, *Vita*, 9: Item librum carminum diversorum, in quo sunt hymni, epitaphia, atque de diversis causis epigrammata numerosa.

690. Felix, *Vita*, 10.

691. Ibid.: Item librum sententiarum, ex decade psalmorum B. Augustini breviter summatimque collectum. Item excerpta de libris S. Augustini contra Julianum haereticum collecta.

692. Hillgarth, *Introduction*, VIII; idem, "St. Julian of Toledo in the Middles Ages," 8.

693. Felix, *Vita*, 10: contra eos qui confugientes ad ecclesiam persequuntur.

694. Felix, *Vita*, 11: Item librum missarum de toto circulo anni, in quatuor partes divisum; in quibus aliquas vetustatis incuria vitiatas ac semiplenas emendavit atque complevit, aliquas vero ex toto composuit.

695. F. J. Simonet, *Historia de los mozárabes Españoles* (Madrid, 1897), 694–95.

696. Hillgarth, "Las fuentes de san Julián de Toledo," 102; see also Janini, "Roma y Toledo," 33–53.

697. *Monumenta Germaniae Historica, Concilia*, 2, 111–12.

698. Ibid., 113.

699. Samson of Cordoba, *Apologeticus* 2, 13. The text is situated at the beginning of the *De comprobatione sextae aetatis*, where it appears in its fullness and equipped with quotations (PL 96, col. 760; Corpus Christianorum, Series Latina, vol. 115, 143–44). The liturgical text, however, is abbreviated and omits some biblical references (PL 85, col. 113).

700. Samson of Cordoba, *Apologeticus*, 2, 23. The text appears, with some differences and additions, in the *Missale mixtum* and constitutes the *Inlatio* of the Holy Mass *In Dominico ante jejunium Kalendarum Novembrium*: Inlatio. Dignum et justum est: nos tibi gratias agere: Domine sancte Pater eterne omnipotens Deus: per Jesum Christum Filium tuum Dominum nostrum. Cujus divinitatis immensitas sic ineffabiliter circumplectitur omnia: ut

in singulis creaturis permaneat tota: et in omnibus habitet universa. Non minoratur in minimis: non augetur in magnis. Non concluditur tempore: non adstringitur quantitate. Non initio cepta: non termino finienda. A quo totus homo et creatus est ad justiciam sine peccato: et reparatus est post ruinam sacrificio ejusdem Christi mundissimo. Per ipsum quem in unitate trine virtutis conlaudant celestia pariter et terrena: hymnum dulci modulatione proclamantia: atque ita dicentia. Sanctus. PL 85, cols. 649D–650A.

701. Férotin, *Le Liber Ordinum*, 331–34. He wondered if the four parts of the Missal that the biographer Felix attributes to Julian were, in reality, the whole Missal, composed, in the Visigothic redaction, of four parts: Advent, Lent, Eastertide, and the Saints. See Férotin, *Le Liber Mozarabicus*, XVI–XVII.

702. Felix, *Vita*, 11.

703. See Flórez, *España Sagrada*, 5:253–54; Férotin, *Le Liber Mozarabicus*, XVIff.; see also Díaz y Díaz, *Index Scriptorum Latinorum*, 639.

704. Felix, *Vita*, 8: Item libellum de remediis blasphemiae cum epistola ad Adrianum abbatem.

705. Ibid.

706. G. Morin, "Un écrit de Saint Julien de Tolède consideré a tort comme perdu," *Revue Bénédectine* 24 (1907): 407–15; idem, *Études, textes, découvertes* (Maredsous-Paris, 1913), 1:53–54.

707. García Villada, *Historia eclesiástica de España*, 2/2, *Apéndice* 3, 267–74.

708. The text is in PL 96, cols. 1379–86. Veiga Valiña (*La doctrina escatológica*, 25–26 nn. 6–8) is in favor of the attribution of the *Tractatus* to Julian, owing to its notable resemblance with some texts of the *Prognosticum*.

709. PL 96, cols. 1379–86.

710. Madoz, "San Julián de Toledo," 62–65, 50.

711. Hillgarth, "El Prognosticon futuri saeculi de San Julián de Toledo," 4; idem, "Las fuentes de San Julián de Toledo," 97, note with asterisk; idem, "The 'Prognosticum futuri saeculi' of St. Julian of Toledo and the 'Tractatus' published by Mai," in *Classica et Iberica: A Festschrift in Honor of the Reverend Joseph M.-F. Marique, S.J.*, ed. P. T. Brannan, SJ, Institute for the Early Christian Iberian Studies, College of the Holy Cross (Worcester, MA, 1975), 338–44; Hillgarth shows that the *Tractatus* was known by Alcuin. See also idem, *Introduction*, XV.

712. Cardinal de Lorenzana published it, attributing it to Julian. PL 96, cols. 703–758A.

713. See A. Wilmart, "Le commentaire sur le prophète Nahum attribué à Julien de Tolède," *Bulletin de littérature ecclésiastiques* (Juillet-Octobre 1922): 253–79; see also G. Morin, "Le commentaire sur Nahum du Pseudo-Julien, une oeuvre de Richard de Saint Victor?," *Revue Bénédectine* 37 (1925): 404–5. Veiga Valiña, *La doctrina escatológica*, 27–29, contains a now obsolete summary

on the question of the attribution to Julian of the *Commentarium* on the prophet Nahum.

714. PL 96, cols. 809–812B.

715. PL 96, cols. 811–814B.

716. PL 96, cols. 813–816B.

717. Veiga Valiña, *La doctrina escatológica*, 30: El poligrafo más fecundo che tuvo la Iglesia Española en el siglo VII.

CHAPTER III

1. G. Mathon, "Julien (Saint) éveque de Tolède," *Catholicisme: Hier, aujourd'hi, demain*, ed. G. Jacquemet (Paris, 1948), vol. 6, cols. 1230–31, here col. 1231.

2. J. N. Hillgarth, "Julian of Toledo," *New Catholic Encyclopedia* (San Francisco, 1967; Detroit, 2003), 8:50.

3. See J. de Ghellinck, "En marge des catalogues des Bibliothèques médiévales," in *Miscellanea Francesco Ehrle: scritti di storia e paleografia pubblicati sotto gli auspici di S.S. Pio XI in occasione dell'ottantesimo natalizio dell'E.mo Cardinale Francesco Ehrle*, 5 vols., Studi e testi 42 (Rome, 1924), 5:353. Similar remarks from the same author can be found in *Le mouvement théologique du XIIe siècle*, 2nd ed. (Bruges, 1948), 116ff. According to N. P. Stork ("A Spanish Bishop Remembers the Future: Oral Traditions and Purgatory in Julian of Toledo," *Oral Tradition* 23 [2008]: 43–70), here 43, Julian of Toledo "creates a work that is *sui generis*: a model of clarity, consolation, and good sense."

4. J. N. Hillgarth, "El Prognosticon futuri saeculi de San Julián de Toledo," *Analecta Sacra Tarraconiensia* 30 (1957): 1–57, here 14.

5. Ibid.

6. Felix, *Vita*, 7: Conscripsit etenim librum Prognosticorum futuri sae-culi ad beatae memoriae Idalium episcopum directum, habentem in capite epistolam, quae ipsi est directa, et orationem.

7. Ibid.: Ex quibus primus de origine mortis humanae est editus; secundus de animabus defunctorum, quomodo sese habeant ante suorum corporum resurrectionem; tertius de suprema corporum resurrection.

8. J. N. Hillgarth, *Introduction* to the critical edition of the works of Julian of Toledo, Corpus Christianorum, Series Latina 115 (Turnhout, 1976), XVIII.

9. Ibid.

10. M. C. Díaz y Díaz, "La obra literaria de los obispos visigóticos toledanos," in *La patrología toledano-visigoda: XXVII Semana Española de Teología* (Madrid, 1970), 55–58.

11. Hillgarth, *Introduction*, XIX.

12. Hillgarth, "El Prognosticon futuri saeculi de San Julián de Toledo," 1–57.

13. Concerning the probability that Bede knew the *Prognosticum* and used the solutions or its eschatological thought, see Hillgarth, *Introduction*, XX n. 3: "Bede might have had *Prog.* III, i, or *De comprobatione*, III.X.34 (p. 211, 115–17) in mind...."

14. A. Bonjour, ed., *Dialogue de Saint-Julien et son disciple: poème anglo-normand du XIIIe siècle*, Anglo-Norman Texts Series 8 (Oxford, 1949).

15. M. Sehlmeyer, "Giuliano di Toledo," *Dizionario di Letteratura Cristiana Antica*, ed. Siegmar Döpp and Wilhelm Geerlings; Italian edition edited by Celestino Noce (Rome, 2006), 447–48, here 447.

16. See J. N. Hillgarth, "El Prognosticon futuri saeculi de San Julián de Toledo," 17–18.

17. According to Hillgarth (*Introduction*, XXIV), apart from the case of Isidore of Seville, whose works, particularly the *Etymologiae*, were circulated in thousands of copies across the whole of medieval Europe, no other seventh-century Spanish author "was so well represented in the libraries of the Middle Ages" as Julian of Toledo with his *Prognosticum*. Hillgarth provides a long list of manuscripts of the *Prognosticum* (pp. XXV–XXXVI) with their relative explanations (pp. XXXVI–LVII). It is interesting to note that some manuscripts of the *Prognosticum* (two or three, Hillgarth says) are illustrated with exquisite and rather naïve miniatures showing the contents of some chapters (p. XLII).

18. See the full explanation and the *stemma codicum* in Hillgarth, *Introduction*, XLV–LVII.

19. Ibid., LIII.

20. According to another hypothesis, it could have been Idalius of Barcelona who sent one of the first copies of the *Prognosticum* to Spassandus, the bishop of Tarragona. See M. C. Díaz y Díaz, "Scrittori della penisola iberica," in *Patrologia*, vol. 4, *Dal Concilio di Calcedonia (451) a Beda: I Padri Latini*, ed. A. Di Berardino (Genoa, 1996), 114.

21. J. N. Hillgarth, "Towards a Critical Edition of the Works of St. Julian of Toledo," *Studia Patristica* 1 (1957): 37–43, here 41.

22. Entitled *Sanctorum Patrum Toletanorum quotquot extant opera* (Madrid, 1785).

23. Hillgarth, "Towards a Critical Edition," 37.

24. Ibid., 42.

25. For example, *Praefatio*, 94–110.

26. Cicero, *De inventione*, 1.20.28.

27. The *Prognosticum* shares this goal with other works of the sixth and seventh centuries, for example, some of the works of Isidore of Seville (the *Sententiae*, the *De ecclesiasticis officiis*) and of Ildephonse of Toledo. These works are born out of the bishops' pastoral concern for the formation of the clergy, which was so often recommended by the Toledan councils.

28. J. Madoz, "San Julián de Toledo," *Estudios Eclesiásticos*, 26 (1952): 39–69, here 56: "Obra dogmática, en tre libros, es el primer tratado 'De novissimis' che conocemos. Del género de las 'Sententias,' elaborado con autoritades patrísticas."

29. A. Veiga Valiña, *La doctrina escatológica de San Julián de Toledo* (Lugo, 1940), 131–35.

30. J. N. Hillgarth, "Eschatological and Political Concepts in the Seventh Century," in *Le septième siècle: changements et continuités. Actes du colloque bilatéral franco-britannique tenu au Warburg Institute les 8–9 juillet 1988*, ed. Jacques Fontaine and J. N. Hillgarth (London, 1992), 226; the interesting *post relationem* debate can be found on pp. 231–35.

31. Ibid., 226.

32. Taio of Saragossa indicates the doubts of theologians of the time: Sunt nonnulli qui de resurrectione carnis incerti sunt, et dum carnem in putredinem ossaque in pulverem redigi per sepulcra conspiciunt, reparari ex pulvere carnem et ossa diffidunt (PL 80, col. 983B). The same alarm about those who recount tales (*fabulantur*) of hypothetical aerial bodies of the risen ones can be found in the texts of Eugene II on the resurrection, inserted in *Prognosticum*, II, xvii.

33. J. N. Hillgarth, "Las fuentes de san Julián de Toledo," *Anales Toledanos* 3 (1971): 97–118, here 111.

34. *Sanctorum Patrum Toletanorum quotquot extant Opera*, 1:X–XI.

35. Veiga Valiña (*La doctrina escatológica*, 135) is of this opinion.

36. Hillgarth, "Las fuentes de san Julián de Toledo," 111.

37. Madoz, "San Julián de Toledo," 68.

38. Veiga Valiña, *La doctrina escatológica*, 40.

39. Vincent of Lerins, *Commonitorium*, chap. 2.

40. Hillgarth, "Las fuentes de san Julián de Toledo," 112.

41. G. García Herrero, "Notas sobre el papel del Prognosticum futuri saeculi de Julián de Toledo en la evolución de la idea medieval del purgatorio," *Antigüedad y cristianismo: Monografías históricas sobre la Antigüedad tardia* 23 (2006), 503–14, here 505–6.

42. C. Pozo, "La doctrina escatológica del 'Prognosticon futuri saeculi' de S. Julián de Toledo," *Estudios Eclesiásticos* 45 (1970): 173–201, here 177. The text is also published in *La Patrología toledano-visigoda* (Madrid, 1970), 215–43.

43. G. García Herrero, "Notas sobre el papel del Prognosticum," 506.

44. Ibid., 507.

45. As is known, one of the principal theses of J. Le Goff in *La naissance du Purgatoire* (Paris, 1981) is that the Christian idea of purgatory came about because of medieval social changes in order to give an eschatological place to the merchant middle class, which had, in the meantime, become a key element of medieval society, from the twelfth century onward. The use of the noun *purgatorium* would therefore mean the objectivized structuring of the

theological hypothesis, a sort of display of ecclesiastical power in the establishment of a reflection of the world in the afterlife. García Herrero criticizes this "hipernominalismo" of Le Goff and affirms that the substance of purgatory (though without its technical name, which is irrelevant to the theological conception of Christian purification) ought to be attributed to Julian of Toledo and to the seventh century of the Christian era, that is, a good five centuries before the writings of Peter Lombard, who was generally considered the father of Christian purgatory. This interpretation would create difficulties for the principal thesis of Le Goff; see G. García Herrero, "Notas sobre el papel del Prognosticum futuri saeculi de Julián de Toledo en la evolución de la idea medieval del purgatorio," *Antigüedad y cristianismo: Monografías históricas sobre la Antigüedad tardía* 23 (2006): 503–14, here 511.

46. Le Goff, *La naissance du Purgatoire*, 110.

47. *Passionis dominicae festum*, Julian says in the *Praefatio* of the *Prognosticum.* These words unequivocally refer to the Friday of the Passion of the Lord or Good Friday. Some authors, for example, J. Madoz, identify the day of retreat and dialogue between the two bishops as Passion or Palm Sunday; see Madoz, "San Julián de Toledo," 55.

48. In the *Praefatio* to the *Prognosticum* (80–84), Julian states that he wrote the three books of the work when the prince—that is, the king—was departing for war and the city of Toledo was entirely calm, this peace favoring intellectual work. Since history tells us that Ervig fought no wars, this statement of Julian refers to the reign of Egica, who ascended to the throne in 687.

49. See a possible account of that holy day of theological dialogue and a detailed description of the internal structure of the *Prognosticum* in J. F. Rivera Recio, *San Julián arzobispo de Toledo (s. VII): Epoca y personalidad* (Barcelona, 1944), 200–205; see also García Herrero, "Notas sobre el papel del Prognosticum," 505.

50. In actual fact we do not know the age of Bishop Idalius, but since his signature appears among the first in the list of bishops who participated in the Fifteenth Council of Toledo (to be exact, his was the fifth name after that of Julian, president of the council), it is probable that he was among the oldest bishops of the synodal assembly; see PL 84, col. 0524C; also Rivera Recio, *San Julián arzobispo de Toledo*, 195.

51. Rivera Recio, *San Julián arzobispo de Toledo*, 195.

52. *Prognosticum, Praefatio*, 35.

53. It should be remembered that in the time of Julian the codices that contain the works of the fathers of the church, and above all the biblical texts, had only internal divisions, that is, they were divided into books alone. This was the case for centuries, at least up to the thirteenth century when, thanks to Bishop Stephen Langton, the biblical texts were divided into sections, chapters, and verses.

54. *Prognosticum, Praefatio*, 50.

55. Ibid., 60.

56. Ibid., 65.

57. Ibid., 70.

58. See Rivera Recio, *San Julián arzobispo de Toledo*, 202.

59. *Prognosticum, Praefatio*, 80.

60. Hillgarth, *Introduction*, LVII.

61. Ibid.

62. There is no lack of opinions contrary to that of Hillgarth. For example, Ananya Jahanara Kabir (*Paradise, Death, and Doomsday in Anglo-Saxon Literature* [Cambridge, 2001], 44 n. 94) wrote: "I retain the title 'Prognosticon' rather than 'Prognosticum,' preferred by Hillgarth, as Gatch and other Anglo-Saxon scholars use the former."

63. Felix, *Vita*, 7 (Felice Toletano, Auctore, *Sancti Juliani Toletani Episcopi vita seu elogium*, PL 96, cols. 444–52 [Paris, 1851]).

64. *Epistola Idalii ad Iulianum, Prognosticum*, 58–59.

65. Ibid., 9.

66. *Prognosticum, Praefatio*, 91.

67. Hillgarth, *Introduction*, LVII.

68. The Migne edition contains the term *Prognosticon* in Greek capital letters in the title (PL 96, col. 453).

69. A. Bengt, *Die Hippokratische Schrift Prognostikon: Uberlieferung und Text*, Acta Universitatis Gothoburgensis, Studia graeca et latina Gothoburgensia 17 (Gothenburg, Sweden, 1963).

70. Cicero, *Prognostica*, fragm, 4, v. 5. The work is known by Isidore of Seville and quoted in his *Etymologiae* (12.7.37) when he speaks of the expressive names of the nightingale.

71. Arab philosopher, physician, and encyclopedist (980–1037).

72. Isidore of Seville, *Etymologiae* 4.10.1: Prognostica praevisio aegritudinum, vocata a praenoscendo.

73. Honorius Augustudunensis, *De scriptoribus ecclesiasticis* 2.14 in PL 172, col. 223A, having described at length the eight books of the important, but lost, *De animae natura*, the last book of which discusses "de his quae in fine mundi futura sunt: vel de quaestionibus quae solent de resurrectione proponi, sive de finibus bonorum atque malorum," adds that the same author "Condidit etiam...alios quoque tres prognosticos De futurae vitae contemplatione, vel actuali conversatione." Since Julian esteemed this author and used the *De animae natura dialogus*, it is possible that he also knew these *tres prognosticos* and was inspired by them in the choice of the title of his own eschatological work. On the contrary, Julian does not quote this work of Julian Pomerius.

74. This is evident in the explanation of the term that Isidore of Seville gives in his *Etymologiae* (4.10.1), which will often be quoted by medieval scribes at the beginning of the manuscripts of the *Prognosticum*: Prognostica praevisio aegritudinum, vocata a praenoscendo.

75. Hillgarth, "El Prognosticon futuri saeculi de San Julián de Toledo," 14.

76. J. Madoz, *Historia General de las literaturas Hispánicas* (Barcelona, 1949), 1:131.

77. J. N. Hillgarth ("St. Julian of Toledo in the Middles Ages," *Journal of the Warburg and Courtauld Institutes* 29 [1958]: 7–26, here 15) quoting a magisterial article of the Rev. J. de Ghellinck, alludes, for example, to works as Visions, Revelations, and Prophecies—or, better, imaginary Apocalypses, such as that attributed to Pseudo Methodius. Written in the time of Julian of Toledo (644–691), the *Apocalypse of Pseudo Methodius* had a notable circulation in the Middle Ages. The work, written in Syriac but then translated into Greek, Latin, and other languages, including Arabic, and of which different editions exist, was attributed by pseudonym to Methodius of Olympus (fourth century) and probably sought to be a political-religious reaction to the Muslim conquest of the Near East.

78. Hillgarth, "El Prognosticon futuri saeculi de San Julián de Toledo," 16, quoting P. Champagne de Labriolle, *Histoire de la littérature latine chrétienne*, 3rd ed. (Paris, 1947).

79. Hillgarth proposes "Foreknowledge of the future life" as the English translation of the title of the work *Prognosticum futuri saeculi* ("St. Julian of Toledo in the Middles Ages," 15).

80. PL 84, cols. 512D–513A.

81. Concerning the following considerations, see W. Berschin, *Greek Letters and the Latin Middle Ages: From Jerome to Nicholas of Cusa*, trans. Jerold C. Frakes, rev. and expanded ed. (Washington, DC, 1988); see also M. C. Díaz y Díaz, "Le latin du Haut Moyen Age espagnol," in *La lexicographie du latin médiéval et ses rapports avec les recherches actuelles sur la civilisation du Moyen Age* (Paris, 1981), 106–14.

82. W. M. Lindsay, "The Philoxenus Glossary," *Classical Review* 31, no. 7 (1917): 158–63. The precious manuscript can be found at the Bibliothèque Nationale and is classified as Lat. 7651.

83. See the elogium of the Greek language written by Isidore of Seville, drawing inspiration from Augustine: Graeca autem lingua inter ceteras gentium clarior habetur. Est enim et Latinis et omnibus linguis sonantior cuius varietas in quinque partibus discernitur. Quarum prima dicitur "koiné," id est mixta, sive communis quam omnes utuntur. Secunda "Attica," videlicet "Atheniensis," qua usi sunt omnes Graeciae auctores. Tertia "Dorica," quam habent Aegyptii et Syri. Quarta "Ionica," quinta "Aeolica," quas Aiolistì locutos dixerunt. Et sunt in observatione Graecae linguae eiusmodi certa discrimina; sermo enim eorum ita est dispertitus. Isidore of Seville, *Etymologiae*, 9.1.4–5.

84. F. Lot, "A quelle époque a-t-on cessé de parler latin?," *Archivum Latinitatis Medii Aevi* 6 (1931): 97–159, here 115 n. 1.

85. As we have already seen, even the subtlety of his particular christo-

logical language will be misunderstood by Pope Benedict II and the Roman curia.

86. So unusual as to arouse manifold suspicions with the theologians of the Roman curia.

87. According to J. Madoz ("Fuentes teológico-literarias de San Julián de Toledo," *Gregorianum* 33 [1952]: 399–400), in this particular christological and trinitarian teaching of Julian, formulated during the important epoch of the councils of Toledo, he seems to be deeply influenced by Greek patristic theology.

88. Madoz, "Fuentes teológico-literarias de San Julián de Toledo," 412. The text is in *Ars grammatica* I, 16 and is taken from the *Etymologiae* 9.1.4–5.

89. See Augustine, *De civitate Dei*, 8.2.

90. For example, P. B. Gams, *Die Kirchengeschichte von Spanien*, 3 vols. (Regensburg, 1874), 2/2:229; Veiga Valiña, *La doctrina escatológica*, 152; J. de Ghellinck, *Littérature latine au Moyen Age, depuis les origines jusq'à la fin de la renaissance carolingienne*, vol. 1 (Paris, 1938), 52–53; idem, *Le mouvement théologique du XIIe siècle*, 473–74, suggesting at least some knowledge of the Greek language for Julian.

91. Madoz, "Fuentes teológico-literarias de San Julián de Toledo," 400. To quote some illustrious names, he recalls the *Bucolics* and the *Georgics* of Virgil, the *Metamorphoses* of Ovid, and the *Satyricon* of Petronius Arbiter. Madoz also quotes Christian authors, who were no less numerous in following this intellectual trait of giving a Greek title to their works even as knowledge of the Greek language was decreasing in the Latin West.

92. Madoz, "Fuentes teológico-literarias de San Julián de Toledo," 400–401.

93. Felix, *Vita*, 9: librum de contrariis, quod Graece Antikeimenon voluit titulo adnotari.

94. Felix (*Vita*, 7) does not use the term *Prognosticum* (that is, *Prognosticum* in the singular nominative case) to denote the eschatological work of Julian of Toledo, but rather the term declined in the plural genitive case: *Librum Prognosticorum futuri saeculi*.

95. Undoubtly the term *Apologeticum* was a rather common and already Latinized term.

96. See Madoz, "Fuentes teológico-literarias de San Julián de Toledo," 406–14.

97. Ibid.; see also J.-P. Bouhot, "Une homélie de Jean Chrysostome citée par Julien de Tolède," *Revue des Etudes Augustiniennes* 23, nos. 1–2 (1977): 122–23.

98. Madoz, "Fuentes teológico-literarias de San Julián de Toledo," 405. See also Bouhot, "Une homélie de Jean Chrysostome," 122–23.

99. Madoz, "Fuentes teológico-literarias de San Julián de Toledo," 399–417.

100. Hillgarth, "Towards a Critical Edition," 42 n. 2.

101. P. Goubert, "Byzance et l'Espagne Wisigothique," *Revue des Etudes Byzantines* 3 (1945): 127–42.

102. Hillgarth, "St. Julian of Toledo in the Middle Ages,"16 n. 68.

103. Ibid.

104. Hillgarth, "Las fuentes de san Julián de Toledo," 100–101.

105. Hillgarth, "St. Julian of Toledo in the Middle Ages," 15. Julian himself says this in the *Praefatio* of the *Prognosticum*, when, turning to the bishop of Barcelona, he affirms, "non mea sed maiorum exempla doctrinamque reperies" (*Praefatio*, 92).

106. De Ghellinck, *Le mouvement théologique au XIIe siècle*, 117ff.

107. For example, the (all too) brief eschatology found in some works of Isidore of Seville and Taio of Saragossa.

108. Hillgarth, "El Prognosticon futuri saeculi de San Julián de Toledo," 14–15.

109. Hillgarth, "St. Julian of Toledo in the Middles Ages," 15.

110. Ibid.

111. According to Hillgarth ("El Prognosticon futuri saeculi de San Julián de Toledo," 14), Idalius's gratitude to Julian for the conciseness of his work will translate into the gratitude of the many readers of the *Prognosticum* in the centuries to come.

112. It does not appear to exclude that the *Prognosticum* was born as a scholastic work, that is, one addressed to the students of the Episcopal School, and therefore to the clergy in formation for the Church of Toledo. See Hillgarth ("St. Julian of Toledo in the Middles Ages," 16), who seems to have no doubt regarding this aim of the work. This shows the bishop's praiseworthy care for the theological formation of his clergy.

113. Hillgarth, "St. Julian of Toledo in the Middles Ages," 15.

114. Hillgarth, "Las fuentes de san Julián de Toledo," 106.

115. Pozo, "La doctrina escatológica del 'Prognosticum futuri saeculi,'" 74.

116. An example is the incredible, almost embarrassing, brevity of *Prognosticum* I, i, where in only three lines and with only one quotation (Rom 5:12), Julian handles the huge theme of the origin of human death in the sin of the progenitors. He could have quoted other texts of St. Paul, the Book of Wisdom, or others, or indeed have added patristic texts and his personal observations. Instead he preferred to limit himself to the main point, perhaps also considering that the reader, just beginning the reading of the *Prognosticum*, would be favorably impressed by the conciseness of the author.

117. Anthologies of patristic texts predating that of Julian already existed in the fifth century, and Julian had also gathered, in his youth and perhaps for personal use, a collection of texts of St. Augustine: the *Excerptas de libris S. Augustini*.

118. Hillgarth, "St. Julian of Toledo in the Middles Ages," 15. He also maintains (p. 16) that Julian could have had as his model for the *Prognosticum* the *Sententiae* of Isidore of Seville, considered, according to the definition of D. Stout, quoted by Hillgarth in the same study (p. 16, n. 71), "the first Latin compendium of faith and morals."

119. *Epistula Idalii ad Iulianum,* 69–73.

120. Ibid., 73.

121. F. X. Murphy, "Julian of Toledo and the Condemnation of Monothelitism in Spain," in *Mélanges Joseph de Ghellinck, S.J.,* vol. 1, *Antiquité* (Gembloux, 1951), 361–73, here 362.

122. Hillgarth, *Introduction,* XVI; idem, "Las fuentes de san Julián de Toledo," 97–118; Madoz, "Fuentes teológico-literarias de San Julián de Toledo," 399–417.

123. The *De civitate Dei* is quoted forty-five times in the three books that constitute the *Prognosticum,* especially in the third book, which is devoted to the resurrection. The *Enchiridion* is also quoted often in book III. The *De cura gerenda pro mortuis* is quoted a few times in book I, which is devoted to death; other works of Augustine are quoted less frequently. Augustine is, therefore, the most quoted patristic author in the *Prognosticum* and represents for Julian the highest theological authority, together with Cyprian of Carthage, to whom he gives the exclusive titles *Doctor beatissimus* or *sanctissimus* or *egregius.* See Hillgarth, "Las fuentes de san Julián de Toledo," 109–10. On the contrary, J. de Ghellinck (*Le mouvement théologique au XIIe siècle,* 34) highlights Gregory the Great as the greatest authority to whom Julian refers in the *Prognosticum.*

124. Hillgarth, "Las fuentes de san Julián de Toledo," 109–10.

125. Particularly the quotation of the *armisonae* (resounding weapons) of *Prognosticum* III, 5, has been considered by Madoz as a Virgilian reference; see Madoz, "Fuentes teológico-literarias de San Julián de Toledo," 405.

126. The passage is situated toward the end of the preface, where Julian says: "Therefore, it has seemed right to me that this work be compiled not so much to reveal to the readers the things almost unknown, since I do not doubt that there be many of these things about which I obtained knowledge from the volumes of many books; but, rather, so that the discourse about the future things, collected here in unity, might touch in a more intense way the minds of the mortals, because, here reunited, they could read them without effort, and, so their composed reason could bear fruit in due time, by the fact that they are offered food here without effort" (*Praefatio,* 107–9). The Virgilian reference mentioned by Hillgarth (*Introduction,* XVII) is taken from the *Aeneid* 5.462, where the poet says that human beings are touched by the sorrows of life. Showing intelligence and a clear familiarity with Virgilian language, Julian transforms human beings touched by the sorrows of life into human beings touched by reflection on the last things. This Virgilian adaptation indicates, particularly in a symbolic sense, a substantial change in the

structure of the culture itself, from pagan to Christian, which Julian both records and effects.

127. Hillgarth, "Las fuentes de san Julián de Toledo," 97–98.

128. PL 69, cols. 225–74.

129. Licinian of Carthage, *Epistola* I. Of Licinian only three letters have reached us, one of which was addressed to Gregory the Great. The text of the letter can be found in PL 72, cols. 689–692B; the quotation on the authority of the fathers of the church is in col. 689C; see also PL 77, cols. 599B–602C. The letter was written to congratulate Gregory for his *Regula pastoralis*, but above all to express to him the desire to read the *Moralia in Job* (*tua legere delectamur*) and, therefore, to ask him to send him a copy of the work. Licinian saw the work in the hands of Leander of Seville when he was returning home from Constantinople, where he had met Gregory, but he did not have occasion to copy it. In view of Licinian's fame as a bibliophile it is not difficult to imagine how much he desired to possess a copy of the *Moralia*.

130. Hillgarth, "Las fuentes de san Julián de Toledo," 103.

131. *Venanti Honori Clementiani Fortunati carminum epistularum expositionum libri undecim, Liber quintus I, Ad Martinum episcopum Galliciae*, in *Monumenta Germaniae Historica, Auctores Antiquissimi*, IV, 102.

132. Out of a total of 121 paragraphs or chapters in the *Prognosticum*, only thirteen have not already had a patristic source identified; see Hillgarth, "Las fuentes de san Julián de Toledo," 109.

133. If in the *Prognosticum* the quotations are abundant, those found in the so-called second *Apologeticum* are superabundant and meticulous. The reason behind this is easily understood: knowing that the work would be carefully scrutinized by Roman theologians, Julian compiled the work with great care and attention before he sent it to Rome to show the orthodoxy of his Christology, which had been called into question by Pope Benedict II and his curia.

134. PL 84, col. 421C–D, evidently a throwback to the times when the word *doctors* referred solely to the authority of the apostles.

135. *Apologeticum de tribus capitulis*, XV, 6–9.

136. PL 84, cols. 421C–D.

137. *Prognosticum*, III, 43. The title of the chapter (*Contra illos qui*) leads one to think that Julian wants to polemicize against these "physicist" eschatologians (they were not lacking in his time, nor are they in ours) who seek to satisfy, at all costs, all curiosity regarding the themes of eschatology and claim to know, for example, the nature of the fire of hell. Julian's conclusion leaves no doubt: he bases himself on the authority of the *Maiores*, concretely on the authority of Augustine, since the science of the *Minores*, compared to that of the greatest, must be considered to be idleness. Accordingly, it would be very dangerous and even superfluous for someone to attempt to define matters that the *Maiores* have cautioned us to leave unanswered. Even the blessed

Augustine shows his "learned ignorance" (*docta ignorantia*) on this matter when he says that nobody can know anything of the nature of that fire.

138. Hillgarth, "Las fuentes de san Julián de Toledo," 98, which extends the qualification of compilers and encyclopedists not only to Julian of Toledo but also to Isidore of Seville, Cassiodorus, Gregory the Great, and Boethius.

139. Hillgarth, "St. Julian of Toledo in the Middles Ages," 18.

140. *Prognosticum futuri saeculi, Praefatio*, 91–95.

141. Ibid., 94–95.

142. PL 84, col. 421B: Beatus etiam papa Gregorius et libris et meritis honorandus, atque in ethicis assertionibus pene cunctis merito praeferendus.

143. Hillgarth, "Las fuentes de san Julián de Toledo," 99.

144. Hillgarth ("Las fuentes de san Julián de Toledo," 100 n. 10) observes that Julian quotes a fragment of work of Athanasius that has not been identified.

145. Quoted from Latin translations, according to Hillgarth, "Las fuentes de san Julián de Toledo," 101.

146. In his *De comprobatione sextae aetatis*, Julian quotes very freely a work of Epiphanius (*De mensuris et ponderibus*), of which a Latin translation is not known. Accordingly, the translation is to be attributed, until proven to the contrary, to Julian of Toledo.

147. Quoted through the works of Jerome; see Hillgarth, "Las fuentes de san Julián de Toledo," 100 n. 10.

148. According to Hillgarth and Madoz, this quotation in *Prognosticum* III, 5, is rather a free translation of a homily of Chrysostom, the *Homilia secunda de cruce et latrone*. The translation is probably by Julian himself, because there is no evidence of a complete Latin translation of this homily of Chrysostom. See Hillgarth, "Las fuentes de san Julián de Toledo," 101; Madoz, "Fuentes teológico-literarias de San Julián de Toledo," 405. In this case one would have to attribute to the primate of Toledo a more than elementary knowledge of Greek. See also Bouhot, "Une homélie de Jean Chrysostome," 122–23.

149. Quoted from Latin translations, according to Hillgarth, "Las fuentes de san Julián de Toledo," 101. Madoz is of the same opinion about the quotation of *Homilia VII in Leviticum* of Origen, found in the translation of Rufinus in *Prognosticum* II, xxviii; see Madoz, "Fuentes teológicos-literarias en San Julián de Toledo," 405.

150. Hillgarth, "Las fuentes de san Julián de Toledo," 100 n. 10.

151. Ibid., 100–101; Madoz, "Fuentes teológico-literarias de San Julián de Toledo," 414, where the author admits that Julian had a sufficient knowledge of Greek but certainly not a mastery of it.

152. In PL 80, col. 674B–C, in which Braulio asks the presbyter and abbot Emilianus to help him find a loan copy of a commentary on the Book of the Apocalypse that he desires to read and possess, but which he has not been able to find (*quaero et not invenio*). He promises to copy the book imme-

diately and then return it as soon as possible (*citius enim et transcribetur et remit-tetur*). See Hillgarth, "Las fuentes de san Julián de Toledo," 102; J. Madoz, *Epistolario de S. Braulio de Zaragoza*, ed. crit. según el códice 22 del Archivo Capitular de León, Estudios onienses: Facultades de Teologia y de Filosofia del Colegio Maximo de Oña, 1/2 (Madrid, 1941), 141ff.

153. Felix, *Vita*, 10: Item librum sententiarum, ex decade psalmorum B. Augustini breviter summatimque collectum. Item excerpta de libris S. Augustini contra Julianum haereticum collecta.

154. Hillgarth, *Introduction*, VIII.

155. Díaz y Díaz, "Scrittori della penisola iberica," 110.

156. *Prognosticum*, II, xxvi.

157. *Prognosticum, Praefatio*, 17–19.

158. Ibid., 48–51.

159. García Herrero, "Notas sobre el papel del Prognosticum," 506.

160. Stork, *A Spanish Bishop Remembers the Future*, 44; García Herrero, "Notas sobre el papel del Prognosticum," 506.

161. *Prognosticum, Praefatio*, 84–85.

162. Hillgarth, *Introduction*, LIX–LXIII.

163. Hillgarth, *Introduction*, LIX–LXII. The letter of Idalius to Suntfredus is present in only seven manuscripts, while it is absent from other codices.

164. See the whole title of the work in Hillgarth, *Introduction*, XXII n. 5. Hillgarth expresses his suspicion that the edition of Cochlaeus has touched on the text of the *Prognosticum* at some point, as well as on the letters of Idalius.

165. De Lorenzana, *Sanctorum Patrum Toletanorum quotquot extant opera* (Madrid, 1785), 2:6–9. The publishers knew that in the edition of Boethius Epo or of Douai the letter of Idalius to Julian of Toledo was missing.

166. PL 96, cols. 457–59.

167. PL 96, cols. 815–18.

168. D'Achery published the letters of Idalius in the *Specilegium*, 2nd ed. (Paris, 1665), 1:313–17.

169. Hillgarth, *Introduction*, LXII–LXIII; see E. Flórez, *España Sagrada*, vol. 29, apéndice X, 815–18.

170. See Rivera Recio, "San Julián arzobispo de Toledo," 217.

171. See the list of manuscripts in Hillgarth, *Introduction*, LIX–LXII.

172. Ibid., LXI. Only seven manuscripts contain the short letter.

173. M. A. W. [Mrs. Humphrey Ward], "Julianus (63)," *A Dictionary of Christian Biography*, ed. W. Smith, DCL, LLD, and H. Wace, BD (London, 1882), 3:477–81, here 480, affirms that "of his literary and theological influence over the Spanish churchmen of his own day on both sides of the Pyrenees, the letters of Idalius of Barcelona to him and to Suntfredus metropolitan of Narbonne...are a sufficient proof."

174. *Epistula Idalii*, 46–47: is qui caduca mercimonia vectare solitus erat.

175. E. Gozalbes Cravioto, "Una aproximación al estudio de las vías en la Hispania visigótica," in *Actas del II Congreso Internacional de Caminería Hispánica— Guadalajara (España) 4–9 Julio 1994*, vol. 1 (Guadalajara, 1998), 85–94.

176. Hillgarth, *Introduction*, LXI–LXII. Only seven manuscripts of the letter to Suntfredus have survived.

177. S. A. Bennet, "Zuntfredus," *A Dictionary of Christian Biography*, 4:1227.

178. Flórez, *España Sagrada*, 5:288: "inviandole los libros del santo que con impaciencia le pidió el Narbonense."

179. R. Ceillier, *Histoire générale des auteurs sacrés et ecclésiastiques* (Paris, 1729–63), 17:735.

180. M. A. W. [Mrs. Humphrey Ward], "Julianus (63)," 479.

181. Felix, *Vita*, 7, 8, and 10.

182. The second of these works was dedicated to Ervig before he had ascended to the Visigothic imperial throne; see Felix, *Vita*, 8.

183. Ibid.

184. Hillgarth, *Introduction*, LVIII–LIX.

185. It is fair to think that this is one of the first manuscript copies of the work, perhaps even the first one after the one made by the copyist for the author.

186. Hillgarth, *Introduction*, LVIII.

187. Ibid., LVIII–LIX; Hillgarth, "El Prognosticon futuri saeculi de San Julián de Toledo," 17–18.

188. For example, no indication of this second dedication of the *Prognosticum* can be found in the numerous entries devoted to Julian of Toledo in the historical, theological, and patristic dictionaries consulted. The hypothesis is, therefore, proper to Hillgarth, who by his own admission owes the identification of Bishop Spassandus to the Italian scholar Prof. Campana. See Hillgarth, "El Prognosticon futuri saeculi de San Julián de Toledo," 18 n. 21.

189. Hillgarth, "Towards a Critical Edition," 41.

190. This dedication is at the beginning of the preface that Julian wrote addressing it to Idalius; the full form says: *In Christi nomine* (but also *In nomine Domini et Salvatoris nostri Iesu Christi), incipit Prognosticum futuri saeculi. Utere feliciter Spassande papa iugiter per saecula longa. Prognosticum, Introduction*, LVIII.

191. See Flórez, *España Sagrada*, 7:189–90.

192. The university city of Alcalá de Henares is practically in the center of Spain, thirty kilometers from Madrid and twenty-five kilometers from Guadalajara.

193. The signature of Spassandus is in the fourth place at the end of the acts of the Fifteenth Council of Toledo (688), a sign of his episcopal seniority among the twenty-six bishops present (PL 84, col. 525C). At the Sixteenth

Council of Toledo the name of Spassandus is in sixteenth place, out of a total of fifty-nine bishops present (PL 84, col. 550).

194. PL 84, col. 521A

195. Hillgarth, *Introduction*, LIX.

196. The list of the manuscripts is in Hillgarth, *Introduction*, LIX n. 1.

197. PL 84, cols. 408D–409.

198. The Councils of Lyons (1274), Ferrara-Florence (1439ff.), and Trent (1547ff.), which will dogmatically pronounce on the eschatological truths of the Catholic faith, are still many centuries in the future.

199. Idumea is the name with which the Septuagint translates the Jewish term *'ĕdōm*, which in the Greek-Roman epoch designated the region located to the south of Palestine. The territory was occupied by the Idumeans after the conquest of Jerusalem by Nebuchadnezzar in 587 BC. In the Seleucid epoch, Idumea constituted a satrapy commanded by a strategist such as Gorgias in the Second Book of Maccabees (12:32). Its governor was Antipater, the father of Herod. The hatred and rivalry between the Jews and the Edomites can be considered traditional, an extension of the rivalry between Jacob and Esau. During the Jewish War it was devastated by the legionaries of Vespasian. In a figurative sense, the term *Idumea* indicates a hostile, inhospitable, desertlike place, impassable and without water, roads, or footpaths (Psalm 62:2 Vulg. stigmatizes Idumea as *inaquosa et invia*). For Julian, it is a desolate image that well represents the idea of being distant from one's own country, that is, in a situation of exile in which he roams around sick and blind.

200. Probably calling to mind Matt 7:8 and Luke 11:10, where believers are urged to pray because *pulsanti aperietur.*

201. Hillgarth, "Las fuentes de san Julián de Toledo," 107.

202. *Prognostiucm, Praefatio,* 111–12.

203. *Prognosticum, Praefatio,* 91–92. Hillgarth reports the similar expression of Isidore, who in the *Quaestiones in Vetus Testamentum* says, more elegantly than Julian, lector non nostra leget, sed veterum releget. Quod enim ego loquor, illi dicunt, et vox mea ipsorum est lingua. PL 83, col. 209A.

204. *Prognosticum, Praefatio,* 94–95.

205. *Prognosticum, Praefatio,* 104–5: Hoc igitur opus, non ad hoc tantum formari mihi perplacuit ut quasi incognita legentibus demonstrarem.

206. Ibid., 104–11.

207. J. Forget, "Julien de Tolède (Saint)," in *Dictionnaire de Théologie Catholique* (Paris, 1903–50), vol. 8, cols. 1940–42, here 1941.

208. J. Fontaine, *Isidore de Séville et la culture classique dans l'Espagne wisigothique,* 2 vols. (Paris, 1959), 1:737.

209. For example, in the important texts of the Missal, used daily in the liturgy and in pastoral ministry; in the hymns; in the sacramental rituals used by the clergy in all the parishes of the kingdom; in hagiographies; and so on.

210. Think, for example, of the collections of texts such as the *Hispana*, that is, the doctrinal and canonical collection that gathered the acts of the numerous Hispanic-Visigothic councils, in addition to the most important texts of the ecumenical councils of antiquity and many documents of the Church of Rome. To this collection must also be added another important document compiled in Latin and of royal character, the legal collection called *Lex visigothorum*. See M. C. Díaz y Díaz, "El Latín de España en el siglo VII: Lengua y escritura según los textos documentales," in *Le septième siècle: changements et continuités*, ed. Jacques Fontaine and J. N. Hillgarth (London, 1992), 25–37, here 25.

211. Also some royal diplomatic documents, the minting of coins, and many epigraphs on stones compiled for public occasions and events; see Díaz y Díaz, "El Latín de España," 25.

212. Rivera Recio, "San Julián arzobispo de Toledo," 211.

213. R. Menéndez Pidal, *Orígenes del español*, 7th ed. (Madrid, 1972), 503 n. 10.

214. Cellier, *Histoire des Auteurs sacrés et ecclésiastiques* 17:739: "Son style est clair, et sa latinité plus pure que de beaucoup d'autres Ecrivains de son siècle."

215. L. Holtz, "Continuité et discontinuité de la tradition grammaticale au VIIe siècle," in *Le septième siècle: changements et continuités*, ed. Jacques Fontaine and J. N. Hillgarth (London, 1992), 41–54, and the discussion on 54–57.

216. Madoz, "San Julián de Toledo," 69.

217. Hillgarth, "St. Julian of Toledo in the Middles Ages," 16; idem, "El Prognosticon futuri saeculi de San Julián de Toledo," 14, where the author repeats the same praise, but in Spanish: Julian "tenía una biblioteca excelente y supo utilizarla."

218. See T. Marín, "Bibliotecas Eclesiasticas," *Diccionario de Historia Eclesiástica de España* (Madrid, 1972–75), 1:250–62, here 251.

219. U. Domínguez Del Val, "Julián de Toledo," *Diccionario de Historia Eclesiástica de España* (Madrid, 1972–75), 2:1259–60, here 1260.

220. Hillgarth, "Julian of Toledo," 50.

221. De Ghellinck, "En marge des catalogues," 342; Hillgarth, "Julian of Toledo," 50.

222. The precious codex, kept in the Diocesan Museum of Sacred Art of Rossano (Cosenza, Italy), dates back to the sixth century. It was produced in a Greek-oriental style and is rich in chromatic Byzantine miniatures; the uncial text is written in gold and silver letters. Originally, it must have been four hundred pages long, containing the four Gospels. Now the codex, which has lost more than half of its sheets, contains the whole Gospel of Matthew and almost all that of Mark, as well as part of the letter of Eusebius to Carpian on the agreement of the Gospels. The text of the Gospel is written in two

columns, each of twenty lines on purple parchment and is preceded by fifteen full-page illustrations.

223. Hillgarth, *Introduction*, XLIII n. 3. He refers to M. C. Díaz y Díaz, "Aspectos de la cultura literaria en la España visigotica," *Anales Toledanos* 3 (1971): 33–58.

224. Iohannes Trithemius, *De scriptoribus Ecclesiasticis*, 79.

225. Substantially the *Afra versio*, the biblical versions that came from Latin Africa, and the so-called *Itala*, the version that came from western Europe.

226. Hillgarth (*Introduction*, XLIII n. 3) maintains that Julian makes an "ultra-literal" intepretation of the Bible. We do not completely agree with this judgment. See B. Bischoff, "Turning Points in the History of Latin Exegesis in the Early Middle Ages," in *Biblical Studies: The Medieval Irish Contribution*, ed. Martin McNamara, Proceedings of the Irish Biblical Association 1 (Dublin, 1976), 74–160.

227. J. Madoz, SJ, *Segundo Decennio de Estudios sobre Patrística Española*, Estudios Onienses 5 (Madrid, 1951), 147. See also de Ghellinck, *Le mouvement théologique XIIe siècle*, 116–17.

228. M. A. W. [Mrs. Humphrey Ward], "Julianus (63)," 477.

229. Hillgarth, *Introduction*, LXX.

230. Madoz, "San Julián de Toledo," 56.

231. Hillgarth, "St. Julian of Toledo in the Middles Ages," 16.

232. De Ghellinck, *Le mouvement théologique du XIIe siècle*, 117–18; see also idem, "En marge des catalogues," 354.

233. Hillgarth, "Towards a Critical Edition," 41.

234. De Ghellink, "En marge des catalogues," 354.

235. *Epistola* 10, in PL 121, cols. 467–73.

236. The letter was published by J. Madoz, *Epistolario de Alvaro de Cordoba*, Epistola 14, 2–6 (Madrid, 1947), 194. The didactic title of the letter is: *Epistola Episcopi (Anonymi) ad alterum episcopum directa, inter epistolas Albari Cordubensis*, 10, 3.

237. Hillgarth, "St. Julian of Toledo in the Middles Ages," 11: the speech of Julian is defined as *venerandum*, and he himself is referred to as "egregius doctor," emulating the way in which Julian refers to Augustine when quoting his authority.

238. Hillgarth, *Introduction*, XXI.

239. For example, Samson, *Apologeticum* 2: ut beatus ait Iulianus, pro fide nolle asserere id ipsum est quod negare.

240. See Hillgarth, *Introduction*, XX n. 4.

241. A. Werminghoff, ed., *Monumenta Germaniae Historica, Concilia Aevi Karolini (742–842)* I, T. I (Hannover, 1906), 113 nn. 10–18.

242. *Epistula ad Alcuinum*, in E. Dümmler, ed., *Monumenta Germaniae*

Historica, Epistolae Karolini Aevi, II (Berlin, 1895), n. 182, 305, 12, 30–34, and 306, 36–37.

243. Elipandus was archbishop of Toledo for almost two decades toward the end of the eighth century, when the city was under Arab rule; he was the founder of the heretical doctrine of adoptionism condemned by the Councils of Ratisbon (792) and Frankfurt (798). The heresy maintained that Christ had had two births, corresponding to his two natures, one for nature and one for adoption. This christological doctrine was surely inspired by Nestorius and would have horrified the experienced Christologian Julian, author of the two *Apologetica,* and Elipandus's predecessor on the primatial see of Toledo. Elipandus elaborated his Christology when he was already an octogenarian, under the influence of Felix of Urgel, but elements of his doctrine were present already in some of his earlier remarks on the Trinity. Condemned on many occasions, he obstinately maintained his position.

244. For example, the confused definitions referred to Christ as *Homo Dominicus et Humanatus Deus* (PL 96, col. 880). Such a definition is not present in the known works of Julian. It might have been inserted into one of his lost works or perhaps been invented by Elipandus himself, as he was wont, as Alcuin of York reproaches him (*Adversus Elipandum,* book 2; PL 101, col. 266).

245. E. Dümmler, ed., *Monumenta Germaniae Historica, Epistolae Karolini Aevi* (Berlin, 1895), II, n. 182, 306, 36–37.

246. A. Werminghoff, ed., *Monumenta Germaniae Historica, Concilia Aevi Karolini (742–842)* I, T. I, 145, nn. 35–40: Et melius est testimonio Dei patris credere de suo filio quam Hildephonsi vestri, qui tales vobis composuit preces in missarum sollemniis, quale universalis et sancta Dei non habet ecclesia.

247. Ibid.

248. PL 101, cols. 231A–270D: Beati Alcuini contra epistolam sibi ab Elipando directam libri quattuor.

249. PL 101, col. 266B: Juliani quoque Pomerii Prognostica ex sanctorum floribus collecta Patrum consideravimus, nec ibi aliquid hujus vestrae invenimus sectae depictum.

250. To definitively show his positive judgment of the great theologians of Toledo, he adds that in the writings of the venerable toledan fathers he *nihil novi, vel antiquis contrarium Patribus; sed omnia catholico stylo perscripta agnovimus* ("has not found anything to report, or something opposite to the ancient fathers; but we verified everything explained with Catholic words").

251. *Elucidarium sive dialogus de summa totius christianae Theologiae,* in PL 172, cols. 1109–1176D. See Hillgarth, *Introduction,* XXI, and the reference in n. 3 to the work of V. Lefèvre *L'Elucidarium et les lucidaires: Contribution par l'histoire d'un texte, à l'histoire des croyances religieuses en France au Moyen Age* (Paris, 1954).

252. Haymo was a fellow student of Rabanus Maurus and a disciple of Alcuin, whose lectures he heard at the Monastery of Saint Martin of Tours.

Even if all the works attributed to him in vols. 116–18 of Migne are not really his, Haymo was, in any case, a prolific writer.

253. PL 118, cols. 875A–958D.

254. *Burchardi Wormaciensis Ecclesiae Episcopi Decretorum Libri Viginti*, in PL 140, cols. 537–1058C; see J. N. Hillgarth, "The Position of Isidorian Studies: A Critical Review of the Literature since 1935," *Isidoriana* [León] 32, no. 58 (1961): 11–74.

255. The *Liber floridus* ("the book full of flowers or in flower") is an encyclopedia, a kind of compilation, which treats various themes: Sacred Scripture, chronology, astronomy, geography, theology, philosophy, and natural history. In its compilation Lambert used the writings of different authors, among them the *Prognosticum* of Julian of Toledo. Originally written in Latin, the work was later translated into French bearing the title *Livre fleurissant*. The work is thus titled because the author sees his compilation as a bouquet of flowers picked from the celestial meadows of which the believer, like a bee, can taste the mellifluous sweetness, if he feeds on them. The work has a respectable collection of nine manuscripts, some of which are splendidly illustrated and decorated with maps and polychromatic drawings of every kind. One of these manuscripts is regarded as the original, written by Lambert himself, and it is kept at the Library of the University of Gent (Belgium). It is this manuscript that Hillgarth used for his study.

256. J. N. Hillgarth, "Julian of Toledo in the 'Liber Floridus,'" *Journal of the Warburg and Courtauld Institutes* 26 (1963): 192–96.

257. Now at Boulogne-sur-Mer (northern France), MS 63, sec. XI, fols. 1–10.

258. E. M. Raynes, "MS. Boulogne-sur-Mer 63 and Ælfric," *Medium Aevum* 26 (1957): 65–73. On the same theme, see also "Ælfric's 'Excerpts' from the 'Prognosticon futuri saeculi' of Julian of Toledo," in *Preaching and Theology in Anglo-Saxon England*, ed. M. McC. Gatch (Toronto, 1977), 127–46; A. L. Meaney, "Ælfric's Use of His Sources in His Homily on Auguries," *English Studies* 66 (1985): 477–95.

259. "Ælfric based this homily on Julian of Toledo's *Prognosticon futuri saeculi*, a rigorously Augustinian commentary on eschatology that counseled that worldly events could not be interpreted as signs of the approaching apocalypse." *The Apocalyptic Year 1000: Religious Expectation and Social Change, 950–1050*, ed. R. Landes, A. Gow, and D. C. Van Meter (Oxford: Oxford University Press, 2003), 301.

260. *Apocalyptic Year 1000*, 301 n. 74. On Julian's antiapocalyptic commentary, see R. Landes, *Relics, Apocalypse, and the Deceits of History: Ademar of Chabannes (989–1034)* (Cambridge, MA, 1995), 92–93. For a discussion of Ælfric's use of *Prognosticum*, see Gatch, *Preaching and Theology*, 96–101, 129–46.

261. Hillgarth, "Julian of Toledo in the 'Liber Floridus,'" 193.

262. N. Wicki, "Das 'Prognosticon futuri saeculi' Julians von Toledo als

Quellenwerken der Sentenzen des Petrus Lombardus," *Divus Thomas* (Fr.) 31 (1953): 351–54; see also Hillgarth, "El Prognosticon futuri saeculi de San Julián de Toledo," 44–47; on pp. 48–61 the complete list of the catalogues that mention the *Prognosticum* can be found, divided by nation.

263. *Magistri Petri Lombardi, Parisiensis Episcopi, Sententiae in IV libris distinctae*, Editio tertia, Ad fidem Codicum Antiquiorum, Tomus II, Liber III et IV, Editiones Collegii S. Bonaventurae Ad Claras Aquas (Grottaferrata, 1981), Dist. XLIV, c. 7, 2. See also J. G. Bougerol, "The Church Fathers and the Sentences of Peter Lombard," in *The Reception of the Church Fathers in the West: From the Carolingians to the Maurists*, ed. Irena Backus, 2 vols. (Leiden/New York, 1997), 1:113–63. The author of the study recognizes that Peter Lombard quotes, under the name of Augustine, an extract of the *Prognosticum futuri saeculi* of Julian of Toledo (II, 11) (p. 122). Analogous considerations are seen in the study of N. Wicki, "Das 'Prognosticon futuri saeculi' Julians von Toledo," 349–60, where the author affirms that Peter Lombard directly and indirectly used the *Prognosticum* in the editing of his *Sententiae*. What made the *Magister Sententiarum* rely so heavily on the *Prognosticum* was probably the fact that Lombard discovered that it had also been used in the works of earlier theologians or jurists (which in some cases he himself had used), for example, those of Burchard of Worms and the *Sic et non* of Peter Abelard. Finally, the author shows the extraordinary resemblance, almost word for word, between the prologue of the *Sententiae* and a text contained in the *Praefatio* to the *Prognosticum*; see pp. 59–60 and n. 2.

264. R. Aubert, "Julien (Saint), évêque de Tolède," *Dictionnaire d'histoire et de géographie ecclésiastiques* (Paris, 1912–), vol. 28, cols. 534–35; see also Hillgarth, *Introduction*, XXI.

265. Hillgarth, "Julian of Toledo in the Middle Ages," 23–24.

266. Bonjour, *Dialogue de Saint-Julien et son disciple.*

267. Hillgarth, "St. Julian of Toledo in the Middles Ages," 14.

268. Le Goff, *La naissance du Purgatoire*, 135–37. We naturally express reserve with regard to the main thesis of Le Goff, which considers purgatory an intellectual creation, the fruit of the sociological transformation of medieval Christianity (p. 256). In any case he recognized the importance and role of the *Prognosticum* in medieval theology.

269. Ibid., 110.

270. Ibid.

271. Hillgarth, "El Prognosticon futuri saeculi de San Julián de Toledo," 16. Hillgarth ("St. Julian of Toledo in the Middle Ages") does not generally use emphatic prose, but when he speaks of the circulation of the work of Julian in the early Middle Ages, as a historian who knows the extraordinary number of manuscripts of the *Prognosticum* spread across Europe, he cannot help but use expressions like, "extraordinary" (p. 14), "phenomenal" (p. 18), "immense popularity" (p. 21). As for the geographical route followed

by the first manuscripts of the *Prognosticum*, it is very likely that the work was introduced to the rest of Europe by Irish and Anglo-Saxon monks; see Hillgarth, "El Prognosticon futuri saeculi de San Julián de Toledo," 15.

272. This important assertion is by E. Lesne, *Le livres, "scriptoria" et bibliothèques du commencement du VIIIe à la fin du XIe siècle* (Lille, 1938), 775.

273. Hillgarth, "St. Julian of Toledo in the Middles Ages," 20 nn. 98, 99.

274. Ibid., 21 n. 100. The author quotes an interesting detail: the *Prognosticum* appears in a list of books to be read during Lent of 1252 in the Abbey of Cluny. We know also that the *Prognosticum* was looked at by monk Hugh and monk Robertus, *infirmarius* of the monastery.

275. F. Brunhölzl, *Histoire de la littérature latine du Moyen Âge*, vol. I/2, *L'époque Carolingienne* (Louvain, 1991), 103–10, 263–64.

276. Hillgarth, "St. Julian of Toledo in the Middles Ages," 19; idem, *Introduction*, XLIII. Hillgarth says that although "the Prognosticum was clearly a work found in every monastic library of any importance as a manual containing an excellent anthology of patristic opinions on everything connected with the Last Thing, it was not allowed to remain on the shelves. It was read and re-read and often the text must have appeared obscure to the Carolingian readers."

277. In his letter to Suntfredus, bishop of Narbonne, Idalius, bishop of Barcelona, expressly says that it was truly Julian who chose a title for his work and that he wished to call it (*appellare…procuravit*) *Prognosticum futuri saeculi* (*Epistula Idalii ad Suntfredum*, 9–10). Moreover, in the preface to the *Prognosticum*, Julian clearly says that he gave the title *Prognosticum futuri saeculi* to the three books previously listed (*Praefatio*, 88–91).

278. *Epistula Idalii*, 58–59: "Appellatur enim Prognosticum futuri saeculi, quod latine 'Praescientia futuri saeculi' dici non incongrue potest."

279. In some cases, however, the cataloguers of the medieval libraries misunderstood the title of the work of Julian of Toledo, mistaking it for a book of prophecies or visions; for example, in the catalogue of the library of Reichenau, the *Prognosticum* was situated together with collections of visions and prophecies on the future. See Hillgarth, "St. Julian of Toledo in the Middle Ages," 15 n. 62. But, despite the sensationalism of such books of visions, which were widely read, one can say without doubt that the *Prognosticum* was more successful than any book that promised to disclose the knowledge of secrets. A typical example is the book of the *Prophecies* of Pseudo Methodius, recalled both by Hillgarth (ibid.) and by de Ghellinck ("En marge des catalogues," 354).

280. Hillgarth, "St. Julian of Toledo in the Middles Ages," 17.

281. Ibid., 18.

282. Ibid.

283. Ibid.

284. Ibid., 18–19 n. 89. Hillgarth observes that eight of the thirteen

manuscripts of the ninth century containing the works of Julian were written in France.

285. Ibid., 18–19 n. 90.

286. Ibid., 18–19 nn. 91 and 92.

287. Ibid., 19.

288. The words of Cyprian of Carthage, quoted by Julian in his *Prognosticum*, are extremely famous: Mundus ecce nutat et labitur, et ruinam sui non senectute rerum, sed fine testatur.

289. Augustine, *Sermo* LXXXI, 8; PL 38, col. 505.

290. Gregory the Great, *In Evangelia*, I, 19, 1–2; PL 76, col. 1155.

291. See F. H. Dudde, *Gregory the Great, His Place in History and Thought*, vol. 2 (London, 1905), 366; he quotes some selected passages of the *Moralia in Iob* related to the Antichrist. See also *Gregoire le Grande, Colloques Internationaux du CNRS*, ed. J. Fontaine et al. (Paris, 1986), 389, 404.

292. See C. Dagens, "La fin des temps et l'Église selon saint Grégoire le Grand," *Recherches de science religieuse* 458 (1970): 273–88.

293. For example in his *Historia Gothorum*.

294. See the "discussion" in Hillgarth, "Eschatological and Political Concepts in the Seventh Century," 234.

295. "In 681 Julian of Toledo attempted to prove that the year 6000 had already passed six years earlier in 675, *De comprobatione sextae aetatis*, 3.10, ll. 100–148, ed. J. Hillgarth, *Corpus Christianorum, Series* Latina, Vol. CXV." *Apocalyptic Year 1000*, 265.

296. J. Fontaine, contribution to the "discussion" in Hillgarth, "Eschatological and Political Concepts in the Seventh Century," 234.

297. *Idalius ad Iulianum*, 94–96.

298. PL 96, col. 193D.

299. Similar expressions are found in the great works of the Latin fathers, for example, the *Moralia in Job* of Gregory the Great (*termino propinquante turbata sunt*); PL 75, cols. 511BC. See Hillgarth, "St. Julian of Toledo in the Middles Ages," 17, which, besides recalling the fundamental importance of a biblical text such as Sir 7:36 ("In all you do, remember the end of your life, and then you will never sin" [*novissima tua*, according to the *Vulgata*]), quotes (n. 81) the judgment of the contemporary historian J. Pérez de Urbel, according to whom the issue of the end of the world obsessed the Spanish bishops and some ecclesiastical writers from the end of the patristic epoch. It is not the case of Julian of Toledo. As N. P. Stork says, the *Prognosticum* is "a surprisingly rational and intimate approach to Judgment Day and the last things. In this work Julian does not offer typical medieval "prognostications" ("Spanish Bishop Remembers the Future," 43).

300. *Apocalyptic Year 1000*, 247: "...chiliasm deserved mention only as a condemned popular belief: Julian of Toledo (687), Bede (724), Remi of

Auxerre (ca. 940), and Byrhtferth (1011) all openly speak of the 'vulgar' belief in the Millennium, to which they oppose their Augustinian teachings."

301. Visions, revelations, and imaginary prophecies were very common at the time of Julian of Toledo, as can be seen from the rich narration of the "journey into the afterlife" described in the *Visio Baronti*, in which the saintly Benedictine monk narrates with a wealth of detail his "out-of-body experience." See W. Levison, ed., *Monumenta Germaniae Historica, Scriptores rerum merovingicarum*, 5, 377–94. This work, written in the years when Julian was presbyter of the Church of Toledo (668–679), is exaggeratedly descriptive of the places, the characters, and even the "time" of the afterlife and can be considered a "daughter" of the visions contained in the works of Gregory the Great (for example, the *Dialogi*). Even if this work was contemporary to Julian, he steers clear, apart from some edifying examples inserted in the *Prognosticum*, of similar descriptions of the places, characters, and times of the afterlife. The Latin text of the *Visio* of the monk Barontius, with a parallel Italian translation and commentary, is available in *Visioni dell'aldilà in Occidente*, Fonti modelli e testi, a cura di Maria Pia Ciccarese (Florence, 1987), 231–75. Another series of visions of the afterlife comes from the Hispanic-Visigothic environment of the seventh century and is therefore contemporary to Julian of Toledo. It deals with the *Dicta ab beatum Donadeum scripta*, which tells of the visions of the afterlife collected by the tormented ascetic monk St. Valerius of Bierzo (d. 695, five years after the death of Julian). There is a hypothesis that attributes the visions to Valerius himself. Also in this work, the geographical and topographical descriptions of the afterlife are abundant and reach heights of realism, but also of surrealism, never reached before. Julian, with his work of theological and dogmatic eschatology, dissociates himself from these kinds of visions and dreams, not surrendering to the temptation of a "material representation" of the two states of damnation and glory. For this extraordinary text of St. Valerius of Bierzo, see *Visioni dell'aldilà in Occidente*, 276–301. See also C. Carozzi: "La géographie de l'au-delà et sa signification pendant le haut moyen âge," in *Popoli e paesi nella cultura altomedievale*, 2 vols., Settimane di studio del Centro Italiano di studi sull'alto medioevo 29 (Spoleto, 1983), 1:423–81; idem, *Le voyage de l'âme dans l'au-delà d'après la littérature latine (Ve-XIIIe siècle)* (Rome, 1994).

302. Landes, *Relics, Apocalypse, and the Deceits of History*, esp. chapter 4.

303. M.-D. Chenu, *Introduction à l'étude de Saint Thomas* (Montréal, 1954), 258; idem, *La théologie au douzième siècle* (Paris, 1957).

304. L. Ott and E. Naab, *Eschatologie in der Scholastik*, Handbuch der Dogmengeschichte, vol. 4, fascicle 7b (Freiburg, 1990), 85–258.

305. For example, the importance in medieval theology of the ideas of *substantia, accidens*, and the fourfold causality (*materialis, efficiens, formalis*, and *finalis*), and so on.

306. L. F. Ladaria, "Fin de l'homme et fin des temps," in *Histoire des*

dogmes, vol. 2, *L'homme et son salut* (Paris, 1995), 450–65. The author attributes to the medieval epoch the "systématisation de l'eschatologie personnelle."

307. See 1 Corinthians 15.

308. G. Gozzelino, *Nell'attesa della beata speranza: saggio di escatologia cristiana* (Turin, 1993), 206–13.

309. On the influence of the *Prognosticum* on the eschatological section of the *De Sacramentis* of Hugh of St. Victor, and also on some of the works of Haymo of Halbertstadt and others, see Veiga Valiña, *La doctrina escatológica*, 36. He does not, however, exclude the possibility that the resemblance of the theses of Hugh of St. Victor to some eschatological texts of Julian of Toledo is due to the fact that both the authors had the same source: the *Moralia* of Gregory the Great.

310. This is how the *Prognosticum futuri saeculi* is often defined by the majority of historians of medieval thought and by scholars of the history of theology.

311. Hillgarth, "St. Julian of Toledo in the Middle Ages," 7–26.

312. Wicki, "Das 'Prognosticum futuri saeculi' Julians von Toledo," 351–54.

313. In particular, the *Sententiae* of Peter Lombard and the immense influence that this work would have on the great Scholastic theologians.

314. We interpret the term *scholastic* in the way described by Chenu in his *Introduction à l'étude de Saint Thomas*, 56: "a rational form of thought which is elaborated by consciously and voluntarily starting from a text to which the value of authority is attributed." With this meaning, Julian of Toledo can be considered a "scholastic" since he did exactly what is written by Chenu, starting from many texts of authors (the fathers of the church) whom he considered to be theological authorities.

315. The magisterial and conciliar documents of an eschatological character are the following: the profession of faith of the emperor Michael Paleologus during the Second Council of Lyons (1274) (DS 856–59); the Apostolic Constitution *Benedictus Deus* (1336) of Pope Benedict XII (DS 1000–1002), the declarations of the Council of Florence-Ferrara (1439) (DS 1304–6) and the Council of Trent (1563) (DS 1820). Documents of the modern magisterium include the Letter of the Sacred Congregation of the Doctrine of the Faith *Recentiores episcoporum synodi* of May 17, 1979, and the official document, even if it is not magisterial, of the International Theological Commission entitled *De quibusdam quaestionibus actualibus circa eschatologiam*, published in March 1992, having received the *placet* of Pope John Paul II. This Catholic eschatological doctrine is confirmed by numerous assertions of the *Catechism of the Catholic Church* (1992). To this list we add also the synthetic eschatological exposition of chapter 7 of the Dogmatic Constitution on the Church *Lumen Gentium* of the Second Vatican Council

and some paragraphs from the Pastoral Constitution on the Church in the Modern World, *Gaudium et Spes* (nos. 14, 18, 39, and so on).

316. Hillgarth, "Towards a Critical Edition," 40; see also idem, "Julian of Toledo in the 'Liber Floridus,'" 192–96, here 192. The quoted critical study is of 1955. But already by 1957, in another essay of Hillgarth ("El Prognosticon futuri saeculi de San Julián de Toledo," 1–57), the number of the codices of the *Prognosticum* consulted by the author had grown to 153 complete and 23 partial. In the critical edition of the *Prognosticum* of 1976 for the Corpus Christianorum, Series Latina, the number of codices had grown once again, to 186 complete and twenty-four fragmentary codices!

317. The most ancient manuscripts of the *Prognosticum* in our possession are the third and the fortieth on the list compiled by Hillgarth (*Introduction*, XXV, XXVII). The two codices (Angers 275 and Kassel THeol.) both date back to the beginning of the ninth century and were written by copyists already accustomed to the reformed orthography of the scriptoria of the Carolingian age.

318. See the long list of the catalogues of the medieval libraries in Hillgarth, "El Prognosticon futuri saeculi de San Julián de Toledo," 44–57; see also idem, *Introduction*, XX–XXI.

319. Hillgarth, "St. Julian of Toledo in the Middle Ages," 14–15 nn. 57–59.

320. Ibid., 15.

321. De Ghellinck, "En marge des catalogues," 354.

322. Hillgarth, "Julian of Toledo in the 'Liber Floridus,'" 192 n. 4.

323. These come from the Monastery of San Millán de la Cogolla and are now in Madrid. See Hillgarth, "St. Julian of Toledo in the Middles Ages," 13–14.

324. Which come from Burgo de Osma.

325. Hillgarth, *Introduction*, XLIII n. 3.

326. Ibid., n. 4, where he says that Manuscript 161 appears to have been written by ten different copyists between the middle and end of the ninth century.

327. Hillgarth, *Introduction*, XLIV.

328. The complex and hypothetical explanations of the various passages of the codices and the resemblance (or lack thereof) of the catalogues can be found in Hillgarth, "St. Julian of Toledo in the Middle Ages," 12–13.

329. Ibid., 14 n. 52.

330. Hillgarth, "El Prognosticon futuri saeculi de San Julián de Toledo," 15.

331. It can be assumed that there were around ten thousand manuscript copies of the *Etymologiae* of Isidore of Seville spread across Europe; see Hillgarth, "El Prognosticon futuri saeculi de San Julián de Toledo," 13 n. 2.

332. Ibid.; see also C. H. Beeson, "The Ars Grammatica of Julian of

Toledo," in *Miscellanea Francesco Ehrle*, Scritti di Storia Paleografia (Rome, 1924), 50.

333. Hillgarth, "El Prognosticon futuri saeculi de San Julián de Toledo," 15.

334. Aubert, "Julien (Saint) évêque de Tolède," 534–35.

335. Hillgarth ("El Prognosticon futuri saeculi de San Julián de Toledo," 15 n. 19) says that the two incunabula copies of the *Prognosticum* are to be found at the British Museum in London; see also 43 n. 10; and idem, *Introduction*, LVI.

336. For these details, see Hillgarth, *Introduction*, LVI n. 1, where the author gives a list of the places in which the two incunabula of the *Prognosticum* are preserved.

337. Hillgarth, *Introduction*, LVI.

338. The nickname Cochlaeus is his own Latinization of the place of his birth, Wendelstein, which means "cochlea." On the humanist and controversialist Johannes Cochlaeus, see C. Toussaint, "Cochlée, Jean," *Dictionnaire de Théologie Catholique* (Paris, 1903–50), vol. 3.1, cols. 264–65.

339. It is virtually impossible to find historical details of Nicholaus Bugnee. From the title page of his edition of the *Prognosticum*, presented by Hillgarth, it would seem that he was a Dominican, a doctor of theology, and a publisher. See Hillgarth, *Introduction*, LVI n. 2: PRONOSTI/CORUM FUTURI SAECULI AE/ternaeque vitae foeliciter sperandae. Per vener-abi/lem virum ac dominum, Dominum Iulianum,/ Toletanae Ecclesiae Episcopum a multis annis edi/tus. Nunc autem opere atque diligentia reli-gio/si patris, Fratris Nicolai Bugnee, compen/diensis, Doctoris Theologi ordinis prae/dicatorum, in lucem proditus. /Parisiis. / Apud Poncetum le Preux, sub insigni /Lupi, via ad D. Iacobum. / 1554. Hillgarth speaks of two existing copies of this edition that are known to him: the first being in Cambridge and the second in Paris (ibid.). A third copy is at the Biblioteca Centrale di Firenze and is partially digitized (n. Inventario/Access number: CF005651830).

340. Hillgarth ("El Prognosticon futuri saeculi de San Julián de Toledo," 15 n. 20; idem, *Introduction*, XXIV) reports the significant and expressly instrumental thought of Cochlaeus, who considers the *Prognosticum* useful in treating *de mortuorum sepolturis exequiisq. et de animarum statu post mortem ac de purgatorio igne*. Bugnee expresses the same idea: *agit nempe adversus Lutheranorum atq. Atheistarum perversa dogmata*; see Hillgarth, *Introduction*, LVI.

341. See the long title page of the work, given by Hillgarth, *Introduction*, XXII n. 5: PROGNOSTI / CON FUTURI SAECULI, / Sancto Iuliano, Episcopo Toletano, an- /te annos DCC. Scriptum, in / Hispaniis. / TRES HABET LIBROS. / I. De morte et transitu ex hoc saeculo. / II. De receptac-ulis animarum post mortem. / III. De resurrectione mortuorum, et Extre-/mo iudicio. / I.C. /Armis, ingeniis, virtute Hispania pollet. / Cui Imperii

Rector Rex modo ibiq. valet. Lipsiae / M.D.XXXVI. The volume, in octavo (19 cm. x 13.5 cm.), consists of 102 pages, numbered A2–N3. The printer is named in the colophon as Michaelis Blum. The letter that serves as prologue is dated *Ex Misnia civitate. Quarto nonas Ianuarii. Anno Domini. M.D.XXXVI.*

342. A. Resendus, "Epistola ad Bart. Quevedo," in Schott, *Hispania Illustrata*, II, quoted in Hillgarth, *Introduction*, LVI. The letter is quoted by Nicolas Antonio in PL 96, col. 430.

343. Hillgarth, *Introduction*, LVI and n. 3.

344. Ibid., LVII.

345. Boëtius Epo (1529–99) was professor at the counter-reformist University of Douai since its establishment in 1562; his works mainly concern canon law.

346. This volume is also in octavo (17 cm. x 10 cm.), and consists of 224 pages. Pages 1–16 contain the *Praefatio* dedicated to the king of France, Philip II; pages 17–207 contain the text of the work. At the end of the volume are reported the *quaedam fragmenta Isidori*. The printer is Loys de Winde from Douai. The title page given by Hillgarth (*Introduction*, XXII–XXIII) is as follows: ANTIQUI SCRIPTORIS ECCLESIASTICI IULIANI / Archiepiscopi olim Toletani / ΠΡΩΓΝΩΣΤΙΚΩΝ / SIVE De futuro seculo libri tres, / à Boëtio Epône Rordahusano Fri- / sio IV. Professore Regio et ordinario in Aca- / demia Duacena, ex vetustissimis / membranis in Marchianensis bi- / blio- theca repertis, in lucem prolati. / Cum eiusdem Boetii Epônis ad DN. PHILIP- / PUM Regem Catholicum Praefatione (Woodcut) Duaci. An. 1564 / Typis Lodovici de Winde Typ. Iur. / Cum Gratia et Privilegio ad quadrien- nium. Hillgarth knows of three existing copies of the work, one at the Bodleian Library (Oxford), one at the Bibliothèque Nationale de Paris, and one at the British Museum (ibid.).

347. A famous doctor of the Sorbonne, Margarin de la Bigne, is known for his significant work *Sacra Bibliotheca SS. Patrum* published in 1575, in eight volumes in folio.

348. Paris, 1575.

349. Hillgarth, *Introduction*, LVII.

350. Lyons, 1677.

351. Madrid, 1785. See Hillgarth, *Introduction*, XXII.

352. See Hillgarth, *Introduction*, XXII–XXIV.

353. For a more detailed explanation, see Hillgarth, "El Prognosticon futuri saeculi de San Julián de Toledo," 16–17.

354. Hillgarth, *Introduction*, XXII.

355. In 1956, Hillgarth defended his doctoral thesis, which was devoted to the establishment of a critical edition of the *Prognosticum futuri saeculi*. The title of the thesis was "A Critical Edition of the 'Prognosticum futuri saeculi' of St. Julian of Toledo" (Cambridge, Queen's College).

356. See the book review by E. Ann Matter on the *editio critica* of the works of Julian of Toledo in *Speculum* 55, no. 3 (1980): 624–25.

357. *Religion, Text, and Society in Medieval Spain and Northern Europe: Essays in Honor of J. N. Hillgarth*, ed. Thomas E. Burman, Mark D. Meyerson, and Leah Shopkow (Toronto, 2002), preface, ix.

358. Ibid. For a further intellectual biography of Hillgarth, see M. D. Meyerson, "El Professor Jocelyn N. Hillgarth," *Anuario de Estudios Medievales* 26, no. 1 (1996): 489–501.

359. Burman et al., *Religion, Text, and Society in Medieval Spain*, xiii–xix.

360. Cambridge, Queens College, 1956.

361. Hillgarth, *Introduction*, I.

362. Robles Sierra had already published some essays leading to the establishment of a critical edition of the *Antikeimenon*. See A. Robles, "Prolegómenos a la edición crítica del Antikeimenon de Julián de Toledo," *Analecta Sacra Tarraconensa* 42 (1969): 111–42; idem, "Fuentes del Antikeimenon de Julián de Toledo," *Escritos del Vedat* 1 (1971): 59–135.

363. Published in *Monumenta Germaniae Historica, Scriptorum rerum merovingicarum*, 5 (1910), 486–535.

364. Published initially as B. Bischoff, "Ein Brief Julians von Toledo über Rhytmen, metrisches Dichtung und Prosa," *Hermes* 87 (1959): 251–52, reprinted in idem, *Mittelalterliche Studien*, 1 (Stuttgart, 1966), 293–94.

365. Hillgarth, *Introduction*, XV: "Although not mentioned by Felix, [it] is unquestionably Julian's."

366. J. Madoz published the *Elogium* in *San Ildefonso de Toledo a través de la pluma del Arcipreste de Talavera* (Madrid, 1943). The *editio critica* is by U. Domínguez Del Val and was published as "Elogium," *Revista española de Teologia* 31 (1971): 138–39.

367. Hillgarth, *Introduction*, XLV.

368. J. N. Hillgarth, ed., *Opera S. Iuliani Toletani*, I, Corpus Christianorum, Series Latina, vol. 115 (Turnhout, 1976), I–LXXIV, 1–126. The volume also contains three other works of Julian of Toledo: the *De comprobatione sextae aetatis*, the *Apologeticum de tribus capitulis*, and the two letters of Idalius, bishop of Barcelona to Julian of Toledo and to the bishop Suntfredus, metropolitan of Narbonne (the last of which can be found in the doctoral thesis of the author). In the same volume there is also a re-edition of the *Versus to Modoenum* by Prof. B. Bischoff and Julian's early *Historia Wambae*, edited by W. Levison.

CHAPTER IV

1. *Praefatio*, 69.

2. *Praefatio*, 73–75.

3. Pastoral Constitution on the Church in the Modern World, *Gaudium et Spes*, §18: "...that bodily death from which man would have been immune had he not sinned will be vanquished." The notes cite the biblical foundations of this teaching: Wis 1:13; 2:23–24; Rom 5:21; 6:23; Jas 1:15.

4. *Catechism of the Catholic Church*, §1008: "Death is a consequence of sin. The Church's Magisterium, as authentic interpreter of the affirmations of Scripture and Tradition, 'teaches' that death entered the world on account of man's sin. Even though man's nature is mortal, God had destined him not to die. Death was therefore contrary to the plans of God the Creator and entered the world as a consequence of sin. 'Bodily death, from which man would have been immune had he not sinned' is thus 'the last enemy' of man left to be conquered." The text quotes in its turn *Gaudium et Spes* §18.

5. On this topic, see the interesting historical considerations of J. Orlandis in *La Iglesia en la España visigótica y medieval* (Pamplona, 1976), 257–306, devoted to the theme: "La elección de sepoltura en la España medieval."

6. C. Pozo ("La doctrina escatológical del 'Prognosticon futuri saeculi' de S. Julián de Toledo," in *La Patrología toledano-visigoda* [Madrid, 1970], 215–43) underlines the optimal balance in the *Prognosticum* between collective and individual eschatology.

7. For example, A. Veiga Valiña (*La doctrina escatológica de San Julián de Toledo* [Lugo, 1940], 43) takes for granted that Julian was also the author of the *Tractatus* or *De remediis blasphemiae* edited by Cardinal Mai and later inserted into the Latin Migne: "Utrum animae de humanis corporibus exeuntes mox deducantur ad gloriam vel ad poenam, an exspectent diem judicii sine gloria et poena" (PL 96, cols. 1379–1386B). It has already been noted that the attribution of this work to Julian has been seriously doubted and denied, with good reason, by J. Madoz and by J. N. Hillgarth, who consider it prudent to continue to attribute this interesting treatise, of very similar matter to book II of the *Prognosticum*, to an anonymous author. The *De remediis blasphemiae* of Julian, with which the *Tractatus* was claimed to be identified, is still to be considered a "lost work" of Bishop Julian of Toledo.

8. *Praefatio*, 45–52.

9. Pozo, "La doctrina escatológica del 'Prognosticum futuri saeculi' de S. Julián de Toledo," *Estudios Eclesiásticos* 45 (1970): 173–201, here 178.

10. Congregatio Pro Doctrina Fidei, "Epistola de quibusdam quaestionibus ad Eschatologiam spectantibus," May 17, 1979, *AAS* 71 (1979): 939–43. "Letter on certain questions regarding Eschatology," *Recentiores episcoporum Synodi*.

11. International Theological Commission, "De quibusdam quaestionibus actualibus circa eschatologiam," published in March 1992.

12. Ibid.

13. Ibid.

14. Vatican II, *Lumen Gentium*, 2.

15. Cassian, *Conlationes* I, 14.

16. J. N. Hillgarth, "Eschatological and Political Concepts in the Seventh Century," in *Le septième siècle: changements et continuités*, ed. J. Fontaine and J. N. Hillgarth (London, 1992), 212–31, here 227.

17. Ibid. See the historian J. Le Goff's appreciation of the work and thought of Julian of Toledo. While he belongs to a nontheological environment and even declares himself a secular scientist, he expresses a noteworthy esteem for and a flattering judgment of the work of Julian in one of his very successful publications (J. Le Goff, *La naissance du Purgatoire* [Paris, 1981]). Neither a theologian nor a professed Christian, Le Goff succeeded in understanding the importance of the work and thought of Julian of Toledo, citing it as a step of exceptional historical significance. Indeed, he opportunely puts the work of Julian in the early Middle Ages, together with that of two other great Spanish bishops, Taio of Saragossa and Isidore of Seville, with whom, in his opinion, Julian forms a theological triad of notable importance. For Le Goff, therefore, Julian not only no longer belongs to the epoch of the fathers of the church, but is indeed to be considered and qualified as a theologian, and his work should be seen as an out-and-out detailed treatise on eschatology (*un véritable traité détaillé d'eschatologie* [p. 135]). He fails, however, to appreciate the innovative character of Julian's work, particularly on the methodological level, rather saying that Julian simply repeats what has already been expressed in the eschatology of Augustine. From what has been said up to this point, we know things to be somewhat different!

18. *Prognosticum*, II, xiii.

19. *Oratio ad Deum*, 29–37.

20. For example, see the *Breviarium Gothicum, feria VI post Dominicam II Adventus*.

21. *Prognosticum*, II, viii.

22. *Prognosticum*, I, xiii.

23. Tertullian, *De monogamia* 10; PL 2, col. 992.

24. See T. Stancati, "Benedictus Deus," in *Lexicon, Dizionario Teologico Enciclopedico* (Casale Monferrato, 1993), 121; G. Greshake, "Benedictus Deus," in *Lexikon für Theologie und Kirche* (1994), vol. 2, cols. 198–200.

25. We quote in its fullness Tertullian's stupendous hymn to the flesh, followed by our own translation: ...quam Deus manibus suis ad imaginem Dei struxit, quam de suo adflatu ad similitudinem suae vivacitatis animavit, quam incolatui, fructui, dominatui, totius suae operationis praeposuit, quam sacramentis suis disciplinisque vestivit: cujus munditias amat, cujus castigationes

probat, cujus passiones sibi adpretiat; haeccine non resurget totiens Dei? Absit, absit, ut Deus manuum suarum operam ingenii sui curam, adflatus sui vaginam, molitionis suae reginam, liberalitatis suae haeredem, religionis suae sacerdotem, testimonii sui militem, Christi sui sororem, in aeternum destituat interitum! Bonum Deum novimus; solum optimum a Christo ejus addiscimus; qui dilectionem mandans, post suam, in proximum, faciet et ipse quod praecepit: diliget carnem, tot modis sibi proximam, etsi infirmam (Matt 26:41)....that which [the flesh] God has made with his hands in the image of God, that which God has animated by his breath into the likeness of his vitality, that which God has put at the head to dwell, to enjoy, to dominate the whole his work of creation, that which he has dressed with his sacraments and his knowledge, of which he has given to prefer sobriety, of which he approves the sacrifices, of which he considers precious the pains, will this flesh, therefore, not rise again, it that has been so many times a thing of God? God forbid! God forbid that God destined to allow to be dispersed forever the work of his hands, the promptness of his mind, the vessel of his breath, the queen of his construction, the inheritor of his nobility, the priestess of his religion, the soldier of his testimony, the sister of his Christ. We know that God is good: that he alone is perfect, we learn it best from his Christ; he who commanded love toward neighbor, after the love of him, will also perform that which he prescribes: he will love the flesh, which is, in so many aspects, so near to him, even though weak (Matt 26:41). Tertullian, *De resurrectione carnis*; PL 2, cols. 807–8.

26. Luke 24:42: "They gave him a piece of broiled fish, and he took it and ate in their presence." See also John 21:9–13. The astonishing observation of Isidore of Seville on this meal of the risen Christ, according to which *Piscem sane, quia eum post resurrectionem accepit Dominus (Joh. 21), possumus manducare* (Isidorus Hispaliensis, *De Ecclesiasticis Officiis* XLV; PL 83, col. 778A), is entirely typical of the simplicity and greatness of the patristic genius.

BOOK I

1. Augustinus, *De Civitate Dei*, XIII, 1 (CSEL 40.1, p. 615, 9–13; CC 48, p. 385, 5–10).

2. Ibid., 3 (CSEL 40.1, p. 617, 22–28; CC 48, p. 386, 11–387, 18).

3. See Gregorius, *Moralia in Iob*, IV, XXVIII (PL 75, col. 664C).

4. The bite to which Julian refers is the one, according to the Bible, of the fruit from the tree of knowledge of good and evil: "So she [Eve] took some of its fruit and ate it; and she also gave some to her husband, who was with her, and he ate it" (see Gen 3:6).

5. See Isidorus, *Etymologiae*, XI, II, 31: "Mors dicta, quod sit amara, vel a Marte, qui est effector mortium (sive mors a morsu hominis primi, quod

vetitiae arbores pomum mordens mortem incurrit)." Isidore of Sevilla, *Etymologiarum sive originum libri XX*, ed. W. M. Lindsay, 2 vols. (Oxford, 1911).

6. Julian's play on words here between the terms *death* (in Latin, *mors*) and bite or morsel (in Latin, *morsus*) is impossible in English. However, it is phonetically effective in Latin: *mors a morsu*, death from a bite (or morsel).

7. Isidorus, *Etymologiae*, XI, II, 32.

8. Augustinus, *De Civitate Dei*, XIII, 6 (CSEL 40.1 p. 622, 4–12; CC 48, p. 389, 1–19).

9. Ibid. (CSEL 40.1, p. 622, 12–19; CC 48, p. 389, 9–16).

10. Gregorius, *Dialogi*, IV, 24 (ed. Moricca, p. 262, 21–263, 7).

11. Ibid., 25 (p. 306, 21–307, 1).

12. Isidorus, *Sententiarum libri III*, LXII, 7–8 (PL 83, cols. 737–38); see Gregorius, *Moralia in Iob*, XXIV, xi, 34 (PL 76, col. 306C).

13. Augustinus, *De Civitate Dei*, XIII, 4 (CSEL 40.1, p. 620, 15–18; CC 48, p. 388, 37–40).

14. Ibid. (CSEL 40.1, p. 619, 8–9; CC 48, p. 387, 1–2).

15. Ibid. (CSEL 40.1, p. 619, 11–27; CC 48, p. 387, 4–388, 20).

16. Iulianus Pomerius, *De animae natura vel qualitate eius*, VIII (lost work); see Gennadius, *De viris illustribus*, 98; Isidorus, *De viris illustribus*, 25.

17. Augustinus, *De cura pro mortuis gerenda*, XV, 18 (CSEL 41, p. 651, 4–9; see below II, 29).

18. Augustinus, *De Trinitate*, XIV, 17, 23 (CC LA, p. 454, 20–455, 22, 26, 31).

19. Augustinus, *In Iohannis Evangelium tractatus*, XLIX, 2, 11–37 (CC 36, p. 420).

20. Augustinus, *De Civitate Dei*, I, 11 (CC 40.1, p. 22, 19–p. 23, 11; CC 47, p. 13, 8–25).

21. Augustinus, *In Iohannis Evangelium tractatus*, XLIII, 11, 9–12, 19 (CC 36, pp. 377–78).

22. Ibid., 12, 35–37 (p. 378).

23. Ibid., XLIX, 15, 5–8 (p. 427).

24. Ibid., XLIII, 13, 11–13 (p. 378).

25. Ibid., XLIX, 15, 1–2; 17–19 (pp. 427–28).

26. Cyprianus, *De mortalitate*, 2–3 (CSEL 3.2, p. 298, 13–p. 299, 9).

27. Ibid., 2 (CSEL 3.2, p. 298, 7–13).

28. Ibid., 4–7 (CSEL 3.2, p. 299, 10–p. 301, 6).

29. Ibid., 21–22 (CSEL 3.2, p. 310, 18–p. 311, 2).

30. Ibid., 22 (CSEL 3.2, p. 311, 11–15).

31. Ibid., 24 (CSEL 3.2, p. 312, 4–8).

32. Ibid., 24–25 (CSEL 3.2, p. 312, 18–p. 313, 10).

33. Ibid., 26 (CSEL 3.2, p. 313, 13–p. 314, 2, 7–11).

34. Ibid., 18–19 (CSEL 3.2, p. 308, 12–p. 309, 10).

35. See Augustinus, *In Iohannis Evangelium tractatus*, CXXIII, 5, 72–77 (CC 36, p. 679).

36. Ibid., 5, 81–83, 84–88 (p. 679).

37. Ibid., 5, 92–96 (p. 680).

38. The theme of chapters XIX-XXI generally concerns the grave (its preparation, burial in the church, burial in the church next to the grave of the martyr, thus guaranteeing the martyr's patronage to the person who has died). The modern reader should not be surprised by so much insistence on this subject, because the grave was one of the themes that aroused most interest in the medieval mentality. The choice of the place of burial (in the church hall, near the grave of a martyr, of a saint, in a monastery, etc.) became particularly important as belief in the resurrection of the body grew, because the place that was chosen with so much care would be the eschatological place where the dead person would await the day of his resurrection.

39. Augustinus, *De cura pro mortuis gerenda*, II, 4 (CSEL 41, p. 626, 14–16); see also *De Civitate Dei*, 12 (CSEL 40.1, p. 24, 16–18; CC 47, p. 14, 27–29).

40. Augustinus, *De cura pro mortuis gerenda*, III, 5 (p. 627, 13–20); see also *De Civitate Dei*, I, 13 (p. 25, 12–19; CC 47, p. 14, 1–8).

41. Augustinus, *De cura pro mortuis gerenda*, XVIII, 22 (p. 658, 19–p. 659, 5).

42. Ibid., III, 5 (p. 627, 22–p. 628, 14); see also *De Civitate Dei*, I, 13 (p. 25, 21–p. 26, 11; CC 47, p. 14, 10–15, 25).

43. Augustinus, *De cura pro mortuis gerenda*, XVIII, 22 (CSEL 41, p. 659, 5–8).

44. Ibid., IV, 6 (p. 630, 17–p. 631, 2); see also Gregorius, *Dialogi*, IV, 52 (ed. Moricca, p. 311).

45. See Gregorius, *Dialogi*, IV, 57 (ed. Moricca, p. 315, 3–4).

46. Augustinus, *De cura pro mortuis gerenda*, V, 7 (CSEL 41, p. 631, 13–21).

47. See Gregorius, *Dialogi*, IV, 52 (p. 311, 11ff.).

48. Augustinus, *De cura pro mortuis gerenda*, I, 2 (CSEL 41, p. 623, 6–8, 12–14).

49. Ibid., I, 3 (CSEL 41, p. 623, 17–p. 624, 2).

BOOK II

1. Isidorus, *Differentiarum libri II*, II, xii, 32 (PL 83, col. 75A–B).

2. Iulianus Pomerius, *De animae natura dialogus*, lib. VIII.

3. Ibid.

4. Augustinus, *De Genesi ad litteram*, XII, 34 (CSEL 28.3.2, p. 432, 1–12).

5. Ambrosius, *Expositio Evangelii Lucae*, VIII, 13 (CSEL 32.4, p. 397, 15–16); see Augustinus, *Sermo Mai XIII* (ed. Morin, Miscellanea Agostiniana I,

p. 290, 24–25); idem, *De Genesi ad litteram,* XII, 33; 34 (CSEL 28.3.2, p. 429, 5–6; p. 430, 23); Gregorius, *Dialogi,* 34 (ed. Moricca, pp. 278–80).

6. Julian makes a literal translation of Ps 86:13, which in the New Revised Standard Version reads: "You have delivered my soul from the depths of Sheol."

7. Augustinus, *Enarratio in Psalmum LXXXV,* 13, n. 17, 36–38 (CC 38, p. 1190).

8. Ibid. (p. 1190, 7–13).

9. Ibid., 13, n. 18, 1–2; 1–19 (pp. 1190–91); see idem, *De Genesi ad litteram,* 12, 33 (CSEL 28.3.2, p. 428, 20–21).

10. The Latin name for hell is *infernus* (situated below) or *inferi* (low): both terms indicate an underground place (*infra* = under), as suggested by the English adjective "infernal."

11. Augustinus, *De Genesi ad litteram,* XII, 34 (CSEL 28.3.2, p. 431, 9–14); Isidorus, *Etymologiae,* XIV, ix, 10 (ed. Lindsay).

12. Augustinus, *De Genesi ad litteram,* XII, 32–33 (CSEL 28.3.2, p. 427, 27–p. 428, 5).

13. Augustinus, *Retractationum libri II,* II, 50 (CSEL 36, p. 160, 13–16).

14. Augustinus, *De Genesi ad litteram,* XII, 33–34 (CSEL 28.3.2, p. 428, 7–10; p. 431, 4–9).

15. Gregorius, *Dialogi,* IV, 25 (ed. Moricca, p. 263, 14–264, 6).

16. Augustinus, *Enchiridion,* 109 (CC 46, p. 108). See Ildephonse, *De cognitione baptismi,* 90 (PL 96, col. 144C).

17. Iulianus Pomerius, *De animae natura dialogus,* lib. VIII.

18. That is, the highest heavens.

19. That is, natural.

20. Augustinus, *De Genesi ad litteram,*12, 35 (CSEL 28.3.2, p. 432, 15–p. 433, 11).

21. Gregorius, *Homiliarum in Evangelia libri II,* I, 19, 4 (PL 76, col. 1156c).

22. Gregorius, *Dialogi,* IV, 29 (ed. Moricca, p. 272, 3–9).

23. See Gregorius, *Moralia in Iob,* VIII, xv (PL 75, col. 819B).

24. Cassianus, *Conlationes XXIII,* I, 14 (CSEL 13, p. 22, 22–24).

25. Ibid. (p. 22, 27–p. 23, 1; p. 23, 5–8).

26. Ibid. (p. 23, 20–26; p. 23, 29–p. 24, 21)

27. Augustinus, *De Genesi ad litteram,* XII, 33 (CSEL 28.3.2., p. 428, 11–19).

28. Gregorius, *Dialogi,* IV, 30 (ed. Moricca, p. 272, 12–14, 19–p. 273, 8).

29. Ibid., IV, 45 (ed. Moricca, p. 303, 1–9).

30. Augustinus, *Enarratio in Psalmum XXXVII,* nn. 3, 34–35 (CC 38, p. 384).

31. Augustinus, *De Civitate Dei,* XXI, 24 (CSEL 40.2, p. 559, 17–20; CC 48, p. 790, 55–56).

32. Gregorius, *Dialogi*, IV, 41 (ed. Moricca, p. 296, 11–p. 297, 17); see Taio of Saragossa, *Sententiarum libri V*, V, xxi (PL 80, col. 975).

33. Augustinus, *De Civitate Dei*, XXI, 26 (CSEL 40.2, p. 570, 12–p. 571, 13; CC 48, p. 798, 70–101).

34. Ibid., 13 (CSEL 40.2, p. 543, 2–3, 14–21; CC 48, p. 779, 28–30, 41–p. 780, 47).

35. Ibid., 16 (CSEL 40.2, p. 548, 5–9; CC 48, p. 782, 40–p. 783, 44).

36. Augustinus, *Enchiridion*, 69 (CC 46, p. 87, 74–81).

37. Augustinus, *De Civitate Dei*, XXI, 26 (CSEL 40.2, p. 571, 26–p. 572, 6; CC 48, p. 799, 113–22).

38. Gregorius, *Dialogi*, IV, 34 (ed. Moricca, p. 279, 17–p. 280, 18).

39. Ibid., IV, 46 (ed. Moricca, p. 305, 1–24). See Augustinus, *De Civitate Dei*, XXI, 24 (CSEL 40.2, pp. 558ff.; CC 48, p. 790).

40. Augustinus, *De cura pro mortuis gerenda*, XIV, 17 (CSEL 41, p. 649, 18).

41. Ibid., XI, 13 (p. 641, 19–p. 642, 12).

42. Origenes, *Homilia VII in Leviticum* (GCS 29, p. 377, 17–p. 379, 1).

43. Augustinus, *De cura pro mortuis gerenda*, XV, 18 (CSEL 41, p. 650, 19–p. 651, 8, 9–15).

44. See Augustinus, *De diversis quaestionibus ad Simplicianum*, II, 3, 1 (CC 44, p. 81).

45. See Augustinus, *De doctrina christiana*, II, 8, 13 (CC 32, p. 39–40).

46. For the whole chapter, see Augustinus, *De cura pro mortuis gerenda*, XV, 18 (CSEL 41, p. 651, 15–p. 652, 9).

47. Gregorius, *Moralia in Iob*, XII, 21 (PL 75, 999B–C).

48. Gregorius, *Homiliarum in Evangelia*, II, 40, n. 8 (PL 76, col. 1308D–1309B).

49. Cassianus, *Conlationes*, I, 14 (CSEL 13, p. 22, 11–22).

50. Augustinus, *Epistola CLIX ad Evodium*, 3–4 (CSEL 44, p. 500, 6, 7, 9–10).

51. Augustinus, *De Genesi ad litteram*, XII, 32 (CSEL 28.3.2, p. 427, 15–27).

52. See Gregorius, *Dialogi*, IV, 26 (ed. Moricca, p. 264, 7–21).

53. Cyprianus, *Ad Fortunatum de exhortatione martyrii*, 13 (CC 3, p. 215, 31–37).

54. This title could seem obvious, but in the body of the chapter Julian says that not only the martyrs, for whom the doors of heaven immediately open wide, but also people who are "simply saints," already reign with Christ in eternity, after their bodily death.

55. Iulianus quotes Ps 9:38 *Antiqua Vulgata*.

56. Augustinus, *De Civitate Dei*, XX, 9 (CSEL 40.2, p. 451, 22–p. 452, 7; CC 48, p. 717, 81–718, 91).

BOOK III

1. Isidorus, *Sententiarum libri III*, I, xxvii, I (PL 83, col. 595).

2. Hieronymus, *Commentarium in Ioelem liber unus* (CC 76, pp. 198–99): see also Isidorus, *Etymologiae*, VII, vi, p. 69 (ed. Lindsay): Iosaphat Domini Iudicium.

3. Hieronymus, *Commentarium in Ioelem liber unus* (CC 76, pp. 198–99).

4. Augustinus, *De Civitate Dei*, XX, I (CSEL 40.2, p. 425, 3–7; CC 48, p. 699, 15–19).

5. See Augustinus, *Enarratio in Psalmum XLIX*, 6 (CC 38, p. 579); idem, *Sermones post Maurinos reperti, Sermo Guelferb, XXI* (ed. Morin, p. 508, 2ff.).

6. See Isidorus, *Etymologiae*, VII, v, 16 (ed. Lindsay).

7. For the whole chapter, see Ioannes Chrysostomus, *Homilia prima de cruce et latrone*, 3–4 (PG 49, 404, cols. 1–43; ibid., 56–65); see Hom. II (ibid., col. 413–14).

8. Ibid., 3–4 (PG 49, 404, cols. 1–43; ibid., cols. 46–65. See Hom II (ibid., col. 416–17).

9. Isidorus, *Sententiarum libri III*, xxix, 6 (PL 83, col. 598). See Gregorius, *Moralia in Iob*, XXXIV, vii (PL 76, col. 724).

10. Isidorus, *Sententiarum libri III*, xxvii, 9 (PL 83, col. 596). See also Gregorius, *Moralia in Iob*, XXXV, v, vi; vii, xiii (PL 76, cols. 322–23; 326–27).

11. Isidorus, *Sententiarum libri III*, xxvii, 8 (PL 83, col. 596B).

12. Augustinus, *In Ioannis Evangelium tractatus*, XIX, 16, 14–20 (CC 36, p. 199).

13. Augustinus, *De Civitate Dei*, XX, 30 (CSEL 40.2, p. 509, 17–24; CC 48, p. 756, 108–15).

14. Augustinus, *Enchiridion*, 54 (CC 46, p. 78).

15. Ibid., 55 (CC 46, p. 79).

16. This etymology is probably drawn from the *Etymologiae* of Isidore of Seville (20, 11, 9). See J. Madoz, "Fuentes teológico-literarias de San Julián de Toledo," *Gregorianum* 33 (1952): 405.

17. See Augustinus, *Enarratio in Psalmum XCIII*, 3, 25–26 (CC 39, p. 1380); Isidorus, *Etymologiae*, XX, xi, 9; VII, 5, 26.

18. See Augustinus, *De Civitate Dei*, XX, 5 (CSEL 40.2, p. 432, 16–20; CC 48, p. 704, 37–40; idem, *Enarratio in Psalmum CXXI*, 9, 28–42 (CC 40, p. 1810).

19. The Latin text contains the expression *vir eius*, which Julian interprets as "man of God." In reality in the Book of Proverbs the expression refers to the fact that beginning from 31:10, the author is speaking of the perfect woman and of her numerous virtues, and of the fortunate husband of whom she is the bride. Therefore, the English translation "her husband" is both possible and pertinent. Evidently Julian drew this text from the ancient *Vulgata*.

20. Augustinus, *De Civitate Dei*, XX, 5 (CSEL 40.2 pp. 432, 23–433, 17;

CC 48, pp. 704, 43–705, 64); see idem, *Enarratio in Psalmum XLIX*, 9, 10 (CC 38, pp. 582, 584).

21. Augustinus, *Enchiridion*, 84 (CC 46, p. 95, 5–8).

22. For this whole paragraph the reference is to Hieronymus, *Epistola CXIX ad Minervium*, 5, 2 (CSEL 55, p. 451, 14–21; p. 448, 10–12; p. 450, 12–15, 21–p. 451, 4).

23. See Augustinus, *Sermo CCLVI*, 2 (PL 38, col. 1192); idem, *Enchiridion*, 92 (CC 46, p. 98).

24. Hieronymus, *Epistola CXIX ad Minervium*, 5, 2 (CSEL 55, p. 458).

25. Iulianus Pomerius, *De natura animae vel qualitate eius*, VIII.

26. Eugenius Toletanus (d. 657), *Fragmentum de aliquo opere suo deperditum* (see Vollmer, *Monumenta Germaniae Historica, Auctores Antiquissimi*, XIV, p. 291); see also *Symbolum Concili XI Toletani* (675) 6 D (PL 84, col. 457B). See also J. Madoz, *Le symbole du XIe Concile de Tolède*, p. 25.21–23; pp. 101–3: "nec in aerea vel qualibet alia carne, ut quidam delirant, resurrecturos nos credimus, sed in ista, qua vivimus, consistimus et movemur." See *Symbolum Concili XVI Toletani* (a. 693) (PL 84, col. 535C). See also J. Madoz, *El Simbolo del XVI Concilio de Toledo*, p. 28. 22–24; pp. 77–79.

27. Augustinus, *Enchiridion*, 91 (CC 46, p. 98, 93–99).

28. The quoted text is 1 Cor 15:51, but according to the ancient *Vulgata*: "omnes quidem resurgemus sed non omnes inmutabimur." The modern version of 1 Cor 15:51, rather, says: "We will not all die, but we will all be changed."

29. Iulianus Pomerius, *De natura animae vel qualitate eius*, VIII.

30. The text of Eph 4:13, according to the translation of the New Revised Standard Version, says: "to the measure of the full stature of Christ."

31. Augustinus, *De Civitate Dei*, XXII, 15 (CSEL 40.2, p. 623, 24–p. 624, 4; CC 48, p. 834, 16–24).

32. Ibid., 16 (CSEL 40.2, p. 624, 19–22; CC 48, p. 835, 11–15).

33. Ibid. (CSEL 40.2, p. 624, 23–25; CC 48, p. 835, 15–18).

34. Iulianus Pomerius, *De natura animae vel qualitate eius*, VIII.

35. Ibid.

36. Ibid.

37. Augustinus, *Enchiridion*, 90 (CC 46 p. 97, 78–90); see Ildefonsus of Toledo, *De cognitione baptismi*, 86 (PL 96, col. 143A–B).

38. Augustinus, *Enchiridion*, 91 (CC 46 p. 98, 93–95); see also idem, *Sermo CCXL*, 3 (PL 38, col. 1131).

39. Augustinus, *De Civitate Dei*, XXII, 19 (CSEL 40.2, p. 631, 9.10–12; CC 48, p. 839, 68, 69–71).

40. The source quoted by Julian is unknown; see Hillgarth, *Editio critica*, XXIII 8/9, p. 97.

41. The full text of Eph 4:13, both in the ancient and in the new *Vulgata*, is as follows: "Donec occurramus omnes in unitatem fidei et agnitionis Filii Dei in virum perfectum in mensuram aetatis plenitudinis Christi."

The full text of the New Revised Standard Version of Eph 4:13 says: "Until all of us come to the unity of the faith and of the knowledge of the Son of God, to maturity, to the measure of the full stature of Christ."

42. Hieronymus, *Comm. In epist. ad Ephesios*, V, 28, (PL 26, col. 533); see *Contra Iovinianum*, I, 36 (PL 23, col. 261); see also Augustinus, *De Civitate Dei*, XXII, 17 (CSEL 40.2, p. 625, 4–9; CC 48, p. 835, 1–6).

43. The text of Matt 22:30 says: "For in the resurrection they neither marry nor are given in marriage, but are like angels in heaven." The text of both the ancient and the new *Vulgata* says: "In resurrectione enim neque nubent neque nubentur sed sunt sicut angeli Dei in caelo." Evidently Julian quotes from memory or uses a different version of the New Testament.

44. Augustinus, *De Civitate Dei*, XXII, 17 (CSEL 40.2, p. 625, 9–15; CC 48, p. 835, 6–12).

45. Eugenius Toletanus (d. 657), *Fragmentum de aliquo opere suo deperditum* (see Vollmer, *Monumenta Germaniae Historica, Auctores Antiquissimi*, XIV, p. 291).

46. Iulianus Pomerius, *De natura animae vel qualitate eius*, VIII.

47. Ibid. See Augustinus, *De Civitate Dei*, XIII, 22 (CSEL 40.1, p. 646; CC 48, p. 405).

48. Iulianus Pomerius, *De natura animae vel qualitate eius*, VIII.

49. Ibid.

50. Eugenius Toletanus (d. 657), *Fragmentum de aliquo opere suo deperditum* (see Vollmer, *Monumenta Germaniae Historica, Auctores Antiquissimi*, XIV, p. 291).

51. Iulianus Pomerius, *De natura animae vel qualitate eius*, VIII.

52. Augustinus, *Enchiridion*, 86 (CC 46, p. 96, 25, 30–33); see idem, *De Civitate Dei*, XXII, 13 (CSEL 40.2, p. 621; CC 48, p. 833).

53. Iulianus Pomerius, *De natura animae vel qualitate eius*, VIII.

54. Hieronymus, *Epistula LXXII ad Vitalem* (CSEL 55, pp. 8ff.). See Augustinus, *De Civitate Dei*, XVI, 8 (CSEL 40.2, pp. 138ff.; CC 48, p. 508.)

55. Augustinus, *Enchiridion*, 87 (CC 46, p. 96).

56. Iulianus Pomerius, *De natura animae vel qualitate eius*, VIII.

57. Augustinus, *Enchiridion*, 88 (CC 46, p. 96); see Ildephonse, *De cognitione baptismi*, 84 (PL 96, col. 142B).

58. Gregorius, *Homiliarum in Ezechielem libri II*, II, 8, 8 (CC 142, p. 342, 237–57); see Augustinus, *De Civitate Dei*, XXII, 12 (CSEL 40.2, p. 620; CC 48, p. 832).

59. Augustinus, *De Civitate Dei*, XXII, 19 (CSEL 40.2, p. 630, 7–16; CC 48, p. 838, 39–840, 48).

60. Ibid. (CSEL 40.2, p. 629, 15–17; CC 48, p. 838, 19–21).

61. Augustinus, *Enchiridion*, 89 (CC 46, p. 97, 58–66); see Ildefonsus of Toledo, *De cognitione baptismi*, 85 (PL 96, col. 142C).

62. Augustinus, *De Civitate Dei*, XXII, 19 (CSEL 40.2, p. 629, 7–15; CC 48, p. 838, 11–19).

63. Ibid. (CSEL 40.2, p. 628, 24–p. 629; CC 48, p. 837, 1–p. 838, 11).

64. Augustinus, *Enchiridion*, 89 (CC 46, p. 97, 74–77); see Ildefonsus of Toledo, *De cognitione baptismi*, 85 (PL 96, col. 142C).

65. Augustinus, *Enchiridion*, 92 (CC 46, p. 98–99); see Ildefonsus of Toledo, *De cognitione baptismi*, 88 (PL 96, cols. 143D–144B).

66. For the whole chapter, see Gregorius, *Moralia in Iob*, XXVI, xxvii, 50 (PL 76, cols. 378–79) and Isidorus, *Sententiarum libri III*, I, xxvii, 10 (PL 83, cols. 596–97).

67. Augustinus, *Enarratio in Psalmum XLIX*, II (CC 38, p. 585).

68. Augustinus, *De Civitate Dei*, XX, 24 (CSEL 40.2, p. 494, 25ff.; CC 48, p. 746, 110ff.).

69. The New Revised Standard Version of Ps 50:5 says: "Gather to me my faithful ones."

70. Augustinus, *De Civitate Dei*, XX, 24 (CSEL 40.2, p. 494, 26–495, 1; CC 48, p. 746, 111–13); see idem, *Enarratio in Psalmum XLIX*, 12 (CC 38, pp. 585–86).

71. Augustinus, *De Civitate Dei*, XX, 14 (CSEL 40.2, p. 461, 18–27; CC 48, p. 724, 26–35).

72. Ibid. (CSEL 40.2, p. 461, 27–p. 462, 10; CC 48, p. 724, 35–49).

73. For the whole chapter, see Augustinus, *Enarratio in Psalmum XXXV*, 5 (CC 38, p. 324).

74. The New Revised Standard Version of Rev 20:15 says: "And anyone whose name was not found written in the book of life was thrown into the lake of fire." For the whole chapter, see Augustinus, *De Civitate Dei*, XX, 15 (CSEL 40.2, p. 464, 8–16; CC 48, p. 726, 35–42).

75. Augustinus, *De Civitate Dei*, XX, 15 (CSEL 40.2, p. 464, 20–25; CC 48, p. 726, 45–50).

76. Augustinus, *De Civitate Dei*, XXI, 2 (CSEL 40.2, p. 513, 15–18; CC 48, p. 759, 1–4).

77. Ibid., 3 (CSEL 40.2, p. 515, 17–21; CC 48, p. 760, 37–41).

78. Ibid., 4 (CSEL 40.2, p. 517, 12–15; CC 48, p. 761, 7–p. 762, 1).

79. Ibid., 10 (CSEL 40.2, p. 537, 24–p. 538, 1, and p. 538, 23–p. 539, 2; CC 48, p. 776, 14–19 and 40–46).

80. Ibid.

81. Augustinus, *Enchiridion*, 93 (CC 46, p. 99, 133–37). See Ildefonsus of Toledo, *De cognitione baptismi*, 89 (PL 96, col. 144B).

82. Augustinus, *De Civitate Dei*, XXI, 16 (CSEL 40.2, p. 548, 9–14; CC 48, p. 783, 44–48).

83. In the Latin text the comparison is between the *Minores* and *Maiores*. As an analogous expression does not exist in English, we have preferred to call the *Minores* "contemporaries" and the *Maiores*, the ancient "masters," "fathers."

84. Augustinus, *De Civitate Dei*, XX, 16 (CSEL 40.2, p. 465, 8–12; CC 48, p. 726, 9–13); see idem, *Enchiridion*, 92 (CC 46, p. 98–99).

85. For the whole chapter, see Augustinus, *De Civitate Dei*, XX, 16; XXI, 1 (CSEL 40.2, pp. 464–65; pp. 512–13; CC 48, p. 726, 1–6; pp. 758ff).

86. Gregorius, *Homiliarum in Evangelia I*, 13, 4 (PL 76, col. 1125A).

87. Augustinus, *De Civitate Dei*, XX, 14 (CSEL 40.2, p. 461, 10–13; CC 48, p. 724, 19–22).

88. Ibid., 16 (CSEL 40.2, p. 465, 12–20; CC 48, p. 726, 13–p. 727, 21).

89. Ibid., 14 (CSEL 40.2, p. 461, 10–13; CC 48, p. 724, 19–22).

90. Ibid., 14 (CSEL 40.2, p. 461, 10–16; CC 48, p. 724, 19–24).

91. The New Revised Standard Version of 1 Cor 15:51 says: "We will not all die, but we will all be changed."

92. Augustinus, *De Civitate Dei*, XX, 18 (CSEL 40.2, p. 470, 10–21; CC 48, p. 730, 43–54).

93. The New Revised Standard Version of John 14:21 says: "They who have my commandments and keep them are those who love me; and those who love me will be loved by my Father, and I will love them and reveal myself to them."

94. Gregorius, *Homiliarum in Evangelia*, I, 13, 4 (PL 76, col. 1125A).

95. Augustinus, *De Civitate Dei*, XX, 22 (CSEL 40.2, p. 486, 4–12; CC 48, p. 741, 11–19).

96. Ibid. (CSEL 40.2, p. 485, 25; CC 48, p. 740, 5).

97. Ibid. (CSEL 40.2, p. 486, 4–12; CC 48, p. 741, 11–19).

98. See ibid., 11 (CSEL 40.2 pp. 615–18; CC 48, pp. 829–31).

99. The New Revised Standard Version of John 17:24 says: "I desire that those also, whom you have given me, may be with me where I am."

100. Isidorus, *Sententiarum libri III*, I, xxx, 4 (PL 83, col. 600).

101. Augustinus, *De Civitate Dei*, XXII, 30 (CSEL 40.2, p. 665, 7–12; CC 48, p. 862, 15–21).

102. The New Revised Standard Version of Ps 116:10 says: "I kept my faith, even when I said, 'I am greatly afflicted.'"

103. Augustinus, *De Civitate Dei*, XXII, 29 (CSEL 40.2, p. 658, 7–16; p. 660, 4–13; CC 48, p. 857, 46–p. 858, 55; p. 859, 95–104).

104. For these considerations of Julian, see Rom 1:20 and 1 Cor 13:12.

105. The New Revised Standard Version of 1 Cor 4:5 says: "Therefore do not pronounce judgment before the time, before the Lord comes, who will bring to light the things now hidden in darkness and will disclose the purposes of the heart. Then each one will receive commendation from God."

106. Augustinus, *De Civitate Dei*, XXII, 29 (CSEL 40.2, pp. 656–57; CC 48, pp. 856–57).

107. The source quoted by Julian is unknown.

108. The New Revised Standard Version of Ps 89:2 says: "I declare that your steadfast love is established for ever; your faithfulness is as firm as the

heavens." For the chapter, see Augustinus, *De Civitate Dei*, XXII, 30 (CSEL 40.2, p. 667, 24–p. 668, 15; CC 48, p. 864, 79–97).

109. Ibid. (CSEL 40.2, p. 666, 9–19; CC 48, p. 863, 38–48).

110. Ibid.

111. Ibid. (CSEL 40.2, p. 664, 23–24; CC 48, p. 862, 5–6).

112. Ibid., XXII, 30 (CSEL 40.2, p. 665, 17–18; CC 48, p. 863, 26).

113. Ibid., XXII, 30 (CSEL 40.2, p. 666, 4–7; CC 48, p. 863, 33–36).

114. Ibid., XXII, 30 (CSEL 40.2, p. 665, 19–p. 666, 4; CC 48, p. 863, 27–33).

115. Ibid., XXII, 30 (CSEL 40.2, p. 668, 19–26; CC 48, p. 864, 100–p. 865, 107).

116. Ibid., XXII, 30 (CSEL 40.2, p. 668, 17–18; CC 48, p. 864, 99–100).

117. Ibid., XXII, 30 (CSEL 40.2, p. 670, 9–16; CC 48, p. 866, 142–48).

BIBLIOGRAPHY

Spain in the Seventh Century

Aigrain, R. "La Spagna cristiana." In *Storia della Chiesa,* vol. 5, *San Gregorio Magno, gli stati barbarici e la conquista araba (590-757),* 315–52. Rome/Turin, 1980.

Ambrosio de Morales. *Crónica General de España.* Alcalá de Henares, 1577.

Carr, R., ed. *Spain: A History.* Oxford, 2000.

Collins, R. *The Arab Conquest of Spain, 710–797.* Oxford/Cambridge, MA, 1989.

————. *Early Medieval Europe, 300–1000.* London, 1991.

————. *Early Medieval Spain: Unity in Diversity, 400–1000.* 3rd ed. London, 1991.

————. *Law, Culture and Regionalism in Early Medieval Spain.* Aldershot, 1992.

————. *Los Visigodos: Historia y Civilización.* Murcia: 1987.

————. *Visigothic Spain, 409–711.* Malden, MA/Oxford, 2004.

Coumert, M. *Origines des peuples: Les récits du Haut Moyen Âge occidental (550–850).* Paris, 2007.

Crocker, R., and D. Hiley, eds. *The Early Middle Ages to 1300.* Oxford, 1990.

De Palol, P. "Demografía y arqueología hispánicas: Siglos IV–VIII. Ensayo de cartografía." *Boletín del Seminario de Estudios de Arte y Arqueología* [Valladolid] 32 (1966): 5–67.

De Palol, P., and G. Ripoll. *Los godos en el occidente europeo: Ostrogodos y visigodos en los siglos V–VIII.* Madrid, 1988.

Díaz y Díaz, M. C. "La cultura de la España visigótica del siglo VII." In *Caratteri del secolo VII in Occidente,* 2:813–44. Settimane di Studio del Centro Italiano di Studi sull'alto medioevo 5. Spoleto, 1958.

Ferreiro, A. *The Visigoths in Gaul and Spain A.D. 418–711: A Bibliography.* Leiden, 1988.

Fontaine, J. "Conversion et culture chez les Visigoths d'Espagne." In *La conversione al cristianesimo nell'Europa dell'alto Medio Evo,* 87–147. Settimane di Studio del Centro Italiano di Studi sull'alto medioevo 14. Spoleto, 1967.

————. *Culture et spiritualité en Espagne du IVe au VIIe siècle.* London, 1986.

————. *Isidore de Seville et la culture classique dans l'Espagne wisigothique*. 2 vols. Paris, 1959.

Fontaine, J., and C. Pellistrandi, eds. *L'Europe héritiére de l'Espagne wisigothique*. Madrid, 1992.

García Moreno, L. A. "El campesino hispano-visigodo entre bajos rendimientos y catástrofes naturales" In *Los Visigodos: Historia y Civilización*, 171–87. Murcia, 1986.

————. "La Ciudad Visigoda." In *A Cidade: Jornadas inter e pluridisciplinares*, edited by Mª J. Ferro, 95–119. Lisbon, 1993.

————. "España Visigoda. Las invasiones. Las sociedades." In *Historia de España*, vol. III.1, *La Iglesia*, edited by R. Menéndez Pidal, 61–404. Madrid, 1991.

————. "Las Españas de los siglos V–X: invasiones, religiones, reinos y estabilidad familiar." In *VII Semana de Estudios Medievales. Nájera, 29 de Julio al 2 de Agosto 1996*, 217–33. Logroño, 1997.

————. "Estudios sobre la organización administrativa del Reino visigodo de Toledo." *Anuario de Historia del Derecho Español* 44 (1974): 5–155.

————. *El fin del reino visigodo de Toledo: Decadencia y catástrofe*. Madrid, 1975.

————. "Hispania: del dominio imperial al visigodo." *Historia* 16, 15 (1977): 63–67.

————. *Historia de España visigoda*. Madrid, 1989.

————. "Organización y estructura de la fuerza de trabajo humana en la Península Ibérica durante la Antigüedad Tardía." *Memorias de Historia Antigua* 1 (1977): 247–55.

————. "El paisaje rural y algunos problemas ganaderos en España durante la Antigüedad Tardía (SS. V–VII)." In *Estudios en Homenaje a D. Claudio Sánchez Albornoz en sus 90 años*, 1:401–20. Buenos Aires, 1983.

————. *Prosopographía del Reino Visigodo de Toledo*. Salamanca, 1974.

————. "Rome, Constantinople and the Barbarians." *American Historical Review* 86 (1981): 275–306.

————. "La sociedad de la Península Ibérica entre el Reino de Tolosa y el de Toledo." In *Actas del V Congreso Español de Estudios Clásicos*, 680–95. Madrid, 1978.

————. "La tecnología en España durante la Antigüedad Tardía (SS. V–VII)." *Memorias de Historia Antigua* 3 (1979): 217–37.

————. "La vid y el vino en la España tardoantigua (SS. V–VII d.C.)." In *VIII Jornadas de Viticultura y Enología de Tierra de Barros*, 467–77. Badajoz, 1987.

————. "I Visigoti nella penisola iberica: Inquadramento storico." In *I Goti*, edited by V. Bierbrauer, 292–97. Milan, 1994.

García Moreno, L. A., and S. Rascón Marqués. *Complutum y las ciudades hispanas en la Antigüedad Tardía*. Acta Antiqua Complutensia 1. Alcalá de Henares, 1999.

García Villada, Z. *Historia eclesiástica de España*. Madrid, 1929.

—————. "La Iglesia y la monarquía en la época visigoda." *Razón y Fe* 97 (1932): 69–88.

—————. "La organización de la Iglesia Visigoda en el siglo VII." *Razón y Fe* 38 (1914): 59–68.

García Villoslada, R., ed. *Historia de la Iglesia en España*. Madrid, 1979.

González, T. "La Iglesia desde la conversión de Recaredo hasta la invasion arabe." In *Historia de la Iglesia en España*, vol. 1, *La Iglesia en la España romana y visigoda (siglos I–VIII)*, edited by R. García Villoslada, 400–727. Madrid, 1979.

Goubert, P. "Byzance et l'Espagne Wisigothique." *Revue des Etudes Byzantines* 3 (1945): 127–42.

Heather, P., ed. *The Visigoths: From the Migration Period to the Seventh Century. An Ethnographic Perspective*. San Marino, 1999.

Hillgarth, J. N. *Christianity and Paganism, 350–750: The Conversion of Western Europe*. Philadelphia, 1986.

—————. "La conversión de los Visigotos: notas críticas." *Analecta Sacra Tarraconensia* 34 (1961): 21–46.

—————. "Eschatological and Political Concepts in the Seventh Century." In *Le septième siècle: changements et continuités. Actes du colloque bilatéral franco-britannique tenu au Warburg Institute les 8–9 juillet 1988* [The Seventh Century: Change and Continuity. Proceedings of a Joint French and British Colloquium Held at the Warburg Institute 8–9 July 1988], edited by Jacques Fontaine and J. N. Hillgarth. London, 1992.

—————. "Historiography in Visigothic Spain." In *La storiografia altomedievale*, 261–311. Settimane di Studio del Centro Italiano di Studi sull'alto medioevo 17. Spoleto, 1970.

—————. "Popular Religion in Visigothic Spain." In *Visigothic Spain: New Approaches*, edited by E. James, 3–60. Oxford, 1980.

—————. "St. Julian of Toledo in the Middle Ages." In *Visigothic Spain, Byzantium and the Irish*. London, 1985.

Innovación y continuidad en la España visigótica. Toledo, 1981.

Konstam, A. *Atlas of Medieval Europe*. New York, 2000.

Laterculus regum Visigothorum legum corpori praemissus. In *Chronica minora saec. iv, v, vi, vii*, edited by T. Mommsen, vol. 3. *Monumenta Germaniae Historica, Auctores Antiquissimi*, 13.3. Berlin, 1898.

Leges visigothorum, edited by K. Zeumer. *Monumenta Germaniae Historica, Leges nationum germanicarum*, 1.1. Hanover, 1902.

Momigliano, A. *The Conflict between Paganism and Christianity in the Fourth Century*. Oxford, 1963.

Murphy, F. X. "Julian of Toledo and the Fall of the Visogothic Kingdom in Spain." *Speculum* 27 (1952): 1–27.

O'Callaghan, J. *A History of Medieval Spain*. Ithaca, NY, 1975.

Orlandis Rovira, J. "El Cristianismo en la España Visigótica." In idem, *Historia de España: La España Visigótica*, 1:13–31. Madrid, 1977.

―――. *Historia de España*, vol. 3, *La España Visigótica*. Madrid, 1977.

―――. *Historia de la Iglesia*, vol. 1, *La Iglesia Antigua y Medieval*. Madrid, 1989.

―――. *Historia del reino visigodo español*. Madrid, 1988.

―――. *Historia del Reino visigodo español: Los Acontecimientos, Las Instituciones*. Madrid, 2003.

―――. "La Iglesia visigoda y los problemas de la sucesión al trono en el siglo VII." In *Le chiese nei regni dell'Europa occidentale e i loro rapporti con Roma sino all'800*. 2 vols. Settimane di studio del Centro italiano di studi sull'alto medioevo, 7, Spoleto, 1960.

―――. "El poder real y la sucesión al trono en la monarquía visigotica." *Estudios visigoticos*, vol. 3. Rome/Madrid, 1962.

―――. *La vida en España en tiempo de los Godos*. Madrid, 1991.

―――. "Die westgotische lateinische Literatur: Probleme und Perspektiven." *Antike und Abendland* 12 (1966): 64–87.

Pidal, R. M., ed. *Historia de España: España visigoda*. Vol. III, 1/3. Reedición. Madrid, 1985.

Retamero, F. "As Coins Go Home: Towns, Merchants, Bishops and Kings in Visigothic Hispania." In *The Visigoths: From the Migration Period to the Seventh Century. An Ethnographic Perspective*, edited by P. Heather, 271–320. San Marino, 1999.

Ripoll López, G. "The Arrival of the Visigoths in Hispania." In *Strategies of Distinction: The Construction of Ethnic Communities, 300–800*, edited by W. Pohl and H. Reimitz, 153–79. Leiden, 1998.

Robles, L. "La cultura religiosa de la España Visigótica." *Escritos del Vedat* 5 (1975): 9–54.

Sotomayor M., et al. *Historia de la Iglesia en España. I, La Iglesia en la España romana y visigoda (siglos I al VIII)*. Madrid, 1979.

Thompson, E. A. *Los Godos en España*. Madrid, 1979. First English edition, Oxford, 1969.

Torres López, M. *Historia de España*, vol. 3, *España visigoda*. Madrid, 1976.

―――. "El reino hispanovisigodo." In *Historia de España*, edited by R. Menéndez Pidal, 3:103. Madrid, 1976–91.

Zamorano Herrera, I. "Caracteres del arte visigodo en Toledo." *Anales Toledanos* 10 (1974): 3–149 (with 125 pictures).

THE CHURCH IN VISIGOTHIC SPAIN

Aparicio Bastardo, J. Á. "Notas para la aproximación al estudio de las Iglesias de mozárabes en la urbe toledana." *Anaquel de Estudios Árabes* (1993): 10–24.

Díaz y Díaz, M. C. "El eremitismo en la España visigótica." *Revista Portuguesa de Historia* 6 (1955): 217–37.

Duchesne, L. *Origines du culte chrétien: étude sur la liturgie latine avant Charlemagne.* Paris, 1908.

Férotin, L. *Le Liber Mozarabicus Sacramentorum et les manuscrits mozarabes.* Paris, 1912. Reprint of the 1912 edition and general bibliography on the Hispanic liturgy, prepared and presented by Anthony Ward, SM, and Cuthbert Johnson, OSB, Bibliotheca Ephemerides Liturg. Subsidia, Rome, 1995.

————. *Le Liber Ordinum en usage dans l'Église wisigothique et mozarabe d'Espagne du cinquième au onzième siècle.* Paris, 1904. Reprint of the 1904 edition and general bibliography on the Hispanic liturgy, prepared and presented by Anthony Ward, SM, and Cuthbert Johnson, OSB, Bibliotheca Ephemerides Liturg. Subsidia, Rome, 1996.

Ferrer Grenesche, J. M. *Curso de liturgía hispano-mozárabe.* Toledo, 1995.

————. "La eucharistía en el rito hispano-mozárabe." *Toletana, questiones de teología e Historia* 1 (1999): 59–88.

————. "El legado de la Liturgía Hispano-Mozárabe." *Cronica Mozárabe* 65 (2006): 1–17.

————. *Los santos del nuevo misal hispano-mozárabe.* Toledo, 1995.

Fuente, V. de la. *Historia eclesiástica de España,* vol. 2. Madrid, 1873.

García Moreno, L. A., "Disidencia religiosa y poder episcopal en la España tardoantigua (SS. V–VII)." In *De Constantino a Carlomagno: Disidentes, heterodoxos, marginados,* edited by F. J. Lomas and F. Devís, 135–58. Cádiz, 1992.

————. "Los monjes y monasterios en las ciudades de las Españas tardorromanas y visigodas." *Habis* 24 (1993): 179–92

García Villada, Z. "La Iglesia y la monarquía en la época visigoda." *Razón y Fe* 97 (1932): 69–88.

————. "La organización de la Iglesia Visigoda en el siglo VII." *Razón y Fe* 38 (1914): 59–68.

González Echegaray, J. "El monacato en la España nórdica en su confrontación con el paganismo (ss. VI–VII)." In *Semana de historia del monacato cántabro-astur-leonés,* 35–56. Oviedo, 1982.

Janini, J. "Roma y Toledo." In *Nuevos estudios sobre la litúrgia mozárabe* (Toledo, 1965).

Magnin, E. *La discipline de l'Église wisigothique au VIIe siècle.* Paris, 1912.

————. *L'église visigothique,* 23–31. Paris, 1912.

Mansilla, D. "Orígines de la organización metropolitana en la Iglesia española." *Hispania Sacra* 12 (1959): 255–90.

Martínez Díez, G. "Función de Inspección y Vigilancia del Episcopado sobre las Autoridades seculares en el periodo Visigodo-católico." *Revista Española de Derecho Canónico* 15 (1960): 579–89.

———. "El patrimonio eclesiástico en la España visigoda." Estudio histórico-jurídico. *Miscelánea Comillas: Revista de teología y ciencias humanas* 17 (1959): 5–200.

Menéndez y Pelayo, M. *Historia de los Heterodoxos Españoles.* 2nd ed. Madrid, 1917.

———. *Historia de los Heterodoxos Españoles. I, España romana y visigoda: Período de la Reconquista. Erasmistas y protestantes.* 5th ed. Madrid, 1998.

Orlandis, J. *Historia del reino visigodo español.* Madrid, 1988.

———. *La iglesia en la España Visigótica y medieval.* Pamplona, 1976.

———. "La Iglesia visigoda y los problemas de la sucesión al trono en el siglo VII." In *Le chiese nei regni dell'Europa occidentale e i loro rapporti con Roma sino all'800.* 2 vols. Settimane di studio del Centro italiano di studi sull'alto medioevo 7. Spoleto, 1960.

———. "El poder real y la sucesión al trono en la monarquía visigotica." *Estudios Visigoticos,* vol. 3. Rome/Madrid, 1962.

———. "Las relaciones intereclesiales en la Hispania visigótica." In *Historia de España,* vol. 3, *La España Visigótica,* 59–93. Madrid, 1977.

Puertas Tricas, R. *Iglesias hispánicas (ss. IV–VIII): Testimonios literarios.* Madrid, 1975.

Rivera Recio, J. F. *Los Arzobispos de Toledo desde sus orígenes hasta fines del siglo XI.* Toledo, 1972.

———. "Los arzobispos de Toledo en el siglo VII." *Anales Toledanos* 3 (1971): 181–217.

———. *Estudios sobre la liturgia mozárabe.* Toledo, 1965.

Robles, L. "La cultura religiosa de la España Visigótica." *Escritos del Vedat* 5 (1975): 9–54.

Sánchez Salor, E. *Jerarquías eclesiásticas y monacales en época visigoda.* Salamanca, 1976.

Septième siècle: Le changements et continuités. Actes du colloque bilatéral franco-britannique tenu au Warburg Institute les 8–9 juillet 1988 [The Seventh Century: Change and Continuity. Proceedings of a Joint French and British Colloquium Held at the Warburg Institute 8–9 July 1988], edited by Jacques Fontaine and J. N. Hillgarth. London, 1992.

Simonet, F. J. *Historia de los mozárabes Españoles.* Madrid, 1897.

Simonetti, M. *La produzione letteraria latina fra romani e barbari (sec. V–VIII).* Rome, 1986.

———. *Profilo storico dell'esegesi patristica.* Rome, 1981.

Sotomayor, M., et al. *Historia de la Iglesia en España. I, La Iglesia en la España romana y visigoda (siglos I al VIII).* Madrid, 1979.

T. A. [T. Arnold]. "Isidorus (23) Pacensis." *A Dictionary of Christian Biography*, edited by W. Smith, DCL, LLD, and H. Wace, BD, 3:313–15. London, 1882.

Ziegler, A. K. "Church and State in Visigothic Spain." PhD diss., Catholic University of America, 1930.

TOLEDO, THE ROYAL CITY AND THE PRIMATIAL CHURCH OF SPAIN

Fernández Collado, Á. *Guía del Archivo y Biblioteca Capitulares de la Catedral de Toledo.* Toledo, 2007.

Flórez, E. *España Sagrada.* 56 vols. Madrid, 1750–. Reprint, 2000–. Estudio preliminar: *El P. Enrique Flórez y la España Sagrada*, by F. J. Campos y Férnandez de Sevilla, Edición de Rafael Lazcano (Madrid, 2000–). Vols. 5 and 6 are devoted to the Church of Toledo and ecclesiastical province of Cartagena.

García Martín, F. "La cripta de Santa Leocadia en el Alcázar." *Anales Toledanos* 41 (2005): 413–30.

García Moreno, L.A. *El fin del reino visigodo de Toledo: Decadencia y catástrofe.* Madrid, 1975.

Görres, F. "Der Primas Julian von Toledo (680–690): Eine Kirchen-cultur, und literargeschichtliche Studie." *Zeitschrift für wissenschaftliche Theologie* 46 (1902–3): 524–53.

Mansilla, D. "Orígines de la organización metropolitana en la Iglesia española." *Hispania Sacra* 12 (1959): 255–90.

Martín Gamero, A. *Historia de la ciudad de Toledo: Sus claros varones y monumentos.* Toledo, 1862.

Martínez, G. "Toledo." *Diccionario de Historia Eclesiástica de España*, 1:568. Madrid, 1972.

Rivera Recio, J. F. *Los arzobispos de Toledo en la Alta Edad Media.* Toledo, 1965.

―――. "Cisma episcopal de la Iglesia toledano-visigoda." *Hispania Sacra* 1 (1948): 259–68.

―――. "Encumbramiento de la sede toledana durante la dominación visigótica." *Hispania Sacra* 8 (1955): 3–34.

―――. *Guía de la Catedral de Toledo.* Toledo, 1953.

―――. "Leocadia di Toledo." *Bibliotheca Sanctorum*, 7:1187–88. Rome, 1965.

―――. "Primado de Toledo o primado de las Españas." *Diccionario de Historia Eclesiástica de España*, 3:2024–27. Madrid, 1973.

THE NATIONAL COUNCILS OF TOLEDO

Alberca, I. E. "Toledo, Councils of." *New Catholic Encyclopedia*. 2nd ed., 14:99–101. New York, 2003.

BIBLIOGRAPHY 575

Casado, M. J. "Los concilios nacionales visigodos, iniciación de una política concordatoria." *Boletín de la Universidad de Granada* 18 (1946): 179–223.

XIV Centenario Concilio III de Toledo (589–1989). Toledo, 1991.

Gonzalez, F. *Collectio canonum Ecclesiae Hispanae*, I. Madrid, 1808.

Hillgarth, J. N. "Elvira, Council of." *New Catholic Encyclopaedia*, 5:178. New York, 2003.

Madoz, J. *Le symbole du XI Concile de Tolède: Ses sources, sa date, sa valeur*. Spicilegium Sacrum Lovaniense, fasc. 19, p. 25.21–23; pp. 101.3; Louvain, 1938.

———. *El símbolo del concilio XVI de Toledo: su texto, sus fuentes, su valor teológico*. Estudios Onienses 3. Madrid, 1946.

Marín Martínez, I., and G. T. Martínez Díez. *Concilios Visigóticos e Hispano-Romanos*. España Cristiana, Textos 1. Madrid, 1963.

Martínez, G. *La colección canónica hispana*, vol. 1. Monumenta Hispaniae Sacra, Serie Canónica 1. Madrid, 1966.

———. "Concilios Nacionales y Provinciales, Toledo IV, 633." *Diccionario de Historia Eclesiástica de España*, 1:569. Madrid, 1972.

Martínez Diez, G. "Los Concilios de Toledo." *Anales Toledanos* 3 (1971): 119–37.

Orlandis, J., "Bible et Royauté dans les Conciles de l'Espagne visigotho-catholique." *Annuarium Historiae Conciliorum* 18 (1986): 51–57.

———. *Historia de los concilios de la España romana y visigoda*. Pamplona, 1986.

Rivera Recio, J. F. *Guía de la Catedral de Toledo*. Toledo, 1953.

Sanchez-Albornoz, C. "El 'aula regia' y las asambleas políticas de los Godos." *Cuadernos de historia de España* 5 (1946): 5–110.

Vives, José, ed. *Concilios visigoticos e hispano-romanos*. Barcelona/Madrid, 1963.

JUDAISM AND ANTI-JUDAISM IN VISIGOTHIC SPAIN

Amón-Hernández, P. "La España Visigoda frente al problema de los judíos." *Ciencia Tomista* 14 (1967): 627–85.

Bachrach, B. S. "A Reassessment of Visigothic Jewish Policy 589–711." *American Historical Review* 78 (1973): 16–19.

Baer, Y. *A History of the Jews in Christian Spain*, vol. 1. Philadelphia, 1992.

Blázquez Miguel, J. *Toledot: Historia del Toledo judío*. Toledo, 1989.

Echánove, A. "Precisiones acerca de la legislación conciliar toledana sobre los judíos." *Hispania Sacra* 14 (1961): 259–79.

García Iglesias, L. *Los judíos en la España antigua*. Madrid, 1978.

García Moreno, L. A. *Los judíos de la España antigua. Del primer encuentro al primer repudio*. Madrid, 1993.

————. "La legislación antijudía del reino visigodo de Toledo." *Miscelánea de Estudios Arabes y Hebraicos* 42 (1993): 37–49.

Gil, J. "Judíos y cristianos en la Hispania del siglo VII." *Hispania Sacra* 30 (1980): 9–102.

Guerreiro, R. "La imagen del judío en los textos hagiográficos y patrísticos. Siglos V al VIII." *Espacio, Tiempo y Forma*, Serie II, Historia Antigua 6 (1993): 543–50.

Katz, S. *The Jews in the Visigothic and Frankish Kingdom of Spain and Gaul.* Cambridge, MA, 1937.

Lacave Riaño, José Luis. "La legislación antijudía de los Visigodos." In *Simposio Toledo Judaico, Toledo, 20–22 April 1972*, 1:31–42. Toledo, 1973.

León Tello, P. *Judíos de Toledo.* 2 vols. Madrid, 1979.

Pobres Martín-Cleto, Julio. "Algunas precisiones sobre las juderías toledanas." *Anales Toledanos* 16 (1983): 37–61.

Roth, N. *Jews, Visigoths and Muslims in Medieval Spain: Cooperation and Conflict.* Leiden, 1994.

————. "New Light on the Jews of Mozarabic Toledo." *Association for Jewish Studies Review* 11, no. 2 (1986): 189–220.

Saitta, B. *L'Antisemitismo nella Spagna Visigotica.* Studia Historica 130. Rome, 1995.

Vásquez, I. "Judíos." *Diccionario de Historia Eclesiástica de España*, 3:1255–59. Madrid, 1972–75.

CULTURE AND EDUCATION IN VISIGOTHIC SPAIN

Fontaine, J. *Fins et moyens de l'enseignement ecclésiastique dans l'Espagne wisigothique.* 2 vols. Paris, 1959. New ed. in 3 vols., Paris, 1983.

Lesne, E. *Le livres, "scriptoria" et bibliothèques du commencement du VIIIe à la fin du XIe siècle.* Lille, 1938.

Marín, T. "Bibliotecas Eclesiásticas." *Diccionario de Historia Eclesiástica de España*, 1:250–62. Madrid, 1972–75.

Marrou, H. I. *Historia de la educación en la antigüedad.* 7th ed. Buenos Aires, 1976.

Martínez Fernández, F. "Escuelas de formación del clero en la España visigoda." In *La Patrología toledano-visigoda*, 65–98. Madrid, 1970.

Martín Hernández, F. *Formación del Clero en la Iglesia Visigótico-Mozárabe.* Toledo, 1979.

Piva, Paolo, Antonio Cadei, et al., eds. *L'Arte medievale nel contesto (300–1300): funzioni, iconografia, tecniche.* Milan, 2006.

Riché. P. *Écoles et enseignement dans le Haut Moyen Age.* Paris, 1979.

————. "L'éducation à l'époque Wisigothique: les 'Institutionum disciplinae.'" *Anales Toledanos* 3 (1971): 171–80.

————. *Éducation et culture dans l'occident barbare: VIe–VIIIe siécles*. Paris, 1962.

Scuola nell'occidente latino nell'alto medioevo. Atti della XIX settimana del Centro italiano di studi sull'alto medioevo, 15–21 April 1971. Spoleto, 1973.

Valentinelli, G. *Delle biblioteche della Spagna*, 85–89. Vienna, 1860.

Velázquez, I. "Ambitos y ambientes de la cultura escrita en Hispania (s. VI): De Martín de Braga a Leandro de Sevilla." In *Studia Ephemeridis Augustinianum*, 329–51. Rome, 1994.

Bishops Eugene II and Ildephonse of Toledo

Alberto, P. F. "Notes on Eugenius of Toledo." *Classical Quarterly* New Series 49 (1999): 304–14.

Bardy, G. "Eugene II." *Catholicisme: Hier, aujourd'hui, demain. Encyclopédie*, edited by G. Jacquemet (vol. 7 and following published under the direction of Centre Interdisciplinaire des Facultés catholique de Lille), vol. 4, col. 673. Paris, 1948.

Bertini, F. "Isidoro e Ildefonso, continuatori di Gerolamo biografo." In *Gerolamo e la biografia letteraria*, 105–22. Genoa, 1989.

Codoñer Merino, C. *El De viris illustribus de Ildefonso de Toledo, estudio y ed. crítica*. Salamanca, 1964.

Eugenii Toletani opera omnia. Edited by P. F. Alberto. Corpus Christianorum, Series Latina 114. Turnhout, 2006.

Eugenius II of Toledo. "Carmina." In *Eugenii Toletani episcopi carmina et epistulae*. Edited by F. Vollmer. In *Monumenta Germaniae Historica, Auctores Antiquissimi*. Berlin, 1905.

Fl. Merobaudis reliquiae, Blossii Aemilii Dracontii carmina, Eugenii Toletani episcopi carmina et epistulae, cum appendicula carminum spuriorum. Edited by F. Vollmer. In *Monumenta Germaniae Historica, Auctores Antiquissimi* 14. Berlin, 1905.

Fontaine, J. "El De viris illustribus de San Ildefonso de Toledo." *Anales Toledanos* 3 (1971): 59–96.

Hormaeche Basauri, J. M. *La Pastoral de iniciación cristiana en la España visigoda: Estudio sobre el 'De cognitione baptismi' de San Ildefonso de Toledo*, 149. Toledo, 1983.

Ildefonsus. *De viris illustribus*. Edited and translated by C. Codoñer Merino. Acta Salmanticensia, Filosofía y Letras 65. Salamanca, 1972.

Madoz, J. "Eugenio di Toledo." *Enciclopedia Cattolica*, vol. 5, col. 804. Florence, 1954.

————. *San Ildefonso de Toledo a través de la pluma del Arcipreste de Talavera*. Madrid, 1943.

Rivera Recio, J. F. *Los Arzobispos de Toledo desde sus orígenes hasta fines del siglo XI*. Toledo, 1972.

————. "Los arzobispos de Toledo en el siglo VII." *Anales Toledanos* 3 (1971):181–217.

————. *Estudio hagiográfico sobre san Eugenio I de Toledo (textos-crítica-culto)*. Toledo, 1963.

————. *Estudios sobre la liturgia mozárabe*. Toledo, 1965.

————. "Eugenio II." In *Biblioteca Sanctorum*, vol. 5, col. 1964. Rome, 1965.

————. *San Eugenio de Toledo y su culto*. Toledo, 1963.

————. *San Ildefonso de Toledo: Biografía, época y posteridad*. Madrid/Toledo, 1985.

————. *Los textos hagiográficos más antiguos sobre San Eugenio de Toledo*. Toledo, 1963.

Vega, A. C. "De patrología española: Sobre el opúsculo 'De Sancta Trinitate' de san Eugenio II de Toledo (en torno a una cita de San Julián de Toledo en su 'Prognosticon' 3, 17)." *Boletín de la Real Accademia de la Historia* [Madrid] 166 (1970): 64.

HISTORICAL AND THEOLOGICAL BIOGRAPHY OF JULIAN OF TOLEDO

Ancient and Modern Authors

Acta Sanctorum, martii. Vol. 1, *Vita Sancti Juliani et commentarius*, edited by J. Carnandet, 780–86. Paris/Rome, 1865.

Acta Sanctorum. Vol. 6, part 1, *Martyrologium Usuardi Monachi*, 140. Anversa, 1715.

Baronius, Caesar. *Annales ecclesiastici*, vol. 8, years 657–680. Mainz, 1601.

Bellarminus, R. *De Scriptoribus Ecclesiasticis liber unus. Cum adiunctis indicibus undecim, & brevi Chronologia ab Orbe condito usque ad annum M. DC. XII. Opera Omnia*, 6:7–142. Neapoli, 1862.

Ceillier, R. *Histoire générale des auteurs sacrés et ecclésiastiques, qui contient leur vie, le catalogue, la critique, le jugement, la chronologie, l'Analyse & le dénombrement des différentes éditions de leurs ouvrages*, 17:733ff. Paris, 1729–63.

"Chronicle of Alfonso III." In *Crónicas asturianas*, edited by J. Gil Fernandez. Oviedo, 1985.

Chronicon (or Anonymus Toletanus, Isidorus Pacensis, Anonymus of Cordoba). PL 96, cols. 1253–80.

"Continuatio hispano-mozarabica." Edited by T. Mommsen. In *Monumenta Germaniae Historica, Chronica minora* II. Berlin, 1894.

La Crónica de Alfonso III. Edited by Z. García Villada. Madrid, 1918.

Crónica mozárabe de 754. Edited by J. E. López Pereira. Zaragoza, 1980.

Felice Toletano Auctore. *Sancti Juliani Toletani Episcopi vita seu elogium.* PL 96, cols. 444–52.

Flórez, E. *España Sagrada.* 56 vols. Madrid, 1750–. Reprint, 2000–. Estudio preliminar: *El P. Enrique Flórez y la España Sagrada,* by F. J. Campos y Férnandez de Sevilla, Edición de Rafael Lazcano (Madrid, 2000–). Vols. 5 and 6 are devoted to the Church of Toledo and ecclesiastical province of Cartagena.

Gennadius. *De scriptoribus ecclesiasticis.* PL 58, cols. 1059–1120.

Iohannis abbatis Biclarensis chronica A. DLXVII-DXC. Chronica minora saec. iv, v, vi, vii, Edited by T. Mommsen. *Monumenta Germaniae Historica,* II.2. Berlin, 1894.

Jo. Alberti Fabricii Lipsiensis s. theologiae inter suos d. et prof. publ. *Bibliotheca latina mediae et infimae aetatis /* cum supplemento Christiani Schoettgeni; jam a.p. Joanne Dominico Mansi [...] e mss. editisque codicibus correcta illustrata aucta post editionem patavinam an. 1754, nunc denuo emendata et aucta, indicibus locupletata. 260, 3 :477–79. Florentiae [1858]–1859.

Labbé, P. *Sanctorum Patrum, Theologorum Scriptorumque Ecclesiasticorum Bibliotheca.* Paris, 1659.

Nicolás Antonius, *Bibliotheca Hispana Vetus, sive Hispani Scriptores qui ab Octaviani Augusti aevo ad Nahum Christum MD floruerunt. Auctore D. Nicolao Antonio hispalense I. C. Ordinis S. Iacobi equite, patriae Ecclesiae canonico, Regiorum negotiorum in Urbe et Romana curia Procuratore generali, Consiliario regio. Curante Francisco Perezio Bayerio, Valentino, Sereniss. Hisp. Infantum Carola III. Regis filiorum Institutore primario, Regio Bibliothecae Palatino – Matritensis Praefecto, qui et prologum, & Auctoris vital epitomen, & notulas adiecit. Tomus primus. Ab anno M ad MD. Matriti apud viduam et heredes D. Ioachimi Ibarrae Regii quondam typographi. MDCCLXXXVIII. Tomus secundus. Ab anno M. ad MD. Matriti apud viduam et heredes D. Ioachimi Ibarrae Regii quondam typographi.* 1788. First edition, Rome, 1696. The second edition was edited by Pérez Bayer (Madrid, 1788), 1:413ff. The edition was reprinted by J. P. Migne in his *Patrologia Latina,* vol. 96, cols. 427–44.

Orosius, Paulus. *Historiarum adversus paganos libri VII. Corpus Scriptorum Ecclesiasticorum Latinorum,* 5, 280.

Rodrigus of Toledo. *De rebus Hispaniae. SS.PP. Toletanorum quotquot extant opera.* Madrid, 1785.

Sigebertus Gemblacensis. *De scriptoribus ecclesiasticis,* LVI. PL 160, col 560A.

Trithemius, Ioannes., *De scriptoribus ecclesiasticis Disertissimi viri Iohannis de Trittehem abbatis Spahemesis De Scriptoribus ecclesiasticis collectanea: Additi nonnulli ex recentioribus vitis et nominibus: qui scriptis suis ac nostra tempestate clariores evaserunt. Venudatur Parrhisi A magistro Bertoldo Rembolt (ubi impressus est) Et a Ioane parvo: In vico sancti Iacobi sub sole et lilio aureis: expensas impress. est MDXII.*

Contemporary Authors

Brunhölzl, F. *Histoire de la littérature latine du Moyen Age*, I/2, *L'époque Carolingienne.* Louvain, 1991 (from the original *Geschichte der lateinischen Literatur des Mittelalters*, I, Munich, 1975).

Cayré, F. *Précis de Patrologie*, II. Paris, 1930.

Chevalier, U. *Répertoire des sources historique du Moyen Age: Bio-bibliographie*, vol. 2. Paris, 1907.

Dekkers, E. *Clavis Patrum Latinorum.* Bruges, 1951.

Díaz y Díaz, M. C. "La cultura de la España visigótica del siglo VII." In *Caratteri del secolo VII in Occidente*, 2:813–44. Settimane di Studio del Centro Italiano di Studi sull'alto medioevo 5. Spoleto, 1958.

————. "La fecha de implantación del oracional festivo visigótico." *Boletín Arqueológico* [Tarragona] 113–30 (1971–72): 215–43.

————. *Index scriptorum Latinorum Medii Aevi Hispanorum.* Salamanca, 1968.

————. "La obra literaria de los obispos visigóticos toledanos." In *La patrología toledano-visigoda: XXVII Semana Española de Teología*, 55–58. Madrid, 1970.

————. "Scrittori della penisola iberica." In *Patrologia*, vol. 4, *Dal Concilio di Calcedonia (451) a Beda: I Padri latini*, edited by Angelo Di Berardino, 59–118. Genoa, 1996.

Domínguez Del Val, U. "Caracteristicas de la Patristica Hispana en el siglo VII." In *La patrología toledano-visigoda: XXVII Semana Española de Teología*, 5–36. Madrid, 1970.

————. *Herencia literaria de Padres y escritores españoles de Osio de Córdoba a Julián de Toledo: Repertorio de Historia de la Ciencias Eclesiásticas en España*, I, *Siglos III–XIV*, 85. Salamanca, 1967.

————. *Historia de la antigua literatura latina hispano-cristiana.* 4 vols. Madrid, 1998–2002.

————. *San Julián de Toledo.* In B. Altaner, *Patrologia.* Madrid, 1962.

D'onofrio, G. "Le origini del medioevo teologico (secoli VI-VII), vol. III, 3: Voci teologiche nelle regioni iberiche: dalla fine del regno visigoto a Beato Libana." In *Storia della Teologia nel Medioevo*, vol. 1, *I princìpi*, 83–89. Casale Monferrato, 1996.

García Villada, Z. *Historia eclesiástica de España.* Madrid, 1929.

————. "La Iglesia y la monarquía en la época visigoda." *Razón y Fe* 97 (1932): 69–88.

————. "La organización de la Iglesia Visigoda en el siglo VII." *Razón y Fe* 38 (1914): 59–68.

Ghellinck, J. de. *Littérature latine au Moyen Age, depuis les origines jusq'à la fin de la renaissance carolingienne*, vol. 1. Paris, 1939.

Kayserling, M. "Julian of Toledo." *Jewish Encyclopedia*, on-line version, www.jewishencyclopedia.com/view.jsp?artid=717&letter=J&search=julian%20of%20toledo.

Labriolle, P. Champagne de. *Histoire de la littérature latine chrétienne*. 3rd ed. Paris, 1947.

Madoz, J., SJ. *Historia general de las literaturas Hispánicas*, vol. 1. Barcelona, 1949.

――――. "San Julián de Toledo." *Estudios Eclesiásticos* 26 (1952): 39–69.

――――. *Segundo Decenio de Estudios sobre Patrística Española*. Estudios Onienses 5. Madrid, 1951.

Mariana, J. de. *Historia de rebus Hispaniae* (Toledo, 1592), 278–80.

――――. *Historia General de España*. 2 vols. Barcelona, 1839.

Mathon, G. "Julien (Saint) éveque de Tolède." *Catholicisme: Hier, aujourd'hui, demain. Encyclopédie*, edited by G. Jacquemet (vol. 7 and following published under the direction of Centre Interdisciplinaire des Facultés catholique de Lille), vol. 6, cols. 1230–31. Paris, 1948.

Moliné, E. *Los Padres de la Iglesia: Una guía introductoria I, II, III*. Madrid, 1982.

Morales, A. *Crónica General de España*. Alcalà de Henares, 1577.

Moreschini, C. *Historia de la literatura cristiana antigua griega y latina*. Madrid, 2006.

Polara, G. *Letteratura latina tardoantica e altomedievale*. With a bibliography by A. De Prisco. Rome, 1987.

DICTIONARIES AND STUDIES

Alonso Nuñez, J. M. "Julian von Toledo." *Lexikon des Mittelalters*, 5:802–3. Munich/Zurich, 1977–99.

Andrés, M., ed. *Historia de la Teología española*, 1:335–37. Madrid, 1983.

Aubert, R. "Julien (Saint), évêque de Tolède." *Dictionnaire d'histoire et de géographie ecclésiastiques*, vol. 28, cols. 534–35. Paris, 1912–.

Baloup, D, "Giuliano di Toledo." *Dizionario enciclopedico del Medioevo*, 3:848. Rome, 1998.

Brunhölzl, F. *Histoire de la littérature latine du Moyen Âge*, 103–10, 263–64. Turnhout, 1991.

Collins, R. "Julian of Toledo." In *Key Figures in Medieval Europe. An Encyclopedia*, edited by Richard K. Emmerson and Sandra Clayton-Emmerson, 387–88. New York, 2006.

Díaz y Díaz, M. C. "Giuliano di Toledo." *Dizionario Patristico e di Antichità Cristiane*, vol. 2, cols. 1611–12. Casale Monferrato, 1983.

Domínguez Del Val, U. "Julián de Toledo." *Diccionario de Historia Eclesiástica de España*, 2:1259–60. Madrid, 1972–75.

Domínguez Del Val, U., and E. Cuevas. "San Julián de Toledo." In B. Altaner, *Patrología Española*, Supplement, 115–22. Madrid, 1956.

Engels, O. "Julian, hl., EB v. Toledo." *Lexikon für Theologie und Kirche*, 1200. 2nd ed. Freiburg im Breisgau, 1960.

Fenoglio, M. L. "Giuliano arcivescovo di Toledo." *Dizionario Ecclesiastico*, 191. Turin, 1955.

Forget, J. "Julian de Tolède, Saint." *Dictionnaire de Théologie Catholique, contenant l'exposé des doctrines de la théologie catholique, leurs preuves et leur histoire*, vol. 8, 2, cols. 1940–42. Paris, 1903–50.

Ghellinck, J., de. "En marge des catologues des Bibliothèques médiévales." In *Miscellanea Francesco Ehrle: scritti di storia e paleografia pubblicati sotto gli auspici di S.S. Pio XI in occasione dell'ottantesimo natalizio dell'E.mo Cardinale Francesco Ehrle*, 5:331–63. 5 vols. Studi e testi 42. Rome, 1924.

Gómez, I. "Julián de Toledo, San." *Gran Enciclopedia Rialp*, 13:650–51. Madrid, 1973.

Gonzálvez Ruiz, R. "San Julián de Toledo en el contexto de su tiempo." *Anales Toledanos* 32 (1996): 7–21.

Hillgarth, J. N. "Julian of Toledo, St." *New Catholic Encyclopedia*, 8:50. San Francisco, 1967.

Madoz, J. "Escritores de la época visigótica." In *Historia general de las literaturas hispánica*, edited by G. Díaz Plaja, 1:131f. Barcelona, 1949.

————. "Giuliano da Toledo, Santo." *Enciclopedia Cattolica*, vol. 6, cols. 747–48. Florence, 1954.

————. "San Julián de Toledo." *Estudios Eclesiásticos* 26 (1952): 39–69.

M. A. W. [Mrs. Humphrey Ward]. "Julianus (63)." *A Dictionary of Christian Biography*, edited by W. Smith, DCL, LLD, and H. Wace, BD, 3:477–81. London, 1882.

Morin, G. "Le commentaire sur Nahum du Pseudo-Julien, une oeuvre de Richard de Saint Victor?" *Revue Bénédectine* 37 (1925): 404–5.

————. "Un écrit de Saint Julien de Tolède consideré a tort comme perdu." *Revue Bénédictine* 24 (1907): 407–15.

————. *Études, textes, découvertes*, 1:53f. Maredsous/Paris, 1913.

Rivera Recio, J. F. "Giuliano di Toledo." *Bibliotheca Sanctorum*, 6:1216–18. Rome, 1965.

————. *San Julián arzobispo de Toledo (s. VII): Epoca y personalidad*. Barcelona, 1944.

Robles Sierra, A. "Julien de Tolède (saint)." *Dictionnaire de Spiritualité*, vol. 8, cols. 1600–1602. Paris, 1974.

Ruiz, T. F. "Julian of Toledo." *Dictionary of the Middle Ages*, 7:181. New York, 1986.

Sehlmeyer, M. "Giuliano di Toledo." *Dizionario di Letteratura Cristiana Antica*, edited by Siegmar Döpp and Wilhelm Geerlings, with Peter Bruns,

Georg Röwekamp, Matthias Skeb, OSB, and Bettina Windau. Italian edition edited by Celestino Noce, 447–48. Rome, 2006.

Stancati, T. "Alle origini dell'Escatologia cristiana sistematica: il Prognosticon futuri saeculi di San Giuliano di Toledo (sec. VII)." *Angelicum* 73 (1996): 401–34.

——. "Giuliano di Toledo." *Lexicon–Dizionario dei Teologi*, 579–80. Casale Monferrato, 1998.

Strati, R. "Giuliano di Toledo." *Enciclopedia Virgiliana*, 2:749–51. Rome, 1984–91.

Vincke, J. "Julian von Toledo." *Lexikon für Theologie und Kirche*, 5:711ff. Freiburg im Breisgau, 1933.

SOURCES OF JULIAN OF TOLEDO

La Bibbia nell'alto Medioevo. Settimane di studio del Centro italiano di studi sull' alto Medioevo 10 (26 aprile–2 maggio 1962). Spoleto, 1963.

Bouhot, J.-P. "Une homélie de Jean Chrysostome citée par Julien de Tolède." *Revue des Etudes Augustiniennes* 23, nos. 1–2 (1977):122–23.

Campos, J., "San Agustín y la escatología de San Julián de Toledo." *Augustinus* 25 (1980): 107–15.

Clavis Patrum Latinorum qua in corpus christianorum edendum optimas quasque scriptorum recensiones a Tertulliano ad Bedam commode recludit Eligius Dekkers opera usus qua rem praeparavit et iuvit Aemilius Gaar † vindobonensis. Editio tertia aucta et emendata (Steenbrugis, in Abbatia Sancti Petri, 1995).

Díaz y Díaz, M. C. *Index scriptorum Latinorum Medii Aevi Hispanorum*. Part 1, Filosofia y Letras. Tome XIII, núm. 1, Acta Salmaticensia. Salamanca, 1958.

Domínguez Del Val, U. "Herencia literaria de padres y escritores españoles de Osio de Córdoba a Julián de Toledo." *Repertorio de Historia de las Ciencias eclesiásticas en España*, 1:29–31. Salamanca, 1967.

Gennadius. *De scriptoribus ecclesiasticis*, 98. PL 58, cols. 1117B–1118B.

Hillgarth, J. N. "Las fuentes de san Julián de Toledo." *Anales Toledanos* 3 (1971): 97–118.

Madoz, J. "Fuentes teológico-literarias de San Julián de Toledo." *Gregorianum* 33 (1952): 399–417.

——. "Ovidio en los santos padre españoles." *Estudios Eclesiasticos* 23 (1949): 233–38.

Strati, R. "Presenze virgiliane in Giuliano di Toledo." *Maia* 38 (1986): 41–50.

Vetus latina hispana: La origen, dependencia, derivaciones, valor e influjo universal, reconstrucción...y analisis de sus diversos elementos, coordinacion y edición crit-

ica de su texto, estudio comparativo con los demás elementos de la Vetus latina, los Padres y escritores eclesiásticos..., by T. Ayuso Marazuela. Madrid, 1953–.

LATIN AND GREEK IN THE SEVENTH CENTURY

Berschin, W. *Greek Letters and the Latin Middle Ages: From Jerome to Nicholas of Cusa.* Translated by Jerold C. Frakes. Revised and expanded edition. Washington, DC, 1988.

Díaz y Díaz, M. C. "Aspectos de la cultura literaria en la España visigotica." *Anales Toledanos* 3 (1971): 33–58.

―――――. *De Isidoro al siglo XI: Ocho estudios sobre la vida literaria peninsular.* Barcelona, 1976.

―――――. "El Latín de España en el siglo VII: Lengua y escritura según los textos documentales." In *Le septième siècle: changements et continuités: Actes du colloque bilatéral franco-britannique tenu au Warburg Institute les 8–9 juillet 1988* [The Seventh Century: Change and Continuity: Proceedings of a Joint French and British Colloquium Held at the Warburg Institute 8–9 July 1988], edited by Jacques Fontaine and J. N. Hillgarth, 25–37. London, 1992.

―――――. "Le latin du Haut Moyen Age espagnol." In *La lexicographie du latin médiéval et ses rapports avec les recherches actuelles sur la civilisation du Moyen Age*, 106–14. Paris, 1981.

Domínguez Del Val, U. *Estudios sobre la literatura latina hispano-cristiana, I, 1955–1971*, 118–20. Madrid, 1986.

Fontán, Antonio, and Ana Moure Casas, eds. *Antología del latin medieval: introducción y textos.* Madrid, 1987.

Holtz, L. "Continuité et discontinuité de la tradition grammaticale au VIIe siècle." In *Le septième siècle: changements et continuités: Actes du colloque bilatéral franco-britannique tenu au Warburg Institute les 8-9 juillet 1988* [The Seventh Century: Change and Continuity: Proceedings of a Joint French and British Colloquium Held at the Warburg Institute 8–9 July 1988], edited by Jacques Fontaine and J. N. Hillgarth, 41–54. London, 1992.

Lindsay, W. M. "The Philoxenus Glossary." *Classical Review* 31, no. 7 (1917): 158–63.

Lot, F. "A quelle époque a-t-on cessè de parler latin?" *Archivum Latinitatis Medii Aevi* 6 (1931): 97–159.

Maierù, Alfonso, ed. *Grafia e interpunzione del latino nel medioevo.* Seminario Internazionale, Roma, 27–29 settembre 1984. Rome, 1987.

Menéndez Pidal, R. *Orígenes del español.* 7th ed. Madrid, 1972.

Mohrmann, C. *Études sur le latin des chrétiens.* 4 vols. (I: *Le latin chrétien et liturgique*; II: *Le latin chrétien et médiéval*; III: *Le latin des chrétiens*; IV: *Le latin chrétien et latin médieval*). 2nd ed. Rome, 1961–77. Appendix: J. Schrijnen, *Characteristik des altchristlichen Latein.*

Stiennon, J., with G. Hasenohr. *Paléographie du moyen âge.* Paris, 1973.

POPULAR AND LITURGICAL CULT OF JULIAN OF TOLEDO

Biblioteca hagiographica Latina antiquae et mediae aetatis. 2 vols. Brussels, 1898–1901. Suppl. 2a edit., ibid. 1911. Vol. 1, 575, n. 4554. See also *Vita Sancti Juliani et commentarius, Acta Sanctorum, martii,* vol. 1, edited by J. Carnandet, 780–86. Paris/Rome, 1865.

Bruyne, D. de. "Le plus ancien catalogue des reliques d'Oviedo." *Analecta Bollandiana* 45 (1927): 93–96.

Gaiffier, B. de. "Les notices hispaniques dans le Martyrologie d'Usuard." *Analecta Bollandiana* 55 (1937): 268–83.

———. "Les reliques de l'abbaye de San Millán de la Cogolla au XIII siècle." *Analecta Bollandiana* 53 (1935): 90–96.

García Rodríguez, C. *El culto a los Santos en la España romana y visigoda.* Madrid, 1966.

Hillgarth, J. N. *Introduction* to the critical edition of the works of Julian of Toledo, VIII–LXXIV. Corpus Christianorum, Series Latina 115. Turnhout, 1976.

Rivera Recio, J. F. *Julián arzobispo de Toledo (s. VII): Epoca y personalidad.* Barcelona, 1944.

WRITINGS OF JULIAN OF TOLEDO

For each of the writings of Julian of Toledo see the *Introduction* to the critical edition of his works by J. N. Hillgarth in Corpus Christianorum, Series Latina 115, VIII–LXXIV, and the articles by Hillgarth and by J. Madoz cited in this bibliography.

The Elogium Ildefonsi

Bertini, F. "Isidoro e Ildefonso, continuatori di Gerolamo biografo." In *Gerolamo e la biografia letteraria,* 105–22. Genoa, 1989.

Codoñer Merino, C. *El De viris illustribus de Isidoro de Sevilla, estudio y ed. crítica.* Salamanca, 1964, 1972.

Domínguez Del Val, U. "Elogium." *Revista española de Teologia* 31 (1971): 138–39.

Fontaine, J. *Culture et spiritualité en Espagne du IVe au VIIe siècle.* London, 1986.

———. "El De viris illustribus de San Ildefonso de Toledo." *Anales Toledanos* 3 (1971): 59–96.

Gennadius. *De scriptoribus ecclesiasticis.* PL 58, cols. 1059–1120.

Hillgarth, J. N. *Introduction* to the critical edition of the works of Julian of Toledo. Corpus Christianorum, Series Latina 115, VIII–LXXIV. Turnhout, 1976.

Honorius Augustudunensis. *De scriptoribus ecclesiasticis,* III, 14. PL 172, cols. 197–233C.

Jerome. *De viris illustribus.* PL 23, cols. 597–720A.

Madoz, J. *San Ildefonso de Toledo a través de la pluma del Arcipreste de Talavera.* Madrid, 1943.

The Historia Wambae Regis

Amman, E. "Penitence." *Dictionnaire de Théologie Catholique,* vol. 12, cols. 833–35. Paris, 1903–50.

Collins, R. "Julian of Toledo and the Education of Kings in Late Seventh-Century Spain." Revised version of "Julian of Toledo and the Royal Succession in Late Seventh Century Spain." In *Early Medieval Kingship,* edited by P. H. Sawyer and I. N. Wood. Leeds, 1977.

————. "Julian of Toledo and the Royal Succession in Late Seventh Century Spain." In *Early Medieval Kingship,* edited by P. H. Sawyer and I. N. Wood, 30–49. Leeds, 1977.

Dahn, F. L. J. *Die könige der Germanen.* 11 vols. Leipzig, 1861–1911.

Díaz y Díaz, P. R. "Historia del Rey Wamba: Traducción y notas." *Florentia Iliberritana* 1 (1990): 89–114.

Gams, P. B. *Die Kirchengeschichte von Spanien.* 3 vols. Regensburg, 1874.

García Herrero, G. "La autoría de la Insultatio y la fecha de composición de la Historia Wambae de Julián de Toledo." In *Jornadas Internacionales: Los visigodos y su mundo, Madrid-Toledo, 22–24 de noviembre de 1990,* 156–98. Madrid, 1994.

————. "Influencia de las utopías en la realización de la Historia: El caso de Julián de Toledo." In *Actas de las II Jornadas de Metodología y Didáctica de la Historia,* 27–35. Cáceres, 1984.

————. "Julián de Toledo y la realeza visigoda." In *Antigüedad y Cristianismo VIII,* 201–55. Murcia, 1991.

————. "El reino visigodo en la concepción de Julián de Toledo." In *Antigüedad y Cristianismo XII,* 120–63. Murcia, 1995.

García López, Y. "La cronología de la 'Historia Wambae.'" *Anales de Estudios Medievales* 23 (1993): 121–39.

Görres, F. "Der Primas Julian von Toledo (680–690): Eine Kirchen-cultur, und literargeschichtliche Studie." *Zeitschrift für Wissenschaftliche Theologie* 46 (1902–3): 524–53.

Hellfferich, A. *Entstehung und Geschichte des Westgothenrechts.* Berlin, 1858.

————. *Westgothischen Arianismus.* Berlin, 1860.

Hillgarth, J. N. *Introduction* to the critical edition of the works of Julian of Toledo. Corpus Christianorum, Series Latina 115, VIII–LXXIV. Turnhout, 1976.

Jong, M. de. "Adding Insult to Injury: Julian of Toledo and His Historia Wambae." In *The Visigoths: From the Migration Period to the Seventh Century. An Ethnographic Perspective*, edited by P. Heather, 373–402. San Marino, 1999.

Julian of Toledo. "Historia Wambae regis." In *Passiones vitaeque Sanctorum Merovingici*, edited by W. Levison. *Monumenta Germaniae Historica, Scriptores Rerum Merovingicarum* 5. Berlin, 1910. Reprinted with revised notes and sources references in *Sancti Iuliani Toletanae sedis episcopi opera*, edited by J. N. Hillgarth, vol. 1, Corpus Christianorum, Series Latina 115. Turnhout, 1976.

M. A. W. [Mrs. Humphrey Ward]. "Ervigius (1), Ervig, Ervich." *A Dictionary of Christian Biography*, edited by W. Smith, DCL, LLD, and H. Wace, BD, 2:186–88. London, 1882.

Miranda Calvo, J. "San Julián cronista de guerra." *Anales Toledanos* 3 (1971): 159–70.

Potamius Olisponensis. *Altercatio Ecclesiae et Synagogae*. In *Opera omnia*, edited by M. Conti and J. N. Hillgarth. Corpus Christianorum, Series Latina 69A. Turnhout, 2007.

Powers, Sister Theresa Joseph. "A Translation of Julian of Toledo's 'Historia Wambae regis' with Introduction and Notes." MA thesis. Catholic University of America, 1941.

The Story of Wamba: Julian of Toledo's Historia Wambae Regis. Translated with an introduction and notes by J. Martínez Pizarro. Washington DC, 2005.

Teillet, S. "La déposition de Wamba: Un coup d'état au VIIe siècle." In *De Tertullien aux Mozarabes: Mélanges offerts a Jacques Fontaine à l'occasion de son 70e anniversaire*, edited by L. Holtz and J.-C. Fredouille, 2:99–113. Paris, 1992.

—————. "L'Historia Wambae' est-elle une oeuvre de circonstance?" In *Los visigodos: Historia y civilización*, 415–24. Antigüedad y cristianismo 3. Murcia, 1986.

Wengen, Paul à. *Julianus Erzbischof von Toledo: Seine Leben und seine Wirksamkeit, unter den Königen Erwig und Egica*. St. Gallen, 1891.

The Ars Grammatica

Beeson, C. H. "The Ars Grammatica of Julian of Toledo." In *Miscellanea Francesco Ehrle*, 1:50–70. Scritti di Storia Paleografia. Rome, 1924.

Bischoff, B. "Ein Brief Julians von Toledo über Rhytmen, metrisches Dichtung und Prosa." *Hermes* 87 (1959): 247–56. Reprinted in idem, *Mittelalterliche Studien*, 1:288–98. Stuttgart, 1966.

Bouhot, J. P. "Une homélie de Jean Chrysostome citée par Julien de Tolède." *Revue des Etudes Augustiniennes* 23 (1977): 122–23.

García Villada, Z. "El 'libellus de remediis blasphemiae' de san Julián de Toledo." *Historia eclesiástica de España*, 2.2:267–74. Madrid, 1933.

Giannini S. *Percorsi metalinguistici nell'Alto Medioevo: Giuliano di Toledo e la teoria della grammatica*. Milan, 1996.

Hillgarth, J. N. *Introduction* to the critical edition of the works of Julian of Toledo. Corpus Christianorum, Series Latina 115, VIII–LXXIV. Turnhout, 1976.

Holtz, L. "Edition et tradition des manuels grammaticaux antiques et médiévaux." *Revue des Études Latines* 52 (1974): 75–82.

Lindsay, W. M., ed. *Julian of Toledo De uitiis et figuris*. Oxford, 1922.

Maestre Yenes, M. A. H. *Ars Juliani Toletani Episcopi: Una gramática latina de la España visigoda*. Toledo, 1973.

Munzi, L. "Ancora sulle citazioni di Giuliano di Toledo (Ars grammatica e De partibus orationis)." *AION (filol.)* 2–3 (1980–81): 229–31.

———. "Cipriano in Giuliano Toletano. Ars gramm. 197, 52–54 M.Y." *Rivista di Filologia e d'Istruzione Classica* 108 (1980): 320–21.

———. "Il *De partibus orationis* di Giulano di Toledo." *AION (filol.)* 2–3 (1980–81): 153–228.

———. "Note testuali all'Ars grammatica di Giuliano de Toledo." *Annali dell' Istituto Universitario Orientale di Napoli*. Sezione filologico-letteraria 1 (1979): 171–73.

Schreckenberg, H. *Die christliche Adversus-Judaeos-Texte und ihr literarisches und historisches Umfeld (1.-11. Jh.)*, 459–60, 639. Frankfurt am Main, 1982.

Stratti, R. "Ancora sulle citazione di Giuliano di Toledo (Ars Grammatica e De partibus orationis)." *Rivista di Filologia e d'Istruzione Classica* 112 (1984): 196–99.

———. "Venanzio Fortunato (e altre fonti) nell' Ars grammatica di Giuliano di Toledo." *Rivista di Filologia e d' Istruzione Classica* 110 (1982): 442–45.

The De Comprobatione Sextae Aetatis Mundi

Campos, J. "El *de comprobatione sextae aetatis libri tres* de San Julián de Toledo." *Helmatica* [Revista de filologia clasica y hebrea, Universidad Pontificia de Salamanca] 18 (1967): 297–340.

———. "El *de comprobatione sextae aetatis libri tres* de San Julián de Toledo (Sus fuentes, dependencias y originalidad)." *La patrología toledano-visigota*, 245–59. Madrid, 1970.

Chase, W. J. *The ars minor of Donatus*. Madison, WI: The University of Wisconsin, 1926.

Díaz y Díaz, M. C. *Index scriptorum Latinorum Medii Aevi Hispanorum*, nn. 266–68. Salamanca, 1968.

Hillgarth, J. N. *Introduction* to the critical edition of the works of Julian of Toledo. Corpus Christianorum, Series Latina 115, VIII–LXXIV. Turnhout, 1976.

Mazzagù, C. *La teoria delle sei età del mondo: tarda antichità e alto medioevo. Giubileo delle Università. Convegno Internazionale – Tempo sacro e tempo profano, Visione laica e visione cristiana del tempo e della storia, Università degli Studi – Messina, 5–7 Settembre 2000,* edited by L. de Salvo and A. Sindoni, 110–15. Soveria Mannelli, 2002.

Moreno Garcia, A., and R. Pozas Garza. "Una controversia judeo-cristiana del S. VII: Julián de Toledo." *Helmantica* 53 (2002): 249–69.

Negri. A. M. *Elio Donato. Ars grammatica maior.* Reggio Emilia, 1960.

The Apologeticum *I and II, and the* Querelle *with the Church of Rome*

Barmby, J. [J.B-y]. "Sergius (16)." *A Dictionary of Christian Biography,* edited by W. Smith, DCL, LLD, and H. Wace, BD, 2: 618–20. London, 1882.

Buchanan, T. R. [T.R.B.] "Benedictus II." *A Dictionary of Christian Biography,* edited by W. Smith, DCL, LLD, and H. Wace, BD, 1:311–12. London, 1882.

Cuntz, O. *Itineraria Romana,* vol. 1, *Itineraria Antonini Augusti et Burdigalense.* Stuttgart, 1990.

Gams, P. B. *Die Kirchengeschichte von Spanien.* Regensburg, 1874.

Görres, F. "Der Primas Julian von Toledo (680–690): Eine Kirchen-cultur und literargeschichtliche Studie." *Zeitschrift für Wissenschaftliche Theologie* 46 (1902–3): 524–53.

Gozalbes Cravioto, E. "Una aproximación al estudio de las vías en la Hispania visigótica." In *Actas del II Congreso Internacional de Caminería Hispánica—Guadalajara (España) 4–9 Julio 1994,* 1:85–94. Guadalajara, 1998.

Hellfferich, A. *Entstehung und Geschichte des Westgothenrechts.* Berlin, 1858.

———. *Westgothischen Arianismus.* Berlin, 1860.

Hillgarth, J. N. *Introduction* to the critical edition of the works of Julian of Toledo. Corpus Christianorum, Series Latina 115, VIII–LXXIV. Turnhout, 1976.

Janini, J. "Roma y Toledo." In *Nueva problemática de la Liturgía Visigótica.* Estudios sobre la Liturgia Mozárabe. Toledo, 1965.

Julian of Toledo. *Apologeticum de tribus capitulis.* In *Sancti Iuliani Toletanae sedis episcopi opera.* Edited by J. N. Hillgarth, vol. 1, 127–39. Corpus Christianorum, Series Latina 115. Turnhout, 1976.

Leclercq, H. *L'Espagne chrétienne.* Paris, 1906.

Madoz, J. "El Primado Romano en España en el ciclo isidoriano." *Revista española de Teología* 2 (1942): 229–55.

Murphy, F. X. "Julian of Toledo and the Condemnation of Monothelitism in

Spain." In *Mélanges Joseph de Ghellinck, S.J.* vol. 1, *Antiquité,* 361–73. Gembloux, 1951.

————. "Julian of Toledo and the Fall of the Visogothic Kingdom in Spain." *Speculum* 27 (1952): 1–27.

Orlandis, J. "Las relaciones intereclesiales en la Hispania visigótica." In *Comunione interecclesiale: Collegialità, Primato, Ecumenismo,* 420–21. Rome, 1972.

Strohm, M. "Der Konflikt zwischen Erzbischof Julian von Toledo und Papst Benedikt II: Ein Faktum von ökumenischer Bedeutung." *Annuarium Historiae Conciliorum* 15 (1983): 249–59.

Vega, A. C. "El Primado Romano y la Iglesia española en lo siete primeros siglos." *Ciudad de Dios* 155 (1943): 69–103.

Weber, E. *Tabula Peutingeriana.* Codex Vindobonensis 324. Graz, 1976.

Wengen, Paul à. *Julianus Erzbischof von Toledo: Sein Leben und seine Wirksamkeit unter den Königen Erwig und Egica.* St. Gallen, 1891.

The Antikeimenon libri duo

Amelli, E. *Miscellanea Gerominiana.* Roma, 1920.

Galmés, L. "Tradición manuscrita y fuentes de los Antikeimenon II de San Julián de Toledo." *Studia Patristica* 3 (1961): 47–56.

Julian of Toledo. *Antikeimenon libri duo.* PL 96, cols. 595–704C.

Robles, A. "Fuentes del Antikeimenon de Julián de Toledo." *Escritos del Vedat* 1 (1971): 59–135.

————. "Prolegómenos a la edición crítica del Antikeimenon de Julián de Toledo." *Analecta Sacra Tarraconiensa* 42 (1969): 111–42.

The Prognosticon futuri saeculi:
the historical editions of the Prognosticum

Editio princeps incunabulum

The *editio princeps incunabulum* of the *Prognosticum* is dated circa 1490, in 8°, probably printed in Milan. The title-page states: *Incipiŭt prenosticata Iulia/ni pomerii urbis toletane epis/copi de futuro seculo. Eivv: Explĭcĭŭt prenosticata Juliani pomerii.*

Sixteenth century: Printed Editions

Ioannes Cochlaeus, Lipsia, 1536, in 8°: PROGNOSTI / CON FUTURI SAE-CULI, / Sancto Iuliano, Episcopo Toletano, an-/te annos DCC. Scriptum, in / Hispaniis. / TRES HABET LIBROS. / I. De morte et transitu ex hoc saeculo. / II. De receptaculis animarum post mortem. / III. De resurrectione mortuorum, et Extre-/mo iudicio. / I.C.

/Armis, ingeniis, virtute Hispania pollet. / Cui Imperii Rector Rex modo ibiq. Valet. Lipsiae / M.D.XXXVI.

Nicolas Bugneus, Paris, 1554, in 16: PRONOSTI/CORUM FUTURI SAECULI AE/ternaeque vitae foeliciter sperandae. Per venerabi/lem virum ac dominum, Dominum Iulianum, / Toletanae Ecclesiae Episcopum a multis annis edi/tus. Nunc autem opere atque diligentia religio/si patris, Fratris Nicolai Bugnee, compen/diensis, Doctoris Theologi ordinis prae/dicatorum, in lucem proditus. / Parisiis. / Apud Poncetum le Preux, sub insigni /Lupi, via ad D. Iacobum. / 1554.

Boëtius Epo, Douai, 1564, in 8°: ANTIQUI SCRIPTORIS ECCLESIASTICI IULIANI / Archiepiscopi olim Toletani / ΠΡΩΓΝΩΣΤΙΚΩΝ / SIVE De Futuro Seculo libri tres, / à Boëtio Epône Rordahusano Fri/asio IV. Professore Regio et ordinario in Aca/demia Duacena, ex vetustissimis / membranis in Marchianensis bi/bliotheca repertis, in lucem prolati. / Cum eiusdem Boetii Epônis ad DN. PHILIP-/PUM Regem Catholicum Praefatione (Woodcut) Duaci. An. 1564 / Typis Lodovici de Winde Typ. Iur. / Cum Gratia et Privilegio ad quadriennium.

Seventeenth Century

Boetius Epo's edition was reproduced in various reprints, from 1575 to 1667, of the *Bibliotheca Patrum* of Margarin de la Bigne: *Bibliothecae Veterum Patrum seu Scriptorum Ecclesiasticorum. Per Margarino de la Bigne ex alma Sorbonae Schola Theologum Doctorem Parisiensem. Editione quarta. Parisiis, MDCXXIV cum privilegio regis.*

Eighteenth Century

The *opera omnia* of Julian of Toledo was reproduced in the second volume of the edition of Cardinal de Lorenzana, *SS. PP. Toletanorum quotquot extant opera nunc primum simul edita, ad codices mss. recognita, nonnullis notis illustrata, atque in duos tomos distributa. Tomus primus Montani, S. Eugenii III et S. Ildephonsi Toletanae ecclesiae praesulum opuscula, epistolas, fragmentaque complectens. Opera, auctoritate, et expensis excellentissimi Domini Francisci De Lorenzana, Archiepiscopi Toletani, Hispaniarum Primatis. Matriti 1782. Apud Ioachimum Ibarra S. C. R. M. et dignitatis archiep. Tolet. Typogr. Regio Permissu. (Casanatense C. x. 20 - 21). Tomus secundus. Sancti Iuliani toletani Antistitis, et Sancti Eulogii Cordubensis Martyris, electi archiepiscopi toletani, opuscula, epistolas, fragmentaque complectens.* Matriti, 1785: 1–384.

Cardinal de Lorenzana edited also the *Ars grammatica* (attributed to Julian of Toledo): *Sancti Iuliani episcopi Toletani Ars grammatica, poetica et rhetorica e membranis antiquis bibliothecae Vaticano-Palatinae nunc primum in lucem edita.* Auctarium voluminis 2. Patrum Toletanorum. Opera, auctoritate,

et expensis eminentissimidomini Francisci cardinalis de Lorenzana...
Romae: apud Antonium Fulgonium, 1797.

Nineteenth Century

The *Patrologia Latina* edited by J. P. Migne reproduced the text of Lorenzana's
edition of the works of Julian of Toledo: PL 96, cols. 427–818.

Twentieth Century

Corpus Christianorum, Series Latina, vol. 115, published in 1976, contains
the *editio critica* of almost all the works of Julian of Toledo:

Julian of Toledo. *Opera, pars I: Idalii Barcelonis Episcopi epistulae, Prognosticum
futuri saeculi libri tres, Apologeticum de tribus capitulis, De comprobatione sextae aetatis libri tres,* edited by J. N. Hillgarth. *Histora Wambae Regis,* edited
by W. Levison. *Epistula ad Modoenum,* edited by B. Bischoff. Corpus
Christianorum, Series latina 115. Turnhout, 1976, i–lxxxiv, 1–263. See
the review by E. Ann Matter in *Speculum* 55, no. 3 (1980): 624–25.

Fontaine, J. "Un chaînon visigotique dans la tradition des «Carmina
Triumphalia»? La lettre à Modoenus de Julien de Tolède." In *Spania,
Estudis d'Antiguitat Tardana oferts en homenatge al professor Pere de Palol i
Salellas.* Barcelona, 1996.

THE *PROGNOSTICUM FUTURI SAECULI*

Amat, J. *Songes et visions: L'au-delà dans la littérature latine tardive.* Paris, 1985.

Barm F. *Les routes de l'autre monde: descentes aux infers et voyages dans l'au-delà.*
Paris, 1946.

Becker, E. J. "A Contribution to the Comparative Study of the Medieval
Visions of Heaven and Hell." Dissertation. Baltimore, 1899.

Bennet, S. A., "Zuntfredus." *A Dictionary of Christian Biography,* edited by W.
Smith, DCL, LLD, and H. Wace, BD, 4:1227. London, 1887.

Carozzi, C. "La géographie de l'au-delà et sa signification pendant le haut
moyen âge." In *Popoli e paesi nella cultura altomedievale.* 2 vols. Settimane
di studio del Centro italiano di studi sull'alto medioevo 29, 1:423–81.
Spoleto, 1983.

———. *Le voyage de l'âme dans l'au-delà d'après la littérature latine (Ve–XIIIe siècle).* Rome, 1994.

D'Achery, Luc, ed. *Spicilegium sive collectio veterum aliquot scriptorium qui in
Galliae Bibliothecis delituerant: Collectio antiqua canonum paenitentialium,
Lutetiae Parisiorum 1670.* New edition by L. F. J. de la Barre. 3 vols. with
notes of Baluze and Mertène (repr., Farnborough, 1967). Paris,
1723–35.

Dana, H. W. L. "Medieval Visions of the Other World." Dissertation, Harvard, 1910.

Díaz y Díaz, M. C. "Sanson." *Diccionario de Historia eclesiástica de España*, 4:2179. Madrid, 1972.

Dinzelbacher, P. "Die visionen des Mittelalters: Eine geschichtlicher Umriß." *Zeitschrift für Religions-und Geistesgeschichte* 30 (1978): 116-28.

——. *Vision und Visioliteratur im Mittelalter*. Stuttgart, 1981.

Erickson, C. *The Medieval Vision: Essays in History and Perception*. New York, 1976.

García Herrero, G. "Notas sobre el papel del Prognosticum futuri saeculi de Julián de Toledo en la evolución de la idea medieval del purgatorio." *Antigüedad y cristianismo: Monografías históricas sobre la Antigüedad tardía* 23 (2006): 503–14. (Ejemplar dedicado a: Espacio y tiempo en la percepción de la antigüedad tardía: homenaje al profesor Antonino González Blanco, "In maturitate aetatis ad prudentiam," edited by M. E. Conde Guerri, R. González Fernández, and A. Egea Vivancos.)

Gozzelino, G. *Nell'attesa della beata speranza: saggio di escatologia cristiana*, 206–13. Corso di studi theologici. Turin, 1993.

Graf, A. *Miti, leggende e superstizioni del Medio Evo*. Turin, 1892.

Hillgarth, J. N. *Introduction* to the critical edition of the works of Julian of Toledo. Corpus Christianorum, Series Latina 115. Turnhout, 1976.

——. "El Prognosticon futuri saeculi de San Julián de Toledo." *Analecta Sacra Tarraconensia* 30 (1957): 5–61.

——. "The 'Prognosticum futuri saeculi' of St. Julian of Toledo and the 'Tractatus' published by Mai." In *Classica et Iberica: A Festschrift in Honor of the Reverend Joseph M.-F. Marique, S.J.*, edited by P. T. Brannan, SJ, Institute for the Early Christian Iberian Studies, College of the Holy Cross, 339–44. Worcester, MA, 1975.

——. "Towards a Critical Edition of the Works of St. Julian of Toledo." *Studia Patristica* 1 (1957): 37–43.

Idalius of Barcelona. *Epistulae Idalii Barcenonensis episcopi ad Iulianum Toletanae sedis episcopum. Sancti Iuliani Toletanae sedis episcopi opera*, vol. 1. Edited by J. N. Hillgarth. Corpus Christianorum, Series Latina 115. Turnhout, 1976.

Kabir, Ananya Jahanara. *Paradise, Death, and Doomsday in Anglo-Saxon Literature*. Cambridge, 2001.

Ladaria, L. F. "Fin de l'homme et fin des temps." In *Histoire des dogmes*, vol. 2, *L'homme et son salut*, 450–65. Paris, 1995.

Le Goff, J. *La naissance du Purgatoire*. Paris, 1981.

Lemaire, J. With N. Truong. *Il corpo nel Medioevo*. Translated by Fausta Cataldi Villari. Rome, 2005.

——. "Escatologia." *Enciclopedia Einaudi*, 5:712–46. Turin, 1978.

——. *Introduction a la codicologie*. Louvain-la-Neuve, 1989.

————. *Un lungo medioevo*. Bari, 2006.

Madoz, J. "Fuentes teológico-literarias de san Julián de Toledo." *Gregorianum* 33 (1952): 399–417.

Magistri Petri Lombardi, Parisiensis Episcopi, Sententiae in IV libris distinctae. Editio tertia, Ad fidem Codicum Antiquiorum, Tomus II, Liber III et IV, Editiones Collegii S. Bonaventurae Ad Claras Aquas, Dist. XLIV, c. 7, 2. Grottaferrata, 1981.

Mathon, G. "Julien (Saint) évêque de Tolède." In *Catholicisme: Hier, aujourd' hui, demain. Encyclopédie*, edited by G. Jacquemet (vol. 7 and following published under the direction of Centre Interdisciplinaire des Facultés catholique de Lille), vol. 6, cols. 1230–31. Paris, 1948.

Morin, G. "Un écrit de Saint Julien de Tolède consideré a tort comme perdu." *Revue Bénédictine* 24 (1907): 407–15.

Ott, L., and E. Naab. *Eschatologie in der Scholastik*. Handbuch der Dogmengeschichte, vol. 4, fascicle 7b, 85–258. Freiburg, 1990.

Patch, H. R. *The Other World according to the Description in Medieval Literature*. Cambridge, MA, 1950.

Piazza, O. F. "Escatologia." *Nuovissimo Dizionario di Teologia*, 536–76. Cinisello Balsamo, 2002.

————. *Giuliano di Toledo: Conoscere le ultime realtà*. Palermo, 2005.

————. "Il Prognosticon futuri saeculi di Giuliano di Toledo." In *Sicut flumen pax tua: Studi in onore del Card. M. Giordano*, edited by A. Ascione and M. Gioia, 217–34. Naples, 1997.

Pozo, C. "La doctrina escatológica del 'Prognosticon futuri saeculi' de S. Julián de Toledo." *Estudios Eclesiásticos* 45 (1970): 173–201. The text is also published in *La Patrología toledano-visigoda*, 215–43. Madrid, 1970.

————. *Teologia dell' Aldilà*. 3rd ed. Rome, 1983.

R. T. S. [R. Travers Smith]. "Julianus (72) Pomerius." *A Dictionary of Christian Biography*, edited by W. Smith, DCL, LLD, and H. Wace, BD, 3:482. London, 1882.

Stancati, T. "Alle origini dell'Escatologia cristiana sistematica: il Prognosticon futuri saeculi di San Giuliano di Toledo (sec. VII)." *Angelicum* 73 (1996): 401–34.

Stork, N. P. "A Spanish Bishop Remembers the Future: Oral Traditions and Purgatory in Julian of Toledo." *Oral Tradition* 23 (2008): 43–70.

T. A. [T. Arnold]. "Isidorus (23) Pacensis." *A Dictionary of Christian Biography*, edited by W. Smith, DCL, LLD, and H. Wace, BD, 3:313–15. London, 1882.

Veiga Valiña, A. *La doctrina escatológica de San Julián de Toledo*. Lugo, 1940.

Visioni dell'aldilà in Occidente: Fonti modelli e testi, edited by Maria Pia Ciccarese. Florence, 1987.

Wicki, N. "Das 'Prognosticon futuri saeculi' Julians von Toledo als

Quellenwerken der Sentenzen des Petrus Lombardus." *Divus Thomas* (Fr.) 31 (1953): 351–54.

The Prognosticum *as anti-apocalyptic work*

Dagens, C. "La fin des temps et l'Église selon saint Grégoire le Grand." *Recherches de science religieuse* 458 (1970): 273–88.

García Moreno, L. A. "Expectativas milenaristas y escatológicas en la España tardoantigua (ss. V–VIII)." In *Spania: Estudis d'Antiguitat Tardana oferts en homenatge al professor Pere de Palol i Salellas*, 103–10. Barcelona, 1996. Also published in *Jornadas Internacionales "Los visigodos y sus mundo," Ateneo de Madrid, noviembre de 1990*. Arqueología, Paleontología y Etnografía 4. Madrid, 1997.

Landes, R. A. "Lest the Millennium Be Fulfilled: Apocalyptic Expectations and the Pattern of Western Chronography, 100–800 C.E." In *The Use and Abuse of Eschatology in the Middle Ages*, edited by W. D. F. Verbeke, D. Verhelst, and A. Welkenhysen. Medievalia Lovaniensia ser. 1, studia 15. Louvain, 1988.

———. *Relics, Apocalypse, and the Deceits of History: Ademar of Chabannes (989–1034)*. Cambridge, MA, 1995.

Landes, R. A., A. Gow, and D. C. Van Meter, eds. *The Apocalyptic Year 1000: Religious Expectation and Social Change, 950–1050*. Oxford, 2003.

The Prognosticum *in the Middle Ages*

"Ælfric's 'Excerpts' from the 'Prognosticon futuri saeculi' of Julian of Toledo." In *Preaching and Theology in Anglo-Saxon England*, edited by M. McC. Gatch, 127–46. Toronto, 1977.

Alcuini contra epistolam sibi ab Elipando directam libri quattuor. PL 101, cols. 231A–270D.

Backus, Irena, ed. *The Reception of the Church Fathers in the West: From the Carolingians to the Maurists*. 2 vols. Leiden/New York, 1997.

Bischoff, B. "Turning Points in the History of Latin Exegesis in the Early Middle Ages." In *Biblical Studies: The Medieval Irish Contribution*, edited by Martin McNamara, 74–160. Proceedings of the Irish Biblical Association 1. Dublin, 1976.

Bonjour, A., ed. *Dialogue de Saint-Julien et son disciple: poème anglo-normand du XIIIe siècle*. Anglo-Norman Texts Series 8. Oxford, 1949.

Bougerol, J. G. "The Church Fathers and the Sentences of Peter Lombard." In *The Reception of the Church Fathers in the West: From the Carolingians to the Maurists*, edited by Irena Backus, 1:113–63. 2 vols. Leiden/New York, 1997.

Chenu, M.-D. *Introduction à l'étude de Saint Thomas*. Montréal, 1954.

————. *La théologie au douzième siècle.* Paris, 1957.

Chiesa, P., and L. Castaldi, eds. *La Trasmissione dei testi latini del medioevo: Medieval Latin Texts and Their Transmission.* 2 vols. Florence, 2004, 2005.

Cortesi, M., ed. *Padri sotto il torchio, I: le edizioni dell'antichità cristiana nei secoli XV–XVI: atti del convegno di studi Certosa del Galluzzo, Firenze, 25–26 giugno 1999.* Florence, 2002.

Gatch, M. McC. "Eschatology in the Anonymous Old English Homilies." *Traditio* 21 (1965): 117–65.

————. "Piety and Liturgy in the Old English 'Vision of Leofric.'" In *Studies in Anglo-Saxon Culture Presented to Helmut Gneuss on the Occasion of His Sixty-fifth Birthday,* edited by Michael Korhammer et al., 159–79. Cambridge, 1992.

————. *Preaching and Theology in Anglo-Saxon England: Ælfric and Wulfstan.* Toronto/Buffalo, NY, 1977.

Ghellinck, J. de. *Littérature latine au Moyen Age, depuis les origines jusq'à la fin de la renaissance carolingienne,* vol. 1 (Paris, 1938).

————. *Le mouvement théologique du XIIe siècle.* 2nd ed. Paris, 1948.

————. *Patristique et Moyen Age: Études d'histoire littéraire et doctrinale,* vol. 2. Museum Lessianum, Section Historique 6. Gembloux, 1946.

Gozzelino, G. *Nell'attesa della beata speranza: Saggio di Escatologia cristiana,* 206–13. Turin, 1993.

Hillgarth, J. N. "St. Julian of Toledo in the Middle Ages." *Journal of the Warburg and Courtauld Institutes* 29 (1958): 7–26.

————. "Julian of Toledo in the Liber Floridus." In *Journal of the Warburg and Courtauld Institutes,* 26 (1963): 192–96.

Kleist, A. J., ed. *The Old English Homily: Precedent, Practice, and Appropriation.* Studies in the Early Middle Ages 17. Turnhout, 2007.

Ladaria, L. F. "Fin de l'homme et fin des temps." In *Histoire des Dogmes,* vol. 2, *L'homme et son salut,* 450–65. Paris, 1995.

Laistner, M. L. W. *The Intellectual Heritage of the Early Middle Ages: Selected Essays,* edited by Chester G. Starr. Ithaca, NY, 1957.

Meaney, A. L. "Aelfric's Use of His Sources in His Homily on Auguries." *English Studies* 66 (1985): 477–95.

Ott, L., and E. Naab. *Eschatologie in der Scholastik.* Handbuch der Dogmengeschichte, vol. 4, fascicle 7b. Freiburg, 1990.

Raynes, E. M. "MS. Boulogne-sur-Mer 63 and Aelfric." *Medium Aevum* 26 (1957): 65–73.

Reynolds, L. D. *Texts and Transmission: A Survey of the Latin Classics.* Oxford, 1983.

Wicki, N. "Das 'Prognosticon futuri saeculi' Julians von Toledo als Quellenwerken der Sentenzen des Petrus Lombardus." *Divus Thomas* (Fr.) 31 (1953): 349–60.

Wilmart, A. "Le commentaire sur le prophète Nahum attribué à Julien de

Tolède." *Bulletin de littérature ecclésiastiques* [Toulouse: Institut Catholique] (Juillet–Octobre 1922): 253–79.

ANCIENT AND RECENT DOCUMENTS OF THE MAGISTERIUM OF THE CATHOLIC CHURCH ON ESCHATOLOGY

Benedict XII. Constitutio Apostolica *Benedictus Deus*, 1336: *Bullarum privilegiorum ac diplomatum Romanorum pontificum amplissima collectio cui accessere pontificum omnium vitae, notae, & indices opportuni. Opera et studio Caroli Cocquelines*, vol. 3.2: *Tomus tertius pars secunda a Gregorio X. ad Martinum V. scilicet ab anno 1271. ad 1431*, 214ab. Rome, 1741. *Bullarum diplomatum et privilegiorum sanctorum romanorum pontificum taurinensis editio locupletior facta collectione novissima plurium brevium, epistolarum, decretorum actorumque S. Sedis a S. Leone Magno usque ad praesens / cura et studio r.p.d. Aloysii Tomassett…et collegii adlecti Romae virorum s. theologiae et ss. canonum peritorum quam SS.D.N. Pius Papa IX apostolica benedictione erexit auspicante Francisco Gaude*, vol. 4, *A Gregorio X (an. MCCLXXI) ad Martinum V (an. MCCCCXXXI)*, 346b–347a. Augustae Taurinorum, Seb. Franco, H. Fory et Henrico Dalmazzo editoribus, 1859. *Acta Benedicti XII, (1334–1342) / e regestis Vaticanis aliisque fontibus collegit Aloysius L. Tăutu.* Fontes/ Pontificia Commissio ad redigendum Codicem iuris canonici Orientalis. Series III/8, Civitas Vaticana: Typis Polyglottis Vaticanis, 1958: 12f. X. le Bachelet, "Benoît XII: II: Constitution 'Benedictus Deus' émise par lui le 29 Janvier 1336." *Dictionnaire de Théologie Catholique*, 2:657–96. Paris, Letouzey et Ané, 1903–50.

Congregation for the Doctrine of Faith. *Recentiores episcoporum synodi*. May 17, 1979.

International Theological Commission. "De quibusdam quaestionibus actualibus circa eschatologiam." March 1992.

Temi attuali di Escatologia, Presentazione di S. E. Mons. Tarcisio Bertone, Prefazione di S. Em. Il Cardinale Joseph Ratzinger. Documenti: *Lettera ai Vescovi della Chiesa Cattolica su alcune questioni concernenti l'Escatologia*; traduzione dell'articolo *carnis resurrectionem* del Simbolo Apostolico (Decisioni della Congregazione per la Dottrina della Fede); Commissione Teologica Internazionale, *Alcune questioni attuali riguardanti l'escatologia* (1992), Commenti e Studi: C. Sorgi, S. Maggiolini, C. Pozo, C. Schönborn, W. Kasper. Città del Vaticano: Libreria Editrice Vaticana, 2000.

VARIA

Bengt, A. *Die Hippokratische Schrift Prognostikon: Uberlieferung und Text.* Acta Universitatis Gothoburgensis, Studia graeca et latina Gothoburgensia 17. Gothenburg, Sweden, 1963.

Burchardi Wormaciensis Ecclesiae Episcopi Decretorum Libri Viginti. PL 140, cols. 537–1058C.

Burman, Thomas E., Mark D. Meyerson, and Leah Shopkow, eds. *Religion, Text, and Society in Medieval Spain and Northern Europe: Essays in Honor of J. N. Hillgarth.* Toronto, 2002.

Cabaniss, A. "Bodo-Eleazar: A Famous Jewish Convert." *Jewish Quarterly Review* n.s. 43 (1953): 313–28.

Dudde, F. H. *Gregory the Great: His Place in History and Thought,* vol. 2. London, 1905.

Dümmler, E., ed. *Monumenta Germaniae Historica, Epistolae Karolini Aevi.* Berlin, 1895.

Fernández Alonso, J. "Fruttuoso." *Bibliotheca Sanctorum,* vol. 5, cols. 1295–96. Rome, 1965.

Fitzgerald, Allan D., ed. *Augustine through the Ages: An Encyclopedia.* Grand Rapids, 1999.

Fontaine, J. *Isidore de Seville et la culture classique dans l'Espagne wisigothique.* 2 vols. Paris, 1959.

Fontaine, J., et al., eds. *Gregoire le Grand: Colloques Internationaux du CNRS.* Paris, 1986.

Greshake, G. "Benedictus Deus." Lexikon für Theologie und Kirche (1994), vol. 2, cols. 198–200.

Hillgarth, J. N. "Elvira, Council of." *The New Catholic Encyclopaedia,* 5:178. New York, 2003.

———. "The Position of Isidorian Studies: A Critical Review of the Literature since 1935." *Isidoriana* [León] 32, no. 58 (1961): 11–74.

Isidore of Sevilla. *Historia de regibus Gothorum, Vandalorum et Suevorum.* Patrologia latina. 83, cols. 1057–82. Edited by J.-P. Migne. Paris, 1844–64.

———. *Etymologiarum sive originum libri xx.* Edited by W. M. Lindsay. 2 vols. Oxford, 1911.

———. *Sententiae.* Edited by P. Cazier. Corpus Christianorum, Series Latina 111. Turnhout, 1998.

Lefèvre, V. *L'Elucidarium et les lucidaires: Contribution par l'histoire d'un texte, à l'histoire des croyances religieuses en France au Moyen Age.* Paris, 1954.

Madoz, J. *Epistolario de Alvaro de Cordoba: Epistola 14, 2–6,* 213–20. Madrid, 1947.

———. *Epistolario de San Braulio de Zaragoza.* Ed. crit. según el códice 22 del

Archivo Capitular de León. *Estudios Onienses: Facultades de Teologia y de Filosofia del Colegio Maximo de Oña* 1–2. Madrid, 1941.

————. "Liciniano de Cartagena y sus cartas." *Estudios Onienses*, series 1, vol. 4:83–96. Madrid, 1948.

————. "Tajón de Zaragoza y su viaje a Roma." In *Mélanges J. de Ghellinck*, 1:345–60. Gembloux, 1951.

Menéndez Pidal, R. *Orígenes del español*, 7th ed. Madrid, 1972.

Meyerson, M. D. "El Professor Jocelyn N. Hillgarth." *Anuario de Estudios Medievales* 26, no. 1 (1996): 489–501.

Monumenta Germaniae Historica, Epistolae Karolini Aevi. Edited by E. Dümmler, II. Berlin, 1895.

Monumenta Germaniae Historica, Concilia Aevi Karolini. Edited by A. Werminghoff, I. Hannover, 1906.

Orosius, Paulus. *Histoires (contre le païens)*. Edited by M.-P. Arnaud-Lindet. 3 vols. Paris, 1990–91.

R. T. S. [R. Travers Smith]. "Julianus (72) Pomerius." *A Dictionary of Christian Biography*, edited by W. Smith, D. C. L., LL. D, and H. Wace, B. D., 3:482. London, 1882.

Sesión Académica en Memoria de Don Juan Francisco Rivera Recio, 23 March 1991. Toledo, 1992.

Sierra, L. "Lorenzana, Francisco Antonio de." *Diccionario de Historia Eclesiástica de España*, 2:1346–48. Madrid, 1972–75.

Singer, I., and M. Kayserling. "Paul de Burgos." *Jewish Encyclopedia*, on-line version: www.jewishencyclopedia.com/view.jsp?artid=115&letter=P&search=paul%20of%20burgos.

Stancati, T. "Benedictus Deus." *Lexicon, Dizionario Teologico Enciclopedico*, 121. Casale Monferrato, 1993.

T. A. [T. Arnold]. "Isidorus (23) Pacensis." *A Dictionary of Christian Biography*, edited by W. Smith, DCL, LLD, and H. Wace, BD, 3:313–15. London, 1882.

Tailhan, J. *Anonyme de Cordove*. Paris, 1885.

Toussaint, C. "Jean Cochlée." *Dictionnaire de Théologie Catholique*, vol. III.I, cols. 264–65. Paris, Letouzey et Ané, 1903–1950.

Walafridus Strabo (= the Squinter). *Diario*. Quoted in A. Messer, *Historia de la pedagogía* (Madrid, 1935), vol. 106–7, 109–24.

Werminghoff, A., ed. *Monumenta Germaniae Historica, Concilia Aevi Karolini (742–842)*. Hannover, 1906.

INDEX OF SCRIPTURAL REFERENCES
IN THE *PROGNOSTICUM*

INDEX OF CITATIONS FROM THE FATHERS OF THE CHURCH IN THE *PROGNOSTICUM*

Ambrose II:iii

Augustine I:ii; I:vi; I:vii; I:viii; I:viiii; I:x; I:xi; I:xiii; I:xvii; I:xviiii; I:xx; I:xxi; I:xxii; II:ii; II:iiii; II:v; II:vi; II:vii; II:viiii; II:xi; II:xvi; II:xviiii; II:xx; II:xxi; II:xxii; II:xxiii; II:xxvii; II:xxviiii; II:xxx; II:xxxiii; II:xxxiiii; II:xxxvii; III:iii; III:iv; III:viiii; III:x; III:xi; III:xiii; III:xiiii; III: xvi; III:xviii; III:xx; III:xxi; III:xxii; III:xxiiii; III:xxv; III:xxvii; III:xxviii; III:xxviiii; III:xxx; III:xxxi; III:xxxii; III:xxxiiii; III:xxxv; III:xxxvi; III:xxxvii; III:xxxviii; III:xxxviiii; III:xxxx; III:xxxxi; III:xxxxii; III: xxxxiii; III:xxxxiiii; III:xxxxvi; III:xxxxvii; III:xxxxviiii; III:li; III:lii; III:liii; III:liiii; III:lv; III:lviii; III:lviiii; III:lx; III:lxi; III:lxii

Cassian II:xv; II:xxxiii

Chrysostom III:v

Cyprian I:xiiii; I:xv; I:xvi; II:xxxvi

Eugene of Toledo III:xvii; III:xxiiii; III:xxvi

Gregory the Great I:iii; I:vii; I:xxi; II:viii; II:xii; II:xiii; II:xiiii; II:xvii; II:xviii; II:xviiii; II:xxiv; II:xxv; II:xxxi; II:xxxii; II: xxxv; III:xxviiii; III:xxxiii; III:xxxxv; III:l

Isidore of Seville I:iiii; I:vi; I:vii; II:i; III:i; III:iiii; III:vi; III:vii; III:viii; III:xxxiii; III:lii

Iulianus Pomerius I:viiii; II:i; II:x; III:xvi; III:xviii; III:xx; III:xxv; III:xxvi; III:xxvii; III:xxviii

Jerome III:ii; III:xv; III:xvi; III:xxiiii; III:xxviii

Origen II:xxviii

INDEX OF THE AUTHORS QUOTED
IN THE INTRODUCTION